Culture and Context

An Interdisciplinary Approach to Literature

Volume 1

Edited by Adam Sweeting and Natalie McKnight
Boston University

cognella®
academic publishing

Bassim Hamadeh, CEO and Publisher
Michael Simpson, Vice President of Acquisitions
Jamie Giganti, Managing Editor
Jess Busch, Graphic Design Supervisor
John Remington, Acquisitions Editor
Brian Fahey, Licensing Associate
Sean Adams, Editorial Associate

First published in the United States of America in 2015 by Cognella, Inc.

Trademark Notice: Product or corporate names may be trademarks or registered trademarks, and are used only for identification and explanation without intent to infringe.

Cover image © 2010 Depositphotos /Alaxandr Ozerov; Copyright © 2010 Depositphotos /Janaka Dharmasena

Printed in the United States of America

ISBN: 978-1-62131-726-5 (pbk)/ 978-1-62131-727-2 (br)

www.cognella.com   800-200-3908

CONTENTS

PREFACE

The name of this book seems clear enough: *Culture and Context*. But readers might fairly ask what we mean by such a title. At first, the term "culture" might seem easy enough to understand, but once we begin to try to define it, we are likely to run into difficulties. "Culture" might mean a way of life, a system of traditional practices, or works of literary, artistic, or musical expression. This anthology focuses on the history and development of literary culture. But here, too, we encounter difficulties. Such a definition would include things such as poems, song lyrics, film scripts, novels, and plays, but would exclude certain essays or diary entries. But then we must ask, on what basis do we make this division? How do we decide what forms of expression are literary and which forms are not? How we answer these questions will largely determine what kinds of works are included in an anthology such as this. Our own ideas of what constitutes literature are fairly broad. For our purposes, the term "literature" can be applied to forms of expression that, by creatively manipulating the written word, help reveal the many ways that people have experienced and imagined their worlds. Such a definition naturally includes works of prose fiction, poetry, and drama—and indeed, these forms comprise the vast bulk of selections in *Culture and Context*—but it also includes certain nonfiction essays and aphoristic sayings. "Literature," we assume, can embrace a multitude of forms.

What about "context?" How does this book present literature in context? The word "context" comes from the Latin word *contextus*, "to weave together," and that is what we have tried to do in this anthology—weave together the various strands that influence the cultural products of certain time periods.

In the subsequent units, we examine how exemplary literary works relate to, reflect, or challenge prevailing intellectual and cultural ideas of their times. These ideas include those seen in the visual arts, as well as those that helped shape broader philosophical and cultural trends. (Ideally, we would have liked to present the music of each period, too, but that would have made the book much longer than would be practical for most students' use. Plus, the visual arts are easier to present within the confines of a written text.) Our operating premise is simple: Literary works emerge in a particular time and space. In other words, they have a context. Helping students to understand these contexts is the purpose of this book. We feel that students can understand and appreciate works of literature better if they see how they reflect and affect the cultural context out of which they emerge. Works of literature that may seem off-putting at first become more accessible when their themes and styles can be seen as expressions of a particular worldview that is also expressed in the arts and philosophies of that period.

We hope that our interdisciplinary approach helps students to understand the readings more fully than they would if encountering them in isolation. Even more boldly, we hope to inspire as many students as possible to love what we and others have loved in these works and understand what makes them worthy of study and preservation.

ORGANIZATION

Culture and Context consists of two volumes, divided into six units organized chronologically: Volume I covers the Ancient Mediterranean World, the Middle Ages, and the Renaissance; Volume II covers the Enlightenment and Age of Reason, the Nineteenth Century, and the Twentieth Century. As this outline suggests, we focus primarily on the contexts of Western literary culture, by which we mean the literature that either emerged in or can be traced to the Ancient Mediterranean world, Europe, and the Americas. Such a focus, however, is neither geographically nor culturally exclusive. As we will see, these regions have long been crossroads of cultures. People from around the world have passed through these territories, bringing with them their own languages, literatures, and traditions. Contexts are always complex.

Of course, literary and cultural history cannot be precisely divided into distinct chronological periods, and the text considers several writers and artists whose work straddles these divisions. Nor can we say that all the major works of literature produced during any one of these periods share common themes or styles. A period such as the Middle Ages, for example, lasted nearly 1,000 years, a time frame that makes generalizing about literature and art difficult. The same can be said for the much shorter time frames considered in Units 5 and 6. Nevertheless, the selected readings at the end of each unit suggest that we can trace the expression of certain broad ideas through time. This does not imply that all works produced during a particular era share identical concerns. Far from it. We can, however, identify patterns as we examine the multiple ways that writers and artists experienced and portrayed their worlds. These patterns are part of the context.

Each unit begins with an introductory overview of the broad historical and cultural events of the time period. These introductions emphasize the major intellectual and political developments that helped shape the perspectives of the creative artists included in the subsequent discussions of the visual arts and literature. The art section of each unit includes representative works by major figures of the period. But these works are not included as mere illustrations. At several points, students are invited to consider particular paintings or sculptures, with the aim of developing a vocabulary to discuss the basic outlines of Western art history. Where appropriate, we highlight connections between the forms, as, for example, the near simultaneous emergence of expressionist art and modernist poetry in the early 20th century, which is covered in Unit 6. At the same time, we must understand that literature and art develop according to their own logic and do not always unfold in similar ways. Baroque music, for example, lasted nearly 50 years longer than Baroque art, as we will see in Unit 3. But by examining these art forms within their broader context, we come to understand patterns, as well as divergences. In short, we reach a firmer understanding of our cultural past.

The vast portion of each unit will be found in the selected readings that follow the historical surveys of art and literature. No list of major literary works, however, can ever be complete. Indeed, selecting one work for inclusion in a text such as this inevitably means some other work is excluded. For many years, scholars generally agreed what works belonged in the *canon*, a term used to describe the literary productions most worthy of study. Students were then taught from this list of classics. Over the last four decades, however, the contents of the canon have been significantly reevaluated, as new reading practices and an increased interest in the work of women and nonwhite authors have brought critical attention to previously under-recognized figures. By no means do we intend our selections to amount to a new canon appropriate for the 21st century. Many of the figures included here can be found in traditional lists of the classics. Others, particularly those in the later units, were brought into the modern classroom as a result of recent efforts to revise and expand the reading lists for literature and humanities courses. In general, we looked for works that would excite and challenge students, while also helping them to situate themselves within the broad sweep of Western culture, but space limitations and licensing restrictions prevented us from using all the works we would have liked to include.

With few exceptions, the works included in *Culture and Context* are complete; they are not excerpted from larger wholes. Like all decisions about what to include in an anthology, this one comes with its own biases. As teachers, we have often experienced the frustration of using select passages to reflect an entire work. Students inevitably understand that they are missing important pieces to a puzzle. In places where we believed the overall spirit of a work would not be violated, we reprinted sections of a larger work. **In general, however, we opted to treat works in their entirety.** Such a decision has its trade-offs, of course, but it also allows students and teachers to confront a work as it was intended to be read.

A FINAL NOTE FOR STUDENTS AND TEACHERS

The chronological structure of the book is intended to assist both students and teachers to organize material in a cohesive manner. While the readings may be challenging, the book is meant to be easy to use at home, in a dorm room, or in class. We have tried to place at the fingertips of both students and teachers the materials they will need to have illuminating readings, class discussions, and writing assignments. We have written the art and literature introductions to be as helpful and accessible to as diverse an audience as possible—those with no background in the arts, as well as those more experienced in these areas. The study questions and writing suggestions at the end of the selected readings offer a range of topics for class discussion and possible essay subjects. When we write and talk about literature, we join a conversation among readers that has been going on for thousands of years. In other words, we enter a new context. We hope that the writing and discussion suggestions offered here help students to create new contexts that heighten their appreciation of the literature and arts of the recent and distant past.

THE ANCIENT MEDITERRANEAN

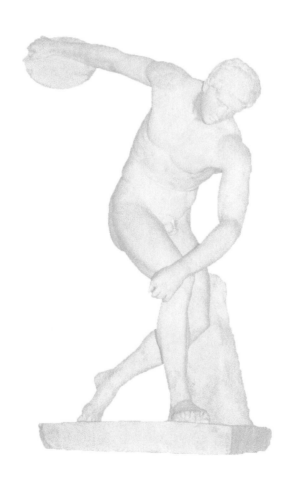

THE HEBREW BIBLE

General Introduction

We begin our exploration of the literature and culture of the ancient Mediterranean with selections from the Hebrew Bible. Unlike the Greeks and Romans discussed later in Unit 1, the Hebrews did not assemble a powerful military or economic force. Nevertheless, they have wielded immeasurable influence over the course of Western history. That influence stems from the remarkable literary and religious power of their Bible.

Very little can be said with certainty about the early Hebrews. Along with the Philistines and the Canaanites, they were one of many groups in the eastern Mediterranean region. But where they came from or how they came together is unclear. The derivation of the term "Hebrew" is also unclear. It was originally used as an ethnic term to distinguish them from other nations residing in far eastern shores of the Mediterranean near the end of the Bronze Age. Later, the geographically based name "Israelites" was more commonly used. In general, biblical writers use the term "Hebrews" only when describing the earliest aspects of the nation's history.

For many years, the emergence of Israel as a distinct political and cultural state was tied to the story of David and Solomon. According to the Bible, around 1,000 BCE,[1] David united the Hebrews into the kingdom of Israel, with Jerusalem as its capital;

these same biblical accounts describe how David's son, Solomon, established the Temple of Jerusalem and ruled over an extensive and luxurious empire. The size, power, and dating of David and Solomon's Jerusalem, however, are subjects of debate. Nonetheless, most scholars assume that the father and son solidified and presided over the Hebrew presence in Jerusalem, even if their kingdom was not as large and powerful as traditional accounts imply. After Solomon's death (traditionally said to be 922 BCE), the kingdom broke into two parts. The larger of the two, the kingdom of Israel, lay to the north; the smaller southern kingdom, Judah, was in the south.

Although it is impossible to date its origins, the most distinctive cultural trait of the Israelites was the practice of monotheism, the belief in one all-powerful and transcendent god. They did not always believe in such a god. Like the Egyptians, Greeks, and other Mediterranean people, the early Hebrews worshipped a pantheon of deities. Such a belief system allowed for a hierarchy of deities or a god who ruled over a particular place. It is possible that such a hierarchical pantheon would lead to belief in a single god. At some point in the history of ancient Israel, the local deity known as Yahweh emerged as the sole god of the Israelites. According to the Book of Exodus, Yahweh revealed himself to Moses on Mount Sinai, promising to deliver the Hebrews safely into Canaan if they promised to worship only Him. But exactly when or how historical Israelites began to worship this god exclusively is unclear. Most likely, such a shift in belief occurred over a period of centuries. Whatever the case, the move to a monotheistic creed

---

1 Like the editors of most modern works, we use the abbreviation BCE to stand for Before the Common Era. For many years, the abbreviation BC—Before Christ—was used when assigning dates to events in the ancient world. BCE does not refer to any single individual or religious identity, so we use the abbreviation throughout this anthology.

marks one of the watershed episodes in Western culture.

The history of ancient Israel is marked by a series of conquests and exiles. In 722 BCE, Assyrians conquered the northern kingdom of Israel, a development that left Judah as the keeper of Hebrew traditions. In 586 BCE, however, the Babylonians in turn conquered Judah. While some remained behind, many of Jerusalem's residents were sent into exile in Babylon. When the Persians conquered Babylon in 539, they allowed the Hebrews to return and rebuild the Temple in Jerusalem. Persia, however, remained firmly in control of all of Israel until it fell to the Macedonian Greeks in 333 BCE.

The Babylonian exile proved to be a pivotal period in the history of the Israelites. Around this time, the term "Jewish," which has roots in the geographical name, Judah, began to be used more commonly. This was also the beginning of the Jewish Diaspora (dispersion). The forced exile from Jerusalem sent Israelites to cities around the Mediterranean, where they practiced their religion, even though they were not physically in the sacred grounds of their ancestors. Many scholars believe that the monotheistic belief in Yahweh firmly took root during the exile, as Israelites may have hoped that His promise to Moses would assure their eventual return home. (Others, however, have argued that monotheism developed well before the exile.) Because the Babylonian experience was central to the formation of Jewish identity, writers typically use the terms preexilic and postexilic when referring to the early history of Judaism.

From 539 to 333 BCE, Israel was controlled by the Persians. When Alexander the Great conquered Persia in 333, most of the eastern Mediterranean, including Israel, was brought under the control of the Macedonian Greeks. The conquest of Israel by the Macedonian Greeks in 333 BCE marks the beginning of the Hellenistic period. Although they resented many aspects of the Greek conquest, the Hellenistic period saw the spread of the Israelite religion throughout the known world. The main vehicle for this spread was the translation of the Hebrew Bible into Greek, a step that helped introduce its ideas to readers outside of Israel. The Hellenistic era ended when the Romans conquered Israel in the first century BCE. By that time, however, the Israelites' seminal ideas about God, ethics, and religion had already reached well beyond their origin in one small corner of the Mediterranean. In the centuries that followed, they would continue to serve as a cornerstone of the Western religious, literary, and cultural traditions.

LITERATURE

The Hebrew Bible

Three major religions have roots in stories told in the Hebrew Bible. For Jews, it is *the* central scriptural document. For this reason, Jews refer to it as either the Hebrew Bible or simply the Bible. Christians identify it as the Old Testament, the first half of the expanded Bible, to which they added the New Testament. For Muslims, figures such as Abraham and Noah are prophets for the one true God. The word "Bible" comes from the Greek for "book." But the Hebrew Bible is not a single book. Rather, it contains 39 separate works that describe the history and religious ideas of the Israelites. Most scholars suggest that they were written over a 500-year period, roughly 750 BCE to 250 BCE. These dates, however, must be understood as speculative.

How the books were arranged into their current form is also a matter of speculation, and indeed, the order of the books has varied over the centuries. Their selection into the canon (the list of books officially accepted as biblical) may be related to the sections into which the books are traditionally divided. The first five books are known as the *Torah* or *Pentateuch*, from the Greek for "five books." The *Torah* begins with the tale of creation in *Genesis* and a description of the early patriarchs of Israel. Subsequent books describe the exodus of the Hebrews from Egypt—where they had been held captive—and the giving of the Law at Mount Sinai. These laws, which God delivered to Moses, provided a code of ethics and regulations for diet, religious practices, and civic life. In return for following the Law, God entered into a covenant with the Hebrews that marked them as His chosen people. In the final book of the *Torah*, Moses, who led the Hebrews during their wanderings and their successful flight from Egypt, announces that he will die before the Hebrews reach their Promised Land in Canaan. Although we cannot know for sure, most scholars believe that the books of the *Torah* were compiled in the seventh century BCE, which places its composition several centuries after the described events.

The second section of the Bible is known as the *Prophets*. Its first six books, known as the *Former Prophets*, complete the historical sequence begun in the *Torah*; they tell the story of the Hebrew conquest of Canaan, the rise of the kingdom of Israel, and its eventual defeat by the Assyrians and the Babylonians. The next 15 books, known as the *Latter Prophets*, offer a mixture of warnings and teachings delivered by figures with special insights into the dangers facing the Hebrews. They are traditionally dated to the period between the end of the exile (539 BCE) and the end of Persian rule (333 BCE).

The 13 books of the *Writings* make up the third and final division of the Hebrew Bible. This unit is less cohesive than the others. It contains books of poems (*Psalms* and *Lamentations*), as well as others that offer prayers, meditations, and examples of devotion, many of which are directed toward particular religious festivals and holidays. The *Writings* also contain historical books (*Chronicles I and II*, *Ezra*, and *Jeremiah*) that are believed to be the last books of the Hebrew Bible to be written. Our Selected Readings contain sections from *Job* and *Ecclesiastes*, two books from the *Writings* often identified as Wisdom Literature.

In most cases, we do not know who wrote the various books of the Hebrew Bible. Traditionally, readers and religious leaders assumed that Moses wrote the five books of the *Torah*. In the 18th and 19th centuries, however, scholars recognized that more than one literary voice could be detected. The best-known example of this occurs in the two stories of man's creation in the Book of Genesis, which contrast in both style and detail. A third distinct style has been identified for *Deuteronomy*, the final book of the *Torah*. Further complicating the question of authorship is that all of the biblical texts were edited when they were assembled into their familiar form. When we read them, then, we enter into a world of history and devotion that has been constructed through layers of revision.

While it is now accepted that individual biblical books may have multiple authors, whether they describe the actual history of the Hebrews is currently the subject of enormous debate. This debate especially revolves around the *Torah* and *Prophets* books that describe the early history of Israel. For nearly 2000 years, the Bible was assumed to provide a reliable account of events, even if the precise time frame could not be determined. Thus, it was taken for granted that there was an actual person named Abraham or that an actual battle marked the Hebrew conquest of Canaan. While most 20th-century scholars understood that the Hebrew Bible should not be read in the way we read a history textbook, they assumed that a rough historic outline could be traced through its pages. This outline, they argued (and continue to argue), was confirmed by evidence in the archaeological record. This remains a popular and well-respected view among specialists in the field. Recently, however, another group of researchers has argued that the Bible offers little insight into the actual history of Israel. For this group, the Bible is foremost a literary and theological work that offers insights into ideas such as liberation, devotion, and our place in the cosmos. Such intricacies of scholarship need not interfere with our enjoyment of these works. For in the Hebrew Bible we find some of the most exalted expressions of human hopes and fears.

GENESIS

Selections

Genesis is the first book of the Bible. It begins with God's creation of the earth and man and the subsequent exile of the first family from the paradise of the Garden of Eden. Like all creation stories, *Genesis* addresses fundamental questions that concern us today. Where are we from? How did the earth and all its living and nonliving material get here? What is the source of human evil and suffering? Scholars refer to these early chapters as the "primeval history," to distinguish them from the patriarchal history of the later sections in *Genesis* that, with the story of Abraham and his descendants, commence the history of the Hebrew people.

Though all-powerful and capable of great mercy, the primeval God is a perplexing figure. We see this in his treatment of Adam and Eve, the first inhabitants of the newly created world. For good or bad, God gives them the immense power of free will, which Adam chooses to use in an act of transgression. The first sin, then, emerges from human choice. The punishment: For Adam, the curse of having to labor to earn his daily bread; for Eve, the pain of childbirth. Both are also expelled from a paradise to which they will never return. We are left to wonder if the misfortunes that ensue from that expulsion were part of God's plan. And if so, why?

The second transgression described in *Genesis*, Cain's murder of Abel, launches the history of human violence, in this case the murderous rage of one brother toward another. God once again chooses exile for his punishment by condemning Cain to spend the rest of his as a "fugitive and vagabond." Yet God also protects Cain by marking and vowing vengeance toward anyone who tries to hurt him. The justice of Cain's punishment is thus tempered by God's mercy. Still, man's wickedness continues until God comes to regret his initial creation of Adam. He unleashes a terrible flood but spares one man, Noah, and his family, from whom new generations of hopefully less wicked men and women will arise. When the floodwaters recede, God makes a covenant with Noah, promising to never again send such a cataclysmic deluge upon the earth. With its mixture of ritualistic cleansing, divine violence, and hopes for a new and better future, the flood story remains one of the most powerful and popular biblical tales.

The Tower of Babel story in Chapter 11 describes why people speak different languages. According to the story, God once again felt compelled to punish His finest creation, even if the punishment is less severe than the previous flood. Angered by human ambition to build a tower to heaven, He makes communication between people difficult by establishing linguistic barriers.

With Abraham, the biblical history of the Hebrews as a distinct people chosen by God begins. He encounters a God whose ways cannot be understood by the rational powers of man, and yet his story is one that we cannot help but try to understand. Told by God that he would become the father of a nation, Abraham can only laugh, for he is nearly 100 and his wife, Sarah, is 90. But God's promise holds true and Isaac, Abraham's son, is born. Later, God tests Abraham's faith by commanding him to do the unimaginable: kill his beloved son—the very person through whom the nation promised to Abraham will descend. At the last moment, God intervenes to save Isaac, but not before Abraham's faith in God's rightness has been tested to the limits. It is a chilling story of devotion that has attracted modern philosophers interested in the difficult moral choices we must sometimes confront. As heirs to the cultures of the ancient Mediterranean world, we have the benefit of hindsight and know that Abraham will become revered as the father of Israel. But to understand the full power of the story, we must put ourselves in Abraham's shoes and try to grasp the enormity of his task.

GENESIS

Chapter 1

1. In the beginning God created the heaven and the earth.

2. And the earth was without form, and void; and darkness *was* upon the face of the deep. And the Spirit of God moved upon the face of the waters.

3. And God said, Let there be light: and there was light.

4. And God saw the light, that *it was* good: and God divided the light from the darkness.

5. And God called the light Day, and the darkness he called Night. And the evening and the morning were the first day.

6. And God said, Let there be a firmament in the midst of the waters, and let it divide the waters from the waters.

7. And God made the firmament, and divided the waters which *were* under the firmament from the waters which *were* above the firmament: and it was so.

8. And God called the firmament Heaven. And the evening and the morning were the second day.

9. And God said, Let the waters under the heaven be gathered together unto one place, and let the dry *land* appear: and it was so.

10. And God called the dry *land* Earth; and the gathering together of the waters called he Seas: and God saw that *it was* good.

11. And God said, Let the earth bring forth grass, the herb yielding seed, *and* the fruit tree yielding fruit after his kind, whose seed *is* in itself, upon the earth: and it was so.

12. And the earth brought forth grass, *and* herb yielding seed after his kind, and the tree yielding fruit, whose seed *was* in itself, after his kind: and God saw that *it was* good.

13. And the evening and the morning were the third day.

14. And God said, Let there be lights in the firmament of the heaven to divide the day from the

night; and let them be for signs, and for seasons, and for days, and years:

15. And let them be for lights in the firmament of the heaven to give light upon the earth: and it was so.

16. And God made two great lights; the greater light to rule the day, and the lesser light to rule the night: *he made* the stars also.

17. And God set them in the firmament of the heaven to give light upon the earth,

18. And to rule over the day and over the night, and to divide the light from the darkness: and God saw that *it was* good.

19. And the evening and the morning were the fourth day.

20. And God said, Let the waters bring forth abundantly the moving creature that hath life, and fowl *that* may fly above the earth in the open firmament of heaven.

21. And God created great whales, and every living creature that moveth, which the waters brought forth abundantly, after their kind, and every winged fowl after his kind: and God saw that *it was* good.

22. And God blessed them, saying, Be fruitful, and multiply, and fill the waters in the seas, and let fowl multiply in the earth.

23. And the evening and the morning were the fifth day.

24. And God said, Let the earth bring forth the living creature after his kind, cattle, and creeping thing, and beast of the earth after his kind: and it was so.

25. And God made the beast of the earth after his kind, and cattle after their kind, and every thing that creepeth upon the earth after his kind: and God saw that *it was* good.

26. And God said, Let us make man in our image, after our likeness: and let them have dominion over the fish of the sea, and over the fowl of the air, and over the cattle, and over all the earth, and over every creeping thing that creepeth upon the earth.

27. So God created man in his *own* image, in the image of God created he him; male and female created he them.

28. And God blessed them, and God said unto them, Be fruitful, and multiply, and replenish the earth, and subdue it: and have dominion over the fish of the sea, and over the fowl of the air, and over every living thing that moveth upon the earth.

29. And God said, Behold, I have given you every herb bearing seed, which *is* upon the face of all the earth, and every tree, in the which *is* the fruit of a tree yielding seed; to you it shall be for meat.

30. And to every beast of the earth, and to every fowl of the air, and to every thing that creepeth upon the earth, wherein *there is* life, *I have given* every green herb for meat: and it was so.

31. And God saw every thing that he had made, and, behold, *it was* very good. And the evening and the morning were the sixth day.

Chapter 2

1. Thus the heavens and the earth were finished, and all the host of them.

2. And on the seventh day God ended his work which he had made; and he rested on the seventh day from all his work which he had made.

3. And God blessed the seventh day, and sanctified it: because that in it he had rested from all his work which God created and made.

4. These *are* the generations of the heavens and of the earth when they were created, in the day that the LORD God made the earth and the heavens,

5. And every plant of the field before it was in the earth, and every herb of the field before it grew: for the LORD God had not caused it to rain upon the earth, and *there was* not a man to till the ground.

6. But there went up a mist from the earth, and watered the whole face of the ground.

7. And the LORD God formed man *of* the dust of the ground, and breathed into his nostrils the breath of life; and man became a living soul.

8. And the LORD God planted a garden eastward in Eden; and there he put the man whom he had formed.

9. And out of the ground made the LORD God to grow every tree that is pleasant to the sight,

and good for food; the tree of life also in the midst of the garden, and the tree of knowledge of good and evil.

10. And a river went out of Eden to water the garden; and from thence it was parted, and became into four heads.

11. The name of the first is Pison: that is it which compasseth the whole land of Havilah, where *there is* gold;

12. And the gold of that land *is* good: there *is* bdellium and the onyx stone.

13. And the name of the second river *is* Gihon: the same *is* it that compasseth the whole land of Ethiopia.

14. And the name of the third river is Hiddekel: that is it which goeth toward the east of Assyria. And the fourth river is Euphrates.

15. And the LORD God took the man, and put him into the garden of Eden to dress it and to keep it.

16. And the LORD God commanded the man, saying, Of every tree of the garden thou mayest freely eat:

17. But of the tree of the knowledge of good and evil, thou shalt not eat of it: for in the day that thou eatest thereof thou shalt surely die.

18. And the LORD God said, *It is* not good that the man should be alone; I will make him an help meet for him.

19. And out of the ground the LORD God formed every beast of the field, and every fowl of the air; and brought *them* unto Adam to see what he would call them: and whatsoever Adam called every living creature, that *was* the name thereof.

20. And Adam gave names to all cattle, and to the fowl of the air, and to every beast of the field; but for Adam there was not found an help meet for him.

21. And the LORD God caused a deep sleep to fall upon Adam, and he slept: and he took one of his ribs, and closed up the flesh instead thereof;

22. And the rib, which the LORD God had taken from man, made he a woman, and brought her unto the man.

23. And Adam said, This *is* now bone of my bones, and flesh of my flesh: she shall be called Woman, because she was taken out of Man.

24. Therefore shall a man leave his father and his mother, and shall cleave unto his wife: and they shall be one flesh.

25. And they were both naked, the man and his wife, and were not ashamed.

Chapter 3

1. Now the serpent was more subtil than any beast of the field which the LORD God had made. And he said unto the woman, Yea, hath God said, Ye shall not eat of every tree of the garden?

2. And the woman said unto the serpent, We may eat of the fruit of the trees of the garden:

3. But of the fruit of the tree which *is* in the midst of the garden, God hath said, Ye shall not eat of it, neither shall ye touch it, lest ye die.

4. And the serpent said unto the woman, Ye shall not surely die:

5. For God doth know that in the day ye eat thereof, then your eyes shall be opened, and ye shall be as gods, knowing good and evil.

6. And when the woman saw that the tree *was* good for food, and that it *was* pleasant to the eyes, and a tree to be desired to make *one* wise, she took of the fruit thereof, and did eat, and gave also unto her husband with her; and he did eat.

7. And the eyes of them both were opened, and they knew that they *were* naked; and they sewed fig leaves together, and made themselves aprons.

8. And they heard the voice of the LORD God walking in the garden in the cool of the day: and Adam and his wife hid themselves from the presence of the LORD God amongst the trees of the garden.

9. And the LORD God called unto Adam, and said unto him, Where *art* thou?

10. And he said, I heard thy voice in the garden, and I was afraid, because I *was* naked; and I hid myself.

11. And he said, Who told thee that thou *wast* naked? Hast thou eaten of the tree, whereof I commanded thee that thou shouldest not eat?

12. And the man said, The woman whom thou gavest *to be* with me, she gave me of the tree, and I did eat.

13. And the LORD God said unto the woman, What *is* this *that* thou hast done? And the woman said, The serpent beguiled me, and I did eat.

14. And the LORD God said unto the serpent, Because thou hast done this, thou *art* cursed above all cattle, and above every beast of the field; upon thy belly shalt thou go, and dust shalt thou eat all the days of thy life:

15. And I will put enmity between thee and the woman, and between thy seed and her seed; it shall bruise thy head, and thou shalt bruise his heel.

16. Unto the woman he said, I will greatly multiply thy sorrow and thy conception; in sorrow thou shalt bring forth children; and thy desire *shall be* to thy husband, and he shall rule over thee.

17. And unto Adam he said, Because thou hast hearkened unto the voice of thy wife, and hast eaten of the tree, of which I commanded thee, saying, Thou shalt not eat of it: cursed *is* the ground for thy sake; in sorrow shalt thou eat *of* it all the days of thy life;

18. Thorns also and thistles shall it bring forth to thee; and thou shalt eat the herb of the field;

19. In the sweat of thy face shalt thou eat bread, till thou return unto the ground; for out of it wast thou taken: for dust thou *art*, and unto dust shalt thou return.

20. And Adam called his wife's name Eve; because she was the mother of all living.

21. Unto Adam also and to his wife did the LORD God make coats of skins, and clothed them.

22. And the LORD God said, Behold, the man is become as one of us, to know good and evil: and now, lest he put forth his hand, and take also of the tree of life, and eat, and live for ever:

23. Therefore the LORD God sent him forth from the garden of Eden, to till the ground from whence he was taken.

24. So he drove out the man; and he placed at the east of the garden of Eden Cherubims, and a flaming sword which turned every way, to keep the way of the tree of life.

Chapter 4

1. And Adam knew Eve his wife; and she conceived, and bare Cain, and said, I have gotten a man from the LORD.

2. And she again bare his brother Abel. And Abel was a keeper of sheep, but Cain was a tiller of the ground.

3. And in process of time it came to pass, that Cain brought of the fruit of the ground an offering unto the LORD.

4. And Abel, he also brought of the firstlings of his flock and of the fat thereof. And the LORD had respect unto Abel and to his offering:

5. But unto Cain and to his offering he had not respect. And Cain was very wroth, and his countenance fell.

6. And the LORD said unto Cain, Why art thou wroth? and why is thy countenance fallen?

7. If thou doest well, shalt thou not be accepted? and if thou doest not well, sin lieth at the door. And unto thee *shall be* his desire, and thou shalt rule over him.

8. And Cain talked with Abel his brother: and it came to pass, when they were in the field, that Cain rose up against Abel his brother, and slew him.

9. And the LORD said unto Cain, Where *is* Abel thy brother? And he said, I know not: *Am* I my brother's keeper?

10. And he said, What hast thou done? the voice of thy brother's blood crieth unto me from the ground.

11. And now *art* thou cursed from the earth, which hath opened her mouth to receive thy brother's blood from thy hand;

12. When thou tillest the ground, it shall not henceforth yield unto thee her strength; a fugitive and a vagabond shalt thou be in the earth.

13. And Cain said unto the LORD, My punishment *is* greater than I can bear.

14. Behold, thou hast driven me out this day from the face of the earth; and from thy face shall I

be hid; and I shall be a fugitive and a vagabond in the earth; and it shall come to pass, *that* every one that findeth me shall slay me.

15. And the LORD said unto him, Therefore whosoever slayeth Cain, vengeance shall be taken on him sevenfold. And the LORD set a mark upon Cain, lest any finding him should kill him.

16. And Cain went out from the presence of the LORD, and dwelt in the land of Nod, on the east of Eden.

17. And Cain knew his wife; and she conceived, and bare Enoch: and he builded a city, and called the name of the city, after the name of his son, Enoch.

18. And unto Enoch was born Irad: and Irad begat Mehujael: and Mehujael begat Methusael: and Methusael begat Lamech.

19. And Lamech took unto him two wives: the name of the one *was* Adah, and the name of the other Zillah.

20. And Adah bare Jabal: he was the father of such as dwell in tents, and *of such as have* cattle.

21. And his brother's name *was* Jubal: he was the father of all such as handle the harp and organ.

22. And Zillah, she also bare Tubalcain, an instructer of every artificer in brass and iron: and the sister of Tubalcain *was* Naamah.

23. And Lamech said unto his wives, Adah and Zillah, Hear my voice; ye wives of Lamech, hearken unto my speech: for I have slain a man to my wounding, and a young man to my hurt.

24. If Cain shall be avenged sevenfold, truly Lamech seventy and sevenfold.

25. And Adam knew his wife again; and she bare a son, and called his name Seth: For God, *said she*, hath appointed me another seed instead of Abel, whom Cain slew.

26. And to Seth, to him also there was born a son; and he called his name Enos: then began men to call upon the name of the LORD.

Chapter 6

1. And GOD saw that the wickedness of man *was* great in the earth, and *that* every imagination of the thoughts of his heart *was* only evil continually.

2. And it repented the LORD that he had made man on the earth, and it grieved him at his heart.

3. And the LORD said, I will destroy man whom I have created from the face of the earth; both man, and beast, and the creeping thing, and the fowls of the air; for it repenteth me that I have made them.

4. But Noah found grace in the eyes of the LORD.

5. These *are* the generations of Noah: Noah was a just man *and* perfect in his generations, *and* Noah walked with God.

6. And Noah begat three sons, Shem, Ham, and Japheth.

7. The earth also was corrupt before God, and the earth was filled with violence.

8. And God looked upon the earth, and, behold, it was corrupt; for all flesh had corrupted his way upon the earth.

9. And God said unto Noah, The end of all flesh is come before me; for the earth is filled with violence through them; and, behold, I will destroy them with the earth.

10. Make thee an ark of gopher wood; rooms shalt thou make in the ark, and shalt pitch it within and without with pitch.

11. And this *is the fashion* which thou shalt make it *of*: The length of the ark *shall be* three hundred cubits, the breadth of it fifty cubits, and the height of it thirty cubits.

12. A window shalt thou make to the ark, and in a cubit shalt thou finish it above; and the door of the ark shalt thou set in the side thereof; *with* lower, second, and third *stories* shalt thou make it.

13. And, behold, I, even I, do bring a flood of waters upon the earth, to destroy all flesh, wherein *is* the breath of life, from under heaven; *and* every thing that *is* in the earth shall die.

14. But with thee will I establish my covenant; and thou shalt come into the ark, thou, and thy sons, and thy wife, and thy sons' wives with thee.

15. And of every living thing of all flesh, two of every *sort* shalt thou bring into the ark, to keep *them* alive with thee; they shall be male and female.

16. Of fowls after their kind, and of cattle after their kind, of every creeping thing of the earth after his kind, two of every *sort* shall come unto thee, to keep *them* alive.

17. And take thou unto thee of all food that is eaten, and thou shalt gather *it* to thee; and it shall be for food for thee, and for them.

18. Thus did Noah; according to all that God commanded him, so did he.

Chapter 7

1. And the LORD said unto Noah, Come thou and all thy house into the ark; for thee have I seen righteous before me in this generation.

2. Of every clean beast thou shalt take to thee by sevens, the male and his female: and of beasts that *are* not clean by two, the male and his female.

3. Of fowls also of the air by sevens, the male and the female; to keep seed alive upon the face of all the earth.

4. For yet seven days, and I will cause it to rain upon the earth forty days and forty nights; and every living substance that I have made will I destroy from off the face of the earth.

5. And Noah did according unto all that the LORD commanded him.

6. And Noah *was* six hundred years old when the flood of waters was upon the earth.

7. And Noah went in, and his sons, and his wife, and his sons' wives with him, into the ark, because of the waters of the flood.

8. Of clean beasts, and of beasts that *are* not clean, and of fowls, and of every thing that creepeth upon the earth,

9. There went in two and two unto Noah into the ark, the male and the female, as God had commanded Noah.

10. And it came to pass after seven days, that the waters of the flood were upon the earth.

11. In the six hundredth year of Noah's life, in the second month, the seventeenth day of the month, the same day were all the fountains of the great deep broken up, and the windows of heaven were opened.

12. And the rain was upon the earth forty days and forty nights.

13. In the selfsame day entered Noah, and Shem, and Ham, and Japheth, the sons of Noah, and Noah's wife, and the three wives of his sons with them, into the ark;

14. They, and every beast after his kind, and all the cattle after their kind, and every creeping thing that creepeth upon the earth after his kind, and every fowl after his kind, every bird of every sort.

15. And they went in unto Noah into the ark, two and two of all flesh, wherein *is* the breath of life.

16. And they that went in, went in male and female of all flesh, as God had commanded him: and the LORD shut him in.

17. And the flood was forty days upon the earth; and the waters increased, and bare up the ark, and it was lift up above the earth.

18. And the waters prevailed, and were increased greatly upon the earth; and the ark went upon the face of the waters.

19. And the waters prevailed exceedingly upon the earth; and all the high hills, that *were* under the whole heaven, were covered.

20. Fifteen cubits upward did the waters prevail; and the mountains were covered.

21. And all flesh died that moved upon the earth, both of fowl, and of cattle, and of beast, and of every creeping thing that creepeth upon the earth, and every man:

22. All in whose nostrils *was* the breath of life, of all that *was* in the dry *land*, died.

23. And every living substance was destroyed which was upon the face of the ground, both man, and cattle, and the creeping things, and the fowl of the heaven; and they were destroyed from the earth: and Noah only remained *alive*, and they that *were* with him in the ark.

24. And the waters prevailed upon the earth an hundred and fifty days.

Chapter 8

1. And God remembered Noah, and every living thing, and all the cattle that *was* with him in the ark: and God made a wind to pass over the earth, and the waters asswaged;

2. The fountains also of the deep and the windows of heaven were stopped, and the rain from heaven was restrained;

3. And the waters returned from off the earth continually: and after the end of the hundred and fifty days the waters were abated.

4. And the ark rested in the seventh month, on the seventeenth day of the month, upon the mountains of Ararat.

5. And the waters decreased continually until the tenth month: in the tenth *month*, on the first *day* of the month, were the tops of the mountains seen.

6. And it came to pass at the end of forty days, that Noah opened the window of the ark which he had made:

7. And he sent forth a raven, which went forth to and fro, until the waters were dried up from off the earth.

8. Also he sent forth a dove from him, to see if the waters were abated from off the face of the ground;

9. But the dove found no rest for the sole of her foot, and she returned unto him into the ark, for the waters *were* on the face of the whole earth: then he put forth his hand, and took her, and pulled her in unto him into the ark.

10. And he stayed yet other seven days; and again he sent forth the dove out of the ark;

11. And the dove came in to him in the evening; and, lo, in her mouth *was* an olive leaf pluckt off: so Noah knew that the waters were abated from off the earth.

12. And he stayed yet other seven days; and sent forth the dove; which returned not again unto him any more.

13. And it came to pass in the six hundredth and first year, in the first *month*, the first *day* of the month, the waters were dried up from off the earth: and Noah removed the covering of the ark, and looked, and, behold, the face of the ground was dry.

14. And in the second month, on the seven and twentieth day of the month, was the earth dried.

15. And God spake unto Noah, saying,

16. Go forth of the ark, thou, and thy wife, and thy sons, and thy sons' wives with thee.

17. Bring forth with thee every living thing that *is* with thee, of all flesh, *both* of fowl, and of cattle, and of every creeping thing that creepeth upon the earth; that they may breed abundantly in the earth, and be fruitful, and multiply upon the earth.

18. And Noah went forth, and his sons, and his wife, and his sons' wives with him:

19. Every beast, every creeping thing, and every fowl, *and* whatsoever creepeth upon the earth, after their kinds, went forth out of the ark.

20. And Noah builded an altar unto the LORD; and took of every clean beast, and of every clean fowl, and offered burnt offerings on the altar.

21. And the LORD smelled a sweet savour; and the LORD said in his heart, I will not again curse the ground any more for man's sake; for the imagination of man's heart *is* evil from his youth; neither will I again smite any more every thing living, as I have done.

22. While the earth remaineth, seedtime and harvest, and cold and heat, and summer and winter, and day and night shall not cease.

Chapter 9

1. And God blessed Noah and his sons, and said unto them, Be fruitful, and multiply, and replenish the earth.

2. And the fear of you and the dread of you shall be upon every beast of the earth, and upon every fowl of the air, upon all that moveth *upon* the earth, and upon all the fishes of the sea; into your hand are they delivered.

3. Every moving thing that liveth shall be meat for you; even as the green herb have I given you all things.

4. But flesh with the life thereof, *which is* the blood thereof, shall ye not eat.

5. And surely your blood of your lives will I require; at the hand of every beast will I require it, and at the hand of man; at the hand of every man's brother will I require the life of man.

6. Whoso sheddeth man's blood, by man shall his blood be shed: for in the image of God made he man.

7. And you, be ye fruitful, and multiply; bring forth abundantly in the earth, and multiply therein.

8. And God spake unto Noah, and to his sons with him, saying,

9. And I, behold, I establish my covenant with you, and with your seed after you;

10. And with every living creature that *is* with you, of the fowl, of the cattle, and of every beast of the earth with you; from all that go out of the ark, to every beast of the earth.

11. And I will establish my covenant with you; neither shall all flesh be cut off any more by the waters of a flood; neither shall there any more be a flood to destroy the earth.

12. And God said, This *is* the token of the covenant which I make between me and you and every living creature that *is* with you, for perpetual generations:

13. I do set my bow in the cloud, and it shall be for a token of a covenant between me and the earth.

14. And it shall come to pass, when I bring a cloud over the earth, that the bow shall be seen in the cloud:

15. And I will remember my covenant, which *is* between me and you and every living creature of all flesh; and the waters shall no more become a flood to destroy all flesh.

16. And the bow shall be in the cloud; and I will look upon it, that I may remember the everlasting covenant between God and every living creature of all flesh that *is* upon the earth.

17. And God said unto Noah, This *is* the token of the covenant, which I have established between me and all flesh that *is* upon the earth.

Chapter 11

1. And the whole earth was of one language, and of one speech.

2. And it came to pass, as they journeyed from the east, that they found a plain in the land of Shinar; and they dwelt there.

3. And they said one to another, Go to, let us make brick, and burn them throughly. And they had brick for stone, and slime had they for morter.

4. And they said, Go to, let us build us a city and a tower, whose top *may reach* unto heaven; and let us make us a name, lest we be scattered abroad upon the face of the whole earth.

5. And the LORD came down to see the city and the tower, which the children of men builded.

6. And the LORD said, Behold, the people *is* one, and they have all one language; and this they begin to do: and now nothing will be restrained from them, which they have imagined to do.

7. Go to, let us go down, and there confound their language, that they may not understand one another's speech.

8. So the LORD scattered them abroad from thence upon the face of all the earth: and they left off to build the city.

9. Therefore is the name of it called Babel; because the LORD did there confound the language of all the earth: and from thence did the LORD scatter them abroad upon the face of all the earth.

Chapter 15

1. After these things the word of the LORD came unto Abram in a vision, saying, Fear not, Abram: I *am* thy shield, *and* thy exceeding great reward.

2. And Abram said, Lord GOD, what wilt thou give me, seeing I go childless, and the steward of my house *is* this Eliezer of Damascus?

3. And Abram said, Behold, to me thou hast given no seed: and, lo, one born in my house is mine heir.

4. And, behold, the word of the LORD *came* unto him, saying, This shall not be thine heir; but he that shall come forth out of thine own bowels shall be thine heir.

5. And he brought him forth abroad, and said, Look now toward heaven, and tell the stars, if thou be able to number them: and he said unto him, So shall thy seed be.

6. And he believed in the LORD; and he counted it to him for righteousness.

7. And he said unto him, I *am* the LORD that brought thee out of Ur of the Chaldees, to give thee this land to inherit it.

8. And he said, Lord GOD, whereby shall I know that I shall inherit it?

9. And he said unto him, Take me an heifer of three years old, and a she goat of three years old, and a ram of three years old, and a turtledove, and a young pigeon.

10. And he took unto him all these, and divided them in the midst, and laid each piece one against another: but the birds divided he not.

11. And when the fowls came down upon the carcases, Abram drove them away.

12. And when the sun was going down, a deep sleep fell upon Abram; and, lo, an horror of great darkness fell upon him.

13. And he said unto Abram, Know of a surety that thy seed shall be a stranger in a land *that is* not theirs, and shall serve them; and they shall afflict them four hundred years;

14. And also that nation, whom they shall serve, will I judge: and afterward shall they come out with great substance.

15. And thou shalt go to thy fathers in peace; thou shalt be buried in a good old age.

16. But in the fourth generation they shall come hither again: for the iniquity of the Amorites *is* not yet full.

17. And it came to pass, that, when the sun went down, and it was dark, behold a smoking furnace, and a burning lamp that passed between those pieces.

18. In the same day the LORD made a covenant with Abram, saying, Unto thy seed have I given this land, from the river of Egypt unto the great river, the river Euphrates:

19. The Kenites, and the Kenizzites, and the Kadmonites,

20. And the Hittites, and the Perizzites, and the Rephaims,

21. And the Amorites, and the Canaanites, and the Girgashites, and the Jebusites.

Chapter 16

1. Now Sarai Abram's wife bare him no children: and she had an handmaid, an Egyptian, whose name *was* Hagar.

2. And Sarai said unto Abram, Behold now, the LORD hath restrained me from bearing: I pray thee, go in unto my maid; it may be that I may obtain children by her. And Abram hearkened to the voice of Sarai.

3. And Sarai Abram's wife took Hagar her maid the Egyptian, after Abram had dwelt ten years in the land of Canaan, and gave her to her husband Abram to be his wife.

4. And he went in unto Hagar, and she conceived: and when she saw that she had conceived, her mistress was despised in her eyes.

5. And Sarai said unto Abram, My wrong *be* upon thee: I have given my maid into thy bosom; and when she saw that she had conceived, I was despised in her eyes: the LORD judge between me and thee.

6. But Abram said unto Sarai, Behold, thy maid *is* in thy hand; do to her as it pleaseth thee. And when Sarai dealt hardly with her, she fled from her face.

7. And the angel of the LORD found her by a fountain of water in the wilderness, by the fountain in the way to Shur.

8. And he said, Hagar, Sarai's maid, whence camest thou? and whither wilt thou go? And she said, I flee from the face of my mistress Sarai.

9. And the angel of the LORD said unto her, Return to thy mistress, and submit thyself under her hands.

10. And the angel of the LORD said unto her, I will multiply thy seed exceedingly, that it shall not be numbered for multitude.

11. And the angel of the LORD said unto her, Behold, thou *art* with child, and shalt bear a son, and shalt call his name Ishmael; because the LORD hath heard thy affliction.

12. And he will be a wild man; his hand *will be* against every man, and every man's hand against him; and he shall dwell in the presence of all his brethren.

13. And she called the name of the LORD that spake unto her, Thou God seest me: for she said, Have I also here looked after him that seeth me?

14. Wherefore the well was called Beerlahairoi; behold, *it is* between Kadesh and Bered.

15. And Hagar bare Abram a son: and Abram called his son's name, which Hagar bare, Ishmael.

16. And Abram *was* fourscore and six years old, when Hagar bare Ishmael to Abram.

Chapter 17

1. And when Abram was ninety years old and nine, the LORD appeared to Abram, and said unto him, I *am* the Almighty God; walk before me, and be thou perfect.
2. And I will make my covenant between me and thee, and will multiply thee exceedingly.
3. And Abram fell on his face: and God talked with him, saying,
4. As for me, behold, my covenant *is* with thee, and thou shalt be a father of many nations.
5. Neither shall thy name any more be called Abram, but thy name shall be Abraham; for a father of many nations have I made thee.
6. And I will make thee exceeding fruitful, and I will make nations of thee, and kings shall come out of thee.
7. And I will establish my covenant between me and thee and thy seed after thee in their generations for an everlasting covenant, to be a God unto thee, and to thy seed after thee.
8. And I will give unto thee, and to thy seed after thee, the land wherein thou art a stranger, all the land of Canaan, for an everlasting possession; and I will be their God.
9. And God said unto Abraham, Thou shalt keep my covenant therefore, thou, and thy seed after thee in their generations.
10. This *is* my covenant, which ye shall keep, between me and you and thy seed after thee; Every man child among you shall be circumcised.
11. And ye shall circumcise the flesh of your foreskin; and it shall be a token of the covenant betwixt me and you.
12. And he that is eight days old shall be circumcised among you, every man child in your generations, he that is born in the house, or bought with money of any stranger, which *is* not of thy seed.
13. He that is born in thy house, and he that is bought with thy money, must needs be circumcised: and my covenant shall be in your flesh for an everlasting covenant.
14. And the uncircumcised man child whose flesh of his foreskin is not circumcised, that soul shall be cut off from his people; he hath broken my covenant.
15. And God said unto Abraham, As for Sarai thy wife, thou shalt not call her name Sarai, but Sarah *shall* her name *be*.
16. And I will bless her, and give thee a son also of her: yea, I will bless her, and she shall be *a mother* of nations; kings of people shall be of her.
17. Then Abraham fell upon his face, and laughed, and said in his heart, Shall *a child* be born unto him that is an hundred years old? and shall Sarah, that is ninety years old, bear?
18. And Abraham said unto God, O that Ishmael might live before thee!
19. And God said, Sarah thy wife shall bear thee a son indeed; and thou shalt call his name Isaac: and I will establish my covenant with him for an everlasting covenant, *and* with his seed after him.
20. And as for Ishmael, I have heard thee: Behold, I have blessed him, and will make him fruitful, and will multiply him exceedingly; twelve princes shall he beget, and I will make him a great nation.
21. But my covenant will I establish with Isaac, which Sarah shall bear unto thee at this set time in the next year.
22. And he left off talking with him, and God went up from Abraham.
23. And Abraham took Ishmael his son, and all that were born in his house, and all that were bought with his money, every male among the men of Abraham's house; and circumcised the flesh of their foreskin in the selfsame day, as God had said unto him.
24. And Abraham *was* ninety years old and nine, when he was circumcised in the flesh of his foreskin.
25. And Ishmael his son *was* thirteen years old, when he was circumcised in the flesh of his foreskin.
26. In the selfsame day was Abraham circumcised, and Ishmael his son.

27. And all the men of his house, born in the house, and bought with money of the stranger, were circumcised with him.

Chapter 18

1. And the LORD appeared unto him in the plains of Mamre: and he sat in the tent door in the heat of the day;

2. And he lift up his eyes and looked, and, lo, three men stood by him: and when he saw *them*, he ran to meet them from the tent door, and bowed himself toward the ground,

3. And said, My Lord, if now I have found favour in thy sight, pass not away, I pray thee, from thy servant:

4. Let a little water, I pray you, be fetched, and wash your feet, and rest yourselves under the tree:

5. And I will fetch a morsel of bread, and comfort ye your hearts; after that ye shall pass on: for therefore are ye come to your servant. And they said, So do, as thou hast said.

6. And Abraham hastened into the tent unto Sarah, and said, Make ready quickly three measures of fine meal, knead *it*, and make cakes upon the hearth.

7. And Abraham ran unto the herd, and fetcht a calf tender and good, and gave *it* unto a young man; and he hasted to dress it.

8. And he took butter, and milk, and the calf which he had dressed, and set *it* before them; and he stood by them under the tree, and they did eat.

9. And they said unto him, Where *is* Sarah thy wife? And he said, Behold, in the tent.

10. And he said, I will certainly return unto thee according to the time of life; and, lo, Sarah thy wife shall have a son. And Sarah heard *it* in the tent door, which *was* behind him.

11. Now Abraham and Sarah *were* old *and* well stricken in age; *and* it ceased to be with Sarah after the manner of women.

12. Therefore Sarah laughed within herself, saying, After I am waxed old shall I have pleasure, my lord being old also?

13. And the LORD said unto Abraham, Wherefore did Sarah laugh, saying, Shall I of a surety bear a child, which am old?

14. Is any thing too hard for the LORD? At the time appointed I will return unto thee, according to the time of life, and Sarah shall have a son.

15. Then Sarah denied, saying, I laughed not; for she was afraid. And he said, Nay; but thou didst laugh.

16. And the men rose up from thence, and looked toward Sodom: and Abraham went with them to bring them on the way.

17. And the LORD said, Shall I hide from Abraham that thing which I do;

18. Seeing that Abraham shall surely become a great and mighty nation, and all the nations of the earth shall be blessed in him?

19. For I know him, that he will command his children and his household after him, and they shall keep the way of the LORD, to do justice and judgment; that the LORD may bring upon Abraham that which he hath spoken of him.

20. And the LORD said, Because the cry of Sodom and Gomorrah is great, and because their sin is very grievous;

21. I will go down now, and see whether they have done altogether according to the cry of it, which is come unto me; and if not, I will know.

22. And the men turned their faces from thence, and went toward Sodom: but Abraham stood yet before the LORD.

23. And Abraham drew near, and said, Wilt thou also destroy the righteous with the wicked?

24. Peradventure there be fifty righteous within the city: wilt thou also destroy and not spare the place for the fifty righteous that *are* therein?

25. That be far from thee to do after this manner, to slay the righteous with the wicked: and that the righteous should be as the wicked, that be far from thee: Shall not the Judge of all the earth do right?

26. And the LORD said, If I find in Sodom fifty righteous within the city, then I will spare all the place for their sakes.

27. And Abraham answered and said, Behold now, I have taken upon me to speak unto the Lord, which *am but* dust and ashes:

28. Peradventure there shall lack five of the fifty righteous: wilt thou destroy all the city for *lack*

of five? And he said, If I find there forty and five, I will not destroy *it*.

29. And he spake unto him yet again, and said, Peradventure there shall be forty found there. And he said, I will not do *it* for forty's sake.

30. And he said *unto him*, Oh let not the Lord be angry, and I will speak: Peradventure there shall thirty be found there. And he said, I will not do *it*, if I find thirty there.

31. And he said, Behold now, I have taken upon me to speak unto the Lord: Peradventure there shall be twenty found there. And he said, I will not destroy *it* for twenty's sake.

32. And he said, Oh let not the Lord be angry, and I will speak yet but this once: Peradventure ten shall be found there. And he said, I will not destroy *it* for ten's sake.

33. And the LORD went his way, as soon as he had left communing with Abraham: and Abraham returned unto his place.

Chapter 21

1. And the LORD visited Sarah as he had said, and the LORD did unto Sarah as he had spoken.

2. For Sarah conceived, and bare Abraham a son in his old age, at the set time of which God had spoken to him.

3. And Abraham called the name of his son that was born unto him, whom Sarah bare to him, Isaac.

4. And Abraham circumcised his son Isaac being eight days old, as God had commanded him.

5. And Abraham was an hundred years old, when his son Isaac was born unto him.

6. And Sarah said, God hath made me to laugh, *so that* all that hear will laugh with me.

7. And she said, Who would have said unto Abraham, that Sarah should have given children suck? for I have born *him* a son in his old age.

8. And the child grew, and was weaned: and Abraham made a great feast the *same* day that Isaac was weaned.

9. And Sarah saw the son of Hagar the Egyptian, which she had born unto Abraham, mocking.

10. Wherefore she said unto Abraham, Cast out this bondwoman and her son: for the son of this bondwoman shall not be heir with my son, *even* with Isaac.

11. And the thing was very grievous in Abraham's sight because of his son.

12. And God said unto Abraham, Let it not be grievous in thy sight because of the lad, and because of thy bondwoman; in all that Sarah hath said unto thee, hearken unto her voice; for in Isaac shall thy seed be called.

13. And also of the son of the bondwoman will I make a nation, because he *is* thy seed.

14. And Abraham rose up early in the morning, and took bread, and a bottle of water, and gave *it* unto Hagar, putting *it* on her shoulder, and the child, and sent her away: and she departed, and wandered in the wilderness of Beersheba.

15. And the water was spent in the bottle, and she cast the child under one of the shrubs.

16. And she went, and sat her down over against *him* a good way off, as it were a bowshot: for she said, Let me not see the death of the child. And she sat over against *him*, and lift up her voice, and wept.

17. And God heard the voice of the lad; and the angel of God called to Hagar out of heaven, and said unto her, What aileth thee, Hagar? fear not; for God hath heard the voice of the lad where he *is*.

18. Arise, lift up the lad, and hold him in thine hand; for I will make him a great nation.

19. And God opened her eyes, and she saw a well of water; and she went, and filled the bottle with water, and gave the lad drink.

20. And God was with the lad; and he grew, and dwelt in the wilderness, and became an archer.

21. And he dwelt in the wilderness of Paran: and his mother took him a wife out of the land of Egypt.

22. And it came to pass at that time, that Abimelech and Phichol the chief captain of his host spake unto Abraham, saying, God *is* with thee in all that thou doest:

23. Now therefore swear unto me here by God that thou wilt not deal falsely with me, nor with my son, nor with my son's son: *but* according to the kindness that I have done unto thee, thou shalt

do unto me, and to the land wherein thou hast sojourned.

24. And Abraham said, I will swear.

25. And Abraham reproved Abimelech because of a well of water, which Abimelech's servants had violently taken away.

26. And Abimelech said, I wot not who hath done this thing: neither didst thou tell me, neither yet heard I *of it*, but to day.

27. And Abraham took sheep and oxen, and gave them unto Abimelech; and both of them made a covenant.

28. And Abraham set seven ewe lambs of the flock by themselves.

29. And Abimelech said unto Abraham, What *mean* these seven ewe lambs which thou hast set by themselves?

30. And he said, For *these* seven ewe lambs shalt thou take of my hand, that they may be a witness unto me, that I have digged this well.

31. Wherefore he called that place Beersheba; because there they sware both of them.

32. Thus they made a covenant at Beersheba: then Abimelech rose up, and Phichol the chief captain of his host, and they returned into the land of the Philistines.

33. And *Abraham* planted a grove in Beersheba, and called there on the name of the LORD, the everlasting God.

34. And Abraham sojourned in the Philistines' land many days.

Chapter 22

1. And it came to pass after these things, that God did tempt Abraham, and said unto him, Abraham: and he said, Behold, *here* I am.

2. And he said, Take now thy son, thine only *son* Isaac, whom thou lovest, and get thee into the land of Moriah; and offer him there for a burnt offering upon one of the mountains which I will tell thee of.

3. And Abraham rose up early in the morning, and saddled his ass, and took two of his young men with him, and Isaac his son, and clave the wood for the burnt offering, and rose up, and went unto the place of which God had told him.

4. Then on the third day Abraham lifted up his eyes, and saw the place afar off.

5. And Abraham said unto his young men, Abide ye here with the ass; and I and the lad will go yonder and worship, and come again to you.

6. And Abraham took the wood of the burnt offering, and laid *it* upon Isaac his son; and he took the fire in his hand, and a knife; and they went both of them together.

7. And Isaac spake unto Abraham his father, and said, My father: and he said, Here *am* I, my son. And he said, Behold the fire and the wood: but where *is* the lamb for a burnt offering?

8. And Abraham said, My son, God will provide himself a lamb for a burnt offering: so they went both of them together.

9. And they came to the place which God had told him of; and Abraham built an altar there, and laid the wood in order, and bound Isaac his son, and laid him on the altar upon the wood.

10. And Abraham stretched forth his hand, and took the knife to slay his son.

11. And the angel of the LORD called unto him out of heaven, and said, Abraham, Abraham: and he said, Here *am* I.

12. And he said, Lay not thine hand upon the lad, neither do thou any thing unto him: for now I know that thou fearest God, seeing thou hast not withheld thy son, thine only *son* from me.

13. And Abraham lifted up his eyes, and looked, and behold behind *him* a ram caught in a thicket by his horns: and Abraham went and took the ram, and offered him up for a burnt offering in the stead of his son.

14. And Abraham called the name of that place Jehovahjireh: as it is said *to* this day, In the mount of the LORD it shall be seen.

15. And the angel of the LORD called unto Abraham out of heaven the second time,

16. And said, By myself have I sworn, saith the LORD, for because thou hast done this thing, and hast not withheld thy son, thine only *son*:

17. That in blessing I will bless thee, and in multiplying I will multiply thy seed as the stars of the heaven, and as the sand which *is* upon the sea shore; and thy seed shall possess the gate of his enemies;

18. And in thy seed shall all the nations of the earth be blessed; because thou hast obeyed my voice.

DISCUSSION QUESTIONS

1. Compare the two versions of the story of creation in *Genesis* Chapters 1 and 2. How do they differ?

2. Consider the role of the serpent. Does its role in the temptation of Eve relieve humankind of responsibility for the expulsion from Eden?

3. What are the implications of the expulsion from Eden?

4. Why would God unleash the flood described in the story of Noah? To what extent does Noah's experience represent a second opportunity?

5. What is the promise God makes to Noah? Why would he make such a promise?

6. Consider God's punishment in the Tower of Babel story. What does it say about the power of human language? Is the existence of many languages, in fact, a punishment?

7. Imagine Abraham's journey with Isaac. What might have he been thinking? What would Isaac think? What would Sarah think?

JOB

Selected Chapters

In the Book of *Job*, perhaps the supreme literary accomplishment in the Hebrew Bible, Job's desire to understand why God works as he does remains unsatisfied. After a lifetime of piety and unquestioned faith in God, Job at first seems to have been rewarded with riches for his exemplary ways. But then one tragedy after another besets him, leaving him without his fortune and family and suffering from a terrible disease. As readers of the book's first chapters, *we* know that God has brought these evils onto Job to prove to Satan that at least one person will retain faith in God no matter how dreadful the situation may be. But Job does not share our knowledge; he never knows why God has tormented him. Rather, he proclaims that his "desire is that the Almighty should answer me, and that mine adversary had written a book."

Job's extended dialogue with his friends contributes to the story's dramatic tension. In many ways, Job's real conflict lies with his orthodox companions, rather than with God. Three of them offer conventional reasons why Job suffers; they assume that misfortune must betray some misdeed or blasphemy for which the evildoer is punished. But Job insists he has done nothing wrong, claiming that God "knowest that I am not wicked." Why, then, does he suffer? A fourth friend, Elihu, suggests that Job misunderstands the nature of God. He "is greater than man," Elihu claims, and "gives no account of his doings." From a whirlwind, God finally speaks to Job, but He does not provide an answer to his faithful servant's plea. Job never understands the reasons for his suffering, but he does come to see that God knows things that he himself will never know. The perennial problem of why people suffer remains a mystery. At the same time, Job's acceptance of that mystery proves fortuitous, as God restores him to his former wealthy state. The orthodox friends who assume that God's behavior can be explained are punished, while Job, who insisted that God's actions did not make sense, is rewarded.

Chapter 1

1. There was a man in the land of Uz, whose name *was* Job; and that man was perfect and upright, and one that feared God, and eschewed evil.
2. And there were born unto him seven sons and three daughters.
3. His substance also was seven thousand sheep, and three thousand camels, and five hundred yoke of oxen, and five hundred she asses, and a very great household; so that this man was the greatest of all the men of the east.
4. And his sons went and feasted *in their* houses, every one his day; and sent and called for their three sisters to eat and to drink with them.
5. And it was so, when the days of *their* feasting were gone about, that Job sent and sanctified them, and rose up early in the morning, and offered burnt offerings *according* to the number of them all: for Job said, It may be that my sons have sinned, and cursed God in their hearts. Thus did Job continually.
6. Now there was a day when the sons of God came to present themselves before the LORD, and Satan came also among them.
7. And the LORD said unto Satan, Whence comest thou? Then Satan answered the LORD, and said, From going to and fro in the earth, and from walking up and down in it.
8. And the LORD said unto Satan, Hast thou considered my servant Job, that *there is* none like him in the earth, a perfect and an upright man, one that feareth God, and escheweth evil?
9. Then Satan answered the LORD, and said, Doth Job fear God for nought?
10. Hast not thou made an hedge about him, and about his house, and about all that he hath on every side? thou hast blessed the work of his hands, and his substance is increased in the land.
11. But put forth thine hand now, and touch all that he hath, and he will curse thee to thy face.
12. And the LORD said unto Satan, Behold, all that he hath *is* in thy power; only upon himself put not forth thine hand. So Satan went forth from the presence of the LORD.
13. And there was a day when his sons and his daughters *were* eating and drinking wine in their eldest brother's house:
14. And there came a messenger unto Job, and said, The oxen were plowing, and the asses feeding beside them:
15. And the Sabeans fell *upon them*, and took them away; yea, they have slain the servants with the edge of the sword; and I only am escaped alone to tell thee.
16. While he *was* yet speaking, there came also another, and said, The fire of God is fallen from heaven, and hath burned up the sheep, and the servants, and consumed them; and I only am escaped alone to tell thee.
17. While he *was* yet speaking, there came also another, and said, The Chaldeans made out three bands, and fell upon the camels, and have carried them away, yea, and slain the servants with the edge of the sword; and I only am escaped alone to tell thee.
18. While he *was* yet speaking, there came also another, and said, Thy sons and thy daughters *were* eating and drinking wine in their eldest brother's house:
19. And, behold, there came a great wind from the wilderness, and smote the four corners of the house, and it fell upon the young men, and they are dead; and I only am escaped alone to tell thee.
20. Then Job arose, and rent his mantle, and shaved his head, and fell down upon the ground, and worshipped,
21. And said, Naked came I out of my mother's womb, and naked shall I return thither: the LORD gave, and the LORD hath taken away; blessed be the name of the LORD.

22. In all this Job sinned not, nor charged God foolishly.

Chapter 2

1. Again there was a day when the sons of God came to present themselves before the LORD, and Satan came also among them to present himself before the LORD.
2. And the LORD said unto Satan, From whence comest thou? And Satan answered the LORD, and said, From going to and fro in the earth, and from walking up and down in it.
3. And the LORD said unto Satan, Hast thou considered my servant Job, that *there is* none like him in the earth, a perfect and an upright man, one that feareth God, and escheweth evil? and still he holdeth fast his integrity, although thou movedst me against him, to destroy him without cause.
4. And Satan answered the LORD, and said, Skin for skin, yea, all that a man hath will he give for his life.
5. But put forth thine hand now, and touch his bone and his flesh, and he will curse thee to thy face.
6. And the LORD said unto Satan, Behold, he *is* in thine hand; but save his life.
7. So went Satan forth from the presence of the LORD, and smote Job with sore boils from the sole of his foot unto his crown.
8. And he took him a potsherd to scrape himself withal; and he sat down among the ashes.
9. Then said his wife unto him, Dost thou still retain thine integrity? curse God, and die.
10. But he said unto her, Thou speakest as one of the foolish women speaketh. What? shall we receive good at the hand of God, and shall we not receive evil? In all this did not Job sin with his lips.
11. Now when Job's three friends heard of all this evil that was come upon him, they came every one from his own place; Eliphaz the Temanite, and Bildad the Shuhite, and Zophar the Naamathite: for they had made an appointment together to come to mourn with him and to comfort him.
12. And when they lifted up their eyes afar off, and knew him not, they lifted up their voice, and wept; and they rent every one his mantle, and sprinkled dust upon their heads toward heaven.
13. So they sat down with him upon the ground seven days and seven nights, and none spake a word unto him: for they saw that *his* grief was very great.

Chapter 3

1. After this opened Job his mouth, and cursed his day.
2. And Job spake, and said,
3. Let the day perish wherein I was born, and the night *in which* it was said, There is a man child conceived.
4. Let that day be darkness; let not God regard it from above, neither let the light shine upon it.
5. Let darkness and the shadow of death stain it; let a cloud dwell upon it; let the blackness of the day terrify it.
6. As *for* that night, let darkness seize upon it; let it not be joined unto the days of the year, let it not come into the number of the months.
7. Lo, let that night be solitary, let no joyful voice come therein.
8. Let them curse it that curse the day, who are ready to raise up their mourning.
9. Let the stars of the twilight thereof be dark; let it look for light, but *have* none; neither let it see the dawning of the day:
10. Because it shut not up the doors of my *mother's* womb, nor hid sorrow from mine eyes.
11. Why died I not from the womb? *why* did I *not* give up the ghost when I came out of the belly?
12. Why did the knees prevent me? or why the breasts that I should suck?
13. For now should I have lain still and been quiet, I should have slept: then had I been at rest,
14. With kings and counsellors of the earth, which built desolate places for themselves;
15. Or with princes that had gold, who filled their houses with silver:
16. Or as an hidden untimely birth I had not been; as infants *which* never saw light.
17. There the wicked cease *from* troubling; and there the weary be at rest.

18. *There* the prisoners rest together; they hear not the voice of the oppressor.
19. The small and great are there; and the servant *is* free from his master.
20. Wherefore is light given to him that is in misery, and life unto the bitter *in* soul;
21. Which long for death, but it *cometh* not; and dig for it more than for hid treasures;
22. Which rejoice exceedingly, *and* are glad, when they can find the grave?
23. *Why is light given* to a man whose way is hid, and whom God hath hedged in?
24. For my sighing cometh before I eat, and my roarings are poured out like the waters.
25. For the thing which I greatly feared is come upon me, and that which I was afraid of is come unto me.
26. I was not in safety, neither had I rest, neither was I quiet; yet trouble came.

Chapter 4

1. Then Eliphaz the Temanite answered and said,
2. *If* we assay to commune with thee, wilt thou be grieved? but who can withhold himself from speaking?
3. Behold, thou hast instructed many, and thou hast strengthened the weak hands.
4. Thy words have upholden him that was falling, and thou hast strengthened the feeble knees.
5. But now it is come upon thee, and thou faintest; it toucheth thee, and thou art troubled.
6. *Is* not *this* thy fear, thy confidence, thy hope, and the uprightness of thy ways?
7. Remember, I pray thee, who *ever* perished, being innocent? or where were the righteous cut off?
8. Even as I have seen, they that plow iniquity, and sow wickedness, reap the same.
9. By the blast of God they perish, and by the breath of his nostrils are they consumed.
10. The roaring of the lion, and the voice of the fierce lion, and the teeth of the young lions, are broken.
11. The old lion perisheth for lack of prey, and the stout lion's whelps are scattered abroad.
12. Now a thing was secretly brought to me, and mine ear received a little thereof.

13. In thoughts from the visions of the night, when deep sleep falleth on men,
14. Fear came upon me, and trembling, which made all my bones to shake.
15. Then a spirit passed before my face; the hair of my flesh stood up:
16. It stood still, but I could not discern the form thereof: an image *was* before mine eyes, *there was* silence, and I heard a voice, *saying,*
17. Shall mortal man be more just than God? shall a man be more pure than his maker?
18. Behold, he put no trust in his servants; and his angels he charged with folly:
19. How much less *in* them that dwell in houses of clay, whose foundation *is* in the dust, *which* are crushed before the moth?
20. They are destroyed from morning to evening: they perish for ever without any regarding *it.*
21. Doth not their excellency *which is* in them go away? they die, even without wisdom.

Chapter 5

1. Call now, if there be any that will answer thee; and to which of the saints wilt thou turn?
2. For wrath killeth the foolish man, and envy slayeth the silly one.
3. I have seen the foolish taking root: but suddenly I cursed his habitation.
4. His children are far from safety, and they are crushed in the gate, neither *is there* any to deliver *them.*
5. Whose harvest the hungry eateth up, and taketh it even out of the thorns, and the robber swalloweth up their substance.
6. Although affliction cometh not forth of the dust, neither doth trouble spring out of the ground;
7. Yet man is born unto trouble, as the sparks fly upward.
8. I would seek unto God, and unto God would I commit my cause:
9. Which doeth great things and unsearchable; marvellous things without number:
10. Who giveth rain upon the earth, and sendeth waters upon the fields:
11. To set up on high those that be low; that those which mourn may be exalted to safety.

12. He disappointeth the devices of the crafty, so that their hands cannot perform *their* enterprise.

13. He taketh the wise in their own craftiness: and the counsel of the froward is carried headlong.

14. They meet with darkness in the daytime, and grope in the noonday as in the night.

15. But he saveth the poor from the sword, from their mouth, and from the hand of the mighty.

16. So the poor hath hope, and iniquity stoppeth her mouth.

17. Behold, happy *is* the man whom God correcteth: therefore despise not thou the chastening of the Almighty:

18. For he maketh sore, and bindeth up: he woundeth, and his hands make whole.

19. He shall deliver thee in six troubles: yea, in seven there shall no evil touch thee.

20. In famine he shall redeem thee from death: and in war from the power of the sword.

21. Thou shalt be hid from the scourge of the tongue: neither shalt thou be afraid of destruction when it cometh.

22. At destruction and famine thou shalt laugh: neither shalt thou be afraid of the beasts of the earth.

23. For thou shalt be in league with the stones of the field: and the beasts of the field shall be at peace with thee.

24. And thou shalt know that thy tabernacle *shall be* in peace; and thou shalt visit thy habitation, and shalt not sin.

25. Thou shalt know also that thy seed *shall be* great, and thine offspring as the grass of the earth.

26. Thou shalt come to *thy* grave in a full age, like as a shock of corn cometh in in his season.

27. Lo this, we have searched it, so it *is*; hear it, and know thou *it* for thy good.

Chapter 6

1. But Job answered and said,

2. Oh that my grief were throughly weighed, and my calamity laid in the balances together!

3. For now it would be heavier than the sand of the sea: therefore my words are swallowed up.

4. For the arrows of the Almighty *are* within me, the poison whereof drinketh up my spirit: the terrors of God do set themselves in array against me.

5. Doth the wild ass bray when he hath grass? or loweth the ox over his fodder?

6. Can that which is unsavoury be eaten without salt? or is there *any* taste in the white of an egg?

7. The things *that* my soul refused to touch *are* as my sorrowful meat.

8. Oh that I might have my request; and that God would grant *me* the thing that I long for!

9. Even that it would please God to destroy me; that he would let loose his hand, and cut me off!

10. Then should I yet have comfort; yea, I would harden myself in sorrow: let him not spare; for I have not concealed the words of the Holy One.

11. What *is* my strength, that I should hope? and what *is* mine end, that I should prolong my life?

12. *Is* my strength the strength of stones? or *is* my flesh of brass?

13. *Is* not my help in me? and is wisdom driven quite from me?

14. To him that is afflicted pity *should be shewed* from his friend; but he forsaketh the fear of the Almighty.

15. My brethren have dealt deceitfully as a brook, *and* as the stream of brooks they pass away;

16. Which are blackish by reason of the ice, *and* wherein the snow is hid:

17. What time they wax warm, they vanish: when it is hot, they are consumed out of their place.

18. The paths of their way are turned aside; they go to nothing, and perish.

19. The troops of Tema looked, the companies of Sheba waited for them.

20. They were confounded because they had hoped; they came thither, and were ashamed.

21. For now ye are nothing; ye see *my* casting down, and are afraid.

22. Did I say, Bring unto me? or, Give a reward for me of your substance?

23. Or, Deliver me from the enemy's hand? or, Redeem me from the hand of the mighty?

24. Teach me, and I will hold my tongue: and cause me to understand wherein I have erred.

25. How forcible are right words! but what doth your arguing reprove?

26. Do ye imagine to reprove words, and the speeches of one that is desperate, *which are* as wind?

27. Yea, ye overwhelm the fatherless, and ye dig *a pit* for your friend.

28. Now therefore be content, look upon me; for *it is* evident unto you if I lie.

29. Return, I pray you, let it not be iniquity; yea, return again, my righteousness *is* in it.

30. Is there iniquity in my tongue? cannot my taste discern perverse things?

Chapter 7

1. *Is there* not an appointed time to man upon earth? *are not* his days also like the days of an hireling?

2. As a servant earnestly desireth the shadow, and as an hireling looketh for *the reward of* his work:

3. So am I made to possess months of vanity, and wearisome nights are appointed to me.

4. When I lie down, I say, When shall I arise, and the night be gone? and I am full of tossings to and fro unto the dawning of the day.

5. My flesh is clothed with worms and clods of dust; my skin is broken, and become loathsome.

6. My days are swifter than a weaver's shuttle, and are spent without hope.

7. O remember that my life *is* wind: mine eye shall no more see good.

8. The eye of him that hath seen me shall see me no *more*: thine eyes *are* upon me, and I *am* not.

9. *As* the cloud is consumed and vanisheth away: so he that goeth down to the grave shall come up no *more*.

10. He shall return no more to his house, neither shall his place know him any more.

11. Therefore I will not refrain my mouth; I will speak in the anguish of my spirit; I will complain in the bitterness of my soul.

12. *Am* I a sea, or a whale, that thou settest a watch over me?

13. When I say, My bed shall comfort me, my couch shall ease my complaint;

14. Then thou scarest me with dreams, and terrifiest me through visions:

15. So that my soul chooseth strangling, *and* death rather than my life.

16. I loathe *it*; I would not live alway: let me alone; for my days *are* vanity.

17. What *is* man, that thou shouldest magnify him? and that thou shouldest set thine heart upon him?

18. And *that* thou shouldest visit him every morning, *and* try him every moment?

19. How long wilt thou not depart from me, nor let me alone till I swallow down my spittle?

20. I have sinned; what shall I do unto thee, O thou preserver of men? why hast thou set me as a mark against thee, so that I am a burden to myself?

21. And why dost thou not pardon my transgression, and take away mine iniquity? for now shall I sleep in the dust; and thou shalt seek me in the morning, but I *shall* not *be*.

Chapter 8

1. Then answered Bildad the Shuhite, and said,

2. How long wilt thou speak these *things*? and *how long shall* the words of thy mouth *be like* a strong wind?

3. Doth God pervert judgment? or doth the Almighty pervert justice?

4. If thy children have sinned against him, and he have cast them away for their transgression;

5. If thou wouldest seek unto God betimes, and make thy supplication to the Almighty;

6. If thou *wert* pure and upright; surely now he would awake for thee, and make the habitation of thy righteousness prosperous.

7. Though thy beginning was small, yet thy latter end should greatly increase.

8. For enquire, I pray thee, of the former age, and prepare thyself to the search of their fathers:

9. (For we *are but of* yesterday, and know nothing, because our days upon earth *are* a shadow:)

10. Shall not they teach thee, *and* tell thee, and utter words out of their heart?

11. Can the rush grow up without mire? can the flag grow without water?

12. Whilst it *is* yet in his greenness, *and* not cut down, it withereth before any *other* herb.

13. So *are* the paths of all that forget God; and the hypocrite's hope shall perish:

14. Whose hope shall be cut off, and whose trust *shall be* a spider's web.

15. He shall lean upon his house, but it shall not stand: he shall hold it fast, but it shall not endure.

16. He *is* green before the sun, and his branch shooteth forth in his garden.

17. His roots are wrapped about the heap, *and* seeth the place of stones.

18. If he destroy him from his place, then *it* shall deny him, *saying*, I have not seen thee.

19. Behold, this *is* the joy of his way, and out of the earth shall others grow.

20. Behold, God will not cast away a perfect *man*, neither will he help the evil doers:

21. Till he fill thy mouth with laughing, and thy lips with rejoicing.

22. They that hate thee shall be clothed with shame; and the dwelling place of the wicked shall come to nought.

Chapter 9

1. Then Job answered and said,

2. I know *it is* so of a truth: but how should man be just with God?

3. If he will contend with him, he cannot answer him one of a thousand.

4. *He is* wise in heart, and mighty in strength: who hath hardened *himself* against him, and hath prospered?

5. Which removeth the mountains, and they know not: which overturneth them in his anger.

6. Which shaketh the earth out of her place, and the pillars thereof tremble.

7. Which commandeth the sun, and it riseth not; and sealeth up the stars.

8. Which alone spreadeth out the heavens, and treadeth upon the waves of the sea.

9. Which maketh Arcturus, Orion, and Pleiades, and the chambers of the south.

10. Which doeth great things past finding out; yea, and wonders without number.

11. Lo, he goeth by me, and I see *him* not: he passeth on also, but I perceive him not.

12. Behold, he taketh away, who can hinder him? who will say unto him, What doest thou?

13. *If* God will not withdraw his anger, the proud helpers do stoop under him.

14. How much less shall I answer him, *and* choose out my words *to reason* with him?

15. Whom, though I were righteous, *yet* would I not answer, *but* I would make supplication to my judge.

16. If I had called, and he had answered me; *yet* would I not believe that he had hearkened unto my voice.

17. For he breaketh me with a tempest, and multiplieth my wounds without cause.

18. He will not suffer me to take my breath, but filleth me with bitterness.

19. If *I speak* of strength, lo, *he is* strong: and if of judgment, who shall set me a time *to plead*?

20. If I justify myself, mine own mouth shall condemn me: *if I say*, I *am* perfect, it shall also prove me perverse.

21. *Though* I *were* perfect, *yet* would I not know my soul: I would despise my life.

22. This *is* one *thing*, therefore I said *it*, He destroyeth the perfect and the wicked.

23. If the scourge slay suddenly, he will laugh at the trial of the innocent.

24. The earth is given into the hand of the wicked: he covereth the faces of the judges thereof; if not, where, *and* who *is* he?

25. Now my days are swifter than a post: they flee away, they see no good.

26. They are passed away as the swift ships: as the eagle *that* hasteth to the prey.

27. If I say, I will forget my complaint, I will leave off my heaviness, and comfort *myself*:

28. I am afraid of all my sorrows, I know that thou wilt not hold me innocent.

29. *If* I be wicked, why then labour I in vain?

30. If I wash myself with snow water, and make my hands never so clean;

31. Yet shalt thou plunge me in the ditch, and mine own clothes shall abhor me.

32. For *he is* not a man, as I *am, that* I should answer him, *and* we should come together in judgment.

33. Neither is there any daysman betwixt us, *that* might lay his hand upon us both.

34. Let him take his rod away from me, and let not his fear terrify me:

35. *Then* would I speak, and not fear him; but *it is* not so with me.

Chapter 10

1. My soul is weary of my life; I will leave my complaint upon myself; I will speak in the bitterness of my soul.

2. I will say unto God, Do not condemn me; shew me wherefore thou contendest with me.

3. *Is it* good unto thee that thou shouldest oppress, that thou shouldest despise the work of thine hands, and shine upon the counsel of the wicked?

4. Hast thou eyes of flesh? or seest thou as man seeth?

5. *Are* thy days as the days of man? *are* thy years as man's days,

6. That thou enquirest after mine iniquity, and searchest after my sin?

7. Thou knowest that I am not wicked; and *there is* none that can deliver out of thine hand.

8. Thine hands have made me and fashioned me together round about; yet thou dost destroy me.

9. Remember, I beseech thee, that thou hast made me as the clay; and wilt thou bring me into dust again?

10. Hast thou not poured me out as milk, and curdled me like cheese?

11. Thou hast clothed me with skin and flesh, and hast fenced me with bones and sinews.

12. Thou hast granted me life and favour, and thy visitation hath preserved my spirit.

13. And these *things* hast thou hid in thine heart: I know that this *is* with thee.

14. If I sin, then thou markest me, and thou wilt not acquit me from mine iniquity.

15. If I be wicked, woe unto me; and *if* I be righteous, *yet* will I not lift up my head. *I am* full of confusion; therefore see thou mine affliction;

16. For it increaseth. Thou huntest me as a fierce lion: and again thou shewest thyself marvellous upon me.

17. Thou renewest thy witnesses against me, and increasest thine indignation upon me; changes and war *are* against me.

18. Wherefore then hast thou brought me forth out of the womb? Oh that I had given up the ghost, and no eye had seen me!

19. I should have been as though I had not been; I should have been carried from the womb to the grave.

20. *Are* not my days few? cease *then, and* let me alone, that I may take comfort a little,

21. Before I go *whence* I shall not return, *even* to the land of darkness and the shadow of death;

22. A land of darkness, as darkness *itself; and* of the shadow of death, without any order, and *where* the light *is* as darkness.

Chapter 11

1. Then answered Zophar the Naamathite, and said,

2. Should not the multitude of words be answered? and should a man full of talk be justified?

3. Should thy lies make men hold their peace? and when thou mockest, shall no man make thee ashamed?

4. For thou hast said, My doctrine *is* pure, and I am clean in thine eyes.

5. But oh that God would speak, and open his lips against thee;

6. And that he would shew thee the secrets of wisdom, that *they are* double to that which is! Know therefore that God exacteth of thee *less* than thine iniquity *deserveth*.

7. Canst thou by searching find out God? canst thou find out the Almighty unto perfection?

8. *It is* as high as heaven; what canst thou do? deeper than hell; what canst thou know?

9. The measure thereof *is* longer than the earth, and broader than the sea.

10. If he cut off, and shut up, or gather together, then who can hinder him?

11. For he knoweth vain men: he seeth wickedness also; will he not then consider *it*?

12. For vain man would be wise, though man be born *like* a wild ass's colt.

13. If thou prepare thine heart, and stretch out thine hands toward him;

14. If iniquity *be* in thine hand, put it far away, and let not wickedness dwell in thy tabernacles.

15. For then shalt thou lift up thy face without spot; yea, thou shalt be stedfast, and shalt not fear:

16. Because thou shalt forget *thy* misery, *and* remember *it* as waters *that* pass away:

17. And *thine* age shall be clearer than the noonday; thou shalt shine forth, thou shalt be as the morning.

18. And thou shalt be secure, because there is hope; yea, thou shalt dig *about thee, and* thou shalt take thy rest in safety.

19. Also thou shalt lie down, and none shall make *thee* afraid; yea, many shall make suit unto thee.

20. But the eyes of the wicked shall fail, and they shall not escape, and their hope *shall be as* the giving up of the ghost.

Chapter 12

1. And Job answered and said,

2. No doubt but ye *are* the people, and wisdom shall die with you.

3. But I have understanding as well as you; I *am* not inferior to you: yea, who knoweth not such things as these?

4. I am *as* one mocked of his neighbour, who calleth upon God, and he answereth him: the just upright *man is* laughed to scorn.

5. He that is ready to slip with *his* feet *is as* a lamp despised in the thought of him that is at ease.

6. The tabernacles of robbers prosper, and they that provoke God are secure; into whose hand God bringeth *abundantly*.

7. But ask now the beasts, and they shall teach thee; and the fowls of the air, and they shall tell thee:

8. Or speak to the earth, and it shall teach thee: and the fishes of the sea shall declare unto thee.

9. Who knoweth not in all these that the hand of the LORD hath wrought this?

10. In whose hand *is* the soul of every living thing, and the breath of all mankind.

11. Doth not the ear try words? and the mouth taste his meat?

12. With the ancient *is* wisdom; and in length of days understanding.

13. With him *is* wisdom and strength, he hath counsel and understanding.

14. Behold, he breaketh down, and it cannot be built again: he shutteth up a man, and there can be no opening.

15. Behold, he withholdeth the waters, and they dry up: also he sendeth them out, and they overturn the earth.

16. With him *is* strength and wisdom: the deceived and the deceiver *are* his.

17. He leadeth counsellors away spoiled, and maketh the judges fools.

18. He looseth the bond of kings, and girdeth their loins with a girdle.

19. He leadeth princes away spoiled, and overthroweth the mighty.

20. He removeth away the speech of the trusty, and taketh away the understanding of the aged.

21. He poureth contempt upon princes, and weakeneth the strength of the mighty.

22. He discovereth deep things out of darkness, and bringeth out to light the shadow of death.

23. He increaseth the nations, and destroyeth them: he enlargeth the nations, and straiteneth them *again*.

24. He taketh away the heart of the chief of the people of the earth, and causeth them to wander in a wilderness *where there is* no way.

25. They grope in the dark without light, and he maketh them to stagger like *a* drunken *man*.

Chapter 13

1. Lo, mine eye hath seen all *this*, mine ear hath heard and understood it.

2. What ye know, *the same* do I know also: I *am* not inferior unto you.

3. Surely I would speak to the Almighty, and I desire to reason with God.

4. But ye *are* forgers of lies, ye *are* all physicians of no value.

5. O that ye would altogether hold your peace! and it should be your wisdom.

6. Hear now my reasoning, and hearken to the pleadings of my lips.

7. Will ye speak wickedly for God? and talk deceitfully for him?

8. Will ye accept his person? will ye contend for God?

9. Is it good that he should search you out? or as one man mocketh another, do ye *so* mock him?

10. He will surely reprove you, if ye do secretly accept persons.

11. Shall not his excellency make you afraid? and his dread fall upon you?

12. Your remembrances *are* like unto ashes, your bodies to bodies of clay.

13. Hold your peace, let me alone, that I may speak, and let come on me what *will*.

14. Wherefore do I take my flesh in my teeth, and put my life in mine hand?

15. Though he slay me, yet will I trust in him: but I will maintain mine own ways before him.

16. He also *shall be* my salvation: for an hypocrite shall not come before him.

17. Hear diligently my speech, and my declaration with your ears.

18. Behold now, I have ordered *my* cause; I know that I shall be justified.

19. Who *is* he *that* will plead with me? for now, if I hold my tongue, I shall give up the ghost.

20. Only do not two *things* unto me: then will I not hide myself from thee.

21. Withdraw thine hand far from me: and let not thy dread make me afraid.

22. Then call thou, and I will answer: or let me speak, and answer thou me.

23. How many *are* mine iniquities and sins? make me to know my transgression and my sin.

24. Wherefore hidest thou thy face, and holdest me for thine enemy?

25. Wilt thou break a leaf driven to and fro? and wilt thou pursue the dry stubble?

26. For thou writest bitter things against me, and makest me to possess the iniquities of my youth.

27. Thou puttest my feet also in the stocks, and lookest narrowly unto all my paths; thou settest a print upon the heels of my feet.

28. And he, as a rotten thing, consumeth, as a garment that is moth eaten.

Chapter 14

1. Man *that is* born of a woman *is* of few days, and full of trouble.

2. He cometh forth like a flower, and is cut down: he fleeth also as a shadow, and continueth not.

3. And dost thou open thine eyes upon such an one, and bringest me into judgment with thee?

4. Who can bring a clean *thing* out of an unclean? not one.

5. Seeing his days *are* determined, the number of his months *are* with thee, thou hast appointed his bounds that he cannot pass;

6. Turn from him, that he may rest, till he shall accomplish, as an hireling, his day.

7. For there is hope of a tree, if it be cut down, that it will sprout again, and that the tender branch thereof will not cease.

8. Though the root thereof wax old in the earth, and the stock thereof die in the ground;

9. *Yet* through the scent of water it will bud, and bring forth boughs like a plant.

10. But man dieth, and wasteth away: yea, man giveth up the ghost, and where *is* he?

11. *As* the waters fail from the sea, and the flood decayeth and drieth up:

12. So man lieth down, and riseth not: till the heavens *be* no more, they shall not awake, nor be raised out of their sleep.

13. O that thou wouldest hide me in the grave, that thou wouldest keep me secret, until thy wrath be past, that thou wouldest appoint me a set time, and remember me!

14. If a man die, shall he live *again*? all the days of my appointed time will I wait, till my change come.

15. Thou shalt call, and I will answer thee: thou wilt have a desire to the work of thine hands.

16. For now thou numberest my steps: dost thou not watch over my sin?

17. My transgression *is* sealed up in a bag, and thou sewest up mine iniquity.

18. And surely the mountain falling cometh to nought, and the rock is removed out of his place.

19. The waters wear the stones: thou washest away the things which grow *out* of the dust of the earth; and thou destroyest the hope of man.

20. Thou prevailest for ever against him, and he passeth: thou changest his countenance, and sendest him away.

21. His sons come to honour, and he knoweth *it* not; and they are brought low, but he perceiveth *it* not of them.

22. But his flesh upon him shall have pain, and his soul within him shall mourn.

Chapter 29

1. Moreover Job continued his parable, and said,

2. Oh that I were as *in* months past, as *in* the days *when* God preserved me;

3. When his candle shined upon my head, *and when* by his light I walked *through* darkness;

4. As I was in the days of my youth, when the secret of God *was* upon my tabernacle;

5. When the Almighty *was* yet with me, *when* my children *were* about me;

6. When I washed my steps with butter, and the rock poured me out rivers of oil;

7. When I went out to the gate through the city, *when* I prepared my seat in the street!

8. The young men saw me, and hid themselves: and the aged arose, *and* stood up.

9. The princes refrained talking, and laid *their* hand on their mouth.

10. The nobles held their peace, and their tongue cleaved to the roof of their mouth.

11. When the ear heard *me*, then it blessed me; and when the eye saw *me*, it gave witness to me:

12. Because I delivered the poor that cried, and the fatherless, and *him that had* none to help him.

13. The blessing of him that was ready to perish came upon me: and I caused the widow's heart to sing for joy.

14. I put on righteousness, and it clothed me: my judgment *was* as a robe and a diadem.

15. I was eyes to the blind, and feet *was* I to the lame.

16. I *was* a father to the poor: and the cause *which* I knew not I searched out.

17. And I brake the jaws of the wicked, and plucked the spoil out of his teeth.

18. Then I said, I shall die in my nest, and I shall multiply *my* days as the sand.

19. My root *was* spread out by the waters, and the dew lay all night upon my branch.

20. My glory *was* fresh in me, and my bow was renewed in my hand.

21. Unto me *men* gave ear, and waited, and kept silence at my counsel.

22. After my words they spake not again; and my speech dropped upon them.

23. And they waited for me as for the rain; and they opened their mouth wide *as* for the latter rain.

24. *If* I laughed on them, they believed *it* not; and the light of my countenance they cast not down.

25. I chose out their way, and sat chief, and dwelt as a king in the army, as one *that* comforteth the mourners.

Chapter 30

1. But now *they that are* younger than I have me in derision, whose fathers I would have disdained to have set with the dogs of my flock.

2. Yea, whereto *might* the strength of their hands *profit* me, in whom old age was perished?

3. For want and famine *they were* solitary; fleeing into the wilderness in former time desolate and waste.

4. Who cut up mallows by the bushes, and juniper roots *for* their meat.

5. They were driven forth from among *men*, (they cried after them as *after* a thief;)

6. To dwell in the clifts of the valleys, *in* caves of the earth, and *in* the rocks.

7. Among the bushes they brayed; under the nettles they were gathered together.

8. *They were* children of fools, yea, children of base men: they were viler than the earth.

9. And now am I their song, yea, I am their byword.

10. They abhor me, they flee far from me, and spare not to spit in my face.

11. Because he hath loosed my cord, and afflicted me, they have also let loose the bridle before me.

12. Upon *my* right *hand* rise the youth; they push away my feet, and they raise up against me the ways of their destruction.

13. They mar my path, they set forward my calamity, they have no helper.

14. They came *upon me* as a wide breaking in *of waters*: in the desolation they rolled themselves *upon me*.

15. Terrors are turned upon me: they pursue my soul as the wind: and my welfare passeth away as a cloud.

16. And now my soul is poured out upon me; the days of affliction have taken hold upon me.

17. My bones are pierced in me in the night season: and my sinews take no rest.

18. By the great force *of my disease* is my garment changed: it bindeth me about as the collar of my coat.

19. He hath cast me into the mire, and I am become like dust and ashes.

20. I cry unto thee, and thou dost not hear me: I stand up, and thou regardest me *not*.

21. Thou art become cruel to me: with thy strong hand thou opposest thyself against me.

22. Thou liftest me up to the wind; thou causest me to ride *upon it*, and dissolvest my substance.

23. For I know *that* thou wilt bring me *to* death, and *to* the house appointed for all living.

24. Howbeit he will not stretch out *his* hand to the grave, though they cry in his destruction.

25. Did not I weep for him that was in trouble? was *not* my soul grieved for the poor?

26. When I looked for good, then evil came *unto me*: and when I waited for light, there came darkness.

27. My bowels boiled, and rested not: the days of affliction prevented me.

28. I went mourning without the sun: I stood up, *and* I cried in the congregation.

29. I am a brother to dragons, and a companion to owls.

30. My skin is black upon me, and my bones are burned with heat.

31. My harp also is *turned* to mourning, and my organ into the voice of them that weep.

Chapter 31

1. I made a covenant with mine eyes; why then should I think upon a maid?

2. For what portion of God *is there* from above? and *what* inheritance of the Almighty from on high?

3. *Is* not destruction to the wicked? and a strange *punishment* to the workers of iniquity?

4. Doth not he see my ways, and count all my steps?

5. If I have walked with vanity, or if my foot hath hasted to deceit;

6. Let me be weighed in an even balance, that God may know mine integrity.

7. If my step hath turned out of the way, and mine heart walked after mine eyes, and if any blot hath cleaved to mine hands;

8. *Then* let me sow, and let another eat; yea, let my offspring be rooted out.

9. If mine heart have been deceived by a woman, or *if* I have laid wait at my neighbour's door;

10. *Then* let my wife grind unto another, and let others bow down upon her.

11. For this *is* an heinous crime; yea, it *is* an iniquity *to be punished by* the judges.

12. For it *is* a fire *that* consumeth to destruction, and would root out all mine increase.

13. If I did despise the cause of my manservant or of my maidservant, when they contended with me;

14. What then shall I do when God riseth up? and when he visiteth, what shall I answer him?

15. Did not he that made me in the womb make him? and did not one fashion us in the womb?

16. If I have withheld the poor from *their* desire, or have caused the eyes of the widow to fail;

17. Or have eaten my morsel myself alone, and the fatherless hath not eaten thereof;

18. (For from my youth he was brought up with me, as *with* a father, and I have guided her from my mother's womb;)

19. If I have seen any perish for want of clothing, or any poor without covering;

20. If his loins have not blessed me, and *if* he were *not* warmed with the fleece of my sheep;

21. If I have lifted up my hand against the fatherless, when I saw my help in the gate:

22. *Then* let mine arm fall from my shoulder blade, and mine arm be broken from the bone.

23. For destruction *from* God *was* a terror to me, and by reason of his highness I could not endure.

24. If I have made gold my hope, or have said to the fine gold, *Thou art* my confidence;

25. If I rejoiced because my wealth *was* great, and because mine hand had gotten much;

26. If I beheld the sun when it shined, or the moon walking *in* brightness;

27. And my heart hath been secretly enticed, or my mouth hath kissed my hand:

28. This also *were* an iniquity *to be punished by* the judge: for I should have denied the God *that is* above.

29. If I rejoiced at the destruction of him that hated me, or lifted up myself when evil found him:

30. Neither have I suffered my mouth to sin by wishing a curse to his soul.

31. If the men of my tabernacle said not, Oh that we had of his flesh! we cannot be satisfied.

32. The stranger did not lodge in the street: *but* I opened my doors to the traveller.

33. If I covered my transgressions as Adam, by hiding mine iniquity in my bosom:

34. Did I fear a great multitude, or did the contempt of families terrify me, that I kept silence, *and* went not out of the door?

35. Oh that one would hear me! behold, my desire *is, that* the Almighty would answer me, and *that* mine adversary had written a book.

36. Surely I would take it upon my shoulder, *and* bind it *as* a crown to me.

37. I would declare unto him the number of my steps; as a prince would I go near unto him.

38. If my land cry against me, or that the furrows likewise thereof complain;

39. If I have eaten the fruits thereof without money, or have caused the owners thereof to lose their life:

40. Let thistles grow instead of wheat, and cockle instead of barley. The words of Job are ended.

Chapter 32

1. So these three men ceased to answer Job, because he *was* righteous in his own eyes.

2. Then was kindled the wrath of Elihu the son of Barachel the Buzite, of the kindred of Ram: against Job was his wrath kindled, because he justified himself rather than God.

3. Also against his three friends was his wrath kindled, because they had found no answer, and *yet* had condemned Job.

4. Now Elihu had waited till Job had spoken, because they *were* elder than he.

5. When Elihu saw that *there was* no answer in the mouth of *these* three men, then his wrath was kindled.

6. And Elihu the son of Barachel the Buzite answered and said, I *am* young, and ye *are* very old; wherefore I was afraid, and durst not shew you mine opinion.

7. I said, Days should speak, and multitude of years should teach wisdom.

8. But *there is* a spirit in man: and the inspiration of the Almighty giveth them understanding.

9. Great men are not *always* wise: neither do the aged understand judgment.

10. Therefore I said, Hearken to me; I also will shew mine opinion.

11. Behold, I waited for your words; I gave ear to your reasons, whilst ye searched out what to say.

12. Yea, I attended unto you, and, behold, *there was* none of you that convinced Job, *or that* answered his words:

13. Lest ye should say, We have found out wisdom: God thrusteth him down, not man.

14. Now he hath not directed *his* words against me: neither will I answer him with your speeches.

15. They were amazed, they answered no more: they left off speaking.

16. When I had waited, (for they spake not, but stood still, *and* answered no more;)

17. *I said*, I will answer also my part, I also will shew mine opinion.

18. For I am full of matter, the spirit within me constraineth me.

19. Behold, my belly *is* as wine *which* hath no vent; it is ready to burst like new bottles.

20. I will speak, that I may be refreshed: I will open my lips and answer.

21. Let me not, I pray you, accept any man's person, neither let me give flattering titles unto man.

22. For I know not to give flattering titles; *in so doing* my maker would soon take me away.

Chapter 33

1. Wherefore, Job, I pray thee, hear my speeches, and hearken to all my words.

2. Behold, now I have opened my mouth, my tongue hath spoken in my mouth.

3. My words *shall be of* the uprightness of my heart: and my lips shall utter knowledge clearly.

4. The Spirit of God hath made me, and the breath of the Almighty hath given me life.

5. If thou canst answer me, set *thy words* in order before me, stand up.

6. Behold, I *am* according to thy wish in God's stead: I also am formed out of the clay.

7. Behold, my terror shall not make thee afraid, neither shall my hand be heavy upon thee.

8. Surely thou hast spoken in mine hearing, and I have heard the voice of *thy* words, *saying,*

9. I am clean without transgression, I *am* innocent; neither *is there* iniquity in me.

10. Behold, he findeth occasions against me, he counteth me for his enemy,

11. He putteth my feet in the stocks, he marketh all my paths.

12. Behold, *in* this thou art not just: I will answer thee, that God is greater than man.

13. Why dost thou strive against him? for he giveth not account of any of his matters.

14. For God speaketh once, yea twice, *yet man* perceiveth it not.

15. In a dream, in a vision of the night, when deep sleep falleth upon men, in slumberings upon the bed;

16. Then he openeth the ears of men, and sealeth their instruction,

17. That he may withdraw man *from his* purpose, and hide pride from man.

18. He keepeth back his soul from the pit, and his life from perishing by the sword.

19. He is chastened also with pain upon his bed, and the multitude of his bones with strong *pain*:

20. So that his life abhorreth bread, and his soul dainty meat.

21. His flesh is consumed away, that it cannot be seen; and his bones *that* were not seen stick out.

22. Yea, his soul draweth near unto the grave, and his life to the destroyers.

23. If there be a messenger with him, an interpreter, one among a thousand, to shew unto man his uprightness:

24. Then he is gracious unto him, and saith, Deliver him from going down to the pit: I have found a ransom.

25. His flesh shall be fresher than a child's: he shall return to the days of his youth:

26. He shall pray unto God, and he will be favourable unto him: and he shall see his face with joy: for he will render unto man his righteousness.

27. He looketh upon men, and *if any* say, I have sinned, and perverted *that which was* right, and it profited me not;

28. He will deliver his soul from going into the pit, and his life shall see the light.

29. Lo, all these *things* worketh God oftentimes with man,

30. To bring back his soul from the pit, to be enlightened with the light of the living.

31. Mark well, O Job, hearken unto me: hold thy peace, and I will speak.

32. If thou hast any thing to say, answer me: speak, for I desire to justify thee.

33. If not, hearken unto me: hold thy peace, and I shall teach thee wisdom.

Chapter 34

1. Furthermore Elihu answered and said,

2. Hear my words, O ye wise *men*; and give ear unto me, ye that have knowledge.

3. For the ear trieth words, as the mouth tasteth meat.

4. Let us choose to us judgment: let us know among ourselves what *is* good.

5. For Job hath said, I am righteous: and God hath taken away my judgment.

6. Should I lie against my right? my wound *is* incurable without transgression.

7. What man *is* like Job, *who* drinketh up scorning like water?

8. Which goeth in company with the workers of iniquity, and walketh with wicked men.

9. For he hath said, It profiteth a man nothing that he should delight himself with God.

10. Therefore hearken unto me, ye men of understanding: far be it from God, *that he should do* wickedness; and *from* the Almighty, *that he should commit* iniquity.

11. For the work of a man shall he render unto him, and cause every man to find according to *his* ways.

12. Yea, surely God will not do wickedly, neither will the Almighty pervert judgment.

13. Who hath given him a charge over the earth? or who hath disposed the whole world?

14. If he set his heart upon man, *if* he gather unto himself his spirit and his breath;

15. All flesh shall perish together, and man shall turn again unto dust.

16. If now *thou hast* understanding, hear this: hearken to the voice of my words.

17. Shall even he that hateth right govern? and wilt thou condemn him that is most just?

18. *Is it fit* to say to a king, *Thou art* wicked? *and* to princes, *Ye are* ungodly?

19. *How much less to him* that accepteth not the persons of princes, nor regardeth the rich more than the poor? for they all *are* the work of his hands.

20. In a moment shall they die, and the people shall be troubled at midnight, and pass away: and the mighty shall be taken away without hand.

21. For his eyes *are* upon the ways of man, and he seeth all his goings.

22. *There is* no darkness, nor shadow of death, where the workers of iniquity may hide themselves.

23. For he will not lay upon man more *than right*; that he should enter into judgment with God.

24. He shall break in pieces mighty men without number, and set others in their stead.

25. Therefore he knoweth their works, and he overturneth *them* in the night, so that they are destroyed.

26. He striketh them as wicked men in the open sight of others;

27. Because they turned back from him, and would not consider any of his ways:

28. So that they cause the cry of the poor to come unto him, and he heareth the cry of the afflicted.

29. When he giveth quietness, who then can make trouble? and when he hideth *his* face, who then can behold him? whether *it be done* against a nation, or against a man only:

30. That the hypocrite reign not, lest the people be ensnared.

31. Surely it is meet to be said unto God, I have borne *chastisement*, I will not offend *any more*:

32. *That which* I see not teach thou me: if I have done iniquity, I will do no more.

33. *Should it be* according to thy mind? he will recompense it, whether thou refuse, or whether thou choose; and not I: therefore speak what thou knowest.

34. Let men of understanding tell me, and let a wise man hearken unto me.

35. Job hath spoken without knowledge, and his words *were* without wisdom.

36. My desire *is that* Job may be tried unto the end because of *his* answers for wicked men.

37. For he addeth rebellion unto his sin, he clappeth *his hands* among us, and multiplieth his words against God.

Chapter 35

1. Elihu spake moreover, and said,

2. Thinkest thou this to be right, *that* thou saidst, My righteousness *is* more than God's?

3. For thou saidst, What advantage will it be unto thee? *and*, What profit shall I have, *if I be cleansed* from my sin?

4. I will answer thee, and thy companions with thee.

5. Look unto the heavens, and see; and behold the clouds *which* are higher than thou.

6. If thou sinnest, what doest thou against him? or *if* thy transgressions be multiplied, what doest thou unto him?

7. If thou be righteous, what givest thou him? or what receiveth he of thine hand?

8. Thy wickedness *may hurt* a man as thou *art*; and thy righteousness *may profit* the son of man.

9. By reason of the multitude of oppressions they make *the oppressed* to cry: they cry out by reason of the arm of the mighty.

10. But none saith, Where *is* God my maker, who giveth songs in the night;

11. Who teacheth us more than the beasts of the earth, and maketh us wiser than the fowls of heaven?

12. There they cry, but none giveth answer, because of the pride of evil men.

13. Surely God will not hear vanity, neither will the Almighty regard it.

14. Although thou sayest thou shalt not see him, *yet* judgment *is* before him; therefore trust thou in him.

15. But now, because *it is* not *so*, he hath visited in his anger; yet he knoweth *it* not in great extremity:

16. Therefore doth Job open his mouth in vain; he multiplieth words without knowledge.

Chapter 36

1. Elihu also proceeded, and said,

2. Suffer me a little, and I will shew thee that *I have* yet to speak on God's behalf.

3. I will fetch my knowledge from afar, and will ascribe righteousness to my Maker.

4. For truly my words *shall* not *be* false: he that is perfect in knowledge *is* with thee.

5. Behold, God *is* mighty, and despiseth not *any: he is* mighty in strength *and* wisdom.

6. He preserveth not the life of the wicked: but giveth right to the poor.

7. He withdraweth not his eyes from the righteous: but with kings *are they* on the throne; yea, he doth establish them for ever, and they are exalted.

8. And if *they be* bound in fetters, *and* be holden in cords of affliction;

9. Then he sheweth them their work, and their transgressions that they have exceeded.

10. He openeth also their ear to discipline, and commandeth that they return from iniquity.

11. If they obey and serve *him*, they shall spend their days in prosperity, and their years in pleasures.

12. But if they obey not, they shall perish by the sword, and they shall die without knowledge.

13. But the hypocrites in heart heap up wrath: they cry not when he bindeth them.

14. They die in youth, and their life *is* among the unclean.

15. He delivereth the poor in his affliction, and openeth their ears in oppression.

16. Even so would he have removed thee out of the strait *into* a broad place, where *there is* no straitness; and that which should be set on thy table *should be* full of fatness.

17. But thou hast fulfilled the judgment of the wicked: judgment and justice take hold *on thee*.

18. Because *there is* wrath, *beware* lest he take thee away with *his* stroke: then a great ransom cannot deliver thee.

19. Will he esteem thy riches? *no*, not gold, nor all the forces of strength.

20. Desire not the night, when people are cut off in their place.

21. Take heed, regard not iniquity: for this hast thou chosen rather than affliction.

22. Behold, God exalteth by his power: who teacheth like him?

23. Who hath enjoined him his way? or who can say, Thou hast wrought iniquity?

24. Remember that thou magnify his work, which men behold.

25. Every man may see it; man may behold *it* afar off.

26. Behold, God *is* great, and we know *him* not, neither can the number of his years be searched out.

27. For he maketh small the drops of water: they pour down rain according to the vapour thereof:

28. Which the clouds do drop *and* distil upon man abundantly.

29. Also can *any* understand the spreadings of the clouds, *or* the noise of his tabernacle?

30. Behold, he spreadeth his light upon it, and covereth the bottom of the sea.

31. For by them judgeth he the people; he giveth meat in abundance.

32. With clouds he covereth the light; and commandeth it *not to shine* by *the cloud* that cometh betwixt.

33. The noise thereof sheweth concerning it, the cattle also concerning the vapour.

Chapter 37

1. At this also my heart trembleth, and is moved out of his place.

2. Hear attentively the noise of his voice, and the sound *that* goeth out of his mouth.

3. He directeth it under the whole heaven, and his lightning unto the ends of the earth.

4. After it a voice roareth: he thundereth with the voice of his excellency; and he will not stay them when his voice is heard.

5. God thundereth marvellously with his voice; great things doeth he, which we cannot comprehend.

6. For he saith to the snow, Be thou *on* the earth; likewise to the small rain, and to the great rain of his strength.

7. He sealeth up the hand of every man; that all men may know his work.

8. Then the beasts go into dens, and remain in their places.

9. Out of the south cometh the whirlwind: and cold out of the north.

10. By the breath of God frost is given: and the breadth of the waters is straitened.

11. Also by watering he wearieth the thick cloud: he scattereth his bright cloud:

12. And it is turned round about by his counsels: that they may do whatsoever he commandeth them upon the face of the world in the earth.

13. He causeth it to come, whether for correction, or for his land, or for mercy.

14. Hearken unto this, O Job: stand still, and consider the wondrous works of God.

15. Dost thou know when God disposed them, and caused the light of his cloud to shine?

16. Dost thou know the balancings of the clouds, the wondrous works of him which is perfect in knowledge?

17. How thy garments *are* warm, when he quieteth the earth by the south *wind*?

18. Hast thou with him spread out the sky, *which is* strong, *and* as a molten looking glass?

19. Teach us what we shall say unto him; *for* we cannot order *our speech* by reason of darkness.

20. Shall it be told him that I speak? if a man speak, surely he shall be swallowed up.

21. And now *men* see not the bright light which *is* in the clouds: but the wind passeth, and cleanseth them.

22. Fair weather cometh out of the north: with God *is* terrible majesty.

23. *Touching* the Almighty, we cannot find him out: *he is* excellent in power, and in judgment, and in plenty of justice: he will not afflict.

24. Men do therefore fear him: he respecteth not any *that are* wise of heart.

Chapter 38

1. Then the LORD answered Job out of the whirlwind, and said,

2. Who *is* this that darkeneth counsel by words without knowledge?

3. Gird up now thy loins like a man; for I will demand of thee, and answer thou me.

4. Where wast thou when I laid the foundations of the earth? declare, if thou hast understanding.

5. Who hath laid the measures thereof, if thou knowest? or who hath stretched the line upon it?

6. Whereupon are the foundations thereof fastened? or who laid the corner stone thereof;

7. When the morning stars sang together, and all the sons of God shouted for joy?

8. Or *who* shut up the sea with doors, when it brake forth, *as if* it had issued out of the womb?

9. When I made the cloud the garment thereof, and thick darkness a swaddlingband for it,

10. And brake up for it my decreed *place*, and set bars and doors,

11. And said, Hitherto shalt thou come, but no further: and here shall thy proud waves be stayed?

12. Hast thou commanded the morning since thy days; *and* caused the dayspring to know his place;

13. That it might take hold of the ends of the earth, that the wicked might be shaken out of it?

14. It is turned as clay *to* the seal; and they stand as a garment.

15. And from the wicked their light is withholden, and the high arm shall be broken.

16. Hast thou entered into the springs of the sea? or hast thou walked in the search of the depth?

17. Have the gates of death been opened unto thee? or hast thou seen the doors of the shadow of death?

18. Hast thou perceived the breadth of the earth? declare if thou knowest it all.

19. Where *is* the way *where* light dwelleth? and *as for* darkness, where *is* the place thereof,

20. That thou shouldest take it to the bound thereof, and that thou shouldest know the paths *to* the house thereof?

21. Knowest thou *it*, because thou wast then born? or *because* the number of thy days *is* great?

22. Hast thou entered into the treasures of the snow? or hast thou seen the treasures of the hail,

23. Which I have reserved against the time of trouble, against the day of battle and war?

24. By what way is the light parted, *which* scattereth the east wind upon the earth?

25. Who hath divided a watercourse for the overflowing of waters, or a way for the lightning of thunder;

26. To cause it to rain on the earth, *where* no man *is; on* the wilderness, wherein *there is* no man;

27. To satisfy the desolate and waste *ground*; and to cause the bud of the tender herb to spring forth?

28. Hath the rain a father? or who hath begotten the drops of dew?

29. Out of whose womb came the ice? and the hoary frost of heaven, who hath gendered it?

30. The waters are hid as *with* a stone, and the face of the deep is frozen.

31. Canst thou bind the sweet influences of Pleiades, or loose the bands of Orion?

32. Canst thou bring forth Mazzaroth in his season? or canst thou guide Arcturus with his sons?

33. Knowest thou the ordinances of heaven? canst thou set the dominion thereof in the earth?

34. Canst thou lift up thy voice to the clouds, that abundance of waters may cover thee?

35. Canst thou send lightnings, that they may go, and say unto thee, Here we *are*?

36. Who hath put wisdom in the inward parts? or who hath given understanding to the heart?

37. Who can number the clouds in wisdom? or who can stay the bottles of heaven,

38. When the dust groweth into hardness, and the clods cleave fast together?

39. Wilt thou hunt the prey for the lion? or fill the appetite of the young lions,

40. When they couch in *their* dens, *and* abide in the covert to lie in wait?

41. Who provideth for the raven his food? when his young ones cry unto God, they wander for lack of meat.

Chapter 39

1. Knowest thou the time when the wild goats of the rock bring forth? *or* canst thou mark when the hinds do calve?

2. Canst thou number the months *that* they fulfil? or knowest thou the time when they bring forth?

3. They bow themselves, they bring forth their young ones, they cast out their sorrows.

4. Their young ones are in good liking, they grow up with corn; they go forth, and return not unto them.

5. Who hath sent out the wild ass free? or who hath loosed the bands of the wild ass?

6. Whose house I have made the wilderness, and the barren land his dwellings.

7. He scorneth the multitude of the city, neither regardeth he the crying of the driver.

8. The range of the mountains *is* his pasture, and he searcheth after every green thing.

9. Will the unicorn be willing to serve thee, or abide by thy crib?

10. Canst thou bind the unicorn with his band in the furrow? or will he harrow the valleys after thee?

11. Wilt thou trust him, because his strength *is* great? or wilt thou leave thy labour to him?

12. Wilt thou believe him, that he will bring home thy seed, and gather *it into* thy barn?

13. *Gavest thou* the goodly wings unto the peacocks? or wings and feathers unto the ostrich?

14. Which leaveth her eggs in the earth, and warmeth them in dust,

15. And forgetteth that the foot may crush them, or that the wild beast may break them.

16. She is hardened against her young ones, as though *they were* not hers: her labour is in vain without fear;

17. Because God hath deprived her of wisdom, neither hath he imparted to her understanding.

18. What time she lifteth up herself on high, she scorneth the horse and his rider.

19. Hast thou given the horse strength? hast thou clothed his neck with thunder?

20. Canst thou make him afraid as a grasshopper? the glory of his nostrils *is* terrible.

21. He paweth in the valley, and rejoiceth in *his* strength: he goeth on to meet the armed men.

22. He mocketh at fear, and is not affrighted; neither turneth he back from the sword.

23. The quiver rattleth against him, the glittering spear and the shield.

24. He swalloweth the ground with fierceness and rage: neither believeth he that *it is* the sound of the trumpet.

25. He saith among the trumpets, Ha, ha; and he smelleth the battle afar off, the thunder of the captains, and the shouting.

26. Doth the hawk fly by thy wisdom, *and* stretch her wings toward the south?

27. Doth the eagle mount up at thy command, and make her nest on high?

28. She dwelleth and abideth on the rock, upon the crag of the rock, and the strong place.

29. From thence she seeketh the prey, *and* her eyes behold afar off.

30. Her young ones also suck up blood: and where the slain *are*, there *is* she.

Chapter 40

1. Moreover the LORD answered Job, and said,

2. Shall he that contendeth with the Almighty instruct *him*? he that reproveth God, let him answer it.

3. Then Job answered the LORD, and said,

4. Behold, I am vile; what shall I answer thee? I will lay mine hand upon my mouth.

5. Once have I spoken; but I will not answer: yea, twice; but I will proceed no further.

6. Then answered the LORD unto Job out of the whirlwind, and said,

7. Gird up thy loins now like a man: I will demand of thee, and declare thou unto me.

8. Wilt thou also disannul my judgment? wilt thou condemn me, that thou mayest be righteous?

9. Hast thou an arm like God? or canst thou thunder with a voice like him?

10. Deck thyself now *with* majesty and excellency; and array thyself with glory and beauty.

11. Cast abroad the rage of thy wrath: and behold every one *that is* proud, and abase him.

12. Look on every one *that is* proud, *and* bring him low; and tread down the wicked in their place.

13. Hide them in the dust together; *and* bind their faces in secret.

14. Then will I also confess unto thee that thine own right hand can save thee.

15. Behold now behemoth, which I made with thee; he eateth grass as an ox.

16. Lo now, his strength *is* in his loins, and his force *is* in the navel of his belly.

17. He moveth his tail like a cedar: the sinews of his stones are wrapped together.

18. His bones *are as* strong pieces of brass; his bones *are* like bars of iron.

19. He *is* the chief of the ways of God: he that made him can make his sword to approach *unto him*.

20. Surely the mountains bring him forth food, where all the beasts of the field play.

21. He lieth under the shady trees, in the covert of the reed, and fens.

22. The shady trees cover him *with* their shadow; the willows of the brook compass him about.

23. Behold, he drinketh up a river, *and* hasteth not: he trusteth that he can draw up Jordan into his mouth.

24. He taketh it with his eyes: *his* nose pierceth through snares.

Chapter 41

1. Canst thou draw out leviathan with an hook? or his tongue with a cord *which* thou lettest down?

2. Canst thou put an hook into his nose? or bore his jaw through with a thorn?

3. Will he make many supplications unto thee? will he speak soft *words* unto thee?

4. Will he make a covenant with thee? wilt thou take him for a servant for ever?

5. Wilt thou play with him as *with* a bird? or wilt thou bind him for thy maidens?

6. Shall the companions make a banquet of him? shall they part him among the merchants?

7. Canst thou fill his skin with barbed irons? or his head with fish spears?

8. Lay thine hand upon him, remember the battle, do no more.

9. Behold, the hope of him is in vain: shall not *one* be cast down even at the sight of him?

10. None *is so* fierce that dare stir him up: who then is able to stand before me?

11. Who hath prevented me, that I should repay *him? whatsoever is* under the whole heaven is mine.

12. I will not conceal his parts, nor his power, nor his comely proportion.

13. Who can discover the face of his garment? *or* who can come *to him* with his double bridle?

14. Who can open the doors of his face? his teeth *are* terrible round about.

15. *His* scales *are his* pride, shut up together *as with* a close seal.

16. One is so near to another, that no air can come between them.

17. They are joined one to another, they stick together, that they cannot be sundered.

18. By his neesings a light doth shine, and his eyes *are* like the eyelids of the morning.

19. Out of his mouth go burning lamps, *and* sparks of fire leap out.

20. Out of his nostrils goeth smoke, as *out* of a seething pot or caldron.

21. His breath kindleth coals, and a flame goeth out of his mouth.

22. In his neck remaineth strength, and sorrow is turned into joy before him.

23. The flakes of his flesh are joined together: they are firm in themselves; they cannot be moved.

24. His heart is as firm as a stone; yea, as hard as a piece of the nether *millstone*.

25. When he raiseth up himself, the mighty are afraid: by reason of breakings they purify themselves.

26. The sword of him that layeth at him cannot hold: the spear, the dart, nor the habergeon.

27. He esteemeth iron as straw, *and* brass as rotten wood.

28. The arrow cannot make him flee: slingstones are turned with him into stubble.

29. Darts are counted as stubble: he laugheth at the shaking of a spear.

30. Sharp stones *are* under him: he spreadeth sharp pointed things upon the mire.

31. He maketh the deep to boil like a pot: he maketh the sea like a pot of ointment.

32. He maketh a path to shine after him; *one* would think the deep *to be* hoary.

33. Upon earth there is not his like, who is made without fear.

34. He beholdeth all high *things*: he *is* a king over all the children of pride.

Chapter 42

1. Then Job answered the LORD, and said,

2. I know that thou canst do every *thing*, and *that* no thought can be withholden from thee.

3. Who *is* he that hideth counsel without knowledge? therefore have I uttered that I understood not; things too wonderful for me, which I knew not.

4. Hear, I beseech thee, and I will speak: I will demand of thee, and declare thou unto me.

5. I have heard of thee by the hearing of the ear: but now mine eye seeth thee.

6. Wherefore I abhor *myself*, and repent in dust and ashes.

7. And it was *so*, that after the LORD had spoken these words unto Job, the LORD said to Eliphaz the Temanite, My wrath is kindled against thee, and against thy two friends: for ye have not spoken of me *the thing that is* right, as my servant Job *hath*.

8. Therefore take unto you now seven bullocks and seven rams, and go to my servant Job, and offer up for yourselves a burnt offering; and my servant Job shall pray for you: for him will I accept: lest I deal with you *after your* folly, in that ye have not spoken of me *the thing which is* right, like my servant Job.

9. So Eliphaz the Temanite and Bildad the Shuhite *and* Zophar the Naamathite went, and did according as the LORD commanded them: the LORD also accepted Job.

10. And the LORD turned the captivity of Job, when he prayed for his friends: also the LORD gave Job twice as much as he had before.

11. Then came there unto him all his brethren, and all his sisters, and all they that had been of his

acquaintance before, and did eat bread with him in his house: and they bemoaned him, and comforted him over all the evil that the LORD had brought upon him: every man also gave him a piece of money, and every one an earring of gold.

12. So the LORD blessed the latter end of Job more than his beginning: for he had fourteen thousand sheep, and six thousand camels, and a thousand yoke of oxen, and a thousand she asses.

13. He had also seven sons and three daughters.

14. And he called the name of the first, Jemima; and the name of the second, Kezia; and the name of the third, Kerenhappuch.

15. And in all the land were no women found *so* fair as the daughters of Job: and their father gave them inheritance among their brethren.

16. After this lived Job an hundred and forty years, and saw his sons, and his sons' sons, *even* four generations.

17. So Job died, *being* old and full of days.

DISCUSSION QUESTIONS

1. What reasons do Job's friends offer to explain the cause of his suffering? Why does Job find these explanations inadequate?

2. Why does Job insist that he is innocent of any wrongdoing? What does his insistence suggest about his faith?

3. Job is typically described as a patient man. To what extent does he display his patience? Does he resist God in any way?

4. What kind of God addresses Job from the whirlwind? How does God answer Job's questions?

5. Why is Job rewarded? Is his reward consistent with what we have learned about both Job and God?

ECCLESIASTES

L ike the Book of *Job*, *Ecclesiastes* falls into the category of "Wisdom Literature." Such works explore the scope of man's knowledge, while also addressing basic questions concerning the meaning of human life. Far more so than Job, the speaker in *Ecclesiastes* resigns himself to an existence that lacks an apparent purpose. We might gain wisdom, but we do not know why we live. The opening chapter announces, "These are the words of the Preacher, the son of David, king in Jerusalem." Most scholars dismiss the notion that one of Solomon's sons wrote the beautiful poetry contained in this book. Instead, they place the composition to the end of the third century BCE, making *Ecclesiastes* one of the latest written books of the Hebrew Bible.

Though often quoted, *Ecclesiastes* does not present a consistent philosophical or theological view. Rather than outlining examples of God's power (as we saw in *Genesis* and *Job*), the Preacher presents a world where our "toils" seem to be futile. We live, we die; the sun comes up; the sun goes down. God has appointed a time for everything: "A time to love, and a time to hate; a time of war and a time of peace." With no greater purpose that we can grasp, "there is nothing better, than that a man should rejoice in his own works; for that is his portion."

Like the other selections from the Hebrew Bible, our selection from *Ecclesiastes* comes from the King James version of the Bible, which was originally published in 1611. Because of its beautiful poetic language, many scholars consider the translations included in the King James version among the great literary achievements of the English Renaissance (See Unit 3). The power of that poetry is captured in this well-known selection from *Ecclesiastes*.

Chapter 3

1. To every *thing there is* a season, and a time to every purpose under the heaven:

2. A time to be born, and a time to die; a time to plant, and a time to pluck up *that which is* planted;

3. A time to kill, and a time to heal; a time to break down, and a time to build up;

4. A time to weep, and a time to laugh; a time to mourn, and a time to dance;

5. A time to cast away stones, and a time to gather stones together; a time to embrace, and a time to refrain from embracing;

6. A time to get, and a time to lose; a time to keep, and a time to cast away;

7. A time to rend, and a time to sew; a time to keep silence, and a time to speak;

8. A time to love, and a time to hate; a time of war, and a time of peace.

9. What profit hath he that worketh in that wherein he laboureth?

10. I have seen the travail, which God hath given to the sons of men to be exercised in it.

11. He hath made every *thing* beautiful in his time: also he hath set the world in their heart, so that no man can find out the work that God maketh from the beginning to the end.

12. I know that *there is* no good in them, but for *a man* to rejoice, and to do good in his life.

13. And also that every man should eat and drink, and enjoy the good of all his labour, it *is* the gift of God.

14. I know that, whatsoever God doeth, it shall be for ever: nothing can be put to it, nor any thing taken from it: and God doeth *it,* that *men* should fear before him.

15. That which hath been is now; and that which is to be hath already been; and God requireth that which is past.

16. And moreover I saw under the sun the place of judgment, *that* wickedness *was* there; and the place of righteousness, *that* iniquity *was* there.

17. I said in mine heart, God shall judge the righteous and the wicked: for *there is* a time there for every purpose and for every work.

18. I said in mine heart concerning the estate of the sons of men, that God might manifest them, and that they might see that they themselves are beasts.

19. For that which befalleth the sons of men befalleth beasts; even one thing befalleth them: as the one dieth, so dieth the other; yea, they have all one breath; so that a man hath no preeminence above a beast: for all *is* vanity.

20. All go unto one place; all are of the dust, and all turn to dust again.

21. Who knoweth the spirit of man that goeth upward, and the spirit of the beast that goeth downward to the earth?

22. Wherefore I perceive that *there is* nothing better, than that a man should rejoice in his own works; for that *is* his portion: for who shall bring him to see what shall be after him?

DISCUSSION QUESTIONS

1.   What are the main points of this famous chapter?

2.   What does the statement "a time for every purpose suggest?"

3.   In verse 9, the Preacher asks "what profit hath he that worketh in that wherein he laboureth?" How does he answer this question?

4.   What does the statement that "there is nothing better than that a man should rejoice in his own works" imply? What are different ways such a claim might be understood?

5.   How does the poetic voice in Ecclesiastes differ from the narrative voice heard in the other selections from the Hebrew Bible?

WRITING SUGGESTIONS

1.   Choose one of the selections from the Hebrew Bible and write a paper comparing it with another mythic or religious story with which you are familiar. To what extent do selections from the Hebrew Bible echo or prefigure motifs found in your chosen story?

2.   Write a paper that discusses how God functions in the stories of Creation and the Garden of Eden. What kind of deity do we encounter in *Genesis*? Why does this God perform the actions that He does? What are the implications of His actions?

THE GREEKS

General Introduction

Between 500 and 350 BCE, Greek writers, artists, and philosophers produced the landmark works upon which many Western cultural and intellectual traditions rest. To the Greeks we owe fundamental components of our culture, such as drama (both comedy and tragedy), moral and political theory, critical historical inquiry, democracy, and, to a lesser extent, naturalistic art. The center of much of this innovation was Athens, the largest city on the Greek mainland. Here—and especially during the height of Athenian power in the middle decades of the fifth century BCE—the architectural and intellectual activity that we identify with Classical Greece took root.

The earliest thriving cultures in Greece emerged on Crete, an island located south of the Greek peninsula in the Mediterranean Sea. From roughly 2200 to 1450 BCE, Crete's inhabitants established an elaborate society that scholars call Minoan Crete, named for its legendary King Minos. Minoan culture centered on a series of towns and cities built around elaborate palaces. At Knossos, the largest palace, archaeologists have uncovered a massive structure containing hundreds of rooms that supported a sophisticated and luxurious culture. At the height of their influence, the Minoans used their palace-based culture to establish extensive trade networks in the eastern Mediterranean and the Aegean seas.

From roughly 1800 to 1200 BCE, the Mycenaeans established the first lasting civilization on the Greek mainland. (The name Mycenaean is derived from one of the principal Greek cities of the time, Mycenaea). They thrived near the end of the Bronze Age, a period that lasted from roughly 4000–1000 BC, during which Mediterranean cultures learned to forge bronze from copper and tin. The technology enabled them to craft elaborate weapons and protective suits of armor, leading historians to assume that military campaigns were central to the development of Mycenaean culture. They also developed a complex pictographic system of writing known as Linear B, which scholars in the early 1950s linked to an early form of spoken Greek.

Around 1200 BCE, the wealthy cities of Mycenaean Greece began a still-mysterious two-century decline. The once-lavish palace communities either collapsed from internal strife or were destroyed by invasion. Whatever the case, the surviving Mycenaeans apparently lost the knowledge of Linear B writing. Consequently, we have no surviving Greek writing for a period of nearly 500 years, a fact that has led most scholars to conclude that literacy vanished from the Greek-speaking world. So, too, did the social organization and craft specialization that allowed the palace cultures to thrive. Only smaller, poorer, and more isolated communities remained. For these reasons, the centuries following the collapse of Mycenaean culture have commonly been known as the Greek Dark Ages.

The Dark Ages came to an end around 800 BCE, when dramatic population increases led to the consolidation of isolated communities into more complex urban centers. The next 300 years (roughly 800–500 BCE) are commonly identified as the Archaic Age. Individual Greeks remained loyal to their respective cities, but the early Archaic Age also saw the origins of several traditions that fostered a heightened sense of Greek identity. Every four years the Olympic Games, commonly dated to 776 BCE, attracted athletes from across the Greek world to compete in contests held during a religious festival at Mount Olympia. The power of literacy also returned, when contact with eastern Mediterranean cultures led Greeks to adopt the Phoenician alphabet to their language. This was a syllabic system, in which each letter corresponded to a particular sound, making it much simpler to master than the pictographic symbols employed in the long-lost Linear B. Although the Greeks added vowels to their adopted alphabet, the Phoenician method of writing is among the most important of the many technologies and concepts that western Mediterranean cultures borrowed from the east.

Aside from helping to facilitate trade with the Phoenicians and others, the new alphabet was used to write the early literary landmarks of ancient Greece. Sometime between 750 and 675 BCE, Homer, a poet for whom we have no biographical details, used it to write the *Iliad* and the *Odyssey*, the two epic poems that stand at the forefront of Greek literature and which formed the cornerstone of education in Classical Athens. Having developed over centuries of oral transmission, the two poems were shaped into their lasting literary form, in part because the poet had mastered the new alphabet. Around 700, another poet, Hesiod, used the new system to write *Theogeny*, a work that traces the history of the gods and their role in the creation of the earth.

The religion described by Hesiod and other Greek writers on the gods was not a formal set of beliefs, such as we find in monotheistic creeds. Rather, it was a pantheistic system that centered on the gods thought to live atop Mount Olympus. Chief among these Olympians were Zeus, Apollo, Athena, Hermes, and Hera. The gods were human in form but were not mortal; they were fascinated by the humans in their midst and readily interfered in the affairs of the world, as they do often in Homer's epic poems. Unlike the deity of Christianity or Judaism, they did not proclaim ethical systems or act as moral guides. Rather, they expected to be honored by appropriate sacrifices and vigils at their temples. Cities and towns typically had a patron protector that needed special devotions from its citizens. Most Greeks, however, believed it wise to honor all the gods. To offend them was a form of sacrilege that could bring harm to an individual or a community.

The dominant form of political organization in both Archaic Age and Classical Greece were the independent city-states known as *polei* (*polis* in the singular). The term *polis* carried multiple meanings for the Greeks. On one level, it referred to a specific place, such as Athens or Sparta. But the residents of a *polis* also shared common religious and historic perspectives that united them as a community. Typically, each *polis* had its own patron deity who protected its citizens. Each *polis* also had its own political structure. Sparta, for example, was ruled by an oligarchy, a small group of men who retained tight control over the city's affairs. Fifth-century Athens, on the other hand, established a radical democracy, in which all male citizens were entitled to speak and vote in the Assembly. Greeks residing in different *polei* understood that they shared aspects of a united culture, such as the Olympic Games, the Olympian gods, and the epic poetry of Hesiod and Homer. But except for rare crises such as the Persian War, this shared culture did not lead to unity among the various city-states. Indeed, they were often at war with each other, a fact that only further encouraged Greeks to locate their political identity within the *polis* rather than the broader Greek-speaking world.

The Persian War of 499–479 BCE is usually said to mark the end of the Archaic Age and the beginning of the Classical Greek era. Twice during this conflict, the much larger Persian army invaded mainland Greece, and both times they were forced to flee. For the Greeks, the first important victory occurred at Marathon in 490, where a small army of Athenians defeated the Persians. A second Persian invasion in 480 was repelled by an alliance of Greek city-states, known as the Hellenic League, who temporarily put aside their differences to defeat a common enemy. At the conclusion of the war, however, Athens and Sparta, the two most powerful Greek city-states, could not retain their alliance, and they soon fell into a protracted round of battles that lasted for most of the fifth century.

Despite the constant threat and reality of war, fifth-century Athens emerged as the center of Greek intellectual and artistic life. For that reason, these years are commonly identified as the Golden Age of Athens, the period when the achievements of Classical Greece reached their peak. Those achievements include the writings of Herodotus and Thucydides, who are credited as the first historians to examine the past by investigating available evidence. This was also the Athens of Aeschylus, Sophocles, and Euripides, the dramatists whose tragic plays defined the Greek stage. The physical manifestations of the Athenian ascendancy were displayed in the several buildings that Pericles in 447 BCE commissioned for the top of the Acropolis. Best exemplified by the graceful monumentality of the Parthenon, the Acropolis structures revealed a culture supremely confident of its place in the world.

One of the most influential and controversial Athenians of the Golden Age was the philosopher Socrates (469–399 BCE). Unlike many of his illustrious contemporaries, Socrates left no writings for us to examine. What we do know of his ideas comes from the writings of others, particularly his disciple, Plato. Socrates was not a teacher in the formal sense; he held no classes and consistently asserted that he had no answers to offer the young Athenian men who gathered around him. He spent most of his time wandering Athens engaging people in discussions about the definitions of ethical terms. But Socrates ultimately angered Athenian leaders, who grew weary of his assertions that they did not understand the ethical terms they employed. In 399 BCE, he stood trial on charges of corrupting the city's young and for not believing in the Athenian gods. Found guilty of the charges, he was executed shortly thereafter. Although Socrates was put to death, he inspired a devotion to philosophy that was one of the hallmarks of Classical Athens. The best-known Athenian thinkers to follow in his wake were Plato (427–347) and Aristotle (384–322), the two major thinkers most responsible for carrying the intellectual achievements of the fifth century into the fourth.

During the fifth century, Athens was governed as a direct participatory democracy, a system that granted all adult male citizens the right to vote and participate in the Assembly. The full promise of democracy, however, was limited by several factors. Women, for instance, were excluded from political affairs, and had only limited abilities to control property. The definition of citizenship also became more restricted over the course of the century. After 451, citizenship was limited to children whose parents were Athenian by birth, a move that negatively affected the large number of people who migrated to Athens to participate in its thriving culture. Athens also had a large number of slaves. Estimates vary, but most scholars suggest that nearly one-third of the people who lived in Athens during the Classical Age were slaves, held either by individuals or the *polis*. Athens, however, was not alone in holding slaves or restricting citizenship; indeed, these were common practices throughout the ancient world.

Although Plato and Aristotle wrote well into the fourth century, the confidence that marked Athenian culture in the middle of the fifth century did not survive the nearly endless conflicts the city waged against its rivals. Athens and Sparta spent much of the second half of the fifth century fighting for influence in the Greek-speaking world, and in 431, full-scale war broke out between the two city-states. Known as the Peloponnesian War, the conflict lasted until 404 BCE, when Sparta finally triumphed over Athens and installed a dictatorship of antidemocratic Athenians. The democracy was soon restored and the dictators expelled, but the Golden Age of Athens had clearly passed.

In the century that followed, Athens fell into the expanding empire of the Macedonians. In the second century BCE, it was absorbed—along with the rest of Greece—into the expanding orbit of Rome. By that time, however, the language, literature, and culture of the Greeks had spread throughout the Mediterranean.

LITERATURE

While the massive size of these works prevents us from including them here, we begin our discussion of Greek literature with a brief consideration of the *Iliad* and the *Odyssey* of Homer, a poet who left no traces for future biographers and historians. The landscape descriptions in his poems suggest that he was familiar with Greek territories in Asia Minor, but we will never know where or when he was born. Greeks of the Classical age believed he was blind, but we have no way to confirm or deny this assumption. What we have, instead, are two epic poems, both containing more than 12,000 lines, which derive from an oral tradition that dates back centuries before the poet wrote his works. The date of composition remains a mystery, although most scholars suggest they were written sometime between 750 and 675 BCE. At some point during this period, the poet we call Homer took advantage of the new Phoenician-derived Greek alphabet, the oldest evidence of which dates to around 750, to write down the words that others had long recited through a combination of memory and improvisation. In so doing, he shaped a centuries-old oral tradition into a cohesive literary artifact.

The events described in the Homeric epics remain a matter of scholarly debate. The Greeks, however, believed that the poems recounted the Trojan War and its aftermath. Fought over a period of ten years, the Trojan War pitted the cities of Greece against the Ionian city of Troy. The *Iliad* describes events near the end of the conflict. For the Greeks, these battles occurred in a distant, more heroic past, in a culture radically different from that of Homer and his contemporaries. The poem provided a mythic beginning to Greek culture by presenting powerful figures, such as Achilles, Ajax, and Hector engaged in battle out of an inflamed sense of honor. The *Odyssey*, on the other hand, describes the difficulty of returning home after battle. At the conclusion of the Trojan War, the Greek hero Odysseus embarks on his journey home, a journey that ultimately takes ten years to complete.

Lyric poetry emerged as a new form of Greek literature in the seventh century BCE. These were quieter, more personal poems that did not contain the grand narrative sweep of epic. The term "lyric" was applied to poetry that could be sung to the lyre, a popular string instrument. (Unfortunately, the music that accompanied these poems has been lost.) Some lyrics were written for a chorus to sing at a formal occasion such as a wedding or funeral; a contrasting style known as monody was written for solo voice.

In the late seventh century and early sixth century, the island of Lesbos, located off the coast of Asia Minor in the Aegean Sea, emerged as a center of lyric poetry. Here, and especially in the city of Mytilene, the poets Alcaeus and Sappho wrote some of the earliest surviving monody. Both are of historic interest, but Sappho has attracted the most critical interest; she remains one of the most frequently read ancient poets. Her deeply personal poems about love and friendship among the young women who apparently gathered around her are striking for their beauty and the depiction of female intimacy. Sadly, except for two complete poems, her poetry survives largely in fragments.

The supreme literary achievements of post-Homeric Greece are the dramatic tragedies initially staged in fifth-century Athens. Like so much of ancient history, the precise origins of drama are unknown. We do know that the form has roots in Greek festivals honoring Dionysus, the god of fertility and wine. Around 530 BCE, Athens inaugurated an annual dramatic competition that was held during a five-day festival known as the City Dionysia. Competing playwrights each wrote and staged three tragic dramas and a satyr play, a humorous and occasionally erotic play intended to relieve the tensions of the tragedies. Most of the plays have been lost. Fortunately, we have seven each from Aeschylus and Sophocles and 19 from Euripides, the three masters of the tragic stage.

We cannot reconstruct the precise structure of the early City Dionysia. Most scholars assume that they included dancing and the singing of choral odes. Tradition holds that a poet named Thespis added a masked actor who interacted with the chorus, thus establishing the tradition of individuals speaking separately from the group chorus. According to Aristotle, Aeschylus (525?–456 BCE) added a second actor, a step that allowed for dialogue between characters. The addition of a third actor by Sophocles (496–401 BCE) further increased the possibilities for dramatic tension and complications. Yet even as the amount of spoken dialogue increased, all tragedians continued to include a chorus in their works. Their odes, sung in ways that have unfortunately been lost, helped establish the emotional mood of the plays. Typically, the chorus functions as a group of townspeople or some other group of interested observers to the action. They could also be used to convey information that could not be portrayed on stage.

Greek dramas were communal events staged in massive theaters subsidized by the *polis*. Some held as many as 15,000 people. The chorus sang their odes in the open center, known as the *orchestra*. The actors performed behind the chorus and in front of a structure known as the *skene*, which was often painted to resemble a castle or other important building. A raised stage, known as the *proskenian*, separated the *skene* from the *orchestra* (see Figure 1-A).

Figure 1-A Greek Theater

The subject matter of tragedies was drawn from Greek myth or the stories connected with the Homeric heroes. Consequently, the audience could be expected to know the basic outlines of the plot. For the audience, the tension stemmed from watching the central character, who is usually a great or powerful person, make either bad or ill-fated decisions that lead to tragic consequences. In tragedies, humans are free to choose certain actions, but they are also subject to the workings of fate, the direction of which was understood only by the gods. The tragic interaction of choice and fate often leads to a sudden moment of reversal, a precise instant when the protagonist realizes what he or she has done or when the direction of their lives are suddenly and dramatically altered. According to Aristotle, when audiences confronted the intense emotion of this reversal, they underwent the experience of catharsis, a cleansing or purging of feelings associated with the crimes committed by the play's hero.

Over the years, the complex interaction of fate and individual responsibility presented by the great tragedians has inspired a range of interpretations. Like the Homeric epics, they have proved to be timeless in their appeal. And yet, we must also remember that Greek tragedy emerged during a specific period of a specific culture's history. Written and performed in Athens during the fifth century BCE, they were first staged when Athenian power and creativity were at their height. But these were also years when Athens and its neighbors engaged in nearly ceaseless hostilities. As the Peloponnesian War unfolded near the end of the fifth century, the institutions of Athenian democracy also came under assault. Many Greek tragedies speak to these tensions. They are concerned with such questions as the nature of effective leadership and with the conflict between legal and divine justice. From these concerns, the future history of Western drama sprang.

Figure 1-B Dipylon Vasse

Although we have fewer surviving examples than we do for tragedies, comedies represent a second significant Greek contribution to the history of the stage. Unfortunately, we know comparatively little of its origins. Most scholars assume that comic plays derived from masquerades and festivals associated with fertility cults. At some point in the late sixth or early fifth century BCE, Athens began holding competitions for comedy, as it did for tragedy. Historians, however, typically use the year 486 BCE as the starting point, as this is the first year for which we can identify the name of the prize-winning comic playwright. Unfortunately, the sole Athenian writer whose comedies have survived is Aristophanes (450–385 BCE). Much of his work addresses issues of immediate concern to fifth-century Athenians, such as the Peloponnesian War. In wildly satiric language that often lampoons well-known Athenian residents, Aristophanes helped inaugurate a tradition that remains vital today: the comedian as social critic. Comedy thus served as the farcical flip side to Athenian tragedy. The tragedians developed their ideas by looking to the culture's mythic past; the comic playwrights, on the other hand, found their material in the present.

VISUAL ARTS

Much of our knowledge of Greek visual arts in the centuries prior to the Classical Age comes from vase paintings executed between 900 and 500 BCE. Although we now place them in museums, Greek vases were commonly used to hold water, oil, wine, and dry goods. For many families, a painted vase was reasonably affordable, making it perhaps the one luxury item that could be brought into the home. Consequently, an extensive industry of vase makers and painters arose to supply the demand. Greek vases have also proved remarkably durable and have been found in archeological sites throughout the Mediterranean.

The first distinctly Greek vase style appears in a mode of decoration known as the Geometric style of the ninth and eighth centuries BCE, the centuries that saw the end of the Dark Ages and the beginning of the Archaic Age. Around 900 BCE, painters began to adorn vases with regular geometric patterns and shapes, such as triangles and rectilinear bands. An earlier style now known as the Protogeometric displayed some of these motifs, but in the Geometric style, vase painters applied their designs to the entire pot, paying particular attention to the shape and form of the vessel. At first, Geometric designs showed few humans or animals. Around 800 BCE, however, painters began to introduce figurative elements, such as we see in the well-known Dipylon Vase (c. 750 BCE, Figure 1-B). The scene depicts a funeral. Human figures, including the horizontal deceased subject and vertical mourners with hands raised to the sky, are placed within the geometric framework. The added human and animal elements such as we see here allowed artists to incorporate narrative elements to their work. Often, these elements were drawn from everyday scenes, as in the mourning scene shown in the Dipylon Vase. But as new styles of vase painting developed in the centuries that followed, painters increasingly relied upon legends and myths familiar to all Greeks. A standard repertoire of subjects, typically drawing from either Homer or images of Olympian gods, emerged.

The narrative possibilities of vase painting increased significantly with the development of the black-figure style, a technique developed in Corinth around 650 BCE. Painters working in this mode used a mixture of clay and water to paint two-dimensional black figures against a background of unpainted red clay. Other colors could be applied to the red for contrasting effect. Details were scratched into the black with a needle. At its best, as in the drinking cup painted by the Athenian artist Exekias,

Figure 1-C Cup in the black figure style

Figure 1-D Red figure style

the artist achieved an elegant silhouette (see Figure 1-C). Made to hold wine, the cup (c. 540 BCE) presents Dionysus, the god of the vine, aboard the vessel upon which he revealed his identity to the pirates who had kidnapped him. (According to Greek legend, the pirates then jumped overboard and were turned into dolphins.)

Near the end of the sixth century, Athenian potters and painters developed the red-figure style, thus reversing the color scheme of the slightly older technique. In these works, the painter covered the pot with black while leaving the unpainted forms to show in red. Now the outlines and details of the human body, which had been incised with a needle in the older style, could be delicately painted in black with a brush. The flowing line of the brush allows for greater naturalism. The folds of clothing, body shape, and muscle become more intricate and realistic, in part because the artist could now show figures overlapping each other. The profile forms of the black-figure style here give way to a less rigidly two-dimensional form (see Figure 1-D).

Greek sculpture followed a similar progression toward naturalistic forms. Around 650 BCE, carvers working with marble began making large freestanding statues of the human figure to dedicate sanctuaries or to mark graves. Statues of males, known as *kouros*, are almost always nude, while females, known as *kore*, are clothed. (The female nude did not appear in Greek statuary for another two centuries.) Greeks most likely developed the appearance of these statues from Egyptian sources. But unlike their Egyptian predecessors, the Greek sculptors

sought to carve bodies that emerged free from the original source of stone. They allowed for the creation of open space. The typical *kouros* presented constricted frontal views; upright and taut, the bodies had been shaped into rigid, almost geometric form. In the well-known life-sized *kouros* (c. 600 BCE) in the Metropolitan Museum of Art, the young man stands alert and ready to move, but he is frozen in space (see Figure 1-E). Like other early *kouros*, the left leg extends outward but both feet remain on the ground. The clenched fists hang just below the hips.

In the sixth century BCE, sculptors using the same basic pose developed a rounder, more naturalistic technique for presenting the human body. In Figure 1-F, we see a fleshier, more engaged depiction of body shape and muscle. Though still standing directly in front of the viewer, they offer a freer and looser sense of the possibilities for movement through space. We have a sense of muscle and bones beneath the skin. Like their earlier counterparts, these later *kouros* were used to mark graves and adorn sanctuaries, but they appear much more like people we might encounter in the real world.

During the Classical Age that followed the Greek defeat of the Persians in 479 BCE, sculptors achieved a still fuller naturalism that prefigures much of later Western representational art. In *Doryphoros* (Spear Bearer), unfortunately known only from a Roman marble copy of the bronze original, Polyclitus presents the male nude gracefully and powerfully moving through space (see Figure 1-G). This is, of course, an idealized view

Figure 1-E Kouros, c. 600 BCE

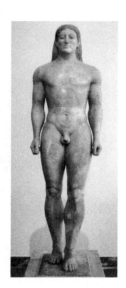

Figure 1-F Kouros

of human beauty, but Polyclitus creates that view by paying particular attention to the lines and contours of the body. The exquisitely balanced movements of the arms, legs, and torso stand in complementary relation to each other, so that the viewer has a sense of proportion and strength. Myron's *Discobolus* (c. 460 BCE) similarly revels in the delicate power of movement through three-dimensional space (see Figure 1-H). Like *Doryphoros*, we know this bronze statue only from its Roman marble copy. Still, we can follow the graceful twists of the body, as each part moves in opposite directions in order to heave the disc. Such idealized naturalism became a hallmark of Classical Age sculpture.

Temple architecture is perhaps the most enduring legacy the Greeks bequeathed to the traditions of Western art. Typically built to honor a particular god or goddess, the Greeks designed temples according to a set of standardized plans that were developed over the course of several centuries. In most plans, the interior room, known as the *cella*, housed a statue to the relevant deity. Immediately adjacent to the *cella* was an interior porch called the *pronaos*. The exterior was defined by either a single or double row of columns collectively known as the *peristyle*. The columns supported a horizontal unit called

the entablature, which in turn supported the roof. Sculptural friezes often adorned the entablature.

When constructing temples, Greek architects relied on columns that fell into one of three systems of decoration and proportion known as the Doric, Ionic, and Corinthian orders. We can readily identify the orders according to their decorative motifs and the relationship between the columns and the floor of the temple (see Figure 1-I). The oldest and simplest was the Doric; its plain but sturdy column sat directly on the floor. The shaft of an Ionic column was thinner but rose higher than its Doric counterpart; its top, known as the capital, was carved into a double spiral called a volute. The most elaborate of the orders was the Corinthian. Developed in Greece around 450 BCE, it later became the favorite architectural order of the Romans. Although they differed in important ways, the standard proportions and motifs of the individual orders enabled architects to design temples that projected a sense of rational and orderly balance.

Without question, the high point of Classical Greek temple architecture was the Parthenon, a structure that symbolized the imperial ambitions of Athens during the age of Pericles. An earlier collection of Acropolis structures had been destroyed during the Persian invasion of 480 BCE. For more than 20 years, Athenian leaders vowed not to rebuild

Figure 1-G Polyclitus' *Doryphoros*

the temples sacked by their invaders. But in 448 BCE, Pericles led Athens into the most significant rebuilding effort in the city's history. The centerpiece of that project was the Parthenon, a temple constructed to honor the goddess Athena.

The Parthenon's simple but elegant columns exemplify the Doric order. The apparent simplicity, however, is accompanied by subtle variations to the typical Doric temple that historians call the Parthenon's refinements. A careful examination of the platform and entablature reveals a slight curve that makes the center stand slightly higher than the two ends (look closely at Figure 1-J). The columns, in turn, lean slightly inward as they rise upward. At the same time, the interval between the corner column and its neighbor is slightly smaller than the space separating the middle ones. These slight refinements from the regular forms of the traditional Doric temple make the Parthenon seem lighter and more vibrant than its counterparts. Like the heroic statues of Myron described above, it combines suppleness with strength. Few buildings have ever stood so ideally poised between power and grace.

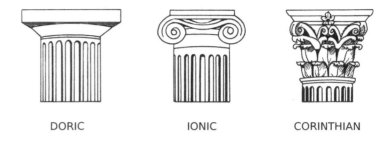

Figure 1-I Greek column orders

Figure 1-J The Parthenon

Figure 1-H Myron's *Discobolus*

SAPPHO (C. 600 BCE)

Selected Poems and Fragments

Sappho is the sole female writer from the Greek Archaic Age whose work survives in any substantial way. Unfortunately, we know little about her beyond the remarkable fragments that identify her as the great lyric poet of ancient Greece. She spent her life on the island of Lesbos, where she apparently married and had a child. That she was sent into exile in Sicily for several years has led several scholars to conclude that either she or her husband was part of a politically important group that angered local leaders. Otherwise, the historical record is silent.

Sappho's poetry suggests that she had a group of young female admirers whom she possibly helped as a teacher, mentor, or poetic guide. There can be little doubt that the relationships among these young women, most of whom probably eventually entered into conventional marriages, contained an erotic element. Many of the surviving fragments suggest that she wrote *epithalamia*—wedding poems—for her young friends as they prepared to leave her circle. In others, the overarching theme is the power of love–love sought, love achieved, love denied.

Scholars in the third century A.D. collected Sappho's poems into nine books, a fact that suggests she produced a significant body of work. Unfortunately, the papyrus rolls on which they were written have been either lost or severely damaged, leaving us with only one complete poem and approximately 150 fragments, some no more than a line. We include the one surviving completed and a second nearly completed poem that is tantalizingly cut off at the start of a new verse.. The first begins as a plea to Aphrodite, the goddess of love, to help the poet obtain the love of someone who has so far proved reluctant. The poet and the goddess are apparently on familiar terms, as the speaker recounts a previous entreaty to Aphrodite, who in turn speaks to the poet directly. The second poem presents a heartbroken speaker overcome with jealousy.

We have also included here several fragments that hint at the richness of Sappho's verse. While we should be careful to avoid reading too much into scattered lines removed from their larger context, for many readers, such fragments contribute to the mystery that surrounds Sappho.

Poem 1

Deathless Aphrodite of the spangled mind,
child of Zeus, who twists lures, I beg you
do not break with hard pains,
        O lady, my heart

but come here if ever before
you caught my voice far off
and listening left your father's
        golden house and came,

yoking your car. And fine birds brought you,
quick sparrows over the black earth
whipping their wings down the sky
        through midair—

they arrived. But you, O blessed one,
smiled in your deathless face
and asked what (now again) I have suffered and why
        (now again) I am calling out

and what I want to happen most of all
in my crazy heart. Whom should I persuade (now
        again)
to lead you back into her love? Who, O
        Sappho, is wronging you?

For if she flees, soon she will pursue.
If she refuses gifts, rather will she give them.
If she does not love, soon she will love
        even unwilling.

Come to me now: loose me from hard
care and all my heart longs
to accomplish, accomplish. You
        be my ally.

Fragment 31

He seems to me equal to gods that man
whoever he is who opposite you
sits and listens close
        to your sweet speaking

and lovely laughing—oh it
puts the heart in my chest on wings
for when I look at you, even a moment, no speaking
        is left in me

no: tongue breaks and thin
fire is racing under skin
and in eyes no sight and drumming
        fills ears

and cold sweat holds me and shaking
grips me all, greener than grass
I am and dead—or almost
        I seem to me.

But all is to be dared, because even a person of poverty

Fragment 33

if only I, O goldcrowned Aphrodite,
could win this lot

Fragment 47

                     Eros shook my
mind like a mountain wind falling on oak trees

Fragment 57

what country girl seduces your wits
wearing a country dress
not knowing how to pull the cloth to her ankles?

Fragment 104A

Evening
     you gather back
          all that dazzling down has put asunder:
              you gather a lamb
            gather a kid
gather a child to its mother

Fragment 107

do I still yearn for my virginity?

Sappho, from *If Not Winter: Fragments of Sappho*, trans. Anne Carson, pp. 3, 5, 63, 67, 99, 119, 213, 219, 221, 261, 285. Copyright © 2002 by Random House, Inc. Reprinted with permission.

Fragment 108

O beautiful O graceful one

Fragment 128

here now
   tender Graces
     and Muses with beautiful hair

Fragment 141

but there a bowl of ambrosia
   had been mixed

and Hermes taking the jug poured wine for
   the gods

and then they all
   held cups
     and poured libation and prayed every
      good thing for the bridegroom

DISCUSSION QUESTIONS

1. How does the speaker address Aphrodite? What does her tone suggest about the relationship between the two? What does she expect from the goddess?

2. Is the speaker's tone consistent throughout the poem?

3. How would you characterize Aphrodite's response? Does she take the speaker's request seriously? Is she amused? Angered?

4. The two complete poems deal with the absence of pending loss of a loved one. How does Sappho convey these ideas? What images does she employ?

5. What is the implication when the speaker in poem #31 states: "for when I look at you, even a moment, no speaking/is left in me?

WRITING SUGGESTION

1. Compare this translation of Sappho with others available in your library. Write an essay that examines the differences in word choice and emphasis in the translations.

SOPHOCLES

Sophocles was alive for most of the fifth century, making him a witness to nearly the entire history of the Athenian golden age. He was also an active participant in the city's affairs, serving as an elected general of the military and briefly as treasurer of the Delian League, a confederacy of Greek city-states that formed after the Persian Wars. In a career that spanned over 60 years, he wrote more than 100 plays, seven of which survive. Unlike Aeschylus and other contemporaries, Sophocles did not appear in his own plays, making him perhaps the first important dramatist to write words entirely for other actors. His other innovations include the reduction of the size of the chorus and the addition of a third actor, a move that Aeschylus adopted in his late plays. With three characters on stage rather than two, Sophocles could expand upon the dramatic possibilities by establishing triangular conversations. As with other Greek authors, his subjects were drawn from well-known myths and Homer. Highly acclaimed in his own day (he was awarded first prize at the annual dramatic festival 24 times), Sophocles is today viewed as the most significant playwright of the Greek stage.

Sophocles' *Oedipus Rex* is the story of a man destroyed by his desire to know. Its protagonist is Oedipus, the king of Thebes, and a figure whose tragic fate had been assigned to him before he was born. As a young man in Corinth, Oedipus mistakenly believed he was the son of Polybus and Merope, who had raised him since he was an infant. After visiting the oracle of Apollo at Delphi, he learns that he is fated to kill his father and marry his mother. Understandably upset at this news and thinking that the oracle refers to Polybus and Merope, he flees Corinth. Oedipus cannot escape his fate, however. At a crossroads he meets and kills a man he later learns was Laius, the king of Thebes and his actual father. After solving the riddle of the Sphinx near Thebes, Oedipus is invited to marry the city's widowed queen—a woman who, in fact, turns out to be his mother. The oracle proves correct. Oedipus, mighty ruler of Thebes, is guilty of horrible crimes against nature: patricide and incest. His sudden and irreversible fall amounts to the definitive example of the tragic reversal of fortune in all of Greek drama.

The play addresses complex topics that continue to fascinate us more than 2,400 years after its first performance. Among the issues is the nature of effective political leadership, a question as important then as it is today. The play begins with Thebes in the midst of a plague; its women produce stillborn infants and its crops lie devastated in the fields. The play also shows the conflicts that may occur when fate collides with the human belief in freedom. Oedipus was fated for his terrible condition even before he was born, so in some ways he cannot be faulted for his actions. At the same time, he makes a series of choices along the way that only strengthens the case against him. Time and again he has the opportunity to act in a way that might save him, only to bluster his way into further difficulty. Though subjected to a horrific curse, he nonetheless remains blind to his own refusal to listen to the counsel of others. Shocked into the recognition of his true condition, he faces a future with more self-knowledge than a human could possibly bear. Such a fate would have troubled Athenians deeply. As the center of Greek philosophical, historical, and scientific inquiry, the city proudly defined itself as a place where the rational pursuit of knowledge thrived. But Oedipus has fallen victim to his understandable desire to know. Exiled from the city he loves, he leaves the stage an isolated and damaged figure.

OEDIPUS THE KING

Dramatis Personae

OEDIPUS
THE PRIEST OF ZEUS
CREON
CHORUS OF THEBAN ELDERS
TEIRESIAS
JOCASTA
MESSENGER
HERD OF LAIUS

Scene

Thebes. Before the Palace of Oedipus. Suppliants of all ages are seated round the altar at the palace doors, at their head a PRIEST OF ZEUS. To them enter OEDIPUS.

Oedipus

My children, latest born to Cadmus old,
Why sit ye here as suppliants, in your hands
Branches of olive filleted with wool?
What means this reek of incense everywhere,
And everywhere laments and litanies?
Children, it were not meet that I should learn
From others, and am hither come, myself,
I Oedipus, your world-renowned king.
Ho! aged sire, whose venerable locks
Proclaim thee spokesman of this company,
Explain your mood and purport. Is it dread
Of ill that moves you or a boon ye crave?
My zeal in your behalf ye cannot doubt;
Ruthless indeed were I and obdurate
If such petitioners as you I spurned.

Priest

Yea, Oedipus, my sovereign lord and king,
Thou seest how both extremes of age besiege
Thy palace altars–fledglings hardly winged,
And greybeards bowed with years, priests, as am I
Of Zeus, and these the flower of our youth.
Meanwhile, the common folk, with wreathed boughs
Crowd our two market-places, or before
Both shrines of Pallas congregate, or where
Ismenus gives his oracles by fire.
For, as thou seest thyself, our ship of State,
Sore buffeted, can no more lift her head,
Foundered beneath a weltering surge of blood.
A blight is on our harvest in the ear,
A blight upon the grazing flocks and herds,
A blight on wives in travail; and withal
Armed with his blazing torch the God of Plague
Hath swooped upon our city emptying
The house of Cadmus, and the murky realm
Of Pluto is full fed with groans and tears.

Therefore, O King, here at thy hearth we sit,
I and these children; not as deeming thee
A new divinity, but the first of men;
First in the common accidents of life,
And first in visitations of the Gods.
Art thou not he who coming to the town
Of Cadmus freed us from the tax we paid
To the fell songs tress? Nor hadst thou received
Prompting from us or been by others schooled;
No, by a god inspired (so all men deem,
And testify) didst thou renew our life.
And now, O Oedipus, our peerless king,
All we thy votaries beseech thee, find
Some succor, whether by a voice from heaven
Whispered, or haply known by human wit.
Tried counselors, methinks, are aptest found
To furnish for the future pregnant rede.
Upraise, O chief of men, upraise our State!
Look to thy laurels! for thy zeal of yore
Our country's savior thou art justly hailed:
O never may we thus record thy reign:–
"He raised us up only to cast us down."
Uplift us, build our city on a rock.
Thy happy star ascendant brought us luck,
O let it not decline! If thou wouldst rule
This land, as now thou reignest, better sure
To rule a peopled than a desert realm.
Nor battlements nor galleys aught avail,
If men to man and guards to guard them tail.

Oedipus

Ah! my poor children, known, ah, known too well,
The quest that brings you hither and your need.
Ye sicken all, well wot I, yet my pain,
How great soever yours, outtops it all.
Your sorrow touches each man severally,
Him and none other, but I grieve at once
Both for the general and myself and you.
Therefore ye rouse no sluggard from day-dreams.
Many, my children, are the tears I've wept,
And threaded many a maze of weary thought.
Thus pondering one clue of hope I caught,
And tracked it up; I have sent Menoeceus' son,
Creon, my consort's brother, to inquire Of Pythian
Phoebus at his Delphic shrine,
How I might save the State by act or word.

And now I reckon up the tale of days
Since he set forth, and marvel how he fares.
'Tis strange, this endless tarrying, passing strange.
But when he comes, then I were base indeed,
If I perform not all the god declares.

Priest

Thy words are well timed; even as thou speakest
That shouting tells me Creon is at hand.

Oedipus

O King Apollo! may his joyous looks
Be presage of the joyous news he brings!

Priest

As I surmise, 'tis welcome; else his head
Had scarce been crowned with berry-laden bays.

Oedipus

We soon shall know; he's now in earshot range.
Enter CREON.
My royal cousin, say, Menoeceus' child,
What message hast thou brought us from the god?

Creon

Good news, for e'en intolerable ills,
Finding right issue, tend to naught but good.

Oedipus

How runs the oracle? thus far thy words
Give me no ground for confidence or fear.

Creon

If thou wouldst hear my message publicly,
I'll tell thee straight, or with thee pass within.

Oedipus

Speak before all; the burden that I bear
Is more for these my subjects than myself.

Creon

Let me report then all the god declared.
King Phoebus bids us straitly extirpate
A fell pollution that infests the land,
And no more harbor an inveterate sore.

Oedipus

What expiation means he? What's amiss?

Creon

Banishment, or the shedding blood for blood.
This stain of blood makes shipwreck of our state.

Oedipus

Whom can he mean, the miscreant thus denounced?

Creon

Before thou didst assume the helm of State,
The sovereign of this land was Laius.

Oedipus

I heard as much, but never saw the man.

Creon

He fell; and now the god's command is plain:
Punish his takers-off, whoe'er they be.

Oedipus

Where are they? Where in the wide world to find
The far, faint traces of a bygone crime?

Creon

In this land, said the god; "who seeks shall find;
Who sits with folded hands or sleeps is blind."

Oedipus

Was he within his palace, or afield,
Or traveling, when Laius met his fate?

Creon

Abroad; he started, so he told us, bound
For Delphi, but he never thence returned.

Oedipus

Came there no news, no fellow-traveler
To give some clue that might be followed up?

Creon

But one escape, who flying for dear life,
Could tell of all he saw but one thing sure.

Oedipus

And what was that? One clue might lead us far,
With but a spark of hope to guide our quest.

Creon

Robbers, he told us, not one bandit but
A troop of knaves, attacked and murdered him.

Oedipus

Did any bandit dare so bold a stroke,
Unless indeed he were suborned from Thebes?

Creon

So 'twas surmised, but none was found to avenge
His murder mid the trouble that ensued.

Oedipus

What trouble can have hindered a full quest,
When royalty had fallen thus miserably?

Creon

The riddling Sphinx compelled us to let slide
The dim past and attend to instant needs.

Oedipus

Well, I will start afresh and once again

Make dark things clear. Right worthy the concern
Of Phoebus, worthy thine too, for the dead;
I also, as is meet, will lend my aid
To avenge this wrong to Thebes and to the god.
Not for some far-off kinsman, but myself,
Shall I expel this poison in the blood;
For whoso slew that king might have a mind
To strike me too with his assassin hand.
Therefore in righting him I serve myself.
Up, children, haste ye, quit these altar stairs,
Take hence your suppliant wands, go summon hither
The Theban commons. With the god's good help
Success is sure; 'tis ruin if we fail.
Exeunt OEDIPUS and CREON.

Priest

Come, children, let us hence; these gracious words
Forestall the very purpose of our suit.
And may the god who sent this oracle
Save us withal and rid us of this pest.
Exeunt PRIEST and SUPPLIANTS.

Chorus

strophe 1

Sweet-voiced daughter of Zeus from thy gold-paved
    Pythian shrine
Wafted to Thebes divine,
What dost thou bring me? My soul is racked and shivers
    with fear.
Healer of Delos, hear!
Hast thou some pain unknown before,
Or with the circling years renewest a penance of yore?
Offspring of golden Hope, thou voice immortal, O tell me.

antistrophe 1

First on Athene I call; O Zeus-born goddess, defend!
Goddess and sister, befriend,
Artemis, Lady of Thebes, high-throned in the midst of
    our mart!
Lord of the death-winged dart!
Your threefold aid I crave
From death and ruin our city to save.

If in the days of old when we nigh had perished, ye drave
From our land the fiery plague, be near us now and
    defend us!

strophe 2

Ah me, what countless woes are mine!
All our host is in decline;
Weaponless my spirit lies.
Earth her gracious fruits denies;
Women wail in barren throes;
Life on life downstriken goes,
Swifter than the wind bird's flight,
Swifter than the Fire-God's might,
To the westering shores of Night.

antistrophe 2

Wasted thus by death on death
All our city perisheth.
Corpses spread infection round;
None to tend or mourn is found.
Wailing on the altar stair
Wives and grandams rend the air–
Long-drawn moans and piercing cries
Blent with prayers and litanies.
Golden child of Zeus, O hear
Let thine angel face appear!

strophe 3

And grant that Ares whose hot breath I feel,
Though without targe or steel
He stalks, whose voice is as the battle shout,
May turn in sudden rout,
To the unharbored Thracian waters sped,
Or Amphitrite's bed.
For what night leaves undone,
Smit by the morrow's sun
Perisheth. Father Zeus, whose hand
Doth wield the lightning brand,
Slay him beneath thy levin bold, we pray,
Slay him, O slay!

antistrophe 3

O that thine arrows too, Lycean King,

From that taut bow's gold string,
Might fly abroad, the champions of our rights;
Yea, and the flashing lights
Of Artemis, wherewith the huntress sweeps
Across the Lycian steeps.
Thee too I call with golden-snooded hair,
Whose name our land doth bear,
Bacchus to whom thy Maenads Evoe shout;
Come with thy bright torch, rout,
Blithe god whom we adore,
The god whom gods abhor.
Enter OEDIPUS.

Oedipus

Ye pray; 'tis well, but would ye hear my words
And heed them and apply the remedy,
Ye might perchance find comfort and relief.
Mind you, I speak as one who comes a stranger
To this report, no less than to the crime;
For how unaided could I track it far
Without a clue? Which lacking (for too late
Was I enrolled a citizen of Thebes)
This proclamation I address to all:–
Thebans, if any knows the man by whom
Laius, son of Labdacus, was slain,
I summon him to make clean shrift to me.
And if he shrinks, let him reflect that thus
Confessing he shall 'scape the capital charge;
For the worst penalty that shall befall him
Is banishment unscathed he shall depart.
But if an alien from a foreign land
Be known to any as the murderer,
Let him who knows speak out, and he shall have
Due recompense from me and thanks to boot.
But if ye still keep silence, if through fear
For self or friends ye disregard my hest,
Hear what I then resolve; I lay my ban
On the assassin whosoe'er he be.
Let no man in this land, whereof I hold
The sovereign rule, harbor or speak to him;
Give him no part in prayer or sacrifice
Or lustral rites, but hound him from your homes.
For this is our defilement, so the god
Hath lately shown to me by oracles.
Thus as their champion I maintain the cause
Both of the god and of the murdered King.

And on the murderer this curse I lay
(On him and all the partners in his guilt):–
Wretch, may he pine in utter wretchedness!
And for myself, if with my privity
He gain admittance to my hearth, I pray
The curse I laid on others fall on me.
See that ye give effect to all my hest,
For my sake and the god's and for our land,
A desert blasted by the wrath of heaven.
For, let alone the god's express command,
It were a scandal ye should leave unpurged
The murder of a great man and your king,
Nor track it home. And now that I am lord,
Successor to his throne, his bed, his wife,
(And had he not been frustrate in the hope
Of issue, common children of one womb
Had forced a closer bond twixt him and me,
But Fate swooped down upon him), therefore I
His blood-avenger will maintain his cause
As though he were my sire, and leave no stone
Unturned to track the assassin or avenge
The son of Labdacus, of Polydore,
Of Cadmus, and Agenor first of the race.
And for the disobedient thus I pray:
May the gods send them neither timely fruits
Of earth, nor teeming increase of the womb,
But may they waste and pine, as now they waste,
Aye and worse stricken; but to all of you,
My loyal subjects who approve my acts,
May Justice, our ally, and all the gods
Be gracious and attend you evermore.

Chorus

The oath thou profferest, sire, I take and swear.
I slew him not myself, nor can I name
The slayer. For the quest, 'twere well, methinks
That Phoebus, who proposed the riddle, himself
Should give the answer–who the murderer was.

Oedipus

Well argued; but no living man can hope
To force the gods to speak against their will.

Chorus

May I then say what seems next best to me?

Oedipus

Aye, if there be a third best, tell it too.

Chorus

My liege, if any man sees eye to eye
With our lord Phoebus, 'tis our prophet, lord
Teiresias; he of all men best might guide
A searcher of this matter to the light.

Oedipus

Here too my zeal has nothing lagged, for twice At
Creon's instance have I sent to fetch him,
And long I marvel why he is not here.

Chorus

I mind me too of rumors long ago—
Mere gossip.

Oedipus

Tell them, I would fain know all.

Chorus

'Twas said he fell by travelers.

Oedipus

So I heard,
But none has seen the man who saw him fall.

Chorus

Well, if he knows what fear is, he will quail
And flee before the terror of thy curse.

Oedipus

Words scare not him who blenches not at deeds.

Chorus

But here is one to arraign him. Lo, at length
They bring the god-inspired seer in whom
Above all other men is truth inborn.

Enter TEIRESIAS, led by a boy.

Oedipus

Teiresias, seer who comprehendest all,
Lore of the wise and hidden mysteries,
High things of heaven and low things of the earth,
Thou knowest, though thy blinded eyes see naught,
What plague infects our city; and we turn
To thee, O seer, our one defense and shield.
The purport of the answer that the God
Returned to us who sought his oracle,
The messengers have doubtless told thee–how
One course alone could rid us of the pest,
To find the murderers of Laius,
And slay them or expel them from the land.
Therefore begrudging neither augury
Nor other divination that is thine,
O save thyself, thy country, and thy king,
Save all from this defilement of blood shed.
On thee we rest. This is man's highest end,
To others' service all his powers to lend.

Teiresias

Alas, alas, what misery to be wise
When wisdom profits nothing! This old lore
I had forgotten; else I were not here.

Oedipus

What ails thee? Why this melancholy mood?

Teiresias

Let me go home; prevent me not; 'twere best
That thou shouldst bear thy burden and I mine.

Oedipus

For shame! no true-born Theban patriot
Would thus withhold the word of prophecy.

Teiresias

Thy words, O king, are wide of the mark, and I
For fear lest I too trip like thee …

Oedipus

Oh speak,
Withhold not, I adjure thee, if thou know'st,
Thy knowledge. We are all thy suppliants.

Teiresias

Aye, for ye all are witless, but my voice
Will ne'er reveal my miseries–or thine.

Oedipus

What then, thou knowest, and yet willst not speak!
Wouldst thou betray us and destroy the State?

Teiresias

I will not vex myself nor thee. Why ask
Thus idly what from me thou shalt not learn?

Oedipus

Monster! thy silence would incense a flint.
Will nothing loose thy tongue? Can nothing melt thee,
Or shake thy dogged taciturnity?

Teiresias

Thou blam'st my mood and seest not thine own
Wherewith thou art mated; no, thou taxest me.

Oedipus

And who could stay his choler when he heard
How insolently thou dost flout the State?

Teiresias

Well, it will come what will, though I be mute.

Oedipus

Since come it must, thy duty is to tell me.

Teiresias

I have no more to say; storm as thou willst,
And give the rein to all thy pent-up rage.

Oedipus

Yea, I am wroth, and will not stint my words,
But speak my whole mind. Thou methinks thou art he,
Who planned the crime, aye, and performed it too,
All save the assassination; and if thou
Hadst not been blind, I had been sworn to boot
That thou alone didst do the bloody deed.

Teiresias

Is it so? Then I charge thee to abide
By thine own proclamation; from this day
Speak not to these or me. Thou art the man,
Thou the accursed polluter of this land.

Oedipus

Vile slanderer, thou blurtest forth these taunts,
And think'st forsooth as seer to go scot free.

Teiresias

Yea, I am free, strong in the strength of truth.

Oedipus

Who was thy teacher? not methinks thy art.

Teiresias

Thou, goading me against my will to speak.

Oedipus

What speech? repeat it and resolve my doubt.

Teiresias

Didst miss my sense wouldst thou goad me on?

Oedipus

I but half caught thy meaning; say it again.

Teiresias

I say thou art the murderer of the man
Whose murderer thou pursuest.

Oedipus

Thou shalt rue it
Twice to repeat so gross a calumny.

Teiresias

Must I say more to aggravate thy rage?

Oedipus

Say all thou wilt; it will be but waste of breath.

Teiresias

I say thou livest with thy nearest kin
In infamy, unwitting in thy shame.

Oedipus

Think'st thou for aye unscathed to wag thy tongue?

Teiresias

Yea, if the might of truth can aught prevail.

Oedipus

With other men, but not with thee, for thou
In ear, wit, eye, in everything art blind.

Teiresias

Poor fool to utter gibes at me which all
Here present will cast back on thee ere long.

Oedipus

Offspring of endless Night, thou hast no power
O'er me or any man who sees the sun.

Teiresias

No, for thy weird is not to fall by me.
I leave to Apollo what concerns the god.

Oedipus

Is this a plot of Creon, or thine own?

Teiresias

Not Creon, thou thyself art thine own bane.

Oedipus

O wealth and empiry and skill by skill
Outwitted in the battlefield of life,
What spite and envy follow in your train!
See, for this crown the State conferred on me.
A gift, a thing I sought not, for this crown
The trusty Creon, my familiar friend,
Hath lain in wait to oust me and suborned
This mountebank, this juggling charlatan,
This tricksy beggar-priest, for gain alone
Keen-eyed, but in his proper art stone-blind.
Say, sirrah, hast thou ever proved thyself
A prophet? When the riddling Sphinx was here
Why hadst thou no deliverance for this folk?
And yet the riddle was not to be solved
By guess-work but required the prophet's art;
Wherein thou wast found lacking; neither birds
Nor sign from heaven helped thee, but I came,
The simple Oedipus; I stopped her mouth
By mother wit, untaught of auguries.
This is the man whom thou wouldst undermine,
In hope to reign with Creon in my stead.
Methinks that thou and thine abettor soon
Will rue your plot to drive the scapegoat out.
Thank thy grey hairs that thou hast still to learn
What chastisement such arrogance deserves.

Chorus

To us it seems that both the seer and thou,
O Oedipus, have spoken angry words.
This is no time to wrangle but consult
How best we may fulfill the oracle.

Teiresias

King as thou art, free speech at least is mine
To make reply; in this I am thy peer.
I own no lord but Loxias; him I serve
And ne'er can stand enrolled as Creon's man.
Thus then I answer: since thou hast not spared
To twit me with my blindness—thou hast eyes,
Yet see'st not in what misery thou art fallen,
Nor where thou dwellest nor with whom for mate.
Dost know thy lineage? Nay, thou know'st it not,
And all unwitting art a double foe
To thine own kin, the living and the dead;
Aye and the dogging curse of mother and sire
One day shall drive thee, like a two-edged sword,
Beyond our borders, and the eyes that now
See clear shall henceforward endless night.
Ah whither shall thy bitter cry not reach,
What crag in all Cithaeron but shall then
Reverberate thy wail, when thou hast found
With what a hymeneal thou wast borne
Home, but to no fair haven, on the gale!
Aye, and a flood of ills thou guessest not
Shall set thyself and children in one line.
Flout then both Creon and my words, for none
Of mortals shall be striken worse than thou.

Oedipus

Must I endure this fellow's insolence?
A murrain on thee! Get thee hence! Begone
Avaunt! and never cross my threshold more.

Teiresias

I ne'er had come hadst thou not bidden me.

Oedipus

I know not thou wouldst utter folly, else
Long hadst thou waited to be summoned here.

Teiresias

Such am I—as it seems to thee a fool,
But to the parents who begat thee, wise.

Oedipus

What sayest thou—"parents"? Who begat me, speak?

Teiresias

This day shall be thy birth-day, and thy grave.

Oedipus

Thou lov'st to speak in riddles and dark words.

Teiresias

In reading riddles who so skilled as thou?

Oedipus

Twit me with that wherein my greatness lies.

Teiresias

And yet this very greatness proved thy bane.

Oedipus

No matter if I saved the commonwealth.

Teiresias

'Tis time I left thee. Come, boy, take me home.

Oedipus

Aye, take him quickly, for his presence irks
And lets me; gone, thou canst not plague me more.

Teiresias

I go, but first will tell thee why I came.
Thy frown I dread not, for thou canst not harm me.
Hear then: this man whom thou hast sought to arrest
With threats and warrants this long while, the wretch

Who murdered Laius–that man is here.
He passes for an alien in the land
But soon shall prove a Theban, native born.
And yet his fortune brings him little joy;
For blind of seeing, clad in beggar's weeds,
For purple robes, and leaning on his staff,
To a strange land he soon shall grope his way.
And of the children, inmates of his home,
He shall be proved the brother and the sire,
Of her who bare him son and husband both,
Co-partner, and assassin of his sire.
Go in and ponder this, and if thou find
That I have missed the mark, henceforth declare
I have no wit nor skill in prophecy.

Exeunt TEIRESIAS and OEDIPUS.

Chorus

strophe 1

Who is he by voice immortal named from Pythia's rocky
    cell,
Doer of foul deeds of bloodshed, horrors that no tongue
    can tell?
A foot for flight he needs
Fleeter than storm-swift steeds,
For on his heels doth follow,
Armed with the lightnings of his Sire, Apollo.
Like sleuth-hounds too
The Fates pursue.

antistrophe 1

Yea, but now flashed forth the summons from Parnassus'
    snowy peak,
"Near and far the undiscovered doer of this murder seek!"
Now like a sullen bull he roves
Through forest brakes and upland groves,
And vainly seeks to fly
The doom that ever nigh
Flits o'er his head,
Still by the avenging Phoebus sped,
The voice divine,
From Earth's mid shrine.

strophe 2

Sore perplexed am I by the words of the master seer.
Are they true, are they false? I know not and bridle my
    tongue for fear,
Fluttered with vague surmise; nor present nor future is clear.
Quarrel of ancient date or in days still near know I none
Twixt the Labdacidan house and our ruler, Polybus' son.
Proof is there none: how then can I challenge our King's
    good name,
How in a blood-feud join for an untracked deed of shame?

antistrophe 2

All wise are Zeus and Apollo, and nothing is hid from
    their ken;
They are gods; and in wits a man may surpass his fellow
    men;
But that a mortal seer knows more than I know—where
Hath this been proven? Or how without sign assured,
    can I blame
Him who saved our State when the winged songstress came,
Tested and tried in the light of us all, like gold assayed?
How can I now assent when a crime is on Oedipus laid?

Creon

Friends, countrymen, I learn King Oedipus
Hath laid against me a most grievous charge,
And come to you protesting. If he deems
That I have harmed or injured him in aught
By word or deed in this our present trouble,
I care not to prolong the span of life,
Thus ill-reputed; for the calumny
Hits not a single blot, but blasts my name,
If by the general voice I am denounced
False to the State and false by you my friends.

Chorus

This taunt, it well may be, was blurted out
In petulance, not spoken advisedly.

Creon

Did any dare pretend that it was I
Prompted the seer to utter a forged charge?

Chorus

Such things were said; with what intent I know not.

Creon

Were not his wits and vision all astray
When upon me he fixed this monstrous charge?

Chorus

I know not; to my sovereign's acts I am blind.
But lo, he comes to answer for himself.

Enter OEDIPUS.

Oedipus

Sirrah, what mak'st thou here? Dost thou presume
To approach my doors, thou brazen-faced rogue,
My murderer and the filcher of my crown?
Come, answer this, didst thou detect in me
Some touch of cowardice or witlessness,
That made thee undertake this enterprise?
I seemed forsooth too simple to perceive
The serpent stealing on me in the dark,
Or else too weak to scotch it when I saw.
This thou art witless seeking to possess
Without a following or friends the crown,
A prize that followers and wealth must win.

Creon

Attend me. Thou hast spoken, 'tis my turn
To make reply. Then having heard me, judge.

Oedipus

Thou art glib of tongue, but I am slow to learn
Of thee; I know too well thy venomous hate.

Creon

First I would argue out this very point.

Oedipus

O argue not that thou art not a rogue.

Creon

If thou dost count a virtue stubbornness,
Unschooled by reason, thou art much astray.

Oedipus

If thou dost hold a kinsman may be wronged,
And no pains follow, thou art much to seek.

Creon

Therein thou judgest rightly, but this wrong
That thou allegest–tell me what it is.

Oedipus

Didst thou or didst thou not advise that I
Should call the priest?

Creon

Yes, and I stand to it.

Oedipus

Tell me how long is it since Laius ...

Creon

Since Laius ...? I follow not thy drift.

Oedipus

By violent hands was spirited away.

Creon

In the dim past, a many years agone.

Oedipus

Did the same prophet then pursue his craft?

Creon

Yes, skilled as now and in no less repute.

Oedipus

Did he at that time ever glance at me?

Creon

Not to my knowledge, not when I was by.

Oedipus

But was no search and inquisition made?

Creon

Surely full quest was made, but nothing learnt.

Oedipus

Why failed the seer to tell his story then?

Creon

I know not, and not knowing hold my tongue.

Oedipus

This much thou knowest and canst surely tell.

Creon

What's mean'st thou? All I know I will declare.

Oedipus

But for thy prompting never had the seer
Ascribed to me the death of Laius.

Creon

If so he thou knowest best; but I
Would put thee to the question in my turn.

Oedipus

Question and prove me murderer if thou canst.

Creon

Then let me ask thee, didst thou wed my sister?

Oedipus

A fact so plain I cannot well deny.

Creon

And as thy consort queen she shares the throne?

Oedipus

I grant her freely all her heart desires.

Creon

And with you twain I share the triple rule?

Oedipus

Yea, and it is that proves thee a false friend.

Creon

Not so, if thou wouldst reason with thyself,
As I with myself. First, I bid thee think,
Would any mortal choose a troubled reign
Of terrors rather than secure repose,
If the same power were given him? As for me,
I have no natural craving for the name
Of king, preferring to do kingly deeds,
And so thinks every sober-minded man.
Now all my needs are satisfied through thee,
And I have naught to fear; but were I king,
My acts would oft run counter to my will.
How could a title then have charms for me
Above the sweets of boundless influence?
I am not so infatuate as to grasp
The shadow when I hold the substance fast.
Now all men cry me Godspeed! wish me well,
And every suitor seeks to gain my ear,
If he would hope to win a grace from thee.
Why should I leave the better, choose the worse?
That were sheer madness, and I am not mad.
No such ambition ever tempted me,
Nor would I have a share in such intrigue.

And if thou doubt me, first to Delphi go,
There ascertain if my report was true
Of the god's answer; next investigate
If with the seer I plotted or conspired,
And if it prove so, sentence me to death,
Not by thy voice alone, but mine and thine.
But O condemn me not, without appeal,
On bare suspicion. 'Tis not right to adjudge
Bad men at random good, or good men bad.
I would as lief a man should cast away
The thing he counts most precious, his own life,
As spurn a true friend. Thou wilt learn in time
The truth, for time alone reveals the just;
A villain is detected in a day.

Chorus

To one who walketh warily his words
Commend themselves; swift counsels are not sure.

Oedipus

When with swift strides the stealthy plotter stalks
I must be quick too with my counterplot.
To wait his onset passively, for him
Is sure success, for me assured defeat.

Creon

What then's thy will? To banish me the land?

Oedipus

I would not have thee banished, no, but dead,
That men may mark the wages envy reaps.

Creon

I see thou wilt not yield, nor credit me.

Oedipus

None but a fool would credit such as thou.

Creon

Thou art not wise.

Oedipus

Wise for myself at least.

Creon

Why not for me too?

Oedipus

Why for such a knave?

Creon

Suppose thou lackest sense.

Oedipus

Yet kings must rule.

Oedipus

Not if they rule ill.

Oedipus

Oh my Thebans, hear him!

Creon

Thy Thebans? am not I a Theban too?

Chorus

Cease, princes; lo there comes, and none too soon,
Jocasta from the palace. Who so fit
As peacemaker to reconcile your feud?

Enter JOCASTA.

Jocasta

Misguided princes, why have ye upraised
This wordy wrangle? Are ye not ashamed,
While the whole land lies stricken, thus to voice
Your private injuries? Go in, my lord;
Go home, my brother, and forebear to make
A public scandal of a petty grief.

Creon

My royal sister, Oedipus, thy lord,
Hath bid me choose (O dread alternative!)
An outlaw's exile or a felon's death.

Oedipus

Yes, lady; I have caught him practicing
Against my royal person his vile arts.

Creon

May I ne'er speed but die accursed, if I
In any way am guilty of this charge.

Jocasta

Believe him, I adjure thee, Oedipus,
First for his solemn oath's sake, then for mine,
And for thine elders' sake who wait on thee.

Chorus

strophe 1

Hearken, King, reflect, we pray thee, but not stubborn
    but relent.

Oedipus

Say to what should I consent?

Chorus

Respect a man whose probity and troth
Are known to all and now confirmed by oath.

Oedipus

Dost know what grace thou cravest?

Chorus

Yea, I know.

Oedipus

Declare it then and make thy meaning plain.

Chorus

Brand not a friend whom babbling tongues assail;
Let not suspicion 'gainst his oath prevail.

Oedipus

Bethink you that in seeking this ye seek
In very sooth my death or banishment?

Chorus

No, by the leader of the host divine!

strophe 2

Witness, thou Sun, such thought was never mine,
Unblest, unfriended may I perish,
If ever I such wish did cherish!
But O my heart is desolate
Musing on our striken State,
Doubly fall'n should discord grow
Twixt you twain, to crown our woe.

Oedipus

Well, let him go, no matter what it cost me,
Or certain death or shameful banishment,
For your sake I relent, not his; and him,
Where'er he be, my heart shall still abhor.

Creon

Thou art as sullen in thy yielding mood
As in thine anger thou wast truculent.
Such tempers justly plague themselves the most.

Oedipus

Leave me in peace and get thee gone.

Creon

I go,

By thee misjudged, but justified by these.

Exeunt CREON.

Chorus

antistrophe 1

Lady, lead indoors thy consort; wherefore longer here
    delay?

Jocasta

Tell me first how rose the fray.

Chorus

Rumors bred unjust suspicious and injustice rankles sore.

Jocasta

Were both at fault?

Chorus

Both.

Jocasta

What was the tale?

Chorus

Ask me no more. The land is sore distressed; 'Twere
    better sleeping ills to leave at rest.

Oedipus

Strange counsel, friend! I know thou mean'st me well,
And yet would'st mitigate and blunt my zeal.

Chorus

antistrophe 2

King, I say it once again,
Witless were I proved, insane,

If I lightly put away
Thee my country's prop and stay,
Pilot who, in danger sought,
To a quiet haven brought
Our distracted State; and now
Who can guide us right but thou?

Jocasta

Let me too, I adjure thee, know, O king,
What cause has stirred this unrelenting wrath.

Oedipus

I will, for thou art more to me than these.
Lady, the cause is Creon and his plots.

Jocasta

But what provoked the quarrel? make this clear.

Oedipus

He points me out as Laius' murderer.

Jocasta

Of his own knowledge or upon report?

Oedipus

He is too cunning to commit himself,
And makes a mouthpiece of a knavish seer.

Jocasta

Then thou mayest ease thy conscience on that score.
Listen and I'll convince thee that no man
Hath scot or lot in the prophetic art.
Here is the proof in brief. An oracle
Once came to Laius (I will not say
'Twas from the Delphic god himself, but from
His ministers) declaring he was doomed
To perish by the hand of his own son,
A child that should be born to him by me.
Now Laius–so at least report affirmed–
Was murdered on a day by highwaymen,

No natives, at a spot where three roads meet.
As for the child, it was but three days old,
When Laius, its ankles pierced and pinned
Together, gave it to be cast away
By others on the trackless mountain side.
So then Apollo brought it not to pass
The child should be his father's murderer,
Or the dread terror find accomplishment,
And Laius be slain by his own son.
Such was the prophet's horoscope. O king,
Regard it not. Whate'er the god deems fit
To search, himself unaided will reveal.

Oedipus

What memories, what wild tumult of the soul
Came o'er me, lady, as I heard thee speak!

Jocasta

What mean'st thou? What has shocked and startled thee?

Oedipus

Methought I heard thee say that Laius
Was murdered at the meeting of three roads.

Jocasta

So ran the story that is current still.

Oedipus

Where did this happen? Dost thou know the place?

Jocasta

Phocis the land is called; the spot is where
Branch roads from Delphi and from Daulis meet.

Oedipus

And how long is it since these things befell?

Jocasta

'Twas but a brief while were thou wast proclaimed

Our country's ruler that the news was brought.

Oedipus

O Zeus, what hast thou willed to do with me!

Jocasta

What is it, Oedipus, that moves thee so?

Oedipus

Ask me not yet; tell me the build and height
Of Laius? Was he still in manhood's prime?

Jocasta

Tall was he, and his hair was lightly strewn
With silver; and not unlike thee in form.

Oedipus

O woe is me! Methinks unwittingly
I laid but now a dread curse on myself.

Jocasta

What say'st thou? When I look upon thee, my king,
I tremble.

Oedipus

'Tis a dread presentiment
That in the end the seer will prove not blind.
One further question to resolve my doubt.

Jocasta

I quail; but ask, and I will answer all.

Oedipus

Had he but few attendants or a train
Of armed retainers with him, like a prince?

Jocasta

They were but five in all, and one of them
A herald; Laius in a mule-car rode.

Oedipus

Alas! 'tis clear as noonday now. But say,
Lady, who carried this report to Thebes?

Jocasta

A serf, the sole survivor who returned.

Oedipus

Haply he is at hand or in the house?

Jocasta

No, for as soon as he returned and found
Thee reigning in the stead of Laius slain,
He clasped my hand and supplicated me
To send him to the alps and pastures, where
He might be farthest from the sight of Thebes.
And so I sent him. 'Twas an honest slave
And well deserved some better recompense.

Oedipus

Fetch him at once. I fain would see the man.

Jocasta

He shall be brought; but wherefore summon him?

Oedipus

Lady, I fear my tongue has overrun
Discretion; therefore I would question him.

Jocasta

Well, he shall come, but may not I too claim
To share the burden of thy heart, my king?

Oedipus

And thou shalt not be frustrate of thy wish.
Now my imaginings have gone so far.
Who has a higher claim that thou to hear
My tale of dire adventures? Listen then.
My sire was Polybus of Corinth, and
My mother Merope, a Dorian;
And I was held the foremost citizen,
Till a strange thing befell me, strange indeed,
Yet scarce deserving all the heat it stirred.
A roisterer at some banquet, flown with wine,
Shouted "Thou art not true son of thy sire."
It irked me, but I stomached for the nonce
The insult; on the morrow I sought out
My mother and my sire and questioned them.
They were indignant at the random slur
Cast on my parentage and did their best
To comfort me, but still the venomed barb
Rankled, for still the scandal spread and grew.
So privily without their leave I went
To Delphi, and Apollo sent me back
Baulked of the knowledge that I came to seek.
But other grievous things he prophesied,
Woes, lamentations, mourning, portents dire;
To wit I should defile my mother's bed
And raise up seed too loathsome to behold,
And slay the father from whose loins I sprang.
Then, lady,—thou shalt hear the very truth–
As I drew near the triple-branching roads,
A herald met me and a man who sat
In a car drawn by colts–as in thy tale–
The man in front and the old man himself
Threatened to thrust me rudely from the path,
Then jostled by the charioteer in wrath
I struck him, and the old man, seeing this,
Watched till I passed and from his car brought down
Full on my head the double-pointed goad.
Yet was I quits with him and more; one stroke
Of my good staff sufficed to fling him clean
Out of the chariot seat and laid him prone.
And so I slew them every one. But if
Betwixt this stranger there was aught in common
With Laius, who more miserable than I,
What mortal could you find more god-abhorred?
Wretch whom no sojourner, no citizen
May harbor or address, whom all are bound
To harry from their homes. And this same curse

Was laid on me, and laid by none but me.
Yea with these hands all gory I pollute
The bed of him I slew. Say, am I vile?
Am I not utterly unclean, a wretch
Doomed to be banished, and in banishment
Forgo the sight of all my dearest ones,
And never tread again my native earth;
Or else to wed my mother and slay my sire,
Polybus, who begat me and upreared?
If one should say, this is the handiwork
Of some inhuman power, who could blame
His judgment? But, ye pure and awful gods,
Forbid, forbid that I should see that day!
May I be blotted out from living men
Ere such a plague spot set on me its brand!

Chorus

We too, O king, are troubled; but till thou
Hast questioned the survivor, still hope on.

Oedipus

My hope is faint, but still enough survives
To bid me bide the coming of this herd.

Jocasta

Suppose him here, what wouldst thou learn of him?

Oedipus

I'll tell thee, lady; if his tale agrees
With thine, I shall have 'scaped calamity.

Jocasta

And what of special import did I say?

Oedipus

In thy report of what the herdsman said
Laius was slain by robbers; now if he
Still speaks of robbers, not a robber, I
Slew him not; "one" with "many" cannot square.
But if he says one lonely wayfarer,
The last link wanting to my guilt is forged.

Jocasta

Well, rest assured, his tale ran thus at first,
Nor can he now retract what then he said;
Not I alone but all our townsfolk heard it.
E'en should he vary somewhat in his story,
He cannot make the death of Laius
In any wise jump with the oracle.
For Loxias said expressly he was doomed
To die by my child's hand, but he, poor babe,
He shed no blood, but perished first himself.
So much for divination. Henceforth I
Will look for signs neither to right nor left.

Oedipus

Thou reasonest well. Still I would have thee send
And fetch the bondsman hither. See to it.

Jocasta

That will I straightway. Come, let us within.
I would do nothing that my lord mislikes.

Exeunt OEDIPUS and JOCASTA.

Chorus

strophe 1

My lot be still to lead
The life of innocence and fly
Irreverence in word or deed,
To follow still those laws ordained on high
Whose birthplace is the bright ethereal sky
No mortal birth they own,
Olympus their progenitor alone:
Ne'er shall they slumber in oblivion cold,
The god in them is strong and grows not old.

antistrophe 1

Of insolence is bred
The tyrant; insolence full blown,
With empty riches surfeited,
Scales the precipitous height and grasps the throne.
Then topples o'er and lies in ruin prone;
No foothold on that dizzy steep.

But O may Heaven the true patriot keep
Who burns with emulous zeal to serve the State.
God is my help and hope, on him I wait.

strophe 2

But the proud sinner, or in word or deed,
That will not Justice heed,
Nor reverence the shrine
Of images divine,
Perdition seize his vain imaginings,
If, urged by greed profane,
He grasps at ill-got gain,
And lays an impious hand on holiest things.
Who when such deeds are done
Can hope heaven's bolts to shun?
If sin like this to honor can aspire,
Why dance I still and lead the sacred choir?

antistrophe 2

No more I'll seek earth's central oracle,
Or Abae's hallowed cell,
Nor to Olympia bring
My votive offering.
If before all God's truth be not bade plain.
O Zeus, reveal thy might,
King, if thou'rt named aright
Omnipotent, all-seeing, as of old;
For Laius is forgot;
His weird, men heed it not;
Apollo is forsook and faith grows cold.

Enter JOCASTA.

Jocasta

My lords, ye look amazed to see your queen
With wreaths and gifts of incense in her hands.
I had a mind to visit the high shrines,
For Oedipus is overwrought, alarmed
With terrors manifold. He will not use
His past experience, like a man of sense,
To judge the present need, but lends an ear
To any croaker if he augurs ill.

Since then my counsels naught avail, I turn
To thee, our present help in time of trouble,
Apollo, Lord Lycean, and to thee
My prayers and supplications here I bring.
Lighten us, lord, and cleanse us from this curse!
For now we all are cowed like mariners
Who see their helmsman dumbstruck in the storm.

Enter Corinthian MESSENGER.

Messenger

My masters, tell me where the palace is
Of Oedipus; or better, where's the king.

Chorus

Here is the palace and he bides within;
This is his queen the mother of his children.

Messenger

All happiness attend her and the house,
Blessed is her husband and her marriage-bed.

Jocasta

My greetings to thee, stranger; thy fair words
Deserve a like response. But tell me why
Thou comest—what thy need or what thy news.

Messenger

Good for thy consort and the royal house.

Jocasta

What may it be? Whose messenger art thou?

Messenger

The Isthmian commons have resolved to make
Thy husband king—so 'twas reported there.

Jocasta

What! is not aged Polybus still king?

Messenger

No, verily; he's dead and in his grave.

Jocasta

What! is he dead, the sire of Oedipus?

Messenger

If I speak falsely, may I die myself.

Jocasta

Quick, maiden, bear these tidings to my lord.
Ye god-sent oracles, where stand ye now!
This is the man whom Oedipus long shunned,
In dread to prove his murderer; and now
He dies in nature's course, not by his hand.

Enter OEDIPUS.

Oedipus

My wife, my queen, Jocasta, why hast thou
Summoned me from my palace?

Jocasta

Hear this man,
And as thou hearest judge what has become
Of all those awe-inspiring oracles.

Oedipus

Who is this man, and what his news for me?

Jocasta

He comes from Corinth and his message this:
Thy father Polybus hath passed away.

Oedipus

What? let me have it, stranger, from thy mouth.

Messenger

If I must first make plain beyond a doubt
My message, know that Polybus is dead.

Oedipus

By treachery, or by sickness visited?

Messenger

One touch will send an old man to his rest.

Oedipus

So of some malady he died, poor man.

Messenger

Yes, having measured the full span of years.

Oedipus

Out on it, lady! why should one regard
The Pythian hearth or birds that scream i' the air?
Did they not point at me as doomed to slay
My father? but he's dead and in his grave
And here am I who ne'er unsheathed a sword;
Unless the longing for his absent son
Killed him and so I slew him in a sense.
But, as they stand, the oracles are dead—
Dust, ashes, nothing, dead as Polybus.

Jocasta

Say, did not I foretell this long ago?

Oedipus

Thou didst: but I was misled by my fear.

Jocasta

Then let I no more weigh upon thy soul.

Oedipus

Must I not fear my mother's marriage bed.

Jocasta

Why should a mortal man, the sport of chance,
With no assured foreknowledge, be afraid?
Best live a careless life from hand to mouth.
This wedlock with thy mother fear not thou.
How oft it chances that in dreams a man
Has wed his mother! He who least regards
Such brainsick phantasies lives most at ease.

Oedipus

I should have shared in full thy confidence,
Were not my mother living; since she lives
Though half convinced I still must live in dread.

Jocasta

And yet thy sire's death lights out darkness much.

Oedipus

Much, but my fear is touching her who lives.

Messenger

Who may this woman be whom thus you fear?

Oedipus

Merope, stranger, wife of Polybus.

Messenger

And what of her can cause you any fear?

Oedipus

A heaven-sent oracle of dread import.

Messenger

A mystery, or may a stranger hear it?

Oedipus

Aye, 'tis no secret. Loxias once foretold
That I should mate with mine own mother, and shed

With my own hands the blood of my own sire.
Hence Corinth was for many a year to me
A home distant; and I trove abroad,
But missed the sweetest sight, my parents' face.

Messenger

Was this the fear that exiled thee from home?

Oedipus

Yea, and the dread of slaying my own sire.

Messenger

Why, since I came to give thee pleasure, King,
Have I not rid thee of this second fear?

Oedipus

Well, thou shalt have due guerdon for thy pains.

Messenger

Well, I confess what chiefly made me come
Was hope to profit by thy coming home.

Oedipus

Nay, I will ne'er go near my parents more.

Messenger

My son, 'tis plain, thou know'st not what thou doest.

Oedipus

How so, old man? For heaven's sake tell me all.

Messenger

If this is why thou dreadest to return.

Oedipus

Yea, lest the god's word be fulfilled in me.

Messenger

Lest through thy parents thou shouldst be accursed?

Oedipus

This and none other is my constant dread.

Messenger

Dost thou not know thy fears are baseless all?

Oedipus

How baseless, if I am their very son?

Messenger

Since Polybus was naught to thee in blood.

Oedipus

What say'st thou? was not Polybus my sire?

Messenger

As much thy sire as I am, and no more.

Oedipus

My sire no more to me than one who is naught?

Messenger

Since I begat thee not, no more did he.

Oedipus

What reason had he then to call me son?

Messenger

Know that he took thee from my hands, a gift.

Oedipus

Yet, if no child of his, he loved me well.

Messenger

A childless man till then, he warmed to thee.

Oedipus

A foundling or a purchased slave, this child?

Messenger

I found thee in Cithaeron's wooded glens.

Oedipus

What led thee to explore those upland glades?

Messenger

My business was to tend the mountain flocks.

Oedipus

A vagrant shepherd journeying for hire?

Messenger

True, but thy savior in that hour, my son.

Oedipus

My savior? from what harm? what ailed me then?

Messenger

Those ankle joints are evidence enow.

Oedipus

Ah, why remind me of that ancient sore?

Messenger

I loosed the pin that riveted thy feet.

Oedipus

Yes, from my cradle that dread brand I bore.

Messenger

Whence thou deriv'st the name that still is thine.

Oedipus

Who did it? I adjure thee, tell me who
Say, was it father, mother?

Messenger

I know not.
The man from whom I had thee may know more.

Oedipus

What, did another find me, not thyself?

Messenger

Not I; another shepherd gave thee me.

Oedipus

Who was he? Would'st thou know again the man?

Messenger

He passed indeed for one of Laius' house.

Oedipus

The king who ruled the country long ago?

Messenger

The same: he was a herdsman of the king.

Oedipus

And is he living still for me to see him?

Messenger

His fellow-countrymen should best know that.

Oedipus

Doth any bystander among you know
The herd he speaks of, or by seeing him
Afield or in the city? answer straight!
The hour hath come to clear this business up.

Oedipus

Methinks he means none other than the hind
Whom thou anon wert fain to see; but that
Our queen Jocasta best of all could tell.

Oedipus

Madam, dost know the man we sent to fetch?
Is the same of whom the stranger speaks?

Jocasta

Who is the man? What matter? Let it be.
'Twere waste of thought to weigh such idle words.

Oedipus

No, with such guiding clues I cannot fail
To bring to light the secret of my birth.

Jocasta

Oh, as thou carest for thy life, give o'er
This quest. Enough the anguish I endure.

Oedipus

Be of good cheer; though I be proved the son
Of a bondwoman, aye, through three descents
Triply a slave, thy honor is unsmirched.

Jocasta

Yet humor me, I pray thee; do not this.

Oedipus

I cannot; I must probe this matter home.

Jocasta

'Tis for thy sake I advise thee for the best.

Oedipus

I grow impatient of this best advice.

Jocasta

Ah mayst thou ne'er discover who thou art!

Oedipus

Go, fetch me here the herd, and
leave yon woman
To glory in her pride of ancestry.

Jocasta

O woe is thee, poor wretch!
With that last word I leave thee, henceforth silent
evermore.

Exit JOCASTA.

Chorus

Why, Oedipus, why stung with passionate grief
Hath the queen thus departed? Much I fear
From this dead calm will burst a storm of woes.

Oedipus

Let the storm burst, my fixed resolve still holds,
To learn my lineage, be it ne'er so low.
It may be she with all a woman's pride
Thinks scorn of my base parentage. But I
Who rank myself as Fortune's favorite child,
The giver of good gifts, shall not be shamed.
She is my mother and the changing moons
My brethren, and with them I wax and wane.
Thus sprung why should I fear to trace my birth?
Nothing can make me other than I am.

Chorus

strophe

If my soul prophetic err not, if my wisdom aught avail,
Thee, Cithaeron, I shall hail,
As the nurse and foster-mother of our Oedipus shall greet
Ere tomorrow's full moon rises, and exalt thee as is meet.
Dance and song shall hymn thy praises, lover of our
    royal race.
Phoebus, may my words find grace!

antistrophe

Child, who bare thee, nymph or goddess? sure thy sure
    was more than man,
Haply the hill-roamer Pan.
Of did Loxias beget thee, for he haunts the upland wold;
Or Cyllene's lord, or Bacchus, dweller on the hilltops cold?
Did some Heliconian Oread give him thee, a new-born joy?
Nymphs with whom he love to toy?

Oedipus

Elders, if I, who never yet before
Have met the man, may make a guess, methinks
I see the herdsman who we long have sought;
His time-worn aspect matches with the years
Of yonder aged messenger; besides
I seem to recognize the men who bring him
As servants of my own. But you, perchance,
Having in past days known or seen the herd,
May better by sure knowledge my surmise.

Chorus

I recognize him; one of Laius' house;
A simple hind, but true as any man.

Enter HERDSMAN.

Oedipus

Corinthian, stranger, I address thee first,
Is this the man thou meanest!

Messenger

This is he.

Oedipus

And now old man, look up and answer all
I ask thee. Wast thou once of Laius' house?

Herdsman

I was, a thrall, not purchased but home-bred.

Oedipus

What was thy business? how wast thou employed?

Herdsman

The best part of my life I tended sheep.

Oedipus

What were the pastures thou didst most frequent?

Herdsman

Cithaeron and the neighboring alps.

Oedipus

Then there
Thou must have known yon man, at least by fame?

Herdsman

Yon man? in what way? what man dost thou mean?

Oedipus

The man here, having met him in past times …

Herdsman

Off-hand I cannot call him well to mind.

Messenger

No wonder, master. But I will revive
His blunted memories. Sure he can recall
What time together both we drove our flocks,
He two, I one, on the Cithaeron range,
For three long summers; I his mate from spring
Till rose Arcturus; then in winter time
I led mine home, he his to Laius' folds.
Did these things happen as I say, or no?

Herdsman

'Tis long ago, but all thou say'st is true.

Messenger

Well, thou mast then remember giving me
A child to rear as my own foster-son?

Herdsman

Why dost thou ask this question? What of that?

Messenger

Friend, he that stands before thee was that child.

Herdsman

A plague upon thee! Hold thy wanton tongue!

Oedipus

Softly, old man, rebuke him not; thy words
Are more deserving chastisement than his.

Herdsman

O best of masters, what is my offense?

Oedipus

Not answering what he asks about the child.

Herdsman

He speaks at random, babbles like a fool.

Oedipus If thou lack'st grace to speak, I'll loose thy tongue.

Herdsman

For mercy's sake abuse not an old man.

Oedipus

Arrest the villain, seize and pinion him!

Herdsman

Alack, alack!
What have I done? what wouldst thou further learn?

Oedipus

Didst give this man the child of whom he asks?

Herdsman

I did; and would that I had died that day!

Oedipus

And die thou shalt unless thou tell the truth.

Herdsman

But, if I tell it, I am doubly lost.

Oedipus

The knave methinks will still prevaricate.

Herdsman

Nay, I confessed I gave it long ago.

Oedipus

Whence came it? was it thine, or given to thee?

Herdsman

I had it from another, 'twas not mine.

Oedipus

From whom of these our townsmen, and what house?

Herdsman

Forbear for God's sake, master, ask no more.

Oedipus

If I must question thee again, thou'rt lost.

Herdsman

Well then—it was a child of Laius' house.

Oedipus

Slave-born or one of Laius' own race?

Herdsman

Ah me!
I stand upon the perilous edge of speech.

Oedipus

And I of hearing, but I still must hear.

Herdsman

Know then the child was by repute his own,
But she within, thy consort best could tell.

Oedipus

What! she, she gave it thee?

Herdsman

'Tis so, my king.

Oedipus

With what intent?

Herdsman

To make away with it.

Oedipus

What, she its mother.

Herdsman

Fearing a dread weird.

Oedipus

What weird?

Herdsman

'Twas told that he should slay his sire.

Oedipus

What didst thou give it then to this old man?

Herdsman

Through pity, master, for the babe. I thought
He'd take it to the country whence he came;
But he preserved it for the worst of woes.
For if thou art in sooth what this man saith,
God pity thee! thou wast to misery born.

Oedipus

Ah me! ah me! all brought to pass, all true!
O light, may I behold thee nevermore!
I stand a wretch, in birth, in wedlock cursed,
A parricide, incestuously, triply cursed! *(Exit Oedipus.)*

Chorus (strophe 1)

Races of mortal man
Whose life is but a span,
I count ye but the shadow of a shade!
For he who most doth know
Of bliss, hath but the show;
A moment, and the visions pale and fade.
Thy fall, O Oedipus, thy piteous fall

Warns me none born of women blest to call.

antistrophe 1

For he of marksmen best,
O Zeus, outshot the rest,
And won the prize supreme of wealth and power.
By him the vulture maid
Was quelled, her witchery laid;
He rose our savior and the land's strong tower.
We hailed thee king and from that day adored
Of mighty Thebes the universal lord.

strophe 2

O heavy hand of fate!
Who now more desolate,
Whose tale more sad than thine, whose lot more dire?
O Oedipus, discrowned head,
Thy cradle was thy marriage bed;
One harborage sufficed for son and sire.
How could the soil thy father eared so long
Endure to bear in silence such a wrong?

antistrophe 2

All-seeing Time hath caught
Guilt, and to justice brought
The son and sire commingled in one bed.
O child of Laius' ill-starred race
Would I had ne'er beheld thy face;
I raise for thee a dirge as o'er the dead.
Yet, sooth to say, through thee I drew new breath,
And now through thee I feel a second death. *(Enter second messenger.)*

Second messenger

Most grave and reverend senators of Thebes,
What Deeds ye soon must hear, what sights behold
How will ye mourn, if, true-born patriots,
Ye reverence still the race of Labdacus!
Not Ister nor all Phasis' flood, I ween,
Could wash away the blood-stains from this house,
The ills it shrouds or soon will bring to light,
Ills wrought of malice, not unwittingly.
The worst to bear are self-inflicted wounds.

Chorus

Grievous enough for all our tears and groans
Our past calamities; what canst thou add?

Second messenger

My tale is quickly told and quickly heard.
Our sovereign lady queen Jocasta's dead.

Chorus

Alas, poor queen! how came she by her death?

Second messenger

By her own hand. And all the horror of it,
Not having seen, yet cannot comprehend.
Nathless, as far as my poor memory serves,
I will relate the unhappy lady's woe.
When in her frenzy she had passed inside
The vestibule, she hurried straight to win
The bridal-chamber, clutching at her hair
With both her hands, and, once within the room,
She shut the doors behind her with a crash.
"Laius," she cried, and called her husband dead
Long, long ago; her thought was of that child
By him begot, the son by whom the sire
Was murdered and the mother left to breed
With her own seed, a monstrous progeny.
Then she bewailed the marriage bed whereon
Poor wretch, she had conceived a double brood,
Husband by husband, children by her child.
What happened after that I cannot tell,
Nor how the end befell, for with a shriek
Burst on us Oedipus; all eyes were fixed
On Oedipus, as up and down he strode,
Nor could we mark her agony to the end.
For stalking to and fro "A sword!" he cried,
"Where is the wife, no wife, the teeming womb
That bore a double harvest, me and mine?"
And in his frenzy some supernal power
(No mortal, surely, none of us who watched him)
Guided his footsteps; with a terrible shriek,
As though one beckoned him, he crashed against
The folding doors, and from their staples forced
The wrenched bolts and hurled himself within.
Then we beheld the woman hanging there,
A running noose entwined about her neck.
But when he saw her, with a maddened roar
He loosed the cord; and when her wretched corpse
Lay stretched on earth, what followed--O 'twas dread!
He tore the golden brooches that upheld
Her queenly robes, upraised them high and smote
Full on his eye-balls, uttering words like these:
"No more shall ye behold such sights of woe,
Deeds I have suffered and myself have wrought;
Henceforward quenched in darkness shall ye see
Those ye should ne'er have seen; now blind to those
Whom, when I saw, I vainly yearned to know."
Such was the burden of his moan, whereto,
Not once but oft, he struck with his hand uplift
His eyes, and at each stroke the ensanguined orbs
Bedewed his beard, not oozing drop by drop,
But one black gory downpour, thick as hail.
Such evils, issuing from the double source,
Have whelmed them both, confounding man and wife.
Till now the storied fortune of this house
Was fortunate indeed; but from this day
Woe, lamentation, ruin, death, disgrace,
All ills that can be named, all, all are theirs.

Chorus

But hath he still no respite from his pain?

Second messenger

He cries, "Unbar the doors and let all Thebes
Behold the slayer of his sire, his mother's--"
That shameful word my lips may not repeat.
He vows to fly self-banished from the land,
Nor stay to bring upon his house the curse
Himself had uttered; but he has no strength
Nor one to guide him, and his torture's more
Than man can suffer, as yourselves will see.
For lo, the palace portals are unbarred,
And soon ye shall behold a sight so sad
That he who must abhorred would pity it. (Enter
oedipus blinded.)

Chorus

Woeful sight! more woeful none
These sad eyes have looked upon.

Whence this madness? None can tell
Who did cast on thee his spell, prowling all thy life around,

Leaping with a demon bound.
Hapless wretch! how can I brook
On thy misery to look?
Though to gaze on thee I yearn,
Much to question, much to learn,
Horror-struck away I turn.

Oedipus

Ah me! ah woe is me!
Ah whither am I borne!
How like a ghost forlorn
My voice flits from me on the air!
On, on the demon goads. The end, ah where?

Chorus

An end too dread to tell, too dark to see.

Oedipus (strophe 1)

Dark, dark! The horror of darkness, like a shroud,
Wraps me and bears me on through mist and cloud.
Ah me, ah me! What spasms athwart me shoot,
What pangs of agonizing memory?

Chorus

No marvel if in such a plight thou feel'st
The double weight of past and present woes.

Oedipus (antistrophe 1)

Ah friend, still loyal, constant still and kind,
Thou carest for the blind.
I know thee near, and though bereft of eyes,
Thy voice I recognize.

Chorus

O doer of dread deeds, how couldst thou mar
Thy vision thus? What demon goaded thee?

Oedipus (strophe 2)

Apollo, friend, Apollo, he it was
That brought these ills to pass;
But the right hand that dealt the blow
Was mine, none other. How,
How, could I longer see when sight
Brought no delight?

Chorus

Alas! 'tis as thou sayest.

Oedipus

Say, friends, can any look or voice
Or touch of love henceforth my heart rejoice?
Haste, friends, no fond delay,
Take the twice cursed away
Far from all ken,
The man abhorred of gods, accursed of men.

Chorus

O thy despair well suits thy desperate case.
Would I had never looked upon thy face!

Oedipus (antistrophe 2)

My curse on him whoe'er unrived
The waif's fell fetters and my life revived!
He meant me well, yet had he left me there,
He had saved my friends and me a world of care.

Chorus

I too had wished it so.

Oedipus

Then had I never come to shed
My father's blood nor climbed my mother's bed;
The monstrous offspring of a womb defiled,
Co-mate of him who gendered me, and child.
Was ever man before afflicted thus,
Like Oedipus.

Chorus

I cannot say that thou hast counseled well,
For thou wert better dead than living blind.
Oedipus What's done was well done. Thou canst never shake
My firm belief. A truce to argument.
For, had I sight, I know not with what eyes
I could have met my father in the shades,
Or my poor mother, since against the twain
I sinned, a sin no gallows could atone.
Aye, but, ye say, the sight of children joys
A parent's eyes. What, born as mine were born?
No, such a sight could never bring me joy;
Nor this fair city with its battlements,
Its temples and the statues of its gods,
Sights from which I, now wretchedst of all,
Once ranked the foremost Theban in all Thebes,
By my own sentence am cut off, condemned
By my own proclamation 'gainst the wretch,
The miscreant by heaven itself declared
Unclean–and of the race of Laius.
Thus branded as a felon by myself,
How had I dared to look you in the face?
Nay, had I known a way to choke the springs
Of hearing, I had never shrunk to make
A dungeon of this miserable frame,
Cut off from sight and hearing; for 'tis bliss to bide in regions
sorrow cannot reach.
Why didst thou harbor me, Cithaeron, why
Didst thou not take and slay me? Then I never
Had shown to men the secret of my birth.
O Polybus, O Corinth, O my home,
Home of my ancestors (so wast thou called)
How fair a nursling then I seemed, how foul
The canker that lay festering in the bud!
Now is the blight revealed of root and fruit.
Ye triple high-roads, and thou hidden glen,
Coppice, and pass where meet the three-branched ways,
Ye drank my blood, the life-blood these hands spilt,
My father's; do ye call to mind perchance
Those deeds of mine ye witnessed and the work
I wrought thereafter when I came to Thebes?
O fatal wedlock, thou didst give me birth,
And, having borne me, sowed again my seed,
Mingling the blood of fathers, brothers, children,
Brides, wives and mothers, an incestuous brood,
All horrors that are wrought beneath the sun,
Horrors so foul to name them were unmeet.

O, I adjure you, hide me anywhere
Far from this land, or slay me straight, or cast me
Down to the depths of ocean out of sight.
Come hither, deign to touch an abject wretch;
Draw near and fear not; I myself must bear
The load of guilt that none but I can share. (Enter creon.)

Creon

Lo, here is Creon, the one man to grant
Thy prayer by action or advice, for he
Is left the State's sole guardian in thy stead.

Oedipus

Ah me! what words to accost him can I find?
What cause has he to trust me? In the past
I have bee proved his rancorous enemy.

Creon

Not in derision, Oedipus, I come
Nor to upbraid thee with thy past misdeeds. (To bystanders.)
But shame upon you! if ye feel no sense
Of human decencies, at least revere
The Sun whose light beholds and nurtures all.
Leave not thus nakedly for all to gaze at
A horror neither earth nor rain from heaven
Nor light will suffer. Lead him straight within,
For it is seemly that a kinsman's woes
Be heard by kin and seen by kin alone.

Oedipus

O listen, since thy presence comes to me
A shock of glad surprise–so noble thou,
And I so vile–O grant me one small boon.
I ask it not on my behalf, but thine.

Creon

And what the favor thou wouldst crave of me?

Oedipus

Forth from thy borders thrust me with all speed;
Set me within some vasty desert where

No mortal voice shall greet me any more.

Creon

This had I done already, but I deemed
It first behooved me to consult the god.

Oedipus

His will was set forth fully–to destroy
The parricide, the scoundrel; and I am he.

Creon

Yea, so he spake, but in our present plight
'Twere better to consult the god anew.
Oedipus Dare ye inquire concerning such a wretch?

Creon

Yea, for thyself wouldst credit now his word.

Oedipus

Aye, and on thee in all humility
I lay this charge: let her who lies within
Receive such burial as thou shalt ordain;
Such rites 'tis thine, as brother, to perform.
But for myself, O never let my Thebes,
The city of my sires, be doomed to bear
The burden of my presence while I live.
No, let me be a dweller on the hills,
On yonder mount Cithaeron, famed as mine,
My tomb predestined for me by my sire
And mother, while they lived, that I may die
Slain as they sought to slay me, when alive.
This much I know full surely, nor disease
Shall end my days, nor any common chance;
For I had ne'er been snatched from death, unless
I was predestined to some awful doom.
So be it. I reck not how Fate deals with me
But my unhappy children–for my sons
Be not concerned, O Creon, they are men,
And for themselves, where'er they be, can fend.
But for my daughters twain, poor innocent maids,
Who ever sat beside me at the board
Sharing my viands, drinking of my cup,

For them, I pray thee, care, and, if thou willst,
O might I feel their touch and make my moan.
Hear me, O prince, my noble-hearted prince!
Could I but blindly touch them with my hands
I'd think they still were mine, as when I saw.
(ANTIGONE and ISMENE are led in.)
What say I? can it be my pretty ones
Whose sobs I hear? Has Creon pitied me
And sent me my two darlings? Can this be?

Creon

'Tis true; 'twas I procured thee this delight,
Knowing the joy they were to thee of old.

Oedipus

God speed thee! and as meed for bringing them
May Providence deal with thee kindlier
Than it has dealt with me! O children mine,
Where are ye? Let me clasp you with these hands,
A brother's hands, a father's; hands that made
Lack-luster sockets of his once bright eyes;
Hands of a man who blindly, recklessly,
Became your sire by her from whom he sprang.
Though I cannot behold you, I must weep
In thinking of the evil days to come,
The slights and wrongs that men will put upon you.
Where'er ye go to feast or festival,
No merrymaking will it prove for you,
But oft abashed in tears ye will return.
And when ye come to marriageable years,
Where's the bold wooers who will jeopardize
To take unto himself such disrepute
As to my children's children still must cling,
For what of infamy is lacking here?
"Their father slew his father, sowed the seed
Where he himself was gendered, and begat
These maidens at the source wherefrom he sprang."
Such are the gibes that men will cast at you.
Who then will wed you? None, I ween, but ye
Must pine, poor maids, in single barrenness.
O Prince, Menoeceus' son, to thee, I turn,
With the it rests to father them, for we
Their natural parents, both of us, are lost.
O leave them not to wander poor, unwed,
Thy kin, nor let them share my low estate.

O pity them so young, and but for thee
All destitute. Thy hand upon it, Prince.
To you, my children I had much to say,
Were ye but ripe to hear. Let this suffice:
Pray ye may find some home and live content,
And may your lot prove happier than your sire's.

Creon

Thou hast had enough of weeping; pass within.

Oedipus

I must obey,
Though 'tis grievous.

Creon

Weep not, everything must have its day.

Oedipus

Well I go, but on conditions.

Creon

What thy terms for going, say.

Oedipus

Send me from the land an exile.

Creon

Ask this of the gods, not me.

Oedipus

But I am the gods' abhorrence.

Creon

Then they soon will grant thy plea.

Oedipus

Lead me hence, then, I am willing.

Creon

Come, but let thy children go.

Oedipus

Rob me not of these my children!

Creon

Crave not mastery in all,
For the mastery that raised thee was thy bane and
wrought thy fall.

Chorus

Look ye, countrymen and Thebans, this is Oedipus the
great,

He who knew the Sphinx's riddle and was mightiest in
our state.

Who of all our townsmen gazed not on his fame with
envious eyes?

Now, in what a sea of troubles sunk and overwhelmed
he lies!

Therefore wait to see life's ending ere thou count one
mortal blest;

Wait till free from pain and sorrow he has gained his
final rest.

DISCUSSION QUESTIONS

1. What kind of king is Oedipus? Do his efforts to defend Thebes make him a more sympathetic figure?

2. What is the importance of the many references to eyes and seeing in the play, particularly in the exchange between Oedipus and Tiresias? Why does Oedipus eventually blind himself?

3. Consider the choral odes. What emotions do they invoke? Is the chorus consistent in its views?

4. How much is Oedipus a victim of his own decisions? How much is beyond his control?

5. Consider Jocasta's efforts to explain away the workings of prophecy. Why does she do this? What does she discover?

6. How do Oedipus' attempts to solve the problems facing Thebes lead him into deeper forms of self-knowledge?

7. One of the major issues of the play is the driving force of our desire to know. What are the costs of such self-knowledge? Would Oedipus have been better off without such knowledge?

8. At the end of the play, Creon is left in charge. Based on what you know about his character, is Thebes in better hands?

ARISTOPHANES (C 450–385 BCE)

Very little is known about the life of Aristophanes. We know he wrote roughly 40 comedies, of which 11 survive. His work is highly topical and includes characters that were active in Athens during the final decades of the fifth century. *The Clouds*, for example, ridicules Socrates, accusing him of being a shameless teacher who takes advantage of his students while pretending to educate them. Aristophanes wrote many of his works during the long and disastrous Peloponnesian War, a 30-year conflict that finally ended in 404, when Sparta finally conquered Athens. It is not surprising, then, that several of his plays carry an antiwar message. The best known and most frequently produced is *Lysistrata* (411), the work included in our Selected Readings.

When *Lysistrata* was first staged, the war had been raging for 20 years, and there was no sign that it would soon end. In the play, the title character seeks to halt the violence by concocting a plot she knows will get the city's attention: She convinces the women of Athens to refuse to have sex until their husbands vote for peace. The Greek comic stage was a highly bawdy place and the actors in the early performances paraded around the stage with huge phalluses protruding from their waists. Their frustration at being denied sex was thus explicitly lampooned for all to see. Yet, as with so many comedies, the humor of *Lysistrata* raises serious concerns, as the men are forced to choose between love and war.

LYSISTRATA

LYSISTRATA
CALONICE
MYRRHINE
LAMPITO
Stratyllis, etc.
Chorus of Women.
MAGISTRATE
CINESIAS
SPARTAN HERALD
ENVOYS
ATHENIANS
Porter, Market Idlers, etc.
Chorus of old Men.

LYSISTRATA *stands alone with the Propylaea at her back.*

LYSISTRATA

If they were trysting for a Bacchanal,
A feast of Pan or Colias or Genetyllis,
The tambourines would block the rowdy streets,
But now there's not a woman to be seen Except–ah,
yes–this neighbour of mine yonder.
Enter CALONICE.
Good day Calonice.

CALONICE

Good day Lysistrata.
But what has vexed you so? Tell me, child.
What are these black looks for?
It doesn't suit you
To knit your eyebrows up glumly like that.

LYSISTRATA

Calonice, it's more than I can bear,
I am hot all over with blushes for our sex.
Men say we're slippery rogues–

CALONICE

And aren't they right?

LYSISTRATA

Yet summoned on the most tremendous business
For deliberation, still they snuggle in bed.

CALONICE

My dear, they'll come.
It's hard for women, you know,
To get away. There's so much to do;
Husbands to be patted and put in good tempers:
Servants to be poked out: children washed
Or soothed with lullays or fed with mouthfuls of pap.

LYSISTRATA

But I tell you, here's a far more weighty object.

CALONICE

What is it all about, dear Lysistrata,
That you've called the women hither in a troop?
What kind of an object is it?

LYSISTRATA

A tremendous thing!

CALONICE

And long?

LYSISTRATA

Indeed, it may be very lengthy.

CALONICE

Then why aren't they here?

LYSISTRATA

No man's connected with it;
If that was the case, they'd soon come fluttering along.
No, no. It concerns an object I've felt over
And turned this way and that for sleepless nights.

CALONICE

It must be fine to stand such long attention.

LYSISTRATA

So fine it comes to this–Greece saved by Woman!

CALONICE

By Woman? Wretched thing, I'm sorry for it.

LYSISTRATA

Our country's fate is henceforth in our hands:
To destroy the Peloponnesians root and branch–

CALONICE

What could be nobler!

LYSISTRATA

Wipe out the Boeotians–

CALONICE

Not utterly. Have mercy on the eels![1]

LYSISTRATA

But with regard to Athens, note I'm careful
Not to say any of these nasty things;
Still, thought is free. … But if the women join us
From Peloponnesus and Boeotia, then
Hand in hand we'll rescue Greece.

CALONICE

How could we do
Such a big wise deed? We women who dwell
Quietly adorning ourselves in a back-room
With gowns of lucid gold and gawdy toilets
Of stately silk and dainty little slippers. …

LYSISTRATA

These are the very armaments of the rescue.
These crocus-gowns, this outlay of the best myrrh,
Slippers, cosmetics dusting beauty, and robes
With rippling creases of light.

CALONICE

Yes, but how?

LYSISTRATA

No man will lift a lance against another--

CALONICE

I'll run to have my tunic dyed crocus.

LYSISTRATA

Or take a shield–

CALONICE

I'll get a stately gown.

LYSISTRATA

Or unscabbard a sword–

CALONICE

Let me buy a pair of slipper.

LYSISTRATA

Now, tell me, are the women right to lag?

---

1 The Boeotian eels were highly esteemed delicacies in Athens.

CALONICE

They should have turned birds, they should have grown
wings and flown.

LYSISTRATA

My friend, you'll see that they are true Athenians:
Always too late. Why, there's not a woman
From the shoreward demes arrived, not one from Salamis.

CALONICE

I know for certain they awoke at dawn,
And got their husbands up if not their boat sails.

LYSISTRATA

And I'd have staked my life the Acharnian dames
Would be here first, yet they haven't come either!

CALONICE

Well anyhow there is Theagenes' wife
We can expect–she consulted Hecate.
But look, here are some at last, and more behind them.
See … where are they from?

CALONICE

From Anagyra they come.

LYSISTRATA

Yes, they generally manage to come first.
Enter MYRRHINE.

MYRRHINE

Are we late, Lysistrata? … What is that?
Nothing to say?

LYSISTRATA

I've not much to say for you,
Myrrhine, dawdling on so vast an affair.

MYRRHINE

I couldn't find my girdle in the dark.
But if the affair's so wonderful, tell us, what is it?

LYSISTRATA

No, let us stay a little longer till
The Peloponnesian girls and the girls of Bocotia
Are here to listen.

MYRRHINE

That's the best advice.
Ah, there comes Lampito.
Enter LAMPITO.

LYSISTRATA

Welcome Lampito!
Dear Spartan girl with a delightful face,
Washed with the rosy spring, how fresh you look
In the easy stride of your sleek slenderness,
Why you could strangle a bull!

LAMPITO

I think I could.
It's frae exercise and kicking high behint.
[Footnote: The translator has put the speech of the
Spartan characters in Scotch dialect which is related to
English about as was the Spartan dialect to the speech
of Athens. The Spartans, in their character, anticipated
the shrewd, canny, uncouth Scotch highlander of modern
times.]

LYSISTRATA

What lovely breasts to own!

LAMPITO

Oo … your fingers
Assess them, ye tickler, wi' such tender chucks
I feel as if I were an altar-victim.

LYSISTRATA

Who is this youngster?

LAMPITO

A Boeotian lady.

LYSISTRATA

There never was much undergrowth in Boeotia,
Such a smooth place, and this girl takes after it.

CALONICE

Yes, I never saw a skin so primly kept.

LYSISTRATA

This girl?

LAMPITO

A sonsie open-looking jinker!
She's a Corinthian.

LYSISTRATA

Yes, isn't she
Very open, in some ways particularly.

LAMPITO

But who's garred this Council o' Women to meet here?

LYSISTRATA

I have.

LAMPITO

Propound then what you want o' us.

MYRRHINE

What is the amazing news you have to tell?

LYSISTRATA

I'll tell you, but first answer one small question.

MYRRHINE

As you like.

LYSISTRATA

Are you not sad your children's fathers
Go endlessly off soldiering afar
In this plodding war? I am willing to wager
There's not one here whose husband is at home.

CALONICE

Mine's been in Thrace, keeping an eye on Eucrates
For five months past.

MYRRHINE

And mine left me for Pylos
Seven months ago at least.

LAMPITO

And as for mine
No sooner has he slipped out frae the line
He straps his shield and he's snickt off again.

LYSISTRATA

And not the slightest glitter of a lover!
And since the Milesians betrayed us, I've not seen
The image of a single upright man
To be a marble consolation to us.
Now will you help me, if I find a means
To stamp the war out.

MYRRHINE

By the two Goddesses, Yes!
I will though I've to pawn this very dress
And drink the barter-money the same day.

CALONICE

And I too though I'm split up like a turbot
And half is hackt off as the price of peace.

LAMPITO

And I too! Why, to get a peep at the shy thing
I'd clamber up to the tip-top o' Taygetus.

LYSISTRATA

Then I'll expose my mighty mystery.
O women, if we would compel the men
To bow to Peace, we must refrain–

MYRRHINE

From what?
O tell us!

LYSISTRATA

Will you truly do it then?

MYRRHINE

We will, we will, if we must die for it.

LYSISTRATA

We must refrain from every depth of love. …
Why do you turn your backs? Where are you going?
Why do you bite your lips and shake your heads?
Why are your faces blanched? Why do you weep?
Will you or won't you, or what do you mean?

MYRRHINE

No, I won't do it. Let the war proceed.

CALONICE

No, I won't do it. Let the war proceed.

LYSISTRATA

You too, dear turbot, you that said just now

You didn't mind being split right up in the least?

CALONICE

Anything else? O bid me walk in fire
But do not rob us of that darling joy.
What else is like it, dearest Lysistrata?

LYSISTRATA

And you?

MYRRHINE

O please give me the fire instead.

LYSISTRATA

Lewd to the least drop in the tiniest vein,
Our sex is fitly food for Tragic Poets,
Our whole life's but a pile of kisses and babies.
But, hardy Spartan, if you join with me
All may be righted yet. O help me, help me.

LAMPITO

It's a sair, sair thing to ask of us, by the Twa,
A lass to sleep her lane and never fill
Love's lack except wi' makeshifts…. But let it be.
Peace maun be thought of first.

LYSISTRATA

My friend, my friend!
The only one amid this herd of weaklings.

CALONICE

But if–which heaven forbid—we should refrain
As you would have us, how is Peace induced?

LYSISTRATA

By the two Goddesses, now can't you see
All we have to do is idly sit indoors
With smooth roses powdered on our cheeks,
Our bodies burning naked through the folds

Of shining Amorgos' silk, and meet the men
With our dear Venus-platsplucked trim and neat.
Their stirring love will rise up furiously,
They'll beg our arms to open. That's our time!
We'll disregard their knocking, beat them off–
And they will soon be rabid for a Peace.
I'm sure of it.

LAMPITO

Just as Menelaus, they say,
Seeing the bosom of his naked Helen
Flang down the sword.

CALONICE

But we'll be tearful fools
If our husbands take us at our word and leave us.

LYSISTRATA

There's only left then, in Pherecrates' phrase,
To *flay a skinned dog*—flay more our flayed desires.

CALONICE

Bah, proverbs will never warm a celibate.
But what avail will your scheme be if the men
Drag us for all our kicking on to the couch?

LYSISTRATA

Cling to the doorposts.

CALONICE

But if they should force us?

LYSISTRATA

Yield then, but with a sluggish, cold indifference.
There is no joy to them in sullen mating.
Besides we have other ways to madden them;
They cannot stand up long, and they've no delight
Unless we fit their aim with merry succour.

CALONICE

Well if you must have it so, we'll all agree.

LAMPITO

For us I ha' no doubt. We can persuade
Our men to strike a fair an' decent Peace,
But how will ye pitch out the battle-frenzy
O' the Athenian populace?

LYSISTRATA

I promise you
We'll wither up that curse.

LAMPITO

I don't believe it.
Not while they own ane trireme oared an' rigged,
Or a' those stacks an' stacks an' stacks O' siller.

LYSISTRATA

I've thought the whole thing out till there's no flaw.
We shall surprise the Acropolis today:
That is the duty set the older dames.
While we sit here talking, they are to go
And under pretence of sacrificing, seize it.

LAMPITO

Certie, that's fine; all's working for the best.

LYSISTRATA

Now quickly, Lampito, let us tie ourselves
To this high purpose as tightly as the hemp of words
Can knot together.

LAMPITO

Set out the terms in detail
And we'll a' swear to them.

LYSISTRATA

Of course. ... Well then

Where is our Scythianess? Why are you staring?
First lay the shield, boss downward, on the floor
And bring the victim's inwards.

CAILONICE

But, Lysistrata,
What is this oath that we're to swear?

LYSISTRATA

What oath!
In Aeschylus they take a slaughtered sheep
And swear upon a buckler. Why not we?

CALONICE

O Lysistrata, Peace sworn on a buckler!

LYSISTRATA

What oath would suit us then?

CALONICE

Something burden bearing
Would be our best insignia. ... A white horse!
Let's swear upon its entrails.

LYSISTRATA

A horse indeed!

CALONICE

Then what will symbolise us?

LYSISTRATA ⁓

This, as I tell you–
First set a great dark bowl upon the ground
And disembowel a skin of Thasian wine,
Then swear that we'll not add a drop of water.

LAMPITO

Ah, what aith could clink pleasanter than that!

LYSISTRATA

Bring me a bowl then and a skin of wine.

CALONICE

My dears, see what a splendid bowl it is;
I'd not say No if asked to sip it off.

LYSISTRATA

Put down the bowl. Lay hands, all, on the victim.
Skiey Queen who givest the last word in arguments,
And thee, O Bowl, dear comrade, we beseech:
Accept our oblation and be propitious to us.

CALONICE

What healthy blood, la, how it gushes out!

LAMPITO

An' what a leesome fragrance through the air.

LYSISTRATA

Now, dears, if you will let me, I'll speak first.

CALONICE

Only if you draw the lot, by Aphrodite!

LYSISTRATA

SO, grasp the brim, you, Lampito, and all.
You, Calonice, repeat for the rest
Each word I say. Then you must all take oath
And pledge your arms to the same stern conditions—

LYSISTRATA

To husband or lover I'll not open arms

CALONICE

To husband or lover I'll not open arms

LYSISTRATA

Though love and denial may enlarge his charms.

CALONICE

Though love and denial may enlarge his charms.
O, O, my knees are failing me, Lysistrata!

LYSISTRATA

But still at home, ignoring him, I'll stay,

CALONICE

But still at home, ignoring him, I'll stay,

LYSISTRATA

Beautiful, clad in saffron silks all day.

CALONICE

Beautiful, clad in saffron silks all day.

LYSISTRATA

If then he seizes me by dint of force,

CALONICE

If then he seizes me by dint of force,

LYSISTRATA

I'll give him reason for a long remorse.

CALONICE

I'll give him reason for a long remorse.

LYSISTRATA

I'll never lie and stare up at the ceiling,

CALONICE

I'll never lie and stare up at the ceiling,

LYSISTRATA

Nor like a lion on all fours go kneeling.

CALONICE

Nor like a lion on all fours go kneeling.

LYSISTRATA

If I keep faith, then bounteous cups be mine.

CALONICE

If I keep faith, then bounteous cups be mine.

LYSISTRATA

If not, to nauseous water change this wine.

CALONICE

If not, to nauseous water change this wine.

LYSISTRATA

Do you all swear to this?

MYRRHINE

We do, we do.

LYSISTRATA

Then I shall immolate the victim thus.
She drinks.

CALONICE

Here now, share fair, haven't we made a pact?
Let's all quaff down that friendship in our turn.

LAMPITO

Hark, what caterwauling hubbub's that?

LYSISTRATA

As I told you,
The women have appropriated the citadel.
So, Lampito, dash off to your own land
And raise the rebels there. These will serve as hostages,
While we ourselves take our places in the ranks
And drive the bolts right home.

CALONICE

But won't the men
March straight against us?

LYSISTRATA

And what if they do?
No threat shall creak our hinges wide, no torch
Shall light a fear in us; we will come out
To Peace alone.

CALONICE

That's it, by Aphrodite!
As of old let us seem hard and obdurate.

LAMPITO and some go off; the others go up into the Acropolis.

Chorus of OLD MEN enter to attack the captured Acropolis.

Make room, Draces, move ahead; why your shoulder's
    chafed, I see,
With lugging uphill these lopped branches of the
    olive-tree.
How upside-down and wrong-way-round a long life sees
    things grow.
Ah, Strymodorus, who'd have thought affairs could
    tangle so?
The women whom at home we fed,
Like witless fools, with fostering bread,
Have impiously come to this—
They've stolen the Acropolis,
With bolts and bars our orders flout
And shut us out.
    Come, Philurgus, bustle thither; lay our faggots on the
ground,
In neat stacks beleaguering the insurgents all around;
And the vile conspiratresses, plotters of such mischief dire,
Pile and burn them all together in one vast and righteous
    pyre:
Fling with our own hands Lycon's wife to fry in the
    thickest fire.
By Demeter, they'll get no brag while I've a vein to beat!
Cleomenes himself was hurtled out in sore defeat.
His stiff-backed Spartan pride was bent.
Out, stripped of all his arms, he went:
A pigmy cloak that would not stretch
To hide his rump (the draggled wretch),
Six sprouting years of beard, the spilth
Of six years' filth.

That was a siege! Our men were ranged in lines of
    seventeen deep
Before the gates, and never left their posts there, even to sleep.
Shall I not smite the rash presumption then of foes like these,
Detested both of all the gods and of Euripides—
Else, may the Marathon-plain not boast my trophied
    victories!

Ah, now, there's but a little space
To reach the place!
A deadly climb it is, a tricky road
With all this bumping load:
A pack-ass soon would tire ...
How these logs bruise my shoulders! further still
Jog up the hill,
And puff the fire inside,
Or just as we reach the top we'll find it's died.
Ough, phew!
I choke with the smoke.

Lord Heracles, how acrid-hot
Out of the pot
This mad-dog smoke leaps, worrying me
And biting angrily. ...
'Tis Lemnian fire that smokes,
Or else it would not sting my eyelids thus. ...
Haste, all of us;
Athene invokes our aid.
Laches, now or never the assault must be made!
Ough, phew!
I choke with the smoke. ..

Thanked be the gods! The fire peeps up and crackles as
it should.
Now why not first slide off our backs these weary loads
of wood
And dip a vine-branch in the brazier till it glows, then
straight
Hurl it at the battering-ram against the stubborn gate?
If they refuse to draw the bolts in immediate compliance,
We'll set fire to the wood, and smoke will strangle their
defiance.

Phew, what a spluttering drench of smoke! Come, now
from off my back. ...
Is there no Samos-general to help me to unpack?
Ah there, that's over! For the last time now it's galled my
shoulder.
Flare up thine embers, brazier, and dutifully smoulder,
To kindle a brand, that I the first may strike the citadel.
Aid me, Lady Victory, that a triumph-trophy may tell
How we did anciently this insane audacity quell!

Chorus of WOMEN.

What's that rising yonder? That ruddy glare, that smoky
skurry?
O is it something in a blaze? Quick, quick, my comrades,
hurry!
Nicodice, helter-skelter!
Or poor Calyce's in flames
And Cratylla's stifled in the welter.
O these dreadful old men
And their dark laws of hate!
There, I'm all of a tremble lest I turn out to be too late.
I could scarcely get near to the spring though I rose
before dawn,
What with tattling of tongues and rattling of pitchers in
one jostling din
With slaves pushing in! ...

Still here at last the water's drawn
And with it eagerly I run
To help those of my friends who stand
In danger of being burned alive.
For I am told a dribbling band
Of greybeards hobble to the field,
Great faggots in each palsied hand,
As if a hot bath to prepare,

And threatening that out they'll drive
These wicked women or soon leave them charring into
ashes there.

O Goddess, suffer not, I pray, this harsh deed to be done,
But show us Greece and Athens with their warlike acts
repealed!
For this alone, in this thy hold,
Thou Goddess with the helm of gold,
We laid hands on thy sanctuary,
Athene. ... Then our ally be
And where they cast their fires of slaughter
Direct our water!

STRATYLLIS (caught)

Let me go!

WOMEN

You villainous old men, what's this you do?
No honest man, no pious man, could do such things as you.

MEN

Ah ha, here's something most original, I have no doubt:
A swarm of women sentinels to man the walls without.

WOMEN

So then we scare you, do we? Do we seem a fearful host?
You only see the smallest fraction mustered at this post.

MEN

Ho, Phaedrias, shall we put a stop to all these chattering
tricks?
Suppose that now upon their backs we splintered these
our sticks?

WOMEN

Let us lay down the pitchers, so our bodies will be free,
In case these lumping fellows try to cause some injury.

MEN

O hit them hard and hit again and hit until they run away,
And perhaps they'll learn, like Bupalus, not to have too
much to say.

WOMEN

Come on, then–do it! I won't budge, but like a dog I'll bite
At every little scrap of meat that dangles in my sight.

MEN

Be quiet, or I'll bash you out of any years to come.

WOMEN

Now you just touch Stratyllis with the top-joint of your
thumb.

MEN

What vengeance can you take if with my fists your face
I beat?

WOMEN

I'll rip you with my teeth and strew your entrails at your
feet.

MEN

Now I appreciate Euripides' strange subtlety:
Woman is the most shameless beast of all the beasts that be.

WOMEN

Rhodippe, come, and let's pick up our water-jars once more.

MEN

Ah cursed drab, what have you brought this water for?

WOMEN

What is your fire for then, you smelly corpse? Yourself to
burn?

MEN

To build a pyre and make your comrades ready for the urn.

WOMEN

And I've the water to put out your fire immediately.

MEN

What, you put out my fire?

WOMEN

Yes, sirrah, as you soon will see.

MEN

I don't know why I hesitate to roast you with this flame.

WOMEN

If you have any soap you'll go off cleaner than you came.

MEN

Cleaner, you dirty slut?

WOMEN

A nuptial-bath in which to lie!

MEN

Did you hear that insolence?

WOMEN

I'm a free woman, I.

MEN

I'll make you hold your tongue.

WOMEN

Henceforth you'll serve in no more juries.

MEN

Burn off her hair for her.

WOMEN

Now forward, water, quench their furies!

MEN

O dear, O dear!

WOMEN

So … was it hot?

MEN

Hot! … Enough, O hold.

WOMEN

Watered, perhaps you'll bloom again--why not?

MEN

Brrr, I'm wrinkled up from shivering with cold.

WOMEN

   Next time you've fire you'll warm yourself and leave
us to our lot.

MAGISTRATE *enters with attendant* SCYTHIANS.

MAGISTRATE

Have the luxurious rites of the women glittered
Their libertine show, their drumming tapped out crowds,
The Sabazian Mysteries summoned their mob,
Adonis been wept to death on the terraces,
As I could hear the last day in the Assembly?
For Demostratus–let bad luck befoul him–
Was roaring, "We must sail for Sicily,"
While a woman, throwing herself about in a dance
Lopsided with drink, was shrilling out "Adonis,
Woe for Adonis." Then Demostratus shouted,
"We must levy hoplites at Zacynthus,"
And there the woman, up to the ears in wine,
Was screaming "Weep for Adonis" on the house-top,
The scoundrelly politician, that lunatic ox,
Bellowing bad advice through tipsy shrieks:
Such are the follies wantoning in them.

MEN

O if you knew their full effrontery!
All of the insults they've done, besides sousing us
With water from their pots to our public disgrace
For we stand here wringing our clothes like grown-up
   infants.

MAGISTRATE

By Poseidon, justly done! For in part with us
The blame must lie for dissolute behaviour
And for the pampered appetites they learn.
Thus grows the seedling lust to blossoming:
We go into a shop and say, "Here, goldsmith,
You remember the necklace that you wrought my wife;
Well, the other night in fervour of a dance
Her clasp broke open. Now I'm off for Salamis;
If you've the leisure, would you go tonight
And stick a bolt-pin into her opened clasp."
Another goes to a cobbler; a soldierly fellow,
Always standing up erect, and says to him,
"Cobbler, a sandal-strap of my wife's pinches her,
Hurts her little toe in a place where she's sensitive.
Come at noon and see if you can stretch out wider
This thing that troubles her, loosen its tightness."
And so you view the result. Observe my case–
I, a magistrate, come here to draw
Money to buy oar-blades, and what happens?
The women slam the door full in my face.
But standing still's no use. Bring me a crowbar,
And I'll chastise this their impertinence.
What do you gape at, wretch, with dazzled eyes?
Peering for a tavern, I suppose.
Come, force the gates with crowbars, prise them apart!
I'll prise away myself too … (LYSISTRATA *appears.*)

LYSISTRATA

Stop this banging.
I'm coming of my own accord. …Why bars?

It is not bars we need but common sense.

MAGISTRATE

Indeed, you slut! Where is the archer now?
Arrest this woman, tie her hands behind.

LYSISTRATA

If he brushes me with a finger, by Artemis,
The public menial, he'll be sorry for it.

MAGISTRATE

Are you afraid? Grab her about the middle.
Two of you then, lay hands on her and end it.

CALONICE

By Pandrosos I if your hand touches her
I'll spread you out and trample on your guts.

MAGISTRATE

My guts! Where is the other archer gone?
Bind that minx there who talks so prettily.

MYRRHINE

By Phosphor, if your hand moves out her way
You'd better have a surgeon somewhere handy.

MAGISTRATE

You too! Where is that archer? Take that woman.
I'll put a stop to these surprise-parties.

STRATYLLIS

By the Tauric Artemis, one inch nearer
My fingers, and it's a bald man that'll be yelling.

MAGISTRATE

Tut tut, what's here? Deserted by my archers. ...
But surely women never can defeat us;
Close up your ranks, my Scythians. Forward at them.

LYSISTRATA

By the Goddesses, you'll find that here await you
Four companies of most pugnacious women
Armed cap-a-pie from the topmost louring curl
To the lowest angry dimple.

MAGISTRATE

On, Scythians, bind them.

LYSISTRATA

On, gallant allies of our high design,
Vendors of grain-eggs-pulse-and-vegetables,
Ye garlic-tavern-keepers of bakeries,
Strike, batter, knock, hit, slap, and scratch our foes,
Be finely imprudent, say what you think of them. ...
Enough! retire and do not rob the dead.

MAGISTRATE

How basely did my archer-force come off.

LYSISTRATA

Ah, ha, you thought it was a herd of slaves
You had to tackle, and you didn't guess
The thirst for glory ardent in our blood.

MAGISTRATE

By Apollo, I know well the thirst that heats you–
Especially when a wine-skin's close.

MEN

You waste your breath, dear magistrate, I fear, in
    answering back.
What's the good of argument with such a rampageous
    pack?
Remember how they washed us down (these very clothes
    I wore)
With water that looked nasty and that smelt so even more.

WOMEN

What else to do, since you advanced too dangerously nigh.
If you should do the same again, I'll punch you in the eye.
Though I'm a stay-at-home and most a quiet life enjoy,
Polite to all and every (for I'm naturally coy),
Still if you wake a wasps' nest then of wasps you must
    beware.

MEN

How may this ferocity be tamed? It grows too great to bear.
Let us question them and find if they'll perchance declare
The reason why they strangely dare
To seize on Cranaos' citadel,
This eyrie inaccessible,
This shrine above the precipice,
The Acropolis.
Probe them and find what they mean with this idle talk;
    listen,
but watch they don't try to deceive.
You'd be neglecting your duty most certainly if now this
mystery unplumbed you leave.

MAGISTRATE

Women there! Tell what I ask you, directly. …
Come, without rambling, I wish you to state
What's your rebellious intention in barring up thus on
    our noses
our own temple-gate.

LYSISTRATA

To take first the treasury out of your management, and
    so stop the war
through the absence of gold.

MAGISTRATE

Is gold then the cause of the war?

LYSISTRATA

Yes, gold caused it and miseries more, too many to be told.
'Twas for money, and money alone, that Pisander with all
of the army of mob-agitators.
Raised up revolutions. But, as for the future, it won't be

worth while to set up to be traitors.
Not an obol they'll get as their loot, not an obol! while
we have the treasure-chest in our command.

MAGISTRATE

What then is that you propose?

LYSISTRATA

Just this–merely to take the exchequer henceforth in hand.

MAGISTRATE

The exchequer!

LYSISTRATA

Yes, why not? Of our capabilities you have had various
clear evidences.
Firstly remember we have always administered soundly
the budget of all
home-expenses.

MAGISTRATE

But this matter's different.

LYSISTRATA

How is it different?

MAGISTRATE

Why, it deals chiefly with war-time supplies.

LYSISTRATA

But we abolish war straight by our policy.

MAGISTRATE

What will you do if emergencies arise?

LYSISTRATA

Face them our own way.

MAGISTRATE

What *you* will?

LYSISTRATA

Yes *we* will!

MAGISTRATE

Then there's no help for it; we're all destroyed.

LYSISTRATA

No, willy-nilly you must be safeguarded.

MAGISTRATE

What madness is this?

LYSISTRATA

Why, it seems you're annoyed.
It must be done, that's all.

MAGISTRATE

Such awful oppression never,
O never in the past yet I bore.

LYSISTRATA

You must be saved, sirrah–that's all there is to it.

MAGISTRATE

If we don't want to be saved?

LYSISTRATA

All the more.

MAGISTRATE

Why do you women come prying and meddling in matters of state touching war-time and peace?

LYSISTRATA

That I will tell you.

MAGISTRATE

O tell me or quickly I'll–

LYSISTRATA

Hearken awhile and from threatening cease.

MAGISTRATE

I cannot, I cannot; it's growing too insolent.

WOMEN

Come on; you've far more than we have to dread.

MAGISTRATE

Stop from your croaking, old carrion-crow there. ...
Continue.

LYSISTRATA

Be calm then and I'll go ahead.
All the long years when the hopeless war dragged along
    we, unassuming, forgotten in quiet,
Endured without question, endured in our loneliness all
    your incessant child's antics and riot.
Our lips we kept tied, though aching with silence, though
    well all the while in our silence we knew
How wretchedly everything still was progressing by
    listening dumbly the day long to you.
For always at home you continued discussing the war
    and its politics loudly, and we
Sometimes would ask you, our hearts deep with sorrow-
    ing though we spoke lightly, though happy to see,
"What's to be inscribed on the side of the Treaty-stone
What, dear, was said in the Assembly today?"
"Mind your own business," he'd answer me growlingly
"hold your tongue, woman, or else go away."
And so I would hold it.

WOMEN

I'd not be silent for any man living on earth, no, not I!

MAGISTRATE

Not for a staff?

LYSISTRATA

Well, so I did nothing but sit in the house, feeling dreary,
   and sigh,
While ever arrived some fresh tale of decisions more
   foolish by far and presaging disaster.
Then I would say to him, "O my dear husband, why still
   do they rush on destruction the faster?"
At which he would look at me sideways, exclaiming,
   "Keep for your web and your shuttle your care,
Or for some hours hence your cheeks will be sore and
   hot; leave this alone, war is Man's sole affair!"

MAGISTRATE

By Zeus, but a man of fine sense, he.

LYSISTRATA

How sensible?
You dotard, because he at no time had lent
His intractable ears to absorb from our counsel one
   temperate word of advice, kindly meant?
But when at the last in the streets we heard shouted
   (everywhere ringing the ominous cry)
"Is there no one to help us, no saviour in Athens?" and,
   "No, there is no one," come back in reply.
At once a convention of all wives through Hellas here for
   a serious purpose was held,
To determine how husbands might yet back to wisdom
   despite their reluctance in time be compelled.
Why then delay any longer? It's settled. For the future
   you'll take up our old occupation.
Now in turn you're to hold tongue, as we did, and listen
   while we show the way to recover the nation.

MAGISTRATE

You talk to us! Why, you're mad. I'll not stand it.

LYSISTRATA

Cease babbling, you fool; till I end, hold your tongue.

MAGISTRATE

If I should take orders from one who wears veils, may
my neck straightaway be deservedly wrung.

LYSISTRATA

O if that keeps pestering you,
I've a veil here for your hair,
I'll fit you out in everything
As is only fair.

CALONICE

Here's a spindle that will do.

MYRRHINE

I'll add a wool-basket too.

LYSISTRATA

Girdled now sit humbly at home,
Munching beans, while you card wool and comb.
For war from now on is the Women's affair.

WOMEN.

Come then, down pitchers, all,
And on, courageous of heart,
In our comradely venture
Each taking her due part.
I could dance, dance, dance, and be fresher after,
I could dance away numberless suns,
To no weariness let my knees bend.
Earth I could brave with laughter,
Having such wonderful girls here to friend.
O the daring, the gracious, the beautiful ones!
Their courage unswerving and witty
Will rescue our city.

O sprung from the seed of most valiant-wombed grand-
   mothers, scions of savage and dangerous nettles!
Prepare for the battle, all. Gird up your angers. Our way

the wind of sweet victory settles.

LYSISTRATA

O tender Eros and Lady of Cyprus, some flush of beauty
    I pray you devise
To flash on our bosoms and, O Aphrodite, rosily gleam
    on our valorous thighs!
Joy will raise up its head through the legions warring and
    all of the far-serried ranks of mad-love
Bristle the earth to the pillared horizon, pointing in vain
    to the heavens above.
I think that perhaps then they'll give us our title—
Peace-makers.

MAGISTRATE

What do you mean? Please explain.

LYSISTRATA

First, we'll not see you now flourishing arms about into
the Marketing-place clang again.

WOMEN

No, by the Paphian.

LYSISTRATA

Still I can conjure them as past were the herbs stand or
    crockery's sold
Like Corybants jingling (poor sots) fully armoured, they
    noisily round on their promenade strolled.

MAGISTRATE

And rightly; that's discipline, they–

LYSISTRATA

But what's sillier than to go on an errand of buying a fish
Carrying along an immense. Gorgon-buckler instead the
    usual platter or dish?
A phylarch I lately saw, mounted on horse-back, dressed
    for the part with long ringlets and all,
Stow in his helmet the omelet bought steaming from an

old woman who kept a food-stall.
Nearby a soldier, a Thracian, was shaking wildly his
    spear like Tereus in the play,
To frighten a fig-girl while unseen the ruffian filched from
    her fruit-trays the ripest away.

MAGISTRATE

How, may I ask, will your rule re-establish order and
justice in lands so tormented?

LYSISTRATA

Nothing is easier.

MAGISTRATE

Out with it speedily–what is this plan that you boast
you've invented?

LYSISTRATA

If, when yarn we are winding, It chances to tangle, then,
    as perchance you may know, through the skein
This way and that still the spool we keep passing till it is
    finally clear all again:
So to untangle the War and its errors, ambassadors out
    on all sides we will send
This way and that, here, there and round about–soon
    you will find that the War has an end.

MAGISTRATE

So with these trivial tricks of the household, domestic
    analogies of threads, skeins and spools,
You think that you'll solve such a bitter complexity,
    unwind such political problems, you fools!

LYSISTRATA

Well, first as we wash dirty wool so's to cleanse it, so
    with a pitiless zeal we will scrub
Through the whole city for all greasy fellows; burrs too,
    the parasites, off we will rub.
That verminous plague of insensate place-seekers soon
    between thumb and forefinger we'll crack.
All who inside Athens' walls have their dwelling into one

great common basket we'll pack.
Disenfranchised or citizens, allies or aliens, pell-mell the
lot of them in we will squeeze.
Till they discover humanity's meaning. ... As for
disjointed and far colonies,
Them you must never from this time imagine as scattered
about just like lost hanks of wool.
Each portion we'll take and wind in to this centre,
inward to Athens each loyalty pull,
Till from the vast heap where all's piled together at last
can be woven a strong Cloak of State.

MAGISTRATE

How terrible is it to stand here and watch them carding
and winding at will with our fate,
Witless in war as they are.

LYSISTRATA

What of us then, who ever in vain for our children must
weep
Borne but to perish afar and in vain?

MAGISTRATE

Not that, O let that one memory sleep!

LYSISTRATA

Then while we should be companioned still merrily,
happy as brides may, the livelong night,
Kissing youth by, we are forced to lie single. ... But leave
for a moment our pitiful plight,
It hurts even more to behold the poor maidens helpless
wrinkling in staler virginity.

MAGISTRATE

Does not a man age?

LYSISTRATA

Not in the same way. Not as a woman grows withered,
grows he.
He, when returned from the war, though grey-headed, yet

if he wishes can choose out a wife.
But she has no solace save peering for omens, wretched
and lonely the rest of her life.

MAGISTRATE

But the old man will often select–

LYSISTRATA

O why not finish and die?
A bier is easy to buy,
A honey-cake I'll knead you with joy,
This garland will see you are decked.

CALONICE

I've a wreath for you too.

MYRRHINE

I also will fillet you.

LYSISTRATA

What more is lacking? Step aboard the boat.
See, Charon shouts ahoy.
You're keeping him, he wants to shove afloat.

MAGISTRATE

Outrageous insults! Thus my place to flout!
Now to my fellow-magistrates I'll go
And what you've perpetrated on me show.

LYSISTRATA

Why are you blaming us for laying you out?
Assure yourself we'll not forget to make
The third day offering early for your sake.

MAGISTRATE *retires*, LYSISTRATA *returns within.*

OLD MEN.

All men who call your loins your own, awake at last, arise
And strip to stand in readiness. For as it seems to me

Some more perilous offensive in their heads they now devise.
I'm sure a Tyranny
Like that of Hippias
In this I detect. ...
They mean to put us under
Themselves I suspect,
And that Laconians assembling
At Cleisthenes' house have played
A trick-of-war and provoked them
Madly to raid
The Treasury, in which term I include
The Pay for my food.
For is it not preposterous
They should talk this way to us
On a subject such as battle!

And, women as they are, about bronze bucklers dare prattle—
Make alliance with the Spartans—people I for one
Like very hungry wolves would always most sincere shun. ...
Some dirty game is up their sleeve,
I believe.
A Tyranny, no doubt... but they won't catch me, that know.
Henceforth on my guard I'll go,
A sword with myrtle-branches wreathed for ever in my hand,
And under arms in the Public Place I'll take my watchful
  stand,
Shoulder to shoulder with Aristogeiton. Now my staff I'll
  draw
And start at once by knocking
that shocking
Hag upon the jaw.

WOMEN.

Your own mother will not know you when you get back
  to the town.
But first, my friends and allies, let us lay these garments
  down,
And all ye fellow-citizens, hark to me while I tell
What will aid Athens well.
Just as is right, for I
Have been a sharer
In all the lavish splendour
Of the proud city.
I bore the holy vessels
At seven, then
I pounded barley

At the age of ten,
And clad in yellow robes,
Soon after this,
I was Little Bear to
Brauronian Artemis;
Then neckletted with figs,
Grown tall and pretty,
I was a Basket-bearer,
And so it's obvious I should
Give you advice that I think good,
The very best I can.
It should not prejudice my voice that I'm not born a man,
If I say something advantageous to the present situation.
For I'm taxed too, and as a toll provide men for the nation
While, miserable greybeards, you,
It is true,
Contribute nothing of any importance whatever to our
  needs;
But the treasure raised against the Medes
You've squandered, and do nothing in return, save that
  you make
Our lives and persons hazardous by some imbecile mistakes
What can you answer? Now be careful, don't arouse my
  spite,
Or with my slipper I'll take you napping,
faces slapping
Left and right.

MEN.

What villainies they contrive!
Come, let vengeance fall,
You that below the waist are still alive,
Off with your tunics at my call—
Naked, all.
For a man must strip to battle like a man.
No quaking, brave steps taking, careless what's ahead,
  white shoed,
in the nude, onward bold,
All ye who garrisoned Leipsidrion of old. ...
Let each one wag
As youthfully as he can,
And if he has the cause at heart
Rise at least a span.

We must take a stand and keep to it,
For if we yield the smallest bit

To their importunity.

Then nowhere from their inroads will be left to us
immunity.

But they'll be building ships and soon their navies will
attack us,

As Artemisia did, and seek to fight us and to sack us.

And if they mount, the Knights they'll rob

Of a job,

For everyone knows how talented they all are in the saddle,

Having long practised how to straddle;

No matter how they're jogged there up and down,
they're never thrown.

Then think of Myron's painting, and each horse-backed
Amazon

In combat hand-to-hand with men. ... Come, on these
women fall,

And in pierced wood-collars let's stick

quick

The necks of one and all.

WOMEN.

Don't cross me or I'll loose

The Beast that's kennelled here. ...

And soon you will be howling for a truce,

Howling out with fear.

But my dear,

Strip also, that women may battle unhindered. ...

But you, you'll be too sore to eat garlic more, or one
black bean,

I really mean, so great's my spleen, to kick you black and
blue

With these my dangerous legs.

I'll hatch the lot of you,

If my rage you dash on,

The way the relentless Beetle

Hatched the Eagle's eggs.

Scornfully aside I set

Every silly old-man threat

While Lampito's with me.

Or dear Ismenia, the noble Theban girl. Then let decree

Be hotly piled upon decree; in vain will be your labours,

You futile rogue abominated by your suffering neighbour

To Hecate's feast I yesterday went.

Off I sent

To our neighbours in Boeotia, asking as a gift to me

For them to pack immediately

That darling dainty thing ... a good fat eel [1] I meant of
course;

[Footnote 1: *Vide supra*, p. 23.]

But they refused because some idiotic old decree's in force.

O this strange passion for decrees nothing on earth can
check,

Till someone puts a foot out tripping you,

and slipping you

Break your neck.

LYSISTRATA enters in dismay.

WOMEN

Dear Mistress of our martial enterprise,

Why do you come with sorrow in your eyes?

LYSISTRATA

O 'tis our naughty femininity,

So weak in one spot, that hath saddened me.

WOMEN

What's this? Please speak.

LYSISTRATA

Poor women, O so weak!

WOMEN

What can it be? Surely your friends may know.

LYSISTRATA

Yea, I must speak it though it hurt me so.

WOMEN

Speak; can we help? Don't stand there mute in need.

LYSISTRATA

I'll blurt it out then--our women's army's mutinied.

WOMEN

O Zeus!

LYSISTRATA

What use is Zeus to our anatomy?
Here is the gaping calamity I meant:
I cannot shut their ravenous appetites
A moment more now. They are all deserting.
The first I caught was sidling through the postern
Close by the Cave of Pan: the next hoisting herself
With rope and pulley down: a third on the point
Of slipping past: while a fourth malcontent, seated
For instant flight to visit Orsilochus
On bird-back, I dragged off by the hair in time. …
They are all snatching excuses to sneak home.
Look, there goes one. … Hey, what's the hurry?

1ST WOMAN

I must get home. I've some Milesian wool
Packed wasting away, and moths are pushing through it.

LYSISTRATA

Fine moths indeed, I know. Get back within.

1ST WOMAN

By the Goddesses, I'll return instantly.
I only want to stretch it on my bed.

LYSISTRATA

You shall stretch nothing and go nowhere either.

1ST WOMAN

Must I never use my wool then?

LYSISTRATA

If needs be.

2ND WOMAN

How unfortunate I am! O my poor flax!
It's left at home unstript.

LYSISTRATA

So here's another
That wishes to go home and strip her flax.
Inside again!

2ND WOMAN

No, by the Goddess of Light,
I'll be back as soon as I have flayed it properly.

LYSISTRATA

You'll not flay anything. For if you begin
There'll not be one here but has a patch to be flayed.

3RD WOMAN

O holy Eilithyia, stay this birth
Till I have left the precincts of the place!

LYSISTRATA

What nonsense is this?

3RD WOMAN

I'll drop it any minute.

LYSISTRATA

Yesterday you weren't with child.

3RD WOMAN

But I am today.
O let me find a midwife, Lysistrata.
O quickly!

LYSISTRATA

Now what story is this you tell?
What is this hard lump here?

3RD WOMAN

It's a male child.

LYSISTRATA

By Aphrodite, it isn't. Your belly's hollow,
And it has the feel of metal. … Well, I soon can see.
You hussy, it's Athene's sacred helm,
And you said you were with child.

3RD WOMAN

And so I am.

LYSISTRATA

Then why the helm?

3RD WOMAN

So if the throes should take me
Still in these grounds I could use it like a dove
As a laying-nest in which to drop the child.

LYSISTRATA

More pretexts! You can't hide your clear intent,
And anyway why not wait till the tenth day
Meditating a brazen name for your brass brat?

WOMAN

And I can't sleep a wink. My nerve is gone
Since I saw that snake-sentinel of the shrine.

WOMAN

And all those dreadful owls with their weird hooting!
Though I'm wearied out, I can't close an eye.

LYSISTRATA

You wicked women, cease from juggling lies.
You want your men. But what of them as well?
They toss as sleepless in the lonely night,
I'm sure of it. Hold out awhile, hold out,
But persevere a teeny-weeny longer.

An oracle has promised Victory
If we don't wrangle. Would you hear the words?

WOMEN

Yes, yes, what is it?

LYSISTRATA

Silence then, you chatterboxes.
Here–
*When as the swallows flocking in one place from the
    hoopoes
Deny themselves love's gambols any more,
All woes shall then have ending and great Zeus the
    Thunderer
Shall put above what was below before.*

WOMEN

Will the men then always be kept under us?

LYSISTRATA

*But if the swallows squabble among themselves and fly away
Out of the temple, refusing to agree,
Then The Most Wanton Birds in all the World
They shall be named for ever. That's his decree.*

WOMAN

It's obvious what it means.

LYSISTRATA

Now by all the gods
We must let no agony deter from duty,
Back to your quarters. For we are base indeed,
My friends, if we betray the oracle.
She goes out.

OLD MEN.

I'd like to remind you of a fable they used to employ,
When I was a little boy:
How once through fear of the marriage-bed a young man,
Melanion by name, to the wilderness ran,

And there on the hills he dwelt.
For hares he wove a net
Which with his dog he set–
Most likely he's there yet.
For he never came back home, so great was the fear he felt.
I loathe the sex as much as he,
And therefore I no less shall be
As chaste as was Melanion.

MAN

Grann'am, do you much mind men?

WOMAN

Onions you won't need, to cry.

MAN

From my foot you shan't escape.

WOMAN

What thick forests I espy.

MEN

So much Myronides' fierce beard
And thundering black back were feared,
That the foe fled when they were shown–
Brave he as Phormion.

WOMEN.

Well, I'll relate a rival fable just to show to you
A different point of view:
There was a rough-hewn fellow, Timon, with a face
That glowered as through a thorn-bush in a wild, bleak
   place.
He too decided on flight,
This very Furies' son,
All the world's ways to shun
And hide from everyone,
Spitting out curses on all knavish men to left and right.
But though he reared this hate for men,
He loved the women even then,
And never thought them enemies.

WOMAN

O your jaw I'd like to break.

MAN

That I fear do you suppose?

WOMAN

Learn what kicks my legs can make.

MAN

Raise them up, and you'll expose–

WOMAN

Nay, you'll see there, I engage,
All is well kept despite my age,
And tended smooth enough to slip
From any adversary's grip.

LYSISTRATA appears.

LYSISTRATA

Hollo there, hasten hither to me
Skip fast along.

WOMAN

What is this? Why the noise?

LYSISTRATA

A man, a man! I spy a frenzied man!
He carries Love upon him like a staff.
O Lady of Cyprus, and Cythera, and Paphos,
I beseech you, keep our minds and hands to the oath.

WOMAN

Where is he, whoever he is?

LYSISTRATA

By the Temple of Chloe.

WOMAN

Yes, now I see him, but who can he be?

LYSISTRATA

Look at him. Does anyone recognise his face?

MYRRHINE

I do. He is my husband, Cinesias.

LYSISTRATA

You know how to work. Play with him, lead him on,
Seduce him to the cozening-point—kiss him, kiss him,
Then slip your mouth aside just as he's sure of it,
Ungirdle every caress his mouth feels at
Save that the oath upon the bowl has locked.

MYRRHINE

You can rely on me.

LYSISTRATA

I'll stay here to help
In working up his ardor to its height
Of vain magnificence. ... The rest to their quarters.
Enter CINESIAS.
Who is this that stands within our lines?

CINESIAS

I.

LYSISTRATA

A man?

CINESIAS

Too much a man!

LYSISTRATA

Then be off at once.

CINESIAS

Who are you that thus eject me?

LYSISTRATA

Guard for the day.

CINESIAS

By all the gods, then call Myrrhine hither.

LYSISTRATA

So, call Myrrhine hither! Who are you?

CINESIAS

I am her husband Cinesias, son of Anthros.

LYSISTRATA

Welcome, dear friend! That glorious name of yours
Is quite familiar in our ranks. Your wife
Continually has it in her mouth.
She cannot touch an apple or an egg
But she must say, "This to Cinesias!"

CINESIAS

O is that true?

LYSISTRATA

By Aphrodite, it is. If the conversation strikes on men,
your wife
Cuts in with, "All are boobies by Cinesias."

CINESIAS

Then call her here.

LYSISTRATA

And what am I to get?

CINESIAS

This, if you want it. ... See, what I have here.
But not to take away.

LYSISTRATA

Then I'll call her.

CINESIAS

Be quick, be quick. All grace is wiped from life
Since she went away. O sad, sad am I
When there I enter on that loneliness,
And wine is unvintaged of the sun's flavour.
And food is tasteless. But I've put on weight.

MYRRHINE (above)

I love him O so much! but he won't have it.
Don't call me down to him.

CINESIAS

Sweet little Myrrhine!
What do you mean? Come here.

MYRRHINE

O no I won't.
Why are you calling me? You don't want me.

CINESIAS

Not want you! with this week-old strength of love.

MYRRHINE

Farewell.

CINESIAS

Don't go, please don't go, Myrrhine.
At least you'll hear our child. Call your mother, lad.

CHILD

Mummy ... mummy ... mummy!

CINESIAS

There now, don't you feel pity for the child?
He's not been fed or washed now for six days.

MYRRHINE

I certainly pity him with so heartless a father.

CINESIAS

Come down, my sweetest, come for the child's sake.

MYRRHINE

A trying life it is to be a mother!
I suppose I'd better go.   *She comes down.*

CINESIAS

How much younger she looks,
How fresher and how prettier! Myrrhine,
Lift up your lovely face, your disdainful face;
And your ankle ... let your scorn step out its worst;
It only rubs me to more ardor here.

MYRRHINE

(*playing with the child*)
You're as innocent as he's iniquitous.
Let me kiss you, honey-petting, mother's darling.

CINESIAS

How wrong to follow other women's counsel
And let loose all these throbbing voids in yourself
As well as in me. Don't you go throb-throb?

MYRRHINE

Take away your hands.

CINESIAS

Everything in the house
Is being ruined.

MYRRHINE

I don't care at all.

CINESIAS

The roosters are picking all your web to rags.
Do you mind that?

MYRRHINE

Not I.

CINESIAS

What time we've wasted
We might have drenched with Paphian laughter, flung
On Aphrodite's Mysteries. O come here.

MYRRHINE

Not till a treaty finishes the war.

CINESIAS

If you must have it, then we'll get it done.

MYRRHINE

Do it and I'll come home. Till then I am bound.

CINESIAS

Well, can't your oath perhaps be got around?

MYRRHINE

No … no … still I'll not say that I don't love you.

CINESIAS

You love me! Then dear girl, let me also love you.

MYRRHINE

You must be joking. The boy's looking on.

CINESIAS

Here, Manes, take the child home!… There, he's gone.
There's nothing in the way now. Come to the point.

MYRRHINE

Here in the open! In plain sight?

CINESIAS

In Pan's cave.
A splendid place.

MYRRHINE

Where shall I dress my hair again
Before returning to the citadel?

CINESIAS

You can easily primp yourself in the Clepsydra.

MYRRHINE

But how can I break my oath?

CINESIAS

Leave that to me,
I'll take all risk.

MYRRHINE

Well, I'll make you comfortable.

CINESIAS

Don't worry. I'd as soon lie on the grass.

MYRRHINE

No, by Apollo, in spite of all your faults
I won't have you lying on the nasty earth.
(*From here MYRRHINE keeps on going off to fetch things.*)

CINESIAS

Ah, how she loves me.

MYRRHINE

Rest there on the bench,
While I arrange my clothes. O what a nuisance,
I must find some cushions first.

CINESIAS

Why some cushions?
Please don't get them!

MYRRHINE

What? The plain, hard wood?
Never, by Artemis! That would be too vulgar.

CINESIAS

Open your arms!

MYRRHINE

No. Wait a second.

CINESIAS

O. …
Then hurry back again.

MYRRHINE

Here the cushions are. Lie down while I—O dear! But
what a shame,
You need more pillows.

CINESIAS

I don't want them, dear.

MYRRHINE

But I do.

CINESIAS

Thwarted affection mine,
They treat you just like Heracles at a feast
With cheats of dainties, O disappointing arms!

MYRRHINE

Raise up your head.

CINESIAS

There, that's everything at last.

MYRRHINE

Yes, all.

CINESIAS

Then run to my arms, you golden girl.

MYRRHINE

I'm loosening my girdle now. But you've not forgotten?
You're not deceiving me about the Treaty?

CINESIAS

No, by my life, I'm not.

MYRRHINE

Why, you've no blanket.

CINESIAS

It's not the silly blanket's warmth but yours I want.

MYRRHINE

Never mind. You'll soon have both. I'll come straight back.

CINESIAS

The woman will choke me with her coverlets.

MYRRHINE

Get up a moment.

CINESIAS

I'm up high enough.

MYRRHINE

Would you like me to perfume you?

CINESIAS

By Apollo, no!

MYRRHINE

By Aphrodite, I'll do it anyway.

CINESIAS

Lord Zeus, may she soon use up all the myrrh.

MYRRHINE

Stretch out your hand. Take it and rub it in.

CINESIAS

Hmm, it's not as fragrant as might be; that is,
Not before it's smeared. It doesn't smell of kisses.

MYRRHINE

How silly I am: I've brought you Rhodian scents.

CINESIAS

It's good enough, leave it, love.

MYRRHINE

You must be jesting.

CINESIAS

Plague rack the man who first compounded scent!

MYRRHINE

Here, take this flask.

CINESIAS

I've a far better one.
Don't tease me, come here, and get nothing more.

MYRRHINE

I'm coming. … I'm just drawing off my shoes. …
You're sure you will vote for Peace?

CINESIAS

I'll think about it.
She runs off.
I'm dead: the woman's worn me all away.
She's gone and left me with an anguished pulse.

MEN

Baulked in your amorous delight
How melancholy is your plight.
With sympathy your case I view;
For I am sure it's hard on you.
What human being could sustain
This unforeseen domestic strain,
And not a single trace
Of willing women in the place!

CINESIAS

O Zeus, what throbbing suffering!

MEN

She did it all, the harlot, she
With her atrocious harlotry.

WOMEN

Nay, rather call her darling-sweet.

MEN

What, sweet? She's a rude, wicked thing.

CINESIAS

A wicked thing, as I repeat.
O Zeus, O Zeus,
Canst Thou not suddenly let loose
Some twirling hurricane to tear
Her flapping up along the air
And drop her, when she's whirled around,
Here to the ground
Neatly impaled upon the stake
That's ready upright for her sake.
He goes out.
Enter SPARTAN HERALD.
The MAGISTRATE *comes forward.*

HERALD

What here gabs the Senate an' the Prytanes?
I've fetcht despatches for them.

MAGISTRATE

Are you a man
Or a monstrosity?

HERALD

My scrimp-brained lad,
I'm a herald, as ye see, who hae come frae Sparta
Anent a Peace.

MAGISTRATE

Then why do you hide that lance
That sticks out under your arms?

HERALD.

I've brought no lance.

MAGISTRATE

Then why do you turn aside and hold your cloak
So far out from your body? Is your groin swollen
With stress of travelling?

HERALD

By Castor, I'll swear
The man is wud.

MAGISTRATE

Indeed, your cloak is wide,
My rascal fellow.

HERALD

But I tell ye No!
Enow o' fleering!

MAGISTRATE

Well, what is it then?

HERALD

It's my despatch cane.

MAGISTRATE

Of course—a Spartan cane!
But speak right out. I know all this too well.
Are new privations springing up in Sparta?

HERALD

Och, hard as could be: in lofty lusty columns
Our allies stand united. We maun get Pellene.

MAGISTRATE

Whence has this evil come? Is it from Pan?

HERALD

No. Lampito first ran asklent, then the others
Sprinted after her example, and blocked, the hizzies,
Their wames unskaithed against our every fleech.

MAGISTRATE

What did you do?

HERALD

We are broken, and bent double,
Limp like men carrying lanthorns in great winds
About the city. They winna let us even
Wi' lightest neif skim their primsie pretties
Till we've concluded Peace-terms wi' a' Hellas.

MAGISTRATE

So the conspiracy is universal;
This proves it. Then return to Sparta. Bid them
Send envoys with full powers to treat of Peace;
And I will urge the Senate here to choose
Plenipotentiary ambassadors,
As argument adducing this connection.

HERALD

I'm off. Your wisdom none could contravert.
They retire.

MEN

There is no beast, no rush of fire, like woman so untamed.
She calmly goes her way where even panthers would be
    shamed.

WOMEN

And yet you are fool enough, it seems, to dare to war
    with me,
When for your faithful ally you might win me easily.

MEN

Never could the hate I feel for womankind grow less.

WOMEN

Then have your will. But I'll take pity on your nakedness.
For I can see just how ridiculous you look, and so
Will help you with your tunic if close up I now may go.

MEN

Well, that, by Zeus, is no scoundrel-deed, I frankly will admit.
I only took them off myself in a scoundrel raging-fit.

WOMEN

Now you look sensible, and that you're men no one
    could doubt.
If you were but good friends again, I'd take the insect out
That hurts your eye.

MEN

Is that what's wrong? That nasty bitie thing.
Please squeeze it out, and show me what it is that makes
    this sting.
It's been paining me a long while now.

WOMEN

Well I'll agree to that,
Although you're most unmannerly. O what a giant gnat.
Here, look! It comes from marshy Tricorysus, I can tell.

MEN

O thank you. It was digging out a veritable well.
Now that it's gone, I can't hold back my tears. See how
    they fall.

WOMEN

I'll wipe them off, bad as you are, and kiss you after all.

MEN

I won't be kissed.

WOMEN

O yes, you will. Your wishes do not matter.

MEN

O botheration take you all! How you cajole and flatter.
A hell it is to live with you; to live without, a hell:
How truly was that said. But come, these enmities let's quell.
You stop from giving orders and I'll stop from doing wrong.
So let's join ranks and seal our bargain with a choric song.

CHORUS.

Athenians, it's not our intention
To sow political dissension
By giving any scandal mention;
But on the contrary to promote good feeling in the state
By word and deed. We've had enough calamities of late.
So let a man or woman but divulge
They need a trifle, say,
Two minas, three or four,
I've purses here that bulge.
There's only one condition made
(Indulge my whim in this I pray)–
When Peace is signed once more,
On no account am I to be repaid.
And I'm making preparation
For a gay select collation
With some youths of reputation.
I've managed to produce some soup and they're slaugh-
   tering for me
A sucking-pig: its flesh should taste as tender as could be.
I shall expect you at my house today.
To the baths make an early visit,
And bring your children along;
Don't dawdle on the way.
Ask no one; enter as if the place
Was all your own–yours henceforth is it.
If nothing chances wrong,
The door will then be shut bang in your face.
   The SPARTAN AMBASSADORS *approach.*

CHORUS

Here come the Spartan envoys with long, worried beards.
Hail, Spartans how do you fare?
Did anything new arise?

SPARTANS

No need for a clutter o' words. Do ye see our condition?

CHORUS

The situation swells to greater tension.
Something will explode soon.

SPARTANS

It's awfu' truly.
But come, let us wi' the best speed we may
Scribble a Peace.

CHORUS

I notice that our men
Like wrestlers poised for contest, hold their clothes
Out from their bellies. An athlete's malady!
Since exercise alone can bring relief.

ATHENIANS

Can anyone tell us where Lysistrata is?
There is no need to describe our men's condition,
It shows up plainly enough.

CHORUS

It's the same disease.
Do you feel a jerking throbbing in the morning?

ATHENIANS

By Zeus, yes! In these straits, I'm racked all through.
Unless Peace is soon declared, we shall be driven
In the void of women to try Cleisthenes.

CHORUS

Be wise and cover those things with your tunics.
Who knows what kind of person may perceive you?

ATHENIANS

By Zeus, you're right.

SPARTANS

By the Twa Goddesses,
Indeed ye are. Let's put our tunics on.

ATHENIANS

Hail O my fellow-sufferers, hail Spartans.

SPARTANS

O hinnie darling, what a waefu' thing!
If they had seen us wi' our lunging waddies!

ATHENIANS

Tell us then, Spartans, what has brought you here?

SPARTANS

We come to treat o' Peace.

ATHENIANS

Well spoken there!
And we the same. Let us callout Lysistrata
Since she alone can settle the Peace-terms.

SPARTANS

Callout Lysistratus too if ye don't mind.

CHORUS

No indeed. She hears your voices and she comes.
Enter LYSISTRATA
Hail, Wonder of all women! Now you must be in turn
Hard, shifting, clear, deceitful, noble, crafty, sweet, and stern.
The foremost men of Hellas, smitten by your fascination,
Have brought their tangled quarrels here for your sole
    arbitration.

LYSISTRATA

An easy task if the love's raging home-sickness
Doesn't start trying out how well each other
Will serve instead of us. But I'll know at once
If they do. O where's that girl, Reconciliation?
Bring first before me the Spartan delegates,
And see you lift no rude or violent hands–
None of the churlish ways our husbands used.
But lead them courteously, as women should.
And if they grudge fingers, guide them by other methods,

And introduce them with ready tact. The Athenians
Draw by whatever offers you a grip.
Now, Spartans, stay here facing me. Here you,
Athenians. Both hearken to my words.
I am a woman, but I'm not a fool.
And what of natural intelligence I own
Has been filled out with the remembered precepts
My father and the city-elders taught me.
First I reproach you both sides equally
That when at Pylae and Olympia,
At Pytho and the many other shrines
That I could name, you sprinkle from one cup
The altars common to all Hellenes, yet
You wrack Hellenic cities, bloody Hellas
With deaths of her own sons, while yonder clangs
The gathering menace of barbarians.

ATHENIANS

We cannot hold it in much longer now.

LYSISTRATA

Now unto you, O Spartans, do I speak.
Do you forget how your own countryman,
Pericleidas, once came hither suppliant
Before our altars, pale in his purple robes,
Praying for an army when in Messenia
Danger growled, and the Sea-god made earth quaver.
Then with four thousand hoplites Cimon marched
And saved all Sparta. Yet base ingrates now,
You are ravaging the soil of your preservers.

ATHENIANS

By Zeus, they do great wrong, Lysistrata.

SPARTANS

Great wrong, indeed. O! What a luscious wench!

LYSISTRATA

And now I turn to the Athenians.
Have you forgotten too how once the Spartans
In days when you wore slavish tunics, came

And with their spears broke a Thessalian host
And all the partisans of Hippias?
They alone stood by your shoulder on that day.
They freed you, so that for the slave's short skirt
You should wear the trailing cloak of liberty.

SPARTANS

I've never seen a nobler woman anywhere.

ATHENIANS

Nor I one with such prettily jointing hips.

LYSISTRATA

Now, brethren twined with mutual benefactions,
Can you still war, can you suffer such disgrace?
Why not be friends? What is there to prevent you?

SPARTANS

We're agreed, gin that we get this tempting Mole.

LYSISTRATA

Which one?

SPARTANS

That ane we've wanted to get into,
O for sae lang. … Pylos, of course.

ATHENIANS

By Poseidon,
Never!

LYSISTRATA

Give it up.

ATHENIANS

Then what will we do?
We need that ticklish place united to us–

LYSISTRATA

Ask for some other lurking-hole in return.

ATHENIANS

Then, ah, we'll choose this snug thing here, Echinus,
Shall we call the nestling spot? And this backside haven,
These desirable twin promontories, the Maliac,
And then of course these Megarean Legs.

SPARTANS

Not that, O surely not that, never that.

LYSISTRATA

Agree! Now what are two legs more or less?

ATHENIANS

I want to strip at once and plough my land.

SPARTANS

And mine I want to fertilize at once.

LYSISTRATA

And so you can, when Peace is once declared.
If you mean it, get your allies' heads together
And come to some decision.

ATHENIANS

What allies?
There's no distinction in our politics:
We've risen as one man to this conclusion;
Every ally is jumping-mad to drive it home.

SPARTANS

And ours the same, for sure.

ATHENIANS

The Carystians first!
I'll bet on that.

LYSISTRATA

I agree with all of you.
Now off, and cleanse yourselves for the Acropolis,
For we invite you all in to a supper
From our commissariat baskets. There at table
You will pledge good behaviour and uprightness;
Then each man's wife is his to hustle home.

ATHENIANS

Come, as quickly as possible.

SPARTANS

As quick as ye like.
Lead on.

ATHENIANS

O Zeus, quick, quick, lead quickly on.
They hurry off.

CHORUS.

Broidered stuffs on high I'm heaping,
Fashionable cloaks and sweeping
Trains, not even gold gawds keeping.
Take them all, I pray you, take them all (I do not care)
And deck your children–your daughter, if the Basket she's
  to bear.
Come, everyone of you, come in and take
Of this rich hoard a share.
Nought's tied so skilfully
But you its seal can break
And plunder all you spy inside.
I've laid out all that I can spare,
And therefore you will see
Nothing unless than I you're sharper-eyed.
If lacking corn a man should be
While his slaves clamour hungrily
And his excessive progeny,
Then I've a handfull of grain at home which is always to
  be had,
And to which in fact a more-than-life-size loaf I'd gladly add.

Then let the poor bring with them bag or sack
And take this store of food.

Manes, my man, I'll tell
To help them all to pack
Their wallets full. But O take care.
I had forgotten; don't intrude,
Or terrified you'll yell.
My dog is hungry too, and bites–beware!

Some LOUNGERS *from the Market with torches
approach the Banqueting hall. The* PORTER *bars their
entrance.*

1ST MARKET-LOUNGER

Open the door.

PORTER

Here move along.

1ST MARKET-LOUNGER

What's this?
You're sitting down. Shall I singe you with my torch?
That's vulgar! O I couldn't do it … yet
If it would gratify the audience,
I'll mortify myself.

2ND MARKET-LOUNGER

And I will too.
We'll both be crude and vulgar, yes we will.

PORTER

Be off at once now or you'll be wailing
Dirges for your hair. Get off at once,
And see you don't disturb the Spartan envoys
Just coming out from the splendid feast they've had.
The banqueters begin to come out.

1ST ATHENIAN

I've never known such a pleasant banquet before, And
what delightful fellows the Spartans are.
When we are warm with wine, how wise we grow.

2ND ATHENIAN

That's only fair, since sober we're such fools:
This is the advice I'd give the Athenians–
See our ambassadors are always drunk.
For when we visit Sparta sober, then
We're on the alert for trickery all the while
So that we miss half of the things they say,
And misinterpret things that were never said,
And then report the muddle back to Athens.
But now we're charmed with each other. They might cap
With the Telamon-catch instead of the Cleitagora,
And we'd applaud and praise them just the same;
We're not too scrupulous in weighing words.

PORTER

Why, here the rascals come again to plague me.
Won't you move on, you sorry loafers there!

MARKET-LOUNGER

Yes, by Zeus, they're already coming out.

SPARTANS

Now hinnie dearest, please tak' up your pipe
That I may try a spring an' sing my best
In honour o' the Athenians an' oursels.

ATHENIANS

Aye, take your pipe. By all the gods, there's nothing
Could glad my heart more than to watch you dance.

SPARTANS.

Mnemosyne,
Let thy fire storm these younkers,
O tongue wi' stormy ecstasy
My Muse that knows
Our deeds and theirs, how when at sea
Their navies swooped upon
The Medes at Artemision–
Gods for their courage, did they strike
Wrenching a triumph frae their foes;
While at Thermopylae
Leonidas' army stood: wild-boars they were like

Wild-boars that wi' fierce threat
Their terrible tusks whet;
The sweat ran streaming down each twisted face,
Faen blossoming i' strange petals o' death
Panted frae mortal breath,
The sweat drenched a' their bodies i' that place,
For the hurly-burly o' Persians glittered more
Than the sands on the shore.

Come, Hunting Girl, an' hear my prayer–
You whose arrows whizz in woodlands, come an' bless
This Peace we swear.
Let us be fenced wi' age long amity,
O let this bond stick ever firm through thee
In friendly happiness.
Henceforth no guilefu' perjury be seen!
O hither, hither O
Thou wildwood queen.

LYSISTRATA

Earth is delighted now, peace is the voice of earth.
Spartans, sort out your wives: Athenians, yours.
Let each catch hands with his wife and dance his joy,
Dance out his thanks, be grateful in music,
And promise reformation with his heels.

ATHENIANS.

O Dancers, forward. Lead out the Graces,
Call Artemis out;
Then her brother, the Dancer of Skies,
That gracious Apollo.
Invoke with a shout
Dionysus out of whose eyes
Breaks fire on the maenads that follow;
And Zeus with his flares of quick lightning, and call,
Happy Hera, Queen of all,
And all the Daimons summon hither to be
Witnesses of our revelry
And of the noble Peace we have made,
Aphrodite our aid.

Io Paieon, Io, cry–
For victory, leap!
Attained by me, leap!
Euoi Euoi Euai Euai.

SPARTANS

Piper, gie us the music for a new sang.

SPARTANS.

Leaving again lovely lofty Taygetus
Hither O Spartan Muse, hither to greet us,
And wi' our choric voice to raise
To Amyclean Apollo praise,
And Tyndareus' gallant sons whose days
Alang Eurotas' banks merrily pass,
An' Athene o' the House o' Brass.

Now the dance begin;
Dance, making swirl your fringe o' woolly skin,
While we join voices
To hymn dear Sparta that rejoices
I' a beautifu' sang,
An' loves to see

Dancers tangled beautifully;
For the girls i' tumbled ranks
Alang Eurotas' banks
Like wanton fillies thrang,
Frolicking there

An' like Bacchantes shaking the wild air
To comb a giddy laughter through the hair,
Bacchantes that clench thyrsi as they sweep
To the ecstatic leap.

An' Helen, Child o' Leda, come
Thou holy, nimble, gracefu' Queen,
Lead thou the dance, gather thy joyous tresses up i' bands
An' play like a fawn. To madden them, clap thy hands,
And sing praise to the warrior goddess templed i' our lands,
Her o' the House o' Brass.

DISCUSSION QUESTIONS

1. How does Lysistrata subvert traditional views of women? How does she rely on such views to advance her position?

2. How do the Chorus of Old Men and the Chorus of Old Women function in the play? How do their views influence the course of action?

3. What is the effect of the highly sexualized language? Does it contribute to political implications of the play? Does it serve a purely comic role?

4. How does the play characterize the differences between Athens and Sparta? Which characters epitomize these differences?

5. Do the comic elements of the play carry tragic implications? How does the comic treatment of serious issues in this play compare with the presentation of tragedy in other Greek dramas?

WRITING SUGGESTION

1. Research the ways antiwar activists have turned to *Lysistrata* for inspiration. How has Aristophanes' play been used? To what extent might the protests described in his play be limited to the ancient Greek world? To what extent do they reach into our own day?

THE ROMANS

General Introduction

According to a popular Roman legend, Rome was founded on April 21, 753 BCE by the twins Romulus and Remus. Sons of the god Mars and a priestess named Rhea Silva, the twins had been abandoned in the Tiber River as infants. Fortunately, they were found and suckled by a she-wolf before a local shepherd and his wife adopted them. As young men, the brothers established a city near the spot where they had washed ashore. After a dispute, Romulus killed his brother and named the city Rome after himself. Curiously, the story roughly corresponds with archaeological evidence indicating that sometime between 800 and 750 BCE, local people known as the Latins living along the southern bank of the Tiber in central Italy merged their small villages to form what would eventually become Rome. Because the legend so closely matches the available evidence, histories of Rome commonly begin with the year 753. Such a date, however, must be understood as a convention rather than an accepted historical fact.

Whatever the precise origins, Rome began its history from a humble and precarious position. The Tiber River marked the northern border of the Latins, who lived in towns scattered to the south. To the north lay the Etruscans, a highly urbanized and formidable power in the eighth century. Over the next century, Greek colonies expanded in Sicily and southern Italy, a development that placed early Rome between two powerful cultures. Yet its location on the Tiber River also placed Rome in an ideal position to dominate commercial activity in the area. Moreover, the position of the Italian peninsula in the middle of the Mediterranean basin would have encouraged whoever dominated it—as the Romans eventually did—to assert their power throughout the region.

Historians generally divide Roman history into three periods known as the Monarchy, the Republic, and the Empire. The power of the Monarchy, which lasted from c. 753 to 509 BCE, was not absolute. In these years, Rome was ruled by a succession of kings whose power was conferred by an assembly of male citizens. The king received advice from a body of elders known as the Senate, which was made up of leading citizens known as patricians. At first, the Monarchy was controlled by Latins, but around 600 BCE, it fell into the hands of the neighboring Etruscans. Latins regained control of Rome in 509, when a group of aristocrats led a rebellion against the Etruscan king. Afterward, Rome entered the long period of the Republic, which lasted from 509 to 44 BCE. For nearly 500 years, a senate and a system of overlapping assemblies made up of adult male citizens governed the Roman Republic. A pair of elected officials known as consuls, who each served a one-year term, controlled the army and exercised executive power.

The great territorial expansion of Rome occurred during the Republic. At first, Rome worked to protect itself from immediate neighbors such as the Etruscans. Later, it expanded to bring the scattered Latin communities to the south under its control. By 265 BCE, Rome ruled all of Italy. Three separate wars with Carthage, known as the Punic Wars, added Sicily, Sardinia, North Africa, and Spain. In the second century BCE, Rome expanded eastward into Greece and Macedonia. By the end of the first century BCE, its power extended into France and Palestine, bringing virtually all of the Mediterranean world and substantial portions of Europe under its control.

The terms by which these territories were brought into the Roman sphere varied. Some conquered cities, especially those in Italy, were granted the rights of Roman citizenship. Others were given limited rights that eventually evolved into full citizenship. All, however, were required to supply troops to the Roman army. To retain order in conquered areas, Rome paid soldiers with captured land, a policy that assured a continuous presence of loyal troops that extended across its growing empire. Whatever the terms of conquest, the Romans generally allowed the culture of conquered territories to remain intact. They also strengthened their position by readily absorbing aspects of other cultures into their own. Consequently, Rome was a truly international city, where ideas generated in other communities could thrive. Such openness to influence was one of the principal reasons that Rome remained powerful for so long.

No culture had a greater influence on the development of Rome than the Greeks. Many Roman gods and goddesses, for instance, had equivalents in Greek mythology. Roman literature, philosophy, and sculpture also had strong ties to Greek predecessors. Contact between the cultures came early, as Greek colonies were present on the Italian peninsula when the town of Rome was formed in the eighth century BCE. The pace and extent of the Greek influence increased during the third and fourth centuries, as Roman expansion brought them into contact with many of the Greek cultural achievements in the Mediterranean world. After the Romans conquered Corinth and Macedonia in the middle of the second century, they had even further access to Greek literary and artistic works. These contacts led Roman writers such as Catullus and Virgil to adopt Greek models of lyric and epic poetry. Likewise, Roman philosophers adopted the Greek philosophical system of stoicism, which was originally developed in Athens. Occasionally, Romans, such as the statesman Cato (234–149 BCE), denounced the extent of Greek influence as an insult to Roman national pride. Most Roman philosophers and writers, however, drew heavily upon the masterpieces of the Greek world, even as they transformed these materials into distinctly Roman works.

Romans regulated their society and culture with a collection of values known as *mos maiorum*, "the way of the ancestors." As the early Roman playwright and historian Ennius claimed, "'Tis by virtue of her morals and her men of old that Rome abides." These values, which the Romans cherished as their founding ideals, emphasized qualities such as valor, faithfulness, respect for authority, and loyalty. These are, of course, broad terms, but to the Romans, they provided a moral framework that defined acceptable public and private behavior. They also helped foster a habit of mind that encouraged seriousness and practicality, traits for which the Romans were particularly renowned.

While Greece produced intellectual innovators, Rome developed a remarkably practical society. We see this in the many engineering projects that linked conquered territories to the imperial capital. To facilitate the movement of troops, for instance, Roman engineers built a road network that connected the city with the rest of the Italian peninsula. Similarly, massive aqueducts, many of them still standing, supplied outlying districts with fresh water. Rome itself, which at the height of the Empire had a population that approached one million, developed a sophisticated food distribution network and water system. In all these areas, the Roman talent for practical affairs excelled.

By the first century BCE, however, the cultural, political, and military institutions that served the Republic for nearly 500 years broke down as Rome was engulfed in a series of disastrous civil wars. Enriched by treasures ransacked from conquering territories, ambitious generals and politicians raised armies that were more loyal to their individual patrons than to Rome itself. For many Romans, the *mos maiorum*, the ways of the ancestors, had been lost. The situation worsened from 49–44 BCE, when Julius Caesar and his chief rival, Gnaeus Pompey, waged a climactic battle for control of the Empire and its wealth. The violence continued after Caesar was assassinated in 44 BCE and only ended in 27 BCE when the Senate conferred power to Caesar's great nephew, Octavian. Given the title Augustus—meaning "exalted" or "divine"—Octavian at last brought an end to the civil wars. Although he claimed to be the restorer of the Republic, Augustus consolidated his rule by keeping the Roman army and treasury under his personal command. Occasionally, the Senate elected him consul (a title from the Republic), but his true power lay in the title *princeps*, Latin for "first citizen."

With peace restored, Augustus set out to transform Roman culture. During his long years of control (27 BCE–CE 14), the city's art and literature flourished as they never had before, in part because he saw the arts as a way to promote his own image and that of Rome. Under Augustus, an extensive program of public works construction replaced older buildings with new structures made from white marble. Likewise, he commissioned sculptors to carve images of himself that drew on Greek models to reflect the dignified and heroic qualities he hoped to introduce to Rome. In these same years, authors such as Horace, Ovid, and Virgil also produced some of the greatest works of Roman literature. For these reasons, the Augustan era is often identified as the Golden Age of Rome, much as fifth-century Athens was the Golden Age of Greece.

With Augustus, Rome entered a period known as the Empire. After his death, familiar institutions of the Republic such as elected consuls remained, but power was increasingly turned over to emperors selected by a senate eager to maintain the stability that Augustus had achieved. For much of the first and second centuries CE, the emperors managed to keep Rome and its empire in a condition of relative peace. Literature and art still flourished while the Empire remained the central power in Europe. In the middle of the third century CE, however, the difficulties of running such a far-flung territory led to renewed violence in Rome and its provinces. A new series of civil wars decimated the city, a situation made worse by invading bands of foreign armies. In 324, the emperor Constantine established his seat of imperial power in the ancient city of Byzantium, which he renamed Constantinople. The Empire formally split in 395 into an eastern and western half. The western half gradually fell apart after the Sack of Rome by the Visigoths in 410 and the final defeat of the emporer in 476; the eastern half survived until 1453, when the Turks overran Constantinople.

The Roman legacy continued long after the Empire collapsed, however. When Constantine converted to Christianity in the early fourth century, the city became the international center of the Roman Catholic Church, a title it still holds. Similarly, Latin remained the major language of science until the 17th century and continues to supply scientists with names for animal and plant specimens. We can hear traces of Latin in French, Spanish, Italian, and Romanian, all of which are direct descendants of the language of Rome. And as we see in the section on literature, Roman authors such as Virgil and Ovid produced literary works of lasting value. Indeed, until quite recently, they, along with the works of the major Greek authors, were among the central documents that anyone who aspired to a liberal arts education was expected to master.

VISUAL ARTS

Our consideration of Roman visual arts focuses on the last 150 years of the Republic and the first century of the Empire, from roughly 150 BCE to 100 CE. These are the years covered by our Selected Readings, and an understanding of the art during those years can help place those readings into a richer cultural and historical context. In making this distinction, however, we must recognize that Roman art unfolded over a much longer period of time.

For many years, the arts of ancient Rome were seen as unoriginal and derivative of Greek models. In some sense, this was inevitable, as Roman art developed within a Mediterranean world filled with Greek art. Certainly, the Romans admired Greek art and drew upon its legacy. As opportunities for work in their own cities declined, Greek artists also settled in Rome, where they found a ready supply of patrons willing to purchase copies of Greek works. To be sure, the Greeks set powerful standards in the arts, as they did in many fields. Roman artistic borrowing, however, does not necessarily imply imitation. As an imperial people with contacts throughout the Mediterranean, they drew from a rich cultural source. But in certain art forms, most notably architecture, they also made those sources their own.

Figure 1-K *Head of a Roman*

Portrait sculpture offers one example of a distinctly Roman style. At first, Romans imitated the idealization of the human form that characterized the finest Greek work. Eventually, however, they achieved a more realistic style that better conformed to a Roman interest in the depiction of realistic forms. The well-known *Head of a Roman* (c. 75 BCE), for example, shows us a man of many wrinkles; he is a stern, almost frightening figure whose face conveys a hard-earned authority (see Figure 1-K). No effort is made to deny the drooping features and other signs of advancing age. Because of this attention to detail, the style here is sometimes known as hyperrealism or verism. Sculptors of the first century BCE used this style to depict the mature virtues that Romans associated with effective leadership. On one hand, such works presented an intimate look at a particular individual. At the same time, they reflected an ideal that extended beyond the individual. The style of hyperrealism, then, paradoxically helped establish a universal standard for the appearance of the typical Roman male.

The Roman mixture of the type with the specific is seen in works depicting Augustus. Once he had assumed power, sculptors presented their ruler by turning to Greek models, as in the *Augustus of Primaporta* (c. 20 BCE) (see Figure 1-L). The powerful body and gestures suggest the heroic Greek ideal, an ideal that Augustus himself sought to cultivate. But a careful look at the face reveals a naturalistic portrayal that distinguishes this work from more conventional Greek models. Augustus the emperor

is idealized in the Greek-inspired form, but Augustus the Roman human being comes across in the naturalistic presentation of his likeness.

A similar combination of the ideal and the real can be found in the sculpted relief figures that line the *Ara Pacis Augustae* (Altar of the Augustan Peace). Built to mark Rome's final pacification of Spain and Gaul in 13 BCE, the altar's contrasting motifs are shown in two of its best-known reliefs, the Tellus Relief and the Procession (see Figure 1-M). The Tellus panel presents the Roman Mother Earth upon a rock with two children in her arms. Meanwhile, cattle graze at her feet. The idyllic scene suggests a new era of peace and plenty now that the wars in Spain and Gaul have drawn to a close. The

Figure 1-L *Augustus of Primaporta*

Figure 1-M Tellus Relief and Procession

Procession, on the other hand, shows the triumphal parade that greeted Augustus upon his return to Rome at the end of hostilities. For Roman audiences of the day, the panel presented an important event from recent history; it commemorated an actual battle by showing actual people on parade. At the same time, this true-to-life realism also served as propaganda for the Augustan regime.

From roughly 100 BCE to 100 AD, wealthy Romans decorated the interior of their homes by hiring artists to paint murals on the walls. The identity of the individual artists remains obscure; the paintings, however, are among the most compelling surviving works from ancient Rome. Much of what we know of this art form comes from examples that had been buried under layers of volcanic ash after the eruption of Mount Vesuvius in 79 CE. Other paintings have been found in homes excavated in and near Rome. A common motif during the first century BCE was the illusion of architectural space opening into the wall (see Figure 1-N). In the image shown here, found near Naples, the view recedes through columns toward buildings in the distance. At the top, a theatrical mask peers back toward us while we catch a glimpse of some sky in the rear. The effect, of course, is entirely illusory and lacks the consistent perspective and single vanishing point made familiar by Renaissance painters (see Unit 3). But with its theatrical flair and ornate decoration, the painting would have offered visitors to this first-century BCE home an enticing invitation into a make-believe world.

Architecture offers perhaps the definitive example of Roman artistic achievement. In the last century of the Republic and the first centuries of the Empire, Romans constructed large civic buildings to accommodate the city's growing population. As the city grew, it needed housing, government buildings, and places for recreation. Many of these buildings relied on a system of arched vaults; adopted from earlier Greek and Etruscan sources, this technology allowed builders to displace the weight of masonry around curved sides. Greek and Etruscan arches, however, were generally used in small or even underground structures. The Romans were the first to use them on a monumental scale. One of the most

Figure 1-N Roman interior wall painting

Figure 1-O Roman Aqueduct

amphitheater constructed between 72 and 80 CE (see Figure 1-P). Built for gladiator games and other popular entertainments, the Colosseum held more than 50,000 people. Aside from its sheer grandeur, the structure is remarkable for its engineering. Though we cannot see it in this image, the interior contained a network of corridors that allowed for easy and efficient movement throughout the building. The exterior contains three stories of cascading arches, with columns that become lighter and more decorative at each level. At the base, the architects used the Doric; next came the Ionic, and finally the Corinthian, The combination of massive size and dignified, orderly proportions made the Colosseum one of the best-known structures in the ancient world. A model for many future stadiums, it remains one of the most popular attractions in Rome.

LITERATURE

Roman literature does not have the equivalent of Homer; there is no single person or story that serves as the foundation for all later works. Nevertheless, a few writers helped launch the tradition of Roman literature. One figure often credited for taking the first steps toward a uniquely Roman literature is Livius Andronicus (c. 284–c.204 BCE). A well-educated Greek slave brought to Rome, Livius was the first person to translate Homer into Latin. He also translated Greek plays for production on the Roman stage. Little of his work survives, however, beyond a few titles and some scattered lines.

Another writer often identified as the father of Latin literature is Quintus Ennius (239–169 BCE). Born in the southern Italian district of Calabria, Ennius served in the Roman army during the Second

famous examples of the Roman arch is the aqueduct constructed at Nîmes, France, in the first century CE. Still standing after nearly 2,000 years, the aqueduct spans 885 feet and reaches a height of 160 feet. Its elegant and orderly cascade of arches is a monument to Roman ingenuity and graceful design (see Figure 1-O).

Another central element of Roman architecture was concrete, a flexible and strong building material that enabled them to construct on a grand scale. Concrete had several advantages that the Romans readily grasped. Because it was so strong, it could be used to construct the massive arches and spans that their architecture demanded. Concrete could also be cheaply manufactured, thus cutting construction costs. Perhaps most importantly, it was much easier to work with than heavy masonry slabs, which had to be cut and hauled into place. With the perfection of concrete, then, Roman civic architecture assumed its familiar monumental form.

The combination of Roman arches and concrete came together at the Colosseum, the enormous

Punic War against Carthage. He was later brought to Rome by Cato the elder and was granted citizenship in 184 BCE. He is believed to be the author of more than 20 tragic plays. As with the plays of Livius, Ennius drew heavily upon Greek themes. He also wrote at least two comedies and several poems. His most important work was the *Annals*, an 18-book history of Rome written in a Latinized adaptation of hexameter, the standard meter of the Greek epic verse. Virgil would later earn lasting fame for the epic of Rome's origin described in the *Aeneid*. But Ennius was the first writer to collect early Roman traditions and stories and place them into a grand verse narrative. In so doing, he helped establish Roman history as a major literary topic. Unfortunately, only a small portion of this monumental work survives.

The first major Roman authors for whom a significant body of work survives are the comic dramatists Plautus and Terrence. Both wrote in the style of the Greek "New Comedy," which was popular in Athens from roughly 400 to 200 BCE. At least 130 such plays have been attributed to Plautus (254–184 BCE), of which 21 survive. They are characterized by the reliance upon broad farce and improbable comic situations. Interludes of song and dance often contributed to their irreverent spirit. Among his best-known works is *The Menaechmus Twins*, which inspired Shakespeare's *Comedy of Errors*. The plays of Terrence employed a subtler, less farcical mode of humor. Born in North Africa and brought to Rome as a slave, Terrence (185–159 BCE) at first did not enjoy the popularity of Plautus. Later generations, however, have generally found his quieter humor more satisfying than his more boisterous near contemporary.

The arts of oratory and nonfiction prose writing also contributed significantly to the development of Roman literature. An early major voice in these areas was Cato (234–149 BCE), a leading general and politician who used his offices to vigorously promote Roman interests and values. Almost alone among his contemporaries, he also strongly criticized the Roman attraction to Greek culture. Romans knew him from the stern and powerful speeches he delivered in the Senate, where he used his influence to bolster the image of Roman power and moral rectitude. Cato also wrote several books, including the first Roman encyclopedia.

The major orator and prose writer of the first century BCE was Cicero (106–43 BCE). A central figure in the final decades of the Roman Republic, Cicero first earned a reputation as a master of legal oratory; in one notable case, he prosecuted the former governor of Sicily on charges of corruption. He later moved into the political arena, eventually rising to become consul. Aside from his active political life, Cicero wrote widely on the subjects of rhetoric

Figure 1-P Colosseum, Rome

and oratory, paying special attention to how these art forms were central to public life. In these works, he spelled out rules for delivery, for presenting positions, and rebutting arguments. Read widely in their day, Cicero's works remained the cornerstones of classical education well into the 19th century. His several volumes of letters also provide us with an invaluable window into the political life of late Republic Rome.

One of the great writers of Roman prose was the historian Titus Livy (59 BCE– CE 17), whose massive *History of Rome from Its Foundation* is one of the most read works of classical literature. Originally written in 142 books, only 35 survive. Livy was primarily interested in the history of Rome as a moral tale, as a series of lessons and examples that could benefit his contemporaries. Although he occasionally ran afoul of the emperor, such a plan fit comfortably into the moral program of Augustus, who hoped to solidify his power by reestablishing Roman faith in its Republican-era virtues. Despite its service to political ends, Livy's history remains compelling for its legends, its epic sweep, and the opportunity it affords us for entering into the mental world of Augustan Rome.

One of the major genres of Roman literature was satire. Indeed, the first-century rhetorician, Quintillion, claimed it was the one literary form in which the Romans were preeminent. When writing satire, Romans used a mixture of humor and criticism (the term "satire" is most likely derived from the Latin word for mixture) to criticize human follies and weaknesses. Despite the common term, the range of Roman satire was quite broad. The Augustan-era poet Horace, for example, wrote verses that gently skewered foibles such as gluttony and greed, while in the first century CE, Juvenal wrote critiques of Roman luxuriousness and sexual habits; in his hands, Rome seems a city of perversions with little to redeem it.

The high point of Roman poetry occurred during the first BCE and into the Augustan era, which ended with the emperor's death in CE 14. Our Selected Readings include works by three major figures from this period: Catullus, Virgil, and Ovid. Each contributed to what has been called the Golden Age of Roman literature. They each also demonstrate how the finest Roman writers transformed Greek models into literature of lasting value.

Catullus (84–54 BCE) was the great lyric poet of Rome. He did not write much during his short life, only 116 poems. Yet the lyrics written to his mistress, whom he identifies as Lesbia, are some of the finest poems of the ancient world. Catullus was also a master stylist who, in his longer epithalamia— wedding songs—created intricate poetic structures that are as original as they are complex. At times, Catullus descends into pornographic descriptions of sexual acts. But the Lesbia lyrics and epithalamia are moving and often beautiful accounts of love and loss. That they were written during the violent first century BCE, when Rome was in the midst of its prolonged civil wars, only makes them more compelling.

The definitive Augustan poet was Virgil (70–19 BCE). Our Selected Readings include sections from Virgil's *Eclogues*, a series of rural episodes that helped define the Western literary tradition of pastoral writing. The more distinctly Augustan Virgil appears in the the *Aeneid*, his epic poem on the legendary founding of Rome. Written at the urging of one of Augustus's closest advisers, the *Aeneid* tells the tale of a Trojan prince who, according to legend, escaped the destroyed city of Troy and eventually wound up in Italy, where his descendants founded Rome. With its clear echoes of Homer, the *Aeneid* provided Rome with an epic of heroic creation to rival the Greek versions told in the *Iliad* and the *Odyssey*.

Writing slowly over a period of years, Virgil showed newly completed work of the *Aeneid* to Augustus, who was apparently quite pleased with the production. Ovid, on the other hand, managed to anger the emperor. As he completed his major work, *Metamorphoses*, Ovid (43 BCE–18 CE) was ordered to leave Rome by Augustus. The reasons remain mysterious, although it is likely that some of Ovid's earlier semi-comical writings about the arts of seduction upset Augustus's effort to reestablish Rome as a beacon of morality. Whatever the case, both Ovid's banishment and Virgil's celebration indicate the powerful role played by writers in Augustan Rome.

CATULLUS (C. 84–54 BCE)

The Poems and Fragments of Catullus

T he short life of Gaius Valerius Catullus occurred during the final stages of the Roman Republic, when a nearly endless round of civil wars convulsed the city. Born near Verona to a well-connected family, Catullus moved to Rome as a young man and quickly established himself as a leading voice in a group of sophisticated and witty poets known today as the Neoterics. The 116 surviving poems reveal Catullus as a poet who wrote on a wide range of subjects, although as we see in the occasional lines about masturbation and oral sex, not all of them were particularly decent. His work also includes attacks on political figures and messages to friends. Catullus is best remembered, however, for his stunning love poetry and his elegant epithalamia. They remain some of the finest examples of these traditions in the Western literary canon.

Written in the manner of Greek lyrics, the love poetry of Catullus follows his relationship with an older woman he calls Lesbia, a name that suggestively links her with Sappho and the island of Lesbos. While we cannot be certain of her identity, many scholars have suggested that she was Clodia, the daughter of a leading Roman politician who was known for engaging in a series of scandalous affairs. The Lesbia poems reprinted here follow the order they appear in the standard editions of Catullus's work; consequently, they do not present a strict chronological history of the affair. But when read together, they suggest the full range of emotions unleashed during this passionate—but ultimately doomed—affair.

5

Living, Lesbia, we should e'en be loving.
Sour severity, tongue of eld maligning,
   All be to us a penny's estimation.

Suns set only to rise again to-morrow.
We, when sets in a little hour the brief light,
Sleep one infinite age, a night for ever.

Thousand kisses, anon to these an hundred,
Thousand kisses again, another hundred,
Thousand give me again, another hundred.

Then once heedfully counted all the thousands,
We'll uncount them as idly; so we shall not
Know, nor traitorous eye shall envy, knowing
All those myriad happy many kisses.

7

Ask me, Lesbia, what the sum delightful
Of thy kisses, enough to charm, to tire me?

Multitudinous as the grains on even
Lybian sands aromatic of Cyrene;

'Twixt Jove's oracle in the sandy desert
And where royally Battus old reposeth;

Yea a company vast as in the silence
Stars which stealthily gaze on happy lovers;

E'en so many the kisses I to kiss thee
Count, wild lover, enough to charm, to tire me;

These no curious eye can wholly number,
Tongue of jealousy ne'er bewitch nor harm them.

8

Ah poor Catullus, learn to play the fool no more.
Lost is the lost, thou know'st it, and the past is past.

Bright once the days and sunny shone the light on
   thee,
Still ever hasting where she led, the maid so fair,
By me belov'd as maiden is belov'd no more.

Was then enacting all the merry mirth wherein
Thyself delighted, and the maid she said not nay.
Ah truly bright and sunny shone the days on thee.

Now she resigns thee; child, do thou resign no less,
Nor follow her that flies thee, or to bide in woe
Consent, but harden all thy heart, resolve, endure.

Farewell, my love. Catullus is resolv'd, endures,
He will not ask for pity, will not importune.

But thou'lt be mourning thus to pine unask'd alway.
O past retrieval faithless! Ah what hours are thine!
When comes a likely wooer? who protests thou'rt fair?

Who brooks to love thee? who decrees to live thine own?
Whose kiss delights thee? whose the lips that own
   thy bite?
Yet, yet, Catullus, learn to bear, resolve, endure.

11

Furius and Aurelius, O my comrades,
Whether your Catullus attain to farthest
Ind, the long shore lash'd by reverberating
                Surges Eoan;

Hyrcan or luxurious horde Arabian,
Sacan or grim Parthian arrow-bearer,
Fields the rich Nile discolorates, a seven-fold
                River abounding;

Whether o'er high Alps he afoot ascending
Track the long records of a mighty Cæsar,
Rhene, the Gauls' deep river, a lonely Britain
                Dismal in ocean;

Catullus, from *The Poems and Fragments of Catullus*, trans.
Robinson Ellis. Copyright in the Public Domain.

This, or aught else haply the gods determine,
Absolute, you, with me in all to part not;
Bid my love greet, bear her a little errand,
                Scarcely of honour.

Say 'Live on yet, still given o'er to nameless
Lords, within one bosom, a many wooers,
Clasp'd, as unlov'd each, so in hourly change all
                Lewdly disabled.

'Think not henceforth, thou, to recal Catullus'
Love; thy own sin slew it, as on the meadow's
Verge declines, ungently beneath the plough-share
                Stricken, a flower.'

51

He to me like unto the Gods appeareth,
He, if I dare speak it, ascends above them,
Face to face who toward thee attently sitting
                Gazes or hears thee

Lovely in sweet laughter; alas within me
Every lost sense falleth away for anguish;
When as I look'd on thee, upon my lips no
                Whisper abideth,

Straight my tongue froze, Lesbia; soon a subtle
Fire thro' each limb streameth adown; with inward
Sound the full ears tinkle, on either eye night's
                Canopy darkens.

Ease alone, Catullus, alone afflicts thee;
Ease alone breeds error of heady riot;
Ease hath entomb'd princes of old renown and
                Cities of honour.

58

That bright Lesbia, Caelius, the self-same
Peerless Lesbia, she than whom Catullus
Self nor family more devoutly cherish'd,
By foul roads, or in every shameful alley,
Strains the vigorous issue of the people.

60

Hadst thou a Libyan lioness on heights all stone,
A Scylla, barking wolvish at the loins' last verge,
To bear thee, O black-hearted, O to shame forsworn,
That unto supplication in my last sad need
Thou mightst not harken, deaf to ruth, a beast, no
    man?

70

Saith my lady to me, no man shall wed me, but only
Thou; no other if e'en Jove should approach me to woo;
Yea; but a woman's words, when a lover fondly desireth,
Limn them on ebbing floods, write on a wintery gale.

72

Lesbia, thou didst swear thou knewest only Catullus,
Cared'st not, if him thine arms chained, a Jove to retain.
Then not alone I loved thee, as each light lover a mistress,
Lov'd as a father his own sons, or an heir to the name.

Now I know thee aright; so, if more hotly desiring,
Yet must count thee a soul cheaper, a frailty to scorn.
'Friend,' thou say'st, 'you cannot.' Alas! such injury leaveth
Blindly to doat poor love's folly, malignly to will.

83

Lesbia while her lord stands near, rails ever upon me.
This to the fond weak fool seemeth a mighty delight.
Dolt, you see not at all. Could she forget me, to rail not,
Nought were amiss; if now scold she, or if she revile,
'Tis not alone to remember; a shrewder stimulus arms her,
Anger; her heart doth burn verily, thus to revile.

85

Half I hate, half love. How so? one haply requireth.
Nay, I know not; alas feel it, in agony groan.

86

Lovely to many a man is Quintia; shapely, majestic,
Stately, to me; each point singly 'tis easy to grant.
'Lovely' the whole, I grant not; in all that bodily
    largeness,

Lives not a grain of salt, breathes not a charm anywhere.
Lesbia–she is lovely, an even temper of utmost
Beauty, that every charm stealeth of every fair.

107

If to delight man's wish, joy e'er unlook'd for,
    unhop'd for,
Falleth, a joy were such proper, a bliss to the soul.
Then 'tis a joy to the soul, like gold of Lydia precious,
Lesbia mine, that thou com'st to delight me again.

Com'st yet again long-hop'd, long-look'd for vainly,
    returnest

Freely to me. O day white with a luckier hue!
Lives there happier any than I, I only? a fairer
Destiny? Life so sweet know ye, or aught parallel?

109

Think you truly, belov'd, this bond of duty between us,
Lasteth, an ever-new jollity, ne'er to decease?
Grant it, Gods immortal, assure her promise in earnest;
Yea, be the lips sincere; yea, be the words from her heart.
So still rightly remain our lovers' charter, a life-long
Friendship in us, whose faith fades not away to the last.

DISCUSSION QUESTIONS

1. Examine the poems that celebrate the poet's love for Lesbia. Why does he find her so beguiling?
2. Several poems express outright hostility toward Lesbia. How much does the poet blame Lesbia for this hostility? How much does much he recognize as his own?
3. In several poems, the poet speaks directly to himself. What is the effect of this form of self-address? Does it color our view of him? How much of his love for Lesbia is connected to frequent addresses to himself?
4. In poem 51, Catullus reworks aspects of Sappho's poem #31. Compare these two poems. To what extent does Catullus alter the ideas of the earlier poem?

WRITING SUGGESTION

1. Try to arrange the Lesbia poems in what might be a chronological sequence of the affair. Write a paper discussing how the new ordering might suggest a different reading of the poems. Does it alter your sense of the poet and his love?

VIRGIL (70–19 BCE)

Selected Eclogues

P ublius Virgilius Maro, commonly known as Virgil, was the definitive poet of the Augustan age. He was born into a farming family in northern Italy and was educated in Milan and Rome. Although well educated, he opted to return home, where he wrote his first major work, the *Eclogues* (42–37 BCE), a collection of ten dialogues set in pastoral scenes, three of which we include in our selections. His next major work, the *Georgics*, describes traditional agricultural pursuits such as cattle breeding and beekeeping. Virgil's identification with Augustan Rome is based on his final masterwork, the *Aeneid*, which he was just completing when he died following an illness he contracted while traveling with the emperor. Written in 12 books, the *Aeneid* is an epic that tells the story of the legendary prince Aeneas, who, according to a popular Roman legend, fled Troy at the end of the Trojan War and eventually came to Italy, where his descendants founded Rome.

The selections below come from the *Eclogues*, Virgil's first major work. Sometimes known as the *Bucolics*, the ten poems in this collection are examples of pastoral, a literary genre depicting leisured life in the country. (The public domain translation used here presents the poems as prose.) Then, as now, such works often appealed to urban readers, who enjoyed reading about the idyllic life beyond the city walls. They are filled with shepherds who amuse themselves with singing contests and stories about their loves. Occasionally, however, the bucolic scenery serves as the setting for bittersweet emotions. In the first poem (which we include here), Virgil presents a shepherd who has been forced from his pastures to make way for a soldier who had been promised land in return for his service in war (such a fate befell Virgil's family).

The ninth *Eclogue* treats a similar theme, only this time the displaced farmer wanders toward the town, wondering why he can no longer recall the songs he sang as a boy. Desperate for a song that could restore him to the spiritual wholeness he enjoyed on his farm, he finally implores his friend to stop singing so they can arrive in town in silence.

The fourth poem in the collection is commonly known as the Messianic Eclogue, as it predicts the arrival of a savior who will transform the world. We do not know the identity of the infant child whose birth will usher in a golden age when all hostilities will cease. Some have suggested that it may have been written for the son of Pollio, who was Roman consul in 40 BCE and who intervened to help Virgil's family recover its land. The image of the savior child led many Christian readers to credit Virgil with prophesizing the birth of Christ some 40 years before he was born. Because of its enigmatic association to the coming of Christ, the poem remains one of the best known and most frequently read ancient works.

ECLOGUE I.–TITYRUS

Meliboeus–Tityrus

M.–Tityrus, thou where thou liest under the covert of spreading beech, broodest on thy slim pipe over the Muse of the woodland: we leave our native borders and pleasant fields; we fly our native land, while thou, Tityrus, at ease in the shade teachest the woods to echo fair Amaryllis.

T.–O Meliboeus, a god brought us this peace: for a god ever will he be to me: his altar a tender lamb from our sheepfolds shall often stain. He granted that my oxen might stray as thou descriest, and myself play what I would on the rustic reed.

M.–I envy not, I, rather I wonder, so is all the countryside being routed out. See, I myself wearily drive forth my she-goats; and this one, Tityrus, I just drag along: for here among the hazel thickets she has borne twins, the hope of the flock, and left them, alas! on the naked flints. Often, had a mind not infatuate been mine, I remember how lightning-scathed oaks presaged this woe of ours. But yet vouchsafe to us, Tityrus, who is this god of thine.

T.–The city they call Rome, O Meliboeus, I fancied in my foolishness like ours here, whither we shepherds are often wont to drive the tender weanlings of the sheep. Thus I knew the likeness of puppies to dogs, of kids to their mothers: thus would I compare great things with small. But she bears her head as high among all other cities as any cypress will do among trailing hedgerow shoots.

M.–And why might nothing less serve thee than seeing Rome?

T.–For freedom: she at last in spite of all turned her face upon a slothful servant, when now the beard was sprinkled with white that fell under the razor: in spite of all she turned her face and came after long delay, since Amaryllis holds us and Galatea has let us go. For I will confess it, while Galatea kept me, there was no hope of freedom, no thrift of savings: though many a victim went out from my pens, and

rich cheese from my presses for the thankless town, never once did my hand come money-laden home.

M.–I wondered, Amaryllis, why thou calledst sadly on the gods, for whom thine apples were left hanging on the tree: Tityrus was away. The very pines, O Tityrus, the very springs and orchards here cried for thee.

T.–What was I to do? Neither might I free myself from service, nor elsewhere know gods so potent to help. Here I saw the prince, O Meliboeus, to whom yearly for twice six days the steam rises from our altars: here he gave present reply to my prayer: Pasture your oxen as of old, my children, rear your bulls.

M.–Happy in thine old age! so thy fields will remain thine, and ample enough for thee, although all the pastures be covered with bare stone or muddy rush of the fen. No strange fodder will try the breeding ewes, or touch of evil hurt them from any neighbour's flock. Happy in thine old age! here, amid familiar streams and holy springs thou wilt woo the coolness of the shade: here the hedge that ever keeps thy neighbour's boundary, where bees of Hybla feed their fill on the willow-blossom, shall often with light murmuring lull thee into sleep: here under the lofty rock shall rise the leaf-gatherer's song: nor all the while shall the hoarse wood-pigeons, thy delight, or the turtle on the elm's aëry top cease to moan.

T.–Therefore sooner shall light stags feed in the sky and the sea-channels leave the fishes naked on the beach; sooner, over-wandering both their boundaries, shall the exiled Parthian drink of Arar, or Germany of Tigris, than his countenance shall fade from our heart.

M.–But we! some shall pass hence to thirsty Africa, some reach Scythia and Oaxes' clay-laden torrent, and the Britons wholly sundered from all the world. Lo, shall I ever, long in time to come, again in my native borders marvel as I see my realm stink to a poor cabin with turf-heaped roof behind a handful of corn? Shall a lawless soldier possess these trim fallows? a barbarian these cornfields? lo,

Virgil, "Eclogues 1, 4, 9," *Virgil*, vol. I, trans. H. Rushton Fairclough, pp. 3, 5, 7, 9, 29, 31, 33, 65, 67, 69. Copyright in the Public Domain.

to what wretched pass has civil discord brought us! lo, for whose profit we have sown our fields! Engraft thy pear trees now, Meliboeus, set thy vines arow! Go, my she-goats, go, once happy flock: never hereafter shall I, stretched in a green cave, see you afar hanging from the tufted rock: no songs shall I sing; not in my herding shall you, my she-goats, crop the flowering cytisus and bitter willows.

T.–Yet here for to-night thou mightst rest with me on green boughs: we have mellow apples and soft chestnuts, and curdled milk in abundance; and already afar the farm roofs smoke, and the shadows fall larger from the high hills.

ECLOGUE IX.–MOERIS

Lycidas–Moeris

L.–Whither footest thou, Moeris? leads thy way townward?

M.–O Lycidas, we live to have come to this, what we never feared, that an intruder in our little fields should say, These are mine; hence with you, old freeholders! Now crushed and sorrowing, since all goes with Fortune's wheel, these kids (small joy may he have thereof!) we are sending to him.

L.–Surely I had heard that, where the hills begin to retire and lower their ridge in a soft slope, even to the waterside and the old beeches that now moulder atop, your Menalcas had saved all the land by his songs.

M.–You had; and so rumour ran. But songs of ours, Lycidas, have no more power among warring arms than Chaonian doves, as they say, when the eagle comes. Had not a raven from the hollow ilex on my left forewarned me to cut short my young suit as best I could, neither thy Moeris nor Menalcas himself were alive and here.

L.–Alas! can such wickedness come over any one? alas for thee and our comfort in thee, Menalcas, so nearly lost to us! Who would sing the nymphs? who strew the ground with blossoming plants, or train green shade over the springs? or those songs I caught of late from thee on thy way to our darling Amaryllis: Tityrus, while I return, (short is the way,) feed the she-goats; and drive them full-fed to drink,

Tityrus; and amid the work, take heed of crossing the he-goat; he strikes with his horn.

M.–Nay these rather, which yet unfinished he sang to Varus: Varus, thy name, if but our Mantua survive, Mantua, ah too near a neighbour to unhappy Cremona, singing swans shall bear aloft to the stars.

L.–So may thy swarms shun yews of Corsica, so may cytisus pasture swell the udders of thy kine, begin with what thou hast. Me also the maidens of Pieria have made a poet. I also have songs: even me the shepherds call a singer; but I believe them not. For, I think, I utter as yet nothing worthy of Varius or of Cinna, a cackling goose among these swans of song.

M.–So I do, Lycidas, and am thinking over silently with myself if I may avail to remember; and it is no mean song:

Come hither, O Galatea: what sport is among the waves? Here spring glows, here round the streams the ground breaks into many a flower; here the silver-white poplar leans over the cavern and trailing vines weave a covert of shade. Come hither; leave the mad billows to beat on the shore.

L.–How of what I once heard thee singing alone under the clear night? I remember the notes, had I the words sure:

Daphnis, why gaze upward on the ancient risings of the signs? lo the star of Caesar, Dione's child, has advanced, the star whereunder fields should rejoice in corn and the grape gather colour on sunny hills. Engraft thy pear-trees, Daphnis; thy children's children shall pluck their fruit.

M.–Time wastes all things, the mind too: often I remember how in boyhood I outwore long sunlit days in singing: now I have forgotten so many a song: Moeris is losing his voice too; wolves have caught first sight of Moeris; but yet Menalcas will repeat them to thee oft enough.

L.–Thy talking prolongs our desire: and now, see, all the mere is smooth and still, and all the windy murmur of the breeze, look, is sunk away. just from this point is half our road, for Bianor's tomb begins to show: here, where rustics strip the thick-leaved sprays, here, Moeris, let us sing; here set down thy kids; for all that, we shall reach the town. Or if we fear lest night ere then gather to rain, we may go singing all the way; so the road wearies the less: that we may go singing, I will lighten thee of this bundle.

M.–Cease thou further, O boy, and let us do our present business: when he is come himself, we will sing his songs better then.

ECLOGUE IV.–POLLIO

Muses of Sicily, sing we a somewhat ampler strain: not all men's delight is in coppices and lowly tamarisks: if we sing of the woods, let them be woods worthy of a Consul.

Now is come the last age of the Cumaean prophecy: the great cycle of periods is born anew. Now returns the Maid, returns the reign of Saturn: now from high heaven a new generation comes down. Yet do thou at that boy's birth, in whom the iron race shall begin to cease, and the golden to arise over all the world, holy Lucina, be gracious; now thine own Apollo reigns. And in thy consulate, in thine, O Pollio, shall this glorious age enter, and the great months begin their march: under thy rule what traces of our guilt yet remain, vanishing shall free earth for ever from alarm. He shall grow in the life of gods, and shall see gods and heroes mingled, and himself be seen by them, and shall rule the world that his fathers' virtues have set at peace. But on thee, O boy, untilled shall Earth first pour childish gifts, wandering ivy-tendrils and foxglove, and colocasia mingled with the laughing acanthus: untended shall the she-goats bring home their milk-swoln udders, nor shall huge lions alarm the herds: unbidden thy cradle shall break into wooing blossom. The snake too shall die, and die the treacherous poison-plant: Assyrian spice shall grow all up and down. But when once thou shalt be able now to read the glories of heroes and thy father's deeds, and to know Virtue as she is, slowly the plain shall grow golden with the soft corn-spike, and the reddening grape trail from the wild briar, and hard oaks shall drip dew of honey. Nevertheless there shall linger I some few traces of ancient wrong, to bid ships tempt the sea and towns be girt with walls and the earth cloven in furrows. Then shall a second Tiphys be, and a second Argo to sail with chosen heroes: new wars too shall arise, and again a mighty Achilles be sent to Troy. Thereafter, when now strengthening age hath wrought thee into man, the very voyager shall cease out of the sea, nor the sailing pine exchange her merchandise: all lands shall bear all things, the ground shall not suffer the mattock, nor the vine the pruning-hook; now likewise the strong ploughman shall loose his bulls from the yoke. Neither shall wool learn to counterfeit changing hues, but the ram in the meadow himself shall dye his fleece now with soft glowing sea-purple, now with yellow saffron; native scarlet shall clothe the lambs at their pasturage. Run even thus, O ages, said the harmonious Fates to their spindles, by the steadfast ordinance of doom. Draw nigh to thy high honours (even now will the time be come) O dear offspring of gods, mighty germ of Jove! Behold the world swaying her orbed mass, lands and spaces of sea and depth of sky; behold how all things rejoice in the age to come. Ah may the latter end of a long life then yet be mine, and such breath as shall suffice to tell thy deeds! Not Orpheus of Thrace nor Linus shall surpass me in song, though he have his mother and be his father to aid, Orpheus Calliope, Linus beautiful Apollo. If even Pan before his Arcady contend with me, even Pan before his Arcady shall declare himself conquered. Begin, O little boy, to know and smile upon thy mother, thy mother on whom ten months have brought weary longings. Begin, O little boy: of them who have not smiled on a parent, never was one honoured at a god's board or on a goddess' couch.

DISCUSSION QUESTIONS

Eclogue 1

1.   Why is Meliboeus so unhappy? What does he feel he we will be losing? Why are such things important to him?

2.   How does Rome figure in this Eclogue? What are the speakers' relationships to the city? How does its presence and power affect their lives?

3.   What type of landscape does the poem celebrate? Why does it have such a powerful hold on the two speakers?

Eclogue 9

1.   In many ways, Eclogues 9 and 1 address similar concerns. How do these two poems relate to each other? How do the different settings create different moods? Do the poems reach similar conclusions?

2.   What is the role of the son in Eclogue 9? How does singing comfort the speakers? Why does it fail to comfort them completely?

Eclogue 4

1.   Describe the new golden age that the speaker predicts will follow the birth of the child?

2.   How does the paradise described in this poem resemble others you have studied? What are its chief characteristics?

OVID (43 BCE–17 CE)

Publius Ovidius Naso was born almost exactly one year after Julius Caesar was assassinated. He came of age after Augustus finally brought the long Roman civil wars to a close. While still young, he was sent to Rome by his prosperous parents to study rhetoric. His first love, however, was poetry. Once he began writing, he quickly earned a reputation as a poet of urbane and mildly scandalous works such as *The Art of Love*, which, among other things, offers advice to young Romans on the art of seduction. Ovid's life was dramatically transformed in 8 CE when Augustus ordered the poet to leave Rome, a city he loved, and sent him to Tomis, a tiny town on the frontier of the Roman Empire in what is now Romania. The reasons for this banishment remain mysterious. One possible explanation may be that Ovid's poetry of seduction may have upset Augustus, who at the time was trying to reestablish Rome's connection to values from its past. There is also some speculation that the poet was involved in a sexual indiscretion involving the emperor's daughter. Whatever the case, Ovid spent his remaining years trying unsuccessfully to plead his case to return. He died in Tomis in 17 CE.

Metamorphoses, Ovid's masterpiece, was nearly completed at the time of the poet's banishment. It is written in 15 books of hexameter, the standard meter of epic verse. The work, however, is far different than the epics of Homer or Virgil. Rather, Ovid spins a charming tale depicting some of the best-known scenes from Greek and Roman mythology. The connecting theme is transformation, the ongoing processes by which mythological figures and animals change form. The poem offers an anthology of classical mythology linked by an ongoing narrative that connects one story to the next. To enter the poem is to enter a world of transformation, a place where nothing is constant except change itself. With its witty and delightful stories, *Metamorphoses* has offered many later writers, most notably Shakespeare, a rich source of material. Our selection comes from Book I, where the poet describes the creation of the world, the stages of human history, and the well-known story of Apollo and Daphne. In these stories, change is the way of the world.

METAMORPHOSES

Book One

My intention is to tell of bodies changed
To different forms; the gods, who made the changes,
Will help me–or I hope so–with a poem
That runs from the world's beginning to our own days.

The Creation

Before the ocean was, or earth, or heaven,
Nature was all alike, a shapelessness,
Chaos, so–called, all rude and lumpy matter,
Nothing but bulk, inert, in whose confusion
Discordant atoms warred: there was no sun
To light the universe; there was no moon
With slender silver crescents filling slowly;
No earth hung balanced in surrounding air;
No sea reached far along the fringe of shore.
Land, to be sure, there was, and air, and ocean,
But land on which no man could stand, and water
No man could swim in, air no man could breathe,
Air without light, substance forever changing,
Forever at war: within a single body
Heat fought with cold, wet fought with dry, the hard
Fought with the soft, things having weight contended
With weightless things.

　　　　Till God, or kindlier Nature,
Settled all argument, and separated
Heaven from earth, water from land, our air
From the high stratosphere, a liberation
So things evolved, and out of blind confusion
Found each its place, bound in eternal order.
The force of fire, that weightless element,
Leaped up and claimed the highest place in heaven;
Below it, air; and under them the earth
Sank with its grosser portions; and the water,
Lowest of all, held up, held in, the land.

Whatever god it was, who out of chaos
Brought order to the universe, and gave it
Division, subdivision, he molded earth,

In the beginning, into a great globe,
Even on every side, and bade the waters
To spread and rise, under the rushing winds,
Surrounding earth; he added ponds and marshes,
He banked the river–channels, and the waters
Feed earth or run to sea, and that great flood
Washes on shores, not banks. He made the plains
Spread wide, the valleys settle, and the forest
Be dressed in leaves; he made the rocky mountains
Rise to full height, and as the vault of Heaven
Has two zones, left and right, and one between them
Hotter than these, the Lord of all Creation
Marked on the earth the same design and pattern.
The torrid zone too hot for men to live in,
The north and south too cold, but in the middle
Varying climate, temperature and season.
Above all things, the air, lighter than earth,
Lighter than water, heavier than fire,
Towers and spreads; there mist and cloud assemble,
And fearful thunder and lightning and cold winds,
But these, by the Creator's order, held
No general dominion; even as it is,
These brothers brawl and quarrel; though each one
Has his own quarter, still they come near tearing
The universe apart. Eurus is monarch
Of the lands of dawn, the realms of Araby,
The Persian ridges under the rays of morning.
Zephyrus holds the west that glows at sunset,
Boreas, who makes men shiver, holds the north,
Warm Auster governs in the misty southland,
And over them all presides the weightless ether,
Pure without taint of earth.

　　　　These boundaries given,
Behold, the stars, long hidden under darkness,
Broke through and shone, all over the spangled heaven,
Their home forever, and the gods lived there,
And shining fish were given the waves for dwelling
And beasts the earth, and birds the moving air.

But something else was needed, a finer being,
More capable of mind, a sage, a ruler,
So Man was born, it may be, in God's image,

Or Earth, perhaps, so newly separated
From the old fire of Heaven, still retained
Some seed of the celestial force which fashioned
Gods out of living clay and running water.
All other animals look downward; Man,
Alone, erect, can raise his have toward Heaven.

The Four Ages

The Golden Age was first, a time that cherished
Of its own will, justice and right; no law.
No punishment, was called for; fearfulness
Was quite unknown, and the bronze tablets held
No legal threatening; no suppliant throng
Studied a judge's face; there were no judges,
There did not need to be. Trees had no yet
Been cut and hollowed, to visit other shores.
Men were content at home, and had no towns
With moats and walls around them; and no trumpets
Blared out alarums; things like swords and helmets
Had not been heard of. No one needed soldiers.
People were unaggressive, and unanxious;
The years went by in peace. And Earth untroubled,
Unharried by hoe or plowshare, brought forth all
That men had need for, and those men were happy,
Gathering berries from the mountain sides,
Cherries, or blackcaps, and the edible acorns.
Spring was forever, with a west wind blowing
Softly across the flowers no man had planted,
And Earth, unplowed, brought forth rich grain; the field,
Unfallowed, whitened with wheat, and there were rivers
Of milk, and rivers of honey, and golden nectar
Dripped from the dark-green oak-trees.
        After Saturn
Was driven to the shadowy land of death,
And the world was under Jove, the Age of Silver
Came in, lower than gold, better than bronze.
Jove made the springtime shorter, added winter,
Summer, and autumn, the seasons as we know them.
That was the first time when the burnt air glowed
White-hot, or icicles hung down in winter.
And men built houses for themselves; the caverns,
The woodland thickets, and the bark-bound shelters
No longer served; and the seeds of grain were planted
In the long furrows, and the oxen struggled
Groaning and laboring under the heavy yoke.

Then came the age of Bronze, and dispositions

Took on aggressive instincts, quick to arm,
Yet not entirely evil. And last of all
        The Iron Age succeeded, whose base vein
Let loose all evil: modesty and truth
And righteousness fled earth, and in their place
Came trickery and slyness, plotting, swindling,
Violence and the damned desire of having.
Men spread their sails to winds unknown to sailors,
The pines came down their mountain-sides, to revel
And leap in the deep waters, and the ground,
Free, once, to everyone, like air and sunshine,
Was stepped off by surveyors. The rich earth,
Good giver of all the bounty of the harvest,
Was asked for more; they dug into her vitals,
Pried out the wealth a kinder lord had hidden
In Stygian shadow, all that precious metal,
The root of evil. They found the guilt of iron,
And gold more guilty still. And War came forth
That uses both go fight with; bloody hands
Brandished the clashing weapons. Men lived on plunder.
Guest was no safe from host, nor brother from brother,
A man would kill his wife, a wife her husband,
Stepmothers, dire and dreadful, stirred their brews
With poisonous aconite, and sons would hustle
Fathers to death, and Piety lay vanquished,
And the maiden Justice, last of all immortals,
Fled from the bloody earth.
        Heaven was no safer.
Giants attacked the very throne of Heaven,
Piled Pelion on Ossa, mountain on mountain
Up to the very stars. Jove struck them down
With thunderbolts, and the bulk of those huge bodies
Lay on the earth, and bled, and Mother Earth,
Made pregnant by that blood, brought forth new bodies,
And gave them, to recall her older offspring,
The forms of men. And this new stock was also
Contemptuous of gods, and murder–hungry
And violent. You would know they were sons of blood.

Jove's Intervention

And Jove was witness from his lofty throne
Of all this evil, and groaned as he remembered
The wicked revels of Lycaon's table,
The latest guilt, a story still unknown
To the high gods. In awful indignation
He summoned them to council. No one dawdled.
Easily seen when the night skies are clear,

The Milky Way shines white. Along this road
The gods move toward the palace of the Thunderer,
His royal halls, and, right and left, the dwellings
Of other gods are open, and guests come thronging.
The lesser gods live in a meaner section,
An area not reserved, as this one is,
For the illustrious Great Wheels of Heaven.
(Their Palatine Hill, if I might call it so.)

They took their places in the marble chamber
Where high above them all their king was seated,
Holding his ivory sceptre, shaking out
Thrice, and again, his awful locks, the sign
That made the earth and stars and ocean tremble,
And then he spoke, in outrage: "I was troubled
Less for the sovereignty of all the world
In that old time when the snake-footed giants
Laid each his hundred hands on captive Heaven.
Monstrous they were, and hostile, but their warfare
Sprung from one source, on body. Now wherever
The sea-gods roar around the earth, a race
Must be destroyed, the race of men, I swear it!
I swear by all the Stygian rivers gliding
Under the world, I have tried all other measures.
The knife must cut the cancer out, infection
Averted while it can be, from our numbers.
Those demigods, those rustic presences,
Nymphs, fauns, and satyrs, wood and mountain dwellers,
We have not yet honored with a place in Heaven,
But they should have some decent place to dwell in,
In peace and safety. Safety? Do you reckon
The will be safe, when I, who wield the thunder,
Who rule you all as subjects, am subjected
To the plottings of barbarous Lycaon?"

They burned, they trembled. Who was this Lycaon,
Guilty of such rank infamy? They shuddered
In horror, with a fear of sudden ruin,
As the whole world did later, when assassins
Struck Julius Caesar down, and Prince Augustus
Found satisfaction in the great devotion
That cried for vengeance, even as Jove took pleasure,
Then, in the god's response. By word and gesture
He calmed them down, awed them again to silence,
And spoke once more:

The Story of Lycaon

"He has indeed been punished.
On that score have no worry. But what the did,
And how he paid, are things that I must tell you.
I had heard the age was desperately wicked,
I had heard, or so I hoped, a lie, a falsehood,
So I came down, as man, from high Olympus,
Wandered about the world. It would take too long
To tell you how widespread was all that evil.
All I had heard was grievous understatement!
I had crossed Maenala, a country bristling
With dens of animals, and crossed Cyllene,
And cold Lycaeus' pine woods. Then I came
At evening, with the shadows growing longer,
To an Arcadian palace, where the tyrant
Was anything but royal in his welcome.
I gave a sign that a god had come, and people
Began to worship, and Lycaon mocked them,
Laughed at their prayers, and said: 'Watch me find out
Whether this fellow is a god or mortal,
I can tell quickly, and no doubt about it.'
He planned, that night, to kill me while I slumbered;
That was his way to test the truth. Moreover,
And not content with that, he took a hostage,
One sent by the Molossians, cut his throat,
Boiled pieces of his flesh, still warm with life,
Broiled others, and set them before me on the table.
That was enough. I struck, and the bolt of lightning
Blasted the household of that guilty monarch.
He fled in terror, reached the silent fields,
And howled, and tried to speak. No use at all!
Foam dripped from his mouth; bloodthirsty still, he turned
Against the sheep, delighting still in slaughter,
And his arms were legs, and his robes were shaggy hair,
Yet he is still Lycaon, the same grayness,
The same fierce face, the same red eyes, a picture
Of bestial savagery. One house has fallen,
But more then one deserves to. Fury reigns
Over all the fields of Earth. They are sworn to evil,
Believe it. Let them pay for it, and quickly!
So stands my purpose."

Part of them approved
With words and added fuel to his anger,
And part approved with silence, and yet all
Were grieving at the loss of humankind,
Were asking what the world would be, bereft
Of mortals: who would bring their altars incense?

Would earth be given the beasts, to spoil and ravage?
Jove told them not to worry; he would give them
Another race, unlike the first, created
Out of a miracle; he would see to it.

He was about to hurl his thunderbolts
At the whole world, but halted, fearing Heaven
Would burn from fire so vast, and pole to pole
Break out in flame and smoke, and he remembered
The fates had said that some day land and ocean,
The vault of Heaven, he whole world's mighty fortress,
Besieged by fire, would perish. He put aside
The bolts made in Cyclopean workshops; better,
He thought, to drown the world by flooding water.

The Flood

So, in the cave of Aeolus, he prisoned
The North-wind, and the West-wind, and such others
As ever banish cloud, and he turned loose
The South-wind, and the South-wind came out streaming
With dripping wings, and pitch-black darkness veiling
His terrible countenance. His beard is heavy
With rain-cloud, and his hoary locks a torrent,
Mists are his chaplet, and his wings and garments
Run with the rain. His broad hands squeeze together
Low-hanging clouds, and crash and rumble follow
Before the cloudburst, and the rainbow, Iris,
Draws water from the teeming earth, and feeds it
Into the clouds again. The crops are ruined,
The farmers' prayers all wasted, all the labor
Of a long year, comes to nothing.
                    And Jove's anger,
Unbounded by his own domain, was given
Help by his dark-blue brother. Neptune called
His rivers all, and told them, very briefly,
To loose their violence, open their houses,
Pour over embankments, let the river horses
Run wild as ever they would. And they obeyed him.
His trident struck the shuddering earth; it opened
Way for the rush of waters. The leaping rivers
Flood over the great plains. Not only orchards
Are swept away, not only grain and cattle,
Not only men and houses, but altars, temples,
And shrines with holy fires. If any building
Stands firm, the waves keep rising over its roof-top,
Its towers are under water, and land and ocean
Are all alike, and everything is ocean,

An ocean with no shore-line.
                    Some poor fellow
Seizes a hill-top; another, in a dinghy,
Rows where he used to plough, and one goes sailing
Over his fields of grain or over the chimney
Of what was once his cottage. Someone catches
Fish in the top of an elm-tree, or an anchor
Drags in green meadow-land, or the curved keel brushes
Grape-arbors under water. Ugly sea-cows
Float where the slender she-goats used to nibble
The tender grass, and the Nereids come swimming
With curious wonder, looking, under water,
At houses, cities, parks, and groves. The dolphins
Invade the woods and brush against the oak-tree;
The wolf swims with the lamb; lion and tiger
Are borne along together; the wild boar
Finds all his strength is useless, and the deer
Cannot outspeed that torrent; wandering birds
Look long, in vain, for landing-place, and tumble,
Exhausted, into the sea. The deep's great license
Has buried all the hills, and new waves thunder
Against the mountain-tops. The flood has taken
All things, or nearly all, and those whom water,
By chance, has spared, starvation slowly conquers.

Deucalion and Pyrrha

Phocis, a fertile land, while there was land,
Marked off Oetean from Boeotian fields.
It was ocean now, a plain of sudden waters.
There Mount Parnassus lifts its twin peaks skyward,
High, steep, cloud-piercing. And Deucalion came there
Rowing his wife. There was no other land,
The sea had drowned it all. And here they worshipped
First the Corycian nymphs and native powers,
Then Themis, oracle and fate-revealer.
There was no better man than this Deucalion,
No one more fond of right; there was no woman
More scrupulously reverent than Pyrrha.
So, when Jove saw the world was one great ocean,
Only one woman left of all those thousands,
And only one man let of all those thousands,
Both innocent and worshipful, he parted
The clouds, turned loose the North-wind, swept them off,
Showed earth to heaven again, and sky to land,
And the sea's anger dwindled, and King Neptune
Put down his trident, calmed the waves, and Triton,
Summoned from far down under, with his shoulders

Barnacle-strewn, loomed up above the waters,
The blue-green sea-god, whose resounding horn
Is heard from shore to shore. Wet-bearded, Triton
Set lip to that great shell, as Neptune ordered,
Sounding retreat, and all the lands waters
Heard and obeyed. The sea has shores; the rivers,
Still running high, have channels; the floods dwindle,
Hill-tops are seen again; the trees, long buried,
Rise with their leaves still muddy. The world returns.

Deucalion saw that world, all desolation,
All emptiness, all silence, and his tears
Rose as he spoke to Pyrrha: "O my wife,
The only woman, now, on all this earth,
My consort and my cousin and my partner
In these immediate dangers, look! Of all the lands
To East or West, we two, we two alone,
Are all the population. Ocean holds
Everything else; our foothold, our assurance,
Are small as they can be, the clouds still frightful.

Poor woman—well, we are not all alone—
Suppose you had been, how would you bear your fear?
Who would console your grief? My wife, believe me,
Had the sea taken you, I would have followed.
If only I had the power, I would restore
The nations as my father did, bring clay
To life with breathing. As it is, we two
Are all the human race, so Heaven has willed it,
Samples of men, mere specimens."
They wept,
And prayed together, and having wept and prayed,
Resolved to make petition to the goddess
To seek her aid through oracles. Together
They went to the river-water, the stream Cephisus,
Still far from clear, by flowing down its channel,
And they took river-water, sprinkled foreheads,
Sprinkled their garments, and they turned their steps
To the temple of the goddess, where the altars
Stood with the fires gone dead, and ugly moss
Stained pediment and column. At the stairs
They both fell prone, kissed the chill stone in prayer:
"If the gods' anger ever listens
To righteous prayers, O Themis, we implore you,
Tell us by what device our wreck and ruin
May be repaired. Bring aid, most gentle goddess,
To sunken circumstance."

And Themis heard them,
And gave this oracle: "Go from the temple,
Cover your heads, loosen your robes, and throw
Your mother's bones behind you!" Dumb, they stood
In blank amazement, a long silence, broken
By Pyrrha, finally: she would not do it!
With trembling lips she prays whatever pardon
Her disobedience might merit, but this outrage
She dare not risk, insult her mother's spirit
By throwing her bones around. In utter darkness
They voice the cryptic saying over and over,
What can it mean? They wonder. At last Deucalion
Finds the way out: "I might be wrong, but surely
The holy oracles would never counsel
A guilty act. The earth is our great mother,
And I suppose those bones the goddess mentions
Are the stones of earth; the order means to throw them,
The stones, behind us."
She was still uncertain,
And he by no means sure, and both distrustful
Of that command from Heaven; but what damage,
What harm, would there be in trying? They descended,
Covered their heads, loosened their garments, threw
The stones behind them as the goddess ordered.
The stones—who would believe it, had we not
The unimpeachable witness of Tradition? —
Began to lose their hardness, to soften, slowly,
To take on form, to grow in size, a little,
Become less rough, to look like human beigns,
Or anyway as much like human beings
As statues do, when the sculptor is only starting,
Images half blocked out. The earthy portion,
Damp with some moisture, turned to flesh, the solid
Was bone, the veins were as they always had been,
The stones the man had thrown turned into men,
The stones the woman threw turned into women,
Such being the will of God. Hence we derive
The hardness that we have, and our endurance
Gives proof of what we have come from.
Other forms
Of life came into being, generated
Out of the earth: the sun burnt off the dampness,
Heat made the slimy marshes swell; as seed
Swells in mother's womb to shape and substance,
So new forms came to life. When the Nile river
Floods and recedes and the mud is warmed by sunshine,

Men, turning over the earth, find living things,
And some not living, but nearly so, imperfect,
On the verge of life, and often the same substance
Is part alive, part only clay. When moisture
Unites with heat, life is conceived; all things
Come from this union. Fire may fight with water,
But heat and moisture generate all things,
Their discord being productive. So when earth,
After that flood, still muddy, took the heat,
Felt the warm fire of sunlight, she conceived,
Brought for forth, after their fashion, all the creatures,
Some old, some strange and monstrous.
                    One, for instance,
She bore unwanted, a gigantic serpent,
Python by name, whom the new people dreaded,
A huge bulk on the mountain-side. Apollo,
God of the glittering bow, took a long time
To bring him down, with arrow after arrow
He had never used before except in hunting
Deer and the skipping goats. Out of the quiver
Sped arrows by the thousand, till the monster,
Dying, poured poisonous blood on those black wounds.
In memory of this, the sacred games,
Called Pythian, were established, and Apollo
Ordained for all young winners in the races,
On foot or chariot, for victorious fighters,
The crown of oak. That was before the laurel,
That was before Apollo wreathed his forehead
With garlands from that tree, or any other.

Apollo and Daphne

Now the first girl Apollo loved was Daphne,
Whose father was the river-god Peneus,
And this was no blind chance, but Cupid's malice.
Apollo, with pride and glory still upon him
Over the Python slain, saw Cupid bending
His tight-strung little bow. "O silly youngster,"
He said, "What are you doing with such weapons?
Those are for grown-ups! The bow is for my shoulder;
I never fail in wounding beast or mortal,
And not so long ago I slew the Python
With countless darts; his bloated body covered
Acre on endless acre, and I slew him!
The torch, my boy, is enough for you to play with,
To get the love-fires burning. Do not meddle
With honors that are mine!" And Cupid answered:
"Your bow shoots everything, Apollo—maybe—

But mine will fix you! You are far above
All creatures living, and by just that distance
Your glory less than mine." He shook his wings,
Soared high, came down to the shadows of Parnassus,
Drew from his quiver different kinds of arrows,
One causing love, golden and sharp and gleaming,
The other blunt, and tipped with lead, and serving
To drive all love away, and this blunt arrow
He used on Daphne, but he fired the other,
The sharp and golden shaft, piercing Apollo
Through bones, through marrow, and at once he loved
And she at once fled from the name of lover,
Rejoicing in the woodland hiding places
And spoils of beasts which she had taken captive,
A rival of Diana, virgin goddess.
She had many suitors, but she scorned them all;
Wanting no part of any man, she travelled
The pathless groves, and had no care whatever
For husband, love, or marriage. Her father often
Said, "Daughter, give me a son-in-law!" and "Daughter,
Give me some grandsons!" But the marriage torches
Were something hateful, criminal, to Daphne,
So she would blush, and put her arms around him,
And coax him: "Let me be a virgin always;
Diana's father said she might. Dear father!
Dear father—please!" he yielded, but her beauty
Kept arguing against her prayer. Apollo
Loves at first sight; he wants to marry Daphne,
He hopes for what he wants—all wishful thinking! —
Is fooled by his own oracles. As stubble
Burns when the grain is harvested, as hedges
Catch fire from torches that a passer-by
Has brought too near, or left behind in the morning,
So the god burned, with all his heart, and burning
Nourished that futile love of his by hoping.
He sees the long hair hanging down her neck
Uncared for, says, "But what if it were combed?"
He gazes at her eyes—they shine like stars!
He gazes at her lips, and knows that gazing
Is not enough. He marvels at her fingers,
Her hands, her wrists, her arms, bare to the shoulder,
And what he does not see he thinks is better.
But still she flees him, swifter than the wind,
And when he calls she does not even listen:
"Don't run away, dear nymph! Daughter of Peneus,
Don't run away! I am no enemy,
Only your follower: don't run away!

The lamb flees from the wolf, the deer the lion,
The dove, on trembling wing, flees from the eagle.
All creatures flee their foes. But I, who follow,
Am not a foe at all. Love makes me follow,
Unhappy fellow that I am, and fearful
You may fall down, perhaps, or have the briars
Make scratches on those lovely legs, unworthy
To be hurt so, and I would be the reason.
The ground is rough here. Run a little slower,
And I will run, I promise, a little slower.
Or wait a minute: be a little curious
Just who it is you charm. I am no shepherd,
No mountain-dweller, I am not a ploughboy,
Uncouth and stinking of cattle. You foolish girl,
You don't know who it is you run away from,
That must be why you run. I am lord of Delphi
And Tenedos and Claros and Patara.
Jove is my father. I am the revealer
Of present, past and future; through my power
The lyre and song make harmony; my arrow
Is sure in aim—there is only one arrow surer,
The one that wounds my heart. The power of healing
Is my discovery; I am called the Healer
Through all the world: all herbs are subject to me.
Alas for me, love is incurable
With any herb; the arts which cure the others
Do me, their lord, no good!"
        He would have said
Much more than this, but Daphne, frightened, left him
With many words unsaid, and she was lovely
Even in flight, her limbs bare in the wind,
Her garments fluttering, and her soft hair streaming,
More beautiful than ever. But Apollo
Too young a god to waste his time in coaxing,
Came following fast. When a hound stats a rabbit
In an open field, one runs for game, one safety,
He has her, or thinks he has, and she is doubtful
Whether she's caught or not, so close the margin,
So ran the god and girl, one swift in hope,
The other in terror, but he ran more swiftly,
Borne on the wings of love, gave her no rest,
Shadowed her shoulder, breathed on her streaming hair.
Her strength was gone, worn out by the long effort
Of the long flight; she was deathly pale, and seeing
The river of her father, cried "O help me,
If there is any power in the rivers,
Change and destroy the body which has given

Too much delight!" And hardly had she finished,
When her limbs grew numb and heavy, her soft breasts
Were closed with delicate bark, her hair was leaves,
Her arms were branches, and her speedy feet
Rooted and held, and her head became a tree top,
Everything gone except her grace, her shining.
Apollo loved her still. He placed his hand
Where he had hoped and felt the heart still beating
Under the bark; and he embraced the branches
As if they still were limbs, and kissed the wood,
And the wood shrank from his kisses, and the god
Exclaimed: "Since you can never be my bride,
My tree at least you shall be! Let the laurel
Adorn, henceforth, my hair, my lyre, my quiver:
Let Roman victors, in the long procession,
Wear laurel wreaths for triumph and ovation.
Beside Augustus' portals let the laurel
Guard and watch over the oak, and as my head
Is always youthful, let the laurel always
Be green and shining!" He said no more. The laurel,
Stirring, seemed to consent, to be saying *Yes*.

There is a grove in Thessaly, surrounded
By woodlands with steep slopes; men call it Tempe.
Through this the Peneus River's foamy waters
Rise below Pindus mountain. The cascades
Drive a fine smoky mist along the tree tops,
Frail clouds, or so it seems, and the roar of the water
Carries beyond the neighborhood. Here dwells
The mighty god himself, his holy of holies
Is under a hinging rock; it is here he gives
Laws to the nymphs, laws to the very water
And here came first the streams of his own country
Not knowing what to offer, consolation
Or something like rejoicing: crowned with poplars
Sperchios came, and restless Enipeus,
Old Apidanus, aeas, and Amphrysos
The easy-going. And all the other rivers
That take their weary waters into oceans

All over the world, came there, and only one
Was absent, Inachus, hiding in his cavern,
Salting his stream with tears, oh, most unhappy,
Mourning a daughter lost. Her name was Io,
Who might, for all he knew, be dead or living,
But since he can not find her anywhere
He thinks she must be nowhere, and his sorrow

Fears for the worst.

Jove and Io

Jove had seen Io coming
From the river of her father, and had spoken:
"O maiden, worthy of the love of Jove,
And sure to make some lover happy in bed,
Come to the shade of these deep woods" (he showed them)
"Come to the shade, the sun is hot and burning.
No beasts will hurt you there, I will go with you,
If a god is at your side, you will walk safely
In the very deepest woods. I am a god,
And no plebeian godling, either, but the holder
Of Heaven's scepter, hurler of the thunder.
Oh, do not flee me!" She had fled already
Leaving Lyrcea's plains, and Lerna's meadows,
When the god hid the lands in murk and darkness
And stayed her flight, and took her.
                        Meanwhile Juno
Looked down on Argos: what could those clouds be doing
In the bright light of day? They were not mists
Rising from rivers or damp ground. She wondered,
Took a quick look around to see her husband,
Or see where he might be—she knew his cheating!
So when she did not find him in the heaven,
She said, "I am either wrong, or being wronged,"
Came gliding down from Heaven, stood on earth,
Broke up the clouds. But Jove, ahead of time,
Could tell that she was coming; he changed Io
Into a heifer, white and shining, lovely
Even in altered form, and even Juno
Looked on, through hating to, with admiration,
And asked whom she belonged to, from what pasture,
As if she did not know! And Jove, the liar,
To put a stop to questions, said she had sprung
Out of the earth, full-grown. Then Juno asked him,
"Could I have her, as present?" What could he do?
To give his love away was surely cruel,
To keep her most suspicious. Shame on one side
Says *Give her up!* And love says *Don't* and shame
Might have been beaten by love's argument,
But then, if he refused his wife the heifer,
So slight a present—if he should refuse it,
Juno might think perhaps it was no heifer!

Her rival thus disposed of, still the goddess
Did not at once abandon all suspicion.

Afraid of Jove, and worried over his cheating,
She turned her over to the keeping of Argus
Who had a hundred eyes; two at a time,
No more than two, would ever close in slumber,
The rest kept watch. No matter how he stood,
Which way he turned, he always looked at Io,
Always had Io in sight. He let her graze
By daylight, but at sundown locked her in,
Hobbled and haltered. She would feed on leaves
And biter grasses, and her couch, poor creature,
Was ground, not always grassy, and the water
She drank was muddy, often. When she wanted
To reach toward Argus her imploring arms,
She had no arms to reach with; when she tried
To plead, she only lowed, and her own voice
Filled her with terror. When she came to the river,
Her father's, where she used to play, and saw,
Reflected in the stream, her jaws and horns,
She fled in panic. None of her sisters knew her,
And Inachus, her father, did not know her,
But following them, she let them pet and praise her.
Old Inachus pulled grass and gave it to her,
And she licked his hand and tried to give it kissed,
Could not restrain her tears. If she could talk,
She would ask for help, and tell her name and sorrow,
But as it was, all she could do was furrow
The dust with one forefoot, and make an I,
And then an O beside it, spelling her name,
Telling the story of her changed condition.
Her father knew her, cried, "Alas for me!"
Clung to her horns and snowy neck, poor heifer,
Crying, "Alas for me! I have sought you, daughter,
All over the world, and now that I have found you,
I have found a greater grief. You do not answer,
And what you think is sighing comes out mooing!
And what you think I, in my ignorance, counted
On marriage for you, wanting, first a son,
Then, later, grandsons; now your mate must be
Selected from some herd, your son a bullock.
Not even death can end my heavy sorrow.
It hurts to be a god; the door of death,
Shut in my face, prolongs my grief forever."
And both of them were weeping, but their guardian,
Argus the star-eyed, drove her from her father
To different pasture-land, and sat there, watching,
Perched on a mountain-top above the valley.
Jove could not bear her sorrows any longer;

He called his son, born of the shining Pleiad,
Told him *Kill Argus!* And Mercury came flying
On winged sandals, wearing the magic helmet,
Bearing the sleep-producing wand, and lighted
On earth, and put aside the wings and helmet
Keeping the wand. With this he plays the shepherd
Across the pathless countryside, a driver
Of goats, collected somewhere, and he goes
Playing a little tune on a pipe of reeds,
And this new sound is wonderful to Argus.
"Whoever you are, come here and sit beside me,"
He says, "This rock is in the shade; the grass
Is nowhere any better." And Mercury joins him,
Whiling the time away with conversation
And soothing little melodies, and Argus
Has a hard fight with drowsiness; his eyes,
Some of them, close, but some of them stay open.
To keep himself awake by listening,
He asks about the pipe of reeds, how was it
This new invention came about?
          The god
Began the story: "Oh the mountain slopes
Of cool Arcadia, a woodland nymph
Once lived, with many suitors, and her name
Was Syrinx. More than once the satyrs chased her,
And so did other gods of field or woodland,
But always she escaped them, virgin always
As she aspired to be, one like Diana,
Like her in dress and calling, thought her bow
Was made of horn, not gold, but even so,
She might, sometimes, be taken for the goddess.
Pan, with a wreath of pine around his temples,
Once saw her coming back from Mount Lycaeus,
And said—" and Mercury broke off the story
And then went on to tell what Pan had told her,
How she said *No,* and fled, through pathless places,
Until she came to Ladon's river, flowing
Peaceful along the sandy banks, whose water
Halted her flight, and she implored her sisters
To change her form, and so, when Pan had caught her
And thought he held a nymph, it was only reeds
That yielded in his arms, and while he sighed,
The soft air stirring in the reeds made also
The echo of a sigh. Touched by this marvel,
Charmed by the sweetness of the tone, he murmured
This much I have! And took the reeds, and bound them
With wax, a tall and shorter one together,

And called them Syrinx, still.
          And Mercury
Might have told more, but all the eyes of Argus,
He saw, had closed, and he made the slumber deeper
With movements of the wand, and then he struck
The nodding head just where, it joins the shoulder,
Severed it withthe curving blade, and sent it
Bloody and rolling over the rocks. So Argus
Lay low, and all the light in all those eyes
Went out forever, a hundred eyes, one darkness.
And Juno took the eyes and fastened them
On the feathers of a bird of hers, the peacock,
So that the peacock's tail is spread with jewels,
And Juno, very angry, sent a fury
To harass Io, to drive her mad with terror,
In flight all over the world. At last a river
Halted her flight, the Nile, and when she came there
She knelt beside the stream, lifted her head,
The only gesture she could make of praying,
And seemed, with groans and tears and mournful lowing,
To voice complaint to Jove, to end her sorrows,
And he was moved to pity; embracing Juno
He begged her: "End this punishment; hereafter
Io, I swear, will never cause you anguish,"
And what he swore he called she Styx to witness.
And Juno was appeased. Io became
What once she was, again; the bristles vanish,
The horns are gone, the great round eyes grow smaller,
The gaping jows are narrower, the shoulders
Return, she has hands again, and toes and fingers,
The only sign of the heifer is the whiteness.
She stands erect, a nymph again, still fearful
That speech may still be mooing, but she tries
And little by little gains back the use of language.
Now people, robed in linen, pay her homage,
A very goddess, and a son is born,
Named Epaphus, the seed of Jove; his temples
Are found beside his mother's in many cities.
          His boon companion was young Phaethon,
Son of the Sun-god, given to speaking proudly,
Boasting about his parentage, till one day
Epaphus said: "You are a silly fellow,
Believing every word your mother tells you,
And all swelled up about your phony father!"
Phaethon flushed, made no retort, but carried
The insult to his mother, the nymph Clymene,
And told her: "Mother, to make it all the worse,

There was nothing I could answer back. I tell you
It is shameful for a fellow with any spirit,
And I think I have plenty, to have to listen
To such insulting slanders, and have no answer.
Give me some proof that my father was the Sun-god,
Really and truly!" He put his arms about her,
Pleading, imploring, in his own name, his brother's
His married sisiters', for complete assurance.
Clymene, moved, by her son's prayers, or maybe
By anger at her damaged reputation,
Stretched out both arms to Heaven, raised her eyes
To the bright sun, and cried: "By that bright splendor
Which hears and sees us both, I swear, my son,
You are his son too, the son of that great presence
Whom you behold with me, the radiant ruler
Of all the world. If I am lying to you,
May I never see his light again, this day
Be the last time I ever look upon him.
And you can find his house with no great trouble;
His rising is not far from here: go thither,
Ask him yourself!" And Phaethon, delighted,
Already imagining himself in Heaven,
Crosses beyond his own frontiers to India,
The nearest land to the starry fires of Heaven,
And comes, exulting, to his father's palace.

DISCUSSION QUESTIONS

1.   Compare the description of creation and the flood scene early in Book 1 with similar scenes from *Genesis*. Where and how does Ovid diverge from the earlier source?
2.   What are the characteristics of each of the stages of history described early in Book 1? How far removed do the stories stand from the golden age?
3.   Trace the method by which one story is transformed into another? What literary devices and figures of speech does Ovid employ?
4.   How do the processes by which one story merges into another relate to the broader theme of change?

WRITING SUGGESTION

1.   Artists and sculptors have frequently turned to Ovid's stories for inspiration. Identify an artist who does so and write a paper that examines how the work of art compares to Ovid's poem. What has been changed? What details are emphasized in the work of art?

THE NEW TESTAMENT

The final section in our exploration of the ancient Mediterranean world focuses on the New Testament, the second half of the Christian Bible. Compiled during the first century of the Common Era, the New Testament brings together three major cultures of the Mediterranean. It describes events that occurred in Palestine, a territory controlled by the Romans; the original language is Greek, and the story concerns the Jewish community in and around Jerusalem.

Like the Hebrew Bible, the New Testament is a collection of books written by many authors. The first four books are the Gospels of Matthew, Mark, Luke, and John. The term "gospel" is from the Greek for "good news." They describe the life and death of Jesus of Nazareth, a man Christians believe was the Son of God. With its powerful stories of the birth and eventual crucifixion of Jesus, the Gospels contain some of the most memorable and influential stories ever recorded. They also provide the framework for the ethical teachings of Christianity. After the gospels come 21 epistles (letters) written by leaders of the early Christian Church, who tried to explain the teachings of the church that grew up among those who believed that Jesus had been sent to earth as the promised savior of mankind. The final book, known as *Revelations*, describes the future of heaven and earth after most of humanity is punished by an angry God.

Although the Gospels are named for individuals, no authors signed their names to these books. So while we conventionally use the names that have been attached to them, we do not know who wrote the four Gospels. Most scholars believe that Mark was the first written, most likely between 65 and 75 CE. Matthew and Luke were probably written about ten years later, while John was composed around the year 90. These dates thus place the Gospels several decades *after* the death of Jesus, which is thought to have occurred around 30 CE. They were almost certainly written by people who heard stories about Jesus rather than by eyewitnesses to his life. These were not, however, the only early accounts of Jesus' life. Throughout the second and third centuries, other writings circulated within the expanding Christian community. Disputes over which ones most closely reflected the life and teachings of Jesus led some books to ultimately be excluded from the New Testament canon, which was not fixed into its familiar form until the fourth century.

The essential figure of the Gospels is Jesus of Nazareth, a man of humble origins whose life and death became the central narrative of Christianity. For early believers, Jesus was the Messiah, from the Hebrew for "anointed one." The Greek term *christos* carries the same meaning, and for this reason, Jesus, whose life was first recorded in Greek-written Gospels, is often identified as Christ. We have virtually no information about him outside of the New Testament. As the Gospels make clear, he was born into and spent his entire life within the religious world of Judaism, and indeed it is vital that we remember that Jesus was Jewish: He practiced Jewish customs, his early followers were Jewish, and he always identified himself as a Jew.

According to the Gospels, Jesus was marked as a divine figure even before he was born, when his mother received a prophecy that she would bear a special child. The Gospels also describe how as a young man he gathered around him a collection of followers known as disciples. Eventually, the crowds that gathered around him attracted the attention of authorities, who became suspicious of his compelling power over the people. Following a brief trial in Jerusalem, he was executed by Roman officials, who probably thought his death would be soon forgotten. In the years that followed, however, the small group that believed Jesus was, in fact, the son of God expanded; in time, what was at first an obscure Jewish sect spread throughout the Roman world to eventually become one of the major religions of the world. That expansion was possible because of the powerful language and stories contained in the New Testament.

SELECTIONS FROM THE BOOKS OF LUKE, MARK, MATTHEW

Our selections from the Gospels highlight the key moments in the life of Jesus of Nazareth, including his birth, important teachings, and death. The sequence is chronological, but the passages come from different Gospels. We begin with the famous Nativity narrative from *Luke*, which describes the supernatural signs that accompanied the birth of the infant Jesus as his parents traveled through Bethlehem. Next comes the story of his baptism and the gathering of the disciples in the opening chapter of *Mark*.

From *Matthew*, we include the Sermon on the Mount, one of the most famous passages in the New Testament. Here, Jesus outlines the ethical principles he expects his disciples to follow. He begins with a series of blessings known as the Beatitudes that are designed lift up and ennoble those who suffer and to praise those who are "pure of heart." After the Beatitudes, Jesus restates the Laws that were given to Moses, thus affirming his connection to the Jewish past. He makes clear that he has not "come to abolish the law or the prophets," but to uphold and even strengthen them. At the conclusion of his sermon, he offers what is familiarly known as the Golden Rule, which calls upon his followers to "Do unto others as you would have done to you." We end with the events surrounding the Crucifixion of Jesus in Chapters 26–28 of *Matthew*.

THE GOSPELS

Luke, Chapter 2

1. And it came to pass in those days, that there went out a decree from Caesar Augustus, that all the world should be taxed.

2. (*And* this taxing was first made when Cyrenius was governor of Syria.)

3. And all went to be taxed, every one into his own city.

4. And Joseph also went up from Galilee, out of the city of Nazareth, into Judaea, unto the city of David, which is called Bethlehem; (because he was of the house and lineage of David:)

5. To be taxed with Mary his espoused wife, being great with child.

6. And so it was, that, while they were there, the days were accomplished that she should be delivered.

7. And she brought forth her firstborn son, and wrapped him in swaddling clothes, and laid him in a manger; because there was no room for them in the inn.

8. And there were in the same country shepherds abiding in the field, keeping watch over their flock by night.

9. And, lo, the angel of the Lord came upon them, and the glory of the Lord shone round about them: and they were sore afraid.

10. And the angel said unto them, Fear not: for, behold, I bring you good tidings of great joy, which shall be to all people.

11. For unto you is born this day in the city of David a Saviour, which is Christ the Lord.

12. And this *shall be* a sign unto you; Ye shall find the babe wrapped in swaddling clothes, lying in a manger.

13. And suddenly there was with the angel a multitude of the heavenly host praising God, and saying,

14. Glory to God in the highest, and on earth peace, good will toward men.

15. And it came to pass, as the angels were gone away from them into heaven, the shepherds said one to another, Let us now go even unto Bethlehem, and see this thing which is come to pass, which the Lord hath made known unto us.

16. And they came with haste, and found Mary, and Joseph, and the babe lying in a manger.

17. And when they had seen *it*, they made known abroad the saying which was told them concerning this child.

18. And all they that heard *it* wondered at those things which were told them by the shepherds.

19. But Mary kept all these things, and pondered *them* in her heart.

20. And the shepherds returned, glorifying and praising God for all the things that they had heard and seen, as it was told unto them.

21. And when eight days were accomplished for the circumcising of the child, his name was called JESUS, which was so named of the angel before he was conceived in the womb.

22. And when the days of her purification according to the law of Moses were accomplished, they brought him to Jerusalem, to present *him* to the Lord;

23. (As it is written in the law of the Lord, Every male that openeth the womb shall be called holy to the Lord;)

24. And to offer a sacrifice according to that which is said in the law of the Lord, A pair of turtledoves, or two young pigeons.

25. And, behold, there was a man in Jerusalem, whose name *was* Simeon; and the same man *was* just and devout, waiting for the consolation of Israel: and the Holy Ghost was upon him.

26. And it was revealed unto him by the Holy Ghost, that he should not see death, before he had seen the Lord's Christ.

27. And he came by the Spirit into the temple: and when the parents brought in the child Jesus, to do for him after the custom of the law,

28. Then took he him up in his arms, and blessed God, and said,

29. Lord, now lettest thou thy servant depart in peace, according to thy word:

30. For mine eyes have seen thy salvation,

31. Which thou hast prepared before the face of all people;

32. A light to lighten the Gentiles, and the glory of thy people Israel.

33. And Joseph and his mother marvelled at those things which were spoken of him.

34. And Simeon blessed them, and said unto Mary his mother, Behold, this *child* is set for the fall and rising again of many in Israel; and for a sign which shall be spoken against;

35. (Yea, a sword shall pierce through thy own soul also,) that the thoughts of many hearts may be revealed.

36. And there was one Anna, a prophetess, the daughter of Phanuel, of the tribe of Aser: she was of a great age, and had lived with an husband seven years from her virginity;

37. And she *was* a widow of about fourscore and four years, which departed not from the temple, but served *God* with fastings and prayers night and day.

38. And she coming in that instant gave thanks likewise unto the Lord, and spake of him to all them that looked for redemption in Jerusalem.

39. And when they had performed all things according to the law of the Lord, they returned into Galilee, to their own city Nazareth.

40. And the child grew, and waxed strong in spirit, filled with wisdom: and the grace of God was upon him.

41. Now his parents went to Jerusalem every year at the feast of the passover.

42. And when he was twelve years old, they went up to Jerusalem after the custom of the feast.

43. And when they had fulfilled the days, as they returned, the child Jesus tarried behind in Jerusalem; and Joseph and his mother knew not *of it.*

44. But they, supposing him to have been in the company, went a day's journey; and they sought him among *their* kinsfolk and acquaintance.

45. And when they found him not, they turned back again to Jerusalem, seeking him.

46. And it came to pass, that after three days they found him in the temple, sitting in the midst of the doctors, both hearing them, and asking them questions.

47. And all that heard him were astonished at his understanding and answers.

48. And when they saw him, they were amazed: and his mother said unto him, Son, why hast thou thus dealt with us? behold, thy father and I have sought thee sorrowing.

49. And he said unto them, How is it that ye sought me? wist ye not that I must be about my Father's business?

50. And they understood not the saying which he spake unto them.

51. And he went down with them, and came to Nazareth, and was subject unto them: but his mother kept all these sayings in her heart.

52. And Jesus increased in wisdom and stature, and in favour with God and man.

MARK, CHAPTER 1

1. The beginning of the gospel of Jesus Christ, the Son of God;

2. As it is written in the prophets, Behold, I send my messenger before thy face, which shall prepare thy way before thee.

3. The voice of one crying in the wilderness, Prepare ye the way of the Lord, make his paths straight.

4. John did baptize in the wilderness, and preach the baptism of repentance for the remission of sins.

5. And there went out unto him all the land of Judaea, and they of Jerusalem, and were all baptized of him in the river of Jordan, confessing their sins.

6. And John was clothed with camel's hair, and with a girdle of a skin about his loins; and he did eat locusts and wild honey;

7. And preached, saying, There cometh one mightier than I after me, the latchet of whose shoes I am not worthy to stoop down and unloose.

8. I indeed have baptized you with water: but he shall baptize you with the Holy Ghost.

9. And it came to pass in those days, that Jesus came from Nazareth of Galilee, and was baptized of John in Jordan.

10. And straightway coming up out of the water, he saw the heavens opened, and the Spirit like a dove descending upon him:

11. And there came a voice from heaven, *saying*, Thou art my beloved Son, in whom I am well pleased.

12. And immediately the Spirit driveth him into the wilderness.

13. And he was there in the wilderness forty days, tempted of Satan; and was with the wild beasts; and the angels ministered unto him.

14. Now after that John was put in prison, Jesus came into Galilee, preaching the gospel of the kingdom of God,

15. And saying, The time is fulfilled, and the kingdom of God is at hand: repent ye, and believe the gospel.

16. Now as he walked by the sea of Galilee, he saw Simon and Andrew his brother casting a net into the sea: for they were fishers.

17. And Jesus said unto them, Come ye after me, and I will make you to become fishers of men.

18. And straightway they forsook their nets, and followed him.

19. And when he had gone a little further thence, he saw James the *son* of Zebedee, and John his brother, who also were in the ship mending their nets.

20. And straightway he called them: and they left their father Zebedee in the ship with the hired servants, and went after him.

21. And they went into Capernaum; and straightway on the sabbath day he entered into the synagogue, and taught.

22. And they were astonished at his doctrine: for he taught them as one that had authority, and not as the scribes.

23. And there was in their synagogue a man with an unclean spirit; and he cried out,

24. Saying, Let *us* alone; what have we to do with thee, thou Jesus of Nazareth? art thou come to destroy us? I know thee who thou art, the Holy One of God.

25. And Jesus rebuked him, saying, Hold thy peace, and come out of him.

26. And when the unclean spirit had torn him, and cried with a loud voice, he came out of him.

27. And they were all amazed, insomuch that they questioned among themselves, saying, What thing is this? what new doctrine *is* this? for with authority commandeth he even the unclean spirits, and they do obey him.

28. And immediately his fame spread abroad throughout all the region round about Galilee.

29. And forthwith, when they were come out of the synagogue, they entered into the house of Simon and Andrew, with James and John.

30. But Simon's wife's mother lay sick of a fever, and anon they tell him of her.

31. And he came and took her by the hand, and lifted her up; and immediately the fever left her, and she ministered unto them.

32. And at even, when the sun did set, they brought unto him all that were diseased, and them that were possessed with devils.

33. And all the city was gathered together at the door.

34. And he healed many that were sick of divers diseases, and cast out many devils; and suffered not the devils to speak, because they knew him.

35. And in the morning, rising up a great while before day, he went out, and departed into a solitary place, and there prayed.

36. And Simon and they that were with him followed after him.

37. And when they had found him, they said unto him, All *men* seek for thee.

38. And he said unto them, Let us go into the next towns, that I may preach there also: for therefore came I forth.

39. And he preached in their synagogues throughout all Galilee, and cast out devils.

40. And there came a leper to him, beseeching him, and kneeling down to him, and saying unto him, If thou wilt, thou canst make me clean.

41. And Jesus, moved with compassion, put forth *his* hand, and touched him, and saith unto him, I will; be thou clean.

42. And as soon as he had spoken, immediately the leprosy departed from him, and he was cleansed.

43. And he straitly charged him, and forthwith sent him away;

44. And saith unto him, See thou say nothing to any man: but go thy way, shew thyself to the priest, and offer for thy cleansing those things which Moses commanded, for a testimony unto them.

45. But he went out, and began to publish *it* much, and to blaze abroad the matter, insomuch that Jesus could no more openly enter into the city, but was without in desert places: and they came to him from every quarter.

MATTHEW, CHAPTER 5

1. And seeing the multitudes, he went up into a mountain: and when he was set, his disciples came unto him:

2. And he opened his mouth, and taught them, saying,

3. Blessed *are* the poor in spirit: for theirs is the kingdom of heaven.

4. Blessed *are* they that mourn: for they shall be comforted.

5. Blessed *are* the meek: for they shall inherit the earth.

6. Blessed *are* they which do hunger and thirst after righteousness: for they shall be filled.

7. Blessed *are* the merciful: for they shall obtain mercy.

8. Blessed *are* the pure in heart: for they shall see God.

9. Blessed *are* the peacemakers: for they shall be called the children of God.

10. Blessed *are* they which are persecuted for righteousness' sake: for theirs is the kingdom of heaven.

11. Blessed are ye, when *men* shall revile you, and persecute *you*, and shall say all manner of evil against you falsely, for my sake.

12. Rejoice, and be exceeding glad: for great *is* your reward in heaven: for so persecuted they the prophets which were before you.

13. Ye are the salt of the earth: but if the salt have lost his savour, wherewith shall it be salted? it is thenceforth good for nothing, but to be cast out, and to be trodden under foot of men.

14. Ye are the light of the world. A city that is set on an hill cannot be hid.

15. Neither do men light a candle, and put it under a bushel, but on a candlestick; and it giveth light unto all that are in the house.

16. Let your light so shine before men, that they may see your good works, and glorify your Father which is in heaven.

17. Think not that I am come to destroy the law, or the prophets: I am not come to destroy, but to fulfil.

18. For verily I say unto you, Till heaven and earth pass, one jot or one tittle shall in no wise pass from the law, till all be fulfilled.

19. Whosoever therefore shall break one of these least commandments, and shall teach men so, he shall be called the least in the kingdom of heaven: but whosoever shall do and teach *them*, the same shall be called great in the kingdom of heaven.

20. For I say unto you, That except your righteousness shall exceed *the righteousness* of the scribes

and Pharisees, ye shall in no case enter into the kingdom of heaven.

21. Ye have heard that it was said by them of old time, Thou shalt not kill; and whosoever shall kill shall be in danger of the judgment:

22. But I say unto you, That whosoever is angry with his brother without a cause shall be in danger of the judgment: and whosoever shall say to his brother, Raca, shall be in danger of the council: but whosoever shall say, Thou fool, shall be in danger of hell fire.

23. Therefore if thou bring thy gift to the altar, and there rememberest that thy brother hath ought against thee;

24. Leave there thy gift before the altar, and go thy way; first be reconciled to thy brother, and then come and offer thy gift.

25. Agree with thine adversary quickly, whiles thou art in the way with him; lest at any time the adversary deliver thee to the judge, and the judge deliver thee to the officer, and thou be cast into prison.

26. Verily I say unto thee, Thou shalt by no means come out thence, till thou hast paid the uttermost farthing.

27. Ye have heard that it was said by them of old time, Thou shalt not commit adultery:

28. But I say unto you, That whosoever looketh on a woman to lust after her hath committed adultery with her already in his heart.

29. And if thy right eye offend thee, pluck it out, and cast *it* from thee: for it is profitable for thee that one of thy members should perish, and not *that* thy whole body should be cast into hell.

30. And if thy right hand offend thee, cut it off, and cast *it* from thee: for it is profitable for thee that one of thy members should perish, and not *that* thy whole body should be cast into hell.

31. It hath been said, Whosoever shall put away his wife, let him give her a writing of divorcement:

32. But I say unto you, That whosoever shall put away his wife, saving for the cause of fornication, causeth her to commit adultery: and

whosoever shall marry her that is divorced committeth adultery.

33. Again, ye have heard that it hath been said by them of old time, Thou shalt not forswear thyself, but shalt perform unto the Lord thine oaths:

34. But I say unto you, Swear not at all; neither by heaven; for it is God's throne:

35. Nor by the earth; for it is his footstool: neither by Jerusalem; for it is the city of the great King.

36. Neither shalt thou swear by thy head, because thou canst not make one hair white or black.

37. But let your communication be, Yea, yea; Nay, nay: for whatsoever is more than these cometh of evil.

38. Ye have heard that it hath been said, An eye for an eye, and a tooth for a tooth:

39. But I say unto you, That ye resist not evil: but whosoever shall smite thee on thy right cheek, turn to him the other also.

40. And if any man will sue thee at the law, and take away thy coat, let him have *thy* cloke also.

41. And whosoever shall compel thee to go a mile, go with him twain.

42. Give to him that asketh thee, and from him that would borrow of thee turn not thou away.

43. Ye have heard that it hath been said, Thou shalt love thy neighbour, and hate thine enemy.

44. But I say unto you, Love your enemies, bless them that curse you, do good to them that hate you, and pray for them which despitefully use you, and persecute you;

45. That ye may be the children of your Father which is in heaven: for he maketh his sun to rise on the evil and on the good, and sendeth rain on the just and on the unjust.

46. For if ye love them which love you, what reward have ye? do not even the publicans the same?

47. And if ye salute your brethren only, what do ye more *than others*? do not even the publicans so?

48. Be ye therefore perfect, even as your Father which is in heaven is perfect.

MATTHEW, CHAPTER 6

1. Take heed that ye do not your alms before men, to be seen of them: otherwise ye have no reward of your Father which is in heaven.

2. Therefore when thou doest *thine* alms, do not sound a trumpet before thee, as the hypocrites do in the synagogues and in the streets, that they may have glory of men. Verily I say unto you, They have their reward.

3. But when thou doest alms, let not thy left hand know what thy right hand doeth:

4. That thine alms may be in secret: and thy Father which seeth in secret himself shall reward thee openly.

5. And when thou prayest, thou shalt not be as the hypocrites *are*: for they love to pray standing in the synagogues and in the corners of the streets, that they may be seen of men. Verily I say unto you, They have their reward.

6. But thou, when thou prayest, enter into thy closet, and when thou hast shut thy door, pray to thy Father which is in secret; and thy Father which seeth in secret shall reward thee openly.

7. But when ye pray, use not vain repetitions, as the heathen *do*: for they think that they shall be heard for their much speaking.

8. Be not ye therefore like unto them: for your Father knoweth what things ye have need of, before ye ask him.

9. After this manner therefore pray ye: Our Father which art in heaven, Hallowed be thy name.

10. Thy kingdom come. Thy will be done in earth, as *it is* in heaven.

11. Give us this day our daily bread.

12. And forgive us our debts, as we forgive our debtors.

13. And lead us not into temptation, but deliver us from evil: For thine is the kingdom, and the power, and the glory, for ever. Amen.

14. For if ye forgive men their trespasses, your heavenly Father will also forgive you:

15. But if ye forgive not men their trespasses, neither will your Father forgive your trespasses.

16. Moreover when ye fast, be not, as the hypocrites, of a sad countenance: for they disfigure their faces, that they may appear unto men to fast. Verily I say unto you, They have their reward.

17. But thou, when thou fastest, anoint thine head, and wash thy face;

18. That thou appear not unto men to fast, but unto thy Father which is in secret: and thy Father, which seeth in secret, shall reward thee openly.

19. Lay not up for yourselves treasures upon earth, where moth and rust doth corrupt, and where thieves break through and steal:

20. But lay up for yourselves treasures in heaven, where neither moth nor rust doth corrupt, and where thieves do not break through nor steal:

21. For where your treasure is, there will your heart be also.

22. The light of the body is the eye: if therefore thine eye be single, thy whole body shall be full of light.

23. But if thine eye be evil, thy whole body shall be full of darkness. If therefore the light that is in thee be darkness, how great *is* that darkness!

24. No man can serve two masters: for either he will hate the one, and love the other; or else he will hold to the one, and despise the other. Ye cannot serve God and mammon.

25. Therefore I say unto you, Take no thought for your life, what ye shall eat, or what ye shall drink; nor yet for your body, what ye shall put on. Is not the life more than meat, and the body than raiment?

26. Behold the fowls of the air: for they sow not, neither do they reap, nor gather into barns; yet your heavenly Father feedeth them. Are ye not much better than they?

27. Which of you by taking thought can add one cubit unto his stature?

28. And why take ye thought for raiment? Consider the lilies of the field, how they grow; they toil not, neither do they spin:

29. And yet I say unto you, That even Solomon in all his glory was not arrayed like one of these.

30. Wherefore, if God so clothe the grass of the field, which to day is, and to morrow is cast into the oven, *shall he* not much more *clothe* you, O ye of little faith?

31. Therefore take no thought, saying, What shall we eat? or, What shall we drink? or, Wherewithal shall we be clothed?

32. (For after all these things do the Gentiles seek:) for your heavenly Father knoweth that ye have need of all these things.

33. But seek ye first the kingdom of God, and his righteousness; and all these things shall be added unto you.

34. Take therefore no thought for the morrow: for the morrow shall take thought for the things of itself. Sufficient unto the day *is* the evil thereof.

MATTHEW, CHAPTER 7

1. Judge not, that ye be not judged.

2. For with what judgment ye judge, ye shall be judged: and with what measure ye mete, it shall be measured to you again.

3. And why beholdest thou the mote that is in thy brother's eye, but considerest not the beam that is in thine own eye?

4. Or how wilt thou say to thy brother, Let me pull out the mote out of thine eye; and, behold, a beam *is* in thine own eye?

5. Thou hypocrite, first cast out the beam out of thine own eye; and then shalt thou see clearly to cast out the mote out of thy brother's eye.

6. Give not that which is holy unto the dogs, neither cast ye your pearls before swine, lest they trample them under their feet, and turn again and rend you.

7. Ask, and it shall be given you; seek, and ye shall find; knock, and it shall be opened unto you:

8. For every one that asketh receiveth; and he that seeketh findeth; and to him that knocketh it shall be opened.

9. Or what man is there of you, whom if his son ask bread, will he give him a stone?

10. Or if he ask a fish, will he give him a serpent?

11. If ye then, being evil, know how to give good gifts unto your children, how much more shall your Father which is in heaven give good things to them that ask him?

12. Therefore all things whatsoever ye would that men should do to you, do ye even so to them: for this is the law and the prophets.

13. Enter ye in at the strait gate: for wide *is* the gate, and broad *is* the way, that leadeth to destruction, and many there be which go in thereat:

14. Because strait *is* the gate, and narrow *is* the way, which leadeth unto life, and few there be that find it.

15. Beware of false prophets, which come to you in sheep's clothing, but inwardly they are ravening wolves.

16. Ye shall know them by their fruits. Do men gather grapes of thorns, or figs of thistles?

17. Even so every good tree bringeth forth good fruit; but a corrupt tree bringeth forth evil fruit.

18. A good tree cannot bring forth evil fruit, neither *can* a corrupt tree bring forth good fruit.

19. Every tree that bringeth not forth good fruit is hewn down, and cast into the fire.

20. Wherefore by their fruits ye shall know them.

21. Not every one that saith unto me, Lord, Lord, shall enter into the kingdom of heaven; but he that doeth the will of my Father which is in heaven.

22. Many will say to me in that day, Lord, Lord, have we not prophesied in thy name? and in thy name have cast out devils? and in thy name done many wonderful works?

23. And then will I profess unto them, I never knew you: depart from me, ye that work iniquity.

24. Therefore whosoever heareth these sayings of mine, and doeth them, I will liken him unto a wise man, which built his house upon a rock:

25. And the rain descended, and the floods came, and the winds blew, and beat upon that house; and it fell not: for it was founded upon a rock.

26. And every one that heareth these sayings of mine, and doeth them not, shall be likened unto a foolish man, which built his house upon the sand:

27. And the rain descended, and the floods came, and the winds blew, and beat upon that house; and it fell: and great was the fall of it.

28. And it came to pass, when Jesus had ended these sayings, the people were astonished at his doctrine:

29. For he taught them as *one* having authority, and not as the scribes.

MATTHEW, CHAPTER 26

1. And it came to pass, when Jesus had finished all these sayings, he said unto his disciples,

2. Ye know that after two days is *the feast of* the passover, and the Son of man is betrayed to be crucified.

3. Then assembled together the chief priests, and the scribes, and the elders of the people, unto the palace of the high priest, who was called Caiaphas,

4. And consulted that they might take Jesus by subtilty, and kill *him*.

5. But they said, Not on the feast *day*, lest there be an uproar among the people.

6. Now when Jesus was in Bethany, in the house of Simon the leper,

7. There came unto him a woman having an alabaster box of very precious ointment, and poured it on his head, as he sat *at meat*.

8. But when his disciples saw *it*, they had indignation, saying, To what purpose *is* this waste?

9. For this ointment might have been sold for much, and given to the poor.

10. When Jesus understood *it*, he said unto them, Why trouble ye the woman? for she hath wrought a good work upon me.

11. For ye have the poor always with you; but me ye have not always.

12. For in that she hath poured this ointment on my body, she did *it* for my burial.

13. Verily I say unto you, Wheresoever this gospel shall be preached in the whole world, *there* shall also this, that this woman hath done, be told for a memorial of her.

14. Then one of the twelve, called Judas Iscariot, went unto the chief priests,

15. And said *unto them*, What will ye give me, and I will deliver him unto you? And they covenanted with him for thirty pieces of silver.

16. And from that time he sought opportunity to betray him.

17. Now the first *day* of the *feast of* unleavened bread the disciples came to Jesus, saying unto him, Where wilt thou that we prepare for thee to eat the passover?

18. And he said, Go into the city to such a man, and say unto him, The Master saith, My time is at hand; I will keep the passover at thy house with my disciples.

19. And the disciples did as Jesus had appointed them; and they made ready the passover.

20. Now when the even was come, he sat down with the twelve.

21. And as they did eat, he said, Verily I say unto you, that one of you shall betray me.

22. And they were exceeding sorrowful, and began every one of them to say unto him, Lord, is it I?

23. And he answered and said, He that dippeth *his* hand with me in the dish, the same shall betray me.

24. The Son of man goeth as it is written of him: but woe unto that man by whom the Son of man is betrayed! it had been good for that man if he had not been born.

25. Then Judas, which betrayed him, answered and said, Master, is it I? He said unto him, Thou hast said.

26. And as they were eating, Jesus took bread, and blessed *it*, and brake *it*, and gave *it* to the disciples, and said, Take, eat; this is my body.

27. And he took the cup, and gave thanks, and gave *it* to them, saying, Drink ye all of it;

28. For this is my blood of the new testament, which is shed for many for the remission of sins.

29. But I say unto you, I will not drink henceforth of this fruit of the vine, until that day when I drink it new with you in my Father's kingdom.

30. And when they had sung an hymn, they went out into the mount of Olives.

31. Then saith Jesus unto them, All ye shall be offended because of me this night: for it is written, I will smite the shepherd, and the sheep of the flock shall be scattered abroad.

32. But after I am risen again, I will go before you into Galilee.

33. Peter answered and said unto him, Though all *men* shall be offended because of thee, *yet* will I never be offended.

34. Jesus said unto him, Verily I say unto thee, That this night, before the cock crow, thou shalt deny me thrice.

35. Peter said unto him, Though I should die with thee, yet will I not deny thee. Likewise also said all the disciples.

36. Then cometh Jesus with them unto a place called Gethsemane, and saith unto the disciples, Sit ye here, while I go and pray yonder.

37. And he took with him Peter and the two sons of Zebedee, and began to be sorrowful and very heavy.

38. Then saith he unto them, My soul is exceeding sorrowful, even unto death: tarry ye here, and watch with me.

39. And he went a little further, and fell on his face, and prayed, saying, O my Father, if it be possible, let this cup pass from me: nevertheless not as I will, but as thou *wilt.*

40. And he cometh unto the disciples, and findeth them asleep, and saith unto Peter, What, could ye not watch with me one hour?

41. Watch and pray, that ye enter not into temptation: the spirit indeed *is* willing, but the flesh *is* weak.

42. He went away again the second time, and prayed, saying, O my Father, if this cup may not pass away from me, except I drink it, thy will be done.

43. And he came and found them asleep again: for their eyes were heavy.

44. And he left them, and went away again, and prayed the third time, saying the same words.

45. Then cometh he to his disciples, and saith unto them, Sleep on now, and take *your* rest: behold, the hour is at hand, and the Son of man is betrayed into the hands of sinners.

46. Rise, let us be going: behold, he is at hand that doth betray me.

47. And while he yet spake, lo, Judas, one of the twelve, came, and with him a great multitude with swords and staves, from the chief priests and elders of the people.

48. Now he that betrayed him gave them a sign, saying, Whomsoever I shall kiss, that same is he: hold him fast.

49. And forthwith he came to Jesus, and said, Hail, master; and kissed him.

50. And Jesus said unto him, Friend, wherefore art thou come? Then came they, and laid hands on Jesus, and took him.

51. And, behold, one of them which were with Jesus stretched out *his* hand, and drew his sword, and struck a servant of the high priest's, and smote off his ear.

52. Then said Jesus unto him, Put up again thy sword into his place: for all they that take the sword shall perish with the sword.

53. Thinkest thou that I cannot now pray to my Father, and he shall presently give me more than twelve legions of angels?

54. But how then shall the scriptures be fulfilled, that thus it must be?

55. In that same hour said Jesus to the multitudes, Are ye come out as against a thief with swords and staves for to take me? I sat daily with you teaching in the temple, and ye laid no hold on me.

56. But all this was done, that the scriptures of the prophets might be fulfilled. Then all the disciples forsook him, and fled.

57. And they that had laid hold on Jesus led *him* away to Caiaphas the high priest, where the scribes and the elders were assembled.

58. But Peter followed him afar off unto the high priest's palace, and went in, and sat with the servants, to see the end.

59. Now the chief priests, and elders, and all the council, sought false witness against Jesus, to put him to death;

60. But found none: yea, though many false witnesses came, *yet* found they none. At the last came two false witnesses,

61. And said, This *fellow* said, I am able to destroy the temple of God, and to build it in three days.

62. And the high priest arose, and said unto him, Answerest thou nothing? what *is it which* these witness against thee?

63. But Jesus held his peace. And the high priest answered and said unto him, I adjure thee by the living God, that thou tell us whether thou be the Christ, the Son of God.

64. Jesus saith unto him, Thou hast said: nevertheless I say unto you, Hereafter shall ye see the Son of man sitting on the right hand of power, and coming in the clouds of heaven.

65. Then the high priest rent his clothes, saying, He hath spoken blasphemy; what further need have we of witnesses? behold, now ye have heard his blasphemy.

66. What think ye? They answered and said, He is guilty of death.

67. Then did they spit in his face, and buffeted him; and others smote *him* with the palms of their hands,

68. Saying, Prophesy unto us, thou Christ, Who is he that smote thee?

69. Now Peter sat without in the palace: and a damsel came unto him, saying, Thou also wast with Jesus of Galilee.

70. But he denied before *them* all, saying, I know not what thou sayest.

71. And when he was gone out into the porch, another *maid* saw him, and said unto them that were there, This *fellow* was also with Jesus of Nazareth.

72. And again he denied with an oath, I do not know the man.

73. And after a while came unto *him* they that stood by, and said to Peter, Surely thou also art *one* of them; for thy speech bewrayeth thee.

74. Then began he to curse and to swear, *saying*, I know not the man. And immediately the cock crew.

75. And Peter remembered the word of Jesus, which said unto him, Before the cock crow, thou shalt deny me thrice. And he went out, and wept bitterly.

MATTHEW, CHAPTER 27

1. When the morning was come, all the chief priests and elders of the people took counsel against Jesus to put him to death:

2. And when they had bound him, they led *him* away, and delivered him to Pontius Pilate the governor.

3. Then Judas, which had betrayed him, when he saw that he was condemned, repented himself, and brought again the thirty pieces of silver to the chief priests and elders,

4. Saying, I have sinned in that I have betrayed the innocent blood. And they said, What *is that* to us? see thou *to that*.

5. And he cast down the pieces of silver in the temple, and departed, and went and hanged himself.

6. And the chief priests took the silver pieces, and said, It is not lawful for to put them into the treasury, because it is the price of blood.

7. And they took counsel, and bought with them the potter's field, to bury strangers in.

8. Wherefore that field was called, The field of blood, unto this day.

9. Then was fulfilled that which was spoken by Jeremy the prophet, saying, And they took the thirty pieces of silver, the price of him that was valued, whom they of the children of Israel did value;

10. And gave them for the potter's field, as the Lord appointed me.

11. And Jesus stood before the governor: and the governor asked him, saying, Art thou the King of the Jews? And Jesus said unto him, Thou sayest.

12. And when he was accused of the chief priests and elders, he answered nothing.

13. Then said Pilate unto him, Hearest thou not how many things they witness against thee?

14. And he answered him to never a word; insomuch that the governor marvelled greatly.

15. Now at *that* feast the governor was wont to release unto the people a prisoner, whom they would.

16. And they had then a notable prisoner, called Barabbas.

17. Therefore when they were gathered together, Pilate said unto them, Whom will ye that I release unto you? Barabbas, or Jesus which is called Christ?

18. For he knew that for envy they had delivered him.

19. When he was set down on the judgment seat, his wife sent unto him, saying, Have thou nothing to do with that just man: for I have suffered many things this day in a dream because of him.

20. But the chief priests and elders persuaded the multitude that they should ask Barabbas, and destroy Jesus.

21. The governor answered and said unto them, Whether of the twain will ye that I release unto you? They said, Barabbas.

22. Pilate saith unto them, What shall I do then with Jesus which is called Christ? *They* all say unto him, Let him be crucified.

23. And the governor said, Why, what evil hath he done? But they cried out the more, saying, Let him be crucified.

24. When Pilate saw that he could prevail nothing, but *that* rather a tumult was made, he took water, and washed *his* hands before the multitude, saying, I am innocent of the blood of this just person: see ye *to it*.

25. Then answered all the people, and said, His blood *be* on us, and on our children.

26. Then released he Barabbas unto them: and when he had scourged Jesus, he delivered *him* to be crucified.

27. Then the soldiers of the governor took Jesus into the common hall, and gathered unto him the whole band *of soldiers*.

28. And they stripped him, and put on him a scarlet robe.

29. And when they had platted a crown of thorns, they put *it* upon his head, and a reed in his right hand: and they bowed the knee before him, and mocked him, saying, Hail, King of the Jews!

30. And they spit upon him, and took the reed, and smote him on the head.

31. And after that they had mocked him, they took the robe off from him, and put his own raiment on him, and led him away to crucify *him*.

32. And as they came out, they found a man of Cyrene, Simon by name: him they compelled to bear his cross.

33. And when they were come unto a place called Golgotha, that is to say, a place of a skull,

34. They gave him vinegar to drink mingled with gall: and when he had tasted *thereof*, he would not drink.

35. And they crucified him, and parted his garments, casting lots: that it might be fulfilled which was spoken by the prophet, They parted my garments among them, and upon my vesture did they cast lots.

36. And sitting down they watched him there;

37. And set up over his head his accusation written, THIS IS JESUS THE KING OF THE JEWS.

38. Then were there two thieves crucified with him, one on the right hand, and another on the left.

39. And they that passed by reviled him, wagging their heads,

40. And saying, Thou that destroyest the temple, and buildest *it* in three days, save thyself. If thou be the Son of God, come down from the cross.

41. Likewise also the chief priests mocking *him*, with the scribes and elders, said,

42. He saved others; himself he cannot save. If he be the King of Israel, let him now come down from the cross, and we will believe him.

43. He trusted in God; let him deliver him now, if he will have him: for he said, I am the Son of God.

44. The thieves also, which were crucified with him, cast the same in his teeth.

45. Now from the sixth hour there was darkness over all the land unto the ninth hour.

46. And about the ninth hour Jesus cried with a loud voice, saying, Eli, Eli, lama sabachthani? that is to say, My God, my God, why hast thou forsaken me?

47. Some of them that stood there, when they heard *that*, said, This *man* calleth for Elias.

48. And straightway one of them ran, and took a spunge, and filled *it* with vinegar, and put *it* on a reed, and gave him to drink.

49. The rest said, Let be, let us see whether Elias will come to save him.

50. Jesus, when he had cried again with a loud voice, yielded up the ghost.

51. And, behold, the veil of the temple was rent in twain from the top to the bottom; and the earth did quake, and the rocks rent;

52. And the graves were opened; and many bodies of the saints which slept arose,

53. And came out of the graves after his resurrection, and went into the holy city, and appeared unto many.

54. Now when the centurion, and they that were with him, watching Jesus, saw the earthquake, and those things that were done, they feared greatly, saying, Truly this was the Son of God.

55. And many women were there beholding afar off, which followed Jesus from Galilee, ministering unto him:

56. Among which was Mary Magdalene, and Mary the mother of James and Joses, and the mother of Zebedee's children.

57. When the even was come, there came a rich man of Arimathaea, named Joseph, who also himself was Jesus' disciple:

58. He went to Pilate, and begged the body of Jesus. Then Pilate commanded the body to be delivered.

59. And when Joseph had taken the body, he wrapped it in a clean linen cloth,

60. And laid it in his own new tomb, which he had hewn out in the rock: and he rolled a great stone to the door of the sepulchre, and departed.

61. And there was Mary Magdalene, and the other Mary, sitting over against the sepulchre.

62. Now the next day, that followed the day of the preparation, the chief priests and Pharisees came together unto Pilate,

63. Saying, Sir, we remember that that deceiver said, while he was yet alive, After three days I will rise again.

64. Command therefore that the sepulchre be made sure until the third day, lest his disciples come by night, and steal him away, and say unto the people, He is risen from the dead: so the last error shall be worse than the first.

65. Pilate said unto them, Ye have a watch: go your way, make *it* as sure as ye can.

66. So they went, and made the sepulchre sure, sealing the stone, and setting a watch.

MATTHEW, CHAPTER 28

1. In the end of the sabbath, as it began to dawn toward the first *day* of the week, came Mary Magdalene and the other Mary to see the sepulchre.

2. And, behold, there was a great earthquake: for the angel of the Lord descended from heaven, and came and rolled back the stone from the door, and sat upon it.

3. His countenance was like lightning, and his raiment white as snow:

4. And for fear of him the keepers did shake, and became as dead *men*.

5. And the angel answered and said unto the women, Fear not ye: for I know that ye seek Jesus, which was crucified.

6. He is not here: for he is risen, as he said. Come, see the place where the Lord lay.

7. And go quickly, and tell his disciples that he is risen from the dead; and, behold, he goeth before you into Galilee; there shall ye see him: lo, I have told you.

8. And they departed quickly from the sepulchre with fear and great joy; and did run to bring his disciples word.

9. And as they went to tell his disciples, behold, Jesus met them, saying, All hail. And they came and held him by the feet, and worshipped him.

10. Then said Jesus unto them, Be not afraid: go tell my brethren that they go into Galilee, and there shall they see me.

11. Now when they were going, behold, some of the watch came into the city, and shewed unto the chief priests all the things that were done.

12. And when they were assembled with the elders, and had taken counsel, they gave large money unto the soldiers,

13. Saying, Say ye, His disciples came by night, and stole him *away* while we slept.

14. And if this come to the governor's ears, we will persuade him, and secure you.

15. So they took the money, and did as they were taught: and this saying is commonly reported among the Jews until this day.

16. Then the eleven disciples went away into Galilee, into a mountain where Jesus had appointed them.

17. And when they saw him, they worshipped him: but some doubted.

18. And Jesus came and spake unto them, saying, All power is given unto me in heaven and in earth.

19. Go ye therefore, and teach all nations, baptizing them in the name of the Father, and of the Son, and of the Holy Ghost:

20. Teaching them to observe all things whatsoever I have commanded you: and, lo, I am with you alway, *even* unto the end of the world. Amen.

DISCUSSION QUESTIONS

1. According to the Book of *Luke*, what were the circumstances surrounding the birth of Jesus of Nazareth?

2. What are the implications of the baptism episode in *Mark*? Why are the apostles called immediately afterward?

3. What kind of ethical system is presented in the Sermon on the Mount? How does it compare with other ethical systems you have studied?

4. Why does Jesus begin offering a series of parables at the end of the Sermon on the Mount? What are the effects of this kind of teaching and speaking?

5. Describe the events surrounding the Crucifixion in *Matthew*. How does it compare with other versions of the story that you have heard or read?

6. How would you characterize the narrative voice present in the Gospels? How does it compare with the voice encountered in the selections from the Hebrew Bible?

Unit Two

THE MIDDLE AGES

GENERAL INTRODUCTION

The Middle Ages span the period between the Fall of the Roman Empire (476 A.D.) and the beginning of the Renaissance (the early 1400s in Italy, the early 1500s farther north). This time span has been called the Middle Ages because it falls between the Classical Age of Greece and Rome and the Renaissance, two periods noted for extraordinary contributions to literature, art, architecture, and philosophy. The Early Middle Ages, roughly 476–800 A.D., have sometimes been referred to as the Dark Ages because during this time, Europe was ravaged by warring tribal kingdoms and much of classical culture was lost and forgotten for centuries. But many cultural historians shun the "Dark Ages" label, since the early centuries of the Middle Ages produced great works of Byzantine art and architecture, influential European epic tales, elaborately crafted illuminated manuscripts, and the Koran (the scripture of Islam). The Early Middle Ages were certainly not devoid of culture, yet in comparing these years on a cultural time line to the Classical Age or the Renaissance, the relative dearth of cultural activity becomes obvious.

The invasion of the Roman Empire by northern tribes destroyed political stability and resulted in the loss of much of the knowledge and texts that had been produced in ancient Greece and Rome. Fortunately, the Eastern Roman Empire, centered in Constantinople (formerly Byzantium and now Istanbul) and removed from the chaos of western Europe, helped to preserve classical culture, even when it passed beyond the knowledge of most Europeans. Isolated monasteries in Ireland, England, and across Europe also helped to preserve great works

of antiquity until they were rediscovered and more widely disseminated in the late 14th century, thereby contributing to the beginning of the Renaissance.

The rise of Christianity and the growing power of the Catholic Church helped to unify western Europe politically and culturally after centuries of chaos. With the crowning of Charlemagne as emperor of the Romans in 800 A.D., and later the crowning of Otto the Great as the first Holy Roman Emperor in 962, a new age of cultural flourishing began, distinct from the previous Classical Age and the Renaissance by the centrality of the Church in politics and the arts. Charlemagne's efforts to improve the education of the clergy, encourage the copying of texts, and standardize the Catholic liturgy (the words used in church services) played a key role in advancing the domination of medieval culture by the Catholic Church. In many ways, the Middle Ages could also be called the Age of Religion, since most of western European art, architecture, literature, and written music of the period focused on Christianity (even Chaucer's bawdy tales have a Christian frame), and the period gave rise to the newest world religion, Islam.

In spite of the relative stability brought about by the rise of Catholicism, for most of the first half of the Middle Ages, feudalism dominated. Feudalism is a system in which political and economic authority centered on local lords and their castles instead of on a broader reaching, more coherent kingdom or government. Not until the 11th century (the High Middle Ages) did towns begin to be a dominant economic and social force in European life. Agricultural improvements and an increase in trading led to the growth of towns and the formation of a new middle class of merchants and artisans, whose economic power challenged the old feudal system. The Crusades, wars in which Europeans attempted to gain back holy lands from Muslims and Jews, contributed to the decline of feudalism, since many lords gave their lives and their property to support what they felt was a noble cause. The Crusades, lasting from the 11th to the 13th centuries, took their toll on nobility and commoners alike, although some cities, particularly in Italy, benefited financially from the increased travel and trade brought about by the wars.

The status of women improved somewhat during the Crusades, since women were often left in charge of managing estates and other work that had traditionally been allocated to men, many of whom were now absent for years fighting in distant lands. Also enhancing the status of women at this time was the courtly love tradition, which extended reverence for the Virgin Mother to all women, but particularly aristocratic women. In literature, and presumably in daily court behavior, women were treated with great respect and adulation. Such behavior is reflected in medieval romances and lays, such as Marie de France's "Eliduc" (see Selected Readings), in which the knight demonstrates his honor not only in battle, but also by worshipping his lady and exercising restraint in their physical relationship.

While the Crusades were finally over by the 1300s, Europe continued to face numerous crises during this century as famine and plague devastated the continent for decades. Bubonic plague, or the Black Death, struck Italy in 1347 and spread throughout Europe for four years. Another outbreak occurred in 1388–1390. It is estimated that a third of the European population died from the Black Death during this time, making it the worst outbreak of disease in history. The terror and grief brought about by bubonic plague heightened the religious devotion of many, turning some into religious fanatics. Self-flagellators walked from town to town whipping themselves in penance for their sins, hoping to deflect the anger of God, whom they thought had inflicted the plague on them as a punishment. Others went to the opposite extreme and abandoned faith, living only for immediate sensual gratification. Adding to the devastation of famine and plague was the Hundred Years' War between England and France (1337–1453), in which Joan of Arc played a decisive role in spurring the French on to victory. Despite the multiple causes of turmoil—or perhaps because of them—this period gave rise to some of the greatest authors of medieval literature, including Chaucer, the Gawain poet, Petrarch, and Boccaccio (who used the bubonic plague as a backdrop to his *Decameron,* a series of tales bound by a narrative framework). By the end of the 14th century, as plagues abated and classical texts began to be studied more widely, Europe was leaving behind the vestiges of the Middle Ages and moving into the Renaissance.

LITERATURE

Heroic epics of kings, knights, battles, and betrayals dominated the literature of the early Middle Ages. These epic tales were passed along orally for centuries before being written down. The Irish Ulster and Leinster cycles are among the earliest epics, the Ulster originating in the first century (although not recorded until 1100 A.D.) and the Leinster in the third century (with written texts dating back to 700 A.D.). While the Ulster cycle focuses on a fictional figure named Cuchulainn with seven eyes, fourteen fingers, and fourteen toes, the Leinster cycle narrates the romantic and heroic exploits of an actual third-century lord named Finn. The *Mabinogion* is a series of pre-Christian Welsh myths, dating from the early centuries of the first millennium; it is one of the first sources of Arthurian legends. *Beowulf* is one of the most famous medieval epics and the only one to be written down in the Early Middle Ages (the only extant manuscript dates from the late 10th century). Written in unrhymed verse with four accents per line, it chronicles the adventures of the hero, Beowulf, who demonstrates his bravery and honor by attacking a monster that has terrorized the hall of the Danish king Hrothgar every night, killing his warriors. The French epic *Song of Roland* (written in approximately 1150), about the death in battle of Charlemagne's nephew Roland, and the German epic *Nibelungenlied* (dating from the sixth century, but written between 1195 and 1205), focus on similar heroic virtues, although the *Nibelungenlied* is grimmer and more savage in its details.

Marie de France, writing in the late 12th century, produced narratives that combine elements of heroic literature with a didactic Christian element. The two strains can clearly be seen in "Eliduc" (see Selected Readings), in which the hero demonstrates prowess in battle, in romance, and ultimately in religious devotion as well. More exclusively religious in focus are the works of two German nuns, Hroswitha (935–1001), who wrote religious poems, epics and plays, and Hildegard of Bingen (1098–1179), who wrote the lives of the saints, narratives of her mystical visions, religious lyrics, and musical compositions (see Selected Readings).

The literature of the High and Late Middle Ages continued to reflect the influence of Christianity. Romances, narrative poems, mystery plays, morality plays, and ballads are the most common forms of literature from this period. Dante's *Divine Comedy* is one of the most influential works of literature in Western culture, and its tour of hell, purgatory, and heaven clearly reflects the Christian ideals of the times (see Selected Readings). Virgil guides the poet through hell and purgatory, while Beatrice, who serves as an intermediary between Dante and divine grace, guides him through heaven. Dante's masterpiece is a "comedy" in the broadest sense of the term, meaning a literary work in which the protagonist ultimately transcends his troubles (the opposite movement from tragedy). Dante's epic reveals how Christians partake in a divine comedy, not a tragedy, because they are promised salvation from their sins through faith.

While Petrarch lived in the Middle Ages (1304–1374), and his poetry shares many similarities with that of his fellow countryman Dante, his works are in many ways precursors to Renaissance poetry. The unconsummated love he expresses for his idol Laura reflects medieval courtly love traditions, yet Petrarch focuses more on himself and his writings than was customary for poets in the Middle Ages, partly due to his study of classical texts such as Cicero's *Pro Archia*, which glorifies the role of the artist. As a scholar of the classics, Petrarch helped bring forgotten Latin texts to light, thereby aiding in the advent of the Renaissance. In addition, he perfected what has come to be called in his honor the Petrarchan or Italian sonnet, a 14-line poem divided into two quatrains and two tercets (see Selected Readings). This form greatly influenced the famous sonnets of the English Renaissance such as Shakespeare's, and, in fact, the sonnet became the preeminent poetic form of the Renaissance.

Chaucer's *Canterbury Tales*, one of the most famous works of the Middle Ages, contains much frivolous and bawdy subject matter and therefore might not seem to fit the religious focus of the age; it has, however, a religious framework, involving a diverse group of travelers on a religious pilgrimage to the shrine of St. Thomas à Becket in Canterbury. Chaucer concludes the work with a "Retraction," in which he asks for forgiveness for his sins, takes the blame for any faults in his tales, and credits any worth in them to Jesus. The framework, therefore, along with parts of many of the stories, reinforce the *Canterbury Tales*' connection to Christian concerns. Even the very earthy and sensuous Wife of Bath, whose tale is included in this unit, makes numerous displays of her religious devotion, although her chief concerns seem to fall elsewhere. Chaucer tips his hat to religion, but his real interest seems to be in capturing the fundamental humanness and uniqueness of his characters. His Wife of Bath, for instance, defies simplistic labels such as good or bad, moral or immoral—she is, almost literally, a fully fleshed-out woman, who makes, in this 14th century work, one of the most memorable feminist statements in the history of literature. The bawdiness of Chaucer's tales, a characteristic that Shakespeare later imitated, simultaneously creates humor and humanness in a way that prefigures the complex characterizations of the novel form.

Mystery plays and morality plays dominated the dramatic arts of the latter half of the Middle Ages. Mystery plays dramatize specific biblical events such as the birth of Christ, while morality plays allegorize the fundamental moral struggles of all humans. For example, *Everyman*, an anonymous morality play written at the cusp of the Middle Ages, depicts the protagonist, Everyman (a character who symbolizes all human beings) as he faces death and learns that most of the people and things he valued in life can't help him in his final crisis (see Selected Readings). Because the characters in morality plays represent generalized traits, attributes, or people such as "Good Deeds" or "Knowledge," they are by necessity uncomplicated and two-dimensional. Yet the best of these plays still produce powerful dramatic moments because of the starkness and universality of their life and death struggles.

Sir Gawain and the Green Knight, an Arthurian romance written by an anonymous poet referred to as the Gawain poet (or the Pearl poet, after another one of his works), develops themes reminiscent of the heroic tales of the early Middle Ages such as the importance of bravery and honor, but yokes them to Christian themes like man's inherently sinful nature and need of salvation. Sir Thomas Malory's *Morte Darthur*, written at the tail end of the Middle Ages, also returns to Arthurian legends, emphasizing both the honor and the human weaknesses of the knights. Malory's focus on the humanity of the characters and his ability to create naturalistic dialogue prefigures, as does Chaucer, the narrative techniques that would flourish in the 18th and 19th centuries, the Golden Age of the Novel.

THE VISUAL ARTS

As with medieval literature, the art and architecture of the period reflect the dominance of Christianity in western culture during the Middle Ages. Byzantine mosaics, illuminated manuscripts, Romanesque and Gothic cathedrals, stained glass, and religious paintings form the highlights of medieval artistry. These art forms share not only a focus on religion, but also an emphasis on verticality—the towering spires of Gothic cathedrals, the elongated figures in a stained-glass window, or the attenuated forms in a tempera painting of the Madonna and Child. All force the eye upward as opposed to horizontally. Medieval philosophy shunned earthly, corporeal matters as being low, filthy, degrading, and sinful, and theologians encouraged people to look to God for answers instead of focusing on the material world; the arts reflect this worldview in their insistent focus on vertical lines that point heavenward.

Some of the earliest masterpieces of the Middle Ages were the Byzantine mosaics in cathedrals in the

Figure 2-A Theodora and here attendants, mosaic.

capital of the Eastern Roman empire, Constantinople. After the fall of Rome, Byzantium became the center of culture for several centuries, as eastern Europe was not affected by tribal warfare as much as the west. Byzantine mosaics, created from bits of stone, glass, or tile, set the standard for iconic images for centuries. The figures in these mosaics are elongated and insubstantial, underscoring the medieval distaste for the body. The faces share the same masklike features—most peer straight ahead with large, dark eyes, long noses, and little or no expression. The lack of distinguishing details in these images also underscores the humbleness and insignificance of human beings in contrast with the glories of God (see Figure 2-A). Hagia Sophia (532–37 A.D.), the great cathedral of Constantinople, is home to some of the most masterful of the eastern mosaics, and is itself a masterpiece of Byzantine architecture. With its elevated central dome pierced by 40 windows, the cathedral shares the emphasis on verticality and light that characterizes later Gothic architecture.

In western Europe, the first major architectural innovations were Romanesque churches and cathedrals. The Romanesque style derives its name from its use of the rounded arches and vaulted ceilings of Roman architecture. Romanesque cathedrals were designed in the shape of a cross. The nave, the longest arm of the cross, and the one that extended from the front of the cathedral to the altar area in back, was often covered by barrel vaulting, a ceiling composed of a series of arches, as is the case in Saint-Sernin in Toulouse (see Figure 2-B). While Romanesque cathedrals clearly emphasize verticality when compared arch), ribbed groin vaulting, and flying buttresses (see Figure 2-C). Ribbed groin vaulting involved crossing the main arch with diagonal arches and covering the seams of the arches in stone. Flying buttresses are supports on the exterior of the church that extend from the ground to the high vaults. All three innovations allow for a more efficient support of weight, which meant that the cathedrals could reach greater heights, and columns could be thinner and more windows could be opened up, thereby letting in more light. The end result is an awe-inspiring structure of magnificent proportions, filled with light, and with every detail designed to evoke a sense of reverence, spirituality, and personal humility.

Gothic cathedrals included more extensive interior and exterior adornments such as statues and stained glass than their Romanesque counterparts,. Statues were sometimes sculpted as parts of columns and were often elongated, reinforcing the aesthetic emphasis on verticality. Most statues celebrated Mary and Jesus, the apostles, and the saints, but stone-carved gargoyles, usually situated around the outer perimeter of roofs, took the shape of ghouls, animals, and mythological creatures. They serve as drain spouts, so that on rainy days they seem to spit or vomit on those below. Some art historians feel that gargoyles were placed on medieval cathedrals to frighten away evil spirits; others argue that they demonstrate that even grotesque creatures can be subsumed in God's plan and have a role to play in a structure built to show reverence to God.

Almost as inspiring as the architecture of Gothic cathedrals are the stained glass windows executed to flood them with prismatic light, symbolizing the "light" given to humankind by the word of God. Stained glass images, made from bits of colored glass held together by lead, usually depicted biblical scenes, often from the life of Jesus. Many of these would be framed by an arched window, but rose windows followed a symmetrical circle and petal-shaped design, hence the name (see Figure 2-D).

Illuminated manuscripts are one of the distinctive artistic contributions of the Middle Ages. Until the invention of the printing press around 1450,

Figure 2-B The Basilica of Saint-Senin, Toulouse.

to horizontally oriented classical Greek temples, they seem almost stunted in comparison to the Gothic structures that succeeded them. Around 1140, an abbot named Suger (pronounced Soo-zhay) brought about the initial innovations of Gothic architecture in his plans for renovating Saint-Denis, an abbey north of Paris. In his records, Suger emphasizes that the innovations should enhance the structure's glorification of God by increasing both height and light. The innovations that helped to bring about these goals are the pointed arch (called a Gothic

Figure 2-C The Abbey of Saint-Denis.

Cross pages were devoted entirely to designs (see Figure 2-E). As with the Gothic cathedrals, illuminated manuscripts demonstrated reverence for God through the elaborateness of the designs and the time and devotion it took to execute them.

Similarly, paintings in the Middle Ages demonstrated and inspired religious feelings. Since this was the sole purpose of medieval art, paintings were not supposed to glorify the painter; therefore, many works of art from this time period are anonymous until the later Middle Ages, when Cimabue and Giotto, among others, made their mark. Because the artist was at best of secondary importance, self-portraits were unheard of; biblical figures and stories from saints' lives dominate the subject matter of medieval paintings. Gothic altar paintings were done mostly on wood with tempera, an egg-based paint. The works of Cimabue, a Florentine artist who lived approximately between 1250–1300, show the continuing influence of Byzantine icons, with their elongated, flat figures, masklike faces, and lack of perspective (see Figure 2-F). Because the body was seen as lowly and inherently sinful, painters did not attempt to recreate human forms in realistic detail, as had classical Greek and Roman sculptors. Instead, everything about the image, from the attenuation of the forms to the gold-leaf halos and backgrounds, was designed to express reverence and evoke awe.

Giotto (1267?–1336/1337), a pupil of Cimabue, developed the most individualistic style of any major medieval painter. While the Byzantine influence can certainly be seen in his *Madonna Enthroned*, Giotto's faces usually appear more lifelike and expressive, and the forms seem more three-dimensional and less elongated. The sophisticated composition

books had to be copied by hand. Prayer books and copies of the Bible were ornamented with elaborate knot-like designs, with the initial letter of a chapter written and designed to take up almost half a page.

of his *Lamentation over the Body of Jesus* (see Figure 2-G), draws the viewer's eye to the figures of Mary and Christ and creates a more realistic sense of depth than was present in most medieval paintings. Although linear perspective had not yet been developed, so the proportional relationship between figures in the foreground and the background is not exact, Giotto makes more of an effort to create the illusion of depth than any of his predecessors and also uses more realistic colors and less gold leaf, thereby prefiguring Renaissance painting.

Figure 2-E Cross-page from The Lindisfarne gospel.

Figure 2-D Rose window, Basilica of Saint-Remi, Reims.

Figure 2-F The Virgin and Child enthroned with two angels.

Figure 2-G Giotto's *Lamentation over the Body of Jesus.*

THE KORAN

The *Koran* (also *Qur'an*, meaning "the Recital") is the holy book of Islam. According to Muslims, Muhammad received the Koran directly as a divine revelation from the Angel Gabriel, but it is unclear whether or not Muhammad wrote down the revelation himself or whether one or more of his followers did. The book records Muhammad's teaching between the years 610 and 632 A.D. and is written in poetic Arabic prose. It contains 114 chapters, called *surahs*, some of which present ethical and practical advice, while others are hymns in praise of Allah. In the Koran, the *surahs* are organized by length, with the longest appearing first and the shortest appearing last. In most cases, the speaker is God. Included below are four complete *surahs*: "Jonah" (*Surah* 10), which contrasts believers and nonbelievers and presents a brief recounting of the stories of Noah, Moses, and Jonah; "Mary" (*Surah* 19), which conveys the story of Jesus' conception and birth; "The Merciful" (*Surah* 55), which is a poetic prayer of praise (similar to the biblical *Psalms*); and "Oneness' (*Surah* 112), which is a brief pronouncement about the nature of God. While the *Koran* views biblical figures such as Abraham, Moses, and Jesus as prophets, it is clear that there is but one God, Allah, and not a trinity, such as the Father, Son, and Holy Spirit of many Christian denominations.

SURA X.-JONAH, PEACE BE ON HIM! [LXXXIV.]

MECCA.-109 Verses

In the Name of God, the Compassionate, the Merciful

ELIF. LAM. RA.[1] These are the signs of the wise Book!

A matter of wonderment is it to the men of Mecca, that to a person among themselves We revealed, "Bear warnings to the people: and, to those who believe, bear the good tidings that they shall have with their Lord the precedence merited by their sincerity." The unbelievers say, "Verily this is a manifest sorcerer."

Verily your Lord is God who hath made the Heavens and the Earth in six days-then mounted his throne to rule all things: None can intercede with him till after his permission: This is God your Lord: therefore serve him: Will ye not reflect?

Unto Him shall ye return, all together: the promise of God is sure: He produceth a creature, then causeth it to return again-that he may reward those who believe and do the things that are right, with equity: but as for the infidels!-for them the draught that boileth and an afflictive torment-because they have not believed.

It is He who hath appointed the sun for brightness, and the moon for a light, and hath ordained her stations that ye may learn the number of years and the reckoning of time. God hath not created all this but for the truth.[2] He maketh his signs clear to those who understand.

Verily, in the alternations of night and of day, and in all that God hath created in the Heavens and in the Earth are signs to those who fear Him.

Verily, they who hope not to meet Us, and find their satisfaction in this world's life, and rest on it, and who of our signs are heedless;-

These! their abode the fire, in recompense of their deeds!

But they who believe and do the things that are right, shall their Lord direct aright because of their faith. Rivers shall flow at their feet in gardens of delight:

Their cry therein, "Glory be to thee, O God!" and their salutation therein,

"Peace!"

And the close of their cry, "Praise be to God, Lord, of all creatures!"

Should God hasten evil on men as they fain would hasten their good, then were their end decreed! So leave we those who hope not to meet Us, bewildered in their error.

When trouble toucheth a man, he crieth to us, on his side, or sitting, or standing; and when we withdraw his trouble from him, he passeth on as though he had not called on us against the trouble which touched him! Thus are the deeds of transgressors pre-arranged for them.

And of old destroyed we generations before you, when they had acted wickedly, and their Apostles had come to them with clear tokens of their mission, and they would not believe:-thus reward we the wicked.

Then we caused you to succeed them on the earth, that we might see how ye would act.

But when our clear signs are recited to them, they who look not forward to meet Us, say, "Bring a different Koran from this, or make some change in it." SAY: It is not for me to change it as mine own soul prompteth. I follow only what is revealed to me: verily, I fear, if I rebel against my Lord, the punishment of a great day.

SAY: Had God so pleased, I had not recited it to you, neither had I taught it to you. Already have I dwelt among you for years, ere it was revealed to me. Understand ye not?

And who is more unjust than he who coineth a lie against God, or treateth his signs as lies? Surely the wicked shall not prosper!

And they worship beside God, what cannot hurt or help them; and say, "These are our advocates with God!" SAY: Will ye inform God of aught in the Heavens and in the Earth which he knoweth not? Praise be to Him! High be He exalted above the deities they join with Him!

Men were of one religion only:[3] then they fell to variance: and had not a decree (of respite) previously gone forth from thy Lord, their differences had surely been decided between them!

They say: "Unless a sign be sent down to him from his Lord. ..." But SAY: The hidden is only with God: wait therefore: I truly will be with you among those who wait.

And when after a trouble which you befallen them,[4] we caused this people to taste of mercy, lo! a plot on their part against our signs! SAY: Swifter to plot is God! Verily, our messengers note down your plottings.

He it is who enableth you to travel by land and sea, so that ye go on board of ships-which sail on with them, with favouring breeze in which they rejoice. But if a tempestuous gale overtake them, and the billow come on them from every side, and they think that they are encompassed therewith, they call on God, professing sincere religion:-"Wouldst thou but

rescue us from this, then will we indeed be of the thankful."

But when we have rescued them, lo! they commit unrighteous excesses on the earth! O men! assuredly your self-injuring excess is only an enjoyment of this life present: soon ye return to us: and we will let you know what ye have done!

Verily, this present life is like the water which we send down from Heaven, and the produce of the earth, of which men and cattle eat, is mingled with it, till the earth hath received its golden raiment, and is decked out: and they who dwell on it deem that they have power over it! but, Our behest cometh to it by night or by day, and we make it as if it had been mown, as if it had not teemed only yesterday! Thus make we our signs clear to those who consider.

And God calleth to the abode of peace;[5] and He guideth whom He will into the right way.

Goodness[6] itself and an increase of it for those who do good! neither blackness nor shame shall cover their faces! These shall be the inmates of Paradise, therein shall they abide for ever.

And as for those who have wrought out evil, their recompense shall be evil of like degree, and shame shall cover them-no protector shall they have against God: as though their faces were darkened with deep murk of night! These shall be inmates of the fire: therein they shall abide for ever.

And on that day will we gather them all together: then will we say to those who added gods to God, "To your place, ye and those added gods of yours!" Then we will separate between them: and those their gods shall say, "Ye served us not:[7]

And God is a sufficient witness between us and you: we cared not aught for your worship."

There shall every soul make proof of what itself shall have sent on before, and they shall be brought back to God, their true lord, and the deities of their own devising shall vanish from them.

SAY: Who supplieth you from the Heaven and the Earth? Who hath power over hearing and sight? And who bringeth forth the living from the dead, and bringeth forth the dead from the living? And who ruleth all things? They will surely say, "God:" then SAY: "What! will ye not therefore fear him?

This God then is your true Lord: and when the truth is gone, what remaineth but error? How then are ye so perverted?

Thus is the word of thy Lord made good on the wicked, that they shall not believe.

SAY: Is there any of the gods whom ye add to God who produceth a creature, then causeth it to return to him? SAY: God produceth a creature, then causeth it to return to Him: How therefore are ye turned aside?

SAY: Is there any of the gods ye add to God who guideth into the truth? SAY:

God guideth into the truth. Is He then who guideth into the truth the more worthy to be followed, or he who guideth not unless he be himself guided?

What then hath befallen you that ye so judge?

And most of them follow only a conceit:-But a conceit attaineth to nought of truth! Verily God knoweth what they say.

Moreover this Koran could not have been devised by any but God: but it confirmeth what was revealed before it, and is a clearing up of the Scriptures-there is no doubt thereof-from the Lord of all creatures.

Do they say, "He hath devised it himself?" SAY: Then bring a Sura like it; and call on whom ye can beside God, if ye speak truth.

But that which they embrace not in their knowledge have they charged with falsehood, though the explanation of it had not yet been given them. So those who were before them brought charges of imposture: But see what was the end of the unjust!

And some of them believe in it, and some of them believe not in it. But thy

Lord well knoweth the transgressors.

And if they charge thee with imposture, then SAY: My work for me, and your work for you! Ye are clear of that which I do, and I am clear of that which ye do.

And some of them lend a ready ear to thee: But wilt thou make the deaf to hear even though they understand not?

And some of them look at thee: But wilt thou guide the blind even though they see not?

Verily, God will not wrong men in aught, but men will wrong themselves.

Moreover, on that day, He will gather them all together: They shall seem as though they had waited but an hour of the day! They shall recognise one another! Now perish they who denied the meeting with God, and were not guided aright!

Whether we cause thee to see some of our menaces against them fulfilled, or whether we first take thee to Ourself,[8] to us do they return. Then shall God bear witness of what they do.

And every people hath had its apostle.[9] And when their apostle came, a rightful decision took place between them, and they were not wronged.

Yet they say, "When will this menace be made good? Tell us if ye speak truly."

SAY: I have no power over my own weal or woe, but as God pleaseth. Every people hath its time: when their time is come, they shall neither retard nor advance it an hour.
SAY: How think ye? if God's punishment came on you by night or by day, what portion of it would the wicked desire to hasten on?

When it falleth on you, will ye believe it then? Yes! ye will believe it then. Yet did ye challenge its speedy coming.

Then shall it be said to the transgressors, "Taste ye the punishment of eternity! Shall ye be rewarded but as ye have wrought?"

They will desire thee to inform them whether this be true? SAY: Yes! by my Lord it is the truth: and it is not ye who can weaken Him.

And every soul that hath sinned, if it possessed all that is on earth, would assuredly ransom itself therewith; and they will proclaim their repentance when they have seen the punishment: and there shall be a rightful decision between them, and they shall not be unjustly dealt with.

Is not whatever is in the Heavens and the Earth God's? Is not then the promise of God true? Yet most of them know it not.

He maketh alive and He causeth to die, and to Him shall ye return.

O men! now hath a warning come to you from your Lord, and a medicine for what is in your breasts, and a guidance and a mercy to believers.

SAY: Through the grace of God and his mercy! and in this therefore let them rejoice: better is this than all ye amass.

SAY: What think ye? of what God hath sent down to you for food, have ye made unlawful and lawful? SAY: Hath God permitted you? or invent ye on the part of God?

But what on the day of Resurrection will be the thought of those who invent a lie on the part of God? Truly God is full of bounties to man; but most of them give not thanks.

Thou shalt not be employed in affairs, nor shalt thou read a text out of the Koran, nor shall ye work any work, but we will be witnesses over you when ye are engaged therein: and not the weight of an atom on Earth or in Heaven escapeth thy Lord; nor is there aught that is less than this or greater, but it is in the perspicuous Book.

Are not the friends of God, those on whom no fear shall come, nor shall they be put to grief?

They who believe and fear God-

For them are good tidings in this life, and in the next! There is no change in the words of God! This, the great felicity!

And let not their discourse grieve thee: for all might is God's: the Hearer, the Knower, He!

Is not whoever is in the Heavens and the Earth subject to God? What then do they follow who, beside God, call upon deities they have joined with Him? They follow but a conceit, and they are but liars!

It is He who hath ordained for you the night wherein to rest, and the lightsome day. Verily in this are signs for those who hearken.

They say, "God hath begotten children." No! by his glory! He is the self-sufficient. All that is in the Heavens and all that is in the Earth is His! Have ye warranty for that assertion? What! speak ye of God that which ye know not?

SAY: Verily, they who devise this lie concerning God shall fare ill.

A portion have they in this world! Then to us they return! Then make we them to taste the vehement torment, for that they were unbelievers.

Recite to them the history of Noah,[10] when he said to his people,-If, O my people! my abode with you, and my reminding you of the signs of God, be grievous to you, yet in God is my trust: Muster, therefore, your designs and your false gods, and let not your design be carried on by you in the dark: then come to some decision about me, and delay not.

And if ye turn your backs on me, yet ask I no reward from you: my reward is with God alone, and I am commanded to be of the Muslims.

But they treated him as a liar: therefore we rescued him and those who were with him in the ark, and we made them to survive the others; and we drowned those who charged our signs with falsehood. See, then, what was the end of these warned ones!

Then after him, we sent Apostles to their peoples, and they came to them with credentials; but they would not believe in what they had denied aforetime: Thus seal we up the hearts of the transgressors!

Then sent we, after them, Moses and Aaron to Pharaoh and his nobles with our signs; but they acted proudly and were a wicked people:

And when the truth came to them from us, they said, "Verily, this is clear sorcery."

Moses said: "What! say ye of the truth after it hath come to you, 'Is this sorcery?' But sorcerers shall not prosper."

They said: "Art thou come to us to pervert us from the faith in which we found our fathers, and that you twain shall bear rule in this land? But we believe you not."

And Pharaoh said: "Fetch me every skilled magician." And when the magicians arrived, Moses said to them, "Cast down what ye have to cast."

And when they had cast them down, Moses said, "Verily, God will render vain the sorceries which ye have brought to pass: God prospereth not the work of the evildoers.

And by his words will God verify the Truth, though the impious be averse to it.

And none believed on Moses but a race among his own people, through fear of Pharaoh and his nobles, lest he should afflict them: For of a truth mighty was Pharaoh in the land, and one who committed excesses.

And Moses said: "O my people! if ye believe in God, then put your trust in Him-if ye be Muslims."

And they said: "In God put we our trust. O our Lord! abandon us not to trial from that unjust people,

And deliver us by thy mercy from the unbelieving people."

Then thus revealed we to Moses and to his brother: "Provide houses for your people in Egypt, and in your houses make a Kebla, and observe prayer and proclaim good tidings to the believers."

And Moses said: "O our Lord! thou hast indeed given to Pharaoh and his nobles splendour and riches in this present life: O our Lord! that they may err from thy way! O our Lord! confound their riches, and harden their hearts that they may not believe till they see the dolorous torment."

He said: "The prayer of you both is heard: pursue ye both therefore the straight path, and follow not the path of those who have no knowledge."

And we led the children of Israel through the sea; and Pharaoh and his hosts followed them in eager and hostile sort until, when the drowning overtook him, he said, "I believe that there is no God but he on whom the children of Israel believe, and I am one of the Muslims."

"Yes, now," said God: "but thou hast been rebellious hitherto, and wast one of the wicked doers.

But this day will we rescue thee with thy body that thou mayest be a sign to those who shall be after thee:[11] but truly, most men are of our signs regardless!"

Moreover we prepared a settled abode for the children of Israel, and provided them with good things: nor did they fall into variance till the knowledge (the Law) came to them: Truly thy Lord will decide between them on the day of Resurrection concerning that in which they differed.

And if thou art in doubt as to what we have sent down to thee, inquire at those who have read the Scriptures before thee.[12] Now hath the truth come unto thee from thy Lord: be not therefore of those who doubt.

Neither be of those who charge the signs of God with falsehood, lest thou be of those who perish.

Verily they against whom the decree of thy Lord is pronounced, shall not believe,

Even though every kind of sign come unto them, till they behold the dolorous torment!

Were it otherwise, any city, had it believed, might have found its safety in its faith. But it was so, only with the people of JONAS [Jonah]. When they believed,
we delivered them from the penalty of shame in this world, and provided for them for a time.

But if thy Lord had pleased, verily all who are in the earth would have believed together. What! wilt thou compel men to become believers?

No soul can believe but by the permission of God: and he shall lay his wrath on those who will not understand.

SAY: Consider ye whatever is in the Heavens and on the Earth: but neither signs, nor warners, avail those who will not believe!

What then can they expect but the like of such days of wrath as befel those who flourish before them? SAY: WAIT; I too will wait with you:

Then will we deliver our apostles and those who believe. Thus is it binding on us to deliver the faithful. SAY: O men! if ye are in doubt as to my religion, verily I worship not what ye worship beside God; but I worship God who will cause you to die: and I am commanded to be a believer.

And set thy face toward true religion, sound in faith, and be not of those who join other gods with God:

Neither invoke beside God that which can neither help nor hurt thee: for if thou do, thou wilt certainly then be one of those who act unjustly.

And if God lay the touch of trouble on thee, none can deliver thee from it but He: and if He will thee any good, none can keep back his boons. He will confer them on such of his servants as he chooseth: and He is the Gracious, the Merciful!

SAY: O men! now hath the truth come unto you from your Lord. He therefore who will be guided, will be guided only for his own behoof: but he who shall err will err only against it; and I am not your guardian!

And follow what is revealed to thee: and persevere steadfastly till God shall judge, for He is the best of Judges.

Notes

1. See Sura 1xviii. n. 3, p. 32.
2. That is, for a serious end, to manifest the Divine Unity.
3. Gen. xi. 1.
4. This refers to the seven years of scarcity with which Mecca had been visited.
5. Paradise.
6. Verses 27, 28 are to be noted, as defining the proportion to be observed in rewards and punishments, the severity of the latter being only in proportion to the crime, the excellence of the former being above and beyond its strict merits.
7. But rather your own lusts. The Muhammadans believe that idols will be gifted with speech at the day of judgment.
8. The ordinary Arabic word for to die seems to be avoided in speaking of Jesus and Muhammad.
9. This is the doctrine of the Rabbins. Comp. Midrasch Rabba, and Midr. Jalkut on Numb. xxii. 2.
10. The preaching of Noah is mentioned by the Rabbins. Sanhedrin, 108. Comp. Midr. Rabbah on

Gen. Par. 30 and 33, on Eccl. ix. 14, and in the probably sub. Apostolic 2 Pet. ii. 5.

11. This is in accordance with Talmudic legend. "Recognise the power of repentance, in the case of Pharaoh, King of Egypt, who rebelled excessively against the most High; Who is God that I should hearken to his voice? (Ex. v. 2). But with the same tongue that sinned he did penance: Who is like thee, O Lord, among the Gods? (xv. 11). The Holy One, Blessed be He, delivered him from the dead, … so that he should not die (ix. 15, 16).-For now have I stretched forth my hand, and verily thee have I raised up from among the dead, to proclaim my might." Ex. ix. 15, 16. A strange comment! Pirke R. Eliezer, § 43. Comp. Midr. on Ps. cvi. Midr. Jalkut, ch. 238.

12. That is, whether thou art not foretold in the Law and Gospel, and whether the Koran is not in unison with, and confirmatory of, them.

SURA XIX.[1]–MARY [LVIII.]

MECCA.-98 Verses

In the Name of God, the Compassionate, the Merciful

KAF. HA. YA. AIN. SAD.[2] A recital of thy Lord's mercy to his servant Zachariah; When he called upon his Lord with secret calling, and said: "O Lord, verily my bones are weakened, and the hoar hairs glisten on my head, and never, Lord, have I prayed to thee with ill success.

But now I have fears for my kindred after me;[3] and my wife is barren: Give me, then, a successor as thy special gift, who shall be my heir and an heir of the family of Jacob: and make him, Lord, well pleasing to thee."

-"O Zachariah! verily we announce to thee a son,-his name John: That name We have given to none before him."[4]

He said: "O my Lord! how when my wife is barren shall I have a son, and when I have now reached old age, failing in my powers?"

He said: So shall it be. Thy Lord hath said, Easy is this to me, for I created thee aforetime when thou wast nothing."

He said: "Vouchsafe me, O my Lord! a sign."

He said: "Thy sign shall be that for three nights, though sound in health, thou speakest not to man."

And he came forth from the sanctuary to his people, and made signs to them to sing praises morn and even.

We said: "O John! receive the Book with purpose of heart:"[5]-and We bestowed on him wisdom while yet a child; and mercifulness from Ourself, and purity; and pious was he, and duteous to his parents; and not proud, rebellious.

And peace was on him on the day he was born, and the day of his death, and shall be on the day when he shall be raised to life!

And make mention in the Book, of Mary, when she went apart from her family, eastward,[6]

And took a veil to shroud herself from them:[7] and we sent our spirit[8] to her, and he took before her the form of a perfect man.[9]

She said: "I fly for refuge from thee to the God of Mercy! If thou fearest him, begone from me."

He said: "I am only a messenger of thy Lord, that I may bestow on thee a holy son."

She said: "How shall I have a son, when man hath never touched me? and I am not unchaste."

He said: "So shall it be. Thy Lord hath said: 'Easy is this with me;' and we will make him a sign to mankind, and a mercy from us. For it is a thing decreed."

And she conceived him,[10] and retired with him to a far-off place.

And the throes came upon her[11] by the trunk of a palm. She said: "Oh, would that I had died ere this, and been a thing forgotten, forgotten quite!"

And one cried to her from below her:[12] "Grieve not thou, thy Lord hath provided a streamlet at thy feet: And shake the trunk of the palm-tree toward thee:[13] it will drop fresh ripe dates upon thee. Eat then and drink, and be of cheerful eye:[14] and shouldst thou see a man, say,-Verily, I have vowed abstinence to the God of mercy.-To no one will I speak this day."

Then came she with the babe to her people, bearing him. They said, "O Mary! now hast thou done a strange thing!

O sister of Aaron![15] Thy father was not a man of wickedness, nor unchaste thy mother."

And she made a sign to them, pointing towards the babe. They said, "How shall we speak with him who is in the cradle, an infant?"

It said,[16] "Verily, I am the servant of God; He hath given me the Book, and He hath made me a prophet; and He hath made me blessed wherever I may be, and hath enjoined me prayer and almsgiving so long as I shall live; and to be duteous to her that bare me: and he hath not made me proud, depraved. And the peace of God was on me the day I was born, and will be the day I shall die, and the day I shall be raised to life."

This is Jesus, the son of Mary; this is a statement of the truth concerning which they doubt.

It beseemeth not God to beget a son. Glory be to Him! when he decreeth a thing, He only saith to it, Be, and it Is.[17]

And verily, God is my Lord and your Lord; adore Him then. This is the right way.

But the Sects have fallen to variance among themselves about Jesus: but woe, because of the assembly of a great day, to those who believe not!

Make them hear, make them behold the day when they shall come before us! But the offenders this day are in a manifest error.

Warn them of the day of sighing when the decree shall be accomplished, while they are sunk in heedlessness and while they believe not.

Verily, we will inherit the earth and all who are upon it. To us shall they be brought back.

Make mention also in the Book of Abraham; for he was a man of truth, a Prophet.[18] When he said to his Father, "O my Father! why dost thou worship that which neither seeth nor heareth, nor profiteth thee aught?

O my Father! verily now hath knowledge come to me which hath not come to thee. Follow me therefore-I will guide thee into an even path.

O my Father! worship not Satan, for Satan is a rebel against the God of Mercy.

O my Father! indeed I fear lest a chastisement from the God of Mercy light upon thee, and thou become Satan's vassal."

He said, "Castest thou off my Gods, O Abraham? If thou forbear not, I will surely stone thee. Begone from me for a length of time."

He said, "Peace be on thee! I will pray my Lord for thy forgiveness, for he is gracious to me:

But I will separate myself from you, and the gods ye call on beside God, and on my Lord will I call. Haply, my prayers to my Lord will not be with ill success."

And when he had separated himself from them and that which they worshipped beside God, we bestowed on him Isaac and Jacob, and each of them we made a prophet: And we bestowed gifts on them in our mercy, and gave them the lofty tongue of truth."[19]

And commemorate Moses in "the Book;" for he was a man of purity: moreover he was an Apostle, a Prophet:

From the right side of the mountain we called to him, and caused him to draw nigh to us for secret converse:

And we bestowed on him in our mercy his brother Aaron, a Prophet.

And commemorate Ismael in "the Book;" for he was true to his promise, and was an Apostle, a Prophet;

And he enjoined prayer and almsgiving on his people, and was well pleasing to his Lord.

And commemorate Edris[20] in "the Book;" for he was a man of truth, a Prophet:

And we uplifted him to a place on high.[21]

These are they among the prophets of the posterity of Adam, and among those whom we bare with Noah, and among the posterity of Abraham and Israel, and among those whom we have guided and chosen, to whom God hath shewed favour. When the signs of the God of Mercy were rehearsed to them, they bowed them down worshipping and weeping.

But others have come in their place after them: they have made an end of prayer, and have gone after their own lusts; and in the end they shall meet with evil:-

Save those who turn and believe and do that which is right, these shall enter the Garden, and in nought shall they be wronged: The Garden of Eden, which the God of Mercy hath promised to his servants, though yet unseen:[22] for his promise shall come to pass:

No vain discourse shall they hear therein, but only "Peace;" and their food shall be given them at morn and even: This is the Paradise which we will make the heritage of those our servants who fear us.

We[23] come not down from Heaven but by thy Lord's command. His, whatever is before us and whatever is behind us, and whatever is between the two! And thy Lord is not forgetful,-

Lord of the Heavens and of the Earth, and of all that is between them! Worship Him, then, and abide thou steadfast in his worship. Knowest thou any other of the same name?[24]

Man saith: "What! after I am dead, shall I in the end be brought forth alive?"

Doth not man bear in mind that we made him at first, when he was nought?

And I swear by thy Lord, we will surely gather together them and the Satans: then will we set them on their knees round Hell:

Then will we take forth from each band those of them who have been stoutest in rebellion against the God of Mercy: Then shall we know right well to whom its burning is most due:

No one is there of you who shall not go down unto it[25]-This is a settled decree with thy Lord-

Then will we deliver those who had the fear of God, and the wicked will we leave in it on their knees.
And when our clear signs are rehearsed to them, the infidels say to those who believe: "Which of the two parties[26] is in the best plight? and which is the most goodly company?" But how many generations have we brought to ruin before them, who surpassed them in riches and in splendour!

SAY: As to those who are in error, the God of Mercy will lengthen out to them a length of days

Until they see that with which they are threatened, whether it be some present chastisement, or whether it be "the Hour," and they shall then know which is in the worse state, and which the more weak in forces:

But God will increase the guidance of the already guided.

And good works which abide, are in thy Lord's sight better in respect of guerdon, and better in the issue than all worldly good.

Hast thou marked him who believeth not in our signs, and saith, "I shall surely have riches and children bestowed upon me?"

Hath he mounted up into the secrets of God? Hath he made a compact with the God of Mercy?

No! we will certainly write down what he saith, and will lengthen the length of his chastisement:
And we will inherit what he spake of, and he shall come before us all alone.

They have taken other gods beside God to be their help.[27]

But it shall not be. Those gods will disavow their worship and will become their enemies.

Seest thou not that we send the Satans against the Infidels to urge them into sin?

Wherefore be not thou in haste with them;[28] for a small number of days do we number to them.

One day we will gather the God-fearing before the God of Mercy with honours due:[29]

But the sinners will we drive unto Hell, like flocks driven to the watering.

None shall have power to intercede, save he who hath received permission at the hands of the God of Mercy.

They say: "The God of Mercy hath gotten offspring." Now have ye done a monstrous thing!

Almost might the very Heavens be rent thereat, and the Earth cleave asunder, and the mountains fall down in fragments,

That they ascribe a son to the God of Mercy, when it beseemeth not the God of Mercy to beget a son!

Verily there is none in the Heavens and in the Earth but shall approach the God of Mercy as a servant. He hath taken note of them, and numbered them with exact numbering:

And each of them shall come to Him, on the day of Resurrection, singly:

But love will the God of Mercy vouchsafe to those who believe and do the things that be right.

Verily we have made this Koran easy and in thine own tongue, that thou mayest announce glad tidings by it to the God-fearing, and that thou mayest warn the contentious by it.

How many generations have we destroyed before them! Canst thou search out one of them? or canst thou hear a whisper from them?

Notes

1. Comp. the first 37 verses of this Sura with Sura iii. 35-57 with reference to the different style adopted by Muhammad in the later Suras, probably for the purpose of avoiding the imputation of his being merely a poet, a sorcerer, or person possessed. Sura lii. 29, 30; xxi. 5; lxviii. 2, 51. This Sura is one of the fullest and earliest Koranic Gospel Histories, and was recited to the Nagash or King of Æthiopia, in the presence of the ambassadors of the Koreisch. His. 220; Caussin, i. 392; Sprenger (Life of M.) p. 193.

2. See Sura lxviii. I, p. 32. Golius conjectured that these letters represent coh ya'as, thus he counselled, and that they were added by some Jewish scribe. Sprenger (Journ. of As. Soc. of Bengal, xx. 280) arranges them as Ain, Sad, Kaf, Ha, Ya, and supposes them to be taken from the Arabic words for Aisa (Jesus) of the Nazarenes, King of the Jews. But we can hardly imagine that Muhammad would ascribe such a title to our Lord, and the word which Dr. Sprenger uses for Jews is not the form peculiar to the Koran.

3. Lest they should desert the worship of the God of Israel.

4. Ar. Yahia. It may be true that the name in this form had never been given. Otherwise, we have in this passage a misunderstanding of Luke i. 61, as well as ignorance of the Jewish Scriptures. Comp. 2 Kings xxv. 23; 1 Chron. iii. 16; Ezra viii. 12; Jerem. xl. 8. Some commentators try to avoid the difficulty by rendering samiyan, deserving of the name.

5. Or, with firm resolve. See Sura [xcvii.] iii. 36. The speaker is God.

6. To an eastern chamber in the temple to pray. Or it may mean, to some place eastward from Jerusalem, or from the house of her parents.

7. Thus the Protev. Jac. c. 12 says that Mary, although at a later period, [greek text] But Wahl, she laid aside her veil.

8. Gabriel.

9. See Sura [lxxxix.] vi. 9.

10. It is quite clear from this passage, and from verse 36, that Muhammad believed Jesus to have been conceived by an act of the divine will. Comp. Sura [xcvii.] iii. 52; see also note at Sura [xci.] ii. 81.

11. Or, the throes urged her to the trunk of, etc.

12. This was either the Infant which spoke as soon as born, or Gabriel. Comp. Thilo Cod. Apoc. 136-139 on this passage. Beidhawi explains: from behind the palm tree.

13. See Thilo Cod. Apoc. N. T. p. 138, and the Hist. Nat. Mar. c. 20, which connects similar incidents with the flight into Egypt. Thus also Latona, [greek text], Call. H. in Apoll. and [greek text], H. in Delum.

14. Or, settle, calm thine eye, refresh thine eye. The birth of a son is still called korrat ol ain.

15. The anachronism is probably only apparent. See Sura iii. 1, n. Muhammad may have supposed that this Aaron (or Harun) was the son of Imran and Anna. Or, if Aaron the brother of Moses be meant Mary may be called his sister, either because she was of the Levitical race, or by way of comparison.

16. See Sura [cxiv.] v. 109.

17. From the change in the rhyme, and from the more polemical tone of the following five verses, it may be inferred that they were added at a somewhat later period.

18. The title Nabi, prophet, is used of Abraham, Isaac, and Jacob, as depositaries of the worship of the one true God, but with a mission restricted to their own families; whereas Houd, Saleh, Shoaib, etc., are designated as (Resoul) apostles and envoys, charged with a more extended mission to the tribes of Arabia. In Moses, Jesus, and Muhammad, etc., are united the office and gift both of prophet (nabi) and apostle (resoul).

19. Made them to be highly praised. Beidh.

20. Enoch. Beidhawi derives the name Edris from the Ar. darasa, to search out, with reference to his knowledge of divine mysteries. The Heb. Enoch, in like manner, means initiated

21. Comp. Gen. v. 24, and the tract Derek Erez in Midr. Jalkut, c. 42, where Enoch is reckoned among the nine according to other Talmudists, thirteen (Schroeder's Talm. und Rabb. Judenthum)-individuals who were exempted from death and taken straight to Paradise. It should be observed that both here and Sura xxi. 85, Edris is named after Ismael.

22. Maracci and Beidhawi, in absentid. Sale, as an object of faith. Beidhawi ad f. in reward for their secret faith. Ullmann für die verborgene Zukunft.

23. This verse is to be understood as an answer on the part of Gabriel to Muhammad's complaints of the long intervals between the revelations.

24. The idolaters called their deities Gods, but as Polytheists were unused to the singular Allah, God.

25. Even the pious on their way to Paradise are to pass the confines of Hell.

26. The Koreisch, or the Muslims.

27. Or, glory, strength.

28. To call down judgments upon them.

29. As ambassadors come into the presence of a prince. Sale. This is implied in the original

URA LV.-THE MERCIFUL [XLVIII.]

MECCA.-78 Verses

In the Name of God, the Compassionate, the Merciful
The God of MERCY hath taught the Koran,
Hath created man,
Hath taught him articulate speech,
The Sun and the Moon have each their times,
And the plants and the trees bend in adoration.

And the Heaven, He hath reared it on high, and hath appointed the balance; that in the balance ye should not transgress.

Weigh therefore with fairness, and scant not the balance.

And the Earth, He hath prepared it for the living tribes: Therein are fruits, and the palms with sheathed clusters, and the grain with its husk, and the fragrant plants. Which then of the bounties of your Lord will ye twain[1] deny?

He created man of clay like that of the potter. And He created the djinn of pure fire:
Which of the bounties, of your Lord will ye deny?

He is the Lord of the East,[2] He is the Lord of the West: Which, of the bounties of your Lord will ye deny?

He hath let loose the two seas[3] which meet each other: Yet between them is a barrier which they overpass not: Which, of the bounties of your Lord will ye deny?

From each he bringeth up pearls both great and small:
Which, etc.

And His are the ships towering up at sea like mountains:
Which, etc.

All on the earth shall pass away,
But the face of thy Lord shall abide resplendent with majesty and glory:
Which, of the bounties of your Lord will ye deny?

To Him maketh suit all that is in the Heaven and the Earth. Every day doth some new work employ Him:
Which, of the bounties of your Lord will ye deny?

We will find leisure to judge you, O ye men and djinn:[4]
Which, of the bounties of your Lord will ye deny?

O company of djinn and men, if ye can overpass the bounds of the Heavens and the Earth, then overpass them. But by our leave only shall ye overpass them:
Which, of the bounties of your Lord will ye deny?

A bright flash of fire shall be hurled at you both, and molten brass, and ye shall not defend yourselves from it:
Which, of the bounties of your Lord will ye deny?

When the Heaven shall be cleft asunder, and become rose red, like stained Leather:
Which, of the bounties of your Lord will ye deny?

On that day shall neither man nor djinn be asked of his sin:
Which, of the bounties of your Lord will ye deny?

By their tokens shall the sinners be known, and they shall be seized by their forelocks and their feet:
Which, of the bounties of your Lord will ye deny?

"This is Hell which sinners treated as a lie."

To and fro shall they pass between it and the boiling water:
Which, of the bounties of your Lord will ye deny?

But for those who dread the majesty of their Lord shall be two gardens:
Which, of the bounties of your Lord will ye deny?

With o'erbranching trees in each:
Which, of the bounties of your Lord will ye deny?

In each two kinds of every fruit:
Which, of the bounties of your Lord will ye deny?

On couches with linings of brocade shall they recline, and the fruit of the two gardens shall be within
easy reach:
Which, of the bounties of your Lord will ye deny?

Therein shall be the damsels with retiring glances,
whom nor man nor djinn hath touched before them:
Which, of the bounties of your Lord will ye deny?
Like jacynths and pearls:
Which, of the bounties of your Lord will ye deny?

Shall the reward of good be aught but good?
Which, of the bounties of your Lord will ye deny?

And beside these shall be two other gardens:⁵
Which, of the bounties of your Lord will ye deny?

Of a dark green:
Which, of the bounties of your Lord will ye deny?

With gushing fountains in each:
Which, of the bounties of your Lord will ye deny?

In each, fruits and the palm and the pomegranate:
Which, of the bounties of your Lord will ye deny?

In each, the fair, the beauteous ones:
Which, of the bounties of your Lord will ye deny?

With large dark eyeballs, kept close in their pavilions:
Which, of the bounties of your Lord will ye deny?

Whom man hath never touched, nor any djinn:⁶
Which, of the bounties of your Lord will ye deny?

Their spouses on soft green cushions and on beautiful carpets shall recline:
Which, of the bounties of your Lord will ye deny?

Blessed be the name of thy Lord, full of majesty and
glory.

Notes

1. Men and djinn. The verb is in the dual.

2. Lit. of the two easts, of the two wests, i.e., of all
that lies between the extreme points at which
the sun rises and sets at the winter and summer
solstices.

3. Lit. he hath set at large, poured forth over the
earth the masses of fresh and salt water which are
in contact at the mouths of rivers, etc. See Sura
[lxviii.] xxvii. 62; [lxxxvi.] xxxv. 13.

4. Lit. O ye two weights; hence, treasures; and, generally, any collective body of men or things.

5. One for men, the other for the Genii; or, two for
each man and Genius; or, both are for the inferior
classes of Muslims. Beidh.

6. It should be remarked that these promises of the
Houris of Paradise are almost exclusively to be
found in Suras written at a time when Muhammad
had only a single wife of 60 years of age, and that in
all the ten years subsequent to the Hejira, women
are only twice mentioned as part of the reward of
the faithful. Suras ii. 23 and iv. 60. While in Suras
xxxvi. 56; xliii. 70; xiii. 23; xl. 8 the proper wives
of the faithful are spoken of as accompanying their
husbands into the gardens of bliss.

SURA CXII.-THE UNITY (OR ONENESS) [X.]

MECCA.-4 Verses

In the Name of God, the Compassionate, the
Merciful

SAY: He is God alone:

God the eternal!

He begetteth not, and He is not begotten;

And there is none like unto Him.

DISCUSSION QUESTIONS

1. Name some of the characteristics of God (Allah) as depicted in the Koran.

2. According to the opening paragraphs of "Jonah," what two things must one do to reap God's rewards?

3. Name some Old Testament/Hebrew Bible figures who appear in the *Koran*'s "Jonah" *surah*. How do their stories here compare to their biblical treatments?

4. List some of the ethical pronouncements that seem to be shared by both the *Koran* and the *Bible*.

5. How does the account of Jesus' birth in the "Mary" *surah* compare to the account in the Gospel of *Luke* (see Unit 1)? What differences does the Koran emphasize in its account of Jesus' conception and birth?

6. In "The Merciful," what is the effect of the repetition of "Which of the bounties of your Lord will ye deny?" What do you think is the purpose of this *surah*?

7. In "The Merciful," what rewards await those who "dread the majesty of their Lord?" Which images in this section seem particularly evocative to you?

HILDEGARD OF BINGEN (1098–1179)

Selected Excerpts

Hildegard, a Benedictine nun, abbess, writer, and music composer, was born in a noble family in Bermersheim in what is now Germany. At eight years of age, she entered the abbey at Disibodenberg, a Benedictine house devoted to prayer and religious study (but later known for its illuminated manuscripts as well). At the age of 38, Hildegard became the *magistra*, or head, of her religious community. Throughout her life, she suffered much pain and illness. As she writes in her first book, *Scivias* (or *Scito vias Domini*, "Know the ways of the Lord"), bodily pain forced her to record her mystical visions, for writing was all she could do to lessen the physical discomfort. As Hildegard describes it, she was "quelled by the whip of God." Hildegard wrote two other books of visions, *Liber vitae meritorum (The Book of Life's Rewards)* and *Liber divinorum operum (The Book of Divine Works)*. In addition, she wrote books of natural science and medicine, an analysis of the Psalms, a play (*Ordo Virtutum*), treatises of saints' lives, and lyrics and music for *Symphonia harmoniae caelestium revelationum (Symphony of the Harmony of Celestial Revelations)*, some of the lyrics from which are included below.

A SOLEMN DECLARATION CONCERNING THE TRUE VISION FLOWING FROM GOD: SCIVIAS. PROTESTIFICATIO

Lo! In the forty-third year of my temporal course, when I clung to a celestial vision with great fear and tremulous effort, I saw a great splendor. In it came a voice from heaven, saying:

"O frail mortal, both ash of ashes, and rottenness of rottenness, speak and write down what you see and hear. But because you are fearful of speaking, simple at expounding, and unlearned in writing-speak and write, not according to the speech of man or according to the intelligence of human invention, or following the aim of human composition, but according to what you see and hear from the heavens above in the wonders of God! Offer explanations of them, just as one who hears and understands the words of an instructor willingly makes them public, revealing and teaching them according to the sense of the instructor's discourse. You therefore, O mortal, speak also the things you see and hear. Write them, not according to yourself or to some other person, but according to the will of the Knower, Seer and Ordainer of all things in the secrets of their mysteries."

And again I heard the voice from heaven saying to me: "Speak these wonders and write the things taught in this manner—and speak!"

It happened in the year 1141 of the Incarnation of the Son of God, Jesus Christ, when I was forty-two years and seven months old, that a fiery light of the greatest radiance coming from the open heavens flooded through my entire brain. It kindled my whole breast like a flame that does not scorch but warms in the same way the sun warms anything on which it sheds its rays.

Suddenly I understood the meaning of books, that is, the Psalms and the Gospels; and I knew other catholic books of the Old as well as the New Testaments—not the significance of the words of the text, or the division of the syllables, nor did I consider an examination of the cases and tenses.

Indeed, from the age of girlhood, from the time that I was fifteen until the present, I had perceived in myself, just as until this moment, a power of mysterious, secret, and marvelous visions of a miraculous sort. However, I revealed these things to no one, except to a few religious persons who were living under the same vows as I was. But meanwhile, until this time when God in his grace has willed these things to be revealed, I have repressed them in quiet silence.

But I have not perceived these visions in dreams, or asleep, or in a delirium, or with my bodily eyes, or with my external mortal ears, or in secreted places, but I received them awake and looking attentively about me with an unclouded mind, in open places, according to God's will. However this may be, it is difficult for carnal man to fathom.

Once the term of my girlhood was completed, and I had arrived at the age of perfect strength which I mentioned, I heard a voice from heaven saying:

"I am the Living Light who illuminates the darkness. I have, according to my pleasure, wondrously shaken with great marvels this mortal whom I desired, and I have placed her beyond the limit reached by men of ancient times who saw in me many secret things. But I have leveled her to the ground, so that she may not raise herself up with any pride in her own mind. The world, moreover, has not had any joy of her, or sport, or practice in those things belonging to the world. I have freed her from obstinate boldness; she is fearful and anxious in her endeavors. She has suffered pain in her very marrow and in all the veins of her body; her spirit has been fettered; she felt and endured many bodily illnesses. No pervading freedom from care has dwelt within her, but she considers herself culpable in all her undertakings.

"I have hedged round the clefts of her heart, so that her mind will not elevate itself through pride or praise, but so that she will feel more fear and pain in these things then joy or wantonness.

Hildegard of Bingen, from *The Writings of Medieval Women*, trans. Marcelle Thiebaux, pp. 321–328, 332–333, 337–342. Copyright © 1994 by Taylor & Francis Group LLC. Reprinted with permission.

"For the sake of my love, therefore, she has searched in her own mind as to where she might find someone who would run in the path of salvation. And when she found one and loved him, she recognized that he was a faithful man, one similar to herself in some part of that work which pertains to me. Keeping him with her, she strove at the same time with him in all these divine studies, so that my hidden wonders might be revealed. And the same man did not place himself above her. But in an ascent to humility, and with the exertion of goodwill when he came to her, he yielded to her with many sighs.

"You, therefore, O mortal, who receive these things—not in the turmoil of deception but in the clarity of simplicity for the purpose of making hidden things plain—write what you see and hear!"

But although I was seeing and hearing these things, I nevertheless refused to write for such a long time because of doubt and wrong thinking—on account of the various judgments of men—not out of boldness but out of the duty of my humility.

Finally, I fell to my sickbed, quelled by the whip of God. Racked by many infirmities, and with a young girl of noble blood and good character as witness—as well as a man I had secretly sought out and discovered, as I have already said—I put my hand to writing.

While I was doing this, I sensed the profound depth of the narration of these books, as I have said. And despite the strength I experienced when I was raised up from my sickness, I carried out that work with difficulty to the end, completing it after ten years. These visions and these words took place during the days of Heinrich, Archbishop of Mainz; Conrad, Emperor of the Romans; and Kuno, abbot of Mount St. Disibodenburg under Pope Eugenius.

I have spoken and written this, not according to the invention of my heart, or of any man, but as I saw these things in the heavens and heard and perceived them through God's sacred mysteries. And again I heard a voice from the sky saying to me, "Shout, therefore, and write this way!"

THE IRON-COLORED MOUNTAIN AND THE RADIANT ONE: SCIVIAS. BOOK I, VISION 1

I saw what seemed to be a huge mountain having the color of iron. On its height was sitting One of such great radiance that it stunned my vision. On both sides of him extended a gentle shadow like a wing of marvelous width and length. And in front of him at the foot of the same mountain stood a figure full of eyes everywhere. Because of those eyes, I was not able to distinguish any human form.

In front of this figure there was another figure, whose age was that of a boy, and he was clothed in a pale tunic and had so much radiance descended from the One sitting on the mountain. From the One sitting on the mountain a great many living sparks cascaded, which flew around those figures with great sweetness. In this same mountain, moreover, there seemed to be a number of little windows, in which men's heads appeared, some pale and some white.

And see! The One sitting on the mountain shouted in an extremely loud, strong voice, saying: "O frail mortal, you who are of the dust of the earth's dust, and ash of ash, cry out and speak of the way into incorruptible salvation! Do this in order that those people may be taught who see the innermost meaning of Scripture, but who do not wish to tell it or preach it because they are lukewarm and dull in preserving God's justice. Unlock for them the mystical barriers. For they, being timid, are hiding themselves in a remote and barren field. You, therefore, pour yourself forth in a fountain of abundance! Flow with mystical learning, so that those who want you to be scorned because of the guilt of Eve may be inundated by the flood of your refreshment!

"For you do not receive this keenness of insight from man, but from that supernal and awesome judge on high. There amidst brilliant light, this radiance will brightly shine forth among the luminous ones. Arise, therefore, and shout and speak! These things are revealed to you through the strongest power of divine aid. For he who potently and benignly rules his creatures imbues with the radiance of heavenly enlightenment all those who fear him and serve him with sweet love in a spirit of humility. And he leads those who persevere in the path of justice to the joys of everlasting vision!"

THE FALL OF LUCIFER, THE FORMATION OF HELL, AND THE FALL OF ADAM AND EVE: SCIVIAS. BOOK I, VISION 2

Then I saw what seemed to be a great number of living torches, full of brilliance. Catching a fiery gleam, they received a most radiant splendor from it. And see! A lake appeared here, of great length and depth, with a mouth like a well, breathing forth a stinking fiery smoke. From the mouth of the lake a loathsome fog also arose until it touched a thing like a blood vessel that had a deceptive appearance.

And in a certain region of brightness, the fog blew through the blood vessel to a pure white cloud, which had emerged from the beautiful form of a man, and the cloud contained within itself many, many stars. Then the loathsome fog blew and drove the cloud and the man's form out of the region of brightness.

Once this had happened, the most luminous splendor encircled that region. The elements of the world, which previously had held firmly together in great tranquility, now, turning into great turmoil, displayed fearful terrors.

[Hildegard hears a voice explaining the meaning of what she has seen:]

The "great number of living torches, full of brilliance" refers to the numerous. They dwell with much honor and adornment, for they have been created by God. These did not grasp at proudly exalting themselves, but persisted steadfastly in divine love.

"Catching a fiery gleam, they received a most radiant splendor from it" means that when Lucifer and his followers tried to rebel against the heavenly Creator and fell, those others who kept a zealous love of God came to a common agreement, and clothed themselves in the vigilance of divine love.

But Lucifer and his followers had embraced the sluggardly ignorance of those who do not wish to know God. What happened? When who the Devil fell, a great praise arose from those angelic spirits who had persisted in righteousness with God. For they recognized with the keenest vision that God remained unshaken, without any mutable change in his power, and that he will not be overthrown by any warrior. And so they burned fiercely in their love for him, and persevering in righteousness, they scorned all the dust of injustice.

Now "that lake of great length and depth" which appeared to you is Hell. In its length are contained vices, and in its deep abyss is damnation, as you see. Also, "it has a mouth like a well, breathing forth a stinking, fiery smoke" means that drowning souls are swallowed in its voracious greed. For although the lake shows them sweetness and delights, it leads them, through perverse deceit, to a perdition of torments. There the heat of the fire breathes forth with a outpouring of the most loathsome smoke, and with a boiling, death-dealing stench. For these abominable torments were prepared for the Devil and his followers, who turned away from the highest good, which they wanted neither to know nor to understand. For this reason they were cast down from every good thing, not because they do not know them but because they were contemptuous of them in their lofty pride.

"From that same lake a most loathsome fog arose, until it touched a thing like a blood vessel that had a deceptive appearance." This means that the diabolical deceit emanating from deepest perdition entered the poisonous serpent. The serpent contained within itself the crime of a fraudulent intention to deceive man. How? When the Devil saw man in Paradise, he cried out in great agitation, saying, "O who is this that approaches me in the mansion of true blessedness!" He knew himself that the malice he had within him had not yet filled other creatures. But seeing Adam and Eve walking in childlike innocence in the garden of delights, he—in his great stupefaction—set out to deceive them through the serpent.

Why? Because he perceived that the serpent was more like him than was any other animal, and that by striving craftily he could bring about covertly what he could not openly accomplish in his own shape. When, therefore, he saw Adam and Eve turn away, both in body in mind, from the tree that was forbidden to them, he realized that they had had a divine command. He realized that through the first act they attempted, he could overthrow them very easily.

The line "in this same region of brightness he blew on a white cloud, which had emerged from the beautiful form of a man, and the cloud contained within itself many, many stars" means this: In this place of delight, the Devil, by means of the serpent's seductions, attacked Eve and brought about her downfall. Eve had an innocent soul. She had been taken from the side of innocent Adam, bearing within her body the luminous multitude of the human race, as God had preordained it.

Why did the Devil attack her? Because he knew that the woman's softness would be more easily conquered than the man's strength, seeing, indeed, that Adam burned so fiercely with love for Eve that if the devil himself could conquer Eve, Adam would do anything she told him. Therefore the Devil "cast her and that same form of a man out of the region." This means that the ancient seducer, by driving Eve and Adam from the abode of blessedness through his decent, sent them into darkness and ruin.

WORLDLY LOVE AND CELESTIAL LOVE: LIBER VITAE MERITORUM. VISION I, PART 1

The Words of Worldly Love:

The first figure had the form of a man and the blackness of an Ethiopian. Standing naked, he wound his arms and legs around a tree below the branches. From the tree all kinds of flowers were growing. With his hands he was gathering those flowers, and he said:

"I possess all the kingdoms of the world with their flowers and ornaments. How should I wither when I have all the greenness? Why should I live in the condition of old age, since I am blossoming in youth? Why should I lead my beautiful eyes into blindness? Because if I did this I should be ashamed. As long as I am able to possess the beauty of this world, I will gladly hold on to it. I have no knowledge of any other life, although I hear all sorts of stories about it."

When he had spoken, that tree I mentioned withered from the root, and sank into the darkness of which I spoke. And the figure died along with it.

The Reply of Celestial Love:

Then from that turbulent cloud of which I spoke I heard a voice replying to this figure:

"You exist in great folly, because you want to lead a life in the cinders of ashes. You do not seek that life which will never wither in the beauty of youth, and which will never die in old age. Besides, you lack all light and exist in a black fog. You are enveloped in human willfulness as if enwrapped with worms. You are also living as if for the single moment, and afterward you will wither like a worthless thing. You will fall into the lake of perdition, and there you will be surrounded by all its embracing arms, which you with your nature call flowers.

"But I am the column of celestial harmony, and I am attendant upon all the joys of life. I do not scorn life, but trample underfoot all harmful things, just as I despise you. I am indeed a mirror of all the virtues, in which all faithfulness may clearly contemplate itself. You, however, pursue a nocturnal course, and your hands will wreak death."

LYRICS: *SYMPHONIA HARMONIAE CAELESTIUM REVELATIONUM*

O tu, suavissima virga
O you, most delightful branch,
putting forth leaves from the rod of Jesse,
O what a great splendor it is
that Divinity gazed at a most beautiful girl
—just as the eagle fixes his eye on the sun—
when the heavenly Father strove toward
the Virgin's brightness
and he wanted his words to be made flesh in her.

Now when the Virgin's mind was illuminated
by God's mystical mystery,
miraculously a bright flower sprang forth
from that Virgin—
with the celestial!

Glory to the Father and the Son
and to the Holy Spirit,
as it was in the beginning—
with the celestial!

O splendidissima gemma

O brightest jewel,
and serene splendor of the sun,
the fountain springing from the Father's heart
has poured into you.
His unique Word,
by which he created the primal matter of the world
—thrown into confusion by Eve—
the Father has forged this Word, as humanity,
for you.
Because of this, you are that lucent matter, through
which that same Word
breathed all the virtues—
just as it drew forth all creatures
from primal matter.

O dulcissime amator

O sweetest lover,
O sweetest embracing love,
help us to guard our virginity.

We have been born out of the dust, ah! ah!
and in the sin of Adam:
most harsh is it to deny
one's longing for a taste of the apple.
Raise us up, Savior Christ.

Ardently we desire to follow you.
O how difficult it is for us, miserable as we are,
to imitate you, spotless and innocent
king of angels!

Yet we trust you,
for you desire to recover a jewel
from what is rotten.

Now we call on you, our husband and comforter,
who redeemed us on the cross.
We are bound to you through your blood
as the pledge of betrothal.
We have renounced earthly men
and chosen you, the Son of God.

O most beautiful form,
O sweetest fragrance of desirable delights,
we sigh for you always in our sorrowful
banishment!
When may we see you and remain with you?

But we dwell in the world,
and you dwell in our mind,
we embrace you in our heart
as if we had you here with us.
you, bravest lion, have burst through the heavens
and are descending to the house of the virgins.
You have destroyed death, and are building life
in the golden city.

Grant us society in that city,
and let us dwell in you,
O sweetest husband,
who has rescued us from the jaws of the Devil,
seducer of our first mother!

O viriditas digiti Dei

O green life-force of the finger of God,
through which God sets his planting,
you gleam with sublime radiance
like an upright column.
You are full of glory
in the completion of God's work.

O mountain's height,
you will never be overthrown
because of God's indifference.

Solitary you stand
from ancient times as our defense.
Yet there is no armed might
that can drag you down.
You are full of glory.

Glory be to the Father and the Son
and the Holy Spirit.
You are full of glory!

DISCUSSION QUESTIONS

1. What kinds of images does Hildegard use to describe humans and human bodies? Why does she use such images?
2. Name some of the recurring images that Hildegard uses for divine presence and inspiration. What characteristics of divinity do these images imply?
3. In "O dulcissime amator," who is being addressed as a "lover?" Why?
4. In "O viriditas digiti Dei," to what is Hildegard referring when she writes of the "green life-force?" Why is this image effective?

WRITING SUGGESTION

1. Try sketching or painting the physical images from one of Hildegard's poetic visions. Pay close attention to the specific visual details she describes. Then write an analysis of the possible symbolic values of the physical images.

MARIE DE FRANCE (LATE 12TH CENTURY)

Eliduc

A native of France as her name indicates, Marie de France was probably associated with the court of King Henry II and Queen Eleanor of Aquitaine. Eleanor of Aquitaine was partly responsible for the development of the courtly love tradition, a code of behavior disseminated in songs and stories that promoted romance and reverence for court ladies and often focused sympathetically on adulterous love. Elements of the courtly love tradition can be seen in Marie de France's lay (a short narrative romance) "Eliduc," in which the knight Eliduc proves his battle prowess and wins the heart of Princess Guilliadun while he is still married to Guildeluec, who nobly and implausibly sacrifices her marital claim by becoming a nun. Eliduc and the princess marry, but later in life renounce earthly passions and join a monastery and convent. Romance and religion are bound tightly in this lay, as is often the case in the courtly love tradition. The story has traditionally been called "Eliduc" in spite of the fact that the author indicates in the first paragraph that she intended it to be called "Guildeluec and Guilliadun," after the two women characters.

THE LAY OF ELIDUC

Now will I rehearse before you a very ancient Breton Lay. As the tale was told to me, so, in turn, will I tell it over again, to the best of my art and knowledge. Hearken now to my story, its why and its reason.

In Brittany there lived a knight, so courteous and so brave, that in all the realm there was no worthier lord than he. This knight was named Eliduc. He had wedded in his youth a noble lady of proud race and name. They had long dwelt together in peace and content, for their hearts were fixed on one another in faith and loyalty. Now it chanced that Eliduc sought his fortune in a far land, where there was a great war. There he loved a Princess, the daughter of the King and Queen of those parts. Guillardun was the maiden's name, and in all the realm was none more fair. The wife of Eliduc had to name, Guildeluec, in her own country. By reason of these two ladies their story is known as the Lay of Guildeluec and Guillardun, but at first it was rightly called the Lay of Eliduc. The name is a little matter; but if you hearken to me you shall learn the story of these three lovers, in its pity and its truth.

Eliduc had as lord and suzerain, the King of Brittany over Sea. The knight was greatly loved and cherished of his prince, by reason of his long and loyal service. When the King's business took him from his realm, Eliduc was his master's Justice and Seneschal. He governed the country well and wisely, and held it from the foe with a strong hand. Nevertheless, in spite of all, much evil was appointed unto him. Eliduc was a mighty hunter, and by the King's grace, he would chase the stag within the woods. He was cunning and fair as Tristan, and so wise in venery, that the oldest forester might not gainsay him in aught concerning the shaw. But by reason of malice and envy, certain men accused him to the King that he had meddled with the royal pleasaunce. The King bade Eliduc to avoid his Court. He gave no reason for his commandment, and the knight might learn nothing of the cause. Often he prayed the King that he might know whereof he was accused. Often he begged his lord not to heed the specious and crafty words of his foes. He called to mind the wounds he had gained in his master's wars, but was answered never a word. When Eliduc found that he might get no speech with his lord, it became his honour to depart. He returned to his house, and calling his friends around him, opened out to them this business of the King's wrath, in recompense for his faithful service.

"I did not reckon on a King's gratitude; but as the proverb says, it is useless for a farmer to dispute with the horse in his plough. The wise and virtuous man keeps faith to his lord, and bears goodwill to his neighbour, not for what he may receive in return."

Then the knight told his friends that since he might no longer stay in his own country, he should cross the sea to the realm of Logres, and sojourn there awhile, for his solace. His fief he placed in the hands of his wife, and he required of his men, and of all who held him dear, that they would serve her loyally. Having given good counsel to the utmost of his power, the knight prepared him for the road. Right heavy were his friends and kin, that he must go forth from amongst them.

Eliduc took with him ten knights of his household, and set out on his journey. His dame came with him so far as she was able, wringing her hands, and making much sorrow, at the departure of her husband. At the end he pledged good faith to her, as she to him, and so she returned to her own home. Eliduc went his way, till he came to a haven on the sea. He took ship, and sailed to the realm of Totenois, for many kings dwell in that country, and ever there were strife and war. Now, near to Exeter, in this land, there dwelt a King, right rich and strong, but old and very full of years. He had no son of his body, but one maid only, young, and of an age to wed. Since he would not bestow this damsel on a certain prince of his neighbours, this lord made mortal war upon his fellow, spoiling and wasting all his land. The ancient King, for surety, had set his daughter within a castle, fair and very strong. He had charged the sergeants

Marie de France, "The Lay of Eliduc," *The Ebony Tower*, trans. Eugene Mason. Copyright in the Public Domain.

not to issue forth from the gates, and for the rest there was none so bold as to seek to storm the keep, or even to joust about the barriers. When Eliduc was told of this quarrel, he needed to go no farther, and sojourned for awhile in the land. He turned over in his mind which of these princes dealt unjustly with his neighbour. Since he deemed that the agèd king was the more vexed and sorely pressed in the matter, he resolved to aid him to the best of his might, and to take arms in his service. Eliduc, therefore, wrote letters to the King, telling him that he had quitted his own country, and sought refuge in the King's realm. For his part he was willing to fight as a mercenary in the King's quarrel, and if a safe conduct were given him, he and the knights of his company would ride, forthwith, to their master's aid. This letter, Eliduc sent by the hands of his squires to the King. When the ancient lord had read the letter, he rejoiced greatly, and made much of the messengers. He summoned his constable, and commanded him swiftly to write out the safe conduct, that would bring the baron to his side. For the rest he bade that the messengers meetly should be lodged and apparelled, and that such money should be given them as would be sufficient to their needs. Then he sealed the safe conduct with his royal seal, and sent it to Eliduc, straightway, by a sure hand.

When Eliduc came in answer to the summons, he was received with great honour by the King. His lodging was appointed in the house of a grave and courteous burgess of the city, who bestowed the fairest chamber on his guest. Eliduc fared softly, both at bed and board. He called to his table such good knights as were in misease, by reason of prison or of war. He charged his men that none should be so bold as to take pelf or penny from the citizens of the town, during the first forty days of their sojourn. But on the third day, it was bruited about the streets, that the enemy were near at hand. The country folk deemed that they approached to invest the city, and to take the gates by storm. When the noise and clamour of the fearful burgesses came to the ears of Eliduc, he and his company donned their harness, and got to horse, as quickly as they might. Forty horsemen mounted with him; as to the rest, many lay sick or hurt within the city, and others were captives in the hands of the foe. These forty stout sergeants waited for no sounding of trumpets; they hastened to seek their captain at his lodging, and rode at his back through the city gate.

"Sir," said they, "where you go, there we will follow, and what you bid us, that shall we do."

"Friends," made answer the knight, "I thank you for your fellowship. There is no man amongst us but who wishes to molest the foe, and do them all the mischief that he is able. If we await them in the town, we defend ourselves with the shield, and not with the sword. To my mind it is better to fall in the field than to hide behind walls; but if any of you have a wiser counsel to offer, now let him speak."

"Sir," replied a soldier of the company, "through the wood, in good faith, there runs a path, right strict and narrow. It is the wont of the enemy to approach our city by this track. After their deeds of arms before the walls, it is their custom to return by the way they came, helmet on saddle bow, and hauberk unbraced. If we might catch them, unready in the path, we could trouble them very grievously, even though it be at the peril of our lives."

"Friends," answered Eliduc, "you are all the King's men, and are bound to serve him faithfully, even to the death. Come, now, with me where I will go, and do that thing which you shall see me do. I give you my word as a loyal gentleman, that no harm shall hap to any. If we gain spoil and riches from the foe, each shall have his lot in the ransom. At the least we may do them much hurt and mischief in this quarrel."

Eliduc set his men in ambush, near by that path, within the wood. He told over to them, like a cunning captain, the crafty plan he had devised, and taught them how to play their parts, and to call upon his name. When the foe had entered on that perilous path, and were altogether taken in the snare, Eliduc cried his name, and summoned his companions to bear themselves like men. This they did stoutly, and assailed their enemy so fiercely that he was dismayed beyond measure, and his line being broken, fled to the forest. In this fight was the constable taken, together with fifty and five other lords, who owned themselves prisoners, and were given to the keeping of the squires. Great was the spoil in horse and harness, and marvellous was the wealth they gained in gold and ransom. So having done such great deeds in so short a space, they returned to the city, joyous and content.

The King looked forth from a tower. He feared grievously for his men, and made his complaint of Eliduc, who—he deemed—had betrayed him in his need. Upon the road he saw a great company, charged and laden with spoil. Since the number of those who returned was more than those who went forth, the king knew not again his own. He came down from the tower, in doubt and sore trouble, bidding that the gates should be made fast, and that men should mount upon the walls. For such coil as this, there was slender warrant. A squire who was sent out, came back with all speed, and showed him of this adventure. He told over the story of the ambush, and the tale of the prisoners. He rehearsed how the constable was taken, and that many a knight was wounded, and many a brave man slain. When the King might give credence thereto, he had more joy than ever king before. He got him from his tower, and going before Eliduc, he praised him to his face, and rendered him the captives as a gift. Eliduc gave the King's bounty to his men. He bestowed on them besides, all the harness and the spoil; keeping, for his part, but three knights, who had won much honour in the battle. From this day the King loved and cherished Eliduc very dearly. He held the knight, and his company, for a full year in his service, and at the end of the year, such faith had he in the knight's loyalty, that he appointed him Seneschal and Constable of his realm.

Eliduc was not only a brave and wary captain; he was also a courteous gentleman, right goodly to behold.

That fair maiden, the daughter of the King, heard tell of his deeds, and desired to see his face, because of the good men spake of him. She sent her privy chamberlain to the knight, praying him to come to her house, that she might solace herself with the story of his deeds, for greatly she wondered that he had no care for her friendship. Eliduc gave answer to the chamberlain that he would ride forthwith, since much he desired to meet so high a dame. He bade his squire to saddle his destrier, and rode to the palace, to have speech with the lady. Eliduc stood without the lady's chamber, and prayed the chamberlain to tell the dame that he had come, according to her

wish. The chamberlain came forth with a smiling face, and straightway led him in the chamber. When the princess saw the knight, she cherished him very sweetly, and welcomed him in the most honourable fashion. The knight gazed upon the lady, who was passing fair to see. He thanked her courteously, that she was pleased to permit him to have speech with so high a princess. Guillardun took Eliduc by the hand, and seated him upon the bed, near her side. They spake together of many things, for each found much to say. The maiden looked closely upon the knight, his face and semblance; to her heart she said that never before had she beheld so comely a man. Her eyes might find no blemish in his person, and Love knocked upon her heart, requiring her to love, since her time had come. She sighed, and her face lost its fair colour; but she cared only to hide her trouble from the knight, lest he should think her the less maidenly therefore. When they had talked together for a great space, Eliduc took his leave, and went his way. The lady would have kept him longer gladly, but since she did not dare, she allowed him to depart. Eliduc returned to his lodging, very pensive and deep in thought. He called to mind that fair maiden, the daughter of his King, who so sweetly had bidden him to her side, and had kissed him farewell, with sighs that were sweeter still. He repented him right earnestly that he had lived so long a while in the land without seeking her face, but promised that often he would enter her palace now. Then he remembered the wife whom he had left in his own house. He recalled the parting between them, and the covenant he made, that good faith and stainless honour should be ever betwixt the twain. But the maiden, from whom he came, was willing to take him as her knight! If such was her will, might any pluck him from her hand?

All night long, that fair maiden, the daughter of the King, had neither rest nor sleep. She rose up, very early in the morning, and commanding her chamberlain, opened out to him all that was in her heart. She leaned her brow against the casement.

"By my faith," she said, "I am fallen into a deep ditch, and sorrow has come upon me. I love Eliduc, the good knight, whom my father made his Seneschal. I love him so dearly that I turn the whole night upon my bed, and cannot close my eyes, nor sleep. If he assured me of his heart, and loved me again, all my pleasure should be found in his happiness. Great might be his profit, for he would become King of this realm, and little enough is it for his deserts, so courteous is he and wise. If he have nothing better than friendship to give me, I choose death before life, so deep is my distress."

When the princess had spoken what it pleased her to say, the chamberlain, whom she had bidden, gave her loyal counsel.

"Lady," said he, "since you have set your love upon this knight, send him now—if so it please you—some goodly gift-girdle or scarf or ring. If he receive the gift with delight, rejoicing in your favour, you may be assured that he loves you. There is no Emperor, under Heaven, if he were tendered your tenderness, but would go the more lightly for your grace."

The damsel hearkened to the counsel of her chamberlain, and made reply, "If only I knew that he desired my love! Did ever maiden woo her knight before, by asking whether he loved or hated her? What if he make of me a mock and a jest in the ears of his friends! Ah, if the secrets of the heart were but written on the face! But get you ready, for go you must, at once."

"Lady," answered the chamberlain, "I am ready to do your bidding."

"You must greet the knight a hundred times in my name, and will place my girdle in his hand, and this my golden ring."

When the chamberlain had gone upon his errand, the maiden was so sick at heart, that for a little she would have bidden him return. Nevertheless, she let him go his way, and eased her shame with words.

"Alas, what has come upon me, that I should put my heart upon a stranger. I know nothing of his folk, whether they be mean or high; nor do I know whether he will part as swiftly as he came. I have done foolishly, and am worthy of blame, since I have bestowed my love very lightly. I spoke to him yesterday for the first time, and now I pray him for his love. Doubtless he will make me a song! Yet if he be the courteous gentleman I believe him, he will understand, and not deal hardly with me. At least the dice are cast, and if he may not love me, I shall know myself the most woeful of ladies, and never taste of joy all the days of my life."

Whilst the maiden lamented in this fashion, the chamberlain hastened to the lodging of Eliduc. He came before the knight, and having saluted him in his lady's name, he gave to his hand the ring and the girdle. The knight thanked him earnestly for the gifts. He placed the ring upon his finger, and the girdle he girt about his body. He said no more to the chamberlain, nor asked him any questions; save only that he proffered him a gift. This the messenger might not have, and returned the way he came. The chamberlain entered in the palace and found the princess within her chamber. He greeted her on the part of the knight, and thanked her for her bounty.

"Diva, diva," cried the lady hastily, "hide nothing from me; does he love me, or does he not?"

"Lady," answered the chamberlain, "as I deem, he loves you, and truly. Eliduc is no cozener with words. I hold him for a discreet and prudent gentleman, who knows well how to hide what is in his heart. I gave him greeting in your name, and granted him your gifts. He set the ring upon his finger, and as to your girdle, he girt it upon him, and belted it tightly about his middle. I said no more to him, nor he to me; but if he received not your gifts in tenderness, I am the more deceived. Lady, I have told you his words: I cannot tell you his thoughts. Only, mark carefully what I am about to say. If Eliduc had not a richer gift to offer, he would not have taken your presents at my hand."

"It pleases you to jest," said the lady. "I know well that Eliduc does not altogether hate me. Since my only fault is to cherish him too fondly, should he hate me, he would indeed be blameworthy. Never again by you, or by any other, will I require him of aught, or look to him for comfort. He shall see that a maiden's love is no slight thing, lightly given, and lightly taken again—but, perchance, he will not dwell in the realm so long as to know of the matter."

"Lady, the knight has covenanted to serve the King, in all loyalty, for the space of a year. You have full leisure to tell, whatever you desire him to learn."

When the maiden heard that Eliduc remained in the country, she rejoiced very greatly. She was glad that the knight would sojourn awhile in her city, for she knew naught of the torment he endured, since first he looked upon her. He had neither peace nor delight, for he could not get her from his mind. He reproached himself bitterly. He called to remembrance the covenant he made with his wife, when he departed from his own land, that he would never be false to his oath. But his heart was a captive now, in a very strong prison. He desired greatly to be loyal and honest, but he could not deny his love for the maiden—Guillardun, so frank and so fair.

Eliduc strove to act as his honour required. He had speech and sight of the lady, and did not refuse her kiss and embrace. He never spoke of love, and was diligent to offend in nothing. He was careful in this, because he would keep faith with his wife, and would attempt no matter against his King. Very grievously he pained himself, but at the end he might do no more. Eliduc caused his horse to be saddled, and calling his companions about him, rode to the castle to get audience of the King. He considered, too, that he might see his lady, and learn what was in her heart. It was the hour of meat, and the King having risen from table, had entered in his daughter's chamber. The King was at chess, with a lord who had but come from over-sea. The lady sat near the board, to watch the movements of the game. When Eliduc came before the prince, he welcomed him gladly, bidding him to seat himself close at hand. Afterwards he turned to his daughter, and said, "Princess, it becomes you to have a closer friendship with this lord, and to treat him well and worshipfully. Amongst five hundred, there is no better knight than he."

When the maiden had listened demurely to her father's commandment, there was no gayer lady than she. She rose lightly to her feet, and taking the knight a little from the others, seated him at her side. They remained silent, because of the greatness of their love. She did not dare to speak the first, and to him the maid was more dreadful than a knight in mail. At the end Eliduc thanked her courteously for the gifts she had sent him; never was grace so precious and so kind. The maiden made answer to the knight, that very dear to her was the use he had found for her ring, and the girdle with which he had belted his body. She loved him so fondly that she wished him for her husband. If she might not have her wish, one thing she knew well, that she would take no living man, but would die unwed. She trusted he would not deny her hope.

"Lady," answered the knight, "I have great joy in your love, and thank you humbly for the goodwill you bear me. I ought indeed to be a happy man, since you deign to show me at what price you value our friendship. Have you remembered that I may not remain always in your realm? I covenanted with the King to serve him as his man for the space of one year. Perchance I may stay longer in his service, for I would not leave him till his quarrel be ended. Then I shall return to my own land; so, fair lady, you permit me to say farewell."

The maiden made answer to her knight, "Fair friend, right sweetly I thank you for your courteous speech. So apt a clerk will know, without more words, that he may have of me just what he would. It becomes my love to give faith to all you say."

The two lovers spoke together no further; each was well assured of what was in the other's heart. Eliduc rode back to his lodging, right joyous and content. Often he had speech with his friend, and passing great was the love which grew between the twain.

Eliduc pressed on the war so fiercely that in the end he took captive the King who troubled his lord, and had delivered the land from its foes. He was greatly praised of all as a crafty captain in the field, and a hardy comrade with the spear. The poor and the minstrel counted him a generous knight. About this time that King, who had bidden Eliduc avoid his realm, sought diligently to find him. He had sent three messengers beyond the seas to seek his ancient Seneschal. A strong enemy had wrought him much grief and loss. All his castles were taken from him, and all his country was a spoil to the foe. Often and sorely he repented him of the evil counsel to which he had given ear. He mourned the absence of his mightiest knight, and drove from his councils those false lords who, for malice and envy, had defamed him. These he outlawed for ever from his realm. The King wrote letters to Eliduc, conjuring him by the loving friendship that was once between them, and summoning him as a vassal is required of his lord, to hasten to his aid, in that his bitter need. When Eliduc heard these tidings they pressed heavily upon him, by reason of the grievous love he bore the dame. She, too, loved him with a woman's whole heart. Between the two there was nothing but the purest love and tenderness. Never by word or deed had they spoiled their friendship. To speak a little closely together; to give some fond and foolish gift; this was the sum of their love. In her wish and hope the maiden trusted to hold the knight in her land, and to have him as her lord. Naught she deemed that he was wedded to a wife beyond the sea.

"Alas," said Eliduc, "I have loitered too long in this country, and have gone astray. Here I have set my heart on a maiden, Guillardun, the daughter of the King, and she, on me. If, now, we part, there is no help that one, or both, of us, must die. Yet go I must. My lord requires me by letters, and by the oath of fealty that I have sworn. My own honour demands that I should return to my wife. I dare not stay; needs must I go. I cannot wed my lady, for not a priest in Christendom would make us man and wife. All things turn to blame. God, what a tearing asunder will our parting be! Yet there is one who will ever think me in the right, though I be held in scorn of all. I will be guided by her wishes, and what she counsels that will I do. The King, her sire, is troubled no longer by any war. First, I will go to him, praying that I may return to my own land, for a little, because of the need of my rightful lord. Then I will seek out the maiden, and show her the whole business. She will tell me her desire, and I shall act according to her wish."

The knight hesitated no longer as to the path he should follow. He went straight to the King, and craved leave to depart. He told him the story of his lord's distress, and read, and placed in the King's hands, the letters calling him back to his home. When the King had read the writing, and knew that Eliduc purposed to depart, he was passing sad and heavy. He offered the knight the third part of his kingdom, with all the treasure that he pleased to ask, if he would remain at his side. He offered these things to the knight—these, and the gratitude of all his days besides.

"Do not tempt me, sire," replied the knight. "My lord is in such deadly peril, and his letters have come so great a way to require me, that go I must to aid him in his need. When I have ended my task, I will return very gladly, if you care for my services, and

with me a goodly company of knights to fight in your quarrels."

The King thanked Eliduc for his words, and granted him graciously the leave that he demanded. He gave him, moreover, all the goods of his house; gold and silver, hound and horses, silken cloths, both rich and fair, these he might have at his will. Eliduc took of them discreetly, according to his need. Then, very softly, he asked one other gift. If it pleased the King, right willingly would he say farewell to the princess, before he went. The King replied that it was his pleasure, too. He sent a page to open the door of the maiden's chamber, and to tell her the knight's request. When she saw him, she took him by the hand, and saluted him very sweetly. Eliduc was the more fain of counsel than of claspings. He seated himself by the maiden's side, and as shortly as he might, commenced to show her of the business. He had done no more than read her of his letters, than her face lost its fair colour, and near she came to swoon. When Eliduc saw her about to fall, he knew not what he did, for grief. He kissed her mouth, once and again, and wept above her, very tenderly. He took, and held her fast in his arms, till she had returned from her swoon.

"Fair dear friend," said he softly, "bear with me while I tell you that you are my life and my death, and in you is all my comfort. I have bidden farewell to your father, and purposed to go back to my own land, for reason of this bitter business of my lord. But my will is only in your pleasure, and whatever the future brings me, your counsel I will do."

"Since you cannot stay," said the maiden, "take me with you, wherever you go. If not, my life is so joyless without you, that I would wish to end it with my knife."

Very sweetly made answer Sir Eliduc, for in honesty he loved honest maid, "Fair friend, I have sworn faith to your father, and am his man. If I carried you with me, I should give the lie to my troth. Let this covenant be made between us. Should you give me leave to return to my own land I swear to you on my honour as a knight, that I will come again on any day that you shall name. My life is in your hands. Nothing on earth shall keep me from your side, so only that I have life and health."

Then she, who loved so fondly, granted her knight permission to depart, and fixed the term, and named the day for his return. Great was their sorrow that the hour had come to bid farewell. They gave rings of gold for remembrance, and sweetly kissed adieu. So they severed from each other's arms.

Eliduc sought the sea, and with a fair wind, crossed swiftly to the other side. His lord was greatly content to learn the tidings of his knight's return. His friends and his kinsfolk came to greet him, and the common folk welcomed him very gladly. But, amongst them all, none was so blithe at his home-coming as the fair and prudent lady who was his wife. Despite this show of friendship, Eliduc was ever sad, and deep in thought. He went heavily, till he might look upon his friend. He felt no happiness, nor made pretence of any, till he should meet with her again. His wife was sick at heart, because of the coldness of her husband. She took counsel with her soul, as to what she had done amiss. Often she asked him privily, if she had come short or offended in any measure, whilst he was without the realm. If she was accused by any, let him tell her the accusation, that she might purge herself of the offence.

"Wife," answered Eliduc, "neither I, nor any other, charge you with aught that is against your honour to do. The cause of my sorrow is in myself. I have pledged my faith to the King of that country, from whence I come, that I will return to help him in his need. When my lord the King has peace in his realm, within eight days I shall be once more upon the sea. Great travail I must endure, and many pains I shall suffer, in readiness for that hour. Return I must, and till then I have no mind for anything but toil; for I will not give the lie to my plighted word."

Eliduc put his fief once more in the hands of his dame. He sought his lord, and aided him to the best of his might. By the counsel and prowess of the knight, the King came again into his own. When the term appointed by his lady, and the day she named for his return drew near, Eliduc wrought in such fashion that peace was accorded between the foes. Then the knight made him ready for his journey, and took thought to the folk he should carry with him. His choice fell on two of his nephews, whom he loved very dearly, and on a certain chamberlain of his household. These were trusted servitors, who

were of his inmost mind, and knew much of his counsel. Together with these went his squires, these only, for Eliduc had no care to take many. All these, nephew and squire and chamberlain, Eliduc made to promise, and confirm by an oath, that they would reveal nothing of his business.

The company put to sea without further tarrying, and, crossing quickly, came to that land where Eliduc so greatly desired to be. The knight sought a hostel some distance from the haven, for he would not be seen of any, nor have it bruited that Eliduc was returned. He called his chamberlain, and sent him to his friend, bearing letters that her knight had come, according to the covenant that had been made. At nightfall, before the gates were made fast, Eliduc issued forth from the city, and followed after his messenger. He had clothed himself in mean apparel, and rode at a footpace straight to the city, where dwelt the daughter of the King. The chamberlain arrived before the palace, and by dint of asking and prying, found himself within the lady's chamber. He saluted the maiden, and told her that her lover was near. When Guillardun heard these tidings she was astonied beyond measure, and for joy and pity wept right tenderly. She kissed the letters of her friend, and the messenger who brought such welcome tidings. The chamberlain prayed the lady to attire and make her ready to join her friend. The day was spent in preparing for the adventure, according to such plan as had been devised. When dark was come, and all was still, the damsel stole forth from the palace, and the chamberlain with her. For fear that any man should know her again, the maiden had hidden, beneath a riding cloak, her silken gown, embroidered with gold. About the space of a bow shot from the city gate, there was a coppice standing within a fair meadow. Near by this wood, Eliduc and his comrades awaited the coming of Guillardun. When Eliduc saw the lady, wrapped in her mantle, and his chamberlain leading her by the hand, he got from his horse, and kissed her right tenderly. Great joy had his companions at so fair a sight. He set her on the horse, and climbing before her, took bridle in glove, and returned to the haven, with all the speed he might. He entered forthwith in the ship, which put to sea, having on board none, save Eliduc, his men, and his lady, Guillardun. With a fair wind, and a quiet hour, the sailors thought that they would swiftly come to shore. But when their journey was near its end, a sudden tempest arose on the sea. A mighty wind drove them far from their harbourage, so that their rudder was broken, and their sail torn from the mast. Devoutly they cried on St. Nicholas, St. Clement, and Madame St. Mary, to aid them in this peril. They implored the Mother that she would approach her Son, not to permit them to perish, but to bring them to the harbour where they would come. Without sail or oar, the ship drifted here and there, at the mercy of the storm. They were very close to death, when one of the company, with a loud voice began to cry, "What need is there of prayers! Sir, you have with you, her, who brings us to our death. We shall never win to land, because you, who already have a faithful wife, seek to wed this foreign woman, against God and His law, against honour and your plighted troth. Grant us to cast her in the sea, and straightway the winds and the waves will be still."

When Eliduc heard these words he was like to come to harm for rage.

"Bad servant and felon traitor," he cried, "you should pay dearly for your speech, if I might leave my lady."

Eliduc held his friend fast in his arms, and cherished her as well as he was able. When the lady heard that her knight was already wedded in his own realm, she swooned where she lay. Her face became pale and discoloured; she neither breathed nor sighed, nor could any bring her any comfort. Those who carried her to a sheltered place, were persuaded that she was but dead, because of the fury of the storm. Eliduc was passing heavy. He rose to his feet, and hastening to his squire, smote him so grievously with an oar, that he fell senseless on the deck. He haled him by his legs to the side of the ship and flung the body in the sea, where it was swiftly swallowed by the waves. He went to the broken rudder, and governed the nave so skilfully, that it presently drew to land. So, having come to their fair haven, they cast anchor, and made fast their bridge to the shore. Dame Guillardun lay yet in her swoon, and seemed no other than if she were really dead. Eliduc's sorrow was all the more, since he deemed that he had slain her with his hand. He inquired of his companions in what near place they might lay

the lady to her rest, "for I will not bid her farewell, till she is put in holy ground with such pomp and rite as befit the obsequies of the daughter of a King." His comrades answered him never a word, for they were all bemused by reason of what had befallen. Eliduc, therefore, considered within himself to what place he should carry the lady. His own home was so near the haven where he had come, that very easily they could ride there before evening. He called to mind that in his realm there was a certain great forest, both long and deep. Within this wood there was a little chapel, served by a holy hermit for forty years, with whom Eliduc had oftimes spoken.

"To this holy man," he said, "I will bear my lady. In his chapel he shall bury her sweet body. I will endow him so richly of my lands, that upon her chantry shall be founded a mighty abbey. There some convent of monks or nuns or canons shall ever hold her in remembrance, praying God to grant her mercy in His day."

Eliduc got to horse, but first took oath of his comrades that never, by them, should be discovered, that which they should see. He set his friend before him on the palfrey, and thus the living and the dead rode together, till they had entered the wood, and come before the chapel. The squires called and beat upon the door, but it remained fast, and none was found to give them any answer. Eliduc bade that one should climb through a window, and open the door from within. When they had come within the chapel they found a new made tomb, and writ thereon, that the holy hermit having finished his course, was made perfect, eight days before. Passing sad was Eliduc, and esmayed. His companions would have digged a second grave, and set therein, his friend; but the knight would in no wise consent, for—he said—he purposed to take counsel of the priests of his country, as to building some church or abbey above her tomb. "At this hour we will but lay her body before the altar, and commend her to God His holy keeping." He commanded them to bring their mantles and make a bed upon the altar-pace. Thereon they laid the maiden, and having wrapped her close in her lover's cloak, left her alone. When the moment came for Eliduc to take farewell of his lady, he deemed that his own last hour had come. He kissed her eyes and her face.

"Fair friend," said he, "if it be pleasing to God, never will I bear sword or lance again, or seek the pleasures of this mortal world. Fair friend, in an ill hour you saw me! Sweet lady, in a bitter hour you followed me to death! Fairest, now were you a queen, were it not for the pure and loyal love you set upon me? Passing sad of heart am I for you, my friend. The hour that I have seen you in your shroud, I will take the habit of some holy order, and every day, upon your tomb, I will tell over the chaplet of my sorrow."

Having taken farewell of the maiden, Eliduc came forth from the chapel, and closed the doors. He sent messages to his wife, that he was returning to his house, but weary and overborne. When the dame heard these tidings, she was happy in her heart, and made ready to greet him. She received her lord tenderly; but little joy came of her welcome, for she got neither smiles in answer, nor tender words in return. She dared not inquire the reason, during the two days Eliduc remained in the house. The knight heard Mass very early in the morning, and then set forth on the road leading to the chapel where the maiden lay. He found her as he had parted, for she had not come back from her swoon, and there was neither stir in her, nor breath. He marvelled greatly, for he saw her, vermeil and white, as he had known her in life. She had lost none of her sweet colour, save that she was a little blanched. He wept bitterly above her, and entreated for her soul. Having made his prayer, he went again to his house.

On a day when Eliduc went forth, his wife called to her a varlet of her household, commanding him to follow his lord afar off, and mark where he went, and on what business. She promised to give him harness and horses, if he did according to her will. The varlet hid himself in the wood, and followed so cunningly after his lord, that he was not perceived. He watched the knight enter the chapel, and heard the cry and lamentation that he made. When Eliduc came out, the varlet hastened to his mistress, and told her what he had seen, the tears and dolour, and all that befell his lord within the hermitage. The lady summoned all her courage.

"We will go together, as soon as we may, to this hermitage. My lord tells me that he rides presently to the Court to speak with the King. I knew that my husband loved this dead hermit very tenderly, but I little thought that his loss would make him mad with grief."

The next day the dame let her lord go forth in peace. When, about noon, Eliduc rode to the Court to greet his King, the lady rose quickly, and carrying the varlet with her, went swiftly to the hermitage. She entered the chapel, and saw the bed upon the altar-pace, and the maiden thereon, like a new sprung rose. Stooping down the lady removed the mantle. She marked the rigid body, the long arms, and the frail white hands, with their slender fingers, folded on the breast. Thus she learned the secret of the sorrow of her lord. She called the varlet within the chapel, and showed him this wonder.

"Seest thou," she said, "this woman, who for beauty shineth as a gem! This lady, in her life, was the lover of my lord. It was for her that all his days were spoiled by grief. By my faith I marvel little at his sorrow, since I, who am a woman too, will—for pity's sake or love—never know joy again, having seen so fair a lady in the dust."

So the wife wept above the body of the maiden. Whilst the lady sat weeping, a weasel came from under the altar, and ran across Guillardun's body. The varlet smote it with his staff, and killed it as it passed. He took the vermin and flung it away. The companion of this weasel presently came forth to seek him. She ran to the place where he lay, and finding that he would not get him on his feet, seemed as one distraught. She went forth from the chapel, and hastened to the wood, from whence she returned quickly, bearing a vermeil flower beneath her teeth. This red flower she placed within the mouth of that weasel the varlet had slain, and immediately he stood upon his feet. When the lady saw this, she cried to the varlet,

"Throw, man, throw, and gain the flower."

The servitor flung his staff, and the weasels fled away, leaving that fair flower upon the floor. The lady rose. She took the flower, and returned with it swiftly to the altar pace. Within the mouth of the maiden, she set a flower that was more vermeil still. For a short space the dame and the damsel were alike breathless. Then the maiden came to herself, with a sigh. She opened her eyes, and commenced to speak.

"Diva," she said, "have I slept so long, indeed!"

When the lady heard her voice she gave thanks to God. She inquired of the maiden as to her name and degree. The damsel made answer to her, "Lady, I was born in Logres, and am daughter to the King of that realm. Greatly there I loved a knight, named Eliduc, the seneschal of my sire. We fled together from my home, to my own most grievous fault. He never told me that he was wedded to a wife in his own country, and he hid the matter so cunningly, that I knew naught thereof. When I heard tell of his dame, I swooned for pure sorrow. Now I find that this false lover, has, like a felon, betrayed me in a strange land. What will chance to a maiden in so foul a plight? Great is that woman's folly who puts her trust in man."

"Fair damsel," replied the lady, "there is nothing in the whole world that can give such joy to this felon, as to hear that you are yet alive. He deems that you are dead, and every day he beweeps your swoon in the chapel. I am his wife, and my heart is sick, just for looking on his sorrow. To learn the reason of his grief, I caused him to be followed, and that is why I have found you here. It is a great happiness for me to know that you live. You shall return with me to my home, and I will place you in the tenderness of your friend. Then I shall release him of his marriage troth, since it is my dearest hope to take the veil."

When the wife had comforted the maiden with such words, they went together to her own house. She called to her servitor, and bade him seek his lord. The varlet went here and there, till he lighted on Eliduc. He came before him, and showed him of all these things. Eliduc mounted straightway on his horse, and waiting neither for squire or companion, that same night came to his hall. When he found alive, her, who once was dead, Eliduc thanked his wife for so dear a gift. He rejoiced beyond measure, and of all his days, no day was more happy than this. He kissed the maiden often, and very sweetly she gave him again his kiss, for great was the joy between the twain. The dame looked on their happiness, and knew that her lord meetly had bestowed his love. She prayed him, therefore, that he would grant her leave to depart, since she would serve God as a cloistered nun. Of his wealth she craved such a

portion as would permit her to found a convent. He would then be able to wed the maiden on whom his heart was set, for it was neither honest nor seemly that a man should maintain a wife with either hand.

Eliduc could do no otherwise than consent. He gave the permission she asked, and did all according to her will. He endowed the lady of his lands, near by that chapel and hermitage, within the wood. There he built a church with offices and refectory, fair to see. Much wealth he bestowed on the convent, in money and estate. When all was brought to a good end, the lady took the veil upon her head. Thirty other ladies entered in the house with her, and long she ruled them as their Abbess, right wisely and well.

Eliduc wedded with his friend, in great pomp, and passing rich was the marriage feast. They dwelt in unity together for many days, for ever between them was perfect love. They walked uprightly, and gave alms of their goods, till such a time as it became them to turn to God. After much thought, Eliduc built a great church close beside his castle. He endowed it with all his gold and silver, and with the rest of his land. He set priests there, and holy layfolk also, for the business of the house, and the fair services of religion.

When all was builded and ordered, Eliduc offered himself, with them, that he—weak man—might serve the omnipotent God. He set with the Abbess Guildeluec —who once was his dame—that wife whom he loved so dearly well. The Abbess received her as a sister, and welcomed her right honourably. She admonished her in the offices of God, and taught her of the rules and practice of their holy Order. They prayed to God for their friend, that He would grant him mercy in His day. In turn, he entreated God for them. Messages came from convent and monastery as to how they fared, so that each might encourage the other in His way. Each strove painfully, for himself and his, to love God the more dearly, and to abide in His holy faith. Each made a good end, and the mercy of God was abundantly made clear to all.

Of the adventure of these three lovers, the courteous Bretons made this Lay for remembrance, since they deemed it a matter that men should not forget.

DISCUSSION QUESTIONS

1. Why do you think the story has been passed down with the title "Eliduc" instead of Marie de France's intended title, "Guildeluec and Guilliadun"?

2. Why does Eliduc leave Brittany?

3. How does Eliduc prove his battle skills in England?

4. What attracts Guilliadun to Eliduc? What attracts him to her?

5. Do the lovers physically consummate their relationship?

6. What is the wife's reaction when she discovers her husband's mistress? (Quote the exact words). Comment on her reaction—does it seem at all believable?

7. Why do you think Marie de France ended the story on a religious note instead of a romantic one?

DANTE ALIGHIERI (1265–1321)

D ante's *Divine Comedy* has come to be one of the most influential works of literature in Western culture, and it is certainly the most complete expression of medieval philosophy and theology. Dante Alighieri, born Durante, penned the best account we have of his early life, *La Vita Nuova* (meaning the new or early life), in which he narrates his first encounter, at age nine, with Beatrice Portinari, the woman who would inspire much of his life's work. His unfailing love for Beatrice only increased after her death at the age of 25, and she appears as a heavenly guide to him in the *Divine Comedy*.

As a young man, Dante became involved in political activities in Florence and found himself in the middle of a long-standing feud between two families that resulted in his banishment from Florence. He lived the rest of his life in exile, the guest of various patrons. Dante reflects the political strife of his times in *The Inferno*, and peoples hell in part with members of the feuding families.

In the *Divine Comedy*, Dante celebrates the redemption of Christianity, while also anatomizing the sins that trap souls in hell. Dante reflects the work's divine images and themes in the complex structure of the *Comedy*, which he patterns after the Holy Trinity: there are three books (*Inferno*, *Purgatory*, and *Paradise*); each book has 33 cantos (plus one introductory canto); and the rhyme scheme is *terza rima*—three-line stanzas in which the first and third lines rhyme, while the end sound of the second line forms the end rhyme for the first and third lines of the subsequent stanza (aba, bcb, cdc, etc.).

While *The Inferno* technically is an excerpt of a larger whole, it still stands on its own extremely well in its encyclopedic anatomy of sin and its geography of hell. Although readers of the excerpt will miss the majestic sweep of the *Divine Comedy* in its entirety, *The Inferno* mirrors the trajectory of the whole in the rising movement of its concluding lines and its final image of the heavenly stars.

THE INFERNO

Canto I.

In middle [160] of the journey of our days
    I found that I was in a darksome wood[161]—
    The right road lost and vanished in the maze.

Ah me! how hard to make it understood
    How rough that wood was, wild, and terrible:
    By the mere thought my terror is renewed.

More bitter scarce were death. But ere I tell
    At large of good which there by me was found,
    I will relate what other things befell.

Scarce know I how I entered on that ground,
    So deeply, at the moment when I passed
    From the right way, was I in slumber drowned.

But when beneath a hill[162] arrived at last,
    Which for the boundary of the valley stood,
    That with such terror had my heart harassed,

I upwards looked and saw its shoulders glowed,
    Radiant already with that planet's[163] light
    Which guideth surely upon every road.

A little then was quieted by the sight
    The fear which deep within my heart had lain
    Through all my sore experience of the night.

And as the man, who, breathing short in pain,
    Hath 'scaped the sea and struggled to the shore,
    Turns back to gaze upon the perilous main;

Even so my soul which fear still forward bore
    Turned to review the pass whence I egressed,
    And which none, living, ever left before.

My wearied frame refreshed with scanty rest,
    I to ascend the lonely hill essayed;
    The lower foot[164] still that on which I pressed.

And lo! ere I had well beginning made,
    A nimble leopard,[165] light upon her feet,
    And in a skin all spotted o'er arrayed:

Nor ceased she e'er me full in the face to meet,
    And to me in my path such hindrance threw
    That many a time I wheeled me to retreat.

It was the hour of dawn; with retinue
    Of stars[166] that were with him when Love Divine
    In the beginning into motion drew

Those beauteous things, the sun began to shine;
    And I took heart to be of better cheer
    Touching the creature with the gaudy skin,

Seeing 'twas morn,[167] and spring-tide of the year;
    Yet not so much but that when into sight
    A lion[168] came, I was disturbed with fear.

Towards me he seemed advancing in his might,
    Rabid with hunger and with head high thrown:
    The very air was tremulous with fright.

A she-wolf,[169] too, beheld I further on;
    All kinds of lust seemed in her leanness pent:
    Through her, ere now, much folk have misery known.

By her oppressed, and altogether spent
    By the terror breathing from her aspect fell,
    I lost all hope of making the ascent.

And as the man who joys while thriving well,
    When comes the time to lose what he has won
    In all his thoughts weeps inconsolable,

So mourned I through the brute which rest knows none:
    She barred my way again and yet again,
    And thrust me back where silent is the sun.

And as I downward rushed to reach the plain,
    Before mine eyes appeared there one aghast,
    And dumb like those that silence long maintain.

When I beheld him in the desert vast,
    'Whate'er thou art, or ghost or man,' I cried,
    'I pray thee show such pity as thou hast.'

'No man,[170] though once I was; on either side
    Lombard my parents were, and both of them
    For native place had Mantua,' he replied.

'Though late, *sub Julio*,[171] to the world I came,
    And lived at Rome in good Augustus' day,
    While yet false gods and lying were supreme.

Poet I was, renowning in my lay
    Anchises' righteous son, who fled from Troy
    What time proud Ilion was to flames a prey.

But thou, why going back to such annoy?
    The hill delectable why fear to mount,
    The origin and ground of every joy?'

'And thou in sooth art Virgil, and the fount
    Whence in a stream so full doth language flow?'
    Abashed, I answered him with humble front.

Dante, "Inferno," *The Divine Comedy,* trans. James Romanes Sibbald. Copyright in the Public Domain.

'Of other poets light and honour thou!
  Let the long study and great zeal I've shown
  In searching well thy book, avail me now!
My master thou, and author[172] thou, alone!
  From thee alone I, borrowing, could attain
  The style[173] consummate which has made me known.
Behold the beast which makes me turn again:
  Deliver me from her, illustrious Sage;
  Because of her I tremble, pulse and vein.'
'Thou must attempt another pilgrimage,'
  Observing that I wept, he made reply,
  'If from this waste thyself thou 'dst disengage.
Because the beast thou art afflicted by
  Will suffer none along her way to pass,
  But, hindering them, harasses till they die.
So vile a nature and corrupt she has,
  Her raging lust is still insatiate,
  And food but makes it fiercer than it was.
Many a creature[174] hath she ta'en for mate,
  And more she'll wed until the hound comes forth
  To slay her and afflict with torment great.
He will not batten upon pelf or earth;
  But he shall feed on valour, love, and lore;
  Feltro and Feltro[175] 'tween shall be his birth.
He will save humbled Italy, and restore,
  For which of old virgin Camilla[176] died;
  Turnus, Euryalus, Nisus, died of yore.
Her through all cities chasing far and wide,
  He at the last to Hell will thrust her down,
  Whence envy[177] first unloosed her. I decide
Therefore and judge that thou hadst best come on
  With me for guide;[178] and hence I'll lead thee where
  A place eternal shall to thee be shown.
There shalt thou hear the howlings of despair
  In which the ancient spirits make lament,
  All of them fain the second death to share.
Next shalt thou them behold who are content,
  Because they hope some time, though now in fire,
  To join the blessed they will win consent.
And if to these thou later wouldst aspire,
  A soul[179] shall guide thee, worthier far than I;
  When I depart thee will I leave with her.
Because the Emperor[180] who reigns on high
  Wills not, since 'gainst His laws I did rebel,[181]
  That to His city I bring any nigh.
O'er all the world He rules, there reigns as well;
  There is His city and exalted seat:

O happy whom He chooses there to dwell!'
And I to him: 'Poet, I thee entreat,
  Even by that God who was to thee unknown,
  That I may 'scape this present ill, nor meet
With worse, conduct me whither thou hast shown,
  That I may see Saint Peter's gate,[182] and those
  Whom thou reportest in such misery thrown.'
He moved away; behind him held I close.

Footnotes

[160] *Middle*: In his *Convito* (iv. 23), comparing human life to an arch, Dante says that at the age of thirty-five a man has reached the top and begins to go down. As he was born in 1265 that was his own age in 1300, the year in which the action of the poem is laid.

[161] *Darksome wood*: A state of spiritual darkness or despair into which he has gradually drifted, not without fault of his own.

[162] *A hill*: Lower down this hill is termed 'the origin and cause of all joy.' It is symbolical of spiritual freedom—of the peace and security that spring from the practice of virtue. Only, as it seems, by gaining such a vantage-ground can he escape from the wilderness of doubt—the valley of the shadow of death—in which he is lost.

[163] *That planet*: On the Ptolemaic system, which, as perfected by the Arabian astronomers, and with some Christian additions, was that followed by Dante, the sun is reckoned as one of the seven planets; all the others as well as the earth and the fixed stars deriving their light from it. Here the sunlight may signify the Divine help granted to all men in their efforts after virtue.

[164] *The lower foot, etc.*: This describes a cautious, slow ascent.

[165] *A nimble leopard*: The leopard and the lion and wolf that come with it are suggested by Jeremiah v. 6: 'A lion out of the forest shall slay them,' etc. We have Dante's own authority for it, in his letter to Can Grande, that several meanings are often hidden under the incidents of the *Comedy*. But whatever else the beasts may signify, their chief meaning is that of moral hindrances. It is plain that the lion and wolf are the sins of others—pride and avarice. If the leopard agrees with them in this, it most probably stands for the envy of those among whom Dante lived: at *Inf*. vi. 74 we find envy, pride, and avarice classed together as the sins that have corrupted Florence. But from *Inf*. xvi. 106 it appears that Dante hoped to get the better of the leopard by means of a cord which he wore girt about his loins. The cord is emblematical of self-control; and hence the leopard seems best to answer the idea of sensual pleasure in the sense of a temptation that makes difficult the pursuit of virtue. But it will be observed that this hindrance Dante trusts to overcome.

[166] *Stars, etc.*: The sun being then in Aries, as it was believed to have been at the creation.

[167] *Morn, etc.*: It is the morning of Friday the 25th of March in the year 1300, and by the use of Florence, which began the year on the anniversary of the incarnation, it is the first day of the New Year. The Good Friday of 1300 fell a fortnight later; but the 25th of March was held to be the true anniversary of the crucifixion as well as of the incarnation and of the creation of the world. The

date of the action is fixed by *Inf*. xxi. 112. The day was of good omen for success in the struggle with his lower self.

[168] *A lion*: Pride or arrogance; to be taken in its widest sense of violent opposition to all that is good.

[169] *A she-wolf*: Used elsewhere in the *Comedy* to represent avarice. Dante may have had specially in his mind the greed and worldly ambition of the Pope and the Court of Rome, but it is plain from line 110 that the wolf stands primarily for a sin, and not for a person or corporate body.

[170] *No man*: Brunetto Latini, the friend and master of Dante, says 'the soul is the life of man, but without the body is not man.'

[171] *Sub Julio*: Julius was not even consul when Virgil was born. But Dante reckoned Julius as the founder of the Empire, and therefore makes the time in which he flourished his. Virgil was only twenty-five years of age when Cæsar was slain; and thus it was under Augustus that his maturer life was spent.

[172] *Author*: Dante defines an author as 'one worthy to be believed and obeyed' (*Convito* iv. 6). For a guide and companion on his great pilgrimage he chooses Virgil, not only because of his fame as a poet, but also because he had himself described a descent to the Shades—had been already there. The vulgar conception of Virgil was that of a virtuous great magician.

[173] *The style, etc.*: Some at least of Dante's minor works had been given to the world before 1300, certainly the *Vita Nuova* and others of his poems. To his study of Virgil he may have felt himself indebted for the purity of taste that kept him superior to the frigid and artificial style of his contemporaries, He prided himself on suiting his language to his theme, as well as on writing straight from the heart.

[174] *Many a creature, etc.*: Great men and states, infected with avarice in its extended sense of encroachment on the rights of others.

[175] *Feltro and Feltro, etc.*: Who the deliverer was that Dante prophesies the coming of is not known, and perhaps never can be. Against the claims of Can Grande of Verona the objection is that, at any date which can reasonably be assigned for the publication of the *Inferno*, he had done nothing to justify such bright hopes of his future career. There seems proof, too, that till the *Paradiso* was written Dante entertained no great respect for the Scala family (*Purg.* xvi. 118, xviii. 121). Neither is Verona, or the widest territory over which Can Grande ever ruled, at all described by saying it lay between Feltro and Feltro.—I have preferred to translate *nazi-one* as birth rather than as nation or people. 'The birth of the deliverer will be found to have been between feltro and feltro.' Feltro, as Dante wrote it, would have no capital letter; and according to an old gloss the deliverer is to be of humble birth; *feltro* being the name of a poor sort of cloth. This interpretation I give as a curiosity more than anything else; for the most competent critics have decided against it, or ignored it.—Henry of Luxemburg, chosen Emperor in November 1308, is an old claimant for the post of the allegorical *veltro* or greyhound. On him Dante's hopes were long set as the man who should 'save Italy;' and it seems not out of place to draw attention to what is said of him by John Villani, the contemporary and fellow-townsman of Dante: 'He was of a magnanimous nature, though, as regarded his family, of poor extraction' (*Cronica*, ix. 1). Whatever may be made of the Feltros, the description in the text of the deliverer as one superior to all personal ambition

certainly answers better to Dante's ideal of a righteous Emperor than to the character of a partisan leader like Uguccione della Faggiuola, or an ambitious prince like Can Grande.

[176] *Camilla, etc.*: All persons of the *Æneid*.

[177] *Envy*: That of Satan.

[178] *Thou hadst best, etc.*: As will be seen from the next Canto, Virgil has been sent to the relief of Dante; but how that is to be wrought out is left to his own judgment. He might secure a partial deliverance for his ward by conducting him up the Delectable Mount—the peaceful heights familiar to himself, and which are to be won by the practice of natural piety. He chooses the other course, of guiding Dante through the regions of the future state, where the pilgrim's trust in the Divine government will be strengthened by what he sees, and his soul acquire a larger peace.

[179] *A soul*: Beatrice.

[180] *The Emperor*: The attribution of this title to God is significant of Dante's lofty conception of the Empire.

[181] *'Gainst his laws, etc.*: Virgil was a rebel only in the sense of being ignorant of the Christian revelation (*Inf.* iv. 37).

[182] *Saint Peter's gate*: Virgil has not mentioned Saint Peter. Dante names him as if to proclaim that it is as a Christian, though under heathen guidance, that he makes the pilgrimage. Here the gate seems to be spoken of as if it formed the entrance to Paradise, as it was popularly believed to do, and as if it were at that point Virgil would cease to guide him. But they are to find it nearer at hand, and after it has been passed Virgil is to act as guide through Purgatory.

Canto II.

It was the close of day;[183] the twilight brown
    All living things on earth was setting free
    From toil, while I preparing was alone[184]
To face the battle which awaited me,
    As well of ruth as of the perilous quest,
    Now to be limned by faultless memory.
Help, lofty genius! Muses,[185] manifest
    Goodwill to me! Recording what befell,
    Do thou, O mind, now show thee at thy best!
I thus began: 'Poet, and Guide as well,
    Ere trusting me on this adventure wide,
    Judge if my strength of it be capable.
Thou say'st that Silvius' father,[186] ere he died,
    Still mortal to the world immortal went,
    There in the body some time to abide.
Yet that the Foe of evil was content
    That he should come, seeing what high effect,
    And who and what should from him claim descent,
No room for doubt can thoughtful man detect:
    For he of noble Rome, and of her sway
    Imperial, in high Heaven grew sire elect.
And both of these,[187] the very truth to say,

Were founded for the holy seat, whereon
    The Greater Peter's follower sits to-day.
Upon this journey, praised by thee, were known
    And heard things by him, to the which he owed
    His triumph, whence derives the Papal gown.[188]
That path the Chosen Vessel[189] later trod
    So of the faith assurance to receive,
    Which is beginning of salvation's road.
But why should I go? Who will sanction give?
    For I am no Æneas and no Paul;
    Me worthy of it no one can believe,
Nor I myself. Hence venturing at thy call,
    I dread the journey may prove rash. But vain
    For me to reason; wise, thou know'st it all.'
Like one no more for what he wished for fain,
    Whose purpose shares mutation with his thought
    Till from the thing begun he turns again;
On that dim slope so grew I all distraught,
    Because, by brooding on it, the design
    I shrank from, which before I warmly sought.
'If well I understand these words of thine,'
    The shade of him magnanimous made reply,
    'Thy soul 'neath cowardice hath sunk supine,
Which a man often is so burdened by,
    It makes him falter from a noble aim,
    As beasts at objects ill-distinguished shy.
To loose thee from this terror, why I came,
    And what the speech I heard, I will relate,
    When first of all I pitied thee. A dame[190]
Hailed me where I 'mongst those in dubious state[191]
    Had my abode: so blest was she and fair,
    Her to command me I petitioned straight.
Her eyes were shining brighter than the star;[192]
    And she began to say in accents sweet
    And tuneable as angel's voices are:
"O Mantuan Shade, in courtesy complete,
    Whose fame survives on earth, nor less shall grow
    Through all the ages, while the world hath seat;
A friend of mine, with fortune for his foe,
    Has met with hindrance on his desert way,
    And, terror-smitten, can no further go,
But turns; and that he is too far astray,
    And that I rose too late for help, I dread,
    From what in Heaven concerning him they say.
Go, with thy speech persuasive him bestead,
    And with all needful help his guardian prove,
    That touching him I may be comforted.

Know, it is Beatrice seeks thee thus to move.
    Thence come I where I to return am fain:
    My coming and my plea are ruled by love.
When I shall stand before my Lord again,
    Often to Him I will renew thy praise."
    And here she ceased, nor did I dumb remain:
"O virtuous Lady, thou alone the race
    Of man exaltest 'bove all else that dwell
    Beneath the heaven which wheels in narrowest space.[193]
To do thy bidding pleases me so well,
    Though 'twere already done 'twere all too slow;
    Thy wish at greater length no need to tell.
But say, what tempted thee to come thus low,
    Even to this centre, from the region vast,[194]
    Whither again thou art on fire to go?"
"This much to learn since a desire thou hast,"
    She answered, "briefly thee I'll satisfy,
    How, coming here, I through no terrors passed.
We are, of right, such things alarmèd by,
    As have the power to hurt us; all beside
    Are harmless, and not fearful. Wherefore I—
Thus formed by God, His bounty is so wide—
    Am left untouched by all your miseries,
    And through this burning[195] unmolested glide.
A noble lady[196] is in Heaven, who sighs
    O'er the obstruction where I'd have thee go,
    And breaks the rigid edict of the skies.
Calling on Lucia,[197] thus she made her know
    What she desired: 'Thy vassal[198] now hath need
    Of help from thee; do thou then helpful show.'
Lucia, who hates all cruelty, in speed
    Rose, and approaching where I sat at rest,
    To venerable Rachel[199] giving heed,
Me: 'Beatrice, true praise of God,' addressed;
    'Why not help him who had such love for thee,
    And from the vulgar throng to win thee pressed?
Dost thou not hear him weeping pitiably,
    Nor mark the death now threatening him upon
    A flood[200] than which less awful is the sea?'
Never on earth did any ever run,
    Allured by profit or impelled by fear,
    Swifter than I, when speaking she had done,
From sitting 'mong the blest descended here,
    My trust upon thy comely rhetoric cast,
    Which honours thee and those who lend it ear."
When of these words she spoken had the last,
    She turned aside bright eyes which tears[201] did fill,

And I by this was urged to greater haste.

And so it was I joined thee by her will,
    And from that raging beast delivered thee,
    Which barred the near way up the beauteous hill.

What ails thee then? Why thus a laggard be?
    Why cherish in thy heart a craven fear?
    Where is thy franchise, where thy bravery,

When three such blessed ladies have a care
    For thee in Heaven's court, and these words of mine
    Thee for such wealth of blessedness prepare?'

As flowers, by chills nocturnal made to pine
    And shut themselves, when touched by morning bright
    Upon their stems arise, full-blown and fine;

So of my faltering courage changed the plight,
    And such good cheer ran through my heart, it spurred
    Me to declare, like free-born generous wight:

'O pitiful, who for my succour stirred!
    And thou how full of courtesy to run,
    Alert in service, hearkening her true word!

Thou with thine eloquence my heart hast won
    To keen desire to go, and the intent
    Which first I held I now no longer shun.

Therefore proceed; my will with thine is blent:
    Thou art my Guide, Lord, Master;[202] thou alone!'
    Thus I; and with him, as he forward went,

The steep and rugged road I entered on.

Footnotes

[183] *Close of day*: The evening of the Friday. It comes on us with something of a surprise that a whole day has been spent in the attempt to ascend the hill, and in conference with Virgil.

[184] *Alone*: Of earthly creatures, though in company with Virgil, a shade. In these words is to be found the keynote to the Canto. With the sense of deliverance from immediate danger his enthusiasm has died away. After all, Virgil is only a shade; and his heart misgives him at the thought of engaging, in the absence of all human companionship, upon a journey so full of terrors. He is not reassured till Virgil has displayed his commission.

[185] *Muses*: The invocation comes now, the First Canto being properly an introduction. Here it may be pointed out, as illustrating the refinement of Dante's art, that the invocation in the *Purgatorio* is in a higher strain, and that in the *Paradiso* in a nobler still.

[186] *Silvius' father*: Æneas, whose visit to the world of shades is described in the Sixth *Æneid*. He finds there his father Anchises, who foretells to him the fortunes of his descendants down to the time of Augustus.

[187] *Both of these*: Dante uses language slightly apologetic as he unfolds to Virgil, the great Imperialist poet, the final cause of Rome and the Empire. But while he thus exalts the Papal office, making all Roman history a preparation for its establishment, Dante throughout his works is careful to refuse any but a spiritual

or religious allegiance to the Pope, and leaves himself free, as will be frequently seen in the course of the *Comedy*, to blame the Popes as men, while yielding all honour to their great office. In this emphatic mention of Rome as the divinely-appointed seat of Peter's Chair may be implied a censure on the Pope for the transference of the Holy See to Avignon, which was effected in 1305, between the date assigned to the action of the poem and the period when it was written.

[188] *Papal gown*: 'The great mantle' Dante elsewhere terms it; the emblem of the Papal dignity. It was only in Dante's own time that coronation began to take the place of investiture with the mantle.

[189] *Chosen Vessel*: Paul, who like Æneas visited the other world, though not the same region of it. Throughout the poem instances drawn from profane history, and even poetry and mythology, are given as of authority equal to those from Christian sources.

[190] *A dame*: Beatrice, the heroine of the *Vita Nuova*, at the close of which Dante promises some day to say of her what was never yet said of any woman. She died in 1290, aged twenty-four. In the *Comedy* she fills different parts: she is the glorified Beatrice Portinari whom Dante first knew as a fair Florentine girl; but she also represents heavenly truth, or the knowledge of it—the handmaid of eternal life. Theology is too hard and technical a term to bestow on her. Virgil, for his part, represents the knowledge that men may acquire of Divine law by the use of their reason, helped by such illumination as was enjoyed by the virtuous heathen. In other words, he is the exponent of the Divine revelation involved in the Imperial system—for the Empire was never far from Dante's thoughts. To him it meant the perfection of just rule, in which due cognisance is taken of every right and of every duty. The relation Dante bears to these two is that of erring humanity struggling to the light. Virgil leads him as far as he can, and then commits him to the holier rule of Beatrice. But the poem would lose its charm if the allegorical meaning of every passage were too closely insisted on. And, worse than that, it cannot always be found.

[191] *Dubious state*: The limbo of the virtuous heathen (Canto iv.).

[192] *The star*: In the *Vita Nuova* Dante speaks of the star in the singular when he means the stars.

[193] *In narrowest space*: The heaven of the moon, on the Ptolemaic system the lowest of the seven planets. Below it there is only the heaven of fire, to which all the flames of earth are attracted. The meaning is, above all on earth.

[194] *The region vast*: The empyrean, or tenth and highest heaven of all. It is an addition by the Christian astronomers to the heavens of the Ptolemaic system, and extends above the *primum mobile*, which imparts to all beneath it a common motion, while leaving its own special motion to each. The empyrean is the heaven of Divine rest.

[195] *Burning*: 'Flame of this burning,' allegorical, as applied to the limbo where Virgil had his abode. He and his companions suffer only from unfulfilled but lofty desire (*Inf.* iv. 41).

[196] *A noble lady*: The Virgin Mary, of whom it is said (*Parad.* xxxiii. 16) that her 'benignity not only succours those who ask, but often anticipates their demand;' as here. She is the symbol of Divine grace in its widest sense. Neither Christ nor Mary is mentioned by name in the *Inferno*.

[197] *Lucia*: The martyr saint of Syracuse. Witte (*Dante-Forschungen*, vol. ii. 30) suggests that Lucia Ubaldini may be

meant, a thirteenth-century Florentine saint, and sister of the Cardinal (*Inf.* x. 120). The day devoted to her memory was the 30th of May. Dante was born in May, and if it could be proved that he was born on the 30th of the month the suggestion would be plausible. But for the greater Lucy is to be said that she was especially helpful to those troubled in their eyesight, as Dante was at one time of his life. Here she is the symbol of illuminating grace.

[198] *Thy vassal*: Saint Lucy being held in special veneration by Dante; or only that he was one that sought light. The word *fedele* may of course, as it usually is, be read in its primary sense of 'faithful one;' but it is old Italian for vassal; and to take the reference to be to the duty of the overlord to help his dependant in need seems to give force to the appeal.

[199] *Rachel*: Symbol of the contemplative life.

[200]*A flood, etc.*: 'The sea of troubles' in which Dante is involved.

[201] *Tears*: Beatrice weeps for human misery—especially that of Dante—though unaffected by the view of the sufferings of Inferno.

[202] *My Guide, etc.*: After hearing how Virgil was moved to come, Dante accepts him not only for his guide, as he did at the close of the First Canto, but for his lord and master as well.

Canto III.

Through me to the city dolorous lies the way,
    Who pass through me shall pains eternal prove,
    Through me are reached the people lost for aye.

'Twas Justice did my Glorious Maker move;
    I was created by the Power Divine,[203]
    The Highest Wisdom, and the Primal Love.

No thing's creation earlier was than mine,
    If not eternal;[204] I for aye endure:
    Ye who make entrance, every hope resign!

These words beheld I writ in hue obscure
    On summit of a gateway; wherefore I:
    'Hard[205] is their meaning, Master.' Like one sure

Beforehand of my thought, he made reply:
    'Here it behoves to leave all fears behind;
    All cowardice behoveth here to die.

For now the place I told thee of we find,
    Where thou the miserable folk shouldst see
    Who the true good[206] of reason have resigned.'

Then, with a glance of glad serenity,
    He took my hand in his, which made me bold,
    And brought me in where secret things there be.

There sighs and plaints and wailings uncontrolled
    The dim and starless air resounded through;
    Nor at the first could I from tears withhold.

The various languages and words of woe,
    The uncouth accents,[207] mixed with angry cries
    And smiting palms and voices loud and low,

Composed a tumult which doth circling rise

For ever in that air obscured for aye;
    As when the sand upon the whirlwind flies.

And, horror-stricken,[208] I began to say:
    'Master, what sound can this be that I hear,
    And who the folk thus whelmed in misery?'

And he replied: 'In this condition drear
    Are held the souls of that inglorious crew
    Who lived unhonoured, but from guilt kept clear.

Mingled they are with caitiff angels, who,
    Though from avowed rebellion they refrained,
    Disloyal to God, did selfish ends pursue.

Heaven hurled them forth, lest they her beauty stained;
    Received they are not by the nether hell,
    Else triumph[209] thence were by the guilty gained.'

And I: 'What bear they, Master, to compel
    Their lamentations in such grievous tone?'
    He answered: 'In few words I will thee tell.

No hope of death is to the wretches known;
    So dim the life and abject where they sigh
    They count all sufferings easier than their own.

Of them the world endures no memory;
    Mercy and justice them alike disdain.
    Speak we not of them: glance, and pass them by.'

I saw a banner[210] when I looked again,
    Which, always whirling round, advanced in haste
    As if despising steadfast to remain.

And after it so many people chased
    In long procession, I should not have said
    That death[211] had ever wrought such countless waste.

Some first I recognised, and then the shade
    I saw and knew of him, the search to close,
    Whose dastard soul the great refusal[212] made.

Straightway I knew and was assured that those
    Were of the tribe of caitiffs,[213] even the race
    Despised of God and hated of His foes.

The wretches, who when living showed no trace
    Of life, went naked, and were fiercely stung
    By wasps and hornets swarming in that place.

Blood drawn by these out of their faces sprung
    And, mingled with their tears, was at their feet
    Sucked up by loathsome worms it fell among.

Casting mine eyes beyond, of these replete,
    People I saw beside an ample stream,
    Whereon I said: 'O Master, I entreat,

Tell who these are, and by what law they seem
    Impatient till across the river gone;
    As I distinguish by this feeble gleam.'

And he: 'These things shall unto thee be known
  What time our footsteps shall at rest be found
  Upon the woful shores of Acheron.'
Then with ashamèd eyes cast on the ground,
  Fearing my words were irksome in his ear,
  Until we reached the stream I made no sound.
And toward us, lo, within a bark drew near
  A veteran[214] who with ancient hair was white,
  Shouting: 'Ye souls depraved, be filled with fear.
Hope never more of Heaven to win the sight;
  I come to take you to the other strand,
  To frost and fire and everlasting night.
And thou, O living soul, who there dost stand,
  From 'mong the dead withdraw thee.'
  Then, awareThat not at all I stirred at his command,
'By other ways,[215] from other ports thou'lt fare;
  But they will lead thee to another shore,
  And 'tis a skiff more buoyant must thee bear.'
And then my leader: 'Charon, be not sore,
  For thus it has been willed where power ne'er came
  Short of the will; thou therefore ask no more.'
And hereupon his shaggy cheeks grew tame
  Who is the pilot of the livid pool,
  And round about whose eyes glowed wheels of flame.
But all the shades, naked and spent with dool,
  Stood chattering with their teeth, and changing hue
  Soon as they heard the words unmerciful.
God they blasphemed, and families whence they grew;
  Mankind, the time, place, seed in which began
  Their lives, and seed whence they were born. Then drew
They crowding all together, as they ran,
  Bitterly weeping, to the accursed shore
  Predestinate for every godless man.
The demon Charon, with eyes evermore
  Aglow, makes signals, gathering them all;
  And whoso lingers smiteth with his oar.
And as the faded leaves of autumn fall
  One after the other, till at last the bough
  Sees on the ground spread all its coronal;
With Adam's evil seed so haps it now:
  At signs each falls in turn from off the coast,
  As fowls[216] into the ambush fluttering go.
The gloomy waters thus by them are crossed,
  And ere upon the further side they land,
  On this, anew, is gathering a host.
'Son,' said the courteous Master,[217] 'understand,
  All such as in the wrath of God expire,

From every country muster on this strand.
To cross the river they are all on fire;
  Their wills by Heavenly justice goaded on
  Until their terror merges in desire.
This way no righteous soul has ever gone;
  Wherefore[218] of thee if Charon should complain,
  Now art thou sure what by his words is shown.'
When he had uttered this the dismal plain
  Trembled[219] so violently, my terror past
  Recalling now, I'm bathed in sweat again.
Out of the tearful ground there moaned a blast
  Whence lightning flashed forth red and terrible,
  Which vanquished all my senses; and, as cast
In sudden slumber, to the ground I fell.

Footnotes

[203] *Power Divine, etc.*: The Persons of the Trinity, described by their attributes.
[204] *If not eternal*: Only the angels and the heavenly spheres were created before Inferno. The creation of man came later. But from *Inf.* xxxiv. 124 it appears that Inferno was hollowed out of the earth; and at *Parad.* vii. 124 the earth is declared to be 'corruptible and enduring short while;' therefore not eternal.
[205] *Hard, etc.*: The injunction to leave all hope behind makes Dante hesitate to enter. Virgil anticipates the objection before it is fully expressed, and reminds him that the passage through Inferno is to be only one stage of his journey. Not by this gate will he seek to quit it.
[206] *True good, etc.*: Truth in its highest form—the contemplation of God.
[207] *Uncouth accents*: 'Like German,' says Boccaccio.
[208] *Horror-stricken*: 'My head enveloped in horror.' Some texts have 'error,' and this yields a better meaning—that Dante is amazed to have come full into the crowd of suffering shades before he has even crossed Acheron. If with the best texts 'horror' be read, the meaning seems to be that he is so overwhelmed by fear as to lose his presence of mind. They are not yet in the true Inferno, but only in the vestibule or forecourt of it—the flat rim which runs round the edge of the pit.
[209] *Else triumph, etc.*: The satisfaction of the rebel angels at finding that they endured no worse punishment than that of such as remained neutral.
[210] *A banner*: Emblem of the instability of those who would never take a side.
[211] *That death, etc.*: The touch is very characteristic of Dante. He feigns astonishment at finding that such a proportion of mankind can preserve so pitiful a middle course between good and evil, and spend lives that are only 'a kind of—as it were.'
[212] *The great refusal*: Dante recognises him, and so he who made the great refusal must have been a contemporary. Almost beyond doubt Celestine V. is meant, who was in 1294 elected Pope against his will, and resigned the tiara after wearing it a few months; the only Pope who ever resigned it, unless we count Clement I. As he was not canonized till 1326, Dante was free to form his own judgment of his conduct. It has been objected

that Dante would not treat with contumely a man so devout as Celestine. But what specially fits him to be the representative caitiff is just that, being himself virtuous, he pusillanimously threw away the greatest opportunity of doing good. By his resignation Boniface VIII. became Pope, to whose meddling in Florentine affairs it was that Dante owed his banishment. Indirectly, therefore, he owed it to the resignation of Celestine; so that here we have the first of many private scores to be paid off in the course of the *Comedy*. Celestine's resignation is referred to (*Inf.* xxvii. 104).—Esau and the rich young man in the Gospel have both been suggested in place of Celestine. To either of them there lies the objection that Dante could not have recognised him. And, besides, Dante's contemporaries appear at once to have discovered Celestine in him who made the great refusal. In Paradise the poet is told by his ancestor Cacciaguida that his rebuke is to be like the wind, which strikes most fiercely on the loftiest summits (*Parad.* xvii. 133); and it agrees well with such a profession, that the first stroke he deals in the *Comedy* is at a Pope.

[213] *Caitiffs*: To one who had suffered like Dante for the frank part he took in affairs, neutrality may well have seemed the unpardonable sin in politics; and no doubt but that his thoughts were set on the trimmers in Florence when he wrote, 'Let us not speak of them!'

[214] *A veteran*: Charon. In all this description of the passage of the river by the shades, Dante borrows freely from Virgil. It has been already remarked on *Inf.* ii. 28 that he draws illustrations from Pagan sources. More than that, as we begin to find, he boldly introduces legendary and mythological characters among the persons of his drama. With Milton in mind, it surprises, on a first acquaintance with the *Comedy*, to discover how nearly independent of angels is the economy invented by Dante for the other world.

[215] *Other ways, etc.*: The souls bound from earth to Purgatory gather at the mouth of the Tiber, whence they are wafted on an angel's skiff to their destination (*Purg.* ii. 100). It may be here noted that never does Dante hint a fear of one day becoming a denizen of Inferno. It is only the pains of Purgatory that oppress his soul by anticipation. So here Charon is made to see at a glance that the pilgrim is not of those 'who make descent to Acheron.'

[216] *As fowls, etc.*: 'As a bird to its lure'—generally interpreted of the falcon when called back. But a witness of the sport of netting thrushes in Tuscany describes them as 'flying into the vocal ambush in a hurried, half-reluctant, and very remarkable manner.'

[217] *Courteous Master*: Virgil here gives the answer promised at line 76; and Dante by the epithet he uses removes any impression that his guide had been wanting in courtesy when he bade him wait.

[218] *Wherefore*: Charon's displeasure only proves that he feels he has no hold on Dante.

[219] *Trembled, etc.*: Symbolical of the increase of woe in Inferno when the doomed souls have landed on the thither side of Acheron. Hell opens to receive them. Conversely, when any purified soul is released from Purgatory the mountain of purification trembles to its base with joy (*Purg.* xxi. 58).

Canto IV.

Resounding thunder broke the slumber deep
  That drowsed my senses, and myself I shook
  Like one by force awakened out of sleep.

Then rising up I cast a steady look,
  With eyes refreshed, on all that lay around,
  And cognisance of where I found me took.

In sooth, me on the valley's brink I found
  Of the dolorous abyss, where infinite
  Despairing cries converge with thundering sound.[220]

Cloudy it was, and deep, and dark as night;
  So dark that, peering eagerly to find
  What its depths held, no object met my sight.

'Descend we now into this region blind,'
  Began the Poet with a face all pale;
  'I will go first, and do thou come behind.'

Marking the wanness on his cheek prevail,
  I asked, 'How can I, seeing thou hast dread,
  My wonted comforter when doubts assail?'

'The anguish of the people,' then he said,
  'Who are below, has painted on my face
  Pity,[221] by thee for fear interpreted.

Come! The long journey bids us move apace.'
  Then entered he and made me enter too
  The topmost circle girding the abyss.

Therein, as far as I by listening knew,
  There was no lamentation save of sighs,
  Whence throbbed the air eternal through and through.

This, sorrow without suffering made arise
  From infants and from women and from men,
  Gathered in great and many companies.

And the good Master: 'Wouldst thou[222] nothing then
  Of who those spirits are have me relate?
  Yet know, ere passing further, although when

On earth they sinned not, worth however great
  Availed them not, they being unbaptized—
  Part[223] of the faith thou holdest. If their fate

Was to be born ere man was Christianised,
  God, as behoved, they never could adore:
  And I myself am with this folk comprised.

For such defects—our guilt is nothing more—
  We are thus lost, suffering from this alone
  That, hopeless, we our want of bliss deplore.'

Greatly I sorrowed when he made this known,
  Because I knew that some who did excel
  In worthiness were to that limbo[224] gone.

'Tell me, O Sir,' I prayed him, 'Master,[225] tell,'
  —That I of the belief might surety win,
  Victorious every error to dispel—

'Did ever any hence to bliss attain
  By merit of another or his own?'

And he, to whom my hidden drift[226] was plain:
  'I to this place but lately[227] had come down,
    When I beheld one hither make descent;
    A Potentate[228] who wore a victor's crown.
The shade of our first sire forth with him went,
  And his son Abel's, Noah's forth he drew,
    Moses' who gave the laws, the obedient
Patriarch Abram's, and King David's too;
  And, with his sire and children, Israel,
    And Rachel, winning whom such toils he knew;
And many more, in blessedness to dwell.
  And I would have thee know, earlier than these
    No human soul was ever saved from Hell.'
While thus he spake our progress did not cease,
  But we continued through the wood to stray;
    The wood, I mean, with crowded ghosts for trees.
Ere from the summit far upon our way
  We yet had gone, I saw a flame which glowed,
    Holding a hemisphere[229] of dark at bay.
'Twas still a little further on our road,
  Yet not so far but that in part I guessed
    That honourable people there abode.
'Of art and science Ornament confessed!
  Who are these honoured in such high degree,
    And in their lot distinguished from the rest?'
He said: 'For them their glorious memory,
  Still in thy world the subject of renown,
    Wins grace[230] by Heaven distinguished thus to be.'
Meanwhile I heard a voice: 'Be honour shown
  To the illustrious poet,[231] for his shade
    Is now returning which a while was gone.'
When the voice paused nor further utterance made,
  Four mighty shades drew near with one accord,
    In aspect neither sorrowful nor glad.
'Consider that one, armèd with a sword,'[232]
  Began my worthy Master in my ear,
    'Before the three advancing like their lord;
For he is Homer, poet with no peer:
  Horace the satirist is next in line,
    Ovid comes third, and Lucan in the rear.
And 'tis because their claim agrees with mine
  Upon the name they with one voice did cry,
    They to their honour[233] in my praise combine.'
Thus I beheld their goodly company—
  The lords[234] of song in that exalted style
    Which o'er all others, eagle-like, soars high.
Having conferred among themselves a while

They turned toward me and salutation made,
  And, this beholding, did my Master smile.[235]
And honour higher still to me was paid,
  For of their company they made me one;
    So I the sixth part 'mong such genius played.
Thus journeyed we to where the brightness shone,
  Holding discourse which now 'tis well to hide,
    As, where I was, to hold it was well done.
At length we reached a noble castle's[236] side
  Which lofty sevenfold walls encompassed round,
    And it was moated by a sparkling tide.
This we traversed as if it were dry ground;
  I through seven gates did with those sages go;
    Then in a verdant mead people we found
Whose glances were deliberate and slow.
  Authority was stamped on every face;
    Seldom they spake, in tuneful voices low.
We drew apart to a high open space
  Upon one side which, luminously serene,
    Did of them all a perfect view embrace.
Thence, opposite, on the enamel green
  Were shown me mighty spirits; with delight
    I still am stirred them only to have seen.
With many more, Electra was in sight;
  'Mong them I Hector and Æneas spied,
    Cæsar in arms,[237] his eyes, like falcon's, bright.
And, opposite, Camilla I descried;
  Penthesilea too; the Latian King
    Sat with his child Lavinia by his side.
Brutus[238] I saw, who Tarquin forth did fling;
  Cornelia, Marcia,[239] Julia, and Lucrece.
    Saladin[240] sat alone. Considering
What lay beyond with somewhat lifted eyes,
  The Master[241] I beheld of those that know,
    'Mong such as in philosophy were wise.
All gazed on him as if toward him to show
  Becoming honour; Plato in advance
    With Socrates: the others stood below.
Democritus[242] who set the world on chance;
  Thales, Diogenes, Empedocles,
    Zeno, and Anaxagoras met my glance;
Heraclitus, and Dioscorides,
  Wise judge of nature. Tully, Orpheus, were
    With ethic Seneca and Linus.[243] These,
And Ptolemy,[244] too, and Euclid, geometer,
  Galen, Hippocrates, and Avicen,[245]
    Averroes,[246] the same who did prepare

The Comment, saw I; nor can tell again

    The names of all I saw; the subject wide

    So urgent is, time often fails me. Then

Into two bands the six of us divide;

    Me by another way my Leader wise

    Doth from the calm to air which trembles, guide.

I reach a part[247] which all benighted lies.

Footnotes

[220] *Thundering sound*: In a state of unconsciousness, Dante, he knows not how, has been conveyed across Acheron, and is awakened by what seems like the thunder-peal following the lightning-flash which made him insensible. He now stands on the brink of Inferno, where the sounds peculiar to each region of it converge and are reverberated from its rim. These sounds are not again to be heard by him except in their proper localities. No sooner does he actually pass into the First Circle than he hears only sighs.—As regards the topography of Inferno, it is enough, as yet, to note that it consists of a cavity extending from the surface to the centre of the earth; narrowing to its base, and with many circular ledges or terraces, of great width in the case of the upper ones, running round its wall—that is, round the sides of the pit. Each terrace or circle is thus less in circumference than the one above it. From one circle to the next there slopes a bank of more or less height and steepness. Down the bank which falls to the comparatively flat ground of the First Circle they are now about to pass.—To put it otherwise, the Inferno is an inverted hollow cone.

[221] *Pity*: The pity felt by Virgil has reference only to those in the circle they are about to enter, which is his own. See also *Purg.* iii. 43.

[222] *Wouldst thou, etc.*: He will not have Dante form a false opinion of the character of those condemned to the circle which is his own.

[223] *Part*: *parte*, altered by some editors into *porta*; but though baptism is technically described as the gate of the sacraments, it never is as the gate of the faith. A tenet of Dante's faith was that all the unbaptized are lost. He had no choice in the matter.

[224] *Limbo*: Border, or borderland. Dante makes the First Circle consist of the two limbos of Thomas Aquinas: that of unbaptized infants, *limbus puerorum*, and that of the fathers of the old covenant, *limbus sanctorum patrum*. But the second he finds is now inhabited only by the virtuous heathen.

[225] *Sir—Master*: As a delicate means of expressing sympathy, Dante redoubles his courtesy to Virgil.

[226] *Hidden drift*: to find out, at first hand as it were, if the article in the creed is true which relates to the Descent into Hell; and, perhaps, to learn if when Christ descended He delivered none of the virtuous heathen.

[227] *Lately*: Virgil died about half a century before the crucifixion.

[228] *A Potentate*: The name of Christ is not mentioned in the *Inferno*.

[229] *A hemisphere, etc.*: An elaborate way of saying that part of the limbo was clearly lit. The flame is symbolical of the light of genius, or of virtue; both in Dante's eyes being modes of worth.

[230] *Wins grace, etc.*: The thirst for fame was one keenly felt and openly confessed by Dante. See, *e.g. De Monarchia*, i. 1. In this he anticipated the humanists of the following century. Here we find that to be famous on earth helps the case of disembodied souls.

[231] *Poet*: Throughout the *Comedy*, with the exception of *Parad.* i. 29, and xxv. 8, the term 'poet' is confined to those who wrote in Greek and Latin. In *Purg.* xxi. 85 the name of poet is said to be that 'which is most enduring and honourable.'

[232] *A sword*: Because Homer sings of battles. Dante's acquaintance with his works can have been but slight, as they were not then translated into Latin, and Dante knew little or no Greek.

[233] *To their honour*: 'And in that they do well:' perhaps as showing themselves free from jealousy. But the remark of Benvenuto of Imola is: 'Poets love and honour one another, and are never envious and quarrelsome like those who cultivate the other arts and sciences.'—I quote with misgiving from Tamburini's untrustworthy Italian translation. Benvenuto lectured on the *Comedy* in Bologna for some years about 1370. It is greatly to be wished that his commentary, lively and full of side-lights as it is, should be printed in full from the original Latin.

[234] *The lords, etc.*: Not the company of him—Homer or Virgil—who is lord of the great song, and soars above all others; but the company of the great masters, whose verse, etc.

[235] *Did my Master smile*: To see Dante made free of the guild of great poets; or, it may be, to think they are about to discover in him a fellow poet.

[236] *A noble castle*: Where the light burns, and in which, as their peculiar seat, the shades of the heathen distinguished for virtue and genius reside. The seven walls are in their number symbolical of the perfect strength of the castle; or, to take it more pedantically, may mean the four moral virtues and the three speculative. The gates will then stand for the seven liberal arts of grammar, rhetoric, etc. The moat may be eloquence, set outside the castle to signify that only as reflected in the eloquent words of inspired men can the outside world get to know wisdom. Over the stream Dante passes easily, as being an adept in learned speech. The castle encloses a spacious mead enamelled with eternal green.

[237] *Cæsar in arms, etc.*: Suetonius says of Cæsar that he was of fair complexion, but had black and piercing eyes. Brunetto Latini, Dante's teacher, says in his *Tesoro* (v. 11), of the hawk here mentioned—the *grifagno*—that its eyes 'flame like fire.'

[238] *Brutus*: Introduced here that he may not be confounded with the later Brutus, for whom is reserved the lowest place of all in Inferno.

[239] *Marcia*: Wife of Cato; mentioned also in *Purg.* i. *Julia*: daughter of Cæsar and wife of Pompey.

[240] *Saladin*: Died 1193. To the thirteenth and fourteenth centuries he supplied the ideal of a just Mohammedan ruler. Here are no other such. 'He sits apart, because not of gentle birth,' says Boccaccio; which shows what even a man of genius risks when he becomes a commentator.

[241] *The Master*: Aristotle, often spoken of by Dante as the Philosopher, and reverenced by him as the genius to whom the secrets of nature lay most open.

[242] *Democritus, etc.*: According to whom the world owes its form to a chance arrangement of atoms.

[243] *Linus*: Not Livy, into which some have changed it. Linus is mentioned by Virgil along with Orpheus, *Egl.* iv.

[244] *Ptolemy*: Greek geographer of the beginning of the second century, and author of the system of the world believed in by Dante, and freely used by him throughout the poem.

[245] *Avicenna*: A physician, born in Bokhara, and died at Ispahan, 1037. His *Medical Canon* was for centuries used as a text-book in Europe.

[246] *Averroes*: A Mohammedan philosopher of Cordova, died 1198. In his great Commentary on Aristotle he gives and explains every sentence of that philosopher's works. He was himself ignorant of Greek, and made use of Arabic versions. Out of his Arabic the Commentary was translated into Hebrew, and thence into Latin. The presence of the three Mohammedans in this honourable place greatly puzzles the early commentators.

[247] *A part, etc.*: He passes into the darkness of the Limbo out of the brightly-lit, fortified enclosure. It is worth remarking, as one reads, how vividly he describes his first impression of a new scene, while when he comes to leave it a word is all he speaks.

Canto V.

From the First Circle thus I downward went
    Into the Second,[248] which girds narrower space,
    But greater woe compelling loud lament.
Minos[249] waits awful there and snarls, the case
    Examining of all who enter in;
    And, as he girds him, dooms them to their place.
I say, each ill-starred spirit must begin
    On reaching him its guilt in full to tell;
    And he, omniscient as concerning sin,
Sees to what circle it belongs in Hell;
    Then round him is his tail as often curled
    As he would have it stages deep to dwell.
And evermore before him stand a world
    Of shades; and all in turn to judgment come,
    Confess and hear, and then are downward hurled.[250]
'O thou who comest to the very home
    Of woe,' when he beheld me Minos cried,
    Ceasing a while from utterance of doom,
'Enter not rashly nor in all confide;
    By ease of entering be not led astray.'
    'Why also[251] growling?' answered him my Guide;
'Seek not his course predestinate to stay;
    For thus 'tis willed[252] where nothing ever fails
    Of what is willed. No further speech essay.'
And now by me are agonising wails
    Distinguished plain; now am I come outright
    Where grievous lamentation me assails.
Now had I reached a place devoid of light,
    Raging as in a tempest howls the sea
    When with it winds, blown thwart each other, fight.
The infernal storm is raging ceaselessly,
    Sweeping the shades along with it, and them
    It smites and whirls, nor lets them ever be.
Arrived at the precipitous extreme,[253]

In shrieks and lamentations they complain,
    And even the Power Divine itself blaspheme.
I understood[254] that to this mode of pain
    Are doomed the sinners of the carnal kind,
    Who o'er their reason let their impulse reign.
As starlings in the winter-time combined
    Float on the wing in crowded phalanx wide,
    So these bad spirits, driven by that wind,
Float up and down and veer from side to side;
    Nor for their comfort any hope they spy
    Of rest, or even of suffering mollified.
And as the cranes[255] in long-drawn company
    Pursue their flight while uttering their song,
    So I beheld approach with wailing cry
Shades lifted onward by that whirlwind strong.
    'Master, what folk are these,'[256] I therefore said,
    'Who by the murky air are whipped along?
'She, first of them,' his answer thus was made,
    'Of whom thou wouldst a wider knowledge win,
    O'er many tongues and peoples, empire swayed.
So ruined was she by licentious sin
    That she decreed lust should be uncontrolled,
    To ease the shame that she herself was in.
She is Semiramis, of whom 'tis told
    She followed Ninus, and his wife had been.
    Hers were the realms now by the Sultan ruled.
The next[257] is she who, amorous and self-slain,
    Unto Sichæus' dust did faithless show:
    Then lustful Cleopatra.' Next was seen
Helen, for whom so many years in woe
    Ran out; and I the great Achilles knew,
    Who at the last[258] encountered love for foe.
Paris I saw and Tristram.[259] In review
    A thousand shades and more, he one by one
    Pointed and named, whom love from life withdrew.
And after I had heard my Teacher run
    O'er many a dame of yore and many a knight,
    I, lost in pity, was wellnigh undone.
Then I: 'O Poet, if I only might
    Speak with the two that as companions hie,
    And on the wind appear to be so light!'[260]
And he to me: 'When they shall come more nigh
    Them shalt thou mark, and by the love shalt pray
    Which leads them onward, and they will comply.'
Soon as the wind bends them to where we stay
    I lift my voice: 'O wearied souls and worn!
    Come speak with us if none[261] the boon gainsay.'

Then even as doves,[262] urged by desire, return
    On outspread wings and firm to their sweet nest
    As through the air by mere volition borne,
From Dido's[263] band those spirits issuing pressed
    Towards where we were, athwart the air malign;
    My passionate prayer such influence possessed.
'O living creature,[264] gracious and benign,
    Us visiting in this obscurèd air,
    Who did the earth with blood incarnadine;
If in the favour of the King we were
    Who rules the world, we for thy peace[265] would pray,
    Since our misfortunes thy compassion stir.
Whate'er now pleases thee to hear or say
    We listen to, or tell, at your demand;[266]
    While yet the wind, as now, doth silent stay.
My native city[267] lies upon the strand
    Where to the sea descends the river Po
    For peace, with all his tributary band.
Love, in a generous heart set soon aglow,
    Seized him for the fair form was mine above;
    And still it irks me to have lost it so.[268]
Love, which absolves[269] no one beloved from love,
    So strong a passion for him in me wrought
    That, as thou seest, I still its mastery prove.
Love led us where we in one death were caught.
    For him who slew us waits Caïna[270] now.'
    Unto our ears these words from them were brought.
When I had heard these troubled souls, my brow
    I downward bent, and long while musing stayed,
    Until the Poet asked: 'What thinkest thou?'
And when I answered him, 'Alas!' I said,
    'Sweet thoughts how many, and what strong desire,
    These to their sad catastrophe betrayed!'
Then, turned once more to them, I to inquire
    Began: 'Francesca, these thine agonies
    Me with compassion unto tears inspire.
But tell me, at the season of sweet sighs
    What sign made love, and what the means he chose
    To strip your dubious longings of disguise?'
And she to me: 'The bitterest of woes
    Is to remember in the midst of pain
    A happy past; as well thy teacher[271] knows.
Yet none the less, and since thou art so fain
    The first occasion of our love to hear,
    Like one I speak that cannot tears restrain.
As we for pastime one day reading were
    How Lancelot[272] by love was fettered fast—

All by ourselves and without any fear—
Moved by the tale our eyes we often cast
    On one another, and our colour fled;
    But one word was it, vanquished us at last.
When how the smile, long wearied for, we read
    Was kissed by him who loved like none before,
    This one, who henceforth never leaves me, laid
A kiss on my mouth, trembling the while all o'er.
    The book was Galahad,[273] and he as well
    Who wrote the book. That day we read no more.'
And while one shade continued thus to tell,
    The other wept so bitterly, I swooned
    Away for pity, and as dead I fell:
Yea, as a corpse falls, fell I on the ground.

Footnotes

[248] *The Second*: The Second Circle of the Inferno, and the first of punishment. The lower the circle, the more rigorous the penalty endured in it. Here is punished carnal sin.

[249] *Minos*: Son of Jupiter and King of Crete, so severely just as to be made after death one of the judges of the under world. He is degraded by Dante, as many other noble persons of the old mythology are by him, into a demon. Unlike the fallen angels of Milton, Dante's devils have no interest of their own. Their only function is to help in working out human destinies.

[250] *Downward hurled*: Each falls to his proper place without lingering by the way. All through Inferno there is an absence of direct Divine interposition. It is ruled, as it were, by a course of nature. The sinners, compelled by a fatal impulse, advance to hear their doom, just as they fall inevitably one by one into Charon's boat. Minos by a sort of devilish instinct sentences each sinner to his appropriate punishment. In *Inf.* xxvii. 127 we find the words in which Minos utters his judgment. In *Inf.* xxi. 29 a devil bears the sinner to his own place.

[251] *Why also, etc.*: Like Charon. If Minos represents conscience, as some would have it, Dante is here again assailed by misgivings as to his enterprise, and is quieted by reason in the person of Virgil.

[252] *Thus 'tis willed, etc.*: These two lines are the same as those to Charon, *Inf.* iii. 95, 96.

[253] *Precipitous extreme*: Opinions vary as to what is meant by *ruina*. As Dante is certainly still on the outer edge of the Second Circle or terrace, and while standing there hears distinctly the words the spirits say when they reach the *ruina*, it most likely denotes the steep slope falling from the First to the Second Circle. The spirits, driven against the wall which hems them in, burst into sharp lamentations against their irremediable fate.

[254] *I understood, etc.*: From the nature of the punishment, which, like all the others invented by Dante, bears some relation to the sin to which it is assigned. They who on earth failed to exercise self-restraint are beaten hither and thither by every wind that blows; and, as once they were blinded by passion, so now they see nothing plainly in that dim and obscure place. That Dante should assign the least grievous punishment of all to this sin throws light upon his views of life. In his eyes it had

more than any other the excuse of natural bent, and had least of malice. Here, it must be remarked, are no seducers. For them a lower depth is reserved (*Inf.* xviii. See also *Purg.* xxvii. 15).

[255] *The cranes:* 'The cranes are a kind of bird that go in a troop, as cavaliers go to battle, following one another in single file. And one of them goes always in front as their gonfalonier, guiding and leading them with its voice' (Brunetto Latini, *Tesoro,* v. 27).

[256] *What folk are these:* The general crowd of sinners guilty of unlawful love are described as being close packed like starlings. The other troop, who go in single file like cranes, are those regarding whom Dante specially inquires; and they prove to be the nobler sort of sinners—lovers with something tragic or pathetic in their fate.

[257] *The next:* Dido, perhaps not named by Virgil because to him she owed her fame. For love of Æneas she broke the vow of perpetual chastity made on the tomb of her husband.

[258] *At the last, etc.:* Achilles, when about to espouse Polyxena, and when off his guard, was slain.

[259] *Paris … and Tristram:* Paris of Troy, and the Tristram of King Arthur's Table.

[260] *So light:* Denoting the violence of the passion to which they had succumbed.

[261] *If none:* If no Superior Power.

[262] *Doves:* The motion of the tempest-driven shades is compared to the flight of birds—starlings, cranes, and doves. This last simile prepares us for the tenderness of Francesca's tale.

[263] *Dido:* Has been already indicated, and is now named. This association of the two lovers with Virgil's Dido is a further delicate touch to engage our sympathy; for her love, though illicit, was the infirmity of a noble heart.

[264] *Living creature:* 'Animal.' No shade, but an animated body.

[265] *Thy peace:* Peace from all the doubts that assail him, and which have compelled him to the journey: peace, it may be, from temptation to sin cognate to her own. Even in the gloom of Inferno her great goodheartedness is left her—a consolation, if not a grace.

[266] *Your demand:* By a refinement of courtesy, Francesca, though addressing only Dante, includes Virgil in her profession of willingness to tell all they care to hear. But as almost always, he remains silent. It is not for his good the journey is being made.

[267] *Native city:* Ravenna. The speaker is Francesca, daughter of Guido of Polenta, lord of Ravenna. About the year 1275 she was married to Gianciotto (Deformed John) Malatesta, son of the lord of Rimini; the marriage, like most of that time in the class to which she belonged, being one of political convenience. She allowed her affections to settle on Paolo, her husband's handsome brother; and Gianciotto's suspicions having been aroused, he surprised the lovers and slew them on the spot. This happened at Pesaro. The association of Francesca's name with Rimini is merely accidental. The date of her death is not known. Dante can never have set eyes on Francesca; but at the battle of Campaldino in 1289, where he was present, a troop of cavaliers from Pistoia fought on the Florentine side under the command of her brother Bernardino; and in the following year, Dante being then twenty-five years of age, her father, Guido, was Podesta in Florence. The Guido of Polenta, lord of Ravenna, whom Dante had for his last and most generous patron, was grandson of that elder Guido, and nephew of Francesca.

[268] *To have lost it so:* A husband's right and duty were too well defined in the prevalent social code for her to complain that

Gianciotto avenged himself. What she does resent is that she was left no breathing-space for repentance and farewells.

[269] *Which absolves, etc.:* Which compels whoever is beloved to love in return. Here is the key to Dante's comparatively lenient estimate of the guilt of Francesca's sin. See line 39, and *Inf.* xi. 83. The Church allowed no distinctions with regard to the lost. Dante, for his own purposes, invents a scale of guilt; and in settling the degrees of it he is greatly influenced by human feeling—sometimes by private likes and dislikes. The vestibule of the caitiffs, *e.g.,* is his own creation.

[270] *Caïna:* The Division of the Ninth and lowest Circle, assigned to those treacherous to their kindred (*Inf.* xxxii. 58). Her husband was still living in 1300.—May not the words of this line be spoken by Paolo? It is as a fratricide even more than as the slayer of his wife that Gianciotto is to find his place in Caïna. The words are more in keeping with the masculine than the feminine character. They certainly jar somewhat with the gentler censure of line 102. And, immediately after, Dante speaks of what the 'souls' have said.

[271] *Thy teacher:* Boethius, one of Dante's favourite authors (*Convito* ii. 13), says in his *De Consol. Phil.,* 'The greatest misery in adverse fortune is once to have been happy.' But, granting that Dante found the idea in Boethius, it is clearly Virgil that Francesca means. She sees that Dante's guide is a shade, and gathers from his grave passionless aspect that he is one condemned for ever to look back with futile regret upon his happier past.

[272] *Lancelot:* King Arthur's famous knight, who was too bashful to make his love for Queen Guinivere known to her. Galahad, holding the secret of both, persuaded the Queen to make the first declaration of love at a meeting he arranged for between them. Her smile, or laugh, as she 'took Lancelot by the chin and kissed him,' assured her lover of his conquest. The Arthurian Romances were the favourite reading of the Italian nobles of Dante's time.

[273] *Galahad:* From the part played by Galahad, or Galeotto, in the tale of Lancelot, his name grew to be Italian for Pander. The book, says Francesca, was that which tells of Galahad; and the author of it proved a very Galahad to us. The early editions of the *Decameron* bear the second title of 'The Prince Galeotto.'

Canto VI.

When I regained my senses, which had fled
  At my compassion for the kindred two,
  Which for pure sorrow quite had turned my head,
New torments and a crowd of sufferers new
  I see around me as I move again,[274]
  Where'er I turn, where'er I bend my view.
In the Third Circle am I of the rain
  Which, heavy, cold, eternal, big with woe,
  Doth always of one kind and force remain.
Large hail and turbid water, mixed with snow,
  Keep pouring down athwart the murky air;
  And from the ground they fall on, stenches grow.
The savage Cerberus,[275] a monster drear,
  Howls from his threefold throat with canine cries
  Above the people who are whelmèd there.

Oily and black his beard, and red his eyes,
    His belly huge: claws from his fingers sprout.
    The shades he flays, hooks, rends in cruel wise.
Beat by the rain these, dog-like, yelp and shout,
    And shield themselves in turn with either side;
    And oft[276] the wretched sinners turn about.
When we by Cerberus, great worm,[277] were spied,
    He oped his mouths and all his fangs he showed,
    While not a limb did motionless abide.
My Leader having spread his hands abroad,
    Filled both his fists with earth ta'en from the ground,
    And down the ravening gullets flung the load.
Then, as sharp set with hunger barks the hound,
    But is appeased when at his meat he gnaws,
    And, worrying it, forgets all else around;
So with those filthy faces there it was
    Of the fiend Cerberus, who deafs the crowd
    Of souls till they from hearing fain would pause.
We, travelling o'er the spirits who lay cowed
    And sorely by the grievous showers harassed,
    Upon their semblances[278] of bodies trod.
Prone on the ground the whole of them were cast,
    Save one of them who sat upright with speed
    When he beheld that near to him we passed.
'O thou who art through this Inferno led,[279]
    Me if thou canst,' he asked me, 'recognise;
    For ere I was dismantled thou wast made.'
And I to him: 'Thy present tortured guise
    Perchance hath blurred my memory of thy face,
    Until it seems I ne'er on thee set eyes.
But tell me who thou art, within this place
    So cruel set, exposed to such a pain,
    Than which, if greater, none has more disgrace.'
And he: 'Thy city, swelling with the bane
    Of envy till the sack is running o'er,
    Me in the life serene did once contain.
As Ciacco[280] me your citizens named of yore;
    And for the damning sin of gluttony
    I, as thou seest, am beaten by this shower.
No solitary woful soul am I,
    For all of these endure the selfsame doom
    For the same fault.' Here ended his reply.
I answered him, 'O Ciacco, with such gloom
    Thy misery weighs me, I to weep am prone;
    But, if thou canst, declare to what shall come
The citizens[281] of the divided town.
    Holds it one just man? And declare the cause

Why 'tis of discord such a victim grown.
Then he to me: 'After[282] contentious pause
    Blood will be spilt; the boorish party[283] then
    Will chase the others forth with grievous loss.
The former it behoves to fall again
    Within three suns, the others to ascend,
    Holpen[284] by him whose wiles ere now are plain.
Long time, with heads held high, they'll make to bend
    The other party under burdens dire,
    Howe'er themselves in tears and rage they spend.
There are two just[285] men, at whom none inquire.
    Envy, and pride, and avarice, even these
    Are the three sparks have set all hearts on fire.'
With this the tearful sound he made to cease:
    And I to him, 'Yet would I have thee tell—
    And of thy speech do thou the gift increase—
Tegghiaio[286] and Farinata, honourable,
    James Rusticucci,[287] Mosca, Arrigo,
    With all the rest so studious to excel
In good; where are they? Help me this to know;
    Great hunger for the news hath seizèd me;
    Delights them Heaven, or tortures Hell below?'
He said: 'Among the blackest souls they be;
    Them to the bottom weighs another sin.
    Shouldst thou so far descend, thou mayst them see.
But when[288] the sweet world thou again dost win,
    I pray thee bring me among men to mind;
    No more I tell, nor new reply begin.'
Then his straightforward eyes askance declined;
    He looked at me a moment ere his head
    He bowed; then fell flat 'mong the other blind.
'Henceforth he waketh not,' my Leader said,
    'Till he shall hear the angel's trumpet sound,
    Ushering the hostile Judge. By every shade
Its dismal sepulchre shall then be found,
    Its flesh and ancient form it shall resume,
    And list[289] what echoes in eternal round.'
So passed we where the shades and rainy spume
    Made filthy mixture, with steps taken slow;
    Touching a little on the world to come.[290]
Wherefore I said: 'Master, shall torments grow
    After the awful sentence hath been heard,
    Or lesser prove and not so fiercely glow?'
'Repair unto thy Science,'[291] was his word;
    'Which tells, as things approach a perfect state
    To keener joy or suffering they are stirred.
Therefore although this people cursed by fate

Ne'er find perfection in its full extent,

To it they then shall more approximate

Than now.'[292] Our course we round the circle bent,

Still holding speech, of which I nothing say,

Until we came where down the pathway went:

There found we Plutus, the great enemy.

Footnotes

[274] *As I move again*: In his swoon he has been conveyed from the Second Circle down to the Third.

[275] *Cerberus*: In the Greek mythology Cerberus is the watch-dog of the under world. By Dante he is converted into a demon, and with his three throats, canine voracity, and ugly inflamed bulk, is appropriately set to guard the entrance to the circle of the gluttonous and wine-bibbers.

[276] *And oft, etc.*: On entering the circle the shades are seized and torn by Cerberus; once over-nice in how they fed, they are now treated as if they were food for dogs. But their enduring pain is to be subjected to every kind of physical discomfort. Their senses of hearing, touch, and smell are assailed by the opposite of what they were most used to enjoy at their luxurious feasts.

[277] *Great worm*: Though human in a monstrous form, Cerberus is so called as being a disgusting brute.

[278] *Semblances, etc.*: 'Emptiness which seems to be a person.' To this conception of the shades as only seeming to have bodies, Dante has difficulty in remaining true. For instance, at line 101 they mix with the sleet to make a sludgy mass; and cannot therefore be impalpable.

[279] Ciacco at once perceives by the weight of Dante's tread that he is a living man.

[280] *Ciacco*: The name or nickname of a Florentine wit, and, in his day, a great diner-out. Boccaccio, in his commentary, says that, though poor, Ciacco associated with men of birth and wealth, especially such as ate and drank delicately. In the *Decameron*, ix. 8, he is introduced as being on such terms with the great Corso Donati as to be able to propose himself to dinner with him. Clearly he was not a bad fellow, and his pitiful case, perhaps contrasted with the high spirits and jovial surroundings in which he was last met by Dante, almost, though not quite, win a tear from the stern pilgrim.

[281] *The citizens, etc.*: Dante eagerly confers on Florentine politics with the first Florentine he encounters in Inferno.

[282] *After, etc.*: In the following nine lines the party history of Florence for two years after the period of the poem (March 1300) is roughly indicated. The city was divided into two factions—the Whites, led by the great merchant Vieri dei Cerchi, and the Blacks, led by Corso Donati, a poor and turbulent noble. At the close of 1300 there was a bloody encounter between the more violent members of the two parties. In May 1301 the Blacks were banished. In the autumn of that year they returned in triumph to the city in the train of Charles of Valois, and got the Whites banished in April 1302, within three years, that is, of the poet's talk with Ciacco. Dante himself was associated with the Whites, but not as a violent partisan; for though he was a strong politician no party quite answered his views. From the middle of June till the middle of August 1300 he was one of the Priors. In the course of 1301 he is believed to have gone on an embassy to Rome to persuade the Pope to abstain from meddling in Florentine affairs. He never entered Florence again, being condemned virtually to banishment in January 1302.

[283] *The boorish party: la parte selvaggia.* The Whites; but what is exactly meant by *selvaggia* is not clear. Literally it is 'woodland,' and some say it refers to the Cerchi having originally come from a well-wooded district; which is absurd. Nor, taking the word in its secondary meaning of savage, does it apply better to one party than another—not so well, perhaps, to the Whites as to the Blacks. Villani also terms the Cerchi *salvatichi* (viii. 39), and in a connection where it may mean rude, ill-mannered. I take it that Dante here indulges in a gibe at the party to which he once belonged, but which, ere he began the *Comedy*, he had quite broken with. In *Parad.* xvii. 62 he terms the members of it 'wicked and stupid.' The sneer in the text would come well enough from the witty and soft-living Ciacco.

[284] *Holpen, etc.*: Pope Boniface, already intriguing to gain the preponderance in Florence, which for a time he enjoyed, with the greedy and faithless Charles of Valois for his agent.

[285] *Two just*: Dante and another, unknown. He thus distinctly puts from himself any blame for the evil turn things had taken in Florence. How thoroughly he had broken with his party ere he wrote this is proved by his exclusion of the irresolute but respectable Vieri dei Cerchi from the number of the just men. He, in Dante's judgment, was only too much listened to.—It will be borne in mind that, at the time assigned to the action of the *Comedy*, Dante was still resident in Florence.

[286] *Tegghiaio*: See *Inf.* xvi. 42. *Farinata: Inf.* x. 32.

[287] *Rusticucci: Inf.* xvi. 44. *Mosca: Inf.* xxviii. 106. *Arrigo*: Cannot be identified. All these distinguished Florentines we may assume to have been hospitable patrons of Ciacco's.

[288] *But when, etc.*: In the Inferno many such prayers are addressed to Dante. The shades in Purgatory ask to have their friends on earth stirred to offer up petitions for their speedy purification and deliverance; but the only alleviation possible for the doomed spirits is to know that they are not yet forgotten up in the 'sweet world.' A double artistic purpose is served by representing them as feeling thus. It relieves the mind to think that in such misery there is any source of comfort at all. And by making them be still interested on their own account in the thoughts of men, the eager colloquies in which they engage with Dante on such unequal terms gain in verisimilitude.

[289] *And list, etc.*: The final sentence against them is to echo, in its results, through all eternity.

[290] *The world to come*: The life after doomsday.

[291] *Thy Science*: To Aristotle. In the *Convito*, iv. 16, he quotes 'the Philosopher' as teaching that 'everything is then at its full perfection when it thoroughly fulfils its special functions.'

[292] *Than now*: Augustine says that 'after the resurrection of the flesh the joys of the blessed and the sufferings of the wicked will be enhanced.' And, according to Thomas Aquinas, 'the soul, without the body, is wanting in the perfection designed for it by Nature.'

Canto VII.

Pape[293] Satan! Pape Satan! Aleppe!

　　Plutus[294] began in accents rough and hard:

　　And that mild Sage, all-knowing, said to me,

For my encouragement: 'Pay no regard
    Unto thy fear; whatever power he sways
    Thy passage down this cliff shall not be barred.'
Then turning round to that inflamèd face
    He bade: 'Accursed wolf,[295] at peace remain;
    And, pent within thee, let thy fury blaze.
Down to the pit we journey not in vain:
    So rule they where by Michael in Heaven's height
    On the adulterous pride[296] was vengeance ta'en.'
Then as the bellied sails, by wind swelled tight,
    Suddenly drag whenever snaps the mast;
    Such, falling to the ground, the monster's plight.
To the Fourth Cavern so we downward passed,
    Winning new reaches of the doleful shore
    Where all the vileness of the world is cast.
Justice of God! which pilest more and more
    Pain as I saw, and travail manifold!
    Why will we sin, to be thus wasted sore?
As at Charybdis waves are forward rolled
    To break on other billows midway met,
    The people here a counterdance must hold.
A greater crowd than I had seen as yet,
    With piercing yells advanced on either track,
    Rolling great stones to which their chests were set.
They crashed together, and then each turned back
    Upon the way he came, while shouts arise,
    'Why clutch it so?' and 'Why to hold it slack?'
In the dark circle wheeled they on this wise
    From either hand to the opposing part,
    Where evermore they raised insulting cries.
Thither arrived, each, turning, made fresh start
    Through the half circle[297] a new joust to run;
    And I, stung almost to the very heart,
Said, 'O my Master, wilt thou make it known
    Who the folk are? Were these all clerks[298] who go
    Before us on the left, with shaven crown?'
And he replied: 'All of them squinted so
    In mental vision while in life they were,
    They nothing spent by rule. And this they show,
And with their yelping voices make appear
    When half-way round the circle they have sped,
    And sins opposing them asunder tear.
Each wanting thatch of hair upon his head
    Was once a clerk, or pope, or cardinal,
    In whom abound the ripest growths of greed.'
And I: 'O Master, surely among all
    Of these I ought[299] some few to recognise,

Who by such filthy sins were held in thrall.'
And he to me: 'Vain thoughts within thee rise;
    Their witless life, which made them vile, now mocks—
    Dimming[300] their faces still—all searching eyes.
Eternally they meet with hostile shocks;
    These rising from the tomb at last shall stand
    With tight clenched fists, and those with ruined locks.[301]
Squandering or hoarding, they the happy land[302]
    Have lost, and now are marshalled for this fray;
    Which to describe doth no fine words demand.
Know hence, my Son, how fleeting is the play
    Of goods at the dispose of Fortune thrown,
    And which mankind to such fierce strife betray.
Not all the gold which is beneath the moon
    Could purchase peace, nor all that ever was,
    To but one soul of these by toil undone.'
'Master,' I said, 'tell thou, ere making pause,
    Who Fortune is of whom thou speak'st askance,
    Who holds all worldly riches in her claws.'[303]
'O foolish creatures, lost in ignorance!'
    He answer made. 'Now see that the reply
    Thou store, which I concerning her advance.
He who in knowledge is exalted high,
    Framing[304] all Heavens gave such as should them guide,
    That so each part might shine to all; whereby
Is equal light diffused on every side:
    And likewise to one guide and governor,
    Of worldly splendours did control confide,
That she in turns should different peoples dower
    With this vain good; from blood should make it pass
    To blood, in spite of human wit. Hence, power,
Some races failing,[305] other some amass,
    According to her absolute decree
    Which hidden lurks, like serpent in the grass.
Vain 'gainst her foresight yours must ever be.
    She makes provision, judges, holds her reign,
    As doth his power supreme each deity.
Her permutations can no truce sustain;
    Necessity[306] compels her to be swift,
    So swift they follow who their turn must gain.
And this is she whom they so often[307] lift
    Upon the cross, who ought to yield her praise;
    And blame on her and scorn unjustly shift.
But she is blest nor hears what any says,
    With other primal creatures turns her sphere,
    Jocund and glad, rejoicing in her ways.

To greater woe now let us downward steer.

    The stars[308] which rose when I began to guide

    Are falling now, nor may we linger here.'

We crossed the circle to the other side,

    Arriving where a boiling fountain fell

    Into a brooklet by its streams supplied.

In depth of hue the flood did perse[309] excel,

    And we, with this dim stream to lead us on,

    Descended by a pathway terrible.

A marsh which by the name of Styx is known,

    Fed by this gloomy brook, lies at the base

    Of threatening cliffs hewn out of cold grey stone.

And I, intent on study of the place,[310]

    Saw people in that ditch, mud-smeared. In it

    All naked stood with anger-clouded face.

Nor with their fists alone each fiercely hit

    The other, but with feet and chest and head,

    And with their teeth to shreds each other bit.

'Son, now behold,' the worthy Master said,

    'The souls of those whom anger made a prize;

    And, further, I would have thee certified

That 'neath the water people utter sighs,

    And make the bubbles to the surface come;

    As thou mayst see by casting round thine eyes.

Fixed in the mud they say: "We lived in gloom[311]

    In the sweet air made jocund by the day,

    Nursing within us melancholy fume.

In this black mud we now our gloom display."

    This hymn with gurgling throats they strive to sound,

    Which they in speech unbroken fail to say.'

And thus about the loathsome pool we wound

    For a wide arc, between the dry and soft,

    With eyes on those who gulp the filth, turned round.

At last we reached a tower that soared aloft.

Footnotes

[293] *Pape, etc.*: These words have exercised the ingenuity of many scholars, who on the whole lean to the opinion that they contain an appeal to Satan against the invasion of his domain. Virgil seems to have understood them, but the text leaves it doubtful whether Dante himself did. Later on, but there with an obvious purpose, we find a line of pure gibberish (*Inf.* xxxi. 67).

[294] *Plutus*: The god of riches; degraded here into a demon. He guards the Fourth Circle, which is that of the misers and spendthrifts.

[295] *Wolf*: Frequently used by Dante as symbolical of greed.

[296] *Pride*: Which in its way was a kind of greed—that of dominion. Similarly, the avarice represented by the wolf of Canto i. was seen to be the lust of aggrandisement. Virgil here answers

Plutus's (supposed) appeal to Satan by referring to the higher Power, under whose protection he and his companion come.

[297] *The half circle*: This Fourth Circle is divided half-way round between the misers and spendthrifts, and the two bands at set periods clash against one another in their vain effort to pass into the section belonging to the opposite party. Their condition is emblematical of their sins while in life. They were one-sided in their use of wealth; so here they can never complete the circle. The monotony of their employment and of their cries represents their subjection to one idea, and, as in life, so now, their displeasure is excited by nothing so much as by coming into contact with the failing opposite to their own. Yet they are set in the same circle because the sin of both arose from inordinate desire of wealth, the miser craving it to hoard, and the spendthrift to spend. In Purgatory also they are placed together (see *Purg.* xxii. 40). So, on Dante's scheme, liberality is allied to and dependent on a wise and reasonable frugality.—There is no hint of the enormous length of the course run by these shades. Far lower down, when the circles of the Inferno have greatly narrowed, the circuit is twenty-two miles (*Inf.* xxix. 9).

[298] *Clerks*: Churchmen. The tonsure is the sign that a man is of ecclesiastical condition. Many took the tonsure who never became priests.

[299] *I ought, etc.*: Dante is astonished that he can pick out no greedy priest or friar of his acquaintance, when he had known so many.

[300] *Dimming, etc.*: Their original disposition is by this time smothered by the predominance of greed. Dante treats these sinners with a special contemptuous bitterness. Scores of times since he became dependent on the generosity of others he must have watched how at a bare hint the faces of miser and spendthrift fell, while their eyes travelled vaguely beyond him, and their voices grew cold.

[301] *Ruined locks*: 'A spendthrift will spend his very hair,' says an Italian proverb.

[302] *The happy land*: Heaven.

[303] *Her claws*: Dante speaks of Fortune as if she were a brutal and somewhat malicious power. In Virgil's answer there is a refutation of the opinion of Fortune given by Dante himself, in the *Convito* (iv. 11). After describing three ways in which the goods of Fortune come to men he says: 'In each of these three ways her injustice is manifest.' This part of the *Convito* Fraticelli seems almost to prove was written in 1297.

[304] *Framing, etc.*: According to the scholastic theory of the world, each of the nine heavens was directed in its motion by intelligences, called angels by the vulgar, and by the heathen, gods (*Convito* ii. 5). As these spheres and the influences they exercise on human affairs are under the guidance of divinely-appointed ministers, so, Virgil says, is the distribution of worldly wealth ruled by Providence through Fortune.

[305] *Some races failing*: It was long believed, nor is the belief quite obsolete, that one community can gain only at the expense of another. Sir Thomas Browne says: 'All cannot be happy at once; for because the glory of one state depends upon the ruin of another, there is a revolution and vicissitude of their greatness, and all must obey the swing of that wheel, not moved by intelligences, but by the hand of God, whereby all states arise to their zeniths and vertical points according to their predestinated periods.'—*Rel. Med.* i. 17.

[306] *Necessity, etc.*: Suggested, perhaps, by Horace's *Te semper anteit sæva necessitas* (*Od.* i. 35). The question of how men can be free in the face of necessity, here associated with Fortune, more than once emerges in the *Comedy*. Dante's belief on the subject was substantially that of his favourite author Boethius, who holds that ultimately 'it is Providence that turns the wheel of all things;' and who says, that 'if you spread your sails to the wind you will be carried, not where you would, but whither you are driven by the gale: if you choose to commit yourself to Fortune, you must endure the manners of your mistress.'

[307] *Whom they so often, etc.*: Treat with contumely.

[308] *The stars, etc.*: It is now past midnight, and towards the morning of Saturday, the 26th of March 1300. Only a few hours have been employed as yet upon the journey.

[309] *Perse*: 'Perse is a colour between purple and black, but the black predominates' (*Conv.* iv. 20). The hue of the waters of Styx agrees with the gloomy temper of the sinners plunged in them.

[310] *The place*: They are now in the Fifth Circle, where the wrathful are punished.

[311] *In gloom*: These submerged spirits are, according to the older commentators, the slothful—those guilty of the sin of slackness in the pursuit of good, as, *e.g.* neglect of the means of grace. This is, theologically speaking, the sin directly opposed to the active grace of charity. By more modern critics it has been ingeniously sought to find in this circle a place not only for the slothful but for the proud and envious as well. To each of these classes of sinners—such of them as have repented in this life—a terrace of Purgatory is assigned, and at first sight it does seem natural to expect that the impenitent among them should be found in Inferno. But, while in Purgatory souls purge themselves of every kind of mortal sin, Inferno, as Dante conceived of it, contains only such sinners as have been guilty of wicked acts. Drift and bent of heart and mind are taken no account of. The evil seed must have borne a harvest, and the guilt of every victim of Justice must be plain and open. Now, pride and envy are sins indeed, but sins that a man may keep to himself. If they have betrayed the subject of them into the commission of crimes, in those crimes they are punished lower down, as is indicated at xii. 49. And so we find that Lucifer is condemned as a traitor, though his treachery sprang from envy: the greater guilt includes the less. For sluggishness in the pursuit of good the vestibule of the caitiffs seems the appropriate place.—There are two kinds of wrath. One is vehement, and declares itself in violent acts; the other does not blaze out, but is grudging and adverse to all social good—the wrath that is nursed. One as much as the other affects behaviour. So in this circle, as in the preceding, we have represented the two excesses of one sin.—Dante's theory of sins is ably treated of in Witte's *Dante-Forschungen*, vol. ii. p. 121.

Canto VIII.

I say, continuing,[312] that long before
    To its foundations we approachèd nigh
    Our eyes went travelling to the top of the tower;
For, hung out there, two flames[313] we could espy.
    Then at such distance, scarce our eyesight made
    It clearly out, another gave reply.
And, to the Sea of Knowledge turned, I said:

'What meaneth this? and what reply would yield
    That other light, and who have it displayed?'
'Thou shouldst upon the impure watery field,'
    He said, 'already what approaches know,
    But that the fen-fog holds it still concealed.'
Never was arrow yet from sharp-drawn bow
    Urged through the air upon a swifter flight
    Than what I saw a tiny vessel show,
Across the water shooting into sight;
    A single pilot served it for a crew,
    Who shouted: 'Art thou come, thou guilty sprite?'[314]
'O Phlegyas, Phlegyas,[315] this thy loud halloo!
    For once,' my Lord said, 'idle is and vain.
    Thou hast us only till the mud we're through.'
And, as one cheated inly smarts with pain
    When the deceit wrought on him is betrayed,
    His gathering ire could Phlegyas scarce contain.
Into the bark my Leader stepped, and made
    Me take my place beside him; nor a jot,
    Till I had entered, was it downward weighed.
Soon as my Guide and I were in the boat,
    To cleave the flood began the ancient prow,
    Deeper[316] than 'tis with others wont to float.
Then, as the stagnant ditch we glided through,
    One smeared with filth in front of me arose
    And said: 'Thus coming ere thy period,[317] who
Art thou?' And I: 'As one who forthwith goes
    I come; but thou defiled, how name they thee?'
    'I am but one who weeps,'[318] he said. 'With woes,
I answered him, 'with tears and misery,
    Accursèd soul, remain; for thou art known
    Unto me now, all filthy though thou be.'
Then both his hands were on the vessel thrown;
    But him my wary Master backward heaved,
    Saying: 'Do thou 'mong the other dogs be gone!'
Then to my neck with both his arms he cleaved,
    And kissed my face, and, 'Soul disdainful,'[319] said,
    'O blessed she in whom thou wast conceived!
He in the world great haughtiness displayed.
    No deeds of worth his memory adorn;
    And therefore rages here his sinful shade.
And many are there by whom crowns are worn
    On earth, shall wallow here like swine in mire,
    Leaving behind them names o'erwhelmed[320] in scorn.'
And I: 'O Master, I have great desire
    To see him well soused in this filthy tide,
    Ere from the lake we finally retire.'

And he: 'Or ever shall have been descried
   The shore by thee, thy longing shall be met;
   For such a wish were justly gratified.'
A little after in such fierce onset
   The miry people down upon him bore,
   I praise and bless God for it even yet.
'Philip Argenti![321] at him!' was the roar;
   And then that furious spirit Florentine
   Turned with his teeth upon himself and tore.
Here was he left, nor wins more words of mine.
   Now in my ears a lamentation rung,
   Whence I to search what lies ahead begin.
And the good Master told me: 'Son, ere long
   We to the city called of Dis[322] draw near,
   Where in great armies cruel burghers[323] throng.'
And I: 'Already, Master, I appear
   Mosques[324] in the valley to distinguish well,
   Vermilion, as if they from furnace were
Fresh come.' And he: 'Fires everlasting dwell
   Within them, whence appear they glowing hot,
   As thou discernest in this lower hell.'
We to the moat profound at length were brought,
   Which girds that city all disconsolate;
   The walls around it seemed of iron wrought.
Not without fetching first a compass great,
   We came to where with angry cry at last:
   'Get out,' the boatman yelled; 'behold the gate!'[325]
More than a thousand, who from Heaven[326] were cast,
   I saw above the gates, who furiously
   Demanded: 'Who, ere death on him has passed,
Holds through the region of the dead his way?'
   And my wise Master made to them a sign
   That he had something secretly to say.
Then ceased they somewhat from their great disdain,
   And said: 'Come thou, but let that one be gone
   Who thus presumptuous enters on this reign.
Let him retrace his madcap way alone,
   If he but can; thou meanwhile lingering here,
   Through such dark regions who hast led him down.'
Judge, reader, if I was not filled with fear,
   Hearing the words of this accursèd threat;
   For of return my hopes extinguished were.
'Beloved Guide, who more than seven times[327] set
   Me in security, and safely brought
   Through frightful dangers in my progress met,
Leave me not thus undone;' I him besought:
   'If further progress be to us denied,

Let us retreat together, tarrying not.'
The Lord who led me thither then replied:
   'Fear not: by One so great has been assigned
   Our passage, vainly were all hindrance tried.
Await me here, and let thy fainting mind
   Be comforted and with good hope be fed,
   Not to be left in this low world behind.'
Thus goes he, thus am I abandonèd
   By my sweet Father. I in doubt remain,
   With Yes and No[328] contending in my head.
I could not hear what speech he did maintain,
   But no long time conferred he in that place,
   Till, to be first, all inward raced again.
And then the gates were closed in my Lord's face
   By these our enemies; outside stood he;
   Then backward turned to me with lingering pace,
With downcast eyes, and all the bravery
   Stripped from his brows; and he exclaimed with sighs;
   'Who dare[329] deny the doleful seats to me!'
And then he said: 'Although my wrath arise,
   Fear not, for I to victory will pursue,
   Howe'er within they plot, the enterprise.
This arrogance of theirs is nothing new;
   They showed it[330] once at a less secret door
   Which stands unbolted since. Thou didst it view,
And saw the dark-writ legend which it bore.
   Thence, even now, is one who hastens down
   Through all the circles, guideless, to this shore,
And he shall win us entrance to the town.'

Footnotes

[312] *Continuing*: The account of the Fifth Circle, begun in the preceding Canto, is continued in this. It is impossible to adopt Boccaccio's story of how the first seven Cantos were found among a heap of other papers, years after Dante's exile began; and that 'continuing' marks the resumption of his work. The word most probably suggested the invention of the incident, or at least led to the identification of some manuscript that may have been sent to Dante, with the opening pages of the *Comedy*. If the tale were true, not only must Ciacco's prophecy (*Inf.* vi.) have been interpolated, but we should be obliged to hold that Dante began the poem while he was a prosperous citizen.—Boccaccio himself in his Comment on the *Comedy* points out the difficulty of reconciling the story with Ciacco's prophecy.

[313] *Two flames*: Denoting the number of passengers who are to be conveyed across the Stygian pool. It is a signal for the ferryman, and is answered by a light hung out on the battlements of the city of Dis.

[314] *Guilty sprite*: Only one is addressed; whether Virgil or Dante is not clear.

[315] *Phlegyas*: Who burnt the temple of Apollo at Delphi in revenge for the violation of his daughter by the god.

[316] *Deeper, etc.*: Because used to carry only shades.

[317] *Ere thy period*: The curiosity of the shade is excited by the sinking of the boat in the water. He assumes that Dante will one day be condemned to Inferno. Neither Francesca nor Ciacco made a like mistake.

[318] *One who weeps*: He is ashamed to tell his name, and hopes in his vile disguise to remain unknown by Dante, whose Florentine speech and dress, and perhaps whose features, he has now recognised.

[319] *Soul disdainful*: Dante has been found guilty of here glorying in the same sin which he so severely reprobates in others. But, without question, of set purpose he here contrasts righteous indignation with the ignoble rage punished in this circle. With his quick temper and zeal so often kindling into flame, he may have felt a special personal need of emphasising the distinction.

[320] *Names o'erwhelmed, etc.*: 'Horrible reproaches.'

[321] *Philip Argenti*: A Florentine gentleman related to the great family of the Adimari, and a contemporary of Dante's. Boccaccio in his commentary describes him as a cavalier, very rich, and so ostentatious that he once shod his horse with silver, whence his surname. In the *Decameron* (ix. 8) he is introduced as violently assaulting—tearing out his hair and dragging him in the mire—the victim of a practical joke played by the Ciacco of Canto vi. Some, without reason, suppose that Dante shows such severity to him because he was a Black, and so a political opponent of his own.

[322] *Dis*: A name of Pluto, the god of the infernal regions.

[323] *Burghers*: The city of Dis composes the Sixth Circle, and, as immediately appears, is populated by demons. The sinners punished in it are not mentioned at all in this Canto, and it seems more reasonable to apply *burghers* to the demons than to the shades. They are called *gravi*, generally taken to mean sore burdened, and the description is then applicable to the shades; but *grave* also bears the sense of cruel, and may describe the fierceness of the devils. Though the city is inhabited by the subjects of Dis, he is found as Lucifer at the very bottom of the pit. By some critics the whole of the lower Inferno, all that lies beyond this point, is regarded as being the city of Dis. But it is the Sixth Circle, with its minarets, that is the city; its walls, however, serving as bulwarks for all the lower Inferno. The shape of the city is, of course, that of a circular belt. Here it may be noted that the Fifth and Sixth Circles are on the same level; the water of Styx, which as a marsh covers the Fifth, is gathered into a moat to surround the walls of the Sixth.

[324] *Mosques*: The feature of an Infidel city that first struck crusader and pilgrim.

[325] *The gate*: They have floated across the stagnant marsh into the deeper waters of the moat, and up to the gate where Phlegyas is used to land his passengers. It may be a question whether his services are required for all who are doomed to the lower Inferno, or only for those bound to the city.

[326] *From Heaven*: 'Rained from Heaven.' Fallen angels.

[327] *Seven times*: Given as a round number.

[328] *Yes and No*: He will return—He will not return. The demons have said that Virgil shall remain, and he has promised Dante not to desert him.

[329] *Who dare, etc.*: Virgil knows the hindrance is only temporary, but wonders what superior devilish power can have incited the demons to deny him entrance. The incident displays the fallen angels as being still rebellious, and is at the same time skillfully conceived to mark a pause before Dante enters on the lower Inferno.

[330] *They showed it, etc.*: At the gate of Inferno, on the occasion of Christ's descent to Limbo. The reference is to the words in the Missal service for Easter Eve: 'This is the night in which, having burst the bonds of death, Christ victoriously ascended from Hell.'

Canto IX.

The hue which cowardice on my face did paint
    When I beheld my guide return again,
    Put his new colour[331] quicker 'neath restraint.
Like one who listens did he fixed remain;
    For far to penetrate the air like night,
    And heavy mist, the eye was bent in vain.
'Yet surely we must vanquish in the fight;'
    Thus he, 'unless[332]—but with such proffered aid—
    O how I weary till he come in sight!'
Well I remarked how he transition made,
    Covering his opening words with those behind,
    Which contradicted what at first he said.
Nath'less his speech with terror charged my mind,
    For, haply, to the word which broken fell
    Worse meaning than he purposed, I assigned.
Down to this bottom[333] of the dismal shell
    Comes ever any from the First Degree,[334]
    Where all their pain is, stripped of hope to dwell?
To this my question thus responded he:
    'Seldom it haps to any to pursue
    The journey now embarked upon by me.
Yet I ere this descended, it is true,
    Beneath a spell of dire Erichtho's[335] laid,
    Who could the corpse with soul inform anew.
Short while my flesh of me was empty made
    When she required me to o'erpass that wall,
    From Judas' circle[336] to abstract a shade.
That is the deepest, darkest place of all,
    And furthest from the heaven[337] which moves the skies;
    I know the way; fear nought that can befall.
These fens[338] from which vile exhalations rise
    The doleful city all around invest,
    Which now we reach not save in angry wise.'
Of more he spake nought in my mind doth rest,
    For, with mine eyes, my every thought had been
    Fixed on the lofty tower with flaming crest,
Where, in a moment and upright, were seen
    Three hellish furies, all with blood defaced,
    And woman-like in members and in mien.

Hydras of brilliant green begirt their waist;
    Snakes and cerastes for their tresses grew,
    And these were round their dreadful temples braced.
That they the drudges were, full well he knew,
    Of her who is the queen of endless woes,
    And said to me: 'The fierce Erynnyes[339] view!
Herself upon the left Megæra shows;
    That is Alecto weeping on the right;
    Tisiphone's between.' Here made he close.
Each with her nails her breast tore, and did smite
    Herself with open palms. They screamed in tone
    So fierce, I to the Poet clove for fright.
'Medusa,[340] come, that we may make him stone!'
    All shouted as they downward gazed; 'Alack!
    Theseus[341] escaped us when he ventured down.'
'Keep thine eyes closed and turn to them thy back,
    For if the Gorgon chance to be displayed
    And thou shouldst look, farewell the upward track!'
Thus spake the Master, and himself he swayed
    Me round about; nor put he trust in mine
    But his own hands upon mine eyelids laid.
O ye with judgment gifted to divine
    Look closely now, and mark what hidden lore
    Lies 'neath the veil of my mysterious line![342]
Across the turbid waters came a roar
    And crash of sound, which big with fear arose:
    Because of it fell trembling either shore.
The fashion of it was as when there blows
    A blast by cross heats made to rage amain,
    Which smites the forest and without repose
The shattered branches sweeps in hurricane;
    In clouds of dust, majestic, onward flies,
    Wild beasts and herdsmen driving o'er the plain.
'Sharpen thy gaze,' he bade—and freed mine eyes—
    'Across the foam-flecked immemorial lake,
    Where sourest vapour most unbroken lies.'
And as the frogs before the hostile snake
    Together of the water get them clear,
    And on the dry ground, huddling, shelter take;
More than a thousand ruined souls in fear
    Beheld I flee from one who, dry of feet,
    Was by the Stygian ferry drawing near.
Waving his left hand he the vapour beat
    Swiftly from 'fore his face, nor seemed he spent
    Save with fatigue at having this to meet.
Well I opined that he from Heaven[343] was sent,
    And to my Master turned. His gesture taught

I should be dumb and in obeisance bent.
    Ah me, how with disdain appeared he fraught!
    He reached the gate, which, touching with a rod,[344]
    He oped with ease, for it resisted not.
'People despised and banished far from God,
    Upon the awful threshold then he spoke,
    'How holds in you such insolence abode?
Why kick against that will which never broke
    Short of its end, if ever it begin,
    And often for you fiercer torments woke?
Butting 'gainst fate, what can ye hope to win?
    Your Cerberus,[345] as is to you well known,
    Still bears for this a well-peeled throat and chin.'
Then by the passage foul he back was gone,
    Nor spake to us, but like a man was he
    By other cares[346] absorbed and driven on
Than that of those who may around him be.
    And we, confiding in the sacred word,
    Moved toward the town in all security.
We entered without hindrance, and I, spurred
    By my desire the character to know
    And style of place such strong defences gird,
Entering, begin mine eyes around to throw,
    And see on every hand a vast champaign,
    The teeming seat of torments and of woe.
And as at Arles[347] where Rhone spreads o'er the plain,
    Or Pola,[348] hard upon Quarnaro sound
    Which bathes the boundaries Italian,
The sepulchres uneven make the ground;
    So here on every side, but far more dire
    And grievous was the fashion of them found.
For scattered 'mid the tombs blazed many a fire,
    Because of which these with such fervour burned
    No arts which work in iron more require.
All of the lids were lifted. I discerned
    By keen laments which from the tombs arose
    That sad and suffering ones were there inurned.
I said: 'O Master, tell me who are those
    Buried within the tombs, of whom the sighs
    Come to our ears thus eloquent of woes?'
And he to me: 'The lords of heresies[349]
    With followers of all sects, a greater band
    Than thou wouldst think, these sepulchres comprise.
To lodge them like to like the tombs are planned.
    The sepulchres have more or less of heat.'[350]
    Then passed we, turning to the dexter hand,[351]
'Tween torments and the lofty parapet.

Footnotes

[331] *New colour*: Both have changed colour, Virgil in anger and Dante in fear.

[332] *Unless*: To conceal his misgiving from Dante, Virgil refrains from expressing all his thought. The 'unless' may refer to what the lying demons had told him or threatened him with; the 'proffered aid,' to that involved in Beatrice's request.

[333] *This bottom*: The lower depths of Inferno. How much still lies below him is unknown to Dante.

[334] *First Degree*: The limbo where Virgil resides. Dante by an indirect question, seeks to learn how much experience of Inferno is possessed by his guide.

[335] *Erichtho*: A Thessalian sorceress, of whom Lucan (*Pharsalia* vi.) tells that she evoked a shade to predict to Sextus Pompey the result of the war between his father and Cæsar. This happened thirty years before the death of Virgil.

[336] *Judas' circle*: The Judecca, or very lowest point of the Inferno. Virgil's death preceded that of Judas by fifty years. He gives no hint of whose the shade was that he went down to fetch; but Lucan's tale was probably in Dante's mind. In the Middle Ages the memory of Virgil was revered as that of a great sorcerer, especially in the neighbourhood of Naples.

[337] *The heaven, etc.*: The *Primum Mobile*; but used here for the highest heaven. See *Inf.* ii. 83, *note*.

[338] *These fens, etc.*: Virgil knows the locality. They have no choice, but must remain where they are, for the same moat and wall gird the city all around.

[339] *Erynnyes*: The Furies. The Queen of whom they are handmaids is Proserpine, carried off by Dis, or Pluto, to the under world.

[340] *Medusa*: One of the Gorgons. Whoever looked on the head of Medusa was turned into stone.

[341] *Theseus*: Who descended into the infernal regions to rescue Proserpine, and escaped by the help of Hercules.

[342] *Mysterious line*: 'Strange verses:' That the verses are called strange, as Boccaccio and others of the older commentators say, because treating of such a subject in the vulgar tongue for the first time, and in rhyme, is difficult to believe. Rather they are strange because of the meaning they convey. What that is, Dante warns the reader of superior intellect to pause and consider. It has been noted (*Inf.* ii. 28) how he uses the characters of the old mythology as if believing in their real existence. But this is for his poetical ends. Here he bids us look below the surface and seek for the truth hidden under the strange disguise.—The opposition to their progress offered by the powers of Hell perplexes even Virgil, while Dante is reduced to a state of absolute terror, and is afflicted with still sharper misgivings than he had at the first as to the issue of his adventure. By an indirect question he seeks to learn how much Virgil really knows of the economy of the lower world; but he cannot so much as listen to all of his Master's reassuring answer, terrified as he is by the sudden appearance of the Furies upon the tower, which rises out of the city of unbelief. These symbolise the trouble of his conscience, and, assailing him with threats, shake his already trembling faith in the Divine government. How, in the face of such foes, is he to find the peace and liberty of soul of which he is in search? That this is the city of unbelief he has not yet been told, and without knowing it he is standing under the very walls of Doubting Castle. And now, if he chance to let his eyes rest on the Gorgon's head, his soul will be petrified by despair; like the denizens of Hell, he will lose the 'good of the intellect,' and will pass into a state from which Virgil—or reason—will be powerless to deliver him. But Virgil takes him in time, and makes him avert his eyes; which may signify that the only safe course for men is to turn their backs on the deep and insoluble problem of how the reality of the Divine government can be reconciled with the apparent triumph of evil.

[343] *From Heaven*: The messenger comes from Heaven, and his words are holy. Against the obvious interpretation, that he is a good angel, there lies the objection that no other such is met with in Inferno, and also that it is spoken of as a new sight for him when Dante first meets with one in Purgatory. But the obstruction now to be overcome is worthy of angelic interference; and Dante can hardly be said to meet the messenger, who does not even glance in his direction. The commentators have made this angel mean all kind of outlandish things.

[344] *A rod*: A piece of the angelic outfit, derived from the *caduceus* of Mercury.

[345] *Cerberus*: Hercules, when Cerberus opposed his entrance to the infernal regions, fastened a chain round his neck and dragged him to the gate. The angel's speech answers Dante's doubts as to the limits of diabolical power.

[346] *By other cares, etc.*: It is not in Inferno that Dante is to hold converse with celestial intelligences. The angel, like Beatrice when she sought Virgil in Limbo, is all on fire to return to his own place.

[347] *Arles*: The Alyscampo (Elysian Fields) at Arles was an enormous cemetery, of which ruins still exist. It had a circumference of about six miles, and contained numerous sarcophagi dating from Roman times.

[348] *Pola*: In Istria, near the Gulf of Quarnaro, said to have contained many ancient tombs.

[349] *Lords of heresies*: 'Heresiarchs.' Dante now learns for the first time that Dis is the city of unbelief. Each class of heretics has its own great sepulchre.

[350] *More or less of heat*: According to the heinousness of the heresy punished in each. It was natural to associate heretics and punishment by fire in days when Dominican monks ruled the roast.

[351] *Dexter hand*: As they move across the circles, and down from one to the other, their course is usually to the left hand. Here for some reason Virgil turns to the right, so as to have the tombs on the left as he advances. It may be that a special proof of his knowledge of the locality is introduced when most needed—after the repulse by the demons—to strengthen Dante's confidence in him as a guide; or, as some subtly think, they being now about to enter the abode of heresy, the movement to the right signifies the importance of the first step in forming opinion. The only other occasion on which their course is taken to the right hand is at *Inf.* xvii. 31.

Canto X.

And now advance we by a narrow track
   Between the torments and the ramparts high,
   My Master first, and I behind his back.
'O mighty Virtue,[352] at whose will am I
   Wheeled through these impious circles,' then I said,
   'Speak, and in full my longing satisfy.

The people who within the tombs are laid,
　　May they be seen? The coverings are all thrown
　　Open, nor is there[353] any guard displayed.'
And he to me: 'All shall be fastened down
　　When hither from Jehoshaphat[354] they come
　　Again in bodies which were once their own.
All here with Epicurus[355] find their tomb
　　Who are his followers, and by whom 'tis held
　　That the soul shares the body's mortal doom.
Things here discovered then shall answer yield,
　　And quickly, to thy question asked of me;
　　As well as[356] to the wish thou hast concealed.'
And I: 'Good Leader, if I hide from thee
　　My heart, it is that I may little say;
　　Nor only now[357] learned I thus dumb to be.'
'O Tuscan, who, still living, mak'st thy way,
　　Modest of speech, through the abode of flame,
　　Be pleased[358] a little in this place to stay.
The accents of thy language thee proclaim
　　To be a native of that state renowned
　　Which I, perchance, wronged somewhat.' Sudden came
These words from out a tomb which there was found
　　'Mongst others; whereon I, compelled by fright,
　　A little toward my Leader shifted ground.
And he: 'Turn round, what ails thee? Lo! upright
　　Beginneth Farinata[359] to arise;
　　All of him 'bove the girdle comes in sight.'
On him already had I fixed mine eyes.
　　Towering erect with lifted front and chest,
　　He seemed Inferno greatly to despise.
And toward him I among the tombs was pressed
　　By my Guide's nimble and courageous hand,
　　While he, 'Choose well thy language,' gave behest.
Beneath his tomb when I had ta'en my stand
　　Regarding me a moment, 'Of what house
　　Art thou?' as if in scorn, he made demand.
To show myself obedient, anxious,
　　I nothing hid, but told my ancestors;
　　And, listening, he gently raised his brows.[360]
'Fiercely to me they proved themselves adverse,
　　And to my sires and party,' then he said;
　　'Because of which I did them twice disperse.'[361]
I answered him: 'And what although they fled!
　　Twice from all quarters they returned with might,
　　An art not mastered yet by these you[362] led.'
Beside him then there issued into sight
　　Another shade, uncovered to the chin,

Propped on his knees, if I surmised aright.
He peered around as if he fain would win
　　Knowledge if any other was with me;
　　And then, his hope all spent, did thus begin,
Weeping: 'By dint of genius if it be
　　Thou visit'st this dark prison, where my son?
　　And wherefore not found in thy company?'
And I to him: 'I come not here alone:
　　He waiting yonder guides me: but disdain
　　Of him perchance was by your Guido[363] shown.'
The words he used, and manner of his pain,
　　Revealed his name to me beyond surmise;
　　Hence was I able thus to answer plain.
Then cried he, and at once upright did rise,
　　'How saidst thou—was? Breathes he not then the air?
　　The pleasant light no longer smites his eyes?'
When he of hesitation was aware
　　Displayed by me in forming my reply,
　　He fell supine, no more to reappear.
But the magnanimous, at whose bidding I
　　Had halted there, the same expression wore,
　　Nor budged a jot, nor turned his neck awry.
'And if'—resumed he where he paused before—
　　'They be indeed but slow that art to learn,
　　Than this my bed, to hear it pains me more.
But ere the fiftieth time anew shall burn
　　The lady's[364] face who reigneth here below,
　　Of that sore art thou shalt experience earn.
And as to the sweet world again thou'dst go,
　　Tell me, why is that people so without
　　Ruth for my race,[365] as all their statutes show?'
And I to him: 'The slaughter and the rout
　　Which made the Arbia[366] to run with red,
　　Cause in our fane[367] such prayers to be poured out.'
Whereon he heaved a sigh and shook his head:
　　'There I was not alone, nor to embrace
　　That cause was I, without good reason, led.
But there I was alone, when from her place
　　All granted Florence should be swept away.
　　'Twas I[368] defended her with open face.'
'So may your seed find peace some better day,'
　　I urged him, 'as this knot you shall untie
　　In which my judgment doth entangled stay.
If I hear rightly, ye, it seems, descry
　　Beforehand what time brings, and yet ye seem
　　'Neath other laws[369] as touching what is nigh.'
'Like those who see best what is far from them,

We see things,' said he, 'which afar remain;

    Thus much enlightened by the Guide Supreme.

To know them present or approaching, vain

    Are all our powers; and save what they relate

    Who hither come, of earth no news we gain.

Hence mayst thou gather in how dead a state

    Shall all our knowledge from that time be thrown

    When of the future shall be closed the gate.'

Then, for my fault as if repentant grown,

    I said: 'Report to him who fell supine,

    That still among the living breathes his son.

And if I, dumb, seemed answer to decline,

    Tell him it was that I upon the knot

    Was pondering then, you helped me to untwine.'

Me now my Master called, whence I besought

    With more than former sharpness of the shade,

    To tell me what companions he had got.

He answered me: 'Some thousand here are laid

    With me; 'mong these the Second Frederick,[370]

    The Cardinal[371] too; of others nought be said.'

Then was he hid; and towards the Bard antique

    I turned my steps, revolving in my brain

    The ominous words[372] which I had heard him speak.

He moved, and as we onward went again

    Demanded of me: 'Wherefore thus amazed?'

    And to his question I made answer plain.

'Within thy mind let there be surely placed,'

    The Sage bade, 'what 'gainst thee thou heardest say.

    Now mark me well' (his finger here he raised),

'When thou shalt stand within her gentle ray

    Whose beauteous eye sees all, she will make known

    The stages[373] of thy journey on life's way.'

Turning his feet, he to the left moved on;

    Leaving the wall, we to the middle[374] went

    Upon a path that to a vale strikes down,

Which even to us above its foulness sent.

Footnotes

[352] *Virtue*: Virgil is here addressed by a new title, which, with the words of deep respect that follow, marks the full restoration of Dante's confidence in him as his guide.

[353] *Nor is there, etc.*: The gate was found to be strictly guarded, but not so are the tombs.

[354] *Jehoshaphat*: 'I will also gather all nations, and will bring them down into the valley of Jehoshaphat' (Joel iii. 2).

[355] *Epicurus*: The unbelief in a future life, or rather the indifference to everything but the calls of ambition and worldly pleasure, common among the nobles of Dante's age and that preceding it, went by the name of Epicureanism. It is the most radical of

heresies, because adverse to the first principles of all religions. Dante, in his treatment of heresy, dwells more on what affects conduct as does the denial of the Divine government—than on intellectual divergence from orthodox belief.

[356] *As well as, etc.*: The question is: 'May they be seen?' The wish is a desire to speak with them.

[357] *Nor only now, etc.*: Virgil has on previous occasions imposed silence on Dante, as, for instance, at *Inf.* iii. 51.

[358] *Be pleased, etc.*: From one of the sepulchres, to be imagined as a huge sarcophagus, come words similar to the *Siste Viator!* common on Roman tombs.

[359] *Farinata*: Of the great Florentine family of the Uberti, and, in the generation before Dante, leader of the Ghibeline or Imperialist party in Florence. His memory long survived among his fellow-townsmen as that of the typical noble, rough-mannered, unscrupulous, and arrogant; but yet, for one good action that he did, he at the same time ranked in the popular estimation as a patriot and a hero. Boccaccio, misled perhaps by the mention of Epicurus, says that he loved rich and delicate fare. It is because all his thoughts were worldly that he is condemned to the city of unbelief. Dante has already (*Inf.* vi. 79) inquired regarding his fate. He died in 1264.

[360] *His brows*: When Dante tells he is of the Alighieri, a Guelf family, Farinata shows some slight displeasure. Or, as a modern Florentine critic interprets the gesture, he has to think a moment before he can remember on which side the Alighieri ranged themselves—they being of the small gentry, while he was a great noble, But this gloss requires Dante to have been more free from pride of family than he really was.

[361] *Twice disperse*: The Alighieri shared in the exile of the Guelfs in 1248 and 1260.

[362] *You*: See also line 95. Dante never uses the plural form to a single person except when desirous of showing social as distinguished from, or over and above, moral respect.

[363] *Guido*: Farinata's companion in the tomb is Cavalcante Cavalcanti, who, although a Guelf, was tainted with the more specially Ghibeline error of Epicureanism. When in order to allay party rancour some of the Guelf and Ghibeline families were forced to intermarry, his son Guido took a daughter of Farinata's to wife. This was in 1267, so that Guido was much older than Dante. Yet they were very intimate, and, intellectually, had much in common. With him Dante exchanged poems of occasion, and he terms him more than once in the *Vita Nuova* his chief friend. The disdain of Virgil need not mean more than is on the surface. Guido died in 1301. He is the hero of the *Decameron*, vi. 9.

[364] *The Lady*: Proserpine; *i.e.* the moon. Ere fifty months from March 1300 were past, Dante was to see the failure of more than one attempt made by the exiles, of whom he was one, to gain entrance to Florence. The great attempt was in the beginning of 1304.

[365] *Ruth for my race*: When the Ghibeline power was finally broken in Florence the Uberti were always specially excluded from any amnesty. There is mention of the political execution of at least one descendant of Farinata's. His son when being led to the scaffold said, 'So we pay our fathers' debts!'—It has been so long common to describe Dante as a Ghibeline, though no careful writer does it now, that it may be worth while here to remark that Ghibelinism, as Farinata understood it, was practically extinct in Florence ere Dante entered political life.

[366] *The Arbia*: At Montaperti, on the Arbia, a few miles from Siena, was fought in 1260 a great battle between the Guelf Florence and her allies on the one hand, and on the other the Ghibelines of Florence, then in exile, under Farinata; the Sienese and Tuscan Ghibelines in general; and some hundreds of men-at-arms lent by Manfred. Notwithstanding the gallant behaviour of the Florentine burghers, the Guelf defeat was overwhelming, and not only did the Arbia run red with Florentine blood—in a figure—but the battle of Montaperti ruined for a time the cause of popular liberty and general improvement in Florence.

[367] *Our fane*: The Parliament of the people used to meet in Santa Reparata, the cathedral; and it is possible that the maintenance of the Uberti disabilities was there more than once confirmed by the general body of the citizens. The use of the word is in any case accounted for by the frequency of political conferences in churches. And the temple having been introduced, edicts are converted into 'prayers.'

[368] *'Twas I, etc.*: Some little time after the victory of Montaperti there was a great Ghibeline gathering from various cities at Empoli, when it was proposed, with general approval, to level Florence with the ground in revenge for the obstinate Guelfism of the population. Farinata roughly declared that as long as he lived and had a sword he would defend his native place, and in the face of this protest the resolution was departed from. It is difficult to understand how of all the Florentine nobles, whose wealth consisted largely in house property, Farinata should have stood alone in protesting against the ruin of the city. But so it seems to have been; and in this great passage Farinata is repaid for his service, in despite of Inferno.

[369] *Other laws*: Ciacco, in Canto vi., prophesied what was to happen in Florence, and Farinata has just told him that four years later than now he will have failed in an attempt to return from exile: yet Farinata does not know if his family is still being persecuted, and Cavalcanti fears that his son Guido is already numbered with the dead. Farinata replies that like the longsighted the shades can only see what is some distance off, and are ignorant of what is going on, or about to happen; which seems to imply that they forget what they once foresaw. Guido was to die within a few months, and the event was too close at hand to come within the range of his father's vision.

[370] *The Second Frederick*: The Emperor of that name who reigned from 1220 to 1250, and waged a life-long war with the Popes for supremacy in Italy. It is not however for his enmity with Rome that he is placed in the Sixth Circle, but for his Epicureanism—as Dante understood it. From his Sicilian court a spirit of free inquiry spread through the Peninsula. With men of the stamp of Farinata it would be converted into a crude materialism.

[371] *The Cardinal*: Ottaviano, of the powerful Tuscan family of the Ubaldini, a man of great political activity, and known in Tuscany as 'The Cardinal.' His sympathies were not with the Roman Court. The news of Montaperti filled him with delight, and later, when the Tuscan Ghibelines refused him money he had asked for, he burst out with 'And yet I have lost my soul for the Ghibelines—if I have a soul.' He died not earlier than 1273. After these illustrious names Farinata scorns to mention meaner ones.

[372] *Ominous words*: Those in which Farinata foretold Dante's exile.

[373] *The stages, etc.*: It is Cacciaguida, his ancestor, who in Paradise instructs Dante in what his future life is to be—one of poverty and exile (*Parad.*xvii.). This is, however, done at the request of Beatrice.

[374] *To the middle*: Turning to the left they cut across the circle till they reach the inner boundary of the city of tombs. Here there is no wall.

Canto XI.

We at the margin of a lofty steep
  Made of great shattered stones in circle bent,
  Arrived where worser torments crowd the deep.
So horrible a stench and violent
  Was upward wafted from the vast abyss,[375]
  Behind the cover we for shelter went
Of a great tomb where I saw written this:
  'Pope Anastasius[376] is within me thrust,
  Whom the straight way Photinus made to miss.'
'Now on our course a while we linger must,'
  The Master said, 'be but our sense resigned
  A little to it, and the filthy gust
We shall not heed.' Then I: 'Do thou but find
  Some compensation lest our time should run
  Wasted.' And he: 'Behold, 'twas in my mind.
Girt by the rocks before us, O my son,
  Lie three small circles,'[377] he began to tell,
  'Graded like those with which thou now hast done,
All of them filled with spirits miserable.
  That sight[378] of them may thee henceforth suffice.
  Hear how and wherefore in these groups they dwell.
Whate'er in Heaven's abhorred as wickedness
  Has injury[379] for its end; in others' bane
  By fraud resulting or in violent wise.
Since fraud to man alone[380] doth appertain,
  God hates it most; and hence the fraudulent band,
  Set lowest down, endure a fiercer pain.
Of the violent is the circle next at hand
  To us; and since three ways is violence shown,
  'Tis in three several circuits built and planned.
To God, ourselves, or neighbours may be done
  Violence, or on the things by them possessed;
  As reasoning clear shall unto thee make known.
Our neighbour may by violence be distressed
  With grievous wounds, or slain; his goods and lands
  By havoc, fire, and plunder be oppressed.
Hence those who wound and slay with violent hands,
  Robbers, and spoilers, in the nearest round
  Are all tormented in their various bands.
Violent against himself may man be found,
  And 'gainst his goods; therefore without avail

They in the next are in repentance drowned
Who on themselves loss of your world entail,
    Who gamble[381] and their substance madly spend,
    And who when called to joy lament and wail.
And even to God may violence extend
    By heart denial and by blasphemy,
    Scorning what nature doth in bounty lend.
Sodom and Cahors[382] hence are doomed to lie
    Within the narrowest circlet surely sealed;
    And such as God within their hearts defy.
Fraud,[383] 'gainst whose bite no conscience findeth shield,
    A man may use with one who in him lays
    Trust, or with those who no such credence yield.
Beneath this latter kind of it decays
    The bond of love which out of nature grew;
    Hence, in the second circle[384] herd the race
To feigning given and flattery, who pursue
    Magic, false coining, theft, and simony,
    Pimps, barrators, and suchlike residue.
The other form of fraud makes nullity
    Of natural bonds; and, what is more than those,
    The special trust whence men on men rely.
Hence in the place whereon all things repose,
    The narrowest circle and the seat of Dis,[385]
    Each traitor's gulfed in everlasting woes.'
'Thy explanation, Master, as to this
    Is clear,' I said, 'and thou hast plainly told
    Who are the people stowed in the abyss.
But tell why those the muddy marshes hold,
    The tempest-driven, those beaten by the rain,
    And such as, meeting, virulently scold,
Are not within the crimson city ta'en
    For punishment, if hateful unto God;
    And, if not hateful, wherefore doomed to pain?'
And he to me: 'Why wander thus abroad,
    More than is wont, thy wits? or how engrossed
    Is now thy mind, and on what things bestowed?
Hast thou the memory of the passage lost
    In which thy Ethics[386] for their subject treat
    Of the three moods by Heaven abhorred the most—
Malice and bestiality complete;
    And how, compared with these, incontinence
    Offends God less, and lesser blame doth meet?
If of this doctrine thou extract the sense,
    And call to memory what people are
    Above, outside, in endless penitence,
Why from these guilty they are sundered far

Thou shalt discern, and why on them alight
    The strokes of justice in less angry war.'
'O Sun that clearest every troubled sight,
    So charmed am I by thy resolving speech,
    Doubt yields me joy no less than knowing right.
Therefore, I pray, a little backward reach,'
    I asked, 'to where thou say'st that usury
    Sins 'gainst God's bounty; and this mystery teach.'
He said: 'Who gives ear to Philosophy
    Is taught by her, nor in one place alone,
    What nature in her course is governed by,
Even Mind Divine, and art which thence hath grown;
    And if thy Physics[387] thou wilt search within,
    Thou'lt find ere many leaves are open thrown,
This art by yours, far as your art can win,
    Is followed close—the teacher by the taught;
    As grandchild then to God your art is kin.
And from these two—do thou recall to thought
    How Genesis[388] begins—should come supplies
    Of food for man, and other wealth be sought.
And, since another plan the usurer plies,
    Nature and nature's child have his disdain;[389]
    Because on other ground his hope relies.
But come,[390] for to advance I now am fain:
    The Fishes[391] over the horizon line
    Quiver; o'er Caurus now stands all the Wain;
And further yonder does the cliff decline.'

Footnotes

[375] *Vast abyss*: They are now at the inner side of the Sixth Circle, and upon the verge of the rocky steep which slopes down from it into the Seventh. All the lower Hell lies beneath them, and it is from that rather than from the next circle in particular that the stench arises, symbolical of the foulness of the sins which are punished there. The noisome smells which make part of the horror of Inferno are after this sometimes mentioned, but never dwelt upon (*Inf.* xviii. 106, and xxix. 50).

[376] *Pope Anastasius*: The second of the name, elected Pope in 496. Photinus, bishop of Sirenium, was infected with the Sabellian heresy, but he was deposed more than a century before the time of Anastasius. Dante follows some obscure legend in charging Anastasius with heresy. The important point is that the one heretic, in the sense usually attached to the term, named as being in the city of unbelief, is a Pope.

[377] *Three small circles*: The Seventh, Eighth, and Ninth; small in circumference compared with those above. The pilgrims are now deep in the hollow cone.

[378] *That sight, etc.*: After hearing the following explanation Dante no longer asks to what classes the sinners met with belong, but only as to the guilt of individual shades.

[379] *Injury*: They have left above them the circles of those whose sin consists in the exaggeration or misdirection of a wholesome natural instinct. Below them lie the circles filled with such as have been guilty of malicious wickedness. This manifests itself in two ways: by violence or by fraud. After first mentioning in a general way that the fraudulent are set lowest in Inferno, Virgil proceeds to define violence, and to tell how the violent occupy the circle immediately beneath them—the Seventh. For division of the maliciously wicked into two classes Dante is supposed to be indebted to Cicero: 'Injury may be wrought by force or by fraud.... Both are unnatural for man, but fraud is the more hateful.'—*De Officiis*, i. 13. It is remarkable that Virgil says nothing of those in the Sixth Circle in this account of the classes of sinners.

[380] *To man alone, etc.*: Fraud involves the corrupt use of the powers that distinguish us from the brutes.

[381] *Who gamble, etc.*: A different sin from the lavish spending punished in the Fourth Circle (*Inf.* vii.). The distinction is that between thriftlessness and the prodigality which, stripping a man of the means of living, disgusts him with life, as described in the following line. It is from among prodigals that the ranks of suicides are greatly filled, and here they are appropriately placed together. It may seem strange that in his classification of guilt Dante should rank violence to one's self as a more heinous sin than that committed against one's neighbour. He may have in view the fact that none harm their neighbours so much as they who are oblivious of their own true interest.

[382] *Sodom and Cahors*: Sins against nature are reckoned sins against God, as explained lower down in this Canto. Cahors in Languedoc had in the Middle Ages the reputation of being a nest of usurers. These in old English Chronicles are termed Caorsins. With the sins of Sodom and Cahors are ranked the denial of God and blasphemy against Him—deeper sins than the erroneous conceptions of the Divine nature and government punished in the Sixth Circle. The three concentric rings composing the Seventh Circle are all on the same level, as we shall find.

[383] *Fraud, etc.*: Fraud is of such a nature that conscience never fails to give due warning against the sin. This is an aggravation of the guilt of it.

[384] *The second circle*: The second now beneath them; that is, the Eighth.

[385] *Seat of Dis*: The Ninth and last Circle.

[386] *Thy Ethics*: The Ethics of Aristotle, in which it is said: 'With regard to manners, these three things are to be eschewed: incontinence, vice, and bestiality.' Aristotle holds incontinence to consist in the immoderate indulgence of propensities which under right guidance are adapted to promote lawful pleasure. It is, generally speaking, the sin of which those about whom Dante has inquired were guilty.—It has been ingeniously sought by Philalethes (*Gött. Com.*) to show that Virgil's disquisition is founded on this threefold classification of Aristotle's—violence being taken to be the same as bestiality, and malice as vice. But the reference to Aristotle is made with the limited purpose of justifying the lenient treatment of incontinence; in the same way as a few lines further on Genesis is referred to in support of the harsh treatment of usury.

[387] *Physics*: The Physics of Aristotle, in which it is said: 'Art imitates nature.' Art includes handicrafts.

[388] *Genesis*: 'And the Lord God took the man, and put him into the garden to dress it and to keep it.' 'In the sweat of thy face shalt thou eat bread.'

[389] *His disdain*: The usurer seeks to get wealth independently of honest labour or reliance on the processes of nature. This far-fetched argument against usury closes one of the most arid passages of the *Comedy*. The shortness of the Canto almost suggests that Dante had himself got weary of it.

[390] *But come, etc.*: They have been all this time resting behind the lid of the tomb.

[391] *The Fishes, etc.*: The sun being now in Aries the stars of Pisces begin to rise about a couple of hours before sunrise. The Great Bear lies above Caurus, the quarter of the N.N.W. wind. It seems impossible to harmonise the astronomical indications scattered throughout the *Comedy*, there being traces of Dante's having sometimes used details belonging rather to the day on which Good Friday fell in 1300, the 8th of April, than to the (supposed) true anniversary of the crucifixion. That this, the 25th of March, is the day he intended to conform to appears from *Inf.* xxi. 112.—The time is now near dawn on the Saturday morning. It is almost needless to say that Virgil speaks of the stars as he knows they are placed, but without seeing them. By what light they see in Inferno is nowhere explained. We have been told that it was dark as night (*Inf.* iv. 10, v. 28).

Canto XII.

The place of our descent[392] before us lay

    Precipitous, and there was something more

    From sight of which all eyes had turned away.

As at the ruin which upon the shore

    Of Adige[393] fell upon this side of Trent—

    Through earthquake or by slip of what before

Upheld it—from the summit whence it went

    Far as the plain, the shattered rocks supply

    Some sort of foothold to who makes descent;

Such was the passage down the precipice high.

    And on the riven gully's very brow

    Lay spread at large the Cretan Infamy[394]

Which was conceived in the pretended cow.

    Us when he saw, he bit himself for rage

    Like one whose anger gnaws him through and through.

'Perhaps thou deemest,' called to him the Sage,

    'This is the Duke of Athens[395] drawing nigh,

    Who war to the death with thee on earth did wage.

Begone, thou brute, for this one passing by

    Untutored by thy sister has thee found,

    And only comes thy sufferings to spy,'

And as the bull which snaps what held it bound

    On being smitten by the fatal blow,

    Halts in its course, and reels upon the ground,

The Minotaur I saw reel to and fro;

    And he, the alert, cried: 'To the passage haste;

    While yet he chafes 'twere well thou down shouldst go.'

So we descended by the slippery waste[396]

    Of shivered stones which many a time gave way

'Neath the new weight[397] my feet upon them placed.
I musing went; and he began to say:
   'Perchance this ruined slope thou thinkest on,
   Watched by the brute rage I did now allay.
But I would have thee know, when I came down
   The former time[398] into this lower Hell,
   The cliff had not this ruin undergone.
It was not long, if I distinguish well,
   Ere He appeared who wrenched great prey from Dis[399]
   From out the upmost circle. Trembling fell
Through all its parts the nauseous abyss
   With such a violence, the world, I thought,
   Was stirred by love; for, as they say, by this
She back to Chaos[400] has been often brought.
   And then it was this ancient rampart strong
   Was shattered here and at another spot.[401]
But toward the valley look. We come ere long
   Down to the river of blood[402] where boiling lie
   All who by violence work others wrong.'
O insane rage! O blind cupidity!
   By which in our brief life we are so spurred,
   Ere downward plunged in evil case for aye!
An ample ditch I now beheld engird
   And sweep in circle all around the plain,
   As from my Escort I had lately heard.
Between this and the rock in single train
   Centaurs[403] were running who were armed with bows,
   As if they hunted on the earth again.
Observing us descend they all stood close,
   Save three of them who parted from the band
   With bow, and arrows they in coming chose.
'What torment,' from afar one made demand,
   'Come ye to share, who now descend the hill?
   I shoot unless ye answer whence ye stand.'
My Master said: 'We yield no answer till
   We come to Chiron[404] standing at thy side;
   But thy quick temper always served thee ill.'
Then touching me: ''Tis Nessus;[405] he who died
   With love for beauteous Dejanire possessed,
   And who himself his own vendetta plied.
He in the middle, staring on his breast,
   Is mighty Chiron, who Achilles bred;
   And next the wrathful Pholus. They invest
The fosse and in their thousands round it tread,
   Shooting whoever from the blood shall lift,
   More than his crime allows, his guilty head.'
As we moved nearer to those creatures swift

Chiron drew forth a shaft and dressed his beard
   Back on his jaws, using the arrow's cleft.
And when his ample mouth of hair was cleared,
   He said to his companions: 'Have ye seen
   The things the second touches straight are stirred,
As they by feet of shades could ne'er have been?'
   And my good Guide, who to his breast had gone—
   The part where join the natures,[406] 'Well I ween
He lives,' made answer; 'and if, thus alone,
   He seeks the valley dim 'neath my control,
   Necessity, not pleasure, leads him on.
One came from where the alleluiahs roll,
   Who charged me with this office strange and new:
   No robber he, nor mine a felon soul.
But, by that Power which makes me to pursue
   The rugged journey whereupon I fare,
   Accord us one of thine to keep in view,
That he may show where lies the ford, and bear
   This other on his back to yonder strand;
   No spirit he, that he should cleave the air.'
Wheeled to the right then Chiron gave command
   To Nessus: 'Turn, and lead them, and take tent
   They be not touched by any other band.'[407]
We with our trusty Escort forward went,
   Threading the margin of the boiling blood
   Where they who seethed were raising loud lament.
People I saw up to the chin imbrued,
   'These all are tyrants,' the great Centaur said,
   'Who blood and plunder for their trade pursued.
Here for their pitiless deeds tears now are shed
   By Alexander,[408] and Dionysius fell,
   Through whom in Sicily dolorous years were led.
The forehead with black hair so terrible
   Is Ezzelino;[409] that one blond of hue,
   Obizzo[410] d'Este, whom, as rumours tell,
His stepson murdered, and report speaks true.'
   I to the Poet turned, who gave command:
   'Regard thou chiefly him. I follow you.'
Ere long the Centaur halted on the strand,
   Close to a people who, far as the throat,
   Forth of that bulicamë[411] seemed to stand.
Thence a lone shade to us he pointed out
   Saying: 'In God's house[412] ran he weapon through
   The heart which still on Thames wins cult devout.'
Then I saw people, some with heads in view,
   And some their chests above the river bore;
   And many of them I, beholding, knew.

And thus the blood went dwindling more and more,

    Until at last it covered but the feet:

    Here took we passage[413] to the other shore.

'As on this hand thou seest still abate

    In depth the volume of the boiling stream,'

    The Centaur said, 'so grows its depth more great,

Believe me, towards the opposite extreme,

    Until again its circling course attains

    The place where tyrants must lament. Supreme

Justice upon that side involves in pains,

    With Attila,[414] once of the world the pest,

    Pyrrhus[415] and Sextus: and for ever drains

Tears out of Rinier of Corneto[416] pressed

    And Rinier Pazzo[417] in that boiling mass,

    Whose brigandage did so the roads infest.'

Then turned he back alone, the ford to pass.

Footnotes

[392] *Our descent*: To the Seventh Circle.

[393] *Adige*: Different localities in the valley of the Adige have been fixed on as the scene of this landslip. The Lavini di Marco, about twenty miles south of Trent, seem best to answer to the description. They 'consist of black blocks of stone and fragments of a landslip which, according to the Chronicle of Fulda, fell in the year 883 and overwhelmed the valley for four Italian miles' (Gsell-Fels, *Ober. Ital.* i. 35).

[394] *The Cretan Infamy*: The Minotaur, the offspring of Pasiphaë; a half-bovine monster who inhabited the Cretan labyrinth, and to whom a human victim was offered once a year. He lies as guard upon the Seventh Circle—that of the violent (*Inf.* xi. 23, *note*)—and is set at the top of the rugged slope, itself the scene of a violent convulsion.

[395] *Duke of Athens*: Theseus, instructed by Ariadne, daughter of Pasiphaë and Minos, how to outwit the Minotaur, entered the labyrinth in the character of a victim, slew the monster, and then made his way out, guided by a thread he had unwound as he went in.

[396] *The slippery waste*: The word used here, *scarco*, means in modern Tuscan a place where earth or stones have been carelessly shot into a heap.

[397] *The new weight*: The slope had never before been trodden by mortal foot.

[398] *The former time*: When Virgil descended to evoke a shade from the Ninth Circle (*Inf.* ix. 22).

[399] *Prey from Dis*: The shades delivered from Limbo by Christ (*Inf.* iv. 53). The expression in the text is probably suggested by the words of the hymn *Vexilla: Prædamque tulit Tartaris*.

[400] *To Chaos*: The reference is to the theory of Empedocles, known to Dante through the refutation of it by Aristotle. The theory was one of periods of unity and division in nature, according as love or hatred prevailed.

[401] *Another spot*: See *Inf.* xxi. 112. The earthquake at the Crucifixion shook even Inferno to its base.

[402] *The river of blood*: Phlegethon, the 'boiling river.' Styx and Acheron have been already passed. Lethe, the fourth infernal river, is placed by Dante in Purgatory. The first round or circlet of the Seventh Circle is filled by Phlegethon.

[403] *Centaurs*: As this round is the abode of such as are guilty of violence against their neighbours, it is guarded by these brutal monsters, half-man and half-horse.

[404] *Chiron*: Called the most just of the Centaurs.

[405] *Nessus*: Slain by Hercules with a poisoned arrow. When dying he gave Dejanira his blood-stained shirt, telling her it would insure the faithfulness to her of any whom she loved. Hercules wore it and died of the venom; and thus Nessus avenged himself.

[406] *The natures*: The part of the Centaur where the equine body is joined on to the human neck and head.

[407] *Other band*: Of Centaurs.

[408] *Alexander*: It is not known whether Alexander the Great or a petty Thessalian tyrant is here meant. *Dionysius*: The cruel tyrant of Syracuse.

[409] *Ezzelino*: Or Azzolino of Romano, the greatest Lombard Ghibeline of his time. He was son-in-law of Frederick II., and was Imperial Vicar of the Trevisian Mark. Towards the close of Fredrick's life, and for some years after, he exercised almost independent power in Vicenza, Padua, and Verona. Cruelty, erected into a system, was his chief instrument of government, and 'in his dungeons men found something worse than death.' For Italians, says Burckhardt, he was the most impressive political personage of the thirteenth century; and around his memory, as around Frederick's, there gathered strange legends. He died in 1259, of a wound received in battle. When urged to confess his sins by the monk who came to shrive him, he declared that the only sin on his conscience was negligence in revenge. But this may be mythical, as may also be the long black hair between his eyebrows, which rose up stiff and terrible as his anger waxed.

[410] *Obizzo*: The second Marquis of Este of that name. He was lord of Ferrara. There seems little, if any, evidence extant of his being specially cruel. As a strong Guelf he took sides with Charles of Anjou against Manfred. He died in 1293, smothered, it was believed, by a son, here called a stepson for his unnatural conduct. But though Dante vouches for the truth of the rumour it seems to have been an invention.

[411] *That bulicamë*: The stream of boiling blood is probably named from the bulicamë, or hot spring, best known to Dante—that near Viterbo (see *Inf.* xiv. 79). And it may be that the mention of the bulicamë suggests the reference at line 119.

[412] *In God's house*: Literally, 'In the bosom of God.' The shade is that of Guy, son of Simon of Montfort and Vicar in Tuscany of Charles of Anjou. In 1271 he stabbed, in the Cathedral of Viterbo, Henry, son of Richard of Cornwall and cousin of Edward I. of England. The motive of the murder was to revenge the death of his father, Simon, at Evesham. The body of the young prince was conveyed to England, and the heart was placed in a vase upon the tomb of the Confessor. The shade of Guy stands up to the chin in blood among the worst of the tyrants, and alone, because of the enormity of his crime.

[413] *Here took we passage*: Dante on Nessus' back. Virgil has fallen behind to allow the Centaur to act as guide; and how he crosses the stream Dante does not see.

[414] *Attila*: King of the Huns, who invaded part of Italy in the fifth century; and who, according to the mistaken belief of Dante's age, was the devastator of Florence.

[415] *Pyrrhus*: King of Epirus. *Sextus*: Son of Pompey; a great sea-captain who fought against the Triumvirs. The crime of the first, in Dante's eyes, is that he fought with Rome; of the second, that he opposed Augustus.

[416] *Rinier of Corneto*: Who in Dante's time disturbed the coast of the States of the Church by his robberies and violence.

[417] *Rinier Pazzo*: Of the great family of the Pazzi of Val d'Arno, was excommunicated in 1269 for robbing ecclesiastics.

Canto XIII.

Ere Nessus landed on the other shore
  We for our part within a forest[418] drew,
  Which of no pathway any traces bore.
Not green the foliage, but of dusky hue;
  Not smooth the boughs, but gnarled and twisted round;
  For apples, poisonous thorns upon them grew.
No rougher brakes or matted worse are found
  Where savage beasts betwixt Corneto[419] roam
  And Cecina,[419] abhorring cultured ground.
The loathsome Harpies[420] nestle here at home,
  Who from the Strophades the Trojans chased
  With dire predictions of a woe to come.
Great winged are they, but human necked and faced,
  With feathered belly, and with claw for toe;
  They shriek upon the bushes wild and waste.
'Ere passing further, I would have thee know,'
  The worthy Master thus began to say,
  'Thou'rt in the second round, nor hence shalt go
Till by the horrid sand thy footsteps stay.
  Give then good heed, and things thou'lt recognise
  That of my words will prove[421] the verity.'
Wailings on every side I heard arise:
  Of who might raise them I distinguished nought;
  Whereon I halted, smitten with surprise.
I think he thought that haply 'twas my thought
  The voices came from people 'mong the trees,
  Who, to escape us, hiding-places sought;
Wherefore the Master said: 'From one of these
  Snap thou a twig, and thou shalt understand
  How little with thy thought the fact agrees.'
Thereon a little I stretched forth my hand
  And plucked a tiny branch from a great thorn.
  'Why dost thou tear me?' made the trunk demand.
When dark with blood it had begun to turn,
  It cried a second time: 'Why wound me thus?
  Doth not a spark of pity in thee burn?
Though trees we be, once men were all of us;
  Yet had our souls the souls of serpents been
  Thy hand might well have proved more piteous.'

As when the fire hath seized a fagot green
  At one extremity, the other sighs,
  And wind, escaping, hisses; so was seen,
At where the branch was broken, blood to rise
  And words were mixed with it. I dropped the spray
  And stood like one whom terror doth surprise.
The Sage replied: 'Soul vexed with injury,
  Had he been only able to give trust
  To what he read narrated in my lay,[422]
His hand toward thee would never have been thrust.
  'Tis hard for faith; and I, to make it plain,
  Urged him to trial, mourn it though I must.
But tell him who thou wast; so shall remain
  This for amends to thee, thy fame shall blow
  Afresh on earth, where he returns again.'
And then the trunk: 'Thy sweet words charm me so,
  I cannot dumb remain; nor count it hard
  If I some pains upon my speech bestow.
For I am he[423] who held both keys in ward
  Of Frederick's heart, and turned them how I would,
  And softly oped it, and as softly barred,
Till scarce another in his counsel stood.
  To my high office I such loyalty bore,
  It cost me sleep and haleness of my blood.
The harlot[424] who removeth nevermore
  From Cæsar's house eyes ignorant of shame—
  A common curse, of courts the special sore—
Set against me the minds of all aflame,
  And these in turn Augustus set on fire,
  Till my glad honours bitter woes became.
My soul, filled full with a disdainful ire,
  Thinking by means of death disdain to flee,
  'Gainst my just self unjustly did conspire.
I swear even by the new roots of this tree
  My fealty to my lord I never broke,
  For worthy of all honour sure was he.
If one of you return 'mong living folk,
  Let him restore my memory, overthrown
  And suffering yet because of envy's stroke.'
Still for a while the poet listened on,
  Then said: 'Now he is dumb, lose not the hour,
  But make request if more thou'dst have made known.'
And I replied: 'Do thou inquire once more
  Of what thou thinkest[425] I would gladly know;
  I cannot ask; ruth wrings me to the core.'
On this he spake: 'Even as the man shall do,
  And liberally, what thou of him hast prayed,

Imprisoned spirit, do thou further show
How with these knots the spirits have been made
Incorporate; and, if thou canst, declare
If from such members e'er is loosed a shade.'
Then from the trunk came vehement puffs of air;
Next, to these words converted was the wind:
'My answer to you shall be short and clear.
When the fierce soul no longer is confined
In flesh, torn thence by action of its own,
To the Seventh Depth by Minos 'tis consigned.
No choice is made of where it shall be thrown
Within the wood; but where by chance 'tis flung
It germinates like seed of spelt that's sown.
A forest tree it grows from sapling young;
Eating its leaves, the Harpies cause it pain,
And open loopholes whence its sighs are wrung.
We for our vestments shall return again
Like others, but in them shall ne'er be clad:[426]
Men justly lose what from themselves they've ta'en.
Dragged hither by us, all throughout the sad
Forest our bodies shall be hung on high;
Each on the thorn of its destructive shade.'
While to the trunk we listening lingered nigh,
Thinking he might proceed to tell us more,
A sudden uproar we were startled by
Like him who, that the huntsman and the boar
To where he stands are sweeping in the chase,
Knows by the crashing trees and brutish roar.
Upon our left we saw a couple race
Naked[427] and scratched; and they so quickly fled
The forest barriers burst before their face.
'Speed to my rescue, death!' the foremost pled.
The next, as wishing he could use more haste;
'Not thus, O Lano,[428] thee thy legs bested
When one at Toppo's tournament thou wast.'
Then, haply wanting breath, aside he stepped,
Merged with a bush on which himself he cast.
Behind them through the forest onward swept
A pack of dogs, black, ravenous, and fleet,
Like greyhounds from their leashes newly slipped.
In him who crouched they made their teeth to meet,
And, having piecemeal all his members rent,
Haled them away enduring anguish great.
Grasping my hand, my Escort forward went
And led me to the bush which, all in vain,
Through its ensanguined openings made lament.
'James of St. Andrews,'[429] it we heard complain;

'What profit hadst thou making me thy shield?
For thy bad life doth blame to me pertain?'
Then, halting there, this speech my Master held:
'Who wast thou that through many wounds dost sigh,
Mingled with blood, words big with sorrow swelled?'
'O souls that hither come,' was his reply,
'To witness shameful outrage by me borne,
Whence all my leaves torn off around me lie,
Gather them to the root of this drear thorn.
My city[430] for the Baptist changed of yore
Her former patron; wherefore, in return,
He with his art will make her aye deplore;
And were it not some image doth remain
Of him where Arno's crossed from shore to shore,
Those citizens who founded her again
On ashes left by Attila,[431] had spent
Their labour of a surety all in vain.
In my own house[432] I up a gibbet went.'

Footnotes

[418] *A forest*: The second round of the Seventh Circle consists of a belt of tangled forest, enclosed by the river of blood, and devoted to suicides and prodigals.

[419] *Corneto and Cecina*: Corneto is a town on the coast of what used to be the States of the Church; Cecina a stream not far south of Leghorn. Between them lies the Maremma, a district of great natural fertility, now being restored again to cultivation, but for ages a neglected and poisonous wilderness.

[420] *Harpies*: Monsters with the bodies of birds and the heads of women. In the *Æneid* iii., they are described as defiling the feast of which the Trojans were about to partake on one of the Strophades—islands of the Ægean; and on that occasion the prophecy was made that Æneas and his followers should be reduced to eat their tables ere they acquired a settlement in Italy. Here the Harpies symbolise shameful waste and disgust with life.

[421] *Will prove, etc.*: The things seen by Dante are to make credible what Virgil tells (*Æn.* iii.) of the blood and piteous voice that issued from the torn bushes on the tomb of Polydorus.

[422] *My lay*: See previous note. Dante thus indirectly acknowledges his debt to Virgil; and, perhaps, at the same time puts in his claim to an imaginative licence equal to that taken by his master. On a modern reader the effect of the reference is to weaken the verisimilitude of the incident.

[423] *For I am he, etc.*: The speaker is Pier delle Vigne, who from being a begging student of Bologna rose to be the Chancellor of the Emperor FrederickII., the chief councillor of that monarch, and one of the brightest ornaments of his intellectual court. Peter was perhaps the more endeared to his master because, like him, he was a poet of no mean order. There are two accounts of what caused his disgrace. According to one of these he was found to have betrayed Frederick's interests in favour of the Pope's; and according to the other he tried to poison him. Neither is it known whether he committed suicide; though he is said to have done so after being disgraced, by dashing his brains out against a church

wall in Pisa. Dante clearly follows this legend. The whole episode is eloquent of the esteem in which Peter's memory was held by Dante. His name is not mentioned in Inferno, but yet the promise is amply kept that it shall flourish on earth again, freed from unmerited disgrace. He died about 1249.

[424] *The harlot*: Envy.

[425] *Of what thou thinkest, etc.*: Virgil never asks a question for his own satisfaction. He knows who the spirits are, what brought them there, and which of them will speak honestly out on the promise of having his fame refreshed in the world. It should be noted how, by a hint, he has made Peter aware of who he is (line 48); a delicate attention yielded to no other shade in the Inferno, except Ulysses (*Inf.* xxvi. 79), and, perhaps, Brunetto Latini (*Inf.* xv. 99).

[426] *In them shall ne'er be clad*: Boccaccio is here at great pains to save Dante from a charge of contradicting the tenet of the resurrection of the flesh.

[427] *Naked*: These are the prodigals; their nakedness representing the state to which in life they had reduced themselves.

[428] *Lano*: Who made one of a club of prodigals in Siena (*Inf.* xxix. 130) and soon ran through his fortune. Joining in a Florentine expedition in 1288 against Arezzo, he refused to escape from a defeat encountered by his side at Pieve del Toppo, preferring, as was supposed, to end his life at once rather than drag it out in poverty.

[429] *James of St. Andrews*: Jacopo da Sant' Andrea, a Paduan who inherited enormous wealth which did not last him for long. He literally threw money away, and would burn a house for the sake of the blaze. His death has been placed in 1239.

[430] *My city, etc.*: According to tradition the original patron of Florence was Mars. In Dante's time an ancient statue, supposed to be of that god, stood upon the Old Bridge of Florence. It is referred to in *Parad.* xvi. 47 and 145. Benvenuto says that he had heard from Boccaccio, who had frequently heard it from old people, that the statue was regarded with great awe. If a boy flung stones or mud at it, the bystanders would say of him that he would make a bad end. It was lost in the great flood of 1333. Here the Florentine shade represents Mars as troubling Florence with wars in revenge for being cast off as a patron.

[431] *Attila*: A confusion with Totila. Attila was never so far south as Tuscany. Neither is there reason to believe that when Totila took the city he destroyed it. But the legend was that it was rebuilt in the time of Charles the Great.

[432] *My own house, etc.*: It is not settled who this was who hanged himself from the beams of his own roof. One of the Agli, say some; others, one of the Mozzi. Boccaccio and Peter Dante remark that suicide by hanging was common in Florence. But Dante's text seems pretty often to have suggested the invention of details in support or illustration of it.

Canto XIV.

Me of my native place the dear constraint[433]
    Led to restore the leaves which round were strewn,
    To him whose voice by this time was grown faint.
Thence came we where the second round joins on
    Unto the third, wherein how terrible
    The art of justice can be, is well shown.
But, clearly of these wondrous things to tell,

I say we entered on a plain of sand
    Which from its bed doth every plant repel.
The dolorous wood lies round it like a band,
    As that by the drear fosse is circled round.
    Upon its very edge we came to a stand.
And there was nothing within all that bound
    But burnt and heavy sand; like that once trod
    Beneath the feet of Cato[434] was the ground.
Ah, what a terror, O revenge of God!
    Shouldst thou awake in any that may read
    Of what before mine eyes was spread abroad.
I of great herds of naked souls took heed.
    Most piteously was weeping every one;
    And different fortunes seemed to them decreed.
For some of them[435] upon the ground lay prone,
    And some were sitting huddled up and bent,
    While others, restless, wandered up and down.
More numerous were they that roaming went
    Than they that were tormented lying low;
    But these had tongues more loosened to lament.
O'er all the sand, deliberate and slow,
    Broad open flakes of fire were downward rained,
    As 'mong the Alps [436] in calm descends the snow.
Such Alexander[437] saw when he attained
    The hottest India; on his host they fell
    And all unbroken on the earth remained;
Wherefore he bade his phalanxes tread well
    The ground, because when taken one by one
    The burning flakes they could the better quell.
So here eternal fire[438] was pouring down;
    As tinder 'neath the steel, so here the sands
    Kindled, whence pain more vehement was known.
And, dancing up and down, the wretched hands[439]
    Beat here and there for ever without rest;
    Brushing away from them the falling brands.
And I: 'O Master, by all things confessed
    Victor, except by obdurate evil powers
    Who at the gate[440] to stop our passage pressed,
Who is the enormous one who noway cowers
    Beneath the fire; with fierce disdainful air
    Lying as if untortured by the showers?'
And that same shade, because he was aware
    That touching him I of my Guide was fain
    To learn, cried: 'As in life, myself I bear
In death. Though Jupiter should tire again
    His smith, from whom he snatched in angry bout
    The bolt by which I at the last was slain;[441]

Though one by one he tire the others out
　At the black forge in Mongibello[442] placed,
　　While "Ho, good Vulcan, help me!" he shall shout—
The cry he once at Phlegra's[443] battle raised;
　Though hurled with all his might at me shall fly
　　His bolts, yet sweet revenge he shall not taste.'
Then spake my Guide, and in a voice so high
　Never till then heard I from him such tone:
　　'O Capaneus, because unquenchably
Thy pride doth burn, worse pain by thee is known.
　Into no torture save thy madness wild
　　Fit for thy fury couldest thou be thrown.'
Then, to me turning with a face more mild,
　He said: 'Of the Seven Kings was he of old,
　　Who leaguered Thebes, and as he God reviled
Him in small reverence still he seems to hold;
　But for his bosom his own insolence
　　Supplies fit ornament,[444] as now I told.
Now follow; but take heed lest passing hence
　Thy feet upon the burning sand should tread;
　　But keep them firm where runs the forest fence.'[445]
We reached a place—nor any word we said—
　Where issues from the wood a streamlet small;
　　I shake but to recall its colour red.
Like that which does from Bulicamè[446] fall,
　And losel women later 'mong them share;
　　So through the sand this brooklet's waters crawl.
Its bottom and its banks I was aware
　Were stone, and stone the rims on either side.
　　From this I knew the passage[447] must be there.
'Of all that I have shown thee as thy guide
　Since when we by the gateway[448] entered in,
　　Whose threshold unto no one is denied,
Nothing by thee has yet encountered been
　So worthy as this brook to cause surprise,
　　O'er which the falling fire-flakes quenched are seen.'
These were my Leader's words. For full supplies
　I prayed him of the food of which to taste
　　Keen appetite he made within me rise.
'In middle sea there lies a country waste,
　Known by the name of Crete,' I then was told,
　　'Under whose king[449] the world of yore was chaste.
There stands a mountain, once the joyous hold
　Of woods and streams; as Ida 'twas renowned,
　　Now 'tis deserted like a thing grown old.
For a safe cradle 'twas by Rhea found.
　To nurse her child[450] in; and his infant cry,

Lest it betrayed him, she with clamours drowned.
　Within the mount an old man towereth high.
　　Towards Damietta are his shoulders thrown;
　　　On Rome, as on his mirror, rests his eye.
His head is fashioned of pure gold alone;
　Of purest silver are his arms and chest;
　　'Tis brass to where his legs divide; then down
From that is all of iron of the best,
　Save the right foot, which is of baken clay;
　　And upon this foot doth he chiefly rest.
Save what is gold, doth every part display
　A fissure dripping tears; these, gathering all
　　Together, through the grotto pierce a way.
From rock to rock into this deep they fall,
　Feed Acheron[451] and Styx and Phlegethon,
　　Then downward travelling by this strait canal,
Far as the place where further slope is none,
　Cocytus form; and what that pool may be
　　I say not now. Thou'lt see it further on.'
'If this brook rises,' he was asked by me,
　'Within our world, how comes it that no trace
　　We saw of it till on this boundary?'
And he replied: 'Thou knowest that the place
　Is round, and far as thou hast moved thy feet,
　　Still to the left hand[452] sinking to the base,
Nath'less thy circuit is not yet complete.
　Therefore if something new we chance to spy,
　　Amazement needs not on thy face have seat.'
I then: 'But, Master, where doth Lethe lie,
　And Phlegethon? Of that thou sayest nought;
　　Of this thou say'st, those tears its flood supply.'
'It likes me well to be by thee besought;
　But by the boiling red wave,' I was told,
　　'To half thy question was an answer brought.
Lethe,[453] not in this pit, shalt thou behold.
　Thither to wash themselves the spirits go,
　　When penitence has made them spotless souled.'
Then said he: 'From the wood 'tis fitting now
　That we depart; behind me press thou nigh.
　Keep we the margins, for they do not glow,
And over them, ere fallen, the fire-flakes die.'

Footnotes

[433] *Dear constraint*: The mention of Florence has awakened Dante to pity, and he willingly complies with the request of the unnamed suicide (*Inf.* xiii. 142). As a rule, the only service he consents to yield the souls with whom he converses in Inferno is to restore their memory upon earth; a favour he does not feign to

be asked for in this case, out of consideration, it may be, for the family of the sinner.

[434] *Cato*: Cato of Utica, who, after the defeat of Pompey at Pharsalia, led his broken army across the Libyan desert to join King Juba.

[435] *Some of them, etc.*: In this the third round of the Seventh Circle are punished those guilty of sins of violence against God, against nature, and against the arts by which alone a livelihood can honestly be won. Those guilty as against God, the blasphemers, lie prone like Capaneus (line 46), and are subject to the fiercest pain. Those guilty of unnatural vice are stimulated into ceaseless motion, as described in Cantos XV. and XVI. The usurers, those who despise honest industry and the humanising arts of life, are found crouching on the ground (*Inf.* xvii. 43).

[436] *The Alps*: Used here for mountains in general.

[437] *Such Alexander, etc.*: The reference is to a pretended letter of Alexander to Aristotle, in which he tells of the various hindrances met with by his army from snow and rain and showers of fire. But in that narrative it is the snow that is trampled down, while the flakes of fire are caught by the soldiers upon their outspread cloaks. The story of the shower of fire may have been suggested by Plutarch's mention of the mineral oil in the province of Babylon, a strange thing to the Greeks; and of how they were entertained by seeing the ground, which had been sprinkled with it, burst into flame.

[438] *Eternal fire*: As always, the character of the place and of the punishment bears a relation to the crimes of the inhabitants. They sinned against nature in a special sense, and now they are confined to the sterile sand where the only showers that fall are showers of fire.

[439] *The wretched hands*: The dance, named in the original the *tresca*, was one in which the performers followed a leader and imitated him in all his gestures, waving their hands as he did, up and down, and from side to side. The simile is caught straight from common life.

[440] *At the gate*: Of the city of Dis (*Inf.* viii. 82).

[441] *Was slain, etc.*: Capaneus, one of the Seven Kings, as told below, when storming the walls of Thebes, taunted the other gods with impunity, but his blasphemy against Jupiter was answered by a fatal bolt.

[442] *Mongibello*: A popular name of Etna, under which mountain was situated the smithy of Vulcan and the Cyclopes.

[443] *Phlegra*: Where the giants fought with the gods.

[444] *Fit ornament, etc.*: Even if untouched by the pain he affects to despise, he would yet suffer enough from the mad hatred of God that rages in his breast. Capaneus is the nearest approach to the Satan of Milton found in the *Inferno*. From the need of getting law enough by which to try the heathen Dante is led into some inconsistency. After condemning the virtuous heathen to Limbo for their ignorance of the one true God, he now condemns the wicked heathen to this circle for despising false gods. Jupiter here stands for, as need scarcely be said, the Supreme Ruler; and in that sense he is termed God (line 69). But it remains remarkable that the one instance of blasphemous defiance of God should be taken from classical fable.

[445] *The forest fence*: They do not trust themselves so much as to step upon the sand, but look out on it from the verge of the forest which encircles it, and which as they travel they have on the left hand.

[446] *Bulicamë*: A hot sulphur spring a couple of miles from Viterbo, greatly frequented for baths in the Middle Ages; and, it is said, especially by light women. The water boils up into a large pool, whence it flows by narrow channels; sometimes by one and sometimes by another, as the purposes of the neighbouring peasants require. Sulphurous fumes rise from the water as it runs. The incrustation of the bottom, sides, and edges of those channels gives them the air of being solidly built.

[447] *The passage*: On each edge of the canal there is a flat pathway of solid stone; and Dante sees that only by following one of these can a passage be gained across the desert, for to set foot on the sand is impossible for him owing to the falling flakes of fire. There may be found in his description of the solid and flawless masonry of the canal a trace of the pleasure taken in good building by the contemporaries of Arnolfo. Nor is it without meaning that the sterile sands, the abode of such as despised honest labour, is crossed by a perfect work of art which they are forbidden ever to set foot upon.

[448] *The gateway*: At the entrance to Inferno.

[449] *Whose king*: Saturn, who ruled the world in the Golden Age. He, as the devourer of his own offspring, is the symbol of Time; and the image of Time is therefore set by Dante in the island where he reigned.

[450] *Her child*: Jupiter, hidden in the mountain from his father Saturn.

[451] *Feed Acheron, etc.*: The idea of this image is taken from the figure in Nebuchadnezzar's dream in Daniel ii. But here, instead of the Four Empires, the materials of the statue represent the Four Ages of the world; the foot of clay on which it stands being the present time, which is so bad that even iron were too good to represent it. Time turns his back to the outworn civilisations of the East, and his face to Rome, which, as the seat of the Empire and the Church, holds the secret of the future. The tears of time shed by every Age save that of Gold feed the four infernal streams and pools of Acheron, Styx, Phlegethon, and Cocytus. Line 117 indicates that these are all fed by the same water; are in fact different names for the same flood of tears. The reason why Dante has not hitherto observed the connection between them is that he has not made a complete circuit of each or indeed of any circle, as Virgil reminds him at line 124, etc. The rivulet by which they stand drains the boiling Phlegethon—where the water is all changed to blood, because in it the murderers are punished—and flowing through the forest of the suicides and the desert of the blasphemers, etc., tumbles into the Eighth Circle as described in Canto xvi. 103. Cocytus they are afterward to reach. An objection to this account of the infernal rivers as being all fed by the same waters may be found in the difference of volume of the great river of Acheron (*Inf.* iii. 71) and of this brooklet. But this difference is perhaps to be explained by the evaporation from the boiling waters of Phlegethon and of this stream which drains it. Dante is almost the only poet applied to whom such criticism would not be trifling. Another difficult point is how Cocytus should not in time have filled, and more than filled, the Ninth Circle.

[452] *To the left hand*: Twice only as they descend they turn their course to the right hand (*Inf.* ix. 132, and xvii. 31). The circuit of the Inferno they do not complete till they reach the very base.

[453] *Lethe*: Found in the Earthly Paradise, as described in *Purgatorio* xxviii. 130.

Canto XV.

Now lies[454] our way along one of the margins hard;
    Steam rising from the rivulet forms a cloud,
    Which 'gainst the fire doth brook and borders guard.
Like walls the Flemings, timorous of the flood
    Which towards them pours betwixt Bruges and Cadsand,[455]
    Have made, that ocean's charge may be withstood;
Or what the Paduans on the Brenta's strand
    To guard their castles and their homesteads rear,
    Ere Chiarentana[456] feel the spring-tide bland;
Of the same fashion did those dikes appear,
    Though not so high[457] he made them, nor so vast,
    Whoe'er the builder was that piled them here.
We, from the wood when we so far had passed
    I should not have distinguished where it lay
    Though I to see it backward glance had cast,
A group of souls encountered on the way,
    Whose line of march was to the margin nigh.
    Each looked at us—as by the new moon's ray
Men peer at others 'neath the darkening sky—
    Sharpening his brows on us and only us,
    Like an old tailor on his needle's eye.
And while that crowd was staring at me thus,
    One of them knew me, caught me by the gown,
    And cried aloud: 'Lo, this is marvellous!'[458]
And straightway, while he thus to me held on,
    I fixed mine eyes upon his fire-baked face,
    And, spite of scorching, seemed his features known,
And whose they were my memory well could trace;
    And I, with hand[459] stretched toward his face below,
    Asked: 'Ser Brunetto![460] and is this your place?'
'O son,' he answered, 'no displeasure show,
    If now Brunetto Latini shall some way
    Step back with thee, and leave his troop to go.'
I said: 'With all my heart for this I pray,
    And, if you choose, I by your side will sit;
    If he, for I go with him, grant delay.'
'Son,' said he, 'who of us shall intermit
    Motion a moment, for an age must lie
    Nor fan himself when flames are round him lit.
On, therefore! At thy skirts I follow nigh,
    Then shall I overtake my band again,
    Who mourn a loss large as eternity.'
I dared not from the path step to the plain
    To walk with him, but low I bent my head,[461]
    Like one whose steps are all with reverence ta'en.
'What fortune or what destiny,' he said,

'Hath brought thee here or e'er thou death hast seen;
    And who is this by whom thou'rt onward led?'
'Up yonder,' said I, 'in the life serene,
    I in a valley wandered all forlorn
    Before my years had full accomplished been.
I turned my back on it but yestermorn;[462]
    Again I sought it when he came in sight
    Guided by whom[463] I homeward thus return.'
And he to me: 'Following thy planet's light[464]
    Thou of a glorious haven canst not fail,
    If in the blithesome life I marked aright.
And had my years known more abundant tale,
    Seeing the heavens so held thee in their grace
    I, heartening thee, had helped thee to prevail.
But that ungrateful and malignant race
    Which down from Fiesole[465] came long ago,
    And still its rocky origin betrays,
Will for thy worthiness become thy foe;
    And with good reason, for 'mong crab-trees wild
    It ill befits the mellow fig to grow.
By widespread ancient rumour are they styled
    A people blind, rapacious, envious, vain:
    See by their manners thou be not defiled.
Fortune reserves such honour for thee, fain
    Both sides[466] will be to enlist thee in their need;
    But from the beak the herb shall far remain.
Let beasts of Fiesole go on to tread
    Themselves to litter, nor the plants molest,
    If any such now spring on their rank bed,
In whom there flourishes indeed the blest
    Seed of the Romans who still lingered there
    When of such wickedness 'twas made the nest.'
'Had I obtained full answer to my prayer,
    You had not yet been doomed,' I then did say,
    'This exile from humanity to bear.
For deep within my heart and memory
    Lives the paternal image good and dear
    Of you, as in the world, from day to day,
How men escape oblivion you made clear;
    My thankfulness for which shall in my speech
    While I have life, as it behoves, appear.
I note what of my future course you teach.
    Stored with another text[467] it will be glozed
    By one expert, should I that Lady reach.
Yet would I have this much to you disclosed:
    If but my conscience no reproaches yield,
    To all my fortune is my soul composed.

Not new to me the hint by you revealed;

    Therefore let Fortune turn her wheel apace,

    Even as she will; the clown[468] his mattock wield.'

Thereon my Master right about[469] did face,

    And uttered this, with glance upon me thrown:

    'He hears[470] to purpose who doth mark the place.'

And none the less I, speaking, still go on

    With Ser Brunetto; asking him to tell

    Who of his band[471] are greatest and best known.

And he to me: 'To hear of some is well,

    But of the rest 'tis fitting to be dumb,

    And time is lacking all their names to spell.

That all of them were clerks, know thou in sum,

    All men of letters, famous and of might;

    Stained with one sin[472] all from the world are come.

Priscian[473] goes with that crowd of evil plight,

    Francis d'Accorso[474] too; and hadst thou mind

    For suchlike trash thou mightest have had sight

Of him the Slave[475] of Slaves to change assigned

    From Arno's banks to Bacchiglione, where

    His nerves fatigued with vice he left behind.

More would I say, but neither must I fare

    Nor talk at further length, for from the sand

    I see new dust-clouds[476] rising in the air,

I may not keep with such as are at hand.

    Care for my *Treasure*;[477] for I still survive

    In that my work. I nothing else demand.'

Then turned he back, and ran like those who strive

    For the Green Cloth[478] upon Verona's plain;

    And seemed like him that shall the first arrive,

And not like him that labours all in vain.

Footnotes

[454] *Now lies, etc.*: The stream on issuing from the wood flows right across the waste of sand which that encompasses. To follow it they must turn to the right, as always when, their general course being to the left, they have to cross a Circle. But such a veering to the right is a consequence of their leftward course, and not an exception to it.

[455] *Cadsand*: An island opposite to the mouth of the great canal of Bruges.

[456] *Chiarentana*: What district or mountain is here meant has been much disputed. It can be taken for Carinthia only on the supposition that Dante was ignorant of where the Brenta rises. At the source of that river stands the Monte Chiarentana, but it may be a question how old that name is. The district name of it is Canzana, or Carenzana.

[457] *Not so high, etc.*: This limitation is very characteristic of Dante's style of thought, which compels him to a precision that will produce the utmost possible effect of verisimilitude in his description. Most poets would have made the walls far higher and more vast, by way of lending grandeur to the conception.

[458] *Marvellous*: To find Dante, whom he knew, still living, and passing through the Circle.

[459] *With hand, etc.*: 'With my face bent to his' is another reading, but there seems to be most authority for that in the text.— The fiery shower forbids Dante to stoop over the edge of the causeway. To Brunetto, who is some feet below him, he throws out his open hand, a gesture of astonishment mingled with pity.

[460] *Ser Brunetto*: Brunetto Latini, a Florentine, was born in 1220. As a notary he was entitled to be called Ser, or Messer. As appears from the context, Dante was under great intellectual obligations to him, not, we may suppose, as to a tutor so much as to an active-minded and scholarly friend of mature age, and possessed of a ripe experience of affairs. The social respect that Dante owed him is indicated by the use of the plural form of address. See note, *Inf*. x. 51. Brunetto held high appointments in the Republic. Perhaps with some exaggeration, Villani says of him that he was the first to refine the Florentines, teaching them to speak correctly, and to administer State affairs on fixed principles of politics (*Cronica*, viii. 10). A Guelf in politics, he shared in the exile of his party after the Ghibeline victory of Montaperti in 1260, and for some years resided in Paris. There is reason to suppose that he returned to Florence in 1269, and that he acted as prothonotary of the court of Charles of Valois' vicar-general in Tuscany. His signature as secretary to the Council of Florence is found under the date of 1273. He died in 1294, when Dante was twenty-nine, and was buried in the cloister of Santa Maria Maggiore, where his tombstone may still be seen. (Not in Santa Maria Novella.) Villani mentions him in his Chronicle with some reluctance, seeing he was a 'worldly man.' His life must indeed have been vicious to the last, before Dante could have had the heart to fix him in such company. Brunetto's chief works are the *Tesoro* and *Tesoretto*. For the *Tesoro*, see note at line 119. The *Tesoretto*, or *Little Treasure*, is an allegorical poem in Italian rhymed couplets. In it he imagines himself, as he is on his return from an embassy to Alphonso of Castile, meeting a scholar of Bologna of whom he asks 'in smooth sweet words for news of Tuscany.' Having been told of the catastrophe of Montaperti he wanders out of the beaten way into the Forest of Roncesvalles, where he meets with various experiences; he is helped by Ovid, is instructed by Ptolemy, and grows penitent for his sins. In this, it will be seen, there is a general resemblance to the action of the *Comedy*. There are even turns of expression that recall Dante (*e.g.* beginning of *Cap*. iv.); but all together amounts to little.

[461] *Low I bent my head*: But not projecting it beyond the line of safety, strictly defined by the edge of the causeway. We are to imagine to ourselves the fire of Sodom falling on Brunetto's upturned face, and missing Dante's head only by an inch.

[462] *Yestermorn*: This is still the Saturday. It was Friday when Dante met Virgil.

[463] *Guided by whom*: Brunetto has asked who the guide is, and Dante does not tell him. A reason for the refusal has been ingeniously found in the fact that among the numerous citations of the *Treasure* Brunetto seldom quotes Virgil. See also the charge brought against Guido Cavalcanti (*Inf*. x. 63), of holding Virgil in disdain. But it is explanation enough of Dante's omission to name his guide that he is passing through Inferno to gain experience for himself, and not to satisfy the curiosity of the shades he meets. See note on line 99.

[464] *Thy planet's light*: Some think that Brunetto had cast Dante's horoscope. In a remarkable passage (*Parad.* xxii. 112) Dante attributes any genius he may have to the influence of the Twins, which constellation was in the ascendant when he was born. See also *Inf.* xxvi. 23. But here it is more likely that Brunetto refers to his observation of Dante's good qualities, from which he gathered that he was well starred.

[465] *Fiesole*: The mother city of Florence, to which also most of the Fiesolans were believed to have migrated at the beginning of the eleventh century. But all the Florentines did their best to establish a Roman descent for themselves; and Dante among them. His fellow-citizens he held to be for the most part of the boorish Fiesolan breed, rude and stony-hearted as the mountain in whose cleft the cradle of their race was seen from Florence.

[466] *Both sides*: This passage was most likely written not long after Dante had ceased to entertain any hope of winning his way back to Florence in the company of the Whites, whose exile he shared, and when he was already standing in proud isolation from Black and White, from Guelf and Ghibeline. There is nothing to show that his expectation of being courted by both sides ever came true. Never a strong partisan, he had, to use his own words, at last to make a party by himself, and stood out an Imperialist with his heart set on the triumph of an Empire far nobler than that the Ghibeline desired. Dante may have hoped to hold a place of honour some day in the council of a righteous Emperor; and this may be the glorious haven with the dream of which he was consoled in the wanderings of his exile.

[467] *Another text*: Ciacco and Farinata have already hinted at the troubles that lie ahead of him (*Inf.* vi. 65, and x. 79).

[468] *The clown, etc.*: The honest performance of duty is the best defence against adverse fortune.

[469] *Right about*: In traversing the sands they keep upon the right-hand margin of the embanked stream, Virgil leading the way, with Dante behind him on the right so that Brunetto may see and hear him well.

[470] *He hears, etc.*: Of all the interpretations of this some-what obscure sentence that seems the best which applies it to Virgil's *Quicquid erit, superanda omnis fortuna ferendo est*—'Whatever shall happen, every fate is to be vanquished by endurance' (*Æn.* v. 710). Taking this way of it, we have in the form of Dante's profession of indifference to all the adverse fortune that may be in store for him a refined compliment to his Guide; and in Virgil's gesture and words an equally delicate revelation of himself to Brunetto, in which is conveyed an answer to the question at line 48, 'Who is this that shows the way?'—Otherwise, the words convey Virgil's approbation of Dante's having so well attended to his advice to store Farinata's prophecy in his memory (*Inf.* x.127).

[471] *His band*: That is, the company to which Brunetto specially belongs, and from which for the time he has separated himself.

[472] *Stained with one sin*: Dante will not make Brunetto individually confess his sin.

[473] *Priscian*: The great grammarian of the sixth century; placed here without any reason, except that he is a representative teacher of youth.

[474] *Francis d'Accorso*: Died about 1294. The son of a great civil lawyer, he was himself professor of the civil law at Bologna, where his services were so highly prized that the Bolognese forbade him, on pain of the confiscation of his goods, to accept an invitation from Edward I. to go to Oxford.

[475] *Of him the Slave, etc.*: One of the Pope's titles is *Servus Servorum Domini*. The application of it to Boniface, so hated by Dante, may be ironical: 'Fit servant of such a slave to vice!' The priest referred to so contemptuously is Andrea, of the great Florentine family of the Mozzi, who was much engaged in the political affairs of his time, and became Bishop of Florence in 1286. About ten years later he was translated to Vicenza, which stands on the Bacchiglione; and he died shortly afterwards. According to Benvenuto he was a ridiculous preacher and a man of dissolute manners. What is now most interesting about him is that he was Dante's chief pastor during his early manhood, and is consigned by him to the same disgraceful circle of Inferno as his beloved master Brunetto Latini—a terrible evidence of the corruption of life among the churchmen as well as the scholars of the thirteenth century.

[476] *New dust-clouds*: Raised by a band by whom they are about to be met.

[477] *My Treasure*: The *Trésor*, or *Tesoro*, Brunetto's principal work, was written by him in French as being 'the pleasantest language, and the most widely spread.' In it he treats of things in general in the encyclopedic fashion set him by Alphonso of Castile. The first half consists of a summary of civil and natural history. The second is devoted to ethics, rhetoric, and politics. To a great extent it is a compilation, containing, for instance, a translation, nearly complete, of the Ethics of Aristotle—not, of course, direct from the Greek. It is written in a plodding style, and speaks to more industry than genius. To it Dante is indebted for some facts and fables.

[478] *The Green Cloth*: To commemorate a victory won by the Veronese there was instituted a race to be run on the first Sunday of Lent. The prize was a piece of green cloth. The competitors ran naked.—Brunetto does not disappear into the gloom without a parting word of applause from his old pupil. Dante's rigorous sentence on his beloved master is pronounced as softly as it can be. We must still wonder that he has the heart to bring him to such an awful judgment.

Canto XVI.

Now could I hear the water as it fell
    To the next circle[479] with a murmuring sound
    Like what is heard from swarming hives to swell;
When three shades all together with a bound
    Burst from a troop met by us pressing on
    'Neath rain of that sharp torment. O'er the ground
Toward us approaching, they exclaimed each one:
    'Halt thou, whom from thy garb[480] we judge to be
    A citizen of our corrupted town.'
Alas, what scars I on their limbs did see,
    Both old and recent, which the flames had made:
    Even now my ruth is fed by memory.
My Teacher halted at their cry, and said:
    'Await a while:' and looked me in the face;
    'Some courtesy to these were well displayed.
And but that fire—the manner of the place—
    Descends for ever, fitting 'twere to find

Rather than them, thee quickening thy pace.'
When we had halted, they again combined
　　In their old song; and, reaching where we stood,
　　Into a wheel all three were intertwined.
And as the athletes used, well oiled and nude,
　　To feel their grip and, wary, watch their chance,
　　Ere they to purpose strike and wrestle could;
So each of them kept fixed on me his glance
　　As he wheeled round,[481] and in opposing ways
　　His neck and feet seemed ever to advance.
'Ah, if the misery of this sand-strewn place
　　Bring us and our petitions in despite,'
　　One then began, 'and flayed and grimy face;
Let at the least our fame goodwill incite
　　To tell us who thou art, whose living feet
　　Thus through Inferno wander without fright.
For he whose footprints, as thou see'st, I beat,
　　Though now he goes with body peeled and nude,
　　More than thou thinkest, in the world was great.
The grandson was he of Gualdrada good;
　　He, Guidoguerra,[482] with his armèd hand
　　Did mighty things, and by his counsel shrewd.
The other who behind me treads the sand
　　Is one whose name should on the earth be dear;
　　For he is Tegghiaio[483] Aldobrand.
And I, who am tormented with them here,
　　James Rusticucci[484] was; my fierce and proud
　　Wife of my ruin was chief minister.'
If from the fire there had been any shroud
　　I should have leaped down 'mong them, nor have earned
　　Blame, for my Teacher sure had this allowed.
But since I should have been all baked and burned,
　　Terror prevailed the goodwill to restrain
　　With which to clasp them in my arms I yearned.
Then I began: "Twas not contempt but pain
　　Which your condition in my breast awoke,
　　Where deeply rooted it will long remain,
When this my Master words unto me spoke,
　　By which expectancy was in me stirred
　　That ye who came were honourable folk.
I of your city[485] am, and with my word
　　Your deeds and honoured names oft to recall
　　Delighted, and with joy of them I heard.60
To the sweet fruits I go, and leave the gall,
　　As promised to me by my Escort true;
　　But first I to the centre down must fall.'
'So may thy soul thy members long endue

With vital power,' the other made reply,
　　'And after thee thy fame[486] its light renew;
As thou shalt tell if worth and courtesy
　　Within our city as of yore remain,
　　Or from it have been wholly forced to fly.
For William Borsier,[487] one of yonder train,
　　And but of late joined with us in this woe,
　　Causeth us with his words exceeding pain.'
'Upstarts, and fortunes suddenly that grow,
　　Have bred in thee pride and extravagance,[488]
　　Whence tears, O Florence! thou art shedding now.'
Thus cried I with uplifted countenance.
　　The three, accepting it for a reply,
　　Glanced each at each as hearing truth men glance.
And all: 'If others thou shalt satisfy
　　As well at other times[489] at no more cost,
　　Happy thus at thine ease the truth to cry!
Therefore if thou escap'st these regions lost,
　　Returning to behold the starlight fair,
　　Then when "There was I,"[490] thou shalt make thy boast,
Something of us do thou 'mong men declare.'
　　Then broken was the wheel, and as they fled
　　Their nimble legs like pinions beat the air.
So much as one *Amen!* had scarce been said
　　Quicker than what they vanished from our view.
　　On this once more the way my Master led.
I followed, and ere long so near we drew
　　To where the water fell, that for its roar
　　Speech scarcely had been heard between us two.
And as the stream which of all those which pour
　　East (from Mount Viso counting) by its own
　　Course falls the first from Apennine to shore—
As Acquacheta[491] in the uplands known
　　By name, ere plunging to its bed profound;
　　Name lost ere by Forlì its waters run—
Above St. Benedict with one long bound,
　　Where for a thousand[492] would be ample room,
　　Falls from the mountain to the lower ground;
Down the steep cliff that water dyed in gloom
　　We found to fall echoing from side to side,
　　Stunning the ear with its tremendous boom.
There was a cord about my middle tied,
　　With which I once had thought that I might hold
　　Secure the leopard with the painted hide.
When this from round me I had quite unrolled
　　To him I handed it, all coiled and tight;
　　As by my Leader I had first been told.

Himself then bending somewhat toward the right,[493]

    He just beyond the edge of the abyss

    Threw down the cord,[494] which disappeared from sight.

'That some strange thing will follow upon this

    Unwonted signal which my Master's eye

    Thus follows,' so I thought, 'can hardly miss.'

Ah, what great caution need we standing by

    Those who behold not only what is done,

    But who have wit our hidden thoughts to spy!

He said to me: 'There shall emerge, and soon,

    What I await; and quickly to thy view

    That which thou dream'st of shall be clearly known.'[495]

From utterance of truth which seems untrue

    A man, whene'er he can, should guard his tongue;

    Lest he win blame to no transgression due.

Yet now I must speak out, and by the song

    Of this my Comedy, Reader, I swear—

    So in good liking may it last full long!—

I saw a shape swim upward through that air.

    All indistinct with gross obscurity,

    Enough to fill the stoutest heart with fear:

Like one who rises having dived to free

    An anchor grappled on a jagged stone,

    Or something else deep hidden in the sea;

With feet drawn in and arms all open thrown.

Footnotes

[479] *The next circle*: The Eighth.

[480] *Thy garb*: 'Almost every city,' says Boccaccio, 'had in those times its peculiar fashion of dress distinct from that of neighboring cities.'

[481] *As he wheeled round*: Virgil and Dante have come to a halt upon the embankment. The three shades, to whom it is forbidden to be at rest for a moment, clasping one another as in a dance, keep wheeling round in circle upon the sand.

[482] *Guidoguerra*: A descendant of the Counts Guidi of Modigliana. Gualdrada was the daughter of Bellincion Berti de' Ravignani, praised for his simple habits in the *Paradiso*, xv. 112. Guidoguerra was a Guelf leader, and after the defeat of Montaperti acted as Captain of his party, in this capacity lending valuable aid to Charles of Anjou at the battle of Benevento, 1266, when Manfred was overthrown. He had no children, and left the Commonwealth of Florence his heir.

[483] *Tegghiaio*: Son of Aldobrando of the Adimari. His name should be dear in Florence, because he did all he could to dissuade the citizens from the campaign which ended so disastrously at Montaperti.

[484] *James Rusticucci*: An accomplished cavalier of humble birth, said to have been a retainer of Dante's friends the Cavalcanti. The commentators have little to tell of him except that he made an unhappy marriage, which is evident from the text. Of the sins of him and his companions there is nothing known beyond what is to be inferred from the poet's words, and nothing to say, except that when Dante consigned men of their stamp, frank and amiable, to the Infernal Circles, we may be sure that he only executed a verdict already accepted as just by the whole of Florence. And when we find him impartially damning Guelf and Ghibeline we may be equally sure that he looked for the aid of neither party, and of no family however powerful in the State, to bring his banishment to a close. He would even seem to be careful to stop any hole by which he might creep back to Florence. When he did return, it was to be in the train of the Emperor, so he hoped, and as one who gives rather than seeks forgiveness.

[485] *Of your city, etc.*: At line 32 Rusticucci begs Dante to tell who he is. He tells that he is of their city, which they have already gathered from his *berretta* and the fashion of his gown; but he tells nothing, almost, of himself. Unless to Farinata, indeed, he never makes an open breast to any one met in Inferno. But here he does all that courtesy requires.

[486] *Thy fame*: Dante has implied in his answer that he is gifted with oratorical powers and is the object of a special Divine care; and the illustrious Florentine, frankly acknowledging the claim he makes, adjures him by the fame which is his in store to appease an eager curiosity about the Florence which even in Inferno is the first thought of every not ignoble Florentine.

[487] *William Borsiere*: A Florentine, witty and well bred, according to Boccaccio. Being once at Genoa he was shown a fine new palace by its miserly owner, and was asked to suggest a subject for a painting with which to adorn the hall. The subject was to be something that nobody had ever seen. Borsiere proposed liberality as something that the miser at any rate had never yet got a good sight of; an answer of which it is not easy to detect either the wit or the courtesy, but which is said to have converted the churl to liberal ways (*Decam.* i. 8). He is here introduced as an authority on the noble style of manners.

[488] *Pride and extravagance*: In place of the nobility of mind that leads to great actions, and the gentle manners that prevail in a society where there is a due subordination of rank to rank and well-defined duties for every man. This, the aristocratic in a noble sense, was Dante's ideal of a social state; for all his instincts were those of a Florentine aristocrat, corrected though they were by his good sense and his thirst for a reign of perfect justice. During his own time he had seen Florence grow more and more democratic; and he was irritated—unreasonably, considering that it was only a sign of the general prosperity—at the spectacle of the amazing growth of wealth in the hands of low-born traders, who every year were coming more to the front and monopolising influence at home and abroad at the cost of their neighbours and rivals with longer pedigrees and shorter purses. In *Paradiso* xvi. Dante dwells at length on the degeneracy of the Florentines.

[489] *At other times*: It is hinted that his outspokenness will not in the future always give equal satisfaction to those who hear.

[490] *There was I, etc.*: Forsan et hæc olim meminisse juvabit.—Æn. i. 203.

[491] *Acquacheta*: The fall of the water of the brook over the lofty cliff that sinks from the Seventh to the Eighth Circle is compared to the waterfall upon the Montone at the monastery of St. Benedict, in the mountains above Forlì. The Po rises in Monte Viso. Dante here travels in imagination from Monte Viso down through Italy, and finds that all the rivers which rise on the left hand, that is, on the north-east of the Apennine, fall into the Po, till the Montone is reached, that river falling into the Adriatic

by a course of its own. Above Forlì it was called Acquacheta. The Lamone, north of the Montone, now follows an independent course to the sea, having cut a new bed for itself since Dante's time.

[492] *Where for a thousand, etc.*: In the monastery there was room for many more monks, say most of the commentators; or something to the like effect. Mr. Longfellow's interpretation seems better: Where the height of the fall is so great that it would divide into a thousand falls.

[493] *Toward the right*: The attitude of one about to throw.

[494] *The cord*: The services of Geryon are wanted to convey them down the next reach of the pit; and as no voice could be heard for the noise of the waterfall, and no signal be made to catch the eye amid the gloom, Virgil is obliged to call the attention of the monster by casting some object into the depth where he lies concealed. But, since they are surrounded by solid masonry and slack sand, one or other of them must supply something fit to throw down; and the cord worn by Dante is fixed on as what can best be done without. There may be a reference to the cord of Saint Francis, which Dante, according to one of his commentators, wore when he was a young man, following in this a fashion common enough among pious laymen who had no thought of ever becoming friars. But the simile of the cord, as representing sobriety and virtuous purpose, is not strange to Dante. In *Purg.* vii. 114 he describes Pedro of Arragon as being girt with the cord of every virtue; and Pedro was no Franciscan. Dante's cord may therefore be taken as standing for vigilance or self-control. With it he had hoped to get the better of the leopard (*Inf.* i. 32), and may have trusted in it for support as against the terrors of Inferno. But although he has been girt with it ever since he entered by the gate, it has not saved him from a single fear, far less from a single danger; and now it is cast away as useless. Henceforth, more than ever, he is to confide wholly in Virgil and have no confidence in himself. Nor is he to be girt again till he reaches the coast of Purgatory, and then it is to be with a reed, the emblem of humility.—But, however explained, the incident will always be somewhat of a puzzle.

[495] Dante attributes to Virgil full knowledge of all that is in his own mind. He thus heightens our conception of his dependence on his guide, with whose will his will is blent, and whose thoughts are always found to be anticipating his own. Few readers will care to be constantly recalling to mind that Virgil represents enlightened human reason. But even if we confine ourselves to the easiest sense of the narrative, the study of the relations between him and Dante will be found one of the most interesting suggested by the poem—perhaps only less so than that of Dante's moods of wonder, anger, and pity.

Canto XVII.

'Behold the monster[496] with the pointed tail,
    Who passes mountains[497] and can entrance make
    Through arms and walls! who makes the whole world ail,
Corrupted by him!' Thus my Leader spake,
    And beckoned him that he should land hard by,
    Where short the pathways built of marble break.
And that foul image of dishonesty
    Moving approached us with his head and chest,

But to the bank[498] drew not his tail on high.
His face a human righteousness expressed,
    'Twas so benignant to the outward view;
    A serpent was he as to all the rest.
On both his arms hair to the arm-pits grew:
    On back and chest and either flank were knot[499]
    And rounded shield portrayed in various hue;
No Turk or Tartar weaver ever brought
    To ground or pattern a more varied dye;[500]
    Nor by Arachne[501] was such broidery wrought.
As sometimes by the shore the barges lie
    Partly in water, partly on dry land;
    And as afar in gluttonous Germany,[502]
Watching their prey, alert the beavers stand;
    So did this worst of brutes his foreparts fling
    Upon the stony rim which hems the sand.
All of his tail in space was quivering,
    Its poisoned fork erecting in the air,
    Which scorpion-like was armèd with a sting.
My Leader said: 'Now we aside must fare
    A little distance, so shall we attain
    Unto the beast malignant crouching there.'
So we stepped down upon the right,[503] and then
    A half score steps[504] to the outer edge did pace,
    Thus clearing well the sand and fiery rain.
And when we were hard by him I could trace
    Upon the sand a little further on
    Some people sitting near to the abyss.
'That what this belt containeth may be known
    Completely by thee,' then the Master said;
    'To see their case do thou advance alone.
Let thy inquiries be succinctly made.
    While thou art absent I will ask of him,
    With his strong shoulders to afford us aid.'
Then, all alone, I on the outmost rim
    Of that Seventh Circle still advancing trod,
    Where sat a woful folk.[505] Full to the brim
Their eyes with anguish were, and overflowed;
    Their hands moved here and there to win some ease,
    Now from the flames, now from the soil which glowed.
No otherwise in summer-time one sees,
    Working its muzzle and its paws, the hound
    When bit by gnats or plagued with flies or fleas.
And I, on scanning some who sat around
    Of those on whom the dolorous flames alight,
    Could recognise[506] not one. I only found
A purse hung from the throat of every wight,

Each with its emblem and its special hue;
    And every eye seemed feasting on the sight.
As I, beholding them, among them drew,
    I saw what seemed a lion's face and mien
    Upon a yellow purse designed in blue.
Still moving on mine eyes athwart the scene
    I saw another scrip, blood-red, display
    A goose more white than butter could have been.
And one, on whose white wallet blazoned lay
    A pregnant sow[507] in azure, to me said:
    'What dost thou in this pit? Do thou straightway
Begone; and, seeing thou art not yet dead,
    Know that Vitalian,[508] neighbour once of mine,
    Shall on my left flank one day find his bed.
A Paduan I: all these are Florentine;
    And oft they stun me, bellowing in my ear:
    "Come, Pink of Chivalry,[509] for whom we pine,
Whose is the purse on which three beaks appear:"'
    Then he from mouth awry his tongue thrust out[510]
    Like ox that licks its nose; and I, in fear
Lest more delay should stir in him some doubt
    Who gave command I should not linger long,
    Me from those wearied spirits turned about.
I found my Guide, who had already sprung
    Upon the back of that fierce animal:
    He said to me: 'Now be thou brave and strong.
By stairs like this[511] we henceforth down must fall.
    Mount thou in front, for I between would sit
    So thee the tail shall harm not nor appal.'
Like one so close upon the shivering fit
    Of quartan ague that his nails grow blue,
    And seeing shade he trembles every whit,
I at the hearing of that order grew;
    But his threats shamed me, as before the face
    Of a brave lord his man grows valorous too.
On the great shoulders then I took my place,
    And wished to say, but could not move my tongue
    As I expected: 'Do thou me embrace!'
But he, who other times had helped me 'mong
    My other perils, when ascent I made
    Sustained me, and strong arms around me flung,
And, 'Geryon, set thee now in motion!' said;
    'Wheel widely; let thy downward flight be slow;
    Think of the novel burden on thee laid.'
As from the shore a boat begins to go
    Backward at first, so now he backward pressed,
    And when he found that all was clear below,

He turned his tail where earlier was his breast;
    And, stretching it, he moved it like an eel,
    While with his paws he drew air toward his chest.
More terror Phaëthon could hardly feel
    What time he let the reins abandoned fall,
    Whence Heaven was fired,[512] as still its tracts reveal;
Nor wretched Icarus, on finding all
    His plumage moulting as the wax grew hot,
    While, 'The wrong road!' his father loud did call;
Than what I felt on finding I was brought
    Where nothing was but air and emptiness;
    For save the brute I could distinguish nought.
He slowly, slowly swims; to the abyss
    Wheeling he makes descent, as I surmise
    From wind felt 'neath my feet and in my face.
Already on the right I heard arise
    From out the caldron a terrific roar,[513]
    Whereon I stretch my head with down-turned eyes.
Terror of falling now oppressed me sore;
    Hearing laments, and seeing fires that burned,
    My thighs I tightened, trembling more and more.
Earlier I had not by the eye discerned
    That we swept downward; scenes of torment now
    Seemed drawing nearer wheresoe'er we turned.
And as a falcon (which long time doth go
    Upon the wing, not finding lure[514] or prey),
    While 'Ha!' the falconer cries, 'descending so!'
Comes wearied back whence swift it soared away;
    Wheeling a hundred times upon the road,
    Then, from its master far, sulks angrily:
So we, by Geryon in the deep bestowed,
    Were 'neath the sheer-hewn precipice set down:
    He, suddenly delivered from our load,
Like arrow from the string was swiftly gone.

Footnotes

[496] *The monster*: Geryon, a mythical king of Spain, converted here into the symbol of fraud, and set as the guardian demon of the Eighth Circle, where the fraudulent are punished. There is nothing in the mythology to justify this account of Geryon; and it seems that Dante has created a monster to serve his purpose. Boccaccio, in his *Genealogy of the Gods* (Lib. i.), repeats the description of Geryon given by 'Dante the Florentine, in his poem written in the Florentine tongue, one certainly of no little importance among poems;' and adds that Geryon reigned in the Balearic Isles, and was used to decoy travellers with his benignant countenance, caressing words, and every kind of friendly lure, and then to murder them when asleep.

[497] *Who passes mountains, etc.*: Neither art nor nature affords any defence against fraud.

[498] *The bank*: Not that which confines the brook but the inner limit of the Seventh Circle, from which the precipice sinks sheer into the Eighth, and to which the embankment by which the travellers have crossed the sand joins itself on. Virgil has beckoned Geryon to come to that part of the bank which adjoins the end of the causeway.

[499] *Knot and rounded shield*: Emblems of subtle devices and subterfuges.

[500] *Varied dye*: Denoting the various colours of deceit.

[501] *Arachne*: The Lydian weaver changed into a spider by Minerva. See *Purg.* xii. 43.

[502] *Gluttonous Germany*: The habits of the German men-at-arms in Italy, odious to the temperate Italians, explains this gibe.

[503] *The right*: This is the second and last time that, in their course through Inferno, they turn to the right. See *Inf.* ix. 132. The action may possibly have a symbolical meaning, and refer to the protection against fraud which is obtained by keeping to a righteous course. But here, in fact, they have no choice, for, traversing the Inferno as they do to the left hand, they came to the right bank of the stream which traverses the fiery sands, followed it, and now, when they would leave its edge, it is from the right embankment that they have to step down, and necessarily to the right hand.

[504] *A half score steps, etc.*: Traversing the stone-built border which lies between the sand and the precipice. Had the brook flowed to the very edge of the Seventh Circle before tumbling down the rocky wall it is clear that they might have kept to the embankment until they were clear beyond the edge of the sand. We are therefore to figure to ourselves the water as plunging down at a point some yards, perhaps the width of the border, short of the true limit of the circle; and this is a touch of local truth, since waterfalls in time always wear out a funnel for themselves by eating back the precipice down which they tumble. It was into this funnel that Virgil flung the cord, and up it that Geryon was seen to ascend, as if by following up the course of the water he would find out who had made the signal. To keep to the narrow causeway where it ran on by the edge of this gulf would seem too full of risk.

[505] *Woful folk*: Usurers; those guilty of the unnatural sin of contemning the legitimate modes of human industry. They sit huddled up on the sand, close to its bound of solid masonry, from which Dante looks down on them. But that the usurers are not found only at the edge of the plain is evident from *Inf.* xiv. 19.

[506] *Could recognise, etc.*: Though most of the group prove to be from Florence Dante recognises none of them; and this denotes that nothing so surely creates a second nature in a man, in a bad sense, as setting the heart on money. So in the Fourth Circle those who, being unable to spend moderately, are always thinking of how to keep or get money are represented as 'obscured from any recognition' (*Inf.* vii. 44).

[507] *A pregnant sow*: The azure lion on a golden field was the arms of the Gianfigliazzi, eminent usurers of Florence; the white goose on a red ground was the arms of the Ubriachi of Florence; the azure sow, of the Scrovegni of Padua.

[508] *Vitalian*: A rich Paduan noble, whose palace was near that of the Scrovegni.

[509] *Pink of Chivalry*: 'Sovereign Cavalier;' identified by his arms as Ser Giovanni Buiamonte, still alive in Florence in 1301, and if we are to judge from the text, the greatest usurer of all. A northern poet of the time would have sought his usurers in the Jewry of some town he knew, but Dante finds his among the nobles of Padua and Florence. He ironically represents them as wearing purses ornamented with their coats of arms, perhaps to hint that they pursued their dishonourable trade under shelter of their noble names—their shop signs, as it were. The whole passage may have been planned by Dante so as to afford him the opportunity of damning the still living Buiamonte without mentioning his name.

[510] *His tongue thrust out*: As if to say: We know well what sort of fine gentleman Buiamonte is.

[511] *By stairs like this*: The descent from one circle to another grows more difficult the further down they come. They appear to have found no special obstacle in the nature of the ground till they reached the bank sloping down to the Fifth Circle, the pathway down which is described as terrible (*Inf.* vii. 105). The descent into the Seventh Circle is made practicable, and nothing more (*Inf.* xii. I).

[512] *Heaven was fired*: As still appears in the Milky Way. In the *Convito*, ii. 15, Dante discusses the various explanations of what causes the brightness of that part of the heavens.

[513] *A terrific roar*: Of the water falling to the ground. On beginning the descent they had left the waterfall on the left hand, but Geryon, after fetching one or more great circles, passes in front of it, and then they have it on the right. There is no further mention of the waters of Phlegethon till they are found frozen in Cocytus (*Inf.* xxxii. 23). Philalethes suggests that they flow under the Eighth Circle.

[514] *Lure*: An imitation bird used in training falcons. Dante describes the sulky, slow descent of a falcon which has either lost sight of its prey, or has failed to discover where the falconer has thrown the lure. Geryon has descended thus deliberately owing to the command of Virgil.

Canto XVIII.

Of iron colour, and composed of stone,
 A place called Malebolge[515] is in Hell,
 Girt by a cliff of substance like its own.
In that malignant region yawns a well[516]
 Right in the centre, ample and profound;
 Of which I duly will the structure tell.
The zone[517] that lies between them, then, is round—
 Between the well and precipice hard and high;
 Into ten vales divided is the ground.
As is the figure offered to the eye,
 Where numerous moats a castle's towers enclose
 That they the walls may better fortify;
A like appearance was made here by those.
 And as, again, from threshold of such place
 Many a drawbridge to the outworks goes;
So ridges from the precipice's base
 Cutting athwart the moats and barriers run,
 Till at the well join the extremities.[518]
From Geryon's back when we were shaken down
 'Twas here we stood, until the Poet's feet
 Moved to the left, and I, behind, came on.

New torments on the right mine eyes did meet
    With new tormentors, novel woe on woe;
    With which the nearer Bolgia was replete.
Sinners, all naked, in the gulf below,
    This side the middle met us; while they strode
    On that side with us, but more swift did go.[519]
Even so the Romans, that the mighty crowd
    Across the bridge, the year of Jubilee,
    Might pass with ease, ordained a rule of road[520]—
Facing the Castle, on that side should be
    The multitude which to St. Peter's hied;
    So to the Mount on this was passage free.
On the grim rocky ground, on either side,
    I saw horned devils[521] armed with heavy whip
    Which on the sinners from behind they plied.
Ah, how they made the wretches nimbly skip
    At the first lashes; no one ever yet
    But sought from the second and the third to slip.
And as I onward went, mine eyes were set
    On one of them; whereon I called in haste:
    'This one already I have surely met!'
Therefore to know him, fixedly I gazed;
    And my kind Leader willingly delayed,
    While for a little I my course retraced.
On this the scourged one, thinking to evade
    My search, his visage bent without avail,
    For: 'Thou that gazest on the ground,' I said,
'If these thy features tell trustworthy tale,
    Venedico Caccianimico[522] thou!
    But what has brought thee to such sharp regale?'[523]
And he, 'I tell it 'gainst my will, I trow,
    But thy clear accents[524] to the old world bear
    My memory, and make me all avow.
I was the man who Ghisola the fair
    To serve the Marquis' evil will led on,
    Whatever[525] the uncomely tale declare.
Of Bolognese here weeping not alone
    Am I; so full the place of them, to-day
    'Tween Reno and Savena[526] are not known
So many tongues that *Sipa* deftly say:
    And if of this thou'dst know the reason why,
    Think but how greedy were our hearts alway.'
To him thus speaking did a demon cry:
    'Pander, begone!' and smote him with his thong;
    'Here are no women for thy coin to buy.'
Then, with my Escort joined, I moved along.
    Few steps we made until we there had come,

Where from the bank a rib of rock was flung.
With ease enough up to its top we clomb,
    And, turning on the ridge, bore to the right;[527]
    And those eternal circles[528] parted from.
When we had reached where underneath the height
    A passage opes, yielding the scourged a way,
    My Guide bade: 'Tarry, so to hold in sight
Those other spirits born in evil day,
    Whose faces until now from thee have been
    Concealed, because with ours their progress lay.'
Then from the ancient bridge by us were seen
    The troop which toward us on that circuit sped,
    Chased onward, likewise, by the scourges keen.
And my good Master, ere I asked him, said:
    'That lordly one now coming hither, see,
    By whom, despite of pain, no tears are shed.
What mien he still retains of majesty!
    'Tis Jason, who by courage and by guile
    The Colchians of the ram deprived. 'Twas he
Who on his passage by the Lemnian isle,
    Where all of womankind with daring hand
    Upon their males had wrought a murder vile,
With loving pledges and with speeches bland
    The tender-yeared Hypsipyle betrayed,
    Who had herself a fraud on others planned.
Forlorn he left her then, when pregnant made.
    That is the crime condemns him to this pain;
    And for Medea[529] too is vengeance paid.
Who in his manner cheat compose his train.
    Of the first moat sufficient now is known,
    And those who in its jaws engulfed remain.'
Already had we by the strait path gone
    To where 'tis with the second bank dovetailed—
    The buttress whence a second arch is thrown.
Here heard we who in the next Bolgia wailed[530]
    And puffed for breath; reverberations told
    They with their open palms themselves assailed.
The sides were crusted over with a mould
    Plastered upon them by foul mists that rise,
    And both with eyes and nose a contest hold.
The bottom is so deep, in vain our eyes
    Searched it till further up the bridge we went,
    To where the arch o'erhangs what under lies.
Ascended there, our eyes we downward bent,
    And I saw people in such ordure drowned,
    A very cesspool 'twas of excrement.
And while I from above am searching round,

One with a head so filth-smeared I picked out,

I knew not if 'twas lay, or tonsure-crowned.

'Why then so eager,' asked he with a shout,

    'To stare at me of all the filthy crew?'

    And I to him: 'Because I scarce can doubt

That formerly thee dry of hair I knew,

    Alessio Interminei[531] the Lucchese;

    And therefore thee I chiefly hold in view.'

Smiting his head-piece, then, his words were these:

    ''Twas flattery steeped me here; for, using such,

    My tongue itself enough could never please.'

'Now stretch thou somewhat forward, but not much,'

    Thereon my Leader bade me, 'and thine eyes

    Slowly advance till they her features touch

And the dishevelled baggage recognise,

    Clawing her yonder with her nails unclean,

    Now standing up, now squatting on her thighs.

'Tis harlot Thais,[532] who, when she had been

    Asked by her lover, "Am I generous

    And worthy thanks?" said, "Greatly so, I ween."

Enough[533] of this place has been seen by us.'

Footnotes

[515] *Malebolge*: Or Evil Pits; literally, Evil Pockets.

[516] *A well*: The Ninth and lowest Circle, to be described in Canto xxxii., etc.

[517] *The zone*: The Eighth Circle, in which the fraudulent of all species are punished, lies between the precipice and the Ninth Circle. A vivid picture of the enormous height of the enclosing wall has been presented to us at the close of the preceding Canto. As in the description of the Second Circle the atmosphere is represented as malignant, being murky and disturbed with tempest; so the Malebolge is called malignant too, being all of barren iron-coloured rock. In both cases the surroundings of the sinners may well be spoken of as malign, adverse to any thought of goodwill and joy.

[518] *The extremities*: The *Malebolge* consists of ten circular pits or fosses, one inside of another. The outermost lies under the precipice which falls sheer from the Seventh Circle; the innermost, and of course the smallest, runs immediately outside of the 'Well,' which is the Ninth Circle. The Bolgias or valleys are divided from each other by rocky banks; and, each Bolgia being at a lower level than the one that encloses it, the inside of each bank is necessarily deeper than the outside. Ribs or ridges of rock—like spokes of a wheel to the axle-tree—run from the foot of the precipice to the outer rim of the 'Well,' vaulting the moats at right angles with the course of them. Thus each rib takes the form of a ten-arched bridge. By one or other of these Virgil and Dante now travel towards the centre and the base of Inferno; their general course being downward, though varied by the ascent in turn of the hog-backed arches over the moats.

[519] *More swift*: The sinners in the First Bolgia are divided into two gangs, moving in opposite directions, the course of those on

the outside being to the right, as looked at by Dante. These are the shades of panders; those in the inner current are such as seduced on their own account. Here a list of the various classes of sinners contained in the Bolgias of the Eighth Circle may be given:—

1st	Bolgia—Seducers,	CANTO	xviii.
2d	"	Flatterers,	"	"
3d	"	Simoniacs,	"	xix.
4th	"	Soothsayers,	"	xx.
5th	"	Barrators,	"	xxi. xxii.
6th	"	Hypocrites,	"	xxiii.
7th	"	Thieves,	"	xxiv. xxv.
8th	"	Evil Counsellors,	"	xxvi. xxvii.
9th	"	Scandal and Heresy Mongers,	"	xxviii. xxix.
10th	"	Falsifiers,	"	xxix. xxx.

[520] *A rule of road*: In the year 1300 a Jubilee was held in Rome with Plenary Indulgence for all pilgrims. Villani says that while it lasted the number of strangers in Rome was never less than two hundred thousand. The bridge and castle spoken of in the text are those of St. Angelo. The Mount is probably the Janiculum.

[521] *Horned devils*: Here the demons are horned—terrible remembrancers to the sinner of the injured husband.

[522] *Venedico Caccianimico*: A Bolognese noble, brother of Ghisola, whom he inveigled into yielding herself to the Marquis of Este, lord of Ferrara. Venedico died between 1290 and 1300.

[523] *Such sharp regale*: 'Such pungent sauces.' There is here a play of words on the *Salse*, the name of a wild ravine outside the walls of Bologna, where the bodies of felons were thrown. Benvenuto says it used to be a taunt among boys at Bologna: Your father was pitched into the Salse.

[524] *Thy clear accents*: Not broken with sobs like his own and those of his companions.

[525] *Whatever, etc.*: Different accounts seem to have been current about the affair of Ghisola.

[526] *'Tween Reno, etc.*: The Reno and Savena are streams that flow past Bologna. *Sipa* is Bolognese for Maybe, or for Yes. So Dante describes Tuscany as the country where *Si* is heard (*Inf.* xxxiii. 80). With regard to the vices of the Bolognese, Benvenuto says: 'Dante had studied in Bologna, and had seen and observed all these things.'

[527] *To the right*: This is only an apparent departure from their leftward course. Moving as they were to the left along the edge of the Bolgia, they required to turn to the right to cross the bridge that spanned it.

[528] *Those eternal circles*: The meaning is not clear; perhaps it only is that they have now done with the outer stream of sinners in this Bolgia, left by them engaged in endless procession round and round.

[529] *Medea*: When the Argonauts landed on Lemnos, they found it without any males, the women, incited by Venus, having put them all to death, with the exception of Thoas, saved by his daughter Hypsipyle. When Jason deserted her he sailed for Colchis, and with the assistance of Medea won the Golden Fleece. Medea, who accompanied him from Colchis, was in turn deserted by him.

[530] *Who in the next Bolgia wailed*: The flatterers in the Second Bolgia.

[531] *Alessio Interminei*: Of the Great Lucchese family of the Interminelli, to which the famous Castruccio Castrucani

belonged. Alessio is know to have been living in 1295. Dante may have known him personally. Benvenuto says he was so liberal of his flattery that he spent it even on menial servants.
[532] *Thais*: In the *Eunuch* of Terence, Thraso, the lover of that courtesan, asks Gnatho, their go-between, if she really sent him many thanks for the present of a slave-girl he had sent her. 'Enormous!' says Gnatho. It proves what great store Dante set on ancient instances when he thought this worth citing.
[533] *Enough, etc.*: Most readers will agree with Virgil.

Canto XIX.

O Simon Magus![534] ye his wretched crew!
    The gifts of God, ordained to be the bride
    Of righteousness, ye prostitute that you
With gold and silver may be satisfied;
    Therefore for you let now the trumpet[535] blow,
    Seeing that ye in the Third Bolgia 'bide.
Arrived at the next tomb,[536] we to the brow
    Of rock ere this had finished our ascent,
    Which hangs true plumb above the pit below.
What perfect art, O Thou Omniscient,
    Is Thine in Heaven and earth and the bad world found!
    How justly does Thy power its dooms invent!
The livid stone, on both banks and the ground,
    I saw was full of holes on every side,
    All of one size, and each of them was round.
No larger seemed they to me nor less wide
    Than those within my beautiful St. John[537]
    For the baptizers' standing-place supplied;
And one of which, not many years agone,
    I broke to save one drowning; and I would
    Have this for seal to undeceive men known.
Out of the mouth of each were seen protrude
    A sinner's feet, and of the legs the small
    Far as the calves; the rest enveloped stood.
And set on fire were both the soles of all,
    Which made their ankles wriggle with such throes
    As had made ropes and withes asunder fall.
And as flame fed by unctuous matter goes
    Over the outer surface only spread;
    So from their heels it flickered to the toes.
'Master, who is he, tortured more,' I said,
    'Than are his neighbours, writhing in such woe;
    And licked by flames of deeper-hearted red?'
And he: 'If thou desirest that below
    I bear thee by that bank[538] which lowest lies,
    Thou from himself his sins and name shalt know.'
And I: 'Thy wishes still for me suffice:
    Thou art my Lord, and knowest I obey

Thy will; and dost my hidden thoughts surprise.'
To the fourth barrier then we made our way,
    And, to the left hand turning, downward went
    Into the narrow hole-pierced cavity;
Nor the good Master caused me make descent
    From off his haunch till we his hole were nigh
    Who with his shanks was making such lament.
'Whoe'er thou art, soul full of misery,
    Set like a stake with lower end upcast,'
    I said to him, 'Make, if thou canst, reply.'
I like a friar[539] stood who gives the last
    Shrift to a vile assassin, to his side
    Called back to win delay for him fixed fast.
'Art thou arrived already?' then he cried,
    'Art thou arrived already, Boniface?
    By several years the prophecy[540] has lied.
Art so soon wearied of the wealthy place,
    For which thou didst not fear to take with guile,
    Then ruin the fair Lady?'[541] Now my case
Was like to theirs who linger on, the while
    They cannot comprehend what they are told,
    And as befooled[542] from further speech resile.
But Virgil bade me: 'Speak out loud and bold,
    "I am not he thou thinkest, no, not he!"'
    And I made answer as by him controlled.
The spirit's feet then twisted violently,
    And, sighing in a voice of deep distress,
    He asked: 'What then requirest thou of me?
If me to know thou hast such eagerness,
    That thou the cliff hast therefore ventured down,
    Know, the Great Mantle sometime was my dress.
I of the Bear, in sooth, was worthy son:
    As once, the Cubs to help, my purse with gain
    I stuffed, myself I in this purse have stown.
Stretched out at length beneath my head remain
    All the simoniacs[543] that before me went,
    And flattened lie throughout the rocky vein.
I in my turn shall also make descent,
    Soon as he comes who I believed thou wast,
    When I asked quickly what for him was meant.
O'er me with blazing feet more time has past,
    While upside down I fill the topmost room,
    Than he his crimsoned feet shall upward cast;
For after him one viler still shall come,
    A Pastor from the West,[544] lawless of deed:
    To cover both of us his worthy doom.
A modern Jason[545] he, of whom we read

In Maccabees, whose King denied him nought:

    With the French King so shall this man succeed.'

Perchance I ventured further than I ought,

    But I spake to him in this measure free:

    'Ah, tell me now what money was there sought

Of Peter by our Lord, when either key

    He gave him in his guardianship to hold?

    Sure He demanded nought save: "Follow me!"

Nor Peter, nor the others, asked for gold

    Or silver when upon Matthias fell

    The lot instead of him, the traitor-souled.

Keep then thy place, for thou art punished well,[546]

    And clutch the pelf, dishonourably gained,

    Which against Charles[547] made thee so proudly swell.

And, were it not that I am still restrained

    By reverence[548] for those tremendous keys,

    Borne by thee while the glad world thee contained,

I would use words even heavier than these;

    Seeing your avarice makes the world deplore,

    Crushing the good, filling the bad with ease.

'Twas you, O Pastors, the Evangelist bore

    In mind what time he saw her on the flood

    Of waters set, who played with kings the whore;

Who with seven heads was born; and as she would

    By the ten horns to her was service done,

    Long as her spouse[549] rejoiced in what was good.

Now gold and silver are your god alone:

    What difference 'twixt the idolater and you,

    Save that ye pray a hundred for his one?

Ah, Constantine,[550] how many evils grew—

    Not from thy change of faith, but from the gift

    Wherewith thou didst the first rich Pope endue!

While I my voice continued to uplift

    To such a tune, by rage or conscience stirred

    Both of his soles he made to twist and shift.

My Guide, I well believe, with pleasure heard;

    Listening he stood with lips so well content

    To me propounding truthful word on word.

Then round my body both his arms he bent,

    And, having raised me well upon his breast,

    Climbed up the path by which he made descent.

Nor was he by his burden so oppressed

    But that he bore me to the bridge's crown,

    Which with the fourth joins the fifth rampart's crest.

And lightly here he set his burden down,

    Found light by him upon the precipice,

    Up which a goat uneasily had gone.

And thence another valley met mine eyes.

Footnotes

[534] *Simon Magus*: The sin of simony consists in setting a price on the exercise of a spiritual grace or the acquisition of a spiritual office. Dante assails it at headquarters, that is, as it was practised by the Popes; and in their case it took, among other forms, that of ecclesiastical nepotism.

[535] *The trumpet*: Blown at the punishment of criminals, to call attention to their sentence.

[536] *The next tomb*: The Third Bolgia, appropriately termed a tomb, because its manner of punishment is that of a burial, as will be seen.

[537] *St. John*: The church of St. John's, in Dante's time, as now, the Baptistery of Florence. In *Parad.* xxv. he anticipates the day, if it should ever come, when he shall return to Florence, and in the church where he was baptized a Christian be crowned as a Poet. Down to the middle of the sixteenth century all baptisms, except in cases of urgent necessity, were celebrated in St. John's; and, even there, only on the eves of Easter and Pentecost. For protection against the crowd, the officiating priests were provided with standing-places, circular cavities disposed around the great font. To these Dante compares the holes of this Bolgia, for the sake of introducing a defence of himself from a charge of sacrilege. Benvenuto tells that once when some boys were playing about the church one of them, to hide himself from his companions, squeezed himself into a baptizer's standing-place, and made so tight a fit of it that he could not be rescued till Dante with his own hands plied a hammer upon the marble, and so saved the child from drowning. The presence of water in the cavity may be explained by the fact of the church's being at that time lighted by an unglazed opening in the roof; and as baptisms were so infrequent the standing-places, situated as they were in the centre of the floor, may often have been partially flooded. It is easy to understand how bitterly Dante would resent a charge of irreverence connected with his 'beautiful St. John's;' 'that fair sheep-fold' (*Parad.* xxv. 5).

[538] *That bank, etc.*: Of each Bolgia the inner bank is lower than the outer; the whole of Malebolge sloping towards the centre of the Inferno.

[539] *Like a friar, etc.*: In those times the punishment of an assassin was to be stuck head downward in a pit, and then to have earth slowly shovelled in till he was suffocated. Dante bends down, the better to hear what the sinner has to say, like a friar recalled by the felon on the pretence that he has something to add to his confession.

[540] *The prophecy*: 'The writing.' The speaker is Nicholas III., of the great Roman family of the Orsini, and Pope from 1277 to 1280; a man of remarkable bodily beauty and grace of manner, as well as of great force of character. Like many other Holy Fathers he was either a great hypocrite while on his promotion, or else he degenerated very quickly after getting himself well settled on the Papal Chair. He is said to have been the first Pope who practised simony with no attempt at concealment. Boniface VIII., whom he is waiting for to relieve him, became Pope in 1294, and died in 1303. None of the four Popes between 1280 and 1294 were simoniacs; so that Nicholas was uppermost in the hole for twenty-three years. Although ignorant of what is now passing on the earth, he can refer back to his foreknowledge of

some years earlier (see *Inf.* x. 99) as if to a prophetic writing, and finds that according to this it is still three years too soon, it being now only 1300, for the arrival of Boniface. This is the usual explanation of the passage. To it lies the objection that foreknowledge of the present that can be referred back to is the same thing as knowledge of it, and with this the spirits in Inferno are not endowed. But Dante elsewhere shows that he finds it hard to observe the limitation. The alternative explanation, supported by the use of *scritto* (writing) in the text, is that Nicholas refers to some prophecy once current about his successors in Rome.

[541] *The fair Lady*: The Church. The guile is that shown by Boniface in getting his predecessor Celestine v. to abdicate (*Inf.* iii. 60).

[542] *As befooled*: Dante does not yet suspect that it is with a Pope he is speaking. He is dumbfounded at being addressed as Boniface.

[543] *All the simoniacs*: All the Popes that had been guilty of the sin.

[544] *A Pastor from the West*: Boniface died in 1303, and was succeeded by Benedict XI., who in his turn was succeeded by Clement V., the Pastor from the West. Benedict was not stained with simony, and so it is Clement that is to relieve Boniface; and he is to come from the West, that is, from Avignon, to which the Holy See was removed by him. Or the reference may simply be to the country of his birth. Elsewhere he is spoken of as 'the Gascon who shall cheat the noble Henry' of Luxemburg (*Parad.* xvii. 82).—This passage has been read as throwing light on the question of when the *Inferno* was written. Nicholas says that from the time Boniface arrives till Clement relieves him will be a shorter period than that during which he has himself been in Inferno, that is to say, a shorter time than twenty years. Clement died in 1314; and so, it is held, we find a date before which the *Inferno* was, at least, not published. But Clement was known for years before his death to be ill of a disease usually soon fatal. He became Pope in 1305, and the wonder was that he survived so long as nine years. Dante keeps his prophecy safe—if it is a prophecy; and there does seem internal evidence to prove the publication of the *Inferno* to have taken place long before 1314.—It is needless to point out how the censure of Clement gains in force if read as having been published before his death.

[545] *Jason*: Or Joshua, who purchased the office of High Priest from Antiochus Epiphanes, and innovated the customs of the Jews (2 Maccab. iv. 7).

[546] *Punished well*: At line 12 Dante has admired the propriety of the Divine distribution of penalties. He appears to regard with a special complacency that which he invents for the simoniacs. They were industrious in multiplying benefices for their kindred; Boniface, for example, besides Cardinals, appointed about twenty Archbishops and Bishops from among his own relatives. Here all the simoniacal Popes have to be contented with one place among them. They paid no regard to whether a post was well filled or not: here they are set upside down.

[547] *Charles*: Nicholas was accused of taking a bribe to assist Peter of Arragon in ousting Charles of Anjou from the kingdom of Sicily.

[548] *By reverence, etc.*: Dante distinguishes between the office and the unworthy holder of it. So in Purgatory he prostrates himself before a Pope (*Purg.*xix. 131).

[549] *Her spouse*: In the preceding lines the vision of the Woman in the Apocalypse is applied to the corruption of the Church, represented under the figure of the seven-hilled Rome seated in honour among the nations and receiving observance from the kings of the earth till her spouse, the Pope, began to prostitute her by making merchandise of her spiritual gifts. Of the Beast there is no mention here, his qualities being attributed to the Woman.

[550] *Ah, Constantine, etc.*: In Dante's time, and for some centuries later, it was believed that Constantine, on transferring the seat of empire to Byzantium, had made a gift to the Pope of rights and privileges almost equal to those of the Emperor. Rome was to be the Pope's; and from his court in the Lateran he was to exercise supremacy over all the West. The Donation of Constantine, that is, the instrument conveying these rights, was a forgery of the Middle Ages.

Canto XX.

Now of new torment must my verses tell,
    And matter for the Twentieth Canto win
    Of Lay the First,[551] which treats of souls in Hell.

Already was I eager to begin
    To peer into the visible profound,[552]
    Which tears of agony was bathèd in:

And I saw people in the valley round;
    Like that of penitents on earth the pace
    At which they weeping came, nor uttering[553] sound.

When I beheld them with more downcast gaze,[554]
    That each was strangely screwed about I learned,
    Where chest is joined to chin. And thus the face

Of every one round to his loins was turned;
    And stepping backward[555] all were forced to go,
    For nought in front could be by them discerned.

Smitten by palsy although one might show
    Perhaps a shape thus twisted all awry,
    I never saw, and am to think it slow.

As, Reader,[556] God may grant thou profit by
    Thy reading, for thyself consider well
    If I could then preserve my visage dry

When close at hand to me was visible
    Our human form so wrenched that tears, rained down
    Out of the eyes, between the buttocks fell.

In very sooth I wept, leaning upon
    A boss of the hard cliff, till on this wise
    My Escort asked: 'Of the other fools[557] art one?

Here piety revives as pity dies;
    For who more irreligious is than he
    In whom God's judgments to regret give rise?

Lift up, lift up thy head, and thou shalt see
    Him for whom earth yawned as the Thebans saw,
    All shouting meanwhile: "Whither dost thou flee,

Amphiaraüs?[558] Wherefore thus withdraw
    From battle?" But he sinking found no rest

Till Minos clutched him with all-grasping claw.
Lo, how his shoulders serve him for a breast!
    Because he wished to see too far before
    Backward he looks, to backward course addressed.
Behold Tiresias,[559] who was changed all o'er,
    Till for a man a woman met the sight,
    And not a limb its former semblance bore;
And he behoved a second time to smite
    The same two twisted serpents with his wand,
    Ere he again in manly plumes was dight.
With back to him, see Aruns next at hand,
    Who up among the hills of Luni, where
    Peasants of near Carrara till the land,
Among the dazzling marbles[560] held his lair
    Within a cavern, whence could be descried
    The sea and stars of all obstruction bare.
The other one, whose flowing tresses hide
    Her bosom, of the which thou seest nought,
    And all whose hair falls on the further side,
Was Manto;[561] who through many regions sought:
    Where I was born, at last her foot she stayed.
    It likes me well thou shouldst of this be taught.
When from this life her father exit made,
    And Bacchus' city had become enthralled,
    She for long time through many countries strayed.
'Neath mountains by which Germany is walled
    And bounded at Tirol, a lake there lies
    High in fair Italy, Benacus[562] called.
The waters of a thousand springs that rise
    'Twixt Val Camonica and Garda flow
    Down Pennine; and their flood this lake supplies.
And from a spot midway, if they should go
    Thither, the Pastors[563] of Verona, Trent,
    And Brescia might their blessings all bestow.
Peschiera,[564] with its strength for ornament,
    Facing the Brescians and the Bergamese
    Lies where the bank to lower curve is bent.
And there the waters, seeking more of ease,
    For in Benacus is not room for all,
    Forming a river, lapse by green degrees.
The river, from its very source, men call
    No more Benacus—'tis as Mincio known,
    Which into Po does at Governo fall.
A flat it reaches ere it far has run,
    Spreading o'er which it feeds a marshy fen,
    Whence oft in summer pestilence has grown.
Wayfaring here the cruel virgin, when

She found land girdled by the marshy flood,
    Untilled and uninhabited of men,
That she might 'scape all human neighbourhood
    Stayed on it with her slaves, her arts to ply;
    And there her empty body was bestowed.
On this the people from the country nigh
    Into that place came crowding, for the spot,
    Girt by the swamp, could all attack defy,
And for the town built o'er her body sought
    A name from her who made it first her seat,
    Calling it Mantua, without casting lot.[565]
The dwellers in it were in number great,
    Till stupid Casalodi[566] was befooled
    And victimised by Pinamonte's cheat.
Hence, shouldst thou ever hear (now be thou schooled!)
    Another story to my town assigned,
    Let by no fraud the truth be overruled.'
And I: 'Thy reasonings, Master, to my mind
    So cogent are, and win my faith so well,
    What others say I shall black embers find.
But of this people passing onward tell,
    If thou, of any, something canst declare,
    For all my thoughts[567] on that intently dwell.'
And then he said: 'The one whose bearded hair
    Falls from his cheeks upon his shoulders dun,
    Was, when the land of Greece[568] of males so bare
Was grown the very cradles scarce held one,
    An augur;[569] he with Calchas gave the sign
    In Aulis through the first rope knife to run.
Eurypylus was he called, and in some line
    Of my high Tragedy[570] is sung the same,
    As thou know'st well, who mad'st it wholly thine.
That other, thin of flank, was known to fame
    As Michael Scott;[571] and of a verity
    He knew right well the black art's inmost game.
Guido Bonatti,[572] and Asdente see
    Who mourns he ever should have parted from
    His thread and leather; but too late mourns he.
Lo the unhappy women who left loom,
    Spindle, and needle that they might divine;
    With herb and image[573] hastening men's doom.
But come; for where the hemispheres confine
    Cain and the Thorns[574] is falling, to alight
    Underneath Seville on the ocean line.
The moon was full already yesternight;
    Which to recall thou shouldst be well content,
    For in the wood she somewhat helped thy plight.'

Thus spake he to me while we forward went.

Footnotes

[551] *Lay the First*: The *Inferno*.

[552] *The visible profound*: The Fourth Bolgia, where soothsayers of every kind are punished. Their sin is that of seeking to find out what God has made secret. That such discoveries of the future could be made by men, Dante seems to have had no doubt; but he regards the exercise of the power as a fraud on Providence, and also credits the adepts in the black art with ruining others by their spells (line 123).

[553] *Nor uttering, etc.*: They who on earth told too much are now condemned to be for ever dumb. It will be noticed that with none of them does Dante converse.

[554] *More downcast gaze*: Standing as he does on the crown of the arch, the nearer they come to him the more he has to decline his eyes.

[555] *Stepping backward*: Once they peered far into the future; now they cannot see a step before them.

[556] *As, Reader, etc.*: Some light may be thrown on this unusual, and, at first sight, inexplicable display of pity, by the comment of Benvenuto da Imola:—'It is the wisest and most virtuous of men that are most subject to this mania of divination; and of this Dante is himself an instance, as is well proved by this book of his.' Dante reminds the reader how often since the journey began he has sought to have the veil of the future lifted; and would have it understood that he was seized by a sudden misgiving as to whether he too had not overstepped the bounds of what, in that respect, is allowed and right.

[557] *Of the other fools*: Dante, weeping like the sinners in the Bolgia, is asked by Virgil: 'What, art thou then one of them?' He had been suffered, without reproof, to show pity for Francesca and Ciacco. The terrors of the Lord grow more cogent as they descend, and even pity is now forbidden.

[558] *Amphiaraüs*: One of the Seven Kings who besieged Thebes. He foresaw his own death, and sought by hiding to evade it; but his wife revealed his hiding-place, and he was forced to join in the siege. As he fought, a thunderbolt opened a chasm in the earth, into which he fell.

[559] *Tiresias*: A Theban soothsayer whose change of sex is described by Ovid (*Metam.* iii.).

[560] *The dazzling marbles*: Aruns, a Tuscan diviner, is introduced by Lucan as prophesying great events to come to pass in Rome—the Civil War and the victories of Cæsar. His haunt was the deserted city of Luna, situated on the Gulf of Spezia, and under the Carrara mountains (*Phars.* i. 586).

[561] *Manto*: A prophetess, a native of Thebes the city of Bacchus, and daughter of Tiresias.—Here begins a digression on the early history of Mantua, the native city of Virgil. In his account of the foundation of it Dante does not agree with Virgil, attributing to a Greek Manto what his master attributes to an Italian one (*Æn.* x. 199).

[562] *Benacus*: The ancient Benacus, now known as the Lake of Garda.

[563] *The Pastors, etc.*: About half-way down the western side of the lake a stream falls into it, one of whose banks, at its mouth, is in the diocese of Trent, and the other in that of Brescia, while the waters of the lake are in that of Verona. The three Bishops, standing together, could give a blessing each to his own diocese.

[564] *Peschiera*: Where the lake drains into the Mincio. It is still a great fortress.

[565] *Without casting lot*; Without consulting the omens, as was usual when a city was to be named.

[566] *Casalodi*: Some time in the second half of the thirteenth century Alberto Casalodi was befooled out of the lordship of Mantua by Pinamonte Buonacolsi. Benvenuto tells the tale as follows:—Pinamonte was a bold, ambitious man, with a great troop of armed followers; and, the nobility being at that time in bad odour with the people at large, he persuaded the Count Albert that it would be a popular measure to banish the suspected nobles for a time. Hardly was this done when he usurped the lordship; and by expelling some of the citizens and putting others of them to death he greatly thinned the population of the city.

[567] *All my thoughts, etc.*: The reader's patience is certainly abused by this digression of Virgil's, and Dante himself seems conscious that it is somewhat ill-timed.

[568] *The land of Greece, etc.*: All the Greeks able to bear arms being engaged in the Trojan expedition.

[569] *An augur*: Eurypylus, mentioned in the Second *Æneid* as being employed by the Greeks to consult the oracle of Apollo regarding their return to Greece. From the auspices Calchas had found at what hour they should set sail for Troy. Eurypylus can be said only figuratively to have had to do with cutting the cable.

[570] *Tragedy*: The *Æneid*. Dante defines Comedy as being written in a style inferior to that of Tragedy, and as having a sad beginning and a happy ending (Epistle to Can Grande, 10). Elsewhere he allows the comic poet great licence in the use of common language (*Vulg. El.* ii. 4). By calling his own poem a Comedy he, as it were, disarms criticism.

[571] *Michael Scott*: Of Balwearie in Scotland, familiar to English readers through the *Lay of the Last Minstrel*. He flourished in the course of the thirteenth century, and made contributions to the sciences, as they were then deemed, of astrology, alchemy, and physiognomy. He acted for some time as astrologer to the Emperor Frederick II., and the tradition of his accomplishments powerfully affected the Italian imagination for a century after his death. It was remembered that the terrible Frederick, after being warned by him to beware of Florence, had died at a place called Firenzuola; and more than one Italian city preserved with fear and trembling his dark sayings regarding their fate. Villani frequently quotes his prophecies; and Boccaccio speaks of him as a great necromancer who had been in Florence. A commentary of his on Aristotle was printed at Venice in 1496. The thinness of his flanks may refer to a belief that he could make himself invisible at will.

[572] *Guido Bonatti*: Was a Florentine, a tiler by trade, and was living in 1282. When banished from his own city he took refuge at Forlì and became astrologer to Guido of Montefeltro (*Inf.* xxvii.), and was credited with helping his master to a great victory.—*Asdente*: A cobbler of Parma, whose prophecies were long renowned, lived in the twelfth century. He is given in the *Convito* (iv. 16) as an instance that a man may be very notorious without being truly noble.

[573] *Herb and image*: Part of the witch's stock in trade. All that was done to a waxen image of him was suffered by the witch's victim.

[574] *Cain and the Thorns*: The moon. The belief that the spots in the moon are caused by Cain standing in it with a bundle of thorns is referred to at *Parad.* ii. 51. Although it is now the morning of the

Saturday, the 'yesternight' refers to the night of Thursday, when Dante found some use of the moon in the Forest. The moon is now setting on the line dividing the hemisphere of Jerusalem, in which they are, from that of the Mount of Purgatory. According to Dante's scheme of the world, Purgatory is the true opposite of Jerusalem; and Seville is ninety degrees from Jerusalem. As it was full moon the night before last, and the moon is now setting, it is now fully an hour after sunrise. But, as has already been said, it is not possible to reconcile the astronomical indications thoroughly with one another.—Virgil serves as clock to Dante, for they can see nothing of the skies.

Canto XXI.

Conversing still from bridge to bridge[575] we went;
  But what our words I in my Comedy
  Care not to tell. The top of the ascent
Holding, we halted the next pit to spy
  Of Malebolge, with plaints bootless all:
  There, darkness[576] full of wonder met the eye.
As the Venetians[577] in their Arsenal
  Boil the tenacious pitch at winter-tide,
  To caulk the ships with for repairs that call;
For then they cannot sail; and so, instead,
  One builds his bark afresh, one stops with tow
  His vessel's ribs, by many a voyage tried;
One hammers at the poop, one at the prow;
  Some fashion oars, and others cables twine,
  And others at the jib and main sails sew:
So, not by fire, but by an art Divine,
  Pitch of thick substance boiled in that low Hell,
  And all the banks did as with plaster line.
I saw it, but distinguished nothing well
  Except the bubbles by the boiling raised,
  Now swelling up and ceasing now to swell.
While down upon it fixedly I gazed,
  'Beware, beware!' my Leader to me said,
  And drew me thence close to him. I, amazed,
Turned sharply round, like him who has delayed,
  Fain to behold the thing he ought to flee,
  Then, losing nerve, grows suddenly afraid,
Nor lingers longer what there is to see;
  For a black devil I beheld advance
  Over the cliff behind us rapidly.
Ah me, how fierce was he of countenance!
  What bitterness he in his gesture put,
  As with spread wings he o'er the ground did dance!
Upon his shoulders, prominent and acute,
  Was perched a sinner[578] fast by either hip;
  And him he held by tendon of the foot.

He from our bridge: 'Ho, Malebranche![579] Grip
  An Elder brought from Santa Zita's town:[580]
  Stuff him below; myself once more I slip
Back to the place where lack of such is none.
  There, save Bonturo, barrates[581] every man,
  And No grows Yes that money may be won.'
He shot him down, and o'er the cliff began
  To run; nor unchained mastiff o'er the ground,
  Chasing a robber, swifter ever ran.
The other sank, then rose with back bent round;
  But from beneath the bridge the devils cried:
  'Not here the Sacred Countenance[582] is found,
One swims not here as on the Serchio's[583] tide;
  So if thou wouldst not with our grapplers deal
  Do not on surface of the pitch abide.'
Then he a hundred hooks[584] was made to feel.
  'Best dance down there,' they said the while to him,
  'Where, if thou canst, thou on the sly mayst steal.'
So scullions by the cooks are set to trim
  The caldrons and with forks the pieces steep
  Down in the water, that they may not swim.
And the good Master said to me: 'Now creep
  Behind a rocky splinter for a screen;
  So from their knowledge thou thyself shalt keep.
And fear not thou although with outrage keen
  I be opposed, for I am well prepared,
  And formerly[585] have in like contest been.'
Then passing from the bridge's crown he fared
  To the sixth bank,[586] and when thereon he stood
  He needed courage doing what he dared.
In the same furious and tempestuous mood
  In which the dogs upon the beggar leap,
  Who, halting suddenly, seeks alms or food,
They issued forth from underneath the deep
  Vault of the bridge, with grapplers 'gainst him stretched;
  But he exclaimed: 'Aloof, and harmless keep!
Ere I by any of your hooks be touched,
  Come one of you and to my words give ear;
  And then advise you if I should be clutched.'
All cried: 'Let Malacoda then go near;'
  On which one moved, the others standing still.
  He coming said: 'What will this[587] help him here?'
'O Malacoda, is it credible
  That I am come,' my Master then replied,
  'Secure your opposition to repel,
Without Heaven's will, and fate, upon my side?
  Let me advance, for 'tis by Heaven's behest

That I on this rough road another guide.'

Then was his haughty spirit so depressed,

He let his hook drop sudden to his feet,

And, 'Strike him not!' commanded all the rest

My Leader charged me thus: 'Thou, from thy seat

Where 'mid the bridge's ribs thou crouchest low,

Rejoin me now in confidence complete.'

Whereon I to rejoin him was not slow;

And then the devils, crowding, came so near,

I feared they to their paction false might show.

So at Caprona[588] saw I footmen fear,

Spite of their treaty, when a multitude

Of foes received them, crowding front and rear.

With all my body braced I closer stood

To him, my Leader, and intently eyed

The aspect of them, which was far from good.

Lowering their grapplers, 'mong themselves they cried:

'Shall I now tickle him upon the thigh?'

'Yea, see thou clip him deftly,' one replied.

The demon who in parley had drawn nigh

Unto my Leader, upon this turned round;

'Scarmiglione, lay thy weapon by!'

He said; and then to us: 'No way is found

Further along this cliff, because, undone,

All the sixth arch lies ruined on the ground.

But if it please you further to pass on,

Over this rocky ridge advancing climb

To the next rib,[589] where passage may be won.

Yestreen,[590] but five hours later than this time,

Twelve hundred sixty-six years reached an end,

Since the way lost the wholeness of its prime.

Thither I some of mine will straightway send

To see that none peer forth to breathe the air:

Go on with them; you they will not offend.

You, Alichin[591] and Calcabrin, prepare

To move,' he bade; 'Cagnazzo, thou as well;

Guiding the ten, thou, Barbariccia, fare.

With Draghignazzo, Libicocco fell,

Fanged Ciriatto, Graffiacane too,

Set on, mad Rubicant and Farfarel!

Search on all quarters round the boiling glue.

Let these go safe, till at the bridge they be,

Which doth unbroken[592] o'er the caverns go.'

'Alas, my Master, what is this I see?'

Said I, 'Unguided, let us forward set,

If thou know'st how. I wish no company.

If former caution thou dost not forget,

Dost thou not mark how each his teeth doth grind,

The while toward us their brows are full of threat?'

And he: 'I would not fear should fill thy mind;

Let them grin all they will, and all they can;

'Tis at the wretches in the pitch confined.'

They wheeled and down the left hand bank began

To march, but first each bit his tongue,[593] and passed

The signal on to him who led the van.

He answered grossly as with trumpet blast.

Footnotes

[575] *From bridge to bridge*: They cross the barrier separating the Fourth from the Fifth Bolgia, and follow the bridge which spans the Fifth until they have reached the crown of it. We may infer that the conversation of Virgil and Dante turned on foreknowledge of the future.

[576] *Darkness, etc.*: The pitch with which the trench of the Bolgia is filled absorbs most of the scanty light accorded to Malebolge.

[577] *The Venetians*: But for this picturesque description of the old Arsenal, and a passing mention of the Rialto in one passage of the *Paradiso*, and of the Venetian coinage in another, it could not be gathered from the *Comedy*, with all its wealth of historical and geographical references, that there was such a place as Venice in the Italy of Dante. Unlike the statue of Time (*Inf.* xiv.), the Queen of the Adriatic had her face set eastwards. Her back was turned and her ears closed as in a proud indifference to the noise of party conflicts which filled the rest of Italy.

[578] *A sinner*: This is the only instance in the *Inferno* of the arrival of a sinner at his special place of punishment. See *Inf.* v. 15, *note*.

[579] *Malebranche*: Evil Claws, the name of the devils who have the sinners of this Bolgia in charge.

[580] *Santa Zita's town*: Zita was a holy serving-woman of Lucca, who died some time between 1270 and 1280, and whose miracle-working body is still preserved in the church of San Frediano. Most probably, although venerated as a saint, she was not yet canonized at the time Dante writes of, and there may be a Florentine sneer hidden in the description of Lucca as her town. Even in Lucca there was some difference of opinion as to her merits, and a certain unlucky Ciappaconi was pitched into the Serchio for making fun of the popular enthusiasm about her. See Philalethes, *Gött. Com.* In Lucca the officials that were called Priors in Florence, were named Elders. The commentators give a name to this sinner, but it is only guesswork.

[581] *Save Bonturo, barrates, etc.*: It is the barrators, those who trafficked in offices and sold justice, that are punished in this Bolgia. The greatest barrator of all in Lucca, say the commentators, was this Bonturo; but there seems no proof of it, though there is of his arrogance. He was still living in 1314.

[582] *The Sacred Countenance*: An image in cedar wood, of Byzantine workmanship, still preserved and venerated in the cathedral of Lucca. According to the legend, it was carved from memory by Nicodemus, and after being a long time lost was found again in the eighth century by an Italian bishop travelling in Palestine. He brought it to the coast at Joppa, where it was received by a vessel without sail or oar, which, with its sacred

freight, floated westwards and was next seen at the port of Luna. All efforts to approach the bark were vain, till the Bishop of Lucca descended to the seashore, and to him the vessel resigned itself and suffered him to take the image into his keeping. 'Believe what you like of all this,' says Benvenuto; 'it is no article of faith.'—The sinner has come to the surface, bent as if in an attitude of prayer, when he is met by this taunt.

[583] *The Serchio*: The stream which flows past Lucca.

[584] *A hundred hooks*: So many devils with their pronged hooks were waiting to receive the victim. The punishment of the barrators bears a relation to their sins. They wrought their evil deeds under all kinds of veils and excuses, and are now themselves effectually buried out of sight. The pitch sticks as close to them as bribes ever did to their fingers. They misused wards and all subject to them, and in their turn are clawed and torn by their devilish guardians.

[585] *Formerly, etc.*: On the occasion of his previous descent (*Inf.* ix. 22).

[586] *The sixth bank*: Dante remains on the crown of the arch overhanging the pitch-filled moat. Virgil descends from the bridge by the left hand to the bank on the inner side of the Fifth Bolgia.

[587] *What will this, etc.*: As if he said: What good will this delay do him in the long-run?

[588] *At Caprona*: Dante was one of the mounted militia sent by Florence in 1289 to help the Lucchese against the Pisans, and was present at the surrender by the Pisan garrison of the Castle of Caprona. Some make the reference to be to a siege of the same stronghold by the Pisans in the following year, when the Lucchese garrison, having surrendered on condition of having their lives spared, were met as they issued forth with cries of 'Hang them! Hang them!' But of this second siege it is only a Pisan commentator that speaks.

[589] *The next rib*: Malacoda informs them that the arch of rock across the Sixth Bolgia in continuation of that by which they have crossed the Fifth is in ruins, but that they will find a whole bridge if they keep to the left hand along the rocky bank on the inner edge of the pitch-filled moat. But, as appears further on, he is misleading them. It will be remembered that from the precipice enclosing the Malebolge there run more than one series of bridges or ribs into the central well of Inferno.

[590] *Yestreen, etc.*: This is the principal passage in the *Comedy* for fixing the date of the journey. It is now, according to the text, twelve hundred and sixty-six years and a day since the crucifixion. Turning to the *Convito*, iv. 23, we find Dante giving his reasons for believing that Jesus, at His death, had just completed His thirty-fourth year. This brings us to the date of 1300 A.D. But according to Church tradition the crucifixion happened on the 25th March, and to get thirty-four years His life must be counted from the incarnation, which was held to have taken place on the same date, namely the 25th March. It was in Dante's time optional to reckon from the incarnation or the birth of Christ. The journey must therefore be taken to have begun on Friday the 25th March, a fortnight before the Good Friday of 1300; and, counting strictly from the incarnation, on the first day of 1301—the first day of the new century. So we find Boccaccio in his unfinished commentary saying in *Inf.* iii. that it will appear from Canto xxi. that Dante began his journey in MCCCI.—The hour is now five hours before that at which the earthquake happened which took place at the death of Jesus. This is held by Dante (*Convito* iv. 23), who professes to follow the account by

Saint Luke, to have been at the sixth hour, that is, at noon; thus the time is now seven in the morning.

[591] *Alichino, etc.*: The names of the devils are all descriptive: Alichino, for instance, is the Swooper; but in this and the next Canto we have enough of the horrid crew without considering too closely how they are called.

[592] *Unbroken*: Malacoda repeats his lie.

[593] *Each bit his tongue, etc.*: The demons, aware of the cheat played by Malacoda, show their devilish humour by making game of Virgil and Dante.—Benvenuto is amazed that a man so involved in his own thoughts as Dante was, should have been such a close observer of low life as this passage shows him. He is sure that he laughed to himself as he wrote the Canto.

Canto XXII.

Horsemen I've seen in march across the field,
    Hastening to charge, or, answering muster, stand,
    And sometimes too when forced their ground to yield;
I have seen skirmishers upon your land,
    O Aretines![594] and those on foray sent;
    With trumpet and with bell[595] to sound command
Have seen jousts run and well-fought tournament,
    With drum, and signal from the castle shown,
    And foreign music with familiar blent;
But ne'er by blast on such a trumpet blown
    Beheld I horse or foot to motion brought,
    Nor ship by star or landmark guided on.
With the ten demons moved we from the spot;
    Ah, cruel company! but 'with the good
    In church, and in the tavern with the sot.'
Still to the pitch was my attention glued
    Fully to see what in the Bolgia lay,
    And who were in its burning mass imbrued.
As when the dolphins vaulted backs display,
    Warning to mariners they should prepare
    To trim their vessel ere the storm makes way;
So, to assuage the pain he had to bear,
    Some wretch would show his back above the tide,
    Then swifter plunge than lightnings cleave the air.
And as the frogs close to the marsh's side
    With muzzles thrust out of the water stand,
    While feet and bodies carefully they hide;
So stood the sinners upon every hand.
    But on beholding Barbariccia nigh
    Beneath the bubbles[596] disappeared the band.
I saw what still my heart is shaken by:
    One waiting, as it sometimes comes to pass
    That one frog plunges, one at rest doth lie;
And Graffiacan, who nearest to him was,
    Him upward drew, clutching his pitchy hair:

To me he bore the look an otter has.
I of their names[597] ere this was well aware,
   For I gave heed unto the names of all
   When they at first were chosen. 'Now prepare,
And, Rubicante, with thy talons fall
   Upon him and flay well,' with many cries
   And one consent the accursed ones did call.
I said: 'O Master, if in any wise
   Thou canst, find out who is the wretched wight
   Thus at the mercy of his enemies.'
Whereon my Guide drew full within his sight,
   Asking him whence he came, and he replied:
   'In kingdom of Navarre[598] I first saw light.
Me servant to a lord my mother tied;
   Through her I from a scoundrel sire did spring,
   Waster of goods and of himself beside.
As servant next to Thiebault,[599] righteous king,
   I set myself to ply barratorship;
   And in this heat discharge my reckoning.'
And Ciriatto, close upon whose lip
   On either side a boar-like tusk did stand,
   Made him to feel how one of them could rip.
The mouse had stumbled on the wild cat band;
   But Barbariccia locked him in embrace,
   And, 'Off while I shall hug him!' gave command.
Round to my Master then he turned his face:
   'Ask more of him if more thou wouldest know,
   While he against their fury yet finds grace.'
My Leader asked: 'Declare now if below
   The pitch 'mong all the guilty there lies here
   A Latian?'[600] He replied: 'Short while ago
From one[601] I parted who to them lived near;
   And would that I might use him still for shield,
   Then hook or claw I should no longer fear,'
Said Libicocco: 'Too much grace we yield.'
   And in the sinner's arm he fixed his hook,
   And from it clean a fleshy fragment peeled.
But seeing Draghignazzo also took
   Aim at his legs, the leader of the Ten
   Turned swiftly round on them with angry look.
On this they were a little quieted; then
   Of him who still gazed on his wound my Guide
   Without delay demanded thus again:
'Who was it whom, in coming to the side,
   Thou say'st thou didst do ill to leave behind?'
   'Gomita of Gallura,'[602] he replied,
'A vessel full of fraud of every kind,

Who, holding in his power his master's foes,
   So used them him they bear in thankful mind;
For, taking bribes, he let slip all of those,
   He says; and he in other posts did worse,
   And as a chieftain 'mong barrators rose.
Don Michael Zanche[603] doth with him converse,
   From Logodoro, and with endless din
   They gossip[604] of Sardinian characters.
But look, ah me! how yonder one doth grin.
   More would I say, but that I am afraid
   He is about to claw me on the skin.'
To Farfarel the captain turned his head,
   For, as about to swoop, he rolled his eye,
   And, 'Cursed hawk, preserve thy distance!' said.
'If ye would talk with, or would closer spy,'
   The frighted wretch began once more to say,
   'Tuscans or Lombards, I will bring them nigh.
But let the Malebranche first give way,
   That of their vengeance they may not have fear,
   And I to this same place where now I stay
For me, who am but one, will bring seven near
   When I shall whistle as we use to do
   Whenever on the surface we appear.'
On this Cagnazzo up his muzzle threw,
   Shaking his head and saying: 'Hear the cheat
   He has contrived, to throw himself below.'
Then he who in devices was complete:
   'Far too malicious, in good sooth,' replied,
   'When for my friends I plan a sorer fate.'
This, Alichin withstood not but denied
   The others' counsel,[605] saying: 'If thou fling
   Thyself hence, thee I strive not to outstride.
But o'er the pitch I'll dart upon the wing.
   Leave we the ridge,[606] and be the bank a shield;
   And see if thou canst all of us outspring.'
O Reader, hear a novel trick revealed.
   All to the other side turned round their eyes,
   He first[607] who slowest was the boon to yield.
In choice of time the Navarrese was wise;
   Taking firm stand, himself he forward flung,
   Eluding thus their hostile purposes.
Then with compunction each of them was stung,
   But he the most[608] whose slackness made them fail;
   Therefore he started, 'Caught!' upon his tongue.
But little it bested, nor could prevail
   His wings 'gainst fear. Below the other went,
   While he with upturned breast aloft did sail.

And as the falcon, when, on its descent,

> The wild duck suddenly dives out of sight,
>
> Returns outwitted back, and malcontent;

To be befooled filled Calcabrin with spite.

> Hovering he followed, wishing in his mind
>
> The wretch escaping should leave cause for fight.

When the barrator vanished, from behind

> He on his comrade with his talons fell
>
> And clawed him, 'bove the moat with him entwined.

The other was a spar-hawk terrible

> To claw in turn; together then the two
>
> Plunged in the boiling pool. The heat full well

How to unlock their fierce embraces knew;

> But yet they had no power[609] to rise again,
>
> So were their wings all plastered o'er with glue.

Then Barbariccia, mourning with his train,

> Caused four to fly forth to the other side
>
> With all their grapplers. Swift their flight was ta'en.

Down to the place from either hand they glide,

> Reaching their hooks to those who were limed fast,
>
> And now beneath the scum were being fried.

And from them thus engaged we onward passed.

Footnotes

[594] *O Aretines*: Dante is mentioned as having taken part in the campaign of 1289 against Arezzo, in the course of which the battle of Campaldino was fought. But the text can hardly refer to what he witnessed in that campaign, as the field of it was almost confined to the Casentino, and little more than a formal entrance was made on the true Aretine territory; while the chronicles make no mention of jousts and forays. There is, however, no reason to think but that Dante was engaged in the attack made by Florence on the Ghibeline Arezzo in the early summer of the preceding year. In a few days the Florentines and their allies had taken above forty castles and strongholds, and devastated the enemy's country far and near; and, though unable to take the capital, they held all kinds of warlike games in front of it. Dante was then twenty-three years of age, and according to the Florentine constitution of that period would, in a full muster of the militia, be required to serve as a cavalier without pay, and providing his own horse and arms.

[595] *Bell*: The use of the bell for martial music was common in the Italy of the thirteenth century. The great war-bell of the Florentines was carried with them into the field.

[596] *Beneath the bubbles, etc.*: As the barrators took toll of the administration of justice and appointment to offices, something always sticking to their palms, so now they are plunged in the pitch; and as they denied to others what should be the common blessing of justice, now they cannot so much as breathe the air without paying dearly for it to the demons.

[597] *Their names*: The names of all the demons. All of them urge Rubicante, the 'mad red devil,' to flay the victim, shining and sleek with the hot pitch, who is held fast by Graffiacane.

[598] *In kingdom of Navarre, etc.*: The commentators give the name of John Paul to this shade, but all that is known of him is found in the text.

[599] *Thiebault*: King of Navarre and second of that name. He accompanied his father-in-law, Saint Louis, to Tunis, and died on his way back, in 1270.

[600] *A Latian*: An Italian.

[601] *From one, etc.*: A Sardinian. The barrator prolongs his answer so as to procure a respite from the fangs of his tormentors.

[602] *Gomita of Gallura*: 'Friar Gomita' was high in favour with Nino Visconti (*Purg.* viii. 53), the lord of Gallura, one of the provinces into which Sardinia was divided under the Pisans. At last, after bearing long with him, the 'gentle Judge Nino' hanged Gomita for setting prisoners free for bribes.

[603] *Don Michael Zanche*: Enzo, King of Sardinia, married Adelasia, the lady of Logodoro, one of the four Sardinian judgedoms or provinces. Of this province Zanche, seneschal to Enzo, acquired the government during the long imprisonment of his master, or upon his death in 1273. Zanche's daughter was married to Branca d'Oria, by whom Zanche was treacherously slain in 1275 (*Inf.* xxxiii. 137). There seems to be nothing extant to support the accusation implied in the text.

[604] *They gossip, etc.*: Zanche's experience of Sardinia was of an earlier date than Gomita's. It has been claimed for, or charged against, the Sardinians, that more than other men they delight in gossip touching their native country. These two, if it can be supposed that, plunged among and choked with pitch, they still cared for Sardinian talk, would find material enough in the troubled history of their land. In 1300 it belonged partly to Genoa and partly to Pisa.

[605] *The others' counsel*: Alichino, confident in his own powers, is willing to risk an experiment with the sinner. The other devils count a bird in the hand worth two in the bush.

[606] *The ridge*: Not the crown of the great rocky barrier between the Fifth and the Sixth Bolgias, for it is not on that the devils are standing; neither are they allowed to pass over it (*Inf.* xxiii. 55). We are to figure them to ourselves as standing on a ledge running between the fosse and the foot of the enclosing rocky steep—a pathway continued under the bridges and all round the Bolgia for their convenience as guardians of it. The bank adjoining the pitch will serve as a screen for the sinner if the demons retire to the other side of this ledge.

[607] *He first, etc.*: Cagnazzo. See line 106.

[608] *He the most, etc.*: Alichino, whose confidence in his agility had led to the outwitting of the band.

[609] *No power*: The foolish ineptitude of the devils for anything beyond their special function of hooking up and flaying those who appear on the surface of the pitch, and their irrational fierce playfulness as of tiger cubs, convey a vivid impression of the limits set to their diabolical power, and at the same time heighten the sense of what Dante's feeling of insecurity must have been while in such inhuman companionship.

Canto XXIII.

Silent, alone, not now with company

> We onward went, one first and one behind,
>
> As Minor Friars[610] use to make their way.

On Æsop's fable[611] wholly was my mind

Intent, by reason of that contest new—
    The fable where the frog and mouse we find;
For *Mo* and *Issa*[612] are not more of hue
    Than like the fable shall the fact appear,
    If but considered with attention due.
And as from one thought springs the next, so here
    Out of my first arose another thought,
    Until within me doubled was my fear.
For thus I judged: Seeing through us[613] were brought
    Contempt upon them, hurt, and sore despite,
    They needs must be to deep vexation wrought.
If anger to malevolence unite,
    Then will they us more cruelly pursue
    Than dog the hare which almost feels its bite.
All my hair bristled, I already knew,
    With terror when I spake: 'O Master, try
    To hide us quick' (and back I turned to view
What lay behind), 'for me they terrify,
    These Malebranche following us; from dread
    I almost fancy I can feel them nigh.'
And he: 'Were I a mirror backed with lead
    I should no truer glass that form of thine,
    Than all thy thought by mine is answered.
For even now thy thoughts accord with mine,
    Alike in drift and featured with one face;
    And to suggest one counsel they combine.
If the right bank slope downward at this place,
    To the next Bolgia[614] offering us a way,
    Swiftly shall we evade the imagined chase.'
Ere he completely could his purpose say,
    I saw them with their wings extended wide,
    Close on us; as of us to make their prey.
Then quickly was I snatched up by my Guide:
    Even as a mother when, awaked by cries,
    She sees the flames are kindling at her side,
Delaying not, seizes her child and flies;
    Careful for him her proper danger mocks,
    Nor even with one poor shift herself supplies.
And he, stretched out upon the flinty rocks,
    Himself unto the precipice resigned
    Which one side of the other Bolgia blocks.
A swifter course ne'er held a stream confined,
    That it may turn a mill, within its race,
    Where near the buckets 'tis the most declined
Than was my Master's down that rock's sheer face;
    Nor seemed I then his comrade, as we sped,
    But like a son locked in a sire's embrace.

And barely had his feet struck on the bed
    Of the low ground, when they were seen to stand
    Upon the crest, no more a cause of dread.[615]
For Providence supreme, who so had planned
    In the Fifth Bolgia they should minister,
    Them wholly from departure thence had banned.
'Neath us we saw a painted people fare,
    Weeping as on their way they circled slow,
    Crushed by fatigue to look at, and despair.
Cloaks had they on with hoods pulled down full low
    Upon their eyes, and fashioned, as it seemed,
    Like those which at Cologne[616] for monks they sew.
The outer face was gilt so that it gleamed;
    Inside was all of lead, of such a weight
    Frederick's[617] to these had been but straw esteemed.
O weary robes for an eternal state!
    With them we turned to the left hand once more,
    Intent upon their tears disconsolate.
But those folk, wearied with the loads they bore,
    So slowly crept that still new company
    Was ours at every footfall on the floor.
Whence to my Guide I said: 'Do thou now try
    To find some one by name or action known,
    And as we go on all sides turn thine eye.'
And one, who recognised the Tuscan tone,
    Called from behind us: 'Halt, I you entreat
    Who through the air obscure are hastening on;
Haply in me thou what thou seek'st shalt meet.'
    Whereon my Guide turned round and said: 'Await,
    And keep thou time with pacing of his feet.'
I stood, and saw two manifesting great
    Desire to join me, by their countenance;
    But their loads hampered them and passage strait.[618]
And, when arrived, me with an eye askance[619]
    They gazed on long time, but no word they spoke;
    Then, to each other turned, held thus parlance:
'His heaving throat[620] proves him of living folk.
    If they are of the dead, how could they gain
    To walk uncovered by the heavy cloak?'
Then to me: 'Tuscan, who dost now attain
    To the college of the hypocrites forlorn,
    To tell us who thou art show no disdain.'
And I to them: 'I was both bred and born
    In the great city by fair Arno's stream,
    And wear the body I have always worn.
But who are ye, whose suffering supreme
    Makes tears, as I behold, to flood the cheek;

And what your mode of pain that thus doth gleam?'
'Ah me, the yellow mantles,' one to speak
    Began, 'are all of lead so thick, its weight
    Maketh the scales after this manner creak.
We, Merry Friars[621] of Bologna's state,
    I Catalano, Loderingo he,
    Were by thy town together designate,
As for the most part one is used to be,
    To keep the peace within it; and around
    Gardingo,[622] what we were men still may see.'
I made beginning: 'Friars, your profound—'
    But said no more, on suddenly seeing there
    One crucified by three stakes to the ground,
Who, when he saw me, writhed as in despair,
    Breathing into his beard with heavy sigh.
    And Friar Catalan, of this aware,
Said: 'He thus fixed, on whom thou turn'st thine eye,
    Counselled the Pharisees that it behoved
    One man as victim[623] for the folk should die.
Naked, thou seest, he lies, and ne'er removed
    From where, set 'cross the path, by him the weight
    Of every one that passes by is proved.
And his wife's father shares an equal fate,
    With others of the Council, in this fosse;
    For to the Jews they proved seed reprobate.'
Meanwhile at him thus stretched upon the cross
    Virgil,[624] I saw, displayed astonishment—
    At his mean exile and eternal loss.
And then this question to the Friars he sent:
    'Be not displeased, but, if ye may, avow
    If on the right[625] hand there lies any vent
By which we, both of us,[626] from hence may go,
    Nor need the black angelic company
    To come to help us from this valley low.'
'Nearer than what thou think'st,' he made reply,
    'A rib there runs from the encircling wall,[627]
    The cruel vales in turn o'erarching high;
Save that at this 'tis rent and ruined all.
    Ye can climb upward o'er the shattered heap
    Where down the side the piled-up fragments fall.'
His head bent down a while my Guide did keep,
    Then said: 'He warned us[628] in imperfect wise,
    Who sinners with his hook doth clutch and steep.
The Friar: 'At Bologna[629] many a vice
    I heard the Devil charged with, and among
    The rest that, false, he father is of lies.'
Then onward moved my Guide with paces long,

And some slight shade of anger on his face.
I with him parted from the burdened throng,
Stepping where those dear feet had left their trace.

Footnotes

[610] *Minor Friars*: In the early years of their Order the Franciscans went in couples upon their journeys, not abreast but one behind the other.

[611] *Æsop's fable*: This fable, mistakenly attributed to Æsop, tells of how a frog enticed a mouse into a pond, and how they were then both devoured by a kite. To discover the aptness of the simile would scarcely be reward enough for the continued mental effort Dante enjoins. So much was everything Greek or Roman then held in reverence, that the mention even of Æsop is held to give dignity to the page.

[612] *Mo and Issa*: Two words for *now*.

[613] *Through us*: The quarrel among the fiends arose from Dante's insatiable desire to confer with 'Tuscan or Lombard.'

[614] *To the next Bolgia*: The Sixth. They are now on the top of the circular ridge that divides it from the Fifth. From the construction of Malebolge the ridge is deeper on the inner side than on that up which they have travelled from the pitch.

[615] *No more a cause of dread*: There seems some incongruity between Virgil's dread of these smaller devils and the ease with which he cowed Minos, Charon, and Pluto. But his character gains in human interest the more he is represented as sympathising with Dante in his terrors; and in this particular case the confession of fellow-feeling prepares the way for the beautiful passage which follows it (line 38, etc.), one full of an almost modern tenderness.

[616] *Cologne*: Some make it Clugny, the great Benedictine monastery; but all the old commentators and most of the mss. read Cologne. All that the text necessarily carries is that the cloaks had great hoods. If, in addition, a reproach of clumsiness is implied, it would agree well enough with the Italian estimate of German people and things.

[617] *Frederick's, etc.*: The Emperor Frederick II.; but that he used any torture of leaden sheets seems to be a fabrication of his enemies.

[618] *Passage strait*: Through the crowd of shades, all like themselves weighed down by the leaden cloaks. There is nothing in all literature like this picture of the heavily-burdened shades. At first sight it seems to be little of a torture compared with what we have already seen, and yet by simple touch after touch an impression is created of the intolerable weariness of the victims. As always, too, the punishment answers to the sin. The hypocrites made a fair show in the flesh, and now their mantles which look like gold are only of base lead. On earth they were of a sad countenance, trying to seem better than they were, and the load which to deceive others they voluntarily assumed in life is now replaced by a still heavier weight, and one they cannot throw off if they would. The choice of garb conveys an obvious charge of hypocrisy against the Friars, then greatly fallen away from the purity of their institution, whether Franciscans or Dominicans.

[619] *An eye askance*: They cannot turn their heads.

[620] *His heaving throat*: In Purgatory Dante is known for a mortal by his casting a shadow. Here he is known to be of flesh and blood by the act of respiration; yet, as appears from line 113, the shades, too, breathe as well as perform other functions

of living bodies. At least they seem so to do, but this is all only in appearance. They only seem to be flesh and blood, having no weight, casting no shadow, and drawing breath in a way of their own. Dante, as has been said (*Inf.* vi. 36), is hard put to it to make them subject to corporal pains and yet be only shadows.

[621] *Merry Friars*: Knights of the Order of Saint Mary, instituted by Urban IV. in 1261. Whether the name of Frati Godenti which they here bear was one of reproach or was simply descriptive of the easy rule under which they lived, is not known. Married men might, under certain conditions, enter the Order. The members were to hold themselves aloof from public office, and were to devote themselves to the defence of the weak and the promotion of justice and religion. The two monkish cavaliers of the text were in 1266 brought to Florence as Podestas, the Pope himself having urged them to go. There is much uncertainty as to the part they played in Florence, but none as to the fact of their rule having been highly distasteful to the Florentines, or as to the other fact, that in Florence they grew wealthy. The Podesta, or chief magistrate, was always a well-born foreigner. Probably some monkish rule or custom forbade either Catalano or Loderingo to leave the monastery singly.

[622] *Gardingo*: A quarter of Florence, in which many palaces were destroyed about the time of the Podestaship of the Frati.

[623] *One man as victim*: *St. John* xi. 50. Caiaphas and Annas, with the Scribes and Pharisees who persecuted Jesus to the death, are the vilest hypocrites of all. They lie naked across the path, unburdened by the leaden cloak, it is true, but only that they may feel the more keenly the weight of the punishment of all the hypocrites of the world.

[624] *Virgil*: On Virgil's earlier journey through Inferno Caiaphas and the others were not here, and he wonders as at something out of a world to him unknown.

[625] *On the right*: As they are moving round the Bolgia to the left, the rocky barrier between them and the Seventh Bolgia is on their right.

[626] *We, both of us*: Dante, still in the body, as well as Virgil, the shade.

[627] *The encircling wall*: That which encloses all the Malebolge.

[628] *He warned us*: Malacoda (*Inf.* xxi. 109) had assured him that the next rib of rock ran unbroken across all the Bolgias, but it too, like all the other bridges, proves to have been, at the time of the earthquake, shattered where it crossed this gulf of the hypocrites. The earthquake told most on this Bolgia, because the death of Christ and the attendant earthquake were, in a sense, caused by the hypocrisy of Caiaphas and the rest.

[629] *At Bologna*: Even in Inferno the Merry Friar must have his joke. He is a gentleman, but a bit of a scholar too; and the University of Bologna is to him what Marischal College was to Captain Dalgetty.

Canto XXIV.

In season of the new year, when the sun
 Beneath Aquarius[630] warms again his hair,
 And somewhat on the nights the days have won;
When on the ground the hoar-frost painteth fair
 A mimic image of her sister white—
 But soon her brush of colour is all bare—
The clown, whose fodder is consumed outright,

Rises and looks abroad, and, all the plain
 Beholding glisten, on his thigh doth smite.
Returned indoors, like wretch that seeks in vain
 What he should do, restless he mourns his case;
 But hope revives when, looking forth again,
He sees the earth anew has changed its face.
 Then with his crook he doth himself provide,
 And straightway doth his sheep to pasture chase:
So at my Master was I terrified,
 His brows beholding troubled; nor more slow
 To where I ailed[631] the plaster was applied.
For when the broken bridge[632] we stood below
 My Guide turned to me with the expression sweet
 Which I beneath the mountain learned to know.
His arms he opened, after counsel meet
 Held with himself, and, scanning closely o'er
 The fragments first, he raised me from my feet;
And like a man who, working, looks before,
 With foresight still on that in front bestowed,
 Me to the summit of a block he bore
And then to me another fragment showed,
 Saying: 'By this thou now must clamber on;
 But try it first if it will bear thy load.'
The heavy cowled[633] this way could ne'er have gone,
 For hardly we, I holpen, he so light,
 Could clamber up from shattered stone to stone.
And but that on the inner bank the height
 Of wall is not so great, I say not he,
 But for myself I had been vanquished quite.
But Malebolge[634] to the cavity
 Of the deep central pit is planned to fall;
 Hence every Bolgia in its turn must be
High on the out, low on the inner wall;
 So to the summit we attained at last,
 Whence breaks away the topmost stone[635] of all.
My lungs were so with breathlessness harassed,
 The summit won, I could no further go;
 And, hardly there, me on the ground I cast
'Well it befits that thou shouldst from thee throw
 All sloth,' the Master said; 'for stretched in down
 Or under awnings none can glory know.
And he who spends his life nor wins renown
 Leaves in the world no more enduring trace
 Than smoke in air, or foam on water blown.
Therefore arise; o'ercome thy breathlessness
 By force of will, victor in every fight
 When not subservient to the body base.

Of stairs thou yet must climb a loftier flight:[636]
   'Tis not enough to have ascended these.
   Up then and profit if thou hear'st aright.'
Rising I feigned to breathe with greater ease
   Than what I felt, and spake: 'Now forward plod,
   For with my courage now my strength agrees.'
Up o'er the rocky rib we held our road;
   And rough it was and difficult and strait,
   And steeper far[637] than that we earlier trod.
Speaking I went, to hide my wearied state,
   When from the neighbouring moat a voice we heard
   Which seemed ill fitted to articulate.
Of what it said I knew not any word,
   Though on the arch[638] that vaults the moat set high;
   But he who spake appeared by anger stirred.
Though I bent downward yet my eager eye,
   So dim the depth, explored it all in vain;
   I then: 'O Master, to that bank draw nigh,
And let us by the wall descent obtain,
   Because I hear and do not understand,
   And looking down distinguish nothing plain.'
'My sole reply to thee,' he answered bland,
   'Is to perform; for it behoves,' he said,
   'With silent act to answer just demand.'
Then we descended from the bridge's head,[639]
   Where with the eighth bank is its junction wrought;
   And full beneath me was the Bolgia spread.
And I perceived that hideously 'twas fraught
   With serpents; and such monstrous forms they bore,
   Even now my blood is curdled at the thought.
Henceforth let sandy Libya boast no more!
   Though she breed hydra, snake that crawls or flies,
   Twy-headed, or fine-speckled, no such store
Of plagues, nor near so cruel, she supplies,
   Though joined to all the land of Ethiop,
   And that which by the Red Sea waters lies.
'Midst this fell throng and dismal, without hope
   A naked people ran, aghast with fear—
   No covert for them and no heliotrope.[640]
Their hands[641] were bound by serpents at their rear,
   Which in their reins for head and tail did get
   A holding-place: in front they knotted were.
And lo! to one who on our side was set
   A serpent darted forward, him to bite
   At where the neck is by the shoulders met.
Nor O nor I did any ever write
   More quickly than he kindled, burst in flame,

And crumbled all to ashes. And when quite
He on the earth a wasted heap became,
   The ashes[642] of themselves together rolled,
   Resuming suddenly their former frame.
Thus, as by mighty sages we are told,
   The Phœnix[643] dies, and then is born again,
   When it is close upon five centuries old.
In all its life it eats not herb nor grain,
   But only tears that from frankincense flow;
   It, for a shroud, sweet nard and myrrh contain.
And as the man who falls and knows not how,
   By force of demons stretched upon the ground,
   Or by obstruction that makes life run low,
When risen up straight gazes all around
   In deep confusion through the anguish keen
   He suffered from, and stares with sighs profound:
So was the sinner, when arisen, seen.
   Justice of God, how are thy terrors piled,
   Showering in vengeance blows thus big with teen!
My Guide then asked of him how he was styled.
   Whereon he said: 'From Tuscany I rained,
   Not long ago, into this gullet wild.
From bestial life, not human, joy I gained,
   Mule that I was; me, Vanni Fucci,[644] brute,
   Pistoia, fitting den, in life contained.'
I to my Guide: 'Bid him not budge a foot,
   And ask[645] what crime has plunged him here below.
   In rage and blood I knew him dissolute.'
The sinner heard, nor insincere did show,
   But towards me turned his face and eke his mind,
   With spiteful shame his features all aglow;
Then said: 'It pains me more thou shouldst me find
   And catch me steeped in all this misery,
   Than when the other life I left behind.
What thou demandest I can not deny:
   I'm plunged[646] thus low because the thief I played
   Within the fairly furnished sacristy;
And falsely to another's charge 'twas laid.
   Lest thou shouldst joy[647] such sight has met thy view
   If e'er these dreary regions thou evade,
Give ear and hearken to my utterance true:
   The Neri first out of Pistoia fail,
   Her laws and parties Florence shapes anew;
Mars draws a vapour out of Magra's vale,
   Which black and threatening clouds accompany:
   Then bursting in a tempest terrible
Upon Piceno shall the war run high;

The mist by it shall suddenly be rent,

And every Bianco[648] smitten be thereby:

And I have told thee that thou mayst lament.'

Footnotes

[630] *Aquarius*: The sun is in the constellation of Aquarius from the end of January till the end of February; and already, say in the middle of February, the day is nearly as long as the night.

[631] *Where I ailed, etc.*: As the peasant is in despair at seeing the earth white with what he thinks is snow, so was Dante at the signs of trouble on Virgil's face. He has mistaken anger at the cheat for perplexity as to how they are to escape from the Bolgia; and his Master's smile is grateful and reassuring to him as the spectacle of the green earth to the despairing shepherd.

[632] *The broken bridge*: They are about to escape from the bottom of the Sixth Bolgia by climbing the wall between it and the Seventh, at the point where the confused fragments of the bridge Friar Catalano told them of (*Inf.* xxiii. 133) lie piled up against the wall, and yield something of a practicable way.

[633] *The heavy cowled*: He finds his illustration on the spot, his mind being still full of the grievously burdened hypocrites.

[634] *But Malebolge, etc.*: Each Bolgia in turn lies at a lower level than the one before it, and consequently the inner side of each dividing ridge or wall is higher than the outer; or, to put it otherwise, in each Bolgia the wall they come to last—that nearest the centre of the Inferno, is lower than that they first reach—the one enclosing the Bolgia.

[635] *The topmost stone*: The stone that had formed the beginning of the arch at this end of it.

[636] *A loftier flight*: When he ascends the Mount of Purgatory.

[637] *Steeper far, etc.*: Rougher and steeper than the rib of rock they followed till they had crossed the Fifth Bolgia. They are now travelling along a different spoke of the wheel.

[638] *The arch, etc.*: He has gone on hiding his weariness till he is on the top of the arch that overhangs the Seventh Bolgia—that in which thieves are punished.

[639] *Front the bridge's head*: Further on they climb up again (*Inf.* xxvi. 13) by the projecting stones which now supply them with the means of descent. It is a disputed point how far they do descend. Clearly it is further than merely from the bridge to the lower level of the wall dividing the Seventh from the Eighth Bolgia; but not so far as to the ground of the moat. Most likely the stones jut forth at the angle formed by the junction of the bridge and the rocky wall. On one of the lowest of these they find a standing-place whence they can see clearly what is in the Bolgia.

[640] *Heliotrope*: A stone supposed to make the bearer of it invisible.

[641] *Their hands, etc.*: The sinners in this Bolgia are the thieves, not the violent robbers and highwaymen but those crime involves a betrayal of trust. After all their cunning thefts they are naked now; and, though here is nothing to steal, hands are firmly bound behind them.

[642] *The ashes, etc.*: The sufferings of the thieves, if looked closely into, will be found appropriate to their sins. They would fain but cannot steal themselves away, and in addition to the constant terror of being found out they are subject to pains the essence of which consists in the deprivation—the theft from them—of their unsubstantial bodies, which are all that they now have to lose. In the case of this victim the deprivation is only temporary.

[643] *The Phœnix*: Dante here borrows very directly from Ovid (*Metam.* xv.).

[644] *Vanni Fucci*: Natural son of a Pistoiese noble and a poet of some merit, who bore a leading part in the ruthless feuds of Blacks and Whites which distracted Pistoia towards the close of the thirteenth century.

[645] *And ask, etc.*: Dante wishes to find out why Fucci is placed among the thieves, and not in the circle of the violent. The question is framed so as to compel confession of a crime for which the sinner had not been condemned in life; and he flushes with rage at being found among the cowardly thieves.

[646] *I'm plunged, etc.*: Fucci was concerned in the theft of treasure from the Cathedral Church of St. James at Pistoia. Accounts vary as to the circumstances under which the crime was committed, and as to who suffered for it. Neither is it certainly known when Fucci died, though his recent arrival in the Bolgia agrees with the view that he was still active on the side of the Blacks in the last year of the century. In the fierceness of his retort to Dante we have evidence of their old acquaintance and old enmity.

[647] *Lest thou shouldst joy*: Vanni, a *Nero* or Black, takes his revenge for being found here by Dante, who was, as he knew, associated with the *Bianchi* or Whites, by prophesying an event full of disaster to these.

[648] *Every Bianco, etc.*: The Blacks, according to Villani (viii. 45), were driven from Pistoia in May 1301. They took refuge in Florence, where their party, in the following November under the protection of Charles of Valois, finally gained the upper hand, and began to persecute and expel the Whites, among whom was Dante. Mars, the god of war, or, more probably, the planet of war, draws a vapour from the valley of the Magra, a small stream which flows into the Mediterranean on the northern confine of Tuscany. This vapour is said to signify Moroello Malaspina, a noble of that district and an active leader of the Blacks, who here figure as murky clouds. The Campo Piceno is the country west of Pistoia. There Moroello bursts on his foes like a lightning-flash out of its cloud. This seems to refer to a pitched battle that should have happened soon after the Blacks recovered their strength; but the chroniclers tell of none such, though some of the commentators do. The fortress of Seravalle was taken from the Pistoiese, it is true, in 1302, and Moroello is said to have been the leader of the force which starved it into submission. He was certainly present at the great siege of Pistoia in 1305, when the citizens suffered the last rigours of famine.—This prophecy by Fucci recalls those by Farinata and Ciacco.

Canto XXV.

The robber,[649] when his words were ended so,

Made both the figs and lifted either fist,

Shouting: 'There, God! for them at thee I throw.'

Then were the snakes my friends; for one 'gan twist

And coiled itself around the sinner's throat,

As if to say: 'Now would I have thee whist.'

Another seized his arms and made a knot,

Clinching itself upon them in such wise

He had no power to move them by a jot.

Pistoia![650] thou, Pistoia, shouldst devise
    To burn thyself to ashes, since thou hast
    Outrun thy founders in iniquities.[Pg 185]
The blackest depths of Hell through which I passed
    Showed me no soul 'gainst God so filled with spite,
    No, not even he who down Thebes' wall[651] was cast.
He spake no further word, but turned to flight;
    And I beheld a Centaur raging sore
    Come shouting: 'Of the ribald give me sight!'
I scarce believe Maremma[652] yieldeth more
    Snakes of all kinds than what composed the load
    Which on his back, far as our form, he bore.
Behind his nape, with pinions spread abroad,
    A dragon couchant on his shoulders lay
    To set on fire whoever bars his road.
'This one is Cacus,'[653] did my Master say,
    'Who underneath the rock of Aventine
    Watered a pool with blood day after day.
Not with his brethren[654] runs he in the line,
    Because of yore the treacherous theft he wrought
    Upon the neighbouring wealthy herd of kine:
Whence to his crooked course an end was brought
    'Neath Hercules' club, which on him might shower down
    A hundred blows; ere ten he suffered nought.'
While this he said, the other had passed on;
    And under us three spirits forward pressed
    Of whom my Guide and I had nothing known
But that: 'Who are ye?' they made loud request.
    Whereon our tale[655] no further could proceed;
    And toward them wholly we our wits addressed.
I recognised them not, but gave good heed;
    Till, as it often haps in such a case,
    To name another, one discovered need,
Saying: 'Now where stopped Cianfa[656] in the race?'
    Then, that my Guide might halt and hearken well,
    On chin[657] and nose I did my finger place.
If, Reader, to believe what now I tell
    Thou shouldst be slow, I wonder not, for I
    Who saw it all scarce find it credible.
While I on them my brows kept lifted high
    A serpent, which had six feet, suddenly flew
    At one of them and held him bodily.
Its middle feet about his paunch it drew,
    And with the two in front his arms clutched fast,
    And bit one cheek and the other through and through.
Its hinder feet upon his thighs it cast,
    Thrusting its tail between them till behind,

Distended o'er his reins, it upward passed.
The ivy to a tree could never bind
    Itself so firmly as this dreadful beast
    Its members with the other's intertwined.
Each lost the colour that it once possessed,
    And closely they, like heated wax, unite,
    The former hue of neither manifest:
Even so up o'er papyrus,[658] when alight,
    Before the flame there spreads a colour dun,
    Not black as yet, though from it dies the white.
The other two meanwhile were looking on,
    Crying: 'Agnello, how art thou made new!
    Thou art not twain, and yet no longer one.'
A single head was moulded out of two;
    And on our sight a single face arose,
    Which out of both lost countenances grew.
Four separate limbs did but two arms compose;
    Belly with chest, and legs with thighs did grow
    To members such as nought created shows.
Their former fashion was all perished now:
    The perverse shape did both, yet neither seem;
    And, thus transformed, departed moving slow.
And as the lizard, which at fierce extreme
    Of dog-day heat another hedge would gain,
    Flits 'cross the path swift as the lightning's gleam;
Right for the bellies of the other twain
    A little snake[659] quivering with anger sped,
    Livid and black as is a pepper grain,
And on the part by which we first are fed
    Pierced one of them; and then upon the ground
    It fell before him, and remained outspread.
The wounded gazed on it, but made no sound.
    Rooted he stood[660] and yawning, scarce awake,
    As seized by fever or by sleep profound.
It closely watched him and he watched the snake,
    While from its mouth and from his wound 'gan swell
    Volumes of smoke which joined one cloud to make.
Be Lucan henceforth dumb, nor longer tell
    Of plagued Sabellus and Nassidius,[661]
    But, hearkening to what follows, mark it well.
Silent be Ovid: of him telling us
    How Cadmus[662] to a snake, and to a fount
    Changed Arethuse,[663] I am not envious;
For never of two natures front to front
    In metamorphosis, while mutually
    The forms[664] their matter changed, he gives account.
'Twas thus that each to the other made reply:

Its tail into a fork the serpent split;
    Bracing his feet the other pulled them nigh:
And then in one so thoroughly were knit
    His legs and thighs, no searching could divine
    At where the junction had been wrought in it.
The shape, of which the one lost every sign,
    The cloven tail was taking; then the skin
    Of one grew rough, the other's soft and fine.
I by the armpits saw the arms drawn in;
    And now the monster's feet, which had been small,
    What the other's lost in length appeared to win.
Together twisted, its hind feet did fall
    And grew the member men are used to hide:
    For his the wretch gained feet with which to crawl.
Dyed in the smoke they took on either side
    A novel colour: hair unwonted grew
    On one; the hair upon the other died.
The one fell prone, erect the other drew,
    With cruel eyes continuing to glare,
    'Neath which their muzzles metamorphose knew.
The erect to his brows drew his. Of stuff to spare
    Of what he upward pulled, there was no lack;
    So ears were formed on cheeks that erst were bare.
Of that which clung in front nor was drawn back,
    Superfluous, on the face was formed a nose,
    And lips absorbed the skin that still was slack.
His muzzle who lay prone now forward goes;
    Backward into his head his ears he draws
    Even as a snail appears its horns to lose.
The tongue, which had been whole and ready was
    For speech, cleaves now; the forked tongue of the snake
    Joins in the other: and the smoke has pause.[665]
The soul which thus a brutish form did take,
    Along the valley, hissing, swiftly fled;
    The other close behind it spluttering spake,
Then, toward it turning his new shoulders, said
    Unto the third: 'Now Buoso down the way
    May hasten crawling, as I earlier sped.'
Ballast which in the Seventh Bolgia lay
    Thus saw I shift and change. Be my excuse
    The novel theme,[666] if swerves my pen astray.
And though these things mine eyesight might confuse
    A little, and my mind with fear divide,
    Such secrecy they fleeing could not use
But that Puccio Sciancatto plain I spied;
    And he alone of the companions three
    Who came at first, was left unmodified.

For the other, tears, Gaville,[667] are shed by thee.

Footnotes

[649] *The robber, etc.*: By means of his prophecy Fucci has, after a fashion, taken revenge on Dante for being found by him among the cheating thieves instead of among the nobler sinners guilty of blood and violence. But in the rage of his wounded pride he must insult even Heaven, and this he does by using the most contemptuous gesture in an Italian's repertory. The fig is made by thrusting the thumb between the next two fingers. In the English 'A fig for him!' we have a reference to the gesture.

[650] *Pistoia*: The Pistoiese bore the reputation of being hard and pitiless. The tradition was that their city had been founded by such of Catiline's followers as survived his defeat on the Campo Piceno. 'It is no wonder,' says Villani (i. 32) 'that, being the descendants as they are of Catiline and his followers, the Pistoiese have always been ruthless and cruel to strangers and to one another.'

[651] *Who down Thebes' wall*: Capaneus (*Inf.* xiv. 63).

[652] *Maremma*: See note, *Inf.* xiii. 8.

[653] *Cacus*: Dante makes him a Centaur, but Virgil (*Æn.* viii.) only describes him as half human. The pool was fed with the blood of his human victims. The herd was the spoil Hercules took from Geryon. In the *Æneid* Cacus defends himself from Hercules by vomiting a fiery smoke; and this doubtless suggested the dragon of the text.

[654] *His brethren*: The Centaurs who guard the river of blood (*Inf.* xii. 56). In Fucci, as a sinner guilty of blood and violence above most of the thieves, the Centaur Cacus takes a special malign interest.

[655] *Our tale*: Of Cacus. It is interrupted by the arrival of three sinners whom Dante does not at first recognise as he gazes down on them, but only when they begin to speak among themselves. They are three noble citizens of Florence: Agnello Brunelleschi, Buoso degli Abati, and Puccio Sciancatto de' Galigai—all said to have pilfered in private life, or to have abused their tenure of high office by plundering the Commonwealth. What is certainly known of them is that they were Florentine thieves of quality.

[656] *Cianfa*: Another Florentine gentleman, one of the Donati. Since his companions lost sight of him he has been transformed into a six-footed serpent. Immediately appearing, he darts upon Agnello.

[657] *On chin, etc.*: A gesture by which silence is requested. The mention of Cianfa shows Dante that he is among Florentines.

[658] *Papyrus*: The original is *papiro*, the word used in Dante's time for a wick made out of a reed like the papyrus; *papér* being still the name for a wick in some dialects.—(Scartazzini.) It cannot be shown that *papiro* was ever employed for paper in Italian. This, however, does not prove that Dante may not so use it in this instance, adopting it from the Latin *papyrus*. Besides, he says that the brown colour travels up over the *papiro*; while it goes downward on a burning wick. Nor would the simile, if drawn from a slowly burning lamp-wick, agree with the speed of the change described in the text.

[659] *A little snake*: As transpires from the last line of the Canto, this is Francesco, of the Florentine family of the Cavalcanti, to which Dante's friend Guido belonged. He wounds Buoso in the navel, and then, instead of growing into one new monster as was the case with Cianfa and Agnello, they exchange shapes, and

when the transformation is complete Buoso is the serpent and Francesco is the human shade.

[660] *Rooted he stood, etc.*: The description agrees with the symptoms of snake-bite, one of which is extreme drowsiness.

[661] *Sabellus and Nassidius*: Were soldiers of Cato's army whose death by snake-bite in the Libyan desert is described by Lucan, *Pharsal.* ix. Sabbellus was burned up by the poison, bones and all; Nassidius swelled up and burst.

[662] *Cadmus*: Metam. iv.

[663] *Arethusa*: Metam. v.

[664] *The forms, etc.*: The word *form* is here to be taken in its scholastic sense of *virtus formativa*, the inherited power of modifying matter into an organised body. 'This, united to the divinely implanted spark of reason,' says Philalethes, 'constitutes, on Dante's system, a human soul. Even after death this power continues to be an essential constituent of the soul, and constructs out of the elements what seems to be a body. Here the sinners exchange the matter they have thus made their own, each retaining, however, his proper plastic energy as part of his soul.' Dante in his *Convito* (iii. 2) says that 'the human soul is the noblest form of all that are made under the heavens, receiving more of the Divine nature than any other.'

[665] *The smoke has pause*: The sinners have robbed one another of all they can lose. In the punishment is mirrored the sin that plunged them here.

[666] *The novel theme*: He has lingered longer than usual on this Bolgia, and pleads wonder of what he saw in excuse either of his prolixity or of some of the details of his description. The expression is perhaps one of feigned humility, to balance his recent boast of excelling Ovid and Lucan in inventive power.

[667] *Gaville*: The other, and the only one of those five Florentine thieves not yet named in the text, is he who came at first in the form of a little black snake, and who has now assumed the shape of Buoso. In reality he is Francesco Cavalcanti, who was slain by the people of Gaville in the upper Valdarno. Many of them were in their turn slaughtered in revenge by the Cavalcanti and their associates. It should be remarked that some of these five Florentines were of one party, some of the other. It is also noteworthy that Dante recruits his thieves as he did his usurers from the great Florentine families.—As the 'shifting and changing' of this rubbish is apt to be found confusing, the following may be useful to some readers:—There first came on the scene Agnello, Buoso, and Puccio. Cianfa, in the shape of a six-footed serpent, comes and throws himself on Agnello, and then, grown incorporate in a new strange monster, two in one, they disappear. Buoso is next wounded by Francesco, and they exchange members and bodies. Only Puccio remains unchanged.

Canto XXVI.

Rejoice, O Florence, in thy widening fame!
    Thy wings thou beatest over land and sea,
    And even through Inferno spreads thy name.
Burghers of thine, five such were found by me
    Among the thieves; whence I ashamed[668] grew,
    Nor shall great glory thence redound to thee.
But if 'tis toward the morning[669] dreams are true,
    Thou shalt experience ere long time be gone

The doom even Prato[670] prays for as thy due.
And came it now, it would not come too soon.
    Would it were come as come it must with time:
    'Twill crush me more the older I am grown.
Departing thence, my Guide began to climb
    The jutting rocks by which we made descent
    Some while ago,[671] and pulled me after him.
And as upon our lonely way we went
    'Mong splinters[672] of the cliff, the feet in vain,
    Without the hand to help, had labour spent.
I sorrowed, and am sorrow-smit again,
    Recalling what before mine eyes there lay,
    And, more than I am wont, my genius rein
From running save where virtue leads the way;
    So that if happy star[673] or holier might
    Have gifted me I never mourn it may.
At time of year when he who gives earth light
    His face shows to us longest visible,
    When gnats replace the fly at fall of night,
Not by the peasant resting on the hill
    Are seen more fire-flies in the vale below,
    Where he perchance doth field and vineyard[674] till,
Than flamelets I beheld resplendent glow
    Throughout the whole Eighth Bolgia, when at last
    I stood whence I the bottom plain could know.
And as he whom the bears avenged, when passed
    From the earth Elijah, saw the chariot rise
    With horses heavenward reared and mounting fast,
And no long time had traced it with his eyes
    Till but a flash of light it all became,
    Which like a rack of cloud swept to the skies:
Deep in the valley's gorge, in mode the same,
    These flitted; what it held by none was shown,
    And yet a sinner[675] lurked in every flame.
To see them well I from the bridge peered down,
    And if a jutting crag I had not caught
    I must have fallen, though neither thrust nor thrown.
My Leader me beholding lost in thought:
    'In all the fires are spirits,' said to me;
    'His flame round each is for a garment wrought.'
'O Master!' I replied, 'by hearing thee
    I grow assured, but yet I knew before
    That thus indeed it was, and longed to be
Told who is in the flame which there doth soar,
    Cloven, as if ascending from the pyre
    Where with Eteocles[676] there burned of yore
His brother.' He: 'Ulysses in that fire

And Diomedes[677] burn; in punishment
 Thus held together, as they held in ire.
And, wrapped within their flame, they now repent
 The ambush of the horse, which oped the door
 Through which the Romans' noble seed[678] forth went.
For guile Deïdamia[679] makes deplore
 In death her lost Achilles, tears they shed,
 And bear for the Palladium[680] vengeance sore.'
'Master, I pray thee fervently,' I said,
 'If from those flames they still can utter speech—
 Give ear as if a thousand times I pled!
Refuse not here to linger, I beseech,
 Until the cloven fire shall hither gain:
 Thou seest how toward it eagerly I reach.'
And he: 'Thy prayers are worthy to obtain
 Exceeding praise; thou hast what thou dost seek:
 But see that thou from speech thy tongue refrain.
I know what thou wouldst have; leave me to speak,
 For they perchance would hear contemptuously
 Shouldst thou address them, seeing they were Greek.'[681]
Soon as the flame toward us had come so nigh
 That to my Leader time and place seemed met,
 I heard him thus adjure it to reply:
'O ye who twain within one fire are set,
 If what I did your guerdon meriteth,
 If much or little ye are in my debt
For the great verse I built while I had breath,
 By one of you be openly confessed
 Where, lost to men, at last he met with death.
Of the ancient flame the more conspicuous crest
 Murmuring began to waver up and down
 Like flame that flickers, by the wind distressed.
At length by it was measured motion shown,
 Like tongue that moves in speech; and by the flame
 Was language uttered thus: 'When I had gone
From Circe[682] who a long year kept me tame
 Beside her, ere the near Gaeta had
 Receivèd from Æneas that new name;
No softness for my son, nor reverence sad
 For my old father, nor the love I owed
 Penelope with which to make her glad,
Could quench the ardour that within me glowed
 A full experience of the world to gain—
 Of human vice and worth. But I abroad
Launched out upon the high and open main[683]
 With but one bark and but the little band
 Which ne'er deserted me.[684] As far as Spain

I saw the sea-shore upon either hand,
 And as Morocco; saw Sardinia's isle,
 And all of which those waters wash the strand.
I and my comrades were grown old the while
 And sluggish, ere we to the narrows came
 Where Hercules of old did landmarks pile
For sign to men they should no further aim;
 And Seville lay behind me on the right,
 As on the left lay Ceuta. Then to them
I spake: "O Brothers, who through such a fight
 Of hundred thousand dangers West have won,
 In this short watch that ushers in the night
Of all your senses, ere your day be done,
 Refuse not to obtain experience new
 Of worlds unpeopled, yonder, past the sun.
Consider whence the seed of life ye drew;
 Ye were not born to live like brutish herd,
 But righteousness and wisdom to ensue."
My comrades to such eagerness were stirred
 By this short speech the course to enter on,
 They had no longer brooked restraining word.
Turning our poop to where the morning shone
 We of the oars made wings for our mad flight,
 Still tending left the further we had gone.
And of the other pole I saw at night
 Now all the stars; and 'neath the watery plain
 Our own familiar heavens were lost to sight.
Five times afresh had kindled, and again
 The moon's face earthward was illumed no more,
 Since out we sailed upon the mighty main;[685]
Then we beheld a lofty mountain[686] soar,
 Dim in the distance; higher, as I thought,
 By far than any I had seen before.
We joyed; but with despair were soon distraught
 When burst a whirlwind from the new-found world
 And the forequarter of the vessel caught.
With all the waters thrice it round was swirled;
 At the fourth time the poop, heaved upward, rose,
 The prow, as pleased Another,[687] down was hurled;
And then above us did the ocean close.'

Footnotes

[668] *Whence I ashamed, etc.*: There is here a sudden change from irony to earnest. 'Five members of great Florentine families, eternally engaged among themselves in their shameful metamorphoses—nay, but it is too sad!'
[669] *Toward the morning, etc.*: There was a widespread belief in the greater truthfulness of dreams dreamed as the night wears

away. See *Purg.* ix. 13. The dream is Dante's foreboding of what is to happen to Florence. Of its truth he has no doubt, and the only question is how soon will it be answered by the fact. Soon, he says, if it is near to the morning that we dream true dreams—morning being the season of waking reality in which dreams are accomplished.

[670] *Even Prato*: A small neighbouring city, much under the influence of Florence, and somewhat oppressed by it. The commentators reckon up the disasters that afflicted Florence in the first years of the fourteenth century, between the date of Dante's journey and the time he wrote—fires, falls of bridges, and civil strife. But such misfortunes were too much in keeping with the usual course of Florentine history to move Dante thus deeply in the retrospect; and as he speaks here in his own person the 'soon' is more naturally counted from the time at which he writes than from the date assigned by him to his pilgrimage. He is looking forward to the period when his own return in triumph to Florence was to be prepared by grievous national reverses; and, as a patriot, he feels that he cannot be wholly reconciled by his private advantage to the public misfortune. But it was all only a dream.

[671] *Some while ago*: See note, *Inf.* xxiv. 79.

[672] *'Mong splinters, etc.*: They cross the wall or barrier between the Seventh and Eighth Bolgias. From *Inf.* xxiv. 63 we have learned that the rib of rock, on the line of which they are now proceeding, with its arches which overhang the various Bolgias, is rougher and worse to follow than that by which they began their passage towards the centre of Malebolge.

[673] *Happy star*: See note, *Inf.* xv. 55. Dante seems to have been uncertain what credence to give to the claims of astrology. In a passage of the *Purgatorio* (xvi. 67) he tries to establish that whatever influence the stars may possess over us we can never, except with our own consent, be influenced by them to evil.—His sorrow here, as elsewhere, is not wholly a feeling of pity for the suffering shades, but is largely mingled with misgivings for himself. The punishment of those to whose sins he feels no inclination he always beholds with equanimity. Here, as he looks down upon the false counsellors and considers what temptations there are to misapply intellectual gifts, he is smitten with dread lest his lot should one day be cast in that dismal valley and he find cause to regret that the talent of genius was ever committed to him. The memory even of what he saw makes him recollect himself and resolve to be wary. Then, as if to justify the claim to superior powers thus clearly implied, there comes a passage which in the original is of uncommon beauty.

[674] *Field and vineyard*: These lines, redolent of the sweet Tuscan midsummer gloaming, give us amid the horrors of Malebolge something like the breath of fresh air the peasant lingers to enjoy. It may be noted that in Italy the village is often found perched above the more fertile land, on a site originally chosen with a view to security from attack. So that here the peasant is at home from his labour.

[675] *And yet a sinner, etc.*: The false counsellors who for selfish ends hid their true minds and misused their intellectual light to lead others astray are for ever hidden each in his own wandering flame.

[676] *Eteocles*: Son of Œdipus and twin brother of Polynices. The brothers slew one another, and were placed on the same funeral pile, the flame of which clove into two as if to image the discord that had existed between them (*Theb.* xii.).

[677] *And Diomedes*: The two are associated in deeds of blood and guile at the siege of Troy.

[678] *The Romans' noble seed*: The trick of the wooden horse led to the capture of Troy, and that led Æneas to wander forth on the adventures that ended in the settlement of the Trojans in Italy.

[679] *Deïdamia*: That Achilles might be kept from joining the Greek expedition to Troy he was sent by his mother to the court of Lycomedes, father of Deïdamia. Ulysses lured him away from his hiding-place and from Deïdamia, whom he had made a mother.

[680] *The Palladium*: The Trojan sacred image of Pallas, stolen by Ulysses and Diomed (*Æn.* ii.). Ulysses is here upon his own ground.

[681] *They were Greek*: Some find here an allusion to Dante's ignorance of the Greek language and literature. But Virgil addresses them in the Lombard dialect of Italian (*Inf.* xxvii. 21). He acts as spokesman because those ancient Greeks were all so haughty that to a common modern mortal they would have nothing to say. He, as the author of the *Æneid*, has a special claim on their good-nature. It is but seldom that the shades are told who Virgil is, and never directly. Here Ulysses may infer it from the mention of the 'lofty verse.'

[682] *From Circe*: It is Ulysses that speaks.

[683] *The open main*: The Mediterranean as distinguished from the Ægean.

[684] *Which ne'er deserted me*: There seems no reason for supposing, with Philalethes, that Ulysses is here represented as sailing on his last voyage from the island of Circe and not from Ithaca. Ulysses, on the contrary, represents himself as breaking away afresh from all the ties of home. According to Homer, Ulysses had lost all his companions ere he returned to Ithaca; and in the *Odyssey* Tiresias prophesies to him that his last wanderings are to be inland. But any acquaintance that Dante had with Homer can only have been vague and fragmentary. He may have founded his narrative of how Ulysses ended his days upon some floating legend; or, eager to fill up what he took to be a blank in the world of imagination, he may have drawn wholly on his own creative power. In any case it is his Ulysses who, through the version of him given by a living poet, is most familiar to the English reader.

[685] *The mighty main*: The Atlantic Ocean. They bear to the left as they sail, till their course is due south, and crossing the Equator, they find themselves under the strange skies of the southern hemisphere. For months they have seen no land.

[686] *A lofty mountain*: This is the Mountain of Purgatory, according to Dante's geography antipodal to Jerusalem, and the only land in the southern hemisphere.

[687] *As pleased Another*: Ulysses is proudly resigned to the failure of his enterprise, 'for he was Greek.'

Canto XXVII.

Now, having first erect and silent grown

    (For it would say no more), from us the flame,

    The Poet sweet consenting,[688] had moved on;

And then our eyes were turned to one that came[689]

    Behind it on the way, by sounds that burst

    Out of its crest in a confusèd stream.

As the Sicilian bull,[690] which bellowed first

With his lamenting—and it was but right—
    Who had prepared it with his tools accurst,[691]
Roared with the howlings of the tortured wight,
    So that although constructed all of brass
    Yet seemed it pierced with anguish to the height;
So, wanting road and vent by which to pass
    Up through the flame, into the flame's own speech
    The woeful language all converted was.
But when the words at length contrived to reach
    The top, while hither thither shook the crest
    As moved the tongue[692] at utterance of each,
We heard: 'Oh thou, to whom are now addressed
    My words, who spakest now in Lombard phrase:
    "Depart;[693] of thee I nothing more request."
Though I be late arrived, yet of thy grace
    Let it not irk thee here a while to stay:
    It irks not me, yet, as thou seest, I blaze.
If lately to this world devoid of day
    From that sweet Latian land thou art come down
    Whence all my guilt I bring, declare and say
Has now Romagna peace? because my own
    Native abode was in the mountain land
    'Tween springs[694] of Tiber and Urbino town.'
While I intent and bending low did stand,
    My Leader, as he touched me on the side,
    'Speak thou, for he is Latian,' gave command.
Whereon without delay I thus replied—
    Because already[695] was my speech prepared:
    'Soul, that down there dost in concealment 'bide,
In thy Romagna[696] wars have never spared
    And spare not now in tyrants' hearts to rage;
    But when I left it there was none declared.
No change has fallen Ravenna[697] for an age.
    There, covering Cervia too with outspread wing,
    Polenta's Eagle guards his heritage.
Over the city[698] which long suffering
    Endured, and Frenchmen slain on Frenchmen rolled,
    The Green Paws[699] once again protection fling.
The Mastiffs of Verrucchio,[700] young and old,
    Who to Montagna[701] brought such evil cheer,
    Still clinch their fangs where they were wont to hold.
Cities,[702] Lamone and Santerno near,
    The Lion couched in white are governed by
    Which changes party with the changing year.
And that to which the Savio[703] wanders nigh
    As it is set 'twixt mountain and champaign
    Lives now in freedom now 'neath tyranny.

But who thou art I to be told am fain:
    Be not more stubborn than we others found,
    As thou on earth illustrious wouldst remain.'
When first the fire a little while had moaned
    After its manner, next the pointed crest
    Waved to and fro; then in this sense breathed sound:
'If I believed my answer were addressed
    To one that earthward shall his course retrace,
    This flame should forthwith altogether rest.
But since[704] none ever yet out of this place
    Returned alive, if all be true I hear,
    I yield thee answer fearless of disgrace.
I was a warrior, then a Cordelier;[705]
    Thinking thus girt to purge away my stain:
    And sure my hope had met with answer clear
Had not the High Priest[706]—ill with him remain!
    Plunged me anew into my former sin:
    And why and how, I would to thee make plain.
While I the frame of bones and flesh was in
    My mother gave me, all the deeds I wrought
    Were fox-like and in no wise leonine.
Of every wile and hidden way I caught
    The secret trick, and used them with such sleight
    That all the world with fame of it was fraught.
When I perceived I had attainèd quite
    The time of life when it behoves each one
    To furl his sails and coil his cordage tight,
Sorrowing for deeds I had with pleasure done,
    Contrite and shriven, I religious grew.
    Ah, wretched me! and well it was begun
But for the Chieftain of the Pharisees new,[707]
    Then waging war hard by the Lateran,
    And not with Saracen nor yet with Jew;
For Christian[708] were his enemies every man,
    And none had at the siege of Acre been
    Or trafficked in the Empire of Soldàn.
His lofty office he held cheap, and e'en
    His Sacred Orders and the cord I wore,
    Which used[709] to make the wearers of it lean.
As from Soracte[710] Constantine of yore
    Sylvester called to cure his leprosy,
    I as a leech was called this man before
To cure him of his fever which ran high;
    My counsel he required, but I stood dumb,
    For drunken all his words appeared to be.
He said; "For fear be in thy heart no room;
    Beforehand I absolve thee, but declare

How Palestrina I may overcome.
Heaven I unlock, as thou art well aware,
    And close at will; because the keys are twin
    My predecessor[711] was averse to bear."
Then did his weighty reasoning on me win
    Till to be silent seemed the worst of all;
    And, "Father," I replied, "since from this sin
Thou dost absolve me into which I fall—
    The scant performance[712] of a promise wide
    Will yield thee triumph in thy lofty stall."
Francis came for me soon as e'er I died;
    But one of the black Cherubim was there
    And "Take him not, nor rob me of him" cried,
"For him of right among my thralls I bear
    Because he offered counsel fraudulent;
    Since when I've had him firmly by the hair.
None is absolved unless he first repent;
    Nor can repentance house with purpose ill,
    For this the contradiction doth prevent."
Ah, wretched me! How did I shrinking thrill
    When clutching me he sneered: "Perhaps of old
    Thou didst not think[713] I had in logic skill."
He carried me to Minos:[714] Minos rolled
    His tail eight times round his hard back; in ire
    Biting it fiercely, ere of me he told:
"Among the sinners of the shrouding fire!"
    Therefore am I, where thou beholdest, lost;
    And, sore at heart, go clothed in such attire.'
What he would say thus ended by the ghost,
    Away from us the moaning flame did glide
    While to and fro its pointed horn was tossed.
But we passed further on, I and my Guide,
    Along the cliff to where the arch is set
    O'er the next moat, where paying they reside,
As schismatics who whelmed themselves in debt.

Footnotes

[688] *Consenting*: See line 21.
[689] *One that came*: This is the fire-enveloped shade of Guido of Montefeltro, the colloquy with whom occupies the whole of the Canto.
[690] *The Sicilian bull*: Perillus, an Athenian, presented Phalaris, the tyrant of Agrigentum, with a brazen bull so constructed that when it was heated from below the cries of the victim it contained were converted into the bellowing of a bull. The first trial of the invention was made upon the artist.
[691] *Accurst*: Not in the original. 'Rime in English hath such scarcity,' as Chaucer says.

[692] *As moved the tongue, etc.*: The shade being enclosed in the hollow fire all his words are changed into a sound like the roaring of a flame. At last, when an opening has been worked through the crested point, the speech becomes articulate.
[693] *Depart, etc.*: One at least of the words quoted as having been used by Virgil is Lombard. There is something very quaint in making him use the Lombard dialect of Dante's time.
[694] *'Tween springs, etc.*: Montefeltro lies between Urbino and the mountain where the Tiber has its source.
[695] *Already*: Dante knew that Virgil would refer to him for an answer to Guido's question, bearing as it did on modern Italian affairs.
[696] *Romagna*: The district of Italy lying on the Adriatic, south of the Po and east of Tuscany, of which Bologna and the cities named in the text were the principal towns. During the last quarter of the thirteenth century it was the scene of constant wars promoted in the interest of the Church, which claimed Romagna as the gift of the Emperor Rudolf, and in that of the great nobles of the district, who while using the Guelf and Ghibeline war-cries aimed at nothing but the lordship of the various cities. Foremost among these nobles was he with whose shade Dante speaks. Villani calls him 'the most sagacious and accomplished warrior of his time in Italy' (*Cronica*, vii. 80). He was possessed of lands of his own near Forlì and Cesena, and was lord in turn of many of the Romagnese cities. On the whole he appears to have remained true to his Ghibeline colours in spite of Papal fulminations, although once and again he was reconciled to the Church; on the last occasion in 1294. In the years immediately before this he had greatly distinguished himself as a wise governor and able general in the service of the Ghibeline Pisa—or rather as the paid lord of it.
[697] *Ravenna*: Ravenna and the neighbouring town of Cervia were in 1300 under the lordship of members of the Polenta family—the father and brothers of the ill-fated Francesca (*Inf.* v.). Their arms were an eagle, half white on an azure and half red on a gold field. It was in the court of the generous Guido, son of one of these brothers, that Dante was to find his last refuge and to die.
[698] *Over the city, etc.*: Forlì. The reference is to one of the most brilliant feats of war performed by Guido of Montefeltro. Frenchmen formed great part of an army sent in 1282 against Forlì by the Pope, Martin IV., himself a Frenchman. Guido, then lord of the city, led them into a trap and overthrew them with great slaughter. Like most men of his time Guido was a believer in astrology, and is said on this occasion to have acted on the counsel of Guido Bonatti, mentioned among the diviners in the Fourth Bolgia (*Inf.* xx. 118).
[699] *The Green Paws*: In 1300 the Ordelaffi were lords of Forlì. Their arms were a green lion on a gold ground. During the first years of his exile Dante had to do with Scarpetta degli Ordelaffi, under whose command the exiled Florentines put themselves for a time, and there is even a tradition that he acted as his secretary.
[700] *The Mastiffs of Verrucchio*: Verrucchio was the castle of the Malatestas, lords of Rimini, called the Mastiffs on account of their cruel tenacity. The elder was the father of Francesca's husband and lover; the younger was a brother of these.
[701] *Montagna*: Montagna de' Parcitati, one of a Ghibeline family that contested superiority in Rimini with the Guelf Malatestas, was taken prisoner by guile and committed by the old Mastiff to the keeping of the young one, whose fangs were set in him to such purpose that he soon died in his dungeon.

[702] *Cities, etc.*: Imola and Faenza, situated on the rivers named in the text. Mainardo Pagani, lord of these towns, had for arms an azure lion on a white field. During his minority he was a ward of the Commonwealth of Florence. By his cunning and daring he earned the name of the Demon (*Purg.* xiv. 118). He died at Imola in 1302, and was buried in the garb of a monk of Vallombrosa. Like most of his neighbours he changed his party as often as his interest required. He was a Guelf in Florence and a Ghibeline in Romagna, say some.

[703] *Savio*: Cesena, on the Savio, was distinguished among the cities of Romagna by being left more frequently than the others were to manage its own affairs. The Malatestas and Montefeltros were in turn possessed of the tyranny of it.

[704] *But since, etc.*: The shades, being enveloped in fire, are unable to see those with whom they speak; and so Guido does not detect in Dante the signs of a living man, but takes him to be like himself a denizen of Inferno. He would not have the truth regarding his fate to be known in the world, where he is supposed to have departed life in the odour of sanctity. Dante's promise to refresh his fame he either regards as meaningless, or as one made without the power of fulfilling it. Dante leaves him in his error, for he is there to learn all he can, and not to bandy personal confessions with the shades.

[705] *A Cordelier*: In 1296 Guido entered the Franciscan Order. He died in 1298, but where is not known; some authorities say at Venice and others at Assisi. Benvenuto tells: 'He was often seen begging his bread in Ancona, where he was buried. Many good deeds are related of him, and I cherish a sweet hope that he may have been saved.'

[706] *The High Priest*: Boniface VIII.

[707] *The Pharisees new*: The members of the Court of Rome. Saint Jerome calls the dignified Roman clergy of his day 'the Senate of the Pharisees.'

[708] *For Christian, etc.*: The foes of Boniface, here spoken of, were the Cardinals Peter and James Colonna. He destroyed their palace in Rome (1297) and carried the war against them to their country seat at Palestrina, the ancient Præneste, then a great stronghold. Dante here bitterly blames Boniface for instituting a crusade against Christians at a time when, by the recent loss of Acre, the gate of the Holy Land had been lost to Christendom. The Colonnas were innocent, too, of the crime of supplying the Infidel with munitions of war—a crime condemned by the Lateran Council of 1215, and by Boniface himself, who excluded those guilty of it from the benefits of the great Jubilee of 1300.

[709] *Which used, etc.*: In former times, when the rule of the Order was faithfully observed. Dante charges the Franciscans with degeneracy in the *Paradiso*, xi. 124.

[710] *From Soracte*: Referring to the well-known legend. The fee for the cure was the fabulous Donation. See *Inf.* xix. 115.

[711] *My predecessor*: Celestine v. See *Inf.* iii. 60.

[712] *The scant performance, etc.*: That Guido gave such counsel is related by a contemporary chronicler: 'The Pope said: Tell me how to get the better of those mine enemies, thou who art so knowing in these things. Then he answered: Promise much, and perform little; which he did.' But it seems odd that the wily and unscrupulous Boniface should have needed to put himself to school for such a simple lesson.

[713] *Thou didst not think, etc.*: Guido had forgot that others could reason besides the Pope. With regard to the inefficacy of the Papal absolution an old commentator says, following Origen:

'The Popes that walk in the footsteps of Peter have this power of binding and loosing; but only such as do so walk.' But on Dante's scheme of what fixes the fate of the soul absolution matters little to save, or priestly curses to damnify. See *Purg.* iii. 133. It is unfeigned repentance that can help a sinner even at the last; and it is remarkable that in the case of Buonconte, the gallant son of this same Guido, the infernal angel who comes for him as he expires complains that he has been cheated of his victim by one poor tear. See *Purg.* v. 88, etc. Why then is no indulgence shown in Dante's court to Guido, who might well have been placed in Purgatory and made to have repented effectually of this his last sin? That Dante had any personal grudge against him we can hardly think. In the Fourth Book of the *Convito* (written, according to Fraticelli, in 1297), he calls him 'our most noble Guido Montefeltrano;' and praises him as one of the wise and noble souls that refuse to run with full sails into the port of death, but furl the sails of their worldly undertakings, and, relinquishing all earthly pleasures and business, give themselves up in their old age to a religious life. Either, then, he sets Guido here in order that he may have a modern false counsellor worthy to be ranked with Ulysses; or because, on longer experience, he had come to reprobate more keenly the abuse of the Franciscan habit; or, most likely of all, that he might, even at the cost of Guido, load the hated memory of Boniface with another reproach.

[714] *Minos*: Here we have Minos represented in the act of pronouncing judgment in words as well as by the figurative rolling of his tail around his body (*Inf.* v. 11).

Canto XXVIII.

Could any, even in words unclogged by rhyme
    Recount the wounds that now I saw,[715] and blood,
    Although he aimed at it time after time?
Here every tongue must fail of what it would,
    Because our human speech and powers of thought
    To grasp so much come short in aptitude.
If all the people were together brought
    Who in Apulia,[716] land distressed by fate,
    Made lamentation for the bloodshed wrought
By Rome;[717] and in that war procrastinate[718]
    When the large booty of the rings was won,
    As Livy writes whose every word has weight;
With those on whom such direful deeds were done
    When Robert Guiscard[719] they as foes assailed;
    And those of whom still turns up many a bone
At Ceperan,[720] where each Apulian failed
    In faith; and those at Tagliacozzo[721] strewed,
    Where old Alardo, not by arms, prevailed;
And each his wounds and mutilations showed,
    Yet would they far behind by those be left
    Who had the vile Ninth Bolgia for abode.
No cask, of middle stave or end bereft,
    E'er gaped like one I saw the rest among,
    Slit from the chin all downward to the cleft.

Between his legs his entrails drooping hung;
 The pluck and that foul bag were evident
 Which changes what is swallowed into dung.
And while I gazed upon him all intent,
 Opening his breast his eyes on me he set,
 Saying: 'Behold, how by myself I'm rent!
See how dismembered now is Mahomet![722]
 Ali[723] in front of me goes weeping too;
 With visage from the chin to forelock split.
By all the others whom thou seest there grew
 Scandal and schism while yet they breathed the day;
 Because of which they now are cloven through.
There stands behind a devil on the way,
 Us with his sword thus cruelly to trim:
 He cleaves again each of our company
As soon as we complete the circuit grim;
 Because the wounds of each are healed outright
 Or e'er anew he goes in front of him.
But who art thou that peerest from the height,
 It may be putting off to reach the pain
 Which shall the crimes confessed by thee requite?'
'Death has not seized him yet, nor is he ta'en
 To torment for his sins,' my Master said;
 'But, that he may a full experience gain,
By me, a ghost, 'tis doomed he should be led
 Down the Infernal circles, round on round;
 And what I tell thee is the truth indeed.'
A hundred shades and more, to whom the sound
 Had reached, stood in the moat to mark me well,
 Their pangs forgot; so did the words astound.
'Let Fra Dolcin[724] provide, thou mayst him tell—
 Thou, who perchance ere long shalt sunward go—
 Unless he soon would join me in this Hell,
Much food, lest aided by the siege of snow
 The Novarese should o'er him victory get,
 Which otherwise to win they would be slow.'
While this was said to me by Mahomet
 One foot he held uplifted; to the ground
 He let it fall, and so he forward set
Next, one whose throat was gaping with a wound,
 Whose nose up to the brows away was sheared
 And on whose head a single ear was found,
At me, with all the others, wondering peered;
 And, ere the rest, an open windpipe made,
 The outside of it all with crimson smeared.
'O thou, not here because of guilt,' he said;
 'And whom I sure on Latian ground did know

Unless by strong similitude betrayed,
Upon Pier da Medicin[725] bestow
 A thought, shouldst thou revisit the sweet plain
 That from Vercelli[726] slopes to Marcabò.
And make thou known to Fano's worthiest twain—
 To Messer Guido and to Angiolel—
 They, unless foresight here be wholly vain,
Thrown overboard in gyve and manacle
 Shall drown fast by Cattolica, as planned
 By treachery of a tyrant fierce and fell.
Between Majolica[727] and Cyprus strand
 A blacker crime did Neptune never spy
 By pirates wrought, or even by Argives' hand.
The traitor[728] who is blinded of an eye,
 Lord of the town which of my comrades one
 Had been far happier ne'er to have come nigh,
To parley with him will allure them on,
 Then so provide, against Focara's[729] blast
 No need for them of vow or orison.'
And I: 'Point out and tell, if wish thou hast
 To get news of thee to the world conveyed,
 Who rues that e'er his eyes thereon were cast?'
On a companion's jaw his hand he laid,
 And shouted, while the mouth he open prised:
 ''Tis this one here by whom no word is said.
He quenched all doubt in Cæsar, and advised—
 Himself an outlaw—that a man equipped
 For strife ran danger if he temporised.'
Alas, to look on, how downcast and hipped
 Curio,[730] once bold in counsel, now appeared;
 With gorge whence by the roots the tongue was ripped.
Another one, whose hands away were sheared,
 In the dim air his stumps uplifted high
 So that his visage was with blood besmeared,
And, 'Mosca,[731] too, remember!' loud did cry,
 'Who said, ah me! "A thing once done is done!"
 An evil seed for all in Tuscany.'
I added: 'Yea, and death to every one
 Of thine!' whence he, woe piled on woe, his way
 Went like a man with grief demented grown.
But I to watch the gang made longer stay,
 And something saw which I should have a fear,
 Without more proof, so much as even to say,
But that my conscience bids me have good cheer—
 The comrade leal whose friendship fortifies
 A man beneath the mail of purpose clear.
I saw in sooth (still seems it 'fore mine eyes),

A headless trunk; with that sad company
   It forward moved, and on the selfsame wise.
The severed head, clutched by the hair, swung free
   Down from the fist, yea, lantern-like hung down;
   Staring at us it murmured: 'Wretched me!'
A lamp he made of head-piece once his own;
   And he was two in one and one in two;
   But how, to Him who thus ordains is known.
Arrived beneath the bridge and full in view,
   With outstretched arm his head he lifted high
   To bring his words well to us. These I knew:
'Consider well my grievous penalty,
   Thou who, though still alive, art visiting
   The people dead; what pain with this can vie?
In order that to earth thou news mayst bring
   Of me, that I'm Bertrand de Born[732] know well,
   Who gave bad counsel to the Younger King.
I son and sire made each 'gainst each rebel:
   David and Absalom were fooled not more
   By counsels of the false Ahithophel.
Kinsmen so close since I asunder tore,
   Severed, alas! I carry now my brain
   From what[733] it grew from in this trunk of yore:
And so I prove the law of pain for pain.'[734]

Footnotes

[715] *That now I saw*: In the Ninth Bolgia, on which he is look-ing down, and in which are punished the sowers of discord in church and state.

[716] *Apulia*: The south-eastern district of Italy, owing to its situ-ation a frequent battle-field in ancient and modern times.

[717] *Rome*: 'Trojans' in most MSS.; and then the Romans are described as descended from Trojans. The reference may be to the defeat of the Apulians with considerable slaughter by P. Decius Mus, or to their losses in general in the course of the Samnite war.

[718] *War procrastinate*: The second Punic war lasted fully fifteen years, and in the course of it the battle of Cannæ was gained by Hannibal, where so many Roman knights fell that the spoil of rings amounted to a peck.

[719] *Guiscard*: One of the Norman conquerors of the regions which up to our own time constituted the kingdom of Naples. In Apulia he did much fighting against Lombards, Saracens, and Greeks. He is found by Dante in Paradise among those who fought for the faith (*Par.* xviii. 48). His death happened in Cephalonia in 1085, at the age of seventy, when he was engaged on an expedition against Constantinople.

[720] *Ceperan*: In the swift and decisive campaign undertaken by Charles of Anjou against Manfred, King of Sicily and Naples, the first victory was obtained at Ceperano; but it was won owing to the treachery of Manfred's lieutenant, and not by the sword. The true battle was fought at Benevento (*Purg.* iii. 128). Ceperano may be named by Dante as the field where the defeat of Manfred

was virtually begun, and where the Apulians first failed in loy-alty to their gallant king. Dante was a year old at the time of Manfred's overthrow (1266).

[721] *Tagliacozzo*: The crown Charles had won from Manfred he had to defend against Manfred's nephew Conradin (grandson and last representative of Frederick II. and the legitimate heir to the kingdom of Sicily), whom, in 1268, he defeated near Tagliacozzo in the Abruzzi. He made his victory the more complete by acting on the advice of Alardo or Erard de Valery, an old Crusader, to hold good part of his force in reserve. Charles wrote to the Pope that the slaughter was so great as far to exceed that at Benevento. The feet of all the low-born prisoners not slain on the field were cut off, while the gentlemen were beheaded or hanged.

[722] *Mahomet*: It has been objected to Dante by M. Littré that he treats Mahomet, the founder of a new religion, as a mere schismatic. The wonder would have been had he dwelt on the good qualities of the Prophet at a time when Islam still threatened Europe. He goes on the fact that Mahomet and his followers rent great part of the East and South from Christendom; and for this the Prophet is represented as being mutilated in a sorer degree than the other schismatics.

[723] *Ali*: Son-in-law of Mahomet.

[724] *Fra Dolcin*: At the close of the thirteenth century, Boniface being Pope, the general discontent with the corruption of the higher clergy found expression in the north of Italy in the foun-dation of a new sect, whose leader was Fra Dolcino. What he chiefly was—enthusiast, reformer, or impostor—it is impossible to ascertain; all we know of him being derived from writers in the Papal interest. Among other crimes he was charged with that of teaching the lawfulness of telling an Inquisitor a lie to save your life, and with prophesying the advent of a pious Pope. A holy war on a small scale was preached against him. After suffering the extremities of famine, snowed up as he was among the moun-tains, he was taken prisoner and cruelly put to death (1307). It may have been in order to save himself from being suspected of sympathy with him, that Dante, whose hatred of Boniface and the New Pharisees was equal to Dolcino's, provides for him by anticipation a place with Mahomet.

[725] *Pier da Medicin*: Medicina is in the territory of Bologna. Piero is said to have stirred up dissensions between the Polentas of Ravenna and the Malatestas of Rimini.

[726] *From Vercelli, etc.*: From the district of Vercelli to where the castle of Marcabò once stood, at the mouth of the Po, is a distance of two hundred miles. The plain is Lombardy.

[727] *Majolica, etc.*: On all the Mediterranean, from Cyprus in the east to Majorca in the west.

[728] *The traitor, etc.*: The one-eyed traitor is Malatesta, lord of Rimini, the Young Mastiff of the preceding Canto. He invited the two chief citizens of Fano, named in the text, to hold a conference with him, and procured that on their way they should be pitched overboard opposite the castle of Cattolica, which stood between Fano and Rimini. This is said to have happened in 1304.

[729] *Focara*: The name of a promontory near Cattolica, subject to squalls. The victims were never to double the headland.

[730] *Curio*: The Roman Tribune who, according to Lucan—the incident is not historically correct—found Cæsar hesitating whether to cross the Rubicon, and advised him: *Tolle moras: semper nocuit differre paratis*. 'No delay! when men are ready they always suffer by putting off.' The passage of the Rubicon was counted as the beginning of the Civil War.—Curio gets scant

justice, seeing that in Dante's view Cæsar in all he did was only carrying out the Divine purpose regarding the Empire.

[731] *Mosca*: In 1215 one of the Florentine family of the Buondelmonti jilted a daughter of the Amidei. When these with their friends met to take counsel touching revenge for the insult, Mosca, one of the Uberti or of the Lamberti, gave his opinion in the proverb, *Cosa fatta ha capo*: 'A thing once done is done with.' The hint was approved of, and on the following Easter morning the young Buondelmonte, as, mounted on a white steed and dressed in white he rode across the Ponte Vecchio, was dragged to the ground and cruelly slain. All the great Florentine families took sides in the feud, and it soon widened into the civil war between Florentine Guelf and Ghibeline.

[732] *Bertrand de Born*: Is mentioned by Dante in his Treatise *De Vulgari Eloquio*, ii. 2, as specially the poet of warlike deeds. He was a Gascon noble who used his poetical gift very much to stir up strife. For patron he had the Prince Henry, son of Henry II. of England. Though Henry never came to the throne he was, during his father's lifetime, crowned as his successor, and was known as the young King. After the death of the Prince, Bertrand was taken prisoner by the King, and, according to the legend, was loaded with favours because he had been so true a friend to his young master. That he had a turn for fomenting discord is shown by his having also led a revolt in Aquitaine against Richard I.—All the old MSS. and all the earlier commentators read *Re Giovanni*, King John; *Re Giovane*, the young King, being a comparatively modern emendation. In favour of adopting this it may be mentioned that in his poems Bertrand calls Prince Henry *lo Reys joves*, the young King; that it was Henry and not John that was his friend and patron; and that in the old *Cento Novelle* Henry is described as the young King: in favour of the older reading, that John as well as his brother was a rebel to Henry; and that the line is hurt by the change from *Giovanni* to *Giovane*. Considering that Dante almost certainly wrote *Giovanni* it seems most reasonable to suppose that he may have confounded the *Re Giovane* with King John.

[733] *From what, etc.*: The spinal cord, as we should now say, though Dante may have meant the heart.

[734] *Pain for pain*: In the City of Dis we found the heresiarchs, those who lead others to think falsely. The lower depth of the Malebolge is reserved for such as needlessly rend any Divinely-constituted order of society, civil or religious. Conduct counts more with Dante than opinion—in this case.

Canto XXIX.

The many folk and wounds of divers kind
    Had flushed mine eyes and set them on the flow,
    Till I to weep and linger had a mind;
But Virgil said to me: 'Why gazing so?
    Why still thy vision fastening on the crew
    Of dismal shades dismembered there below?
Thou didst not[735] thus the other Bolgias view:
    Think, if to count them be thine enterprise,
    The valley circles twenty miles and two.[736]
Beneath our feet the moon[737] already lies;
    The time[738] wears fast away to us decreed;

And greater things than these await thine eyes.'
I answered swift: 'Hadst thou but given heed
    To why it was my looks were downward bent,
    To yet more stay thou mightest have agreed.'
My Guide meanwhile was moving, and I went
    Behind him and continued to reply,
    Adding: 'Within the moat on which intent
I now was gazing with such eager eye
    I trow a spirit weeps, one of my kin,
    The crime whose guilt is rated there so high.'
Then said the Master: 'Henceforth hold thou in
    Thy thoughts from wandering to him: new things claim
    Attention now, so leave him with his sin.
Him saw I at thee from the bridge-foot aim
    A threatening finger, while he made thee known;
    Geri del Bello[739] heard I named his name.
But, at the time, thou wast with him alone
    Engrossed who once held Hautefort,[740] nor the place
    Didst look at where he was; so passed he on.'
'O Leader mine! death violent and base,
    And not avenged as yet,' I made reply,
    'By any of his partners in disgrace,
Made him disdainful; therefore went he by
    And spake not with me, if I judge aright;
    Which does the more my ruth[741] intensify.'
So we conversed till from the cliff we might
    Of the next valley have had prospect good
    Down to the bottom, with but clearer light.[742]
When we above the inmost Cloister stood
    Of Malebolge, and discerned the crew
    Of such as there compose the Brotherhood,[743]
So many lamentations pierced me through—
    And barbed with pity all the shafts were sped—
    My open palms across my ears I drew.
From Valdichiana's[744] every spital bed
    All ailments to September from July,
    With all in Maremma and Sardinia[745] bred,
Heaped in one pit a sickness might supply
    Like what was here; and from it rose a stink
    Like that which comes from limbs that putrefy.
Then we descended by the utmost brink
    Of the long ridge[746]—leftward once more we fell—
    Until my vision, quickened now, could sink
Deeper to where Justice infallible,
    The minister of the Almighty Lord,
    Chastises forgers doomed on earth[747] to Hell.
Ægina[748] could no sadder sight afford,

As I believe (when all the people ailed

And all the air was so with sickness stored,

Down to the very worms creation failed

And died, whereon the pristine folk once more,

As by the poets is for certain held,

From seed of ants their family did restore),

Than what was offered by that valley black

With plague-struck spirits heaped upon the floor.

Supine some lay, each on the other's back

Or stomach; and some crawled with crouching gait

For change of place along the doleful track.

Speechless we moved with step deliberate,

With eyes and ears on those disease crushed down

Nor left them power to lift their bodies straight.

I saw two sit, shoulder to shoulder thrown

As plate holds plate up to be warmed, from head

Down to the feet with scurf and scab o'ergrown.

Nor ever saw I curry-comb so plied

By varlet with his master standing by,

Or by one kept unwillingly from bed,

As I saw each of these his scratchers ply

Upon himself; for nought else now avails

Against the itch which plagues them furiously.

The scab[749] they tore and loosened with their nails,

As with a knife men use the bream to strip,

Or any other fish with larger scales.

'Thou, that thy mail dost with thy fingers rip,'

My Guide to one of them began to say,

'And sometimes dost with them as pincers nip,

Tell, is there any here from Italy

Among you all, so may thy nails suffice

For this their work to all eternity.'[750]

'Latians are both of us in this disguise

Of wretchedness,' weeping said one of those;

'But who art thou, demanding on this wise?'

My Guide made answer: 'I am one who goes

Down with this living man from steep to steep

That I to him Inferno may disclose.'

Then broke their mutual prop; trembling with deep

Amazement each turned to me, with the rest

To whom his words had echoed in the heap.

Me the good Master cordially addressed:

'Whate'er thou hast a mind to ask them, say.'

And since he wished it, thus I made request:

'So may remembrance of you not decay

Within the upper world out of the mind

Of men, but flourish still for many a day,

As ye shall tell your names and what your kind:

Let not your vile, disgusting punishment

To full confession make you disinclined.'

'An Aretine,[751] I to the stake was sent

By Albert of Siena,' one confessed,

'But came not here through that for which I went

To death. 'Tis true I told him all in jest,

I through the air could float in upward gyre;

And he, inquisitive and dull at best,

Did full instruction in the art require:

I could not make him Dædalus,[752] so then

His second father sent me to the fire.

But to the deepest Bolgia of the ten,

For alchemy which in the world I wrought,

The unerring Minos doomed me.' 'Now were men

E'er found,' I of the Poet asked, 'so fraught

With vanity as are the Sienese?[753]

French vanity to theirs is surely nought.'

The other leper hearing me, to these

My words: 'Omit the Stricca,'[754] swift did shout,

'Who knew his tastes with temperance to please;

And Nicholas,[755] who earliest found out

The lavish custom of the clove-stuffed roast

Within the garden where such seed doth sprout.

Nor count the club[756] where Caccia d' Ascian lost

Vineyards and woods; 'mid whom away did throw

His wit the Abbagliato.[757] But whose ghost

It is, that thou mayst weet, that backs thee so

Against the Sienese, make sharp thine eyes

That thou my countenance mayst surely know.

In me Capocchio's[758] shade thou'lt recognise,

Who forged false coin by means of alchemy:

Thou must remember, if I well surmise,

How I of nature very ape could be.'

Footnotes

[735] *Thou didst not, etc.*: It is a noteworthy feature in the conduct of the Poem that when Dante has once gained sufficient knowledge of any group in the Inferno he at once detaches his mind from it, and, carrying on as little arrear of pity as he can, gives his thoughts to further progress on the journey. The departure here made from his usual behaviour is presently accounted for. Virgil knows why he lingers, but will not seem to approve of the cause.

[736] *Twenty miles and two*: The Ninth Bolgia has a circumference of twenty-two miles, and as the procession of the shades is slow it would indeed involve a protracted halt to wait till all had passed beneath the bridge. Virgil asks ironically if he wishes to count them all. This precise detail, taken along with one of the same kind in the following Canto (line 86), has suggested the

attempt to construct the Inferno to a scale. Dante wisely suffers us to forget, if we will, that—taking the diameter of the earth at 6500 miles, as given by him in the *Convito*—he travels from the surface of the globe to the centre at the rate of more than two miles a minute, counting downward motion alone. It is only when he has come to the lowest rings that he allows himself to give details of size; and probably the mention of the extent of the Ninth Bolgia, which comes on the reader as a surprise, is thrown out in order to impress on the imagination some sense of the enormous extent of the regions through which the pilgrim has already passed. Henceforth he deals in exact measurement.

[737] *The moon*: It is now some time after noon on the Saturday. The last indication of time was at Canto xxi. 112.

[738] *The time, etc.*: Before nightfall they are to complete their exploration of the Inferno, and they will have spent twenty-four hours in it.

[739] *Geri del Bello*: One of the Alighieri, a full cousin of Dante's father. He was guilty of encouraging dissension, say the commentators; which is to be clearly inferred from the place assigned him in Inferno: but they do not agree as to how he met his death, nor do they mention the date of it. 'Not avenged till thirty years after,' says Landino; but does not say if this was after his death or the time at which Dante writes.

[740] *Hautefort*: Bertrand de Born's castle in Gascony.

[741] *My ruth*: Enlightened moralist though Dante is, he yet shows himself man of his age enough to be keenly alive to the extremest claims of kindred; and while he condemns the *vendetta* by the words put into Virgil's mouth, he confesses to a feeling of meanness not to have practised it on behoof of a distant relative. There is a high art in this introduction of Geri del Bello. Had they conferred together Dante must have seemed either cruel or pusillanimous, reproaching or being reproached. As it is, all the poetry of the situation comes out the stronger that they do not meet face to face: the threatening finger, the questions hastily put to Geri by the astonished shades, and his disappearance under the dark vault when by the law of his punishment the sinner can no longer tarry.

[742] *With but clearer light*: They have crossed the rampart dividing the Ninth Bolgia from the Tenth, of which they would now command a view, were it not so dark.

[743] *The Brotherhood*: The word used properly describes the Lay Brothers of a monastery. Philalethes suggests that Dante may regard the devils as the true monks of the monastery of Malebolge. The simile involves no contempt for the monastic life, but is naturally used with reference to those who live secluded and under a fixed rule. He elsewhere speaks of the College of the Hypocrites (*Inf.* xxiii. 91) and of Paradise as the Cloister where Christ is Abbot (*Purg.* xxvi.129).

[744] *Valdichiana*: The district lying between Arezzo and Chiusi; in Dante's time a hotbed of malaria, but now, owing to drainage works promoted by the enlightened Tuscan minister Fossombroni (1823), one of the most fertile and healthy regions of Italy.

[745] *Sardinia*: Had in the middle ages an evil reputation for its fever-stricken air. The Maremma has been already mentioned (*Inf.* xxv.19). In Dante's time it was almost unpeopled.

[746] *The long ridge*: One of the ribs of rock which, like the spokes of a wheel, ran from the periphery to the centre of Malebolge, rising into arches as they crossed each successive Bolgia. The utmost brink is the inner bank of the Tenth and last

Bolgia. To the edge of this moat they descend, bearing as usual to the left hand.

[747] *Doomed on earth, etc.*: 'Whom she here registers.' While they are still on earth their doom is fixed by Divine justice.

[748] *Ægina*: The description is taken from Ovid (*Metam.* vii.).

[749] *The scab, etc.*: As if by an infernal alchemy the matter of the shadowy bodies of these sinners is changed into one loathsome form or another.

[750] *To all eternity*: This may seem a stroke of sarcasm, but is not. Himself a shade, Virgil cannot, like Dante, promise to refresh the memory of the shades on earth, and can only wish for them some slight alleviation of their suffering.

[751] *An Aretine*: Called Griffolino, and burned at Florence or Siena on a charge of heresy. Albert of Siena is said to have been a relative, some say the natural son, of the Bishop of Siena. A man of the name figures as hero in some of Sacchetti's novels, always in a ridiculous light. There seems to be no authentic testimony regarding the incident in the text.

[752] *Dædalus*: Who escaped on wings of his invention from the Cretan Labyrinth he had made and lost himself in.

[753] *The Sienese*: The comparison of these to the French would have the more cogency as Siena boasted of having been founded by the Gauls. 'That vain people,' says Dante of the Sienese in the *Purgatory* (xiii. 151). Among their neighbours they still bear the reputation of light-headedness; also, it ought to be added, of great urbanity.

[754] *The Stricca*: The exception in his favour is ironical, as is that of all the others mentioned.

[755] *Nicholas*: 'The lavish custom of the clove' which he invented is variously described. I have chosen the version which makes it consist of stuffing pheasants with cloves, then very costly.

[756] *The club*: The commentators tell that the two young Sienese nobles above mentioned were members of a society formed for the purpose of living luxuriously together. Twelve of them contributed a fund of above two hundred thousand gold florins; they built a great palace and furnished it magnificently, and launched out into every other sort of extravagance with such assiduity that in a few months their capital was gone. As that amounted to more than a hundred thousand pounds of our money, equal in those days to a million or two, the story must be held to savour of romance. That Dante refers to a prodigal's club that actually existed some time before he wrote we cannot doubt. But it seems uncertain, to say the least, whether the sonnets addressed by the Tuscan poet Folgore da Gemignano to a jovial crew in Siena can be taken as having been inspired by the club Dante speaks of. A translation of them is given by Mr. Rossetti in his *Circle of Dante*. (See Mr. Symonds's *Renaissance*, vol. iv. page 54, *note*, for doubts as to the date of Folgore.)—*Caccia d' Ascian*: Whose short and merry club life cost him his estates near Siena.

[757] *The Abbagliato*: Nothing is known, though a great deal is guessed, about this member of the club. It is enough to know that, having a scant supply of wit, he spent it freely.

[758] *Capocchio*: Some one whom Dante knew. Whether he was a Florentine or a Sienese is not ascertained, but from the strain of his mention of the Sienese we may guess Florentine. He was burned in Siena in 1293.—(Scartazzini.) They had studied together, says the *Anonimo*. Benvenuto tells of him that one Good Friday, while in a cloister, he painted on his nail with marvellous completeness a picture of the crucifixion. Dante came up, and

was lost in wonder, when Capocchio suddenly licked his nail clean—which may be taken for what it is worth.

Canto XXX.

Because of Semele[759] when Juno's ire
    Was fierce 'gainst all that were to Thebes allied,
    As had been proved by many an instance dire;
So mad grew Athamas[760] that when he spied
    His wife as she with children twain drew near,
    Each hand by one encumbered, loud he cried:
'Be now the nets outspread, that I may snare
    Cubs with the lioness at yon strait ground!'
    And stretching claws of all compassion bare
He on Learchus seized and swung him round,
    And shattered him upon a flinty stone;
    Then she herself and the other burden drowned.
And when by fortune was all overthrown
    The Trojans' pride, inordinate before—
    Monarch and kingdom equally undone—
Hecuba,[761] sad and captive, mourning o'er
    Polyxena, when dolorous she beheld
    The body of her darling Polydore
Upon the coast, out of her wits she yelled,
    And spent herself in barking like a hound;
    So by her sorrow was her reason quelled.
But never yet was Trojan fury[762] found,
    Nor that of Thebes, to sting so cruelly
    Brute beasts, far less the human form to wound,
As two pale naked shades were stung, whom I
    Saw biting run, like swine when they escape
    Famished and eager from the empty sty.
Capocchio[763] coming up to, in his nape
    One fixed his fangs, and hauling at him made
    His belly on the stony pavement scrape.
The Aretine[764] who stood, still trembling, said:
    'That imp is Gianni Schicchi,[765] and he goes
    Rabid, thus trimming others.' 'O!' I prayed,
'So may the teeth of the other one of those
    Not meet in thee, as, ere she pass from sight,
    Thou freely shalt the name of her disclose.'
And he to me: 'That is the ancient sprite
    Of shameless Myrrha,[766] who let liking rise
    For him who got her, past all bounds of right.
As, to transgress with him, she in disguise
    Came near to him deception to maintain;
    So he, departing yonder from our eyes,
That he the Lady of the herd might gain,

Bequeathed his goods by formal testament
    While he Buoso Donate's[767] form did feign.'
And when the rabid couple from us went,
    Who all this time by me were being eyed,
    Upon the rest ill-starred I grew intent;
And, fashioned like a lute, I one espied,
    Had he been only severed at the place
    Where at the groin men's lower limbs divide.
The grievous dropsy, swol'n with humours base,
    Which every part of true proportion strips
    Till paunch grows out of keeping with the face,
Compelled him widely ope to hold his lips
    Like one in fever who, by thirst possessed,
    Has one drawn up while the other chinward slips.
'O ye![768] who by no punishment distressed,
    Nor know I why, are in this world of dool,'
    He said; 'a while let your attention rest
On Master Adam[769] here of misery full.
    Living, I all I wished enjoyed at will;
    Now lust I for a drop of water cool.
The water-brooks that down each grassy hill
    Of Casentino to the Arno fall
    And with cool moisture all their courses fill—
Always, and not in vain, I see them all;
    Because the vision of them dries me more
    Than the disease 'neath which my face grows small.
For rigid justice, me chastising sore,
    Can in the place I sinned at motive find
    To swell the sighs in which I now deplore.
There lies Romena, where of the money coined[770]
    With the Baptist's image I made counterfeit,
    And therefore left my body burnt behind.
But could I see here Guido's[771] wretched sprite,
    Or Alexander's, or their brother's, I
    For Fonte Branda[772] would not give the sight.
One is already here, unless they lie—
    Mad souls with power to wander through the crowd—
    What boots it me, whose limbs diseases tie?
But were I yet so nimble that I could
    Creep one poor inch a century, some while
    Ago had I begun to take the road
Searching for him among this people vile;
    And that although eleven miles[773] 'tis long,
    And has a width of more than half a mile.
Because of them am I in such a throng;
    For to forge florins I by them was led,
    Which by three carats[774] of alloy were wrong,'

'Who are the wretches twain,' I to him said,
　　'Who smoke[775] like hand in winter-time fresh brought
　　From water, on thy right together spread?'
'Here found I them, nor have they budged a jot,'
　　He said, 'since I was hurled into this vale;
　　And, as I deem, eternally they'll not.
One[776] with false charges Joseph did assail;
　　False Sinon,[777] Greek from Troy, is the other wight.
　　Burning with fever they this stink exhale.'
Then one of them, perchance o'ercome with spite
　　Because he thus contemptuously was named,
　　Smote with his fist upon the belly tight.
It sounded like a drum; and then was aimed
　　A blow by Master Adam at his face
　　With arm no whit less hard, while he exclaimed:
'What though I can no longer shift my place
　　Because my members by disease are weighed!
　　I have an arm still free for such a case.'
To which was answered: 'When thou wast conveyed
　　Unto the fire 'twas not thus good at need,
　　But even more so when the coiner's trade
Was plied by thee.' The swol'n one: 'True indeed!
　　But thou didst not bear witness half so true
　　When Trojans[778] at thee for the truth did plead.'
'If I spake falsely, thou didst oft renew
　　False coin,' said Sinon; 'one fault brought me here;
　　Thee more than any devil of the crew.'
'Bethink thee of the horse, thou perjurer,'
　　He of the swol'n paunch answered; 'and that by
　　All men 'tis known should anguish in thee stir.'
'Be thirst that cracks thy tongue thy penalty,
　　And putrid water,' so the Greek replied,
　　'Which 'fore thine eyes thy stomach moundeth high.'
The coiner then: 'Thy mouth thou openest wide,
　　As thou art used, thy slanderous words to vent;
　　But if I thirst and humours plump my hide
Thy head throbs with the fire within thee pent.
　　To lap Narcissus' mirror,[779] to implore
　　And urge thee on would need no argument.'
While I to hear them did attentive pore
　　My Master said: 'Thy fill of staring take!
　　To rouse my anger needs but little more.'
And when I heard that he in anger spake
　　Toward him I turned with such a shame inspired,
　　Recalled, it seems afresh on me to break.
And, as the man who dreams of hurt is fired
　　With wish that he might know his dream a dream,

And so what is, as 'twere not, is desired;
So I, struck dumb and filled with an extreme
　　Craving to find excuse, unwittingly
　　The meanwhile made the apology supreme.
'Less shame,' my Master said, 'would nullify
　　A greater fault, for greater guilt atone;
　　All sadness for it, therefore, lay thou by.
But bear in mind that thou art not alone,
　　If fortune hap again to bring thee near
　　Where people such debate are carrying on.
To things like these 'tis shame[780] to lend an ear.'

Footnotes

[759] *Semele*: The daughter of Cadmus, founder and king of Thebes, was beloved by Jupiter and therefore hated by Juno, who induced her to court destruction by urging the god to visit her, as he was used to come to Juno, in all his glory. And in other instances the goddess took revenge (Ovid, *Metam.* iv.).

[760] *Athamas*: Married to a sister of Semele, was made insane by the angry Juno, with the result described in the text.

[761] *Hecuba*: Wife of Priam, king of Troy, and mother of Polyxena and Polydorus. While she was lamenting the death of her daughter, slain as an offering on the tomb of Achilles, she found the corpse of her son, slain by the king of Thrace, to whose keeping she had committed him (Ovid, *Metam.* xiii.).

[762] *Trojan fury, etc.*: It was by the agency of a Fury that Athamas was put out of his mind; but the Trojan and Theban furies here meant are the frenzies of Athamas and Hecuba, wild with which one of them slew his son, and the other scratched out the eyes of the Thracian king.

[763] *Capocchio*: See close of the preceding Canto. Here as elsewhere sinners are made ministers of vengeance on one another.

[764] *The Aretine*: Griffolino, who boasted he could fly; already represented as trembling (*Inf.* xxix. 97).

[765] *Gianni Schicchi*: Giovanni Schicchi, one of the Cavalcanti of Florence.

[766] *Myrrha*: This is a striking example of Dante's detestation of what may be called heartless sins. It is covered by the classification of Canto xi. Yet it is almost with a shock that we find Myrrha here for personation, and not rather condemned to some other circle for another sin.

[767] *Buoso Donati*: Introduced as a thief in the Seventh Bolgia (*Inf.* xxv. 140). Buoso was possessed of a peerless mare, known as the Lady of the herd. To make some amends for his unscrupulous acquisition of wealth, he made a will bequeathing legacies to various religious communities. When he died his nephew Simon kept the fact concealed long enough to procure a personation of him as if on his death-bed by Gianni Schicchi, who had great powers of mimicry. Acting in the character of Buoso, the rogue professed his wish to make a new disposition of his means, and after specifying some trifling charitable bequests the better to maintain his assumed character, named Simon as general legatee, and bequeathed Buoso's mare to himself.

[768] *O ye, etc.*: The speaker has heard and noted Virgil's words of explanation given in the previous Canto, line 94.

[769] *Master Adam*: Adam of Brescia, an accomplished worker in metals, was induced by the Counts Guidi of Romena in the Casentino, the upland district of the upper Arno, to counterfeit the gold coin of Florence. This false coin is mentioned in a Chronicle as having been in circulation in 1281. It must therefore have been somewhat later that Master Adam was burned, as he was by sentence of the Republic, upon the road which led from Romena to Florence. A cairn still existing near the ruined castle bears the name of the 'dead man's cairn.'

[770] *The money coined, etc.*: The gold florin, afterwards adopted in so many countries, was first struck in 1252; 'which florins weighed eight to the ounce, and bore the lily on the one side, and on the other Saint John.'—(Villani, vi. 54.) The piece was thus of about the weight of our half-sovereign. The gold was of twenty-four carats; that is, it had no alloy. The coin soon passed into wide circulation, and to maintain its purity became for the Florentines a matter of the first importance. Villani, in the chapter above cited, tells how the King of Tunis finding the florin to be of pure gold sent for some of the Pisans, then the chief traders in his ports, and asked who were the Florentines that they coined such money. 'Only our Arabs,' was the answer; meaning that they were rough country folk, dependent on Pisa. 'Then what is your coin like?' he asked. A Florentine of Oltrarno named Pera Balducci, who was present, took the opportunity of informing him how great Florence was compared with Pisa, as was shown by that city having no gold coinage of its own; whereupon the King made the Florentines free of Tunis, and allowed them to have a factory there. 'And this,' adds Villani, who had himself been agent abroad for a great Florentine house of business, 'we had at first hand from the aforesaid Pera, a man worthy of credit, and with whom we were associated in the Priorate.'

[771] *Guido, etc.*: The Guidi of Romena were a branch of the great family of the Counts Guidi. The father of the three brothers in the text was grandson of the old Guido that married the Good Gualdrada, and cousin of the Guidoguerra met by Dante in the Seventh Circle (*Inf.* xvi. 38). How the third brother was called is not settled, nor which of the three was already dead in the beginning of 1300. The Alexander of Romena, who for some time was captain of the banished Florentine Whites, was, most probably, he of the text. A letter is extant professing to be written by Dante to two of Alexander's nephews on the occasion of his death, in which the poet excuses himself for absence from the funeral on the plea of poverty. By the time he wrote the *Inferno* he may, owing to their shifty politics, have lost all liking for the family, yet it seems harsh measure that is here dealt to former friends and patrons.

[772] *Fonte Branda*: A celebrated fountain in the city of Siena. Near Romena is a spring which is also named Fonte Branda; and this, according to the view now most in favour, was meant by Master Adam. But was it so named in Dante's time? Or was it not so called only when the *Comedy* had begun to awaken a natural interest in the old coiner, which local ingenuity did its best to meet? The early commentators know nothing of the Casentino Fonte Branda, and, though it is found mentioned under the date of 1539, that does not take us far enough back. In favour of the Sienese fountain is the consideration that it was the richest of any in the Tuscan cities; that it was a great architectural as well as engineering work; and that, although now more than half a century old, it was still the subject of curiosity with people far and near. Besides, Adam has already recalled the brooks of Casentino, and so the mention of the paltry spring at Romena

would introduce no fresh idea like that of the abundant waters of the great fountain which daily quenched the thirst of thousands.

[773] *Eleven miles*: It will be remembered that the previous Bolgia was twenty-two miles in circumference.

[774] *Three carats*: Three carats in twenty-four being of some foreign substance.

[775] *Who smoke, etc.*: This description of sufferers from high fever, like that of Master Adam with his tympanitis, has the merit, such as it is, of being true to the life.

[776] *One, etc.*: Potiphar's wife.

[777] *Sinon*: Called of Troy, as being known through his conduct at the siege. He pretended to have deserted from the Greeks, and by a false story persuaded the Trojans to admit the fatal wooden horse.

[778] *When Trojans, etc.*: When King Priam sought to know for what purpose the wooden horse was really constructed.

[779] *Narcissus' mirror*: The pool in which Narcissus saw his form reflected.

[780] *'Tis shame*: Dante knows that Virgil would have scorned to portray such a scene of low life as this, but he must allow himself a wider licence and here as elsewhere refuses nothing, even in the way of mean detail, calculated to convey to his readers 'a full experience of the Inferno' as he conceived of it—the place 'where all the vileness of the world is cast.'

Canto XXXI.

The very tongue that first had caused me pain,
    Biting till both my cheeks were crimsoned o'er,
    With healing medicine me restored again.
So have I heard, the lance Achilles[781] bore,
    Which earlier was his father's, first would wound
    And then to health the wounded part restore.
From that sad valley[782] we our backs turned round,
    Up the encircling rampart making way
    Nor uttering, as we crossed it, any sound.
Here was it less than night and less than day,
    And scarce I saw at all what lay ahead;
    But of a trumpet the sonorous bray—
No thunder-peal were heard beside it—led
    Mine eyes along the line by which it passed,
    Till on one spot their gaze concentrated.
When by the dolorous rout was overcast
    The sacred enterprise of Charlemagne
    Roland[783] blew not so terrible a blast.
Short time my head was that way turned, when plain
    I many lofty towers appeared to see.
    'Master, what town is this?' I asked. 'Since fain
Thou art,' he said, 'to pierce the obscurity
    While yet through distance 'tis inscrutable, Thou must
    of error needs the victim be.
Arriving there thou shalt distinguish well
    How much by distance was thy sense betrayed;

Therefore to swifter course thyself compel.'
Then tenderly[784] he took my hand, and said:
    'Ere we pass further I would have thee know,
    That at the fact thou mayst be less dismayed,
These are not towers but giants; in a row
    Set round the brink each in the pit abides,
    His navel hidden and the parts below.'
And even as when the veil of mist divides
    Little by little dawns upon the sight
    What the obscuring vapour earlier hides;
So, piercing the gross air uncheered by light,
    As I step after step drew near the bound
    My error fled, but I was filled with fright.
As Montereggion[785] with towers is crowned
    Which from the walls encircling it arise;
    So, rising from the pit's encircling mound,
Half of their bodies towered before mine eyes—
    Dread giants, still by Jupiter defied
    From Heaven whene'er it thunders in the skies.
The face of one already I descried,
    His shoulders, breast, and down his belly far,
    And both his arms dependent by his side.
When Nature ceased such creatures as these are
    To form, she of a surety wisely wrought
    Wresting from Mars such ministers of war.
And though she rue not that to life she brought
    The whale and elephant, who deep shall read
    Will justify her wisdom in his thought;
For when the powers of intellect are wed
    To strength and evil will, with them made one,
    The race of man is helpless left indeed.
As large and long as is St. Peter's cone[786]
    At Rome, the face appeared; of every limb
    On scale like this was fashioned every bone.
So that the bank, which covered half of him
    As might a tunic, left uncovered yet
    So much that if to his hair they sought to climb
Three Frisians[787] end on end their match had met;
    For thirty great palms I of him could see,
    Counting from where a man's cloak-clasp is set.
Rafel[788] *mai amech zabi almi!*
    Out of the bestial mouth began to roll,
    Which scarce would suit more dulcet psalmody.
And then my Leader charged him: 'Stupid soul,
    Stick to thy horn. With it relieve thy mind
    When rage or other passions pass control.
Feel at thy neck, round which the thong is twined

    O puzzle-headed wretch! from which 'tis slung;
    Clipping thy monstrous breast thou shalt it find.
And then to me: 'From his own mouth is wrung
    Proof of his guilt. 'Tis Nimrod, whose insane
    Whim hindered men from speaking in one tongue.
Leave we him here nor spend our speech in vain;
    For words to him in any language said,
    As unto others his, no sense contain.'
Turned to the left, we on our journey sped,
    And at the distance of an arrow's flight
    We found another huger and more dread.
By what artificer thus pinioned tight
    I cannot tell, but his left arm was bound
    In front, as at his back was bound the right,
By a chain which girt him firmly round and round;
    About what of his frame there was displayed
    Below the neck, in fivefold gyre 'twas wound.
'Incited by ambition this one made
    Trial of prowess 'gainst Almighty Jove,'
    My Leader told, 'and he is thus repaid.
'Tis Ephialtes,[789] mightily who strove
    What time the giants to the gods caused fright:
    The arms he wielded then no more will move.'
And I to him: 'Fain would I, if I might,
    On the enormous Briareus set eye,
    And know the truth by holding him in sight.'
'Antæus[790] thou shalt see,' he made reply,
    'Ere long, and he can speak, nor is in chains.
    Us to the depth of all iniquity
He shall let down. The one thou'dst see[791] remains
    Far off, like this one bound and like in make,
    But in his face far more of fierceness reigns.'
Never when earth most terribly did quake
    Shook any tower so much as what all o'er
    And suddenly did Ephialtes shake.
Terror of death possessed me more and more;
    The fear alone had served my turn indeed,
    But that I marked the ligatures he wore.
Then did we somewhat further on proceed,
    Reaching Antæus who for good five ell,[792]
    His head not counted, from the pit was freed.
'O thou who from the fortune-haunted dell[793]—
    Where Scipio of glory was made heir
    When with his host to flight turned Hannibal—
A thousand lions didst for booty bear
    Away, and who, hadst thou but joined the host
    And like thy brethren fought, some even aver

The victory to earth's sons had not been lost,

    Lower us now, nor disobliging show,

    To where Cocytus[794] fettered is by frost.

To Tityus[795] nor to Typhon make us go.

    To grant what here is longed for he hath power,

    Cease them to curl thy snout, but bend thee low.

He can for wage thy name on earth restore;

    He lives, and still expecteth to live long,

    If Grace recall him not before his hour.'

So spake my Master. Then his hands he swung

    Downward and seized my Leader in all haste—

    Hands in whose grip even Hercules once was wrung.

And Virgil when he felt them round him cast

    Said: 'That I may embrace thee, hither tend,'

    And in one bundle with him made me fast.

And as to him that under Carisend[796]

    Stands on the side it leans to, while clouds fly

    Counter its slope, the tower appears to bend;

Even so to me who stood attentive by

    Antæus seemed to stoop, and I, dismayed,

    Had gladly sought another road to try.

But us in the abyss he gently laid,

    Where Lucifer and Judas gulfed remain;

    Nor to it thus bent downward long time stayed,

But like a ship's mast raised himself again.

Footnotes

[781] *Achilles*: The rust upon his lance had virtue to heal the wound.

[782] *From that sad valley*: Leaving the Tenth and last Bolgia they climb the inner bank of it and approach the Ninth and last Circle, which consists of the pit of the Inferno.

[783] *Roland*: Charles the Great, on his march north after defeating the Saracens at Saragossa, left Roland to bring up his rear-guard. The enemy fell on this in superior strength, and slew the Christians almost to a man. Then Roland, mortally wounded, sat down under a tree in Roncesvalles and blew upon his famous horn a blast so loud that it was heard by Charles at a distance of several miles.—The *Chansons de Geste* were familiarly known to Italians of all classes.

[784] *Then tenderly, etc.*: The wound inflicted by his reproof has been already healed, but Virgil still behaves to Dante with more than his wonted gentleness. He will have him assured of his sympathy now that they are about to descend into the 'lowest depth of all wickedness.'

[785] *Montereggioni*: A fortress about six miles from Siena, of which ample ruins still exist. It had no central keep, but twelve towers rose from its circular wall like spikes from the rim of a coronet. They had been added by the Sienese in 1260, and so were comparatively new in Dante's time.—As the towers stood round Montereggioni so the giants at regular intervals stand round the central pit. They have their foothold within the enclosing mound; and thus, to one looking at them from without, they are hidden by it up to their middle. As the embodiment of superhuman impious strength and pride they stand for warders of the utmost reach of Hell.

[786] *St. Peter's cone*: The great pine cone of bronze, supposed to have originally crowned the mausoleum of Hadrian, lay in Dante's time in the forecourt of St Peter's. When the new church was built it was removed to the gardens of the Vatican, where it still remains. Its size, it will be seen, is of importance as helping us to a notion of the stature of the giants; and, though the accounts of its height are strangely at variance with one another, I think the measurement made specially for Philalethes may be accepted as substantially correct. According to that, the cone is ten palms long—about six feet. Allowing something for the neck, down to 'where a man clasps his cloak' (line 66), and taking the thirty palms as eighteen feet, we get twenty-six feet or so for half his height. The giants vary in bulk; whether they do so in height is not clear. We cannot be far mistaken if we assume them to stand from fifty to sixty feet high. Virgil and Dante must throw their heads well back to look up into the giant's face; and Virgil must raise his voice as he speaks.—With regard to the height of the cone it may be remarked that Murray's Handbook for Rome makes it eleven feet high; Gsell-Fels two and a half metres, or eight feet and three inches. It is so placed as to be difficult of measurement.

[787] *Three Frisians*: Three very tall men, as Dante took Frisians to be, if standing one on the head of the other would not have reached his hair.

[788] *Rafel, etc.*: These words, like the opening line of the Seventh Canto, have, to no result, greatly exercised the ingenuity of scholars. From what follows it is clear that Dante meant them to be meaningless. Part of Nimrod's punishment is that he who brought about the confusion of tongues is now left with a language all to himself. It seems strange that commentators should have exhausted themselves in searching for a sense in words specially invented to have none.—In his *De Vulg. El.*, i. 7, Dante enlarges upon the confusion of tongues, and speaks of the tower of Babel as having been begun by men on the persuasion of a giant.

[789] *Ephialtes*: One of the giants who in the war with the gods piled Ossa on Pelion.

[790] *Antæus*: Is to be asked to lift them over the wall, because, unlike Nimrod, he can understand what is said to him, and, unlike Ephialtes, is not bound. Antæus is free-handed because he took no part in the war with the gods.

[791] *The one thou'dst see*: Briareus. Virgil here gives Dante to know what is the truth about Briareus (see line 97, etc.). He is not, as he was fabled, a monster with a hundred hands, but is like Ephialtes, only fiercer to see. Hearing himself thus made light of Ephialtes trembles with anger, like a tower rocking in an earthquake.

[792] *Five ell*: Five ells make about thirty palms, so that Antæus is of the same stature as that assigned to Nimrod at line 65. This supports the view that the 'huger' of line 84 may apply to breadth rather than to height.

[793] *The fortune-haunted dell*: The valley of the Bagrada near Utica, where Scipio defeated Hannibal and won the surname of Africanus. The giant Antæus had, according to the legend, lived in that neighbourhood, with the flesh of lions for his food and his dwelling in a cave. He was son of the Earth, and could not be vanquished so long as he was able to touch the ground; and thus ere Hercules could give him a mortal hug he needed to

swing him aloft. In the *Monarchia*, ii. 10, Dante refers to the combat between Hercules and Antæus as an instance of the wager of battle corresponding to that between David and Goliath. Lucan's *Pharsalia*, a favourite authority with Dante, supplies him with these references to Scipio and Antæus.

[794] *Cocytus*: The frozen lake fed by the waters of Phlegethon. See Canto xiv. at the end.

[795] *Tityus, etc.*: These were other giants, stated by Lucan to be less strong than Antæus. This introduction of their names is therefore a piece of flattery to the monster. A light contemptuous turn is given by Virgil to his flattery when in the following sentence he bids Antæus not curl his snout, but at once comply with the demand for aid. There is something genuinely Italian in the picture given of the giants in this Canto, as of creatures whose intellect bears no proportion to their bulk and brute strength. Mighty hunters like Nimrod, skilled in sounding the horn but feeble in reasoned speech, Frisians with great thews and long of limb, and German men-at-arms who traded in their rude valour, to the subtle Florentine in whom the ferment of the Renaissance was beginning to work were all specimens of Nature's handicraft that had better have been left unmade, were it not that wiser people could use them as tools.

[796] *Carisenda*: A tower still standing in Bologna, built at the beginning of the twelfth century, and, like many others of its kind in the city, erected not for strength but merely in order to dignify the family to whom it belonged. By way of further distinction to their owners, some of these towers were so constructed as to lean from the perpendicular. Carisenda, like its taller neighbour the Asinelli, still supplies a striking feature to the near and distant views of Bologna. What is left of it hangs for more than two yards off the plumb. In the half-century after Dante's time it had, according to Benvenuto, lost something of its height. It would therefore as the poet saw it seem to be bending down even more than it now does to any one standing under it on the side it slopes to, when a cloud is drifting over it in the other direction.

Canto XXXII.

Had I sonorous rough rhymes at command,
    Such as would suit the cavern terrible
    Rooted on which all the other ramparts stand,
The sap of fancies which within me swell
    Closer I'd press; but since I have not these,
    With some misgiving I go on to tell.
For 'tis no task to play with as you please,
    Of all the world the bottom to portray,
    Nor one that with a baby speech[797] agrees.
But let those ladies help me with my lay
    Who helped Amphion[798] walls round Thebes to pile,
    And faithful to the facts my words shall stay.
O 'bove all creatures wretched, for whose vile
    Abode 'tis hard to find a language fit,
    As sheep or goats ye had been happier! While
We still were standing in the murky pit—
    Beneath the giant's feet[799] set far below—
    And at the high wall I was staring yet,

When this I heard: 'Heed to thy steps[800] bestow,
    Lest haply by thy soles the heads be spurned
    Of wretched brothers wearied in their woe.'
Before me, as on hearing this I turned,
    Beneath my feet a frozen lake,[801] its guise
    Rather of glass than water, I discerned.
In all its course on Austrian Danube lies
    No veil in time of winter near so thick,
    Nor on the Don beneath its frigid skies,
As this was here; on which if Tabernicch[802]
    Or Mount Pietrapana[803] should alight
    Not even the edge would answer with a creak.
And as the croaking frog holds well in sight
    Its muzzle from the pool, what time of year[804]
    The peasant girl of gleaning dreams at night;
The mourning shades in ice were covered here,
    Seen livid up to where we blush[805] with shame.
    In stork-like music their teeth chattering were.
With downcast face stood every one of them:
    To cold from every mouth, and to despair
    From every eye, an ample witness came.
And having somewhat gazed around me there
    I to my feet looked down, and saw two pressed
    So close together, tangled was their hair,
'Say, who are you with breast[806] thus strained to breast?'
    I asked; whereon their necks they backward bent,
    And when their upturned faces lay at rest
Their eyes, which earlier were but moistened, sent
    Tears o'er their eyelids: these the frost congealed
    And fettered fast[807] before they further went.
Plank set to plank no rivet ever held
    More firmly; wherefore, goat-like, either ghost
    Butted the other; so their wrath prevailed.
And one who wanted both ears, which the frost
    Had bitten off, with face still downward thrown,
    Asked: 'Why with us art thou so long engrossed?
If who that couple are thou'dst have made known—
    The vale down which Bisenzio's floods decline
    Was once their father Albert's[808] and their own.
One body bore them: search the whole malign
    Caïna,[809] and thou shalt not any see
    More worthy to be fixed in gelatine;
Not he whose breast and shadow equally
    Were by one thrust of Arthur's lance[810] pierced through:
    Nor yet Focaccia;[811] nor the one that me
With his head hampers, blocking out my view,
    Whose name was Sassol Mascheroni:[812] well

Thou must him know if thou art Tuscan too.
And that thou need'st not make me further tell—
　I'm Camicion de' Pazzi,[813] and Carlin[814]
　I weary for, whose guilt shall mine excel.'
A thousand faces saw I dog-like grin,
　Frost-bound; whence I, as now, shall always shake
　Whenever sight of frozen pools I win.
While to the centre[815] we our way did make
　To which all things converging gravitate,
　And me that chill eternal caused to quake;
Whether by fortune, providence, or fate,
　I know not, but as 'mong the heads I went
　I kicked one full in the face; who therefore straight
'Why trample on me?' snarled and made lament,
　'Unless thou com'st to heap the vengeance high
　For Montaperti,[816] why so virulent
'Gainst me?' I said: 'Await me here till I
　By him, O Master, shall be cleared of doubt;[817]
　Then let my pace thy will be guided by.'
My Guide delayed, and I to him spake out,
　While he continued uttering curses shrill:
　'Say, what art thou, at others thus to shout?'
'But who art thou, that goest at thy will
　Through Antenora,[818] trampling on the face
　Of others? 'Twere too much if thou wert still
In life.' 'I live, and it may help thy case,'
　Was my reply, 'if thou renown wouldst gain,
　Should I thy name[819] upon my tablets place.
And he: 'I for the opposite am fain.
　Depart thou hence, nor work me further dool;
　Within this swamp thou flatterest all in vain.'
Then I began him by the scalp to pull,
　And 'Thou must tell how thou art called,' I said,
　'Or soon thy hair will not be plentiful.'
And he: 'Though every hair thou from me shred
　I will not tell thee, nor my face turn round;
　No, though a thousand times thou spurn my head.'
His locks ere this about my fist were wound,
　And many a tuft I tore, while dog-like wails
　Burst from him, and his eyes still sought the ground.
Then called another: 'Bocca, what now ails?
　Is't not enough thy teeth go chattering there,
　But thou must bark? What devil thee assails?'
'Ah! now,' said I, 'thou need'st not aught declare,
　Accursed traitor; and true news of thee
　To thy disgrace I to the world will bear.'
'Begone, tell what thou wilt,' he answered me;

'But, if thou issue hence, not silent keep[820]
　Of him whose tongue but lately wagged so free.
He for the Frenchmen's money[821] here doth weep.
　Him of Duera saw I, mayst thou tell,
　Where sinners shiver in the frozen deep.
Shouldst thou be asked who else within it dwell—
　Thou hast the Beccheria[822] at thy side;
　Across whose neck the knife at Florence fell.
John Soldanieri[823] may be yonder spied
　With Ganellon,[824] and Tribaldell[825] who threw
　Faenza's gates, when slept the city, wide.'
Him had we left, our journey to pursue,
　When frozen in a hole[826] a pair I saw;
　One's head like the other's hat showed to the view.
And, as their bread men hunger-driven gnaw,
　The uppermost tore fiercely at his mate
　Where nape and brain-pan to a junction draw.
No worse by Tydeus[827] in his scornful hate
　Were Menalippus' temples gnawed and hacked
　Than skull and all were torn by him irate.
'O thou who provest by such bestial act
　Hatred of him who by thy teeth is chewed,
　Declare thy motive,' said I, 'on this pact—
That if with reason thou with him hast feud,
　Knowing your names and manner of his crime
　I in the world[828] to thee will make it good;
If what I speak with dry not ere the time.'

Footnotes

[797] *A baby speech*: 'A tongue that cries *mamma* and *papa*' For his present purpose, he complains, he has not in Italian an adequate supply of rough high-sounding rhymes; but at least he will use only the best words that can be found. In another work (*De Vulg. El.* ii. 7) he instances *mamma* and *babbo* as words of a kind to be avoided by all who would write nobly in Italian.
[798] *Amphion*: Who with his music charmed rocks from the mountain and heaped them in order for walls to Thebes.
[799] *The giant's feet*: Antæus. A bank slopes from where the giants stand inside the wall down to the pit which is filled with the frozen Cocytus. This is the Ninth and inmost Circle, and is divided into four concentric rings—Caïna, Antenora, Ptolomæa, and Judecca—where traitors of different kinds are punished.
[800] *Thy steps*: Dante alone is addressed, the speaker having seen him set heavily down upon the ice by Antæus.
[801] *A frozen lake*: Cocytus. See *Inf.* xiv. 119.
[802] *Tabernicch*: It is not certain what mountain is here meant; probably Yavornick near Adelsberg in Carniola. It is mentioned, not for its size, but the harshness of its name.
[803] *Pietrapana*: A mountain between Modena and Lucca, visible from Pisa: Petra Apuana.

[804] *Time of year*: At harvest-time, when in the warm summer nights the wearied gleaner dreams of her day's work.

[805] *To where we blush*: The bodies of the shades are seen buried in the clear glassy ice, out of which their heads and necks stand free—as much as 'shows shame,' that is, blushes.

[806] *With breast, etc.*: As could be seen through the clear ice.

[807] *Fettered fast*: Binding up their eyes. In the punishment of traitors is symbolised the hardness and coldness of their hearts to all the claims of blood, country, or friendship.

[808] *Their father Albert's*: Albert, of the family of the Counts Alberti, lord of the upper valley of the Bisenzio, near Florence. His sons, Alexander and Napoleon, slew one another in a quarrel regarding their inheritance.

[809] *Caïna*: The outer ring of the Ninth Circle, and that in which are punished those treacherous to their kindred.—Here a place is reserved for Gianciotto Malatesta, the husband of Francesca (*Inf.* v. 107).

[810] *Arthur's lance*: Mordred, natural son of King Arthur, was slain by him in battle as a rebel and traitor. 'And the history says that after the lance-thrust Girflet plainly saw a ray of the sun pass through the hole of the wound.'—*Lancelot du Lac.*

[811] *Focaccia*: A member of the Pistoiese family of Cancellieri, in whose domestic feuds the parties of Whites and Blacks took rise. He assassinated one of his relatives and cut off the hand of another.

[812] *Sassol Mascheroni*: Of the Florentine family of the Toschi. He murdered his nephew, of whom by some accounts he was the guardian. For this crime he was punished by being rolled through the streets of Florence in a cask and then beheaded. Every Tuscan would be familiar with the story of such a punishment.

[813] *Camicion de' Pazzi*: To distinguish the Pazzi to whom Camicione belonged from the Pazzi of Florence they were called the Pazzi of Valdarno, where their possessions lay. Like his fellow-traitors he had slain a kinsman.

[814] *Carlin*: Also one of the Pazzi of Valdarno. Like all the spirits in this circle Camicione is eager to betray the treachery of others, and prophesies the guilt of his still living relative, which is to cast his own villany into the shade. In 1302 or 1303 Carlino held the castle of Piano de Trevigne in Valdarno, where many of the exiled Whites of Florence had taken refuge, and for a bribe he betrayed it to the enemy.

[815] *The centre*: The bottom of Inferno is the centre of the earth, and, on the system of Ptolemy, the central point of the universe.

[816] *Montaperti*: See *Inf.* x. 86. The speaker is Bocca, of the great Florentine family of the Abati, who served as one of the Florentine cavaliers at Montaperti. When the enemy was charging towards the standard of the Republican cavalry Bocca aimed a blow at the arm of the knight who bore it and cut off his hand. The sudden fall of the flag disheartened the Florentines, and in great measure contributed to the defeat.

[817] *Cleared of doubt*: The mention of Montaperti in this place of traitors suggests to Dante the thought of Bocca. He would fain be sure as to whether he has the traitor at his feet. Montaperti was never very far from the thoughts of the Florentine of that day. It is never out of Bocca's mind.

[818] *Antenora*: The second ring of the Ninth Circle, where traitors to their country are punished, named after Antenor the Trojan prince who, according to the belief of the middle ages, betrayed his native city to the Greeks.

[819] *Should I thy name, etc.*: 'Should I put thy name among the other notes.' It is the last time that Dante is to offer such a bribe; and here the offer is most probably ironical.

[820] *Not silent keep, etc.*: Like all the other traitors Bocca finds his only pleasure in betraying his neighbours.

[821] *The Frenchmen's money*: He who had betrayed the name of Bocca was Buoso of Duera, one of the Ghibeline chiefs of Cremona. When Guy of Montfort was leading an army across Lombardy to recruit Charles of Anjou in his war against Manfred in 1265 (*Inf.* xxviii. 16 and *Purg.* iii.), Buoso, who had been left to guard the passage of the Oglio, took a bribe to let the French army pass.

[822] *Beccheria*: Tesauro of the Pavian family Beccheria, Abbot of Vallombrosa and legate in Florence of Pope Alexander IV. He was accused of conspiring against the Commonwealth along with the exiled Ghibelines (1258). All Europe was shocked to hear that a great churchman had been tortured and beheaded by the Florentines. The city was placed under Papal interdict, proclaimed by the Archbishop of Pisa from the tower of S. Pietro in Vincoli at Rome. Villani seems to think the Abbot was innocent of the charge brought against him (*Cron.* vi. 65), but he always leans to the indulgent view when a priest is concerned.

[823] *Soldanieri*: Deserted from the Florentine Ghibelines after the defeat of Manfred.

[824] *Ganellon*: Whose treacherous counsel led to the defeat of Roland at Roncesvalles.

[825] *Tribaldello*: A noble of Faenza, who, as one account says, to revenge himself for the loss of a pig, sent a cast of the key of the city gate to John of Apia, then prowling about Romagna in the interest of the French Pope, Martin IV. He was slain at the battle of Forlì in 1282 (*Inf.* xxvii. 43).

[826] *Frozen in a hole, etc.*: The two are the Count Ugolino and the Archbishop Roger.

[827] *Tydeus*: One of the Seven against Thebes, who, having been mortally wounded by Menalippus the Theban, whom he slew, got his friends to bring him the head of his foe and gnawed at it with his teeth. Dante found the incident in his favourite author Statius (*Theb.* viii.).

[828] *I in the world, etc.*: Dante has learned from Bocca that the prospect of having their memory refreshed on earth has no charm for the sinners met with here. The bribe he offers is that of loading the name of a foe with ignominy—but only if from the tale it shall be plain that the ignominy is deserved.

Canto XXXIII.

His mouth uplifting from the savage feast,

 The sinner[829] rubbed and wiped it free of gore

 On the hair of the head he from behind laid waste;

And then began: 'Thou'dst have me wake once more

 A desperate grief, of which to think alone,

 Ere I have spoken, wrings me to the core.

But if my words shall be as seed that sown

 May fructify unto the traitor's shame

 Whom thus I gnaw, I mingle speech[830] and groan.

Of how thou earnest hither or thy name

 I nothing know, but that a Florentine[831]

In very sooth thou art, thy words proclaim.
Thou then must know I was Count Ugolin,
    The Archbishop Roger[832] he. Now hearken well
    Why I prove such a neighbour. How in fine,
And flowing from his ill designs, it fell
    That I, confiding in his words, was caught
    Then done to death, were waste of time[833] to tell.
But that of which as yet thou heardest nought
    Is how the death was cruel which I met:
    Hearken and judge if wrong to me he wrought.
Scant window in the mew whose epithet
    Of Famine[834] came from me its resident,
    And cooped in which shall many languish yet,
Had shown me through its slit how there were spent
    Full many moons,[835] ere that bad dream I dreamed
    When of my future was the curtain rent.
Lord of the hunt and master this one seemed,
    Chasing the wolf and wolf-cubs on the height[836]
    By which from Pisan eyes is Lucca hemmed.
With famished hounds well trained and swift of flight,
    Lanfranchi[837] and Gualandi in the van,
    And Sismond he had set. Within my sight
Both sire and sons—nor long the chase—began
    To grow (so seemed it) weary as they fled;
    Then through their flanks fangs sharp and eager ran.
When I awoke before the morning spread
    I heard my sons[838] all weeping in their sleep—
    For they were with me—and they asked for bread.
Ah! cruel if thou canst from pity keep
    At the bare thought of what my heart foreknew;
    And if thou weep'st not, what could make thee weep?
Now were they 'wake, and near the moment drew
    At which 'twas used to bring us our repast;
    But each was fearful[839] lest his dream came true.
And then I heard the under gate[840] made fast
    Of the horrible tower, and thereupon I gazed
    In my sons' faces, silent and aghast.
I did not weep, for I to stone was dazed:
    They wept, and darling Anselm me besought:
    "What ails thee, father? Wherefore thus amazed?"
And yet I did not weep, and answered not
    The whole day, and that night made answer none,
    Till on the world another sun shone out.
Soon as a feeble ray of light had won
    Into our doleful prison, made aware
    Of the four faces[841] featured like my own,
Both of my hands I bit at in despair;

And they, imagining that I was fain
    To eat, arose before me with the prayer:
"O father, 'twere for us an easier pain
    If thou wouldst eat us. Thou didst us array
    In this poor flesh: unclothe us now again."
I calmed me, not to swell their woe. That day
    And the next day no single word we said.
    Ah! pitiless earth, that didst unyawning stay!
When we had reached the fourth day, Gaddo, spread
    Out at my feet, fell prone; and made demand:
    "Why, O my father, offering us no aid?"
There died he. Plain as I before thee stand
    I saw the three as one by one they failed,
    The fifth day and the sixth; then with my hand,
Blind now, I groped for each of them, and wailed
    On them for two days after they were gone.
    Famine[842] at last, more strong than grief, prevailed,'
When he had uttered this, his eyes all thrown
    Awry, upon the hapless skull he fell
    With teeth that, dog-like, rasped upon the bone.
Ah, Pisa! byword of the folk that dwell
    In the sweet country where the Sì[843] doth sound,
    Since slow thy neighbours to reward thee well
Let now Gorgona and Capraia[844] mound
    Themselves where Arno with the sea is blent,
    Till every one within thy walls be drowned.
For though report of Ugolino went
    That he betrayed[845] thy castles, thou didst wrong
    Thus cruelly his children to torment.
These were not guilty, for they were but young,
    Thou modern Thebes![846] Brigata and young Hugh,
    And the other twain of whom above 'tis sung.
We onward passed to where another crew[847]
    Of shades the thick-ribbed ice doth fettered keep;
    Their heads not downward these, but backward threw.
Their very weeping will not let them weep,
    And grief, encountering barriers at their eyes,
    Swells, flowing inward, their affliction deep;
For the first tears that issue crystallise,
    And fill, like vizor fashioned out of glass,
    The hollow cup o'er which the eyebrows rise.
And though, as 'twere a callus, now my face
    By reason of the frost was wholly grown
    Benumbed and dead to feeling, I could trace
(So it appeared), a breeze against it blown,
    And asked: 'O Master, whence comes this? So low
    As where we are is any vapour[848] known?'

And he replied: 'Thou ere long while shalt go
 Where touching this thine eye shall answer true,
 Discovering that which makes the wind to blow.'
Then from the cold crust one of that sad crew
 Demanded loud: 'Spirits, for whom they hold
 The inmost room, so truculent were you,
Back from my face let these hard veils be rolled,
 That I may vent the woe which chokes my heart,
 Ere tears again solidify with cold.'
And I to him: 'First tell me who thou art
 If thou'dst have help; then if I help not quick
 To the bottom[849] of the ice let me depart.'
He answered: 'I am Friar Alberic[850]—
 He of the fruit grown in the orchard fell—
 And here am I repaid with date for fig.'120
'Ah!' said I to him, 'art thou dead as well?'
 'How now my body fares,' he answered me,
 'Up in the world, I have no skill to tell;
For Ptolomæa[851] has this quality—
 The soul oft plunges hither to its place
 Ere it has been by Atropos[852] set free.
And that more willingly from off my face
 Thou mayst remove the glassy tears, know, soon
 As ever any soul of man betrays
As I betrayed, the body once his own
 A demon takes and governs until all
 The span allotted for his life be run.
Into this tank headlong the soul doth fall;
 And on the earth his body yet may show
 Whose shade behind me wintry frosts enthral.
But thou canst tell, if newly come below:
 It is Ser Branca d'Oria,[853] and complete
 Is many a year since he was fettered so.'
'It seems,' I answered, 'that thou wouldst me cheat,
 For Branca d'Oria never can have died:
 He sleeps, puts clothes on, swallows drink and meat.'
'Or e'er to the tenacious pitchy tide
 Which boils in Malebranche's moat had come
 The shade of Michael Zanche,' he replied,
'That soul had left a devil in its room
 Within its body; of his kinsmen one[854]
 Treacherous with him experienced equal doom.
But stretch thy hand and be its work begun
 Of setting free mine eyes.' This did not I.
 Twas highest courtesy to yield him none.[855]
Ah, Genoese,[856] strange to morality!
 Ye men infected with all sorts of sin!

Out of the world 'tis time that ye should die.
Here, to Romagna's blackest soul[857] akin,
 I chanced on one of you; for doing ill
 His soul o'erwhelmed Cocytus' floods within,
Though in the flesh he seems surviving still.

Note on the Count Ugolino.

Ugolino della Gherardesca, Count of Donoratico, a wealthy noble and a man fertile in political resource, was deeply engaged in the affairs of Pisa at a critical period of her history. He was born in the first half of the thirteenth century. By giving one of his daughters in marriage to the head of the Visconti of Pisa—not to be confounded with those of Milan—he came under the suspicion of being Guelf in his sympathies; the general opinion of Pisa being then, as it always had been, strongly Ghibeline. When driven into exile, as he was along with the Visconti, he improved the occasion by entering into close relations with the leading Guelfs of Tuscany, and in 1278 a free return for him to Pisa was made by them a condition of peace with that city. He commanded one of the divisions of the Pisan fleet at the disastrous battle of Meloria in 1284, when Genoa wrested from her rival thesupremacy of the Western Mediterranean, and carried thousands of Pisan citizens into a captivity which lasted many years. Isolated from her Ghibeline allies, and for the time almost sunk in despair, the city called him to the government with wellnigh dictatorial powers; and by dint of crafty negotiations in detail with the members of the league formed against Pisa, helped as was believed by lavish bribery, he had the glory of saving the Commonwealth from destruction though he could not wholly save it from loss. This was in 1285. He soon came to be suspected of being in a secret alliance with Florence and of being lukewarm in the negotiations for the return of the prisoners in Genoa, all with a view to depress the Ghibeline element in the city that he might establish himself as an absolute tyrant with the greater ease. In order still further to strengthen his position he entered into a family compact with his Guelf grandson Nino (*Purg.* viii. 53), now at the head of the Visconti. But without the support of the people it was impossible for him to hold his ground against the Ghibeline nobles, who resented the arrogance of his manners and were embittered by the loss of their own share in the government; and these contrived that month by month the charges of treachery brought against him should increase in virulence. He had, by deserting his post, caused the defeat at Meloria, it was said; and had bribed the other Tuscan cities to favour him, by ceding to them distant Pisan strongholds. His fate was sealed when, having quarrelled with his grandson Nino, he sought alliance with the Archbishop Roger who now led the Ghibeline opposition. With Ugo's connivance an onslaught was planned upon the Guelfs. To preserve an appearance of impartiality he left the city for a neighbouring villa. On returning to enjoy his riddance from a rival he was invited to a conference, at which he resisted a proposal that he should admit partners with him in the government. On this the Archbishop's party raised the cry of treachery; the bells rang out for a street battle, in which he was worsted; and with his sons he had to take refuge in the Palace of the People. There he stood a short siege against the Ghibeline families and the angry mob; and in the same palace he was kept prisoner for twenty days. Then, with his sons and grandsons, he was carried in chains to the tower of the Gualandi, which stood where seven ways met in the heart of Pisa. This was in July 1288. The imprisonment lasted for months, and seems to have been thus prolonged with the view of extorting a heavy ransom. It was only in the following March that the Archbishop ordered his victims to be starved to death; for, being a churchman, says one account, he would not shed blood. Not even a confessor was allowed to Ugo and his sons. After the door of the tower had been kept closed for eight days it was opened, and the corpses, still fettered, were huddled into a tomb in the Franciscan church.—The original authorities are far from being agreed as to the details of Ugo's overthrow and death.—For the matter of this note I am chiefly indebted to the careful epitome of the Pisan history of that time by Philalethes in his note on this Canto (*Göttliche Comödie*).

Footnotes

[829] *The sinner*: Count Ugolino. See note at the end of the Canto.

[830] *Mingle speech, etc.*: A comparison of these words with those of Francesca (*Inf.* v. 124) will show the difference in moral tone between the Second Circle of Inferno and the Ninth.

[831] *A Florentine*: So Farinata (*Inf.* x. 25) recognises Dante by his Florentine speech. The words heard by Ugo are those at xxxii. 133.

[832] *The Archbishop Roger*: Ruggieri, of the Tuscan family of the Ubaldini, to which the Cardinal of *Inf.* x. 120 also belonged. Towards the end of his life he was summoned to Rome to give an account of his evil deeds, and on his refusal to go was declared a rebel to the Church. Ugolino was a traitor to his country; Roger, having entered into some sort of alliance with Ugolino, was a traitor to him. This has led some to suppose that while Ugolino is in Antenora he is so close to the edge of it as to be able to reach the head of Roger, who, as a traitor to his friend, is fixed in Ptolomæa. Against this view is the fact that they are described as being in the same hole (xxxii. 125), and also that in Ptolomæa the shades are set with head thrown back, and with only the face appearing above the ice, while Ugo is described as biting his foe at where the skull joins the nape. From line 91 it is clear that Ptolomæa lay further on than where Roger is. Like Ugo he is therefore here as a traitor to his country.

[833] *Were waste, etc.*: For Dante knows it already, all Tuscany being familiar with the story of Ugo's fate.

[834] *Whose epithet of Famine*: It was called the Tower of Famine. Its site is now built over. Buti, the old Pisan commentator of Dante, says it was called the Mew because the eagles of the Republic were kept in it at moulting-time. But this may have been an after-thought to give local truth to Dante's verse, which it does at the expense of the poetry.

[835] *Many moons*: The imprisonment having already lasted for eight months.

[836] *The height, etc.*: Lucca is about twelve miles from Pisa, Mount Giuliano rising between them.

[837] *Lanfranchi, etc.*: In the dream, these, the chief Ghibeline families of Pisa, are the huntsmen, Roger being master of the hunt, and the populace the hounds. Ugo and his sons and grandsons are the wolf and wolf-cubs. In Ugo's dream of himself as a wolf there may be an allusion to his having engaged in the Guelf interest.

[838] *My sons*: According to Dante, taken literally, four of Ugo were imprisoned with him. It would have hampered him to explain that two were grandsons—Anselmuccio and Nino, called the Brigata at line 89, grandsons by their mother of King Enzo, natural son of Frederick II.—the sons being Gaddo and Uguccione, the latter Ugo's youngest son.

[839] *Each was fearful, etc.*: All the sons had been troubled by dreams of famine. Had their rations been already reduced?

[840] *The under gate, etc.*: The word translated *made fast* (*chiavare*) may signify either to nail up or to lock. The commentators and chroniclers differ as to whether the door was locked, nailed, or built up. I would suggest that the lower part of the tower was occupied by a guard, and that the captives had not been used to hear the main door locked. Now, when they hear the great key creaking in the lock, they know that the tower is deserted.

[841] *The four faces, etc.*: Despairing like his own, or possibly that, wasted by famine, the faces of the young men had become liker than ever to Ugo's own time-worn face.

[842] *Famine, etc.*: This line, quite without reason, has been held to mean that Ugo was driven by hunger to eat the flesh of his children. The meaning is, that poignant though his grief was it did not shorten his sufferings from famine.

[843] *Where the Sì, etc.*: Italy, *Sì* being the Italian for *Yes*. In his *De Vulg. El.*, i. 8, Dante distinguishes the Latin languages—French, Italian, etc.—by their words of affirmation, and so terms Italian the language of *Sì*. But Tuscany may here be meant, where, as a Tuscan commentator says, the *Sì* is more sweetly pronounced than in any other part of Italy. In Canto xviii. 61 the Bolognese are distinguished as the people who say *Sipa*. If Pisa be taken as being specially the opprobrium of Tuscany the outburst against Genoa at the close of the Canto gains in distinctness and force.

[844] *Gorgona and Capraia*: Islands not far from the mouth of the Arno.

[845] *That he betrayed, etc.*: Dante seems here to throw doubt on the charge. At the height of her power Pisa was possessed of

many hundreds of fortified stations in Italy and scattered over the Mediterranean coasts. The charge was one easy to make and difficult to refute. It seems hard on Ugo that he should get the benefit of the doubt only after he has been, for poetical ends, buried raging in Cocytus.

[846] *Modern Thebes*: As Thebes was to the race of Cadmus, so was Pisa to that of Ugolino.

[847] *Another crew*: They are in Ptolomæa, the third division of the circle, and that assigned to those treacherous to their friends, allies, or guests. Here only the faces of the shades are free of the ice.

[848] *Is any vapour*: Has the sun, so low down as this, any influence upon the temperature, producing vapours and wind? In Dante's time wind was believed to be the exhalation of a vapour.

[849] *To the bottom, etc.*: Dante is going there in any case, and his promise is nothing but a quibble.

[850] *Friar Alberic*: Alberigo of the Manfredi, a gentleman of Faenza, who late in life became one of the Merry Friars. See *Inf.* xxiii. 103. In the course of a dispute with his relative Manfred he got a hearty box on the ear from him. Feigning to have forgiven the insult he invited Manfred with a youthful son to dinner in his house, having first arranged that when they had finished their meat, and he called for fruit, armed men should fall on his guests. 'The fruit of Friar Alberigo' passed into a proverb. Here he is repaid with a date for a fig—gets more than he bargained for.

[851] *Ptolomæa*: This division is named from the Hebrew Ptolemy, who slew his relatives at a banquet, they being then his guests (1 Maccab. xvi.).

[852] *Atropos*: The Fate who cuts the thread of life and sets the soul free from the body.

[853] *Branca d'Oria*: A Genoese noble who in 1275 slew his father-in-law Michael Zanche (*Inf.* xxii. 88) while the victim sat at table as his invited guest.—This mention of Branca is of some value in helping to ascertain when the *Inferno* was finished. He was in imprisonment and exile for some time before and up to 1310. In 1311 he was one of the citizens of Genoa heartiest in welcoming the Emperor Henry to their city. Impartial as Dante was, we can scarcely think that he would have loaded with infamy one who had done what he could to help the success of Henry, on whom all Dante's hopes were long set, and by their reception of whom on his descent into Italy he continued to judge his fellow-countrymen. There is considerable reason to believe that the *Inferno* was published in 1309; this introduction of Branca helps to prove that at least it was published before 1311. If this was so, then Branca d'Oria lived long enough to read or hear that for thirty-five years his soul had been in Hell.—It is significant of the detestation in which Dante held any breach of hospitality, that it is as a treacherous host and not as a treacherous kinsman that Branca is punished—in Ptolomæa and not in Caïna. Cast as the poet was on the hospitality of the world, any disloyalty to its obligations came home to him. For such disloyalty he has invented one of the most appalling of the fierce retributions with the vision of which he satisfied his craving for vengeance upon prosperous sin.—It may be that the idea of this demon-possession of the traitor is taken from the words, 'and after the sop Satan entered into Judas.'

[854] *Of his kinsmen one*: A cousin or nephew of Branca was engaged with him in the murder of Michael Zanche. The vengeance came on them so speedily that their souls were plunged in Ptolomæa ere Zanche breathed his last.

[855] *To yield him none*: Alberigo being so unworthy of courtesy. See note on 117. But another interpretation of the words has been suggested which saves Dante from the charge of cruelty and mean quibbling; namely, that he did not clear the ice from the sinner's eyes because then he would have been seen to be a living man—one who could take back to the world the awful news that Alberigo's body was the dwelling-place of a devil.

[856] *Ah, Genoese, etc.*: The Genoese, indeed, held no good character. One of their annalists, under the date of 1293, describes the city as suffering from all kinds of crime.

[857] *Romagna's blackest soul*: Friar Alberigo.

Canto XXXIV.

'*Vexilla*[858] *Regis prodeunt Inferni*
    Towards where we are; seek then with vision keen,'
    My Master bade, 'if trace of him thou spy.'
As, when the exhalations dense have been,
    Or when our hemisphere grows dark with night,
    A windmill from afar is sometimes seen,
I seemed to catch of such a structure sight;
    And then to 'scape the blast did backward draw
    Behind my Guide—sole shelter in my plight.
Now was I where[859] (I versify with awe)
    The shades were wholly covered, and did show
    Visible as in glass are bits of straw.
Some stood[860] upright and some were lying low,
    Some with head topmost, others with their feet;
    And some with face to feet bent like a bow.
But we kept going on till it seemed meet
    Unto my Master that I should behold
    The creature once[861] of countenance so sweet.
He stepped aside and stopped me as he told:
    'Lo, Dis! And lo, we are arrived at last
    Where thou must nerve thee and must make thee bold,'
How I hereon stood shivering and aghast,
    Demand not, Reader; this I cannot write;
    So much the fact all reach of words surpassed.
I was not dead, yet living was not quite:
    Think for thyself, if gifted with the power,
    What, life and death denied me, was my plight.
Of that tormented realm the Emperor
    Out of the ice stood free to middle breast;
    And me a giant less would overtower
Than would his arm a giant. By such test
    Judge then what bulk the whole of him must show,[862]
    Of true proportion with such limb possessed.
If he was fair of old as hideous now,
    And yet his brows against his Maker raised,

Meetly from him doth all affliction flow.
   O how it made me horribly amazed
      When on his head I saw three faces[863] grew!
      The one vermilion which straight forward gazed;
And joining on to it were other two,
      One rising up from either shoulder-bone,
      Till to a junction on the crest they drew.
'Twixt white and yellow seemed the right-hand one;
      The left resembled them whose country lies
      Where valleywards the floods of Nile flow down.
Beneath each face two mighty wings did rise,
      Such as this bird tremendous might demand:
      Sails of sea-ships ne'er saw I of such size.
Not feathered were they, but in style were planned
      Like a bat's wing:[864] by them a threefold breeze—
      For still he flapped them—evermore was fanned,
And through its depths Cocytus caused to freeze.
      Down three chins tears for ever made descent
      From his six eyes; and red foam mixed with these.
In every mouth there was a sinner rent
      By teeth that shred him as a heckle[865] would;
      Thus three at once compelled he to lament.
To the one in front 'twas little to be chewed
      Compared with being clawed and clawed again,
      Till his back-bone of skin was sometimes nude.[866]
'The soul up yonder in the greater pain
      Is Judas 'Scariot, with his head among
      The teeth,' my Master said, 'while outward strain
His legs. Of the two whose heads are downward hung,
      Brutus is from the black jowl pendulous:
      See how he writhes, yet never wags his tongue.
The other, great of thew, is Cassius:[867]
      But night is rising[868] and we must be gone;
      For everything hath now been seen by us.'
Then, as he bade, I to his neck held on
      While he the time and place of vantage chose;
      And when the wings enough were open thrown
He grasped the shaggy ribs and clutched them close,
      And so from tuft to tuft he downward went
      Between the tangled hair and crust which froze.
We to the bulging haunch had made descent,
      To where the hip-joint lies in it; and then
      My Guide, with painful twist and violent,
Turned round his head to where his feet had been,
      And like a climber closely clutched the hair:
      I thought to Hell[869] that we returned again.
'Hold fast to me; it needs by such a stair,'

Panting, my Leader said, like man foredone,
      'That we from all that wretchedness repair.'
Right through a hole in a rock when he had won,
      The edge of it he gave me for a seat
      And deftly then to join me clambered on.
I raised mine eyes, expecting they would meet
      With Lucifer as I beheld him last,
      But saw instead his upturned legs[870] and feet.
If in perplexity I then was cast,
      Let ignorant people think who do not see
      What point[871] it was that I had lately passed.
'Rise to thy feet,' my Master said to me;
      'The way is long and rugged the ascent,
      And at mid tierce[872] the sun must almost be.'
'Twas not as if on palace floors we went:
      A dungeon fresh from nature's hand was this;
      Rough underfoot, and of light indigent.
'Or ever I escape from the abyss,
      O Master,' said I, standing now upright,
      'Correct in few words where I think amiss.
Where lies the ice? How hold we him in sight
      Set upside down? The sun, how had it skill
      In so short while to pass to morn from night?'[873]
And he: 'In fancy thou art standing, still,
      On yon side of the centre, where I caught
      The vile worm's hair which through the world doth drill.
There wast thou while our downward course I wrought;
      But when I turned, the centre was passed by
      Which by all weights from every point is sought.
And now thou standest 'neath the other sky,
      Opposed to that which vaults the great dry ground
      And 'neath whose summit[874] there did whilom die
The Man[875] whose birth and life were sinless found.
      Thy feet are firm upon the little sphere,
      On this side answering to Judecca's round.
'Tis evening yonder when 'tis morning here;
      And he whose tufts our ladder rungs supplied.
      Fixed as he was continues to appear.
Headlong from Heaven he fell upon this side;
      Whereon the land, protuberant here before,
      For fear of him did in the ocean hide,
And 'neath our sky emerged: land, as of yore[876]
      Still on this side, perhaps that it might shun
      His fall, heaved up, and filled this depth no more.
From Belzebub[877] still widening up and on,
      Far-stretching as the sepulchre,[878] extends
      A region not beheld, but only known

By murmur of a brook[879] which through it wends,

Declining by a channel eaten through

The flinty rock; and gently it descends.

My Guide and I, our journey to pursue

To the bright world, upon this road concealed

Made entrance, and no thought of resting knew.

He first, I second, still ascending held

Our way until the fair celestial train

Was through an opening round to me revealed:

And, issuing thence, we saw the stars[880] again.

Footnotes

[858] *Vexilla, etc.*: 'The banners of the King of Hell advance.' The words are adapted from a hymn of the Cross used in Holy Week; and they prepare us to find in Lucifer the opponent of 'the Emperor who reigns on high' (*Inf.* i. 124). It is somewhat odd that Dante should have put a Christian hymn into Virgil's mouth.

[859] *Now was I where*: In the fourth and inner division or ring of the Ninth Circle. Here are punished those guilty of treachery to their lawful lords or to their benefactors. From Judas Iscariot, the arch-traitor, it takes the name of Judecca.

[860] *Some stood, etc.*: It has been sought to distinguish the degrees of treachery of the shades by means of the various attitudes assigned to them. But it is difficult to make more out of it than that some are suffering more than others. All of them are the worst of traitors, hard-hearted and cold-hearted, and now they are quite frozen in the ice, sealed up even from the poor relief of intercourse with their fellow-sinners.

[861] *The creature once, etc.*: Lucifer, guilty of treachery against the Highest, at *Purg.* xii. 25 described as 'created noble beyond all other creatures.' Virgil calls him Dis, the name used by him for Pluto in the *Æneid*, and the name from which that of the City of Unbelief is taken (*Inf.* viii. 68).

[862] *Judge then what bulk*: The arm of Lucifer was as much longer than the stature of one of the giants as a giant was taller than Dante. We have seen (*Inf.* xxxi. 58) that the giants were more than fifty feet in height—nine times the stature of a man. If a man's arm be taken as a third of his stature, then Satan is twenty-seven times as tall as a giant, that is, he is fourteen hundred feet or so. For a fourth of this, or nearly so—from the middle of the breast upwards—he stands out of the ice, that is, some three hundred and fifty feet. It seems almost too great a height for Dante's purpose; and yet on the calculations of some commentators his stature is immensely greater—from three to five thousand feet.

[863] *Three faces*: By the three faces are represented the three quarters of the world from which the subjects of Lucifer are drawn: vermilion or carnation standing for Europe, yellow for Asia, and black for Africa. Or the faces may symbolise attributes opposed to the Wisdom, Power, and Love of the Trinity (*Inf.* iii. 5). See also note on line 1.

[864] *A bat's wing*: Which flutters and flaps in dark and noisome places. The simile helps to bring more clearly before us the dim light and half-seen horrors of the Judecca.

[865] *A heckle*: Or brake; the instrument used to clear the fibre of flax from the woody substance mixed with it.

[866] *Sometimes nude*: We are to imagine that the frame of Judas is being for ever renewed and for ever mangled and torn.

[867] *Cassius*: It has been surmised that Dante here confounds the pale and lean Cassius who was the friend of Brutus with the L. Cassius described as corpulent by Cicero in the Third Catiline Oration. Brutus and Cassius are set with Judas in this, the deepest room of Hell, because, as he was guilty of high treason against his Divine Master, so they were guilty of it against Julius Cæsar, who, according to Dante, was chosen and ordained by God to found the Roman Empire. As the great rebel against the spiritual authority Judas has allotted to him the fiercer pain. To understand the significance of this harsh treatment of the great Republicans it is necessary to bear in mind that Dante's devotion to the idea of the Empire was part of his religion, and far surpassed in intensity all we can now well imagine. In the absence of a just and strong Emperor the Divine government of the world seemed to him almost at a stand.

[868] *Night is rising*: It is Saturday evening, and twenty-four hours since they entered by the gate of Inferno.

[869] *I thought to Hell, etc.*: Virgil, holding on to Lucifer's hairy sides, descends the dark and narrow space between him and the ice as far as to his middle, which marks the centre of the earth. Here he swings himself round so as to have his feet to the centre as he emerges from the pit to the southern hemisphere. Dante now feels that he is being carried up, and, able to see nothing in the darkness, deems they are climbing back to the Inferno. Virgil's difficulty in turning himself round and climbing up the legs of Lucifer arises from his being then at the 'centre to which all weights tend from every part.' Dante shared the erroneous belief of the time, that things grew heavier the nearer they were to the centre of the earth.

[870] *His upturned legs*: Lucifer's feet are as far above where Virgil and Dante are as was his head above the level of the Judecca.

[871] *What point, etc.*: The centre of the earth. Dante here feigns to have been himself confused—a fiction which helps to fasten attention on the wonderful fact that if we could make our way through the earth we should require at the centre to reverse our posture. This was more of a wonder in Dante's time than now.

[872] °*Mid tierce*: The canonical day was divided into four parts, of which Tierce was the first and began at sunrise. It is now about half-past seven in the morning. The night was beginning when they took their departure from the Judecca: the day is now as far advanced in the southern hemisphere as they have spent time on the passage. The journey before them is long indeed, for they have to ascend to the surface of the earth.

[873] *To morn from night*: Dante's knowledge of the time of day is wholly derived from what Virgil tells him. Since he began his descent into the Inferno he has not seen the sun.

[874] *'Neath whose summit*: Jerusalem is in the centre of the northern hemisphere—an opinion founded perhaps on *Ezekiel* v. 5: 'Jerusalem I have set in the midst of the nations and countries round about her.' In the *Convito*, iii. 5, we find Dante's belief regarding the distribution of land and sea clearly given: 'For those I write for it is enough to know that the Earth is fixed and does not move, and that, with the ocean, it is the centre of the heavens. The heavens, as we see, are for ever revolving around it as a centre; and in these revolutions they must of necessity have two fixed poles. ... Of these one is visible to almost all the dry land of

the Earth; and that is our north pole [star]. The other, that is, the south, is out of sight of almost all the dry land.'

[875] *The Man*: The name of Christ is not mentioned in the *Inferno*.

[876] *Land, as of yore, etc.*: On the fall of Lucifer from the southern sky all the dry land of that hemisphere fled before him under the ocean and took refuge in the other; that is, as much land emerged in the northern hemisphere as sank in the southern. But the ground in the direct line of his descent to the centre of the earth heaped itself up into the Mount of Purgatory—the only dry land left in the southern hemisphere. The Inferno was then also hollowed out; and, as Mount Calvary is exactly antipodal to Purgatory, we may understand that on the fall of the first rebels the Mount of Reconciliation for the human race, which is also that of Purification, rose out of the very realms of darkness and sin.—But, as Todeschini points out, the question here arises of whether the Inferno was not created before the earth. At *Parad.* vii. 124, the earth, with the air and fire and water, is described as 'corruptible and lasting short while;' but the Inferno is to endure for aye, and was made before all that is not eternal (*Inf.* iii. 8).

[877] *Belzebub*: Called in the Gospel the prince of the devils. It may be worth mentioning here that Dante sees in Purgatory (*Purg.* viii. 99) a serpent which he says may be that which tempted Eve. The identification of the great tempter with Satan is a Miltonic, or at any rate a comparatively modern idea.

[878] *The sepulchre*: The Inferno, tomb of Satan and all the wicked.

[879] *A brook*: Some make this to be the same as Lethe, one of the rivers of the Earthly Paradise. It certainly descends from the Mount of Purgatory.

[880] *The stars*: Each of the three divisions of the Comedy closes with 'the stars.' These, as appears from *Purg.* i. are the stars of dawn. It was after sunrise when they began their ascent to the surface of the earth, and so nearly twenty-four hours have been spent on the journey—the time it took them to descend through Inferno. It is now the morning of Easter Sunday—that is, of the true anniversary of the Resurrection although not of the day observed that year by the Church. See *Inf.* xxi. 112.

DISCUSSION QUESTIONS

1. Why does Dante use the "dark wood" in Canto 1 as an image of straying from the proper paths? Analyze the connotations of this image.

2. Why is Virgil a fitting guide for the poet?

3. In *The Inferno*, Dante tends to fit the punishment to the sinner. Which punishments seem particularly suited to the sinners involved?

4. As the poets descend, the sins and the punishments worsen. Does Dante's hierarchy of sins seem reasonable to you? Would you reorder the sins and their corresponding circles of hell in a different way? Why or why not?

5. List two or three of the most gruesome passages. What makes these descriptions effective and memorable? Why might Dante have chosen to make his descriptions of torture in hell so graphic?

6. Why do you think Dante chose to fix sinners in ice in the last circle of hell? Why might he think this is a worse punishment than burning?

7. Why does Virgil take the speaker on this tour of hell?

FRANCIS PETRARCH (1304–1374)

In spite of the fact that Petrarch and Dante were Italian literary men at roughly the same time (Petrarch was 17 years old when Dante finished *The Divine Comedy*), Dante seems to epitomize the voice of the Middle Ages, while Petrarch's poetry heralds the Renaissance. The humanistic and self-conscious spirit of Petrarch's sonnets and his promotion of classical studies better fit the spirit of later centuries than they do the Middle Ages. Even his recurring use of the sonnet yokes him to the Renaissance, as his mastery of what came to be known in his honor as the Italian or Petrarchan sonnet (a fourteen-line poem divided into an eight-line stanza, or octave, and a six-line stanza, or sestet) greatly influenced Renaissance poets such as Shakespeare and Donne. But devotion to medieval religious and courtly love themes and ideals still persists in Petrarch's verse, making him a vital bridge between these two time periods. Consider, for instance, his lifelong but apparently unconsummated passion for Laura, whom he saw for the first time on Good Friday, April 6, 1327, in a church in Avignon (see Sonnet 3, "'Twas on the morn"). He devoted many sonnets to Laura, even after her death by plague exactly 21 years after he first saw her. Petrarch writes of her in spiritual terms, seeing her, as Dante saw Beatrice, as an intermediary between himself and grace.

SONNETS

Sonnet III.

Era 'l giorno ch' al sol si scoloraro.

HE BLAMES LOVE FOR WOUNDING HIM ON
A HOLY DAY (GOOD FRIDAY).

'Twas on the morn, when heaven its blessed ray
In pity to its suffering master veil'd,
First did I, Lady, to your beauty yield,
Of your victorious eyes th' unguarded prey.
Ah! little reck'd I that, on such a day,
Needed against Love's arrows any shield;
And trod, securely trod, the fatal field:
Whence, with the world's, began my heart's dismay.
On every side Love found his victim bare,
And through mine eyes transfix'd my throbbing heart;
Those eyes, which now with constant sorrows flow:
But poor the triumph of his boasted art,
Who thus could pierce a naked youth, nor dare
To you in armour mail'd even to display his bow!

Wrangham.

'Twas on the blessed morning when the sun
In pity to our Maker hid his light,
That, unawares, the captive I was won,
Lady, of your bright eyes which chain'd me quite;
That seem'd to me no time against the blows
Of love to make defence, to frame relief:
Secure and unsuspecting, thus my woes
Date their commencement from the common grief.
Love found me feeble then and fenceless all,
Open the way and easy to my heart
Through eyes, where since my sorrows ebb and flow:
But therein was, methinks, his triumph small,
On me, in that weak state, to strike his dart,
Yet hide from you so strong his very bow.

Macgregor.

Sonnet XXXII.

S' amore o morte non dà qualche stroppio.

HE ASKS FROM A FRIEND THE LOAN OF THE
WORKS OF ST. AUGUSTIN.

IF Love or Death no obstacle entwine
With the new web which here my fingers fold,
And if I 'scape from beauty's tyrant hold
While natural truth with truth reveal'd I join,

Perchance a work so double will be mine
Between our modern style and language old,
That (timidly I speak, with hope though bold)
Even to Rome its growing fame may shine:

But, since, our labour to perfèct at last
Some of the blessed threads are absent yet
Which our dear father plentifully met,
Wherefore to me thy hands so close and fast
Against their use? Be prompt of aid and free,
And rich our harvest of fair things shall be.

MACGREGOR.

Sonnet LXII.

Se bianche non son prima ambe le tempie.
THOUGH NOT SECURE AGAINST THE WILES
OF LOVE, HE FEELS STRENGTH ENOUGH TO
RESIST THEM.

TILL silver'd o'er by age my temples grow,
Where Time by slow degrees now plants his grey,
Safe shall I never be, in danger's way
While Love still points and plies his fatal bowl
Fear no more his tortures and his tricks,
That he will keep me further to ensnare
Nor ope my heart, that, from without, he there
His poisonous and ruthless shafts may fix.
No tears can now find issue from mine eyes,
But the way there so well they know to win,

That nothing now the pass to them denies.
Though the fierce ray rekindle me within,
It burns not all: her cruel and severe
Form may disturb, not break my slumbers here.

MACGREGOR.

Sonnet LXIII.

Occhi, piangete; accompagnate il core.
DIALOGUE BETWEEN THE POET AND HIS EYES.

PLAYNE ye, myne eyes, accompanye my harte,
For, by your fault, lo, here is death at hand!
Ye brought hym first into this bitter band,
And of his harme as yett ye felt no part;
But now ye shall: Lo! here beginnes your smart.
Wett shall you be, ye shall it not withstand
With weepinge teares that shall make dymm your sight,
And mystic clowdes shall hang still in your light.
Blame but yourselves that kyndlyd have this brand,
With suche desyre to strayne that past your might;
But, since by you the hart hath caught his harme,
His flamèd heat shall sometyme make you warme.

HARRINGTON.
P. Weep, wretched eyes, accompany the heart
Which only from your weakness death sustains.
E.   Weep? evermore we weep; with keener pains
For others' error than our own we smart.
P.   Love, entering first through you an easy part,
Took up his seat, where now supreme he reigns.
E.   We oped to him the way, but Hope the veins
First fired of him now stricken by death's dart.
P.   The lots, as seems to you, scarce equal fall
'Tween heart and eyes, for you, at first sight, were
Enamour'd of your common ill and shame
.E. This is the thought which grieves us most of all;
For perfect judgments are on earth so rare
That one man's fault is oft another's blame.

MACGREGOR.

Sonnet LX.

Ite, rime dolenti, al duro sasso.
HE PRAYS THAT SHE WILL BE NEAR HIM AT HIS DEATH, WHICH HE FEELS APPROACHING.

Go, plaintive verse, to the cold marble go,
Which hides in earth my treasure from these eyes;
There call on her who answers from yon skies,
Although the mortal part dwells dark and low.
Of life how I am wearied make her know,
Of stemming these dread waves that round me rise:
But, copying all her virtues I so prize,
Her track I follow, yet my steps are slow.
I sing of her, living, or dead, alone;
(Dead, did I say? She is immortal made!)
That by the world she should be loved, and known.
Oh! in my passage hence may she be near,
To greet my coming that's not long delay'd;
And may I hold in heaven the rank herself holds there!

Nott.

Go, melancholy rhymes! your tribute bring
To that cold stone, which holds the dear remains
Of all that earth held precious;—uttering,
If heaven should deign to hear them, earthly strains.
Tell her, that sport of tempests, fit no more
To stem the troublous ocean,—here at last
Her votary treads the solitary shore;
His only pleasure to recall the past.
Tell her, that she who living ruled his fate,
In death still holds her empire: all his care,
So grant the Muse her aid,—to celebrate
Her every word, and thought, and action fair.
Be this my meed, that in the hour of death
Her kindred spirit may hail, and bless my parting breath!

Woodhouselee.

DISCUSSION QUESTIONS

1. In Petrarch's Sonnet 3, why does the speaker draw attention to the fact that he first saw his "Lady" on Good Friday? Does he see a connection between the two events?

2. What is the main image used in lines 5-8 of Sonnet 3? Does this image continue in any way in stanza 3?

3. What is the speaker praying for in Sonnet 62?

4. Who is the speaker addressing in the first line of Sonnet 60? What is odd about this address, from a medieval viewpoint? In what way might this poem seem more like a Renaissance than a medieval poem?

5. What is the speaker hoping for in the final three lines of Sonnet 60? Does this wish align him more with the Middle Ages or the Renaissance?

GEOFFREY CHAUCER (1343/1344–1400)

Chaucer is the foremost English literary figure of the Middle Ages, but literature did not dominate his work life. He began as a page to Lionel of Antwerp, the son of King Edward III. Later, he served in the English army and was taken prisoner while fighting in France; his ransom was paid in part by the king. He became a court diplomat, traveling on royal missions to Italy, Spain, and France. In 1376, Chaucer conducted several secret service missions to the continent for the king. In addition, he held official positions such as the Controller of Customs for London and later the Clerk of the King's Works.

It is possible that Chaucer met Boccaccio and Petrarch in his sojourns in Italy, and some literary historians have argued that Boccaccio's *Decameron* served as a source for Chaucer's *Canterbury Tales*. While *The Decameron* may have been an influence on Chaucer, the idea of a group of tales bound together by a narrative frame was not original to either man. But Chaucer enriched and complicated the formula by having every member of a diverse band of pilgrims tell tales that reflect on elements of their characters; in addition, the pilgrims converse with one another between tales, adding another layer to the narrative. Chaucer originally planned to have each pilgrim deliver two tales, 120 stories total, but he completed only 22. The frame of *Canterbury Tales* involves pilgrims traveling from the Tabard Inn in London to the shrine of Thomas à Becket in Canterbury, so the purpose of their journey is religious and religious beliefs and prayers are voiced by all the pilgrims, although some, like the Wife of Bath, seem much more interested in human, earthly concerns.

CANTERBURY TALES

General Prologue

When April's gentle rains have pierced the drought
Of March right to the root, and bathed each sprout
Through every vein with liquid of such power
It brings forth the engendering of the flower;
When Zephyrus too with his sweet breath has blown
Through every field and forest, urging on
The tender shoots, and there's a youthful sun,
His second half course through the Ram now run,
And little birds are making melody
And sleep all night, eyes open as can be
(So Nature pricks them in each little heart),
On pilgrimage then folks desire to start.
The palmers long to travel foreign strands
To distant shrines renowned in sundry lands;
And specially, from every shire's end
In England, folks to Canterbury wend:
To seek the blissful martyr is their will,
The one who gave such help when they were ill.
Now in that season it befell one day
In Southwark at the Tabard where I lay,
As I was all prepared for setting out
To Canterbury with a heart devout,
That there had come into that hostelry
At night some twenty-nine, a company
Of sundry folk whom chance had brought to fall
In fellowship, for pilgrims were they all
And onward to Canterbury would ride.
The chambers and the stables there were wide,
We had it easy, served with all the best;
And by the time the sun had gone to rest
I'd spoken with each one about the trip
And was a member of the fellowship.
We made agreement, early to arise
To take our way, of which I shall advise.
But nonetheless, while I have time and space,
Before proceeding further here's the place
Where I believe it reasonable to state
Something about these pilgrims–to relate
Their circumstances as they seemed to me,
Just who they were and each of what degree
And also what array they all were in.
And with a Knight I therefore will begin.

The Wife of Bath's Tale

In the old days of King Arthur, today
Still praised by Britons in a special way,
This land was filled with fairies all about.
The elf-queen with her jolly little rout
In many a green field often danced. Indeed
This was the old belief of which I read;
I speak of many hundred years ago.
But now such elves no one is seeing. No,
For now the prayers and charitable desires
Of limiters and other holy friars
Who wander all the land, by every stream,
As thick as specks of dust in a sunbeam,
To bless our halls, chambers, kitchens, bowers,
Boroughs, cities, castles, lofty towers,
Villages, granaries, stables, dairies,
Have made sure that no longer are there fairies.
For where there once was wont to walk an elf
There's walking now the limiter himself,
Early and late, to give his auspices,
Say matins and his other offices,
Go all about the limit where he's found.
Now women may go safely all around;
In every bush and under every tree
He is the only incubus, and he
Won't do a thing except dishonor them.

It happened that King Arthur had with him
A bachelor in his house; this lusty liver,
While riding from his hawking by the river,
Once chanced upon, alone as she was born,
A maiden who was walking–soon forlorn,
For he, despite all that she did or said,
By force deprived her of her maidenhead.
Because of this, there was such clamoring
And such demand for justice to the king,

This knight was all but numbered with the dead
By course of law, and should have lost his head
(Which may have been the law in that milieu).
But then the queen and other ladies too
Prayed so long that the king might grant him grace,
King Arthur spared him for at least a space;
He left him to the queen to do her will,
To choose to save or order them to kill.

The queen then thanked the king with all her might,
And after this the queen spoke with the knight
When she saw opportunity one day.
"For you," she said, "things stand in such a way
You can't be sure if you're to live or not.
I'll grant you life if you can tell me what
It is that women most desire. Beware
The iron ax, your neckbone now to spare!
And if you cannot tell me right away,
I'll give you leave, a twelvemonth and a day,
That you may go to seek, that you might find
An answer that is of sufficient kind.
I want your word before you take a pace:
You'll bring yourself back to this very place."
This knight with sorrow sighed, was full of woe.
What could he do? Not as he pleased, and so
To go away was what he finally chose,
To come back when his year was at its close
With such an answer as God might provide.
He took his leave and forth he went to ride.

He sought in every house and every place
In hopes he could secure the promised grace
By learning that which women love the most.
But he did not arrive at any coast
Where he could find two people on the matter
Who might agree, if judging by their chatter.
Some said that women all love riches best,
While some said honor, others jolly zest,
Some rich array; some said delights in bed,
And many said to be a widow wed;
Some others said that our hearts are most eased
When we are flattered and when we are pleased—
And he was nigh the truth, if you ask me.
A man shall win us best with flattery;
With much attendance, charm, and application
Can we be caught, whatever be our station.

Some said our love to which we all aspire
Is to be free to do as we desire,
With no reproof of vice but with the rule
That men should say we're wise, not one a fool.
For truly there is none among us all
Who, if a man should claw us on the gall,
Won't kick for being told the truth; he who
Does an assay will find out that it's true.
But though we may have vices kept within,
We like to be called wise and clean of sin.

And some say that we take the most delight
In keeping secrets, keeping our lips tight,
To just one purpose striving to adhere:
Not to betray one thing that we may hear.
That tale's not worth the handle of a rake.
We women can't keep secrets, heaven's sake!
Just look at Midas—would you hear the tale?

Ovid, among the trifles he'd detail,
Said Midas had long hair, for it appears
That on his head had grown two ass's ears.
This defect he had tried as best he might
To keep well as he could from others' sight,
And save his wife there was none who could tell.
He loved her much and trusted her as well
And prayed that not one living creature she
Would ever tell of his deformity.

She swore she'd not, though all the world to win,
Be guilty of such villainy and sin
And make her husband have so foul a name.
To tell it would as well bring her to shame.
But nonetheless she all but nearly died,
So long to have a secret she must hide.
She thought it swelled so sorely in her heart
Some word from out of her was bound to start;
And since she dared to tell it to no man,
Down close beside a marsh the lady ran—
She had to rush, her heart was so afire.
Then like a bittern booming in the mire,
She put her mouth down to the water, saying,
"Water, make no sound, don't be betraying,
For I will tell this to no one but you.
My husband has long ass's ears—it's true!"

She thought, "My heart is cured now, it is out;
I couldn't keep it longer, there's no doubt."
So as you see, we may awhile abide
But it must out, no secret we can hide.
(As for the tale, if you would hear the rest,
Read Ovid, for that's where you'll learn it best.)

This knight of whom my tale is all about,
When seeing that he couldn't find it out—
That is to say, what women love the most—
Felt in his breast already like a ghost;
For home he headed, he could not sojourn,
The day had come when homeward he must turn.
And in this woeful state he chanced to ride
While on his way along a forest side,
And there he saw upon the forest floor
Some ladies dancing, twenty-four or more.
Toward these dancers he was quick to turn
In hope that of some wisdom he might learn;
But all at once, before he'd gotten there,
The dancers disappeared, he knew not where.
He didn't see one creature bearing life,
Save sitting on the green one single wife.
An uglier creature no mind could devise.
To meet him this old wife was to arise,
And said, "You can't get there from here, Sir Knight.
What are you seeking, by your faith? It might
Well be to your advantage, sir, to tell;
Old folks like me know many things, and well."

"Dear mother," said the knight, "it is for sure
That I am dead if I cannot secure
What thing it is that women most desire.
If you could teach me, gladly I would hire."

"Give me your word here in my hand," said she,
"The next thing I request you'll do for me
If it's a thing that lies within your might,
And I will tell you then before it's night."
The knight said, "Here's my oath, I guarantee."

"Then certainly I dare to boast," said she,
"Your life is safe, for I'll be standing by;
Upon my life, the queen will say as I.
Let's see who is the proudest of them all,
With kerchief or with headdress standing tall,

Who shall deny that which I have to teach.
Now let us go, no need to make a speech."
She whispered then a message in his ear
And bade him to be glad and have no fear.

When they had come to court, the knight declared,
"I've come back to the day, and to be spared,
For I am now prepared to give reply."
The noble wives and maidens stood nearby,
And widows too (who were considered wise);
The queen sat like a justice in her guise.
All these had been assembled there to hear,
And then the knight was summoned to appear.

Full silence was commanded in the court
So that the knight might openly report
The thing that worldly women love the best.
He stood not like a beast at one's behest
But quickly gave his answer loud and clear,
With manly voice that all the court might hear.

"My liege and lady, generally," said he,
"What women most desire is sovereignty
Over their husbands or the ones they love,
To have the mastery, to be above.
This is your most desire, though you may kill
Me if you wish. I'm here, do as you will."
No wife or maid or widow in the court
Saw fit to contradict the knight's report;
They all agreed, "He's worthy of his life."
And with that word up started the old wife,
The one the knight had seen upon the green.
"Mercy," she said, "my sovereign lady queen!
Before your court departs, grant me my right.
It's I who taught this answer to the knight,
For which he gave a solemn oath to me:
The first thing I request he'd do for me
If it's a thing that lies within his might.
Before the court I therefore pray, Sir Knight,"
She said, "that you will take me as your wife;
For well you know that I have saved your life.
If I speak falsely, by your faith accuse me."

The knight replied, "Alas, how woes abuse me!
I know I made the promise you've expressed.
For love of God, please choose a new request.

Take all my goods and let my body go."
"No, damn us both then!" she replied. "For though
I may be ugly, elderly, and poor,
I'd give all of the metal and the ore
That lies beneath the earth and lies above
If only I could be your wife and love."

"My love?" he said. "No, rather my damnation!
Alas! that there is any of my nation
Who ever could so foully be disgraced."
But all for naught, the end was that he faced
Constrainment, for he now would have to wed
And take his gray old wife with him to bed.

Now there are some men who might say perhaps
That it's my negligence or else a lapse
That I don't tell you of the joyous way
In which the feast took place that very day.
I'll answer briefly should the question fall:
There wasn't any joy or feast at all,
Just lots of sorrow, things went grievously.
He married her that morning privately,
Then all that day he hid just like an owl,
So woeful, for his wife looked really foul.

Great was the woe the knight had in his head
When with his wife he'd been brought to the bed;
He tossed and then he turned both to and fro.
His old wife lay there smiling at him, though,
And said, "Dear husband, *benedicite!*
Acts every knight toward his wife this way?
Is this the law of great King Arthur's house?
Is every knight of his so distant? Spouse,
I am your own true love and I'm your wife
And I'm the one as well who saved your life,
And I have never done you wrong or spite.
Why do you treat me so on our first night?
You act just like a man who's lost his wit.
What is my guilt? For God's love, tell me it,
And it shall be amended if I may."

"Amended?" asked the knight. "Whatever way?
There's no way it could ever be amended.
You are so old and loathsome–and descended,
To add to that, from such a lowly kind–
No wonder that I toss and turn and wind.

I wish to God my heart would burst, no less!"
"Is this," she said, "the cause of your distress?"

"Why, yes," said he, "and is there any wonder?"

She said, "I could amend the stress you're under,
If you desire, within the next three days,
If you'll treat me more kindly in your ways.

"But when you talk about gentility
Like old wealth handed down a family tree,
That this is what makes of you gentlemen,
Such arrogance I judge not worth a hen.
Take him who's always virtuous in his acts
In public and in private, who exacts
Of himself all the noble deeds he can,
And there you'll find the greatest gentleman.
Christ wills we claim nobility from him,
Not from our elders or the wealth of them;
For though they give us all their heritage
And we claim noble birth by parentage,
They can't bequeath–all else theirs for the giving–
To one of us the virtuous way of living
That made the nobles they were known to be,
The way they bade us live in like degree.

"How well the poet wise, the Florentine
Named Dante, speaks about just what I mean,
And this is how he rhymes it in his story:
'Of men who climb their family trees for glory,
Few will excel, for it is by God's grace
We gain nobility and not by race.'
No, from our elders all that we can claim
Are temporal things such as may hurt and maim.

"All know as I, that if gentility
Were something that was planted naturally
Through all a certain lineage down the line,
In private and in public they'd be fine
And noble people doing what is nice,
Completely free of villainy and vice.

"Take fire into the darkest house or hut
Between here and Mount Caucasus, then shut
The doors, and all men leave and not return;
That fire will still remain as if the burn

Were being watched by twenty thousand souls.
Its function will not cease, its nature holds,
On peril of my life, until it dies.

"Gentility, you then should realize,
Is not akin to things like property;
For people act with much variety,
Not like the fire that always is the same.
God knows that men may often find, for shame,
A lord's son who's involved in villainy.
Who prides himself to have gentility
Because it happens he's of noble birth,
With elders virtuous, of noble worth,
But never tries to do a noble deed
Nor follow in his dead ancestors' lead,
Is not a noble, be he duke or earl;
For bad and sinful deeds just make a churl.
Sir, your gentility is but the fame
Of your ancestors, who earned their good name
With qualities quite foreign to your own.
Gentility can come from God alone,
So true gentility's a thing of grace,
Not something that's bequeathed by rank or place.

"For nobleness, as says Valerius,
Consider Tullius Hostilius:
Though poor, he rose to noble heights. Look in
Boethius or Seneca, and when
You do, don't doubt the truth of what you read:
The noble is the man of noble deed.
And so, dear husband, thus I will conclude:
If it's true my ancestors were so rude,
Yet may the Lord, as I do hope, grant me
The grace to live my life most virtuously;
For I'm a noble when I so begin
To live in virtue and avoid sin.

"For poverty you scold me. By your leave,
The God on high, in whom we both believe,
Chose willfully to live a poor man's life;
And surely every man, maiden, or wife
Can understand that Jesus, heaven's King,
Would not choose sinful living. It's a thing
Of honor to be poor without despair,
As Seneca and other clerks declare.
To be poor yet contented, I assert,
Is to be rich, though having not a shirt.

The one who covets is the poorer man,
For he would have that which he never can;
But he who doesn't have and doesn't crave
Is rich, though you may hold him but a knave.
True poverty's been sung of properly;
As Juvenal said of it, 'Merrily
The poor man, as he goes upon his way,
In front of every thief can sing and play.'
It is a hateful good and, as I guess,
A great promoter of industriousness.
A source of greater wisdom it can be
For one who learns to bear it patiently.
Though it seem wearisome, poverty is
Possession none will take from you as his.
Poverty often makes a fellow know
Himself as well as God when he is low.
Poverty is an eyeglass, I contend,
Through which a man can see a truthful friend.
I bring no harm at all to you, therefore
Do not reprove me, sire, for being poor.

"For being old you've also fussed at me;
Yet surely, sire, though no authority
Were in a book, you gentlemen select
Say men should treat an elder with respect
And call him father, by your courtesy.
I think I could find authors who agree.

"If I am old and ugly, as you've said,
Of cuckoldry you needn't have a dread;
For filthiness and age, as I may thrive,
Are guards that keep one's chastity alive.
But nonetheless, since I know your delight,
I shall fulfill your worldly appetite.
"Choose now," she said, "one of these two: that I
Be old and ugly till the day I die,
And be to you a true and humble wife,
One never to displease you all your life;
Or if you'd rather, have me young and fair,
And take your chance on those who will repair
To your house now and then because of me
(Or to some other place, it may well be).
Choose for yourself the one you'd rather try."

The knight gave it some thought, then gave a sigh,
And finally answered as you are to hear:
"My lady and my love and wife so dear,

I leave to your wise governance the measure;
You choose which one would give the fullest pleasure
And honor to you, and to me as well.
I don't care which you do, you best can tell.
What you desire is good enough for me."

"You've given me," she said, "the mastery?
The choice is mine and all's at my behest?"

"Yes, surely, wife," said he, "I think it best."

"Then kiss me, we'll no longer fight," she said,
"For you've my oath that I'll be both instead—
That is to say, I'll be both good and fair.
I pray to God I die in mad despair
Unless I am to you as good and true
As any wife since this old world was new.
Come dawn, if I'm not as fair to be seen
As any lady, empress, any queen
Who ever lived between the east and west,

Then take my life or do whatever's best.
Lift up the curtains now, see how it is."

And when the knight had truly seen all this,
How she was young and fair in all her charms,
In utter joy he took her in his arms;
His heart was bathing in a bath of bliss,
A thousand kisses he began to kiss,
And she obeyed in each and every way,
Whatever was his pleasure or his play.

And so they lived, till their lives' very end,
In perfect joy. And may Christ Jesus send
Us husbands meek and young and fresh abed,
And then the grace to outlive those we wed;
I also pray that Jesus shorten lives
Of those who won't be governed by their wives;
As for old niggards angered by expense,
God send them soon a mighty pestilence!

DISCUSSION QUESTIONS

1. According to the Wife of Bath, who should wield the authority in a marriage?
2. What is the Wife of Bath's opinion of virginity?
3. How does the Wife of Bath's tale work both with and against the ideals of courtly love?
4. What question does the queen want the knight to answer? What answer does he eventually give her?
5. What choice does the ugly old woman give to the knight when he marries her? What is his decision? Does he make the right decision? How can you tell?
6. How does this tale reflect the self-interestedness of the Wife of Bath?

SUGGESTION FOR WRITING

1. Language differences and historical periods aside, the Wife of Bath in many ways is a truly modern feminist. Compare her views on the roles of women to late-19th- or early-20th-century writers such as Kate Chopin or Virginia Woolf (see Units 5 and 6). How are her views similar? Different? How can you explain the similarities between the Wife and Woolf or Chopin, in spite of the five centuries that stretch between them?

ANONYMOUS

Everyman

The Middle Ages' unparalleled emphasis on religious themes is perhaps best exemplified in the morality plays such as *Everyman* that were popular throughout Europe for centuries. Morality plays, along with mystery plays, which dramatized events from the Bible, were the dominant dramatic forms of the Middle Ages, but to contemporary audiences, they might seem more like sermons broken into dialogue. The morality play, as its name suggests, upheld Christian moral values through allegorical dramatic scenes in which characters represent traits and categories instead of individualized people. In *Everyman*, for instance, the protagonist is called "Everyman" to remind audiences that he stands for all humans. Other characters, such as Fellowship, Kindred, Goods, Beauty, and Good Deeds, represent exactly what their names state, and all desert Everyman as he faces death, except for Good Deeds, who goes with him to the grave. While the starkness of the allegorical form and the heavy-handedness of the preaching may strike modern readers as strange and off-putting, both bring focus and intensity to the play's depiction of a man facing death.

EVERYMAN

CHARACTERS

- Everyman--------------------------Strength
- God: Adonai----------------------Discretion
- Death-----------------------------Five-Wits
- Messenger------------------------Beauty
- Fellowship------------------------Knowledge
- Cousin-----------------------------Confession
- Kindred----------------------------Angel
- Goods------------------------------Doctor
- Good-Deeds

HERE BEGINNETH A TREATISE HOW THE HIGH FATHER OF HEAVEN SENDETH DEATH TO SUMMON EVERY CREATURE TO COME AND GIVE ACCOUNT OF THEIR LIVES IN THIS WORLD AND IS IN MANNER OF A MORAL PLAY.

Messenger
I pray you all give your audience,
And hear this matter with reverence,
By figure a moral play—
The *Summoning of Everyman* called it is,
That of our lives and ending shows
How transitory we be all day.
This matter is wondrous precious,
But the intent of it is more gracious,
And sweet to bear away.
The story saith,–Man, in the beginning,
Look well, and take good heed to the ending,
Be you never so gay!
Ye think sin in the beginning full sweet,
Which in the end causeth thy soul to weep,
When the body lieth in clay.
Here shall you see how *Fellowship* and *Jollity*,
Both *Strength*, *Pleasure*, and *Beauty*,
Will fade from thee as flower in May.
For ye shall hear, how our heaven king
Calleth *Everyman* to a general reckoning:
Give audience, and hear what he doth say.

God
I perceive here in my majesty,
How that all creatures be to me unkind,
Living without dread in worldly prosperity:
Of ghostly sight the people be so blind,
Drowned in sin, they know me not for their God;
In worldly riches is all their mind,
They fear not my rightwiseness, the sharp rod;
My law that I shewed, when I for them died,
They forget clean, and shedding of my blood red;
I hanged between two, it cannot be denied;
To get them life I suffered to be dead;
I healed their feet, with thorns hurt was my head:
I could do no more than I did truly,
And now I see the people do clean forsake me.
They use the seven deadly sins damnable;
As pride, covetise, wrath, and lechery,
Now in the world be made commendable;
And thus they leave of angels the heavenly company;
Everyman liveth so after his own pleasure,
And yet of their life they be nothing sure:
I see the more that I them forbear
The worse they be from year to year;
All that liveth appaireth fast,
Therefore I will in all the haste
Have a reckoning of Everyman's person
For and I leave the people thus alone
In their life and wicked tempests,
Verily they will become much worse than beasts;
For now one would by envy another up eat;
Charity they all do clean forget.
I hoped well that Everyman
In my glory should make his mansion,
And thereto I had them all elect;
But now I see, like traitors deject,
They thank me not for the pleasure that I to them meant,
Nor yet for their being that I them have lent;
I proffered the people great multitude of mercy,
And few there be that asketh it heartily;
They be so cumbered with worldly riches,
That needs on them I must do justice,
On Everyman living without fear.

Where art thou, *Death*, thou mighty messenger?

Death
Almighty God, I am here at your will,
Your commandment to fulfil.

God
Go thou to *Everyman*,
And show him in my name
A pilgrimage he must on him take,
Which he in no wise may escape;
And that he bring with him a sure reckoning
Without delay or any tarrying.

Death
Lord, I will in the world go run over all,
And cruelly outsearch both great and small;
Every man will I beset that liveth beastly
Out of God's laws, and dreadeth not folly:
He that loveth riches I will strike with my dart,
His sight to blind, and from heaven to depart,
Except that alms be his good friend,
In hell for to dwell, world without end.
Lo, yonder I see *Everyman* walking;
Full little he thinketh on my coming;
His mind is on fleshly lusts and his treasure,
And great pain it shall cause him to endure
Before the Lord Heaven King.

Everyman, stand still;
whither art thou going
Thus gaily? Hast thou thy Maker forget?

Everyman
Why askst thou?
Wouldest thou wete?

Death
Yea, sir, I will show you;
In great haste I am sent to thee
From God out of his majesty.

Everyman
What, sent to me?

Death
Yea, certainly.
Though thou have forget him here,
He thinketh on thee in the heavenly sphere,
As, or we depart, thou shalt know.

Everyman
What desireth God of me?

Death
That shall I show thee;
A reckoning he will needs have
Without any longer respite.

Everyman
To give a reckoning longer leisure I crave;
This blind matter troubleth my wit.

Death
On thee thou must take a long journey:
Therefore thy book of count with thee thou bring;
For turn again thou can not by no way,
And look thou be sure of thy reckoning:
For before God thou shalt answer, and show
Thy many bad deeds and good but a few;
How thou hast spent thy life, and in what wise,
Before the chief lord of paradise.
Have ado that we were in that way,
For, wete thou well, thou shalt make none attournay.

Everyman
Full unready I am such reckoning to give.
I know thee not: what messenger art thou?

Death
I am *Death*, that no man dreadeth.
For every man I rest and no man spareth;
For it is God's commandment
That all to me should be obedient.

Everyman
O *Death*, thou comest when I had thee least in mind;
In thy power it lieth me to save,
Yet of my good will I give thee, if ye will be kind,
Yea, a thousand pound shalt thou have,

And defer this matter till another day.

Death
Everyman, it may not be by no way;
I set not by gold, silver, nor riches,
Ne by pope, emperor, king, duke, ne princes.
For and I would receive gifts great,
All the world I might get;
But my custom is clean contrary.
I give thee no respite: come hence, and not tarry.

Everyman
Alas, shall I have no longer respite?
I may say *Death* giveth no warning:
To think on thee, it maketh my heart sick,
For all unready is my book of reckoning.
But twelve year and I might have abiding,
My counting book I would make so clear,
That my reckoning I should not need to fear.
Wherefore, Death, I pray thee, for God's mercy,
Spare me till I be provided of remedy.

Death
Thee availeth not to cry, weep, and pray:
But haste thee lightly that you were gone the journey,
And prove thy friends if thou can.
For, wete thou well, the tide abideth no man,
And in the world each living creature
For *Adam's* sin must die of nature.

Everyman
Death, if I should this pilgrimage take,
And my reckoning surely make,
Show me, for saint *charity*,
Should I not come again shortly?

Death
No, *Everyman*; and thou be once there,
Thou mayst never more come here,
Trust me verily.

Everyman
O gracious God, in the high seat celestial,
Have mercy on me in this most need;
Shall I have no company from this vale terrestrial
Of mine acquaintance that way me to lead?

Death
Yea, if any be so hardy,
That would go with thee and bear thee company.
Hie thee that you were gone to God's magnificence,
Thy reckoning to give before his presence.
What, weenest thou thy life is given thee,
And thy worldly goods also?

Everyman
I had wend so, verily.

Death
Nay, nay; it was but lent thee;
For as soon as thou art go,
Another awhile shall have it, and then go therefor
Even as thou hast done.
Everyman, thou art mad; thou hast thy wits five,
And here on earth will not amend thy life,
For suddenly I do come.

Everyman
O wretched caitiff, whither shall I flee,
That I might scape this endless sorrow!
Now, gentle *Death*, spare me till to-morrow,
That I may amend me
With good advisement.

Death
Nay, thereto I will not consent,
Nor no man will I respite,
But to the heart suddenly I shall smite
Without any advisement.
And now out of thy sight I will me hie;
See thou make thee ready shortly,
For thou mayst say this is the day
That no man living may scape away.

Everyman
Alas, I may well weep with sighs deep;
Now have I no manner of company
To help me in my journey, and me to keep;
And also my writing is full unready.
How shall I do now for to excuse me?
I would to God I had never be gete!
To my soul a full great profit it had be;
For now I fear pains huge and great.
The time passeth; Lord, help that all wrought;

For though I mourn it availeth nought.
The day passeth, and is almost a-go;
I wot not well what for to do.
To whom were I best my complaint do make?
What, and I to *Fellowship* thereof spake,
And showed him of this sudden chance?
For in him is all mine affiance;
We have in the world so many a day
Be on good friends in sport and play.
I see him yonder, certainly;
I trust that he will bear me company;
Therefore to him will I speak to ease my sorrow.
Well met, good *Fellowship*, and good morrow!

Fellowship speaketh
Everyman, good morrow by this day.
Sir, why lookest thou so piteously?
If any thing be amiss, I pray thee, me say,
That I may help to remedy.

Everyman
Yea, good *Fellowship*, yea,
I am in great jeopardy.

Fellowship
My true friend, show to me your mind;
I will not forsake thee, unto my life's end,
In the way of good company.

Everyman
That was well spoken, and lovingly.

Fellowship
Sir, I must needs know your heaviness;
I have pity to see you in any distress;
If any have you wronged ye shall revenged be,
Though I on the ground be slain for thee,–
Though that I know before that I should die.

Everyman
Verily, *Fellowship*, gramercy.

Fellowship
Tush! by thy thanks I set not a straw.
Show me your grief, and say no more.

Everyman
If I my heart should to you break,
And then you to turn your mind from me,
And would not me comfort, when you hear me speak,
Then should I ten times sorrier be.

Fellowship
Sir, I say as I will do in deed.

Everyman
Then be you a good friend at need:
I have found you true here before.

Fellowship
And so ye shall evermore;
For, in faith, and thou go to Hell,
I will not forsake thee by the way!

Everyman
Ye speak like a good friend; I believe you well;
I shall deserve it, and I may.

Fellowship
I speak of no deserving, by this day.
For he that will say and nothing do
Is not worthy with good company to go;
Therefore show me the grief of your mind,
As to your friend most loving and kind.
Everyman. I shall show you how it is;
Commanded I am to go a journey,
A long way, hard and dangerous,
And give a strait count without delay
Before the high judge Adonai.
Wherefore I pray you, bear me company,
As ye have promised, in this journey.

Fellowship
That is mater indeed! Promise is duty,
But, and I should take such a voyage on me,
I know it well, it should be to my pain:
Also it make me afeard, certain.
But let us take counsel here as well as we can,
For your words would fear a strong man.

Everyman
Why, ye said, If I had need,
Ye would me never forsake, quick nor dead,

Though it were to hell truly.

Fellowship
So I said, certainly,
But such pleasures be set aside, thee sooth to say:
And also, if we took such a journey,
When should we come again?

Everyman
Nay, never again till the day of doom.

Fellowship
In faith, then will not I come there!
Who hath you these tidings brought?

Everyman
Indeed, *Death* was with me here.

Fellowship
Now, by God that all hath bought,
If *Death* were the messenger,
For no man that is living to-day
I will not go that loath journey—
Not for the father that begat me!

Everyman
Ye promised other wise, pardie.

Fellowship
I wot well I say so truly;
And yet if thou wilt eat, and rink, and make good cheer,
Or haunt to women, the lusty company,
I would not forsake you, while the day is clear,
Trust me verily!

Everyman
Yea, thereto ye would be ready;
To go to mirth, solace, and play,
Your mind will sooner apply
Than to bear me company in my long journey.

Fellowship
Now, in good faith, I will not that way.
But and thou wilt murder, or any man kill,
In that I will help thee with a good will!

Everyman

O that is a simple advice indeed!
Gentle fellow, help me in my necessity;
We have loved long, and now I need,
And now, gentle Fellowship, remember me.

Fellowship
Whether ye have loved me or no,
By Saint John, I will not with thee go.

Everyman
Yet I pray thee, take the labour, and do so much for me
To bring me forward, for saint charity,
And comfort me till I come without the town.

Fellowship
Nay, and thou would give me a new gown,
I will not a foot with thee go;
But and you had tarried I would not have left thee so.
And as now, God speed thee in thy journey,
For from thee I will depart as fast as I may.

Everyman
Whither away, *Fellowship*? will you forsake me?

Fellowship
Yea, by my fay, to God I betake thee.

Everyman
Farewell, good *Fellowship*; for this my heart is sore;
Adieu for ever, I shall see thee no more.

Fellowship
In faith, *Everyman*, farewell now at the end;
For you I will remember that parting is mourning.

Everyman
Alack! shall we thus depart indeed?
Our Lady, help, without any more comfort,
Lo, Fellowship forsaketh me in my most need:
For help in this world whither shall I resort?
Fellowship herebefore with me would merry make;
And now little sorrow for me doth he take.
It is said, in prosperity men friends may find,
Which in adversity be full unkind.
Now whither for succour shall I flee,
Sith that *Fellowship* hath forsaken me?
To my kinsmen I will truly,

Praying them to help me in my necessity;
I believe that they will do so,
For kind will creep where it may not go.
I will go say, for yonder I see them go.
Where be ye now, my friends and kinsmen?

Kindred

Here be we now at your commandment.
Cousin, I pray you show us your intent
In any wise, and not spare.

Cousin

Yea, Everyman, and to us declare
If ye be disposed to go any whither,
For wete you well, we will live and die together.

Kindred

In wealth and woe we will with you hold,
For over his kin a man may be bold.

Everyman

Gramercy, my friends and kinsmen kind.
Now shall I show you the grief of my mind:
I was commanded by a messenger,
That is an high king's chief officer;
He bade me go a pilgrimage to my pain,
And I know well I shall never come again;
Also I must give a reckoning straight,
For I have a great enemy, that hath me in wait,
Which intendeth me for to hinder.

Kindred

What account is that which ye must render?
That would I know.

Everyman

Of all my works I must show
How I have lived and my days spent;
Also of ill deeds, that I have used
In my time, sith life was me lent;
And of all virtues that I have refused.
Therefore I pray you go thither with me,
To help to make mine account, for saint *charity*.

Cousin

What, to go thither? Is that the matter?
Nay, Everyman, I had liefer fast bread and water

All this five year and more.

Everyman

Alas, that ever I was bore!
For now shall I never be merry
If that you forsake me.

Kindred

Ah, sir; what, ye be a merry man!
Take good heart to you, and make no moan.
But one thing I warn you, by Saint Anne,
As for me, ye shall go alone.

Everyman

My *Cousin*, will you not with me go?

Cousin

No, by our Lady; I have the cramp in my toe.
Trust not to me, for, so God me speed,
I will deceive you in your most need,

Kindred

It availeth not us to tice.
Ye shall have my maid with all my heart;
She loveth to go to feasts, there to be nice,
And to dance, and abroad to start:
I will give her leave to help you in that journey,
If that you and she may agree.

Everyman

Now show me the very effect of your mind.
Will you go with me, or abide behind?

Kindred

Abide behind? yea, that I will and I may!
Therefore farewell until another day.

Everyman

How should I be merry or glad?
For fair promises to me make,
But when I have most need, they me forsake.
I am deceived; that maketh me sad.

Cousin

Cousin Everyman, farewell now,
For verily I will not go with you;
Also of mine own an unready reckoning

I have to account; therefore I make tarrying.
Now, God keep thee, for now I go.

Everyman
Ah, Jesus, is all come hereto?
Lo, fair words maketh fools feign;
They promise and nothing will do certain.
My kinsmen promised me faithfully
For to abide with me steadfastly,
And now fast away do they flee:
Even so Fellowship promised me.
What friend were best me of to provide?
I lose my time here longer to abide.
Yet in my mind a thing there is;–
All my life I have loved riches;
If that my good now help me might,
He would make my heart full light.
I will speak to him in this distress.–
Where art thou, my Goods and riches?

Goods
Who calleth me? *Everyman?* what haste thou hast!
I lie here in corners, trussed and piled so high,
And in chests I am locked so fast,
Also sacked in bags, thou mayst see with thine eye,
I cannot stir; in packs low I lie.
What would ye have, lightly me say.

Everyman
Come hither, Good, in all the haste thou may,
For of counsel I must desire thee.

Goods
Sir, and ye in the world have trouble or adversity,
That can I help you to remedy shortly.

Everyman
It is another disease that grieveth me;
In this world it is not, I tell thee so.
I am sent for another way to go,
To give a straight account general
Before the highest *Jupiter* of all;
And all my life I have had joy and pleasure in thee.
Therefore I pray thee go with me,
For, peradventure, thou mayst before God Almighty
My reckoning help to clean and purify;
For it is said ever among,

That money maketh all right that is wrong.

Goods
Nay, *Everyman*, I sing another song,
I follow no man in such voyages;
For and I went with thee
Thou shouldst fare much the worse for me;
For because on me thou did set thy mind,
Thy reckoning I have made blotted and blind,
That thine account thou cannot make truly;
And that hast thou for the love of me.
Everyman. That would grieve me full sore,
When I should come to that fearful answer.
Up, let us go thither together.

Goods
Nay, not so, I am too brittle, I may not endure;
I will follow no man one foot, be ye sure.

Everyman
Alas, I have thee loved, and had great pleasure
All my life-days on good and treasure.

Goods
That is to thy damnation without lesing,
For my love is contrary to the love everlasting.
But if thou had me loved moderately during,
As, to the poor give part of me,
Then shouldst thou not in this dolour be,
Nor in this great sorrow and care.

Everyman
Lo, now was I deceived or I was ware,
And all I may wyte my spending of time.

Goods
What, weenest thou that I am thine?

Everyman
I had wend so.

Goods
Nay, *Everyman,* I say no;
As for a while I was lent thee,
A season thou hast had me in prosperity;
My condition is man's soul to kill;
If I save one, a thousand I do spill;

Weenest thou that I will follow thee?
Nay, from this world, not verily.

Everyman
I had wend otherwise.

Goods
Therefore to thy soul *Good* is a thief;
For when thou art dead, this is my guise
Another to deceive in the same wise
As I have done thee, and all to his soul's reprief.

Everyman
O false *Good*, cursed thou be!
Thou traitor to God, that hast deceived me,
And caught me in thy snare.

Goods
Marry, thou brought thyself in care,
Whereof I am glad,
I must needs laugh, I cannot be sad.

Everyman
Ah, *Good*, thou hast had long my heartly love;
I gave thee that which should be the Lord's above.
But wilt thou not go with me in deed?
I pray thee truth to say.

Goods
No, so God me speed,
Therefore farewell, and have good day.

Everyman
O, to whom shall I make my moan
For to go with me in that heavy journey?
First *Fellowship* said he would with me gone;
His words were very pleasant and gay,
But afterward he left me alone.
Then spake I to my kinsmen all in despair,
And also they gave me words fair,
They lacked no fair speaking,
But all forsake me in the ending.
Then went I to my *Goods* that I loved best,
In hope to have comfort, but there had I least;
For my *Goods* sharply did me tell
That he bringeth many into hell.
Then of myself I was ashamed,

And so I am worthy to be blamed;
Thus may I well myself hate.
Of whom shall I now counsel take?
I think that I shall never speed
Till that I go to my *Good-Deed*,
But alas, she is so weak,
That she can neither go nor speak;
Yet will I venture on her now.–
My *Good-Deeds*, where be you?

Good-Deeds
Here I lie cold in the ground;
Thy sins hath me sore bound,
That I cannot stir.

Everyman
O, *Good-Deeds*, I stand in fear;
I must you pray of counsel,
For help now should come right well.

Goods-Deeds
Everyman, I have understanding
That ye be summoned account to make
Before *Messias*, of Jerusalem King;
And you do by me that journey what you will I take.

Everyman
Therefore I come to you, my moan to make;
I pray you, that ye will go with me.

Good-Deeds
I would full fain, but I cannot stand verily.

Everyman
Why, is there anything on you fall?

Good-Deeds
Yea, sir, I may thank you of all;
If ye had perfectly cheered me,
Your book of account now full ready had be.
Look, the books of your works and deeds eke;
Oh, see how they lie under the feet,
To your soul's heaviness.

Everyman
Our Lord *Jesus*, help me!
For one letter here I can not see.

Good-Deeds
There is a blind reckoning in time of distress!

Everyman
Good-Deeds, I pray you, help me in this need,
Or else I am for ever damned indeed;
Therefore help me to make reckoning
Before the redeemer of all thing,
That king is, and was, and ever shall.

Good-Deeds
Everyman, I am sorry of your fall,
And fain would I help you, and I were able.

Everyman
Good-Deeds, your counsel I pray you give me.

Good-Deeds
That shall I do verily;
Though that on my feet I may not go,
I have a sister, that shall with you also,
Called *Knowledge*, which shall with you abide,
To help you to make that dreadful reckoning.

Knowledge
Everyman, I will go with thee, and be thy guide,
In thy most need to go by thy side.

Everyman
In good condition I am now in every thing,
And am wholly content with this good thing;
Thanked be God my Creator.

Good-Deeds
And when he hath brought thee there,
Where thou shalt heal thee of thy smart,
Then go you with your reckoning and your *Good-Deeds*
    together
For to make you joyful at heart
Before the blessed Trinity.

Everyman
My *Good-Deeds*, gramercy;
I am well content, certainly,
With your words sweet.

Knowledge
Now go we together lovingly,
To *Confession*, that cleansing river.

Everyman
For joy I weep; I would we were there;
But, I pray you, give me cognition
Where dwelleth that holy man, *Confession*.

Knowledge
In the house of salvation:
We shall find him in that place,
That shall us comfort by God's grace.
Lo, this is *Confession*; kneel down and ask mercy,
For he is in good conceit with God almighty.

Everyman
O glorious fountain that all uncleanness doth clarify,
Wash from me the spots of vices unclean,
That on me no sin may be seen;
I come with *Knowledge* for my redemption,
Repent with hearty and full contrition;
For I am commanded a pilgrimage to take,
And great accounts before God to make.
Now, I pray you, *Shrift*, mother of salvation,
Help my good deeds for my piteous exclamation.

Confession
I know your sorrow well, *Everyman*;
Because with *Knowledge* ye come to me,
I will you comfort as well as I can,
And a precious jewel I will give thee,
Called penance, wise voider of adversity;
Therewith shall your body chastised be,
With abstinence and perseverance in God's service:
Here shall you receive that scourge of me,
Which is penance strong, that ye must endure,
To remember thy Saviour was scourged for thee
With sharp scourges, and suffered it patiently;
So must thou, or thou scape that painful pilgrimage;
Knowledge, keep him in this voyage,
And by that time *Good-Deeds* will be with thee.
But in any wise, be sure of mercy,
For your time draweth fast, and ye will saved be;
Ask God mercy, and He will grant truly,
When with the scourge of penance man doth him bind,
The oil of forgiveness then shall he find.

Everyman
Thanked be God for his gracious work!
For now I will my penance begin;
This hath rejoiced and lighted my heart,
Though the knots be painful and hard within.

Knowledge
Everyman, look your penance that ye fulfil,
What pain that ever it to you be,
And *Knowledge* shall give you counsel at will,
How your accounts ye shall make clearly.

Everyman
O eternal God, O heavenly figure,
O way of rightwiseness, O goodly vision,
Which descended down in a virgin pure
Because he would *Everyman* redeem,
Which *Adam* forfeited by his disobedience:
O blessed Godhead, elect and high-divine,
Forgive my grievous offence;
Here I cry thee mercy in this presence.
O ghostly treasure, O ransomer and redeemer
Of all the world, hope and conductor,
Mirror of joy, and founder of mercy,
Which illumineth heaven and earth thereby,
Hear my clamorous complaint, though it late be;
Receive my prayers; unworthy in this heavy life,
Though I be, a sinner most abominable,
Yet let my name be written in *Moses'* table;
O *Mary*, pray to the Maker of all thing,
Me for to help at my ending,
And save me from the power of my enemy,
For *Death* assaileth me strongly;
And, Lady, that I may by means of thy prayer
Of your Son's glory to be partaker,
By the means of his passion I it crave,
I beseech you, help my soul to save.–
Knowledge, give me the scourge of penance;
My flesh therewith shall give a quittance:
I will now begin, if God give me grace.

Knowledge
Everyman, God give you time and space:
Thus I bequeath you in the hands of our Saviour,
Thus may you make your reckoning sure.

Everyman
In the name of the Holy Trinity,
My body sore punished shall be:
Take this body for the sin of the flesh;
Also thou delightest to go gay and fresh,
And in the way of damnation thou did me bring;
Therefore suffer now strokes and punishing.
Now of penance I will wade the water clear,
To save me from purgatory, that sharp fire.

Good-Deeds
I thank God, now I can walk and go;
And am delivered of my sickness and woe.
Therefore with *Everyman* I will go, and not spare;
His good works I will help him to declare.

Knowledge
Now, *Everyman*, be merry and glad;
Your *Good-Deeds* cometh now; ye may not be sad;
Now is your *Good-Deeds* whole and sound,
Going upright upon the ground.

Everyman
My heart is light, and shall be evermore;
Now will I smite faster than I did before.

Good-Deeds
Everyman, pilgrim, my special friend,
Blessed be thou without end;
For thee is prepared the eternal glory.
Ye have me made whole and sound,
Therefore I will bide by thee in every stound.

Everyman
Welcome, my *Good-Deeds*; now I hear thy voice,
I weep for very sweetness of love.

Knowledge
Be no more sad, but ever rejoice,
God seeth thy living in his throne above;
Put on this garment to thy behove,
Which is wet with your tears,
Or else before God you may it miss,
When you to your journey's end come shall.

Everyman
Gentle *Knowledge*, what do you it call?

Knowledge
It is a garment of sorrow:
From pain it will you borrow;
Contrition it is,
That getteth forgiveness;
It pleaseth God passing well.

Good-Deeds
Everyman, will you wear it for your heal?

Everyman
Now blessed be *Jesu, Mary's* Son!
For now have I on true contrition.
And let us go now without tarrying;
Good-Deeds, have we clear our reckoning?

Good-Deeds
Yea, indeed I have it here.

Everyman
Then I trust we need not fear;
Now, friends, let us not part in twain.

Knowledge
Nay, *Everyman*, that will we not, certain.

Good-Deeds
Yet must thou lead with thee
Three persons of great might.

Everyman
Who should they be?

Good-Deeds
Discretion and *Strength* they hight,
And thy *Beauty* may not abide behind.

Knowledge
Also ye must call to mind
Your *Five-wits* as for your counsellors.

Good-Deeds
You must have them ready at all hours.

Everyman
How shall I get them hither?

Knowledge
You must call them all together,
And they will hear you incontinent.

Everyman
My friends, come hither and be present
Discretion, *Strength*, my *Five-wits*, and *Beauty*.

Beauty
Here at your will we be all ready.
What will ye that we should do?

Good-Deeds
That ye would with *Everyman* go,
And help him in his pilgrimage,
Advise you, will ye with him or not in that voyage?

Strength
We will bring him all thither,
To his help and comfort, ye may believe me.

Discretion
So will we go with him all together.

Everyman
Almighty God, loved thou be,
I give thee laud that I have hither brought
Strength, *Discretion*, *Beauty*, and *Five-wits*; lack I nought;
And my *Good-Deeds*, with *Knowledge* clear,
All be in my company at my will here;
I desire no more to my business.

Strength
And I, *Strength*, will by you stand in distress,
Though thou would in battle fight on the ground.

Five-wits
And though it were through the world round,
We will not depart for sweet nor sour.

Beauty
No more will I unto death's hour,
Whatsoever thereof befall.

Discretion
Everyman, advise you first of all;
Go with a good advisement and deliberation;

We all give you virtuous monition
That all shall be well.

Everyman
My friends, hearken what I will tell:
I pray God reward you in his heavenly sphere.
Now hearken, all that be here,
For I will make my testament
Here before you all present.
In alms half my good I will give with my hands twain
In the way of charity, with good intent,
And the other half still shall remain
In quiet to be returned there it ought to be.
This I do in despite of the fiend of hell
To go quite out of his peril
Ever after and this day.

Knowledge
Everyman, hearken what I say;
Go to priesthood, I you advise,
And receive of him in any wise
The holy sacrament and ointment together;
Then shortly see ye turn again hither;
We will all abide you here.

Five-Wits
Yea, *Everyman*, hie you that ye ready were,
There is no emperor, king, duke, ne baron,
That of God hath commission,
As hath the least priest in the world being;
For of the blessed sacraments pure and benign,
He beareth the keys and thereof hath the cure
For man's redemption, it is ever sure;
Which God for our soul's medicine
Gave us out of his heart with great pine;
Here in this transitory life, for thee and me
The blessed sacraments seven there be,
Baptism, confirmation, with priesthood good,
And the sacrament of God's precious flesh and blood,
Marriage, the holy extreme unction, and penance;
These seven be good to have in remembrance,
Gracious sacraments of high divinity.

Everyman
Fain would I receive that holy body
And meekly to my ghostly father I will go.

Five-wits
Everyman, that is the best that ye can do:
God will you to salvation bring,
For priesthood exceedeth all other thing;
To us Holy Scripture they do teach,
And converteth man from sin heaven to reach;
God hath to them more power given,
Than to any angel that is in heaven;
With five words he may consecrate
God's body in flesh and blood to make,
And handleth his maker between his hands;
The priest bindeth and unbindeth all bands,
Both in earth and in heaven;
Thou ministers all the sacraments seven;
Though we kissed thy feet thou were worthy;
Thou art surgeon that cureth sin deadly:
No remedy we find under God
But all only priesthood.
Everyman, God gave priests that dignity,
And setteth them in his stead among us to be;
Thus be they above angels in degree.

Knowledge
If priests be good it is so surely;
But when Jesus hanged on the cross with great smart
There he gave, out of his blessed heart,
The same sacrament in great torment:
He sold them not to us, that Lord Omnipotent.
Therefore Saint Peter the apostle doth say
That Jesu's curse hath all they
Which God their Saviour do buy or sell,
Or they for any money do take or tell.
Sinful priests giveth the sinners example bad;
Their children sitteth by other men's fires, I have heard;
And some haunteth women's company,
With unclean life, as lusts of lechery
These be with sin made blind.

Five-wits
I trust to God no such may we find;
Therefore let us priesthood honour,
And follow their doctrine for our souls' succour;
We be their sheep, and they shepherds be
By whom we all be kept in surety.
Peace, for yonder I see *Everyman* come,
Which hath made true satisfaction.

Good-Deeds
Methinketh it is he indeed.

Everyman
Now Jesu be our alder speed.
I have received the sacrament for my redemption,
And then mine extreme unction:
Blessed be all they that counselled me to take it!
And now, friends, let us go without longer respite;
I thank God that ye have tarried so long.
Now set each of you on this rod your hand,
And shortly follow me:
I go before, there I would be; God be our guide.

Strength
Everyman, we will not from you go,
Till ye have gone this voyage long.

Discretion
I, *Discretion*, will bide by you also.

Knowledge
And though this pilgrimage be never so strong,
I will never part you fro:
Everyman, I will be as sure by thee
As ever I did by Judas Maccabee.

Everyman
Alas, I am so faint I may not stand,
My limbs under me do fold;
Friends, let us not turn again to this land,
Not for all the world's gold,
For into this cave must I creep
And turn to the earth and there to sleep.

Beauty
What, into this grave? alas!

Everyman
Yea, there shall you consume more and less.

Beauty
And what, should I smother here?

Everyman
Yea, by my faith, and never more appear.
In this world live no more we shall,

But in heaven before the highest Lord of all.

Beauty
I cross out all this; adieu by Saint *John*;
I take my cap in my lap and am gone.

Everyman
What, *Beauty*, whither will ye?

Beauty
Peace, I am deaf; I look not behind me,
Not and thou would give me all the gold in thy chest.

Everyman
Alas, whereto may I trust?
Beauty goeth fast away hie;
She promised with me to live and die.

Strength
Everyman, I will thee also forsake and deny;
Thy game liketh me not at all.

Everyman
Why, then ye will forsake me all.
Sweet *Strength*, tarry a little space.

Strength
Nay, sir, by the rood of grace
I will hie me from thee fast,
Though thou weep till thy heart brast.

Everyman
Ye would ever bide by me, ye said.

Strength
Yea, I have you far enough conveyed;
Ye be old enough, I understand,
Your pilgrimage to take on hand;
I repent me that I hither came.

Everyman
Strength, you to displease I am to blame;
Will you break promise that is debt?

Strength
In faith, I care not;
Thou art but a fool to complain,

You spend your speech and waste your brain;
Go thrust thee into the ground.

Everyman
I had wend surer I should you have found.
He that trusteth in his *Strength*
She him deceiveth at the length.
Both *Strength* and *Beauty* forsaketh me,
Yet they promised me fair and lovingly.

Discretion
Everyman, I will after *Strength* be gone,
As for me I will leave you alone.

Everyman
Why, *Discretion*, will ye forsake me?

Discretion
Yea, in faith, I will go from thee,
For when *Strength* goeth before
I follow after evermore.

Everyman
Yet, I pray thee, for the love of the Trinity,
Look in my grave once piteously.

Discretion
Nay, so nigh will I not come.
Farewell, every one!

Everyman
O all thing faileth, save God alone;
Beauty, *Strength*, and *Discretion*;
For when *Death* bloweth his blast,
They all run from me full fast.

Five-wits
Everyman, my leave now of thee I take;
I will follow the other, for here I thee forsake.

Everyman
Alas! then may I wail and weep,
For I took you for my best friend.

Five-wits
I will no longer thee keep;
Now farewell, and there an end.

Everyman
O Jesu, help, all hath forsaken me!

Good-Deeds
Nay, *Everyman*, I will bide with thee,
I will not forsake thee indeed;
Thou shalt find me a good friend at need.

Everyman
Gramercy, *Good-Deeds*; now may I true friends see;
They have forsaken me every one;
I loved them better than my *Good-Deeds* alone.
Knowledge, will ye forsake me also?

Knowledge
Yea, *Everyman*, when ye to death do go:
But not yet for no manner of danger.

Everyman
Gramercy, *Knowledge*, with all my heart.

Knowledge
Nay, yet I will not from hence depart,
Till I see where ye shall be come.

Everyman
Methinketh, alas, that I must be gone,
To make my reckoning and my debts pay,
For I see my time is nigh spent away.
Take example, all ye that this do hear or see,
How they that I loved best do forsake me,
Except my *Good-Deeds* that bideth truly.

Good-Deeds
All earthly things is but vanity:
Beauty, *Strength*, and *Discretion*, do man forsake,
Foolish friends and kinsmen, that fair spake,
All fleeth save *Good-Deeds*, and that am I.

Everyman
Have mercy on me, God most mighty;
And stand by me, thou Mother and Maid, holy *Mary*.

Good-Deeds
Fear not, I will speak for thee.

Everyman
Here I cry God mercy.

Good-Deeds
Short our end, and minish our pain;
Let us go and never come again.

Everyman
Into thy hands, Lord, my soul I commend;
Receive it, Lord, that it be not lost;
As thou me boughtest, so me defend,
And save me from the fiend's boast,
That I may appear with that blessed host
That shall be saved at the day of doom.
In manus tuas–of might's most
For ever–*commendo spiritum meum*.

Knowledge
Now hath he suffered that we all shall endure;
The *Good-Deeds* shall make all sure.
Now hath he made ending;
Methinketh that I hear angels sing
And make great joy and melody,
Where *Everyman's* soul received shall be.

Angel
Come, excellent elect spouse to Jesu:
Hereabove thou shalt go
Because of thy singular virtue:
Now the soul is taken the body fro;

Thy reckoning is crystal-clear.
Now shalt thou into the heavenly sphere,
Unto the which all ye shall come
That liveth well before the day of doom.

Doctor
This moral men may have in mind;
Ye hearers, take it of worth, old and young,
And forsake pride, for he deceiveth you in the end,
And remember *Beauty*, *Five-wits*, *Strength*, and *Discretion*,
They all at the last do *Everyman* forsake,
Save his *Good-Deeds*, there doth he take.
But beware, and they be small
Before God, he hath no help at all.
None excuse may be there for *Everyman*:
Alas, how shall he do then?
For after death amends may no man make,
For then mercy and pity do him forsake.
If his reckoning be not clear when he do come,
God will say–*ite maledicti in ignem æternum*.
And he that hath his account whole and sound,
High in heaven he shall be crowned;
Unto which place God bring us all thither
That we may live body and soul together.
Thereto help the Trinity,
Amen, say ye, for saint *Charity*.

THUS ENDETH THIS MORALL PLAY OF EVERYMAN.

DISCUSSION QUESTIONS

1. According to the Messenger in the opening speech, what is the purpose of the play? Does that purpose remind you of any other works of medieval literature or art?
2. What is God angry about in the opening of the play? What does he plan to do?
3. What does Everyman turn to in his attempt to make his journey toward death less fearful?
4. Why does "Goods" feel that he would make matters worse for Everyman if he went along with him?
5. Which two characters willingly accompany Everyman?
6. What does Everyman do to strengthen Good Deeds?
7. What is the purpose of the Doctor's closing speech?

WRITING SUGGESTION

1. Write an essay in which you describe the kind of set and costumes you would design if you were to direct *Everyman*. Also discuss what characteristics you would look for when casting actors, and how you would stage the final descent into the grave.

THE RENAISSANCE AND THE BAROQUE ERA

GENERAL INTRODUCTION

The period we now refer to as the Renaissance (from roughly the early 1400s to the early 1600s) did not get that name until the mid-19th century. Yet educated men and women of the 15th and 16th centuries certainly recognized that they were living in a time of extraordinary human accomplishments in arts, sciences, and in geographical discovery, even though they did not use the term "Renaissance" (meaning "rebirth") to describe their age. The term certainly fits the times, however, since the rebirth of classical learning helped to inspire many of the advances accomplished in these two centuries. With trade increasing with the East and the fall of Constantinople in 1453, scholars brought to Italy classical manuscripts that had been preserved in the Eastern Roman Empire but lost in the West. These rediscovered works sparked an interest in all aspects of Greek and Roman culture, inspiring artists, architects, philosophers, and scientists to build from classical models. In the mid-1400s, Johann Gutenberg's development of a movable type printing press allowed for a much wider dissemination of both classical and contemporary texts.

Other factors contributed to the acceleration of cultural activity we refer to as the Renaissance. The terrible plagues of the mid and late 1300s had unsettled traditional religious beliefs, which made way for the advent of new ideas. The cessation of the plagues also gave people the luxury to turn their attention to matters beyond simply surviving, and the end of the Hundred Years' War between France and England in 1453 had a similar effect. In addition, the growth of city-states and the wealthy individuals in these locales helped to fuel the cultural rebirth by providing alternative sources of patronage, other than the Church and the nobility. The Medici family in particular patronized the arts for generations and made Florence the epicenter of the Renaissance artistic revolution. Cosimo de Medici founded the Platonic Academy of Philosophy in Florence in 1462, which advocated Neoplatonism, an adoption of Plato's philosophy in conjunction with Christian ideology. Cosimo's grandson, Lorenzo, himself a poet and musician, spent liberally in improving Florence with parks, palaces, and festivals.

"Humanism" is a term that defines the dominant spirit of the times: It is a philosophy that emphasizes the dignity and potential of humans and the importance of classical learning. It is important to recognize that Renaissance humanists did not abandon the Christian beliefs that dominated the Middle Ages; rather, they included these beliefs in an expanded range of interests and concerns. Because "Renaissance" means "rebirth," some students mistakenly think that culture was dead in the Middle Ages. As we demonstrate in Unit 2, that is certainly not the case, and, in fact, culture was flourishing in the late medieval period. The Renaissance can best be distinguished from the Middle Ages by the widespread interest in humans and their potential, the adoption of classical ideas and aesthetics, and an increasing focus on close observation of humans and the natural world, both in the arts and the sciences. One could say that the Renaissance marks the shift between a culture focused on faith in God to a culture focused on faith in humans. Instead of the vertical emphasis of the medieval period, with paintings and cathedrals characterized by lines that point heavenward, the

Renaissance emphasized horizontal lines, leading the eye outward to humankind instead of upward to God, with depth being created in paintings through linear perspective and architecture following the lower, longer lines reminiscent of the Parthenon and other classical structures.

The horizontal emphasis of Renaissance advancements can also be seen in the geographical explorations that extended the known world by opening up new routes and discovering whole new continents. Just as humanists were looking outward at the potential of human beings, so were explorers looking outward at the potential of the globe. Christopher Columbus discovered the Bahamas in 1492; in 1497, Vasco da Gama found a route to India around the Cape of Good Hope; and from 1519 to 1522, Magellan and his crew proved the world was round by circumnavigating the globe. These men, and others, radically altered basic perceptions of the earth and Europe's position in it, while vastly extending the range of territories to be explored. The number and rate of these discoveries must have been dumbfounding—it would be the equivalent of our discovering life on another planet in our own times. It is hardly surprising that references to these discoveries frequently occur in the art and literature of the age (see Shakespeare's *The Tempest*, or Donne's "The Good-Morrow," both printed below, or Rembrandt's *Man in Oriental Costume*, which you can view at http://commons.wikimedia.org/wiki/File:Rembrandt_-_Man_in_Oriental_Costume.JPG).

Changing understandings of the cosmos paralleled changing perceptions of geography. In *On the Revolutions of Celestial Bodies*, Copernicus in 1543 argued that the earth revolved around the sun instead of vice versa, which shook people's faith that Earth was the center of the universe. The idea was widely shunned and the book was banned, but Galileo, who invented the telescope and proved that light takes time to travel, confirmed Copernicus's theory, although he was later forced to recant his arguments. Francis Bacon contributed to scientific advances by arguing for the use of a "scientific method" that involved close observation and experimentation to test hypotheses, instead of the tendency toward abstract contemplation of ideas that typified medieval thought.

While perceptions of the globe and cosmos were changing, so were perceptions of religion. The Catholic Church still played a dominant role in Renaissance culture, but less so than in the Middle Ages, due to the growing power of cities and the growing interest in human affairs and pre-Christian philosophy and art. The Church permanently lost its exclusive control over Christianity with the Protestant Reformation of the 16th century, which began when Martin Luther nailed his Ninety-five Theses to the entrance of Wittenberg's Castle Church on October 31,1517. Luther's Ninety-five Theses protested various corruptions of the Catholic Church, such as the granting of indulgences by priests to sinners, who paid the priests for forgiveness. Luther's protest set in motion a series of rebellions against the corruption of the Church. Protestantism, or the belief in Christianity—but not in the authority of the Catholic Church—was born out of these rebellions, and it led to the development of many new Christian-based religions, such as Lutheran, Calvinism, Methodist, and Presbyterian. The loosening of the Catholic Church's stranglehold on religion let some air into theological and philosophical debates, which further fueled the cultural developments of the Renaissance.

Art and music of the baroque era extend many of the developments brought about in the Renaissance. While some cultural historians, particularly art historians, refer to the baroque era as a separate period from the Renaissance, others see it more as a continuation of Renaissance interests and values, as we do here. Certainly the art and music of the baroque era were not in direct opposition to Renaissance arts, as some cultural periods seem to be reactions against their predecessors. Rather, baroque music, art, and architecture built on the advances of the Renaissance, often by increasing the drama, ornamentation, or complexity of the works. During the baroque period, the Church attempted to regain its cultural dominance by patronizing the arts even more than it had in the past. Increasing art patronage was an important aspect of the Counter-Reformation, which was the Church's response to Luther's attack on its authority. The Council of Trent, which met between 1545 and 1563 to organize the Church's response to the Reformation, decided that paintings and other artworks that depicted "the mysteries of our Redemption" would help inspire the people's awe of the Church.[1] The council particularly emphasized the importance of clarity and emotion in art, an emphasis which influenced some of the baroque artists and architects discussed below, such as Caravaggio and Artemisia Gentileschi.

Much baroque art and architecture falls outside the influence of the Church, however. The extravagant ornamentation of Versailles and the evocative depictions of light in Rembrandt's and Vermeer's paintings, for instance, stem more from aesthetic than religious concerns. And in the case of Versailles, high ornamentation was also motivated by a desire to demonstrate the power and majesty of King Louis the XIV. In baroque music, Monteverdi composed the first opera, *Orfeo*; the opera form itself clearly reflects the baroque age's focus on drama and ornamentation. Other new types of musical compositions such as concertos and oratorios also emphasize music's dramatic potential.

In 1616, both Shakespeare and Cervantes died—in fact, they both died on the same day, April 23, 1616; the year is often seen as marking the end of the Renaissance. And the end of the baroque age has often been seen as 1650, the year that Bach died. But such precise demarcations can never be entirely accurate. Numerous influential artists, writers, and musicians produced works in both time periods, and it would be absurd to say that the Renaissance came to an abrupt halt one year, giving way immediately to the baroque age.

THE VISUAL ARTS

The new ideas and classical influences that dominate the Renaissance first affected the visual arts most strikingly. One of the most important advances in the visual arts in the Renaissance was the development of linear perspective by Filippo Brunelleschi (1377–1446). The principles of linear perspective were later systematized by the architect

Figure 3-A Linear perspective diagram.

Leon Battista Alberti in *De Pictura* in 1435. Linear perspective is a method for depicting depth and accurate proportions in a drawing or painting by using a vanishing point with lines radiating outward from it (See Figure 3-A). Brunelleschi developed linear perspective so that he could execute his architectural drawings more accurately, but the method was soon adopted by painters as well. Masaccio was probably the first to use it accurately in painting his *Holy Trinity*, c. 1425–1428 (see Figure 3-B). Note how the vaulted ceiling seems to recede into the background of the painting, and the figures are realistically proportionate, unlike most medieval paintings, which compress the picture into two dimensions and ignore exact proportions among figures. The development of linear perspective both reflects and affects the Renaissance interest in close observation and capturing realistic details. Unlike medieval artists, Renaissance artists no longer eschewed the earthly; instead, they celebrated humans and their accomplishments by rendering them as accurately as possible in paintings and sculptures. It's not just

1   Quoted in *Arts and Culture: An Introduction to the Humanities*. Vol. II, p. 156. Eds. Janetta Rebold Benton and Robert DiYanni. Upper Saddle River, NJ: Prentice Hall, 1998.

Figure 3-B Masaccio's *Holy Trinity*.

Figure 3-C Il Duomo, Florence.

that a new technique was developed by Brunelleschi: A new perspective on earthly and human matters came along with it.

Brunelleschi also contributed to the growing influence of Classicism in the Italian Renaissance. After carefully observing the remnants of classical structures in Rome, Brunelleschi began incorporating elements of classical architecture such as arches and domes in his designs, adding his own innovations for a more dramatic effect. His greatest achievement is the octagonal dome of the cathedral in Florence (Il Duomo). The cathedral dome has both an inner and outer shell and uses principles of Gothic architecture, such as ribbing and pointed arches to allow for its great width (see Figure 3-C). Renaissance architects also adopted the classical use of columns and structures with more horizontal than vertical emphasis. The awe-inspiring towers of Gothic cathedrals gave way to structures that more closely resemble Greek or Roman temples. The shift to more horizontal lines in architecture reaches its culmination in the baroque age with the design of Versailles, which has a length of 1,903 feet (see Figure 3-D) and includes the Hall of Mirrors, with a length of 240 feet, but a width of only 34 feet.

Renaissance developments in painting extend beyond the use of linear perspective, however. While tempera paint on wooden panels had been the norm in the Middle Ages, Renaissance painters began using more frescoes (paintings made on wet plaster) and oil paints, which allowed for greater naturalism in art. In the Early Renaissance, along with Masaccio, Sandro Botticelli (1445–1510) also captured more lifelike forms in his works. The realistic flesh tones and proportions of the women in Botticelli's *Primavera* are particularly noteworthy, as is his allusion to classical antiquity with his depiction of Cupid and the allusion to a Roman festival of spring (see Figure 3-E).

Figure 3-D The Palace of Versailles.

meticulous execution of small details such as the fringe on the wife's dress and the reflection of the couple and the artist in the mirror behind them (see Figure 3-F).

The Italian High Renaissance is characterized by the works of Leonardo da Vinci, Michelangelo, and Raphael. These three artists extended the use of perspective begun in the Early Renaissance, often creating elaborate backgrounds for their subjects to draw the viewer's attention to the depths of their paintings. All three artists made advances in the realistic depiction of the human form; in fact, both da Vinci and Michelangelo studied anatomy scientifically and observed autopsies in order to more accurately render the skeleton and musculature of a human body.

While the Early Renaissance was flourishing in Italy, the Northern Renaissance was getting underway with Flemish painter Jan van Eyck (c.1390–1441), who is credited with introducing the use of oil paints on canvas, one of the most significant innovations of the Renaissance. Like his counterparts in Italy, van Eyck desired to observe closely and capture carefully the realistic details of his subjects. His famous painting, *Giovanni Arnolfini and His Wife Giovanna Cenami* (1434), demonstrates his

Leonardo da Vinci (1452–1519) helped to develop the techniques of chiaroscuro and sfumato. Chiaroscuro (*chiaro* means "light" and *scuro* means "dark) is the painting technique of juxtaposing light and dark areas to create a rounded effect. Sfumato (meaning "smoky") is a painting technique that involves applying multiple layers of glaze to a canvas to create a smoky, atmospheric effect. Da Vinci's use of linear perspective and his elaboration of the background of his painting, and his use of chiaroscuro and sfumato, can all be seen in his *Mona Lisa* (c.1503), one of the most famous paintings of all time, and certainly one of the most often reprinted (see Figure 3-G). But the painting has not captured the imaginations of so many because of its perspective, chiaroscuro, or sfumato techniques alone. What seems most to intrigue viewers is Mona Lisa's mysterious half-smile and her knowing glance. This painting, more than any others of its time, epitomizes the Renaissance artists' interest in human nature, in individuals and their unique personalities.

Figure 3-E Botticelli's *Primavera..*

Figure 3–F Van Eyck's *Giovanni Arnolfini and His Wife Giovanna Cenami.*

Figure 3-G Da Vinci's *Mona Lisa*.

Figure 3-H Michelangelo's *Moses*.

Mona Lisa's intelligent expression makes one feel the presence of a thinking, feeling human being on a two-dimensional canvas. If da Vinci had done nothing but paint *Mona Lisa* and *The Last Supper* (1495–1498), he still would be considered one of the great artists of the Renaissance. But da Vinci was also a sculptor, an engineer, and an inventor—he epitomized what we would now call a "Renaissance man," someone gifted in a wide range of disciplines.

Michelangelo Buonarroti (1475–1564) was another "Renaissance man," a gifted sculptor, painter, architect, and poet, although he considered himself primarily a sculptor. Michelangelo believed that when he sculpted, he was, in essence, removing excess marble to uncover the perfect figure lying within. His mastery in sculpting the human physique can best be seen in his *David* (1501–1504). Michelangelo's *Moses* (1515) similarly captures an eerie sense of motion just about to happen (see Figure 3-H). Both *David* and *Moses* create a commanding presence, not just because of their size or the perfection of their marble musculature, but also because of their intense expressions. They seem taut with energy, focus, and intelligence; no previous sculptor had managed to create figures so lifelike out of stone.

But Michelangelo is equally well known for his painting of the Sistine Chapel in the Vatican, a papal commission he tried to avoid. His design was ambitious—Old Testament history, featuring in the center the famous "Creation of Adam," in which God reaches his finger toward Adam's extended forefinger, ready to convey to Adam the spark of the divine. The expulsion of Adam and Eve from Eden is another famous panel in this awe-inspiring ceiling. In this panel, Michelangelo paradoxically depicts the expelled couple in more light than when they are crouching in Eden, thereby suggesting that the Fall was indeed fortunate, as some theologians have argued, because it brought humankind greater understanding and illumination, a sentiment certainly befitting a Renaissance humanist artist.

Figure 3-I Raphael's *School of Athens.*

Raphael (Raffaello Santi of Urbino, 1483–1520) benefited from studying the works of both Leonardo and Michelangelo. Georgio Vasari, the 16th-century author of *Lives of the Most Eminent Painters, Sculptors, and Architects,* records that Raphael's techniques improved immeasurably after he came to Rome and viewed Michelangelo's painting on the Sistine Chapel ceiling. Raphael later paid tribute to the master by placing him in the central foreground, leaning against a marble block in his painting, *The School of Athens* (1510–1511), which he executed for Pope Julius II for a room in the Vatican Palace (see Figure 3-I). The painting, as its name suggests, celebrates the thriving intellectual activity in ancient Athens; it includes, among other figures, Plato and Aristotle in the center of the top level, and their gestures summarize the focus of their philosophies: Plato, holding his *Timaeus,* points upward toward his ideal forms, while Aristotle, holding his *Ethics,* points outward toward the real forms surrounding them. Euclid, Ptolemy, Zoroaster, and Raphael himself appear in a grouping in the right foreground. The painting embodies the spirit of Renaissance humanism in its celebration of classical antiquity and all branches of learning. Raphael epitomizes the horizontal focus of Renaissance artists and philosophers by emphasizing the painting's illusion of depth

Figure 3-J El Greco's *The Burial of the Count of Orgaz*.

Figure 3-K Bruegel's *Peasant Wedding*.

through the mathematically accurate application of linear perspective in the series of receding arches.

By the late Renaissance, painters and sculptors felt that the pinnacle of realism had been reached. It did not seem possible to portray humans more realistically than Michelangelo or Raphael, so a new style or technique needed to be developed for artists to make their mark. Mannerism is the artistic style that evolved to fill the void. Mannerist art is distinguished by a heightened sense of drama—both in subject and in technique; the name comes from the Italian *di maniera*, which indicates art that emphasizes style more than a realistic portrayal of nature. Highly emotional subjects predominate, and Mannerist painters often used heightened contrasts of light and dark and distorted figures to reflect the emotions of the scene. This increasing emphasis on drama is a natural response to a century or more of focusing on reason, realism, and classical balance and harmony, but Mannerism also reflects the instability of the times. In 1494, France invaded Italy, and

in 1527, Rome was sacked by Spain. Between these two events, Martin Luther began his attack on the Church, which started the Reformation. Suddenly the stability of Italy and the dominance of the Church both came into question. The balanced compositions of the High Renaissance gave way to off-center paintings with writhing bodies and bold—sometimes even garish—lighting.

Domenikos Theotocopoulos (1541–1614), nicknamed El Greco (meaning "the Greek" in Spanish) developed the most distinctive style of the Mannerist painters. While he was born in Crete and studied in Venice, he executed his major paintings primarily in Spain. His works can be easily identified even at a distance because of his use of elongated bodies, sharp light/dark contrasts, bold colors, and the bluish-gray flesh color of many of his figures. El Greco's paintings reflect the heightened focus on spirituality in Spain at the time, in response to the Reformation's challenge to the Church. The preponderance of saints and angels in his famous *The*

Burial of the Count of Orgaz, along with El Greco's disregard for mathematically proportionate spatial relations and his elongation of bodies, all hark back to prevailing styles of painting in the Middle Ages (see Figure 3-J). It is likely he adopted these medieval techniques as a way of reminding viewers of a time in the not-too-distant past when Europeans had focused more exclusively and unanimously on spiritual matters.

In Brussels, during the late Renaissance, Pieter Bruegel the Elder, although not typically considered a Mannerist, similarly developed an approach to painting that emphasized style over realism. Like other Mannerists, Bruegel paid less attention to portraying details and proportions realistically, and instead painted somewhat simplified figures in a highly distinctive manner that emphasizes an overall pattern of shape and color more than a precise reflection of nature, as in his *Peasant Wedding*, c. 1566–1567 (see Figure 3-K). While El Greco elongated his figures, Bruegel exaggerated the roundedness of his, which emphasizes the comfort and harmony of the gathering. These are not the twisted bodies of most Mannerist art, distorted by either religious agony or ecstasy; Bruegel's subjects exude a sense of contentedness with themselves and the world around them. Yet, in their highly stylized

look, they do not fit in with the patterns of earlier Renaissance art or later baroque art.

Baroque art and architecture continued the Mannerist emphasis on emotion and drama, as well as the technical innovations and the classical focus of the Renaissance. Baroque, initially a term used to refer to irregular pearls, has come to signify elaborate ornamentation, but this connotation ignores its deeper roots and purpose. Baroque arts stemmed in part from the Catholic Church's Counter-Reformation, its response to the Reformation, as mentioned in the general introduction to this unit. Having lost its monopoly on European religious affairs, the Catholic Church decided to use the arts to win back those who had strayed and strengthen the faith of those who had stayed. It particularly encouraged artists to depict religious stories clearly, realistically, and emotionally. The works of Caravaggio, Gentileschi, and Bernini reflect this impulse.

Caravaggio (1573–1610) depicted dramatic religious moments such as *The Calling of Saint Matthew* (ca. 1599–1602), and heightened the intensity of the scene by using stark contrasts of light and dark areas, also known as tenebrism (see Figure

Figure 3-L Caravaggio's *The Calling of Saint Matthew.*

Figure 3-M Gentileschi's *Judith Slaying Holofernes.*

3-L). Note how Caravaggio positions the three fingers that are pointing toward Matthew so that they parallel the diagonal shaft of light illuminating the faces, while the left and right extremes of the canvas fall into deep shadow. The composition of the scene works with the lighting to enhance the painting's drama and tension.

Artemisia Gentileschi uses a similar tenebristic style in *Judith Slaying Holofernes*, c.1620 (see Figure 3-M). In this painting, the sword that is about to slice Holofernes' throat is at the center foreground of the canvas, with the radiating lines of the women's arms all directing the eye to Holofernes' throat. With all three figures compressed into the foreground of the painting, looking as if they were lit by a strong light with the background in complete darkness, the horror of the moment is intensified. Gentileschi frequently turned to the story of Judith from the Old Testament, perhaps finding Judith's violence against an invading enemy appealing, since Gentileschi herself was raped when she was 15 and then tortured with a thumb-screw in court when she brought charges against her attacker.

Gianlorenzo Bernini (1598–1680) epitomized baroque style in both his architectural designs and his sculptures. Bernini designed the sweeping colonnade in front of St. Peter's Basilica in Rome, as well as St. Peter's ornate, 100-foot high baldacchino, a canopy-like structure that goes over a church altar. Bernini's dramatic style and the baroque emphasis on drama in general can perhaps best be exemplified by his sculpture, *David*. Compare Bernini's *David* to the Davids of Donatello and Michelangelo (see Figure 3-N). Donatello's *David* appears relaxed, Michelangelo's appears primed for action, but Bernini's is in mid-throw, his body twisted back ready to swing the slingshot forward, without a doubt the most action oriented of the three figures. Bernini's *David* seems to embody the fierceness of the Catholic Church's Counter-Reformation response to the threatening giant of Protestantism.

Not all baroque art was inspired by Counter-Reformation politics, however. In northern Protestant countries such as England and Holland, religious art was seen as promoting idolatry, so artists turned more to nonreligious subjects in their works. Instead of the Church, the growing mercantile classes, fed by the wealth of new colonies, patronized the arts, as did the aristocracy in both Catholic and non-Catholic countries. Patronizing the arts became a symbol of status. Consequently, portraits of merchants, aristocracy, and even peasants became increasingly popular. Classical and religious figures no longer predominated in the works of northern, Protestant artists such as Rembrandt and Vermeer. And even in Catholic Spain, Velázquez achieved fame primarily through his portraits of royalty, not his depictions of religious subjects.

Rembrandt van Rijn (1606–1669), a Dutch painter, was one of the greatest artists of the baroque period, and, indeed, one of the greatest in history. His paintings and sketches cover a wide range of subjects, from historical and religious scenes, to autopsies, portraits of humble scholars, and numerous self-portraits. From Caravaggio, Rembrandt took and developed the use of tenebristic lighting, heightening even more dramatically the striking contrast between the lit portions of his subjects and those that fall into deep shadow, as can be seen in *The Anatomy Lesson of Dr. Tulp* (see Figure 3-O). Note how the lighting emphasizes and symbolizes a source of illumination—the corpse being dissected. Rembrandt uses light to give an almost holy resonance to secular subjects. This technique, along with his choice of subject matter, reflects the Renaissance spirit of humanism, with its emphasis on learning and its faith in human potential. In his later paintings, Rembrandt used more subtle lighting and coloring and coarser brushstrokes. While the light effects are less dramatic, the emotional and psychological complexity captured in his portraits deepens in these later works, particularly in the self-portraits.

Jan Vermeer (1632–1675), another Dutch master painter, developed his own unique style of capturing the effects of light. Focusing on mostly domestic subjects, Vermeer frequently depicts his figures in a warm swath of light pouring through a side window, as in *Young Woman with a Water Pitcher*, c.1664–1665 (see Figure 3-P). While not as dramatic as Rembrandt's lighting, Vermeer's still seems to hallow his figures, to suggest something holy even in the humble. Vermeer seems to delight in accurately portraying the smallest domestic details, such as the

a. Donatello's *David*

c. Bernini's *David*

Figure 3-N (a,b,c)

b. Michelangelo's *David*

pattern of the tablecloth, the etchings on the window, and the glint of light off the pitcher.

In Spain, Diego Velázquez (1599–1660) focused on more aristocratic subjects in his position as royal painter to Philip IV. One of his most famous paintings is *Las Meninas* (Maids of Honor, 1656), which depicts the five-year-old Princess Margarita, her servants, a nun, a dwarf, a dog, and the painter himself, most of whom seem to be staring out at us, as if we were the subjects of the painting that the figure of Velázquez is working on in the left foreground of the canvas (see Figure 3-Q). But in the background, a mirror shows the reflection of the king and queen, apparently the real subjects being studied by the figure of Velázquez. As a painting of a painting in progress, the work is highly self-referential and thought provoking, particularly since it places the viewer in the position of the subject. Velázquez maximizes the potential of linear perspective to suggest depth by having a figure in the far central background opening a door that leads further back into the palace. And of course the reflection of the king and queen in the mirror suggests a foreground that would be in front of the actual painting, giving the work an unusually strong horizontal emphasis.

LITERATURE

The late Renaissance produced two of the greatest literary figures of all time—Miguel de Cervantes and William Shakespeare. Both men transcended the confines of their times and of literary traditions, creating works that continue to influence literature today. In the exuberance, generosity, and virtuosity of their writings, both men pushed out the boundaries of literature, just as artists, musicians, scientists, and explorers were pushing out the boundaries of their fields. Cervantes (1547–1616), a native of Spain, led the kind

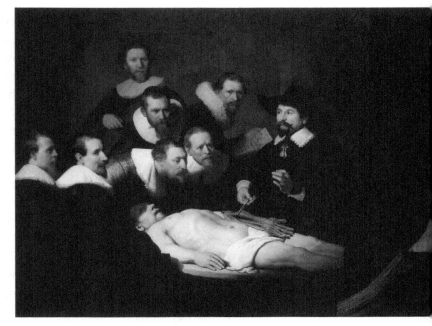

Figure 3-O Rembrandt's *The Anatomy Lesson of Dr. Tule.*

Figure 3-P Vermeer's *Young Woman with a Water Pitcher.*

Figure 3-Q Velázquez's *Las Meninas.*

of adventurous life that would have appealed to his most famous character, Don Quixote. As a young man, he fought in Italy as a mercenary soldier and lost the use of his left hand from a battle wound. In 1575, he was taken captive by pirates and served as a galley slave for five years. At the age of 37, he was ransomed; soon after he married a 19-year-old girl and began his career as a writer and business-man. He wrote his masterpiece, *The Most Ingenious Knight, Don Quixote of La Mancha*, between 1603 and 1605. Many consider it to be the first novel, and certainly in its boisterous complexity and its richly drawn characters—particularly Quixote him-self—Cervantes takes the narrative form a quantum leap ahead. Don Quixote, simultaneously noble and foolish, satirized and honored, displays the kind of three-dimensionality of characterization that Shakespeare is famous for in his plays. The work is too long to be contained within our anthology, and we do not want to shortchange it by excerpting it here, but we fervently recommend reading it in its entirety.

William Shakespeare (1564–1616), considered one of the greatest playwrights and poets of all time, demonstrates the Renaissance spirit of exploration and interest in human complexity by delving more deeply into the psyches of characters than had

ever been done before. His characters' soliloquies (speeches that reveal a character's thoughts) enable readers and audiences to explore the fluctuations of the human mind in a way that had not previously been attempted, as can be seen particularly well in *Hamlet*. In his plays, Shakespeare initiated the mod-ern sense of characterization that continues to affect both drama and fiction today. Shakespeare also pushed out the boundaries of poetic language more than any previous poet, by using a greater density of metaphors, puns, allusions, and rhyme and rhythmic effects than any other writer of his time. Consider the verbal pyrotechnics of his sonnet "That Time of Year Thou Mayst in Me Behold" (see Selected Readings), where he uses three separate images, all richly devel-oped, to describe his own aging and fear of death, but also to offer simultaneously some consolation for mortality—all within 14 lines. Like Petrarch before him, Shakespeare made the sonnet form his own, so much so that the English sonnet, with three quatrains followed by a couplet, is also known as the Shakespearean sonnet. When both Cervantes and Shakespeare died on April 23, 1616, an age really did end, but new understandings of human nature had begun.

Shakespeare and Cervantes were certainly not the only significant writers of the Renaissance, however. Machiavelli (1469–1527) was one of the first to cap-ture the bold and independent Renaissance spirit in his writings, albeit in a cynical fashion. His book *The Prince*, written in 1513 and published posthumously in 1532, presents guidelines for leaders to gain and keep power. "It is better to be feared than loved," is one of Machiavelli's ideas that sums up his cyni-cal view of human nature. Humans are greedy and untrustworthy, Machiavelli felt, so a leader should always operate independently, trust no one, and use whatever means possible, regardless of ethics, to gain and maintain power. Having been arrested, tortured, and jailed by the Medici family because they thought he was a conspirator, Machiavelli knew firsthand how fickle rulers could be and the precariousness of the fates of those ruled. It is little wonder that he characterizes the successful prince as ruthless. While Machiavelli's approach disregards the idealism of humanism, it does reflect the human-centered focus of the times. Christian ethics, cosmic justice, the will of God—these matter little to Machiavelli, and many subsequent leaders have used his writings to justify their quest for power.

Michel de Montaigne (1533–1592), a humanist writer from Bordeaux, France, did for essay writing what Cervantes did for fiction and Shakespeare for drama and poetry. In his *Essays*, Montaigne developed the genre of essay writing, creating a personal, exploratory style that has influenced writers for centuries, perhaps most notably Virginia Woolf, and continues to shape nonfiction writers today. While Montaigne clearly reflects his humanist education in his essays, his primary focus seems to be an exploration of himself and his society, an exploration that does not always lead to answers. The name he used to describe his writings, *essai*, is French for "an attempt" and comes from the verb *essayer*, which means "to try"; the name itself, then, indicates the lack of certainty and closure that characterizes his works. In his use of writing to probe his own thoughts and push out the boundaries of his ideas, Montaigne prefigures contemporary approaches to composition used by writing teachers today.

While men dominate the literary world of the Renaissance, aristocratic women (and some women raised in the homes of aristocrats) often received excellent humanistic educations like their male counterparts and then produced their own poetry, fiction, drama, and translations. Marguerite de Navarre in France and Mary Sidney in England are notable examples of the aristocratic woman of letters—the "Renaissance woman." Marguerite de Navarre (1492–1549) was one of the leading cultural figures in the French court. As the daughter of the count of Angoulême, the sister of King Francis I, and the wife of Charles, Duke of Alençon, she invited leading writers and artists of the time such as Leonardo da Vinci to come to the French court. With her second marriage to Henri d'Albret, she became queen of Navarre, although not much territory came along with the kingdom, since much of the region had been taken by Spain. Still, Marguerite presided over their castles at Pau and Nerac and continued her friendships with artists and writers such as Rabelais, Erasmus, and Calvin. While she sympathized with Protestant intellectuals and agreed that the Church needed to reform, she seems to have remained

devoted to Catholicism all her life. Perhaps because of this, her writings have more of a medieval flavor than those of most other Renaissance authors; concern for Christian ethics reverberates throughout her works. In 1547, she published *Les Marguerites de la Marguerite des Princesses* (Marguerite referring to both her name and its original meaning, "pearl"), which included poetry and dramatic pieces. She is best known, however, for the *Heptameron*, published posthumously in 1558. The *Heptameron* is a framed series of tales like Chaucer's *Canterbury Tales* and Boccaccio's *Decameron*, told by a group of aristocrats whose journey is hindered by a flood. The *Heptameron*'s narrators must tell of situations they have observed themselves or have heard of through reliable witnesses. This restriction reflects the same Renaissance concerns for close observation and for naturalistic portrayals of human beings that inspired the visual artists of the time to perfect their rendering of human forms in paintings and sculptures. With the *Heptameron*, Marguerite de Navarre gives the framed tale a Renaissance voice.

Later in the 16th century, Mary Sidney made her mark on the English Renaissance with her poetry and translations, as well as her completion and editing of the works of her brother, Sir Philip Sidney, whose heroic death from battle wounds at the age of 31 brought about a remarkable display of public mourning. Much of Mary Sidney's literary work stems from a desire to honor her lost brother. She wrote elegies for him, encouraged other poets to elegize him, published his poetry, and finished his collection of Psalm paraphrases.[2] When she was not praising her brother, she was praising her queen, Elizabeth I, who was also a poet and patron of the arts, as can be seen in the readings below. Mary Sidney's self-deprecating attitude toward her own literary merits and her celebration of the merits of her brother and her queen enabled her to transcend some of the social, intellectual, and literary limitations placed on women at the time. In other words, she did not publish to glorify herself, which would

2   See *The Collected Works of Mary Sidney Herbert, Countess of Pembroke*. Vol. 1, p. 6. Ed. by Margaret P. Hannay, Noel J. Kinnamon, and Michael G. Brennan. Oxford: Clarendon Press, 1998.

have been unseemly, but to glorify her brother and Elizabeth, an appropriate action for a dutiful sister and subject. Like Navarre, Sidney's friendships with and patronage of numerous male authors also aided her literary reputation by giving her a ready and learned audience, such as Edmund Spenser, who was both a friend and a literary influence. Many of these connections would be eager to please a possible patron.

John Donne (1572–1631) is a transitional literary figure between the Renaissance and the baroque age. Like Shakespeare, Donne loved rich, complex metaphors and metaphors that reflect contemporary discoveries in science and geographic exploration. But while Shakespeare worked primarily with the restrictive and contained sonnet form in his poetry, Donne experimented with somewhat looser and lengthier structures (although he, too, wrote sonnets, and they are some of the most powerful in the history of the form—see Holy Sonnet 14, "Batter My Heart," for instance). Donne and his family were persecuted for being Catholics during the reign of the Protestant Elizabeth I; when he converted to Anglicanism, he began a successful career in the Church of England that led to his being dean of St. Paul's Cathedral in London. Donne struggled with his religious feelings, partly because of his abandonment of the Catholic faith and partly because they conflicted with his earthly desires. He gives voice to these struggles in his poetry and in the sermons he wrote. Donne's passionate, expressive nature makes every poem he writes dramatic, whether he is discussing God or his mistress (see "To His Mistress Going to Bed"). It is the drama of his poetry that allies Donne with the baroque aesthetic.

Anne Dudley Bradstreet (1612–1672) was the first American poet to achieve popular and critical acclaim. Having emigrated to America in 1630 (her husband worked for the Massachusetts Bay Company), Bradstreet helped to establish a fledgling colony. At the same time, she gave poetry a new voice and direction. Her poems often revolve around domestic life and relationships, such as "Before the Birth of One of Her Children." Even when she writes about her role as a poet, as she does in "Author to Her Book," she uses maternal metaphors to characterize her relationship to her literary works. In doing so, Bradstreet defines not just new territory for women writers to explore, but the beginnings of a distinctively American literary style.

Paradise Lost, by John Milton (1608–1674), embodies the baroque sense of splendor, vastness, drama, and ornamentation more than any other literary work of the period. A cosmic epic encompassing Heaven, Hell, Earth, and the origins and future of humankind, Milton's most famous work could not be grander in its conception or execution. *Paradise Lost*, like any great epic, really should be read from beginning to end to appreciate its richness, but Book 1, included below, will give the reader a sense of its narrative arc and its poetic magnificence. Milton's powerful writing can also be witnessed in shorter works such as his sonnets and the influential elegy *Lycidas* (see Selected Readings). In his sonnets, Milton clearly has been influenced by Shakespeare, but still he marks them with his own style, sometimes placing the sonnet's "turn" (the point at which the tone of the speaker changes and moves toward resolution) right in the middle of a line (often the eighth line or earlier), instead of at the beginning of the ninth line, which would be typical of Italian sonnets, or at the beginning of the thirteenth line, as in English sonnets. This disruption of a line adds to the sonnet's dramatic effect.

In *Lycidas*, an elegy written to honor a young friend who drowned, Milton borrows from the pastoral elegy tradition of classical antiquity, using the tradition's metaphors of shepherds, sheep, fields, and streams to characterize a 17th-century university man. In doing so, Milton reflects the Renaissance interest in classicism and the baroque interest in ornamentation; yet at the same time, the poem's attack on clergy and bishops reflects Milton's Puritan distaste for contemporary clerical abuses.

MARGUERITE DE NAVARRE (1492–1549)

Marguerite de Navarre contributed to Renaissance letters through her writings and through her patronage of artists and other writers. As the sister of the French king Francis I, the wife of the Duke of Alençon, and later as the queen of Navarre, Marguerite de Navarre befriended such notable Renaissance figures as Leonardo da Vinci, Erasmus, and John Calvin. She made the French court and then her own court major cultural centers. While critical of abuses in the Catholic Church and sympathetic to the Protestant call for reform, she appears to have remained a loyal Catholic all her life. In 1547, she published *Les Marguerites de la Marguerite des Princesses*, a collection of poetry and drama (the title plays on her name and its literal meaning, "pearl"). Her best-known work, the *Heptameron*, published posthumously in 1558, presents a series of tales bound together by a narrative frame, like Chaucer's *Canterbury Tales* or Boccaccio's *Decameron*. Although there is some dispute over whether or not she wrote all the tales, Navarre seems at least to have been the grand designer and editor of the whole. Her tales are told by a band of aristocrats who are hindered in their journey by a flood and decide to entertain each other by storytelling (she planned ten days of storytelling, but completed only seven, hence the preface "Hepta" in the title, meaning "seven"). But her narrators must operate under greater restrictions than Chaucer's or Boccaccio's: They agree only to tell stories they have witnessed themselves or have heard from a reliable witness. As mentioned in the "Literature" section of the introductory essay to this unit, this restriction matches the aesthetic concerns of the Renaissance by emphasizing, as did the visual artists of the time, the importance of observation and accurate portrayal of reality. But in spite of the restriction and its emphasis on realism, Navarre still includes some outlandish situations in her tales, such as the possible, if not plausible, series of unfortunate mishaps in "Tale 30."

HEPTAMERON

Tale XXX.

A young gentleman, of from fourteen to fifteen years of age, thought to lie with one of his mother's maids, but lay with his mother herself; and she, in consequence thereof, was, nine months afterwards, brought to bed of a daughter, who, twelve or thirteen years later, was wedded by the son; he being ignorant that she was his daughter and sister, and she, that he was her father and brother.[1]

In the time of King Louis the Twelfth, the Legate at Avignon being then a scion of the house of Amboise, nephew to George, Legate of France,[2] there lived in the land of Languedoc a lady who had an income of more than four thousand ducats a year, and whose name I shall not mention for the love I bear her kinsfolk.

While still very young, she was left a widow with one son; and, both by reason of her regret for her husband and her love for her child, she determined never to marry again. To avoid all opportunity of doing so, she had fellowship only with the devout, for she imagined that opportunity makes the sin, not knowing that sin will devise the opportunity.

This young widow, then, gave herself up wholly to the service of God, and shunned all worldly assemblies so completely that she scrupled to be present at a wedding, or even to listen to the organs playing in a church. When her son was come to the age of seven years, she chose for his schoolmaster a man of holy life, so that he might be trained up in all piety and devotion.

When the son was reaching the age of fourteen or fifteen, Nature, who is a very secret schoolmaster, finding him in good condition and very idle, taught him a different lesson to any he had learned from his tutor. He began to look at and desire such things as he deemed beautiful, and among others a maiden who slept in his mother's room. No one had any suspicion of this, for he was looked upon as a mere child, and, moreover, in that household nothing save godly talk was ever heard.

This young gallant, however, began secretly soliciting the girl, who complained of it to her mistress. The latter had so much love for her son and so high an opinion of him, that she thought the girl spoke as she did in order to make her hate him; but, being strongly urged by the other, she at last said—

"I shall find out whether it is true, and will punish him if it be as you say. But if, on the other hand, you are bringing an untruthful accusation against him, you shall suffer for it."

Then, in order to test the matter, she bade the girl make an appointment with her son that he might come and lie with her at midnight, in the bed in which she slept alone, beside the door of his mother's room.

The maid obeyed her mistress, who, when night came, took the girl's place, resolved, if the story were true, to punish her son so severely that he would never again lie with a woman without remembering it.

While she was thinking thus wrathfully, her son came and got into the bed, but although she beheld him do so, she could not yet believe that he meditated any unworthy deed. She therefore refrained

---

1 This story is based on an ancient popular tradition common to many parts of France, and some particulars of which, with a list of similar tales in various European languages, will be found in the Appendix, D.—En

2 The Papal Legate in France here alluded to is the famous George, Cardinal d'Amboise, favourite minister of Louis XII. His nephew, the Legate at Avignon, is Louis d'Amboise, fourth son of Peter d'Amboise, Lord of Chaumont, and brother of the Grand-Master of Chaumont. Louis d'Amboise became bishop of Albi, and lieutenant-general of the King of France in Burgundy, Languedoc and Roussillon, and played an important part in the public affairs of his time. He died in 1505.—See *Gallia Christiana*, vol. i. p. 34.—L. and R. J.

Marguerite de Navarre, "Tale XXX," *Heptaméron*, trans. George Saintsbury. Copyright in the Public Domain.

from speaking to him until he had given her some token of his evil intent, for no trifling matters could persuade her that his desire was actually a criminal one. Her patience, however, was tried so long, and her nature proved so frail that, forgetting her motherhood, her anger became transformed into an abominable delight. And just as water that has been restrained by force rushes onward with the greater vehemence when it is released, so was it with this unhappy lady who had so prided herself on the constraint she had put upon her body. After taking the first step downwards to dishonour, she suddenly found herself at the bottom, and thus that night she became pregnant by him whom she had thought to restrain from acting in similar fashion towards another.

No sooner was the sin accomplished than such remorse of conscience began to torment her as filled the whole of her after-life with repentance. And so keen was it at the first, that she rose from beside her son—who still thought that she was the maid—and entered a closet, where, dwelling upon the goodness of her intention and the wickedness of its execution, she spent the whole night alone in tears and lamentation.

But instead of humbling herself, and recognising the powerlessness of our flesh, without God's assistance, to work anything but sin, she sought by her own tears and efforts to atone for the past, and by her own prudence to avoid mischief in the future, always ascribing her sin to circumstances and not to wickedness, for which there is no remedy save the grace of God. Accordingly she sought to act so as never again to fall into such wrongdoing; and as though there were but one sin that brought damnation in its train, she put forth all her strength to shun that sin alone.

But the roots of pride, which acts of sin ought rather to destroy, grew stronger and stronger within her, so that in avoiding one evil she wrought many others. Early on the morrow, as soon as it was light, she sent for her son's preceptor, and said—

"My son is beginning to grow up, it is time to send him from home. I have a kinsman, Captain Monteson,[3] who is beyond the mountains with my lord the Grand-Master of Chaumont, and he will be very glad to admit him into his company. Take him, therefore, without delay, and to spare me the pain of parting do not let him come to bid me farewell."

So saying, she gave him money for the journey, and that very morning sent the young man away, he being right glad of this, for, after enjoying his sweetheart, he asked nothing better than to set off to the wars.

The lady continued for a great while in deep sadness and melancholy, and, but for the fear of God, had many a time longed that the unhappy fruit of her womb might perish. She feigned sickness, in order that she might wear a cloak and so conceal her condition; and having a bastard brother, in whom she had more trust than in any one else, and upon whom she had conferred many benefits, she sent for him when the time of her confinement was drawing nigh, told him her condition (but without mentioning her son's part in it), and besought him to help her save her honour. This he did, and, a few days before the time when she expected to be delivered, he begged her to try a change of air and remove to his house, where she would recover her health more quickly than at home. Thither she went with but a very small following, and found there a midwife who had been summoned as for her brother's wife, and who one night, without recognising her, delivered her of a fine little girl. The gentleman gave the child to a nurse, and caused it to be cared for as his own.

After continuing there for a month, the lady returned in sound health to her own house, where she lived more austerely than ever in fasts and disciplines. But when her son was grown up, he sent to beg his mother's permission to return home, as there was at that time no war in Italy. She, fearing lest she should fall again into the same misfortune, would not at first allow him, but he urged her so earnestly that at last she could find no reason for

---

3 Monteson was one of the bravest captains of his time; as the comrade of Bayard, he greatly distinguished himself by his intrepidity in Louis XII.'s Italian campaigns. Some particulars concerning him will be found in M. Lacroix's edition of Les Chroniques de Jean d'Anton.—B. J. Respecting the Grand-Master of Chaumont, also mentioned above, see ante, vol ii., notes to Tale XIV.

refusing him. However, she instructed him that he was not to appear before her until he was married to a woman whom he dearly loved; but to whose fortune he need give no heed, for it would suffice if she were of gentle birth.

Meanwhile her bastard brother, finding that the daughter left in his charge had grown to be a tall maiden of perfect beauty, resolved to place her in some distant household where she would not be known, and by the mother's advice she was given to Catherine, Queen of Navarre.[4] The maiden thus came to the age of twelve or thirteen years, and was so beautiful and virtuous that the Queen of Navarre had great friendship for her, and much desired to marry her to one of wealth and station. Being poor, however, she found no husband, though she had lovers enough and to spare.

Now it happened one day that the gentleman who was her unknown father came to the house of the Queen of Navarre on his way back from beyond the mountains, and as soon as he had set eyes on his daughter he fell in love with her, and having license from his mother to marry any woman that might please him, he only inquired whether she was of gentle birth, and, hearing that she was, asked her of the Queen in marriage. The Queen willingly

consented, for she knew that the gentleman was not only rich and handsome, but worshipful to boot.

When the marriage had been consummated, the gentleman again wrote to his mother, saying that she could no longer close her doors against him, since he was bringing with him as fair a daughter-in-law as she could desire. The lady inquired to whom he had allied himself, and found that it was to none other than their own daughter. Thereupon she fell into such exceeding sorrow that she nearly came by a sudden death, seeing that the more she had striven to hinder her misfortune, the greater had it thereby become.

Not knowing what else to do, she went to the Legate of Avignon, to whom she confessed the enormity of her sin, at the same time asking his counsel as to how she ought to act. The Legate, to satisfy his conscience, sent for several doctors of theology, and laid the matter before them, without, however, mentioning any names; and their advice was that the lady should say nothing to her children, for they, being in ignorance, had committed no sin, but that she herself should continue doing penance all her life without allowing it to become known.

Accordingly, the unhappy lady returned home, where not long afterwards her son and daughter-in-law arrived. And they loved each other so much that never were there husband and wife more loving, nor yet more resembling each other; for she was his daughter, his sister and his wife, while he was her father, her brother and her husband. And this exceeding love between them continued always; and the unhappy and deeply penitent lady could never see them in dalliance together without going apart to weep.

"You see, ladies, what befalls those who think that by their own strength and virtue they may subdue Love and Nature and all the faculties that God has given them. It were better to recognise their own weakness, and instead of running a-tilt against such an adversary, to betake themselves to Him who is their true Friend, saying to Him in the words of the Psalmist, 'Lord, I am afflicted very much; answer Thou for me.'"[5]

---

4 This is Catherine, daughter of Gaston and sister of Francis Phoebus de Foix. On her brother's death, in 1483, she became Queen of Navarre, Duchess of Nemours and Countess of Foix and Bigorre, and in the following year espoused John, eldest son of Alan, Sire d'Albret. Catherine at this time was fourteen years old, and her husband, who by the marriage became King of Navarre, was only one year her senior. Their title to the crown was disputed by a dozen pretenders, for several years they exercised but a precarious authority, and eventually, in July 1512, Ferdinand the Catholic despatched the Duke of Alva to besiege Pamplona. On the fourth day of the siege John and Catherine succeeded in escaping from their capital, which, three days later, surrendered. Ferdinand, having sworn to maintain the fueros, was thereupon acknowledged as sovereign. However, it was only in 1516 that the former rulers were expelled from Navarrese territory. "Had I been Don Juan and you Donna Catherine," said the Queen to her pusillanimous husband, as they crossed the Pyrenees, "we should not have lost our kingdom." From this time forward the d'Albrets, like their successors the Bourbons, were sovereigns of Navarre in name only, for an attempt made in 1521 to reconquer the kingdom resulted in total failure, and their dominions were thenceforth confined to Beam, Bigorre, and Foix on the French side of the Pyrenees. Queen Catherine died in 1517, aged 47, leaving several children, the eldest of whom was Henry, Queen Margaret's second husband.—M., B. J., D. and Ed.

---

5 We have failed to find this sentence in the Psalms. Probably the reference is to Isaiah xxxviii. 14, "O Lord, I am oppressed; undertake for me."—Eu.

"It were impossible," said Oisille "to hear a stranger story than this. Methinks every man and woman should bend low in the fear of God, seeing that in spite of a good intention so much mischief came to pass."

"You may be sure," said Parlamente, "that the first step a man takes in self-reliance, removes him so far from reliance upon God."

"A man is wise," said Geburon, "when he knows himself to be his greatest enemy, and holds his own wishes and counsels in suspicion."

"Albeit the motive might seem to be a good and holy one," said Longarine, "there were surely none, howsoever worthy in appearance, that should induce a woman to lie beside a man, whatever the kinship between them, for fire and tow may not safely come together."

"Without question," said Ennasuite, "she must have been some self-sufficient fool, who, in her friar-like dreaming, deemed herself so saintly as to be incapable of sin, just as many of the Friars would have us believe that we can become, merely by our own efforts, which is an exceeding great error."

"Is it possible, Longarine," asked Oisille, "that there are people foolish enough to hold such an opinion?"

"They go further than that," replied Longarine. "They say that we ought to accustom ourselves to the virtue of chastity; and in order to try their strength they speak with the prettiest women they can find and whom they like best, and by kissing and touching them essay whether their fleshly nature be wholly dead. When they find themselves stirred by such pleasure, they desist, and have recourse to fasts and grievous discipline. Then, when they have so far mortified their flesh that neither speech nor kiss has power to move them, they make trial of the supreme temptation, that, namely, of lying together and embracing without any lustfulness.[6] But for one who has escaped, so many have come to mischief, that the Archbishop of Milan, where this religious practice used to be carried on,[7] was obliged to separate them and place the women in convents and the men in monasteries."

"Truly," said Geburon, "it were the extremity of folly to seek to become sinless by one's own efforts, and at the same time to seek out opportunities for sin."

"There are some," said Saffredent, "who do the very opposite, and flee opportunities for sin as carefully as they are able; nevertheless, concupiscence pursues them. Thus the good Saint Jerome, after scourging and hiding himself in the desert, confessed that he could not escape from the fire that consumed his marrow. We ought, therefore, to recommend ourselves to God, for unless He uphold us by His power, we are greatly prone to fall."

"You do not notice what I do," said Hircan. "While we were telling our stories, the monks behind the hedge here heard nothing of the vesper-bell; whereas, now that we have begun to speak about God, they have taken themselves off, and are at this moment ringing the second bell."

"We shall do well to follow them," said Oisille, "and praise God for enabling us to spend this day in the happiest manner imaginable."

Hereat they rose and went to the church, where they piously heard vespers; after which they went to supper, discussing the discourses they had heard, and calling to mind divers adventures that had come to pass in their own day, in order to determine which of them were worthy to be recounted. And after spending the whole evening in gladness, they betook themselves to their gentle rest, hoping on the morrow to continue this pastime which was so agreeable to them.

And so was the Third Day brought to an end.

---

6 Robert d'Arbrissel, the founder of the abbey of Fontevrault (see ante, p. 74), was accused of this practice.—See the article Fontevraud in Desoer's edition of Bayle's Dictionary, vi. 508, 519.—M.

7 Queen Margaret possibly refers to some incidents which occurred at Milan in the early part of the fourteenth century, when Matteo and Galeazzo Visconti ruled the city. In Signor Tullio Dandolo's work, Sui xxiii. libri delta Histories Patrice di Giuseppe Ripamonti ragionamento (Milano, 1856, pp. 52-60), will be found the story of a woman of the people, Guglielmina, and her accomplice, Andrea Saramita, who under some religious pretext founded a secret society of females. The debauchery practised by its members being discovered, Saramita was burnt alive, and Guglielmina's bones were disinterred and thrown into the fire. The Bishop of Milan at this time (1296-1308) was Francesco Fontana.—M.

DISCUSSION QUESTIONS

1. According to Saffredent, what is the lesson to be learned from this story? Do you agree?

2. Clearly, "Tale 30" shares many similarities with the play *Oedipus*, in that both deal with the disastrous results of a son sleeping with his mother. Yet the effect the story produces is much different from the play. Describe the difference in the story's effect, and list important differences between the two works in terms of situation, genre, and use of language.

3. Whose duplicitous action sets in motion the horrendous sequence of events in "Tale 30?" What was the motivation for this action?

4. According to the first listeners to respond, what is the moral of this story? Do you agree? In what ways could this "moral" be seen as a warning to fellow Renaissance humanists, excited by their own potential and the many advances being made in their times?

MICHEL DE MONTAIGNE (1533–1592)

The descendant of a wealthy merchant family that had constructed a chateau in Montaigne, Michel de Montaigne received an excellent humanistic education, partly directed by his father, who, in addition to steeping him in Latin, also encouraged him to be contemplative and analytical, qualities that would manifest themselves in his famous *Essays*. He studied law and served as counselor in the Cour des Aides of Périgueux and later counselor of Bordeaux's Parlement. But by 1571, at the age of 38, Montaigne decided to retire from professional life to focus on literary pursuits and the management of his estate. His favorite haunt was his vast library, lined with a thousand books, where he spent much of his time reading and taking notes, with occasional absences for military service and travel for pleasure. In 1580, he published the first two volumes of the *Essays*. He was elected mayor of Bordeaux in 1581 and reelected in 1583. In this position, he served as an arbiter in a dispute between the king of France and the king of Navarre; it is testament to his skills in diplomacy that he managed to stay on friendly terms with both. In 1588, he completed a third volume of essays and published a revised edition of the earlier essays.

Poor health forced Montaigne to live a quiet, retired life on his estate, although his love of reading and writing would probably have led him to the same choice. His *Essays*, on such diverse topics as cannibals, friendship, idleness, solitude, cruelty, and fathers, created and gave a name to a whole new literary form, whose popularity continues to this day. Montaigne's probing, reflective, and highly personal analyses of topics that struck his fancy introduced a whole new approach to writing and to the relationship between author and reader. Montaigne saw writing as a means to explore ideas and observations, and he did not feel that his essays needed to come to a firm conclusion or offer the last word on a subject. His willingness to share with readers not only a rational examination of external subjects, but also his personal thoughts and feelings, helped to forge a more intimate connection between author and audience than was traditional. Numerous essayists in subsequent centuries have imitated Montaigne's appealing mix of rational analysis, emotion, and personal observations in their writings. He created a form as well as a style that has been highly influential and seems distinctly modern in its tone.

OF CANNIBALS

When King Pyrrhus invaded Italy, having viewed and considered the order of the army the Romans sent out to meet him; "I know not," said he, "what kind of barbarians" (for so the Greeks called all other nations) "these may be; but the disposition of this army that I see has nothing of barbarism in it."—[Plutarch, Life of Pyrrhus, c. 8.]—As much said the Greeks of that which Flaminius brought into their country; and Philip, beholding from an eminence the order and distribution of the Roman camp formed in his kingdom by Publius Sulpicius Galba, spake to the same effect. By which it appears how cautious men ought to be of taking things upon trust from vulgar opinion, and that we are to judge by the eye of reason, and not from common report.

I long had a man in my house that lived ten or twelve years in the New World, discovered in these latter days, and in that part of it where Villegaignon landed,—[At Brazil, in 1557.]—which he called Antarctic France. This discovery of so vast a country seems to be of very great consideration. I cannot be sure, that hereafter there may not be another, so many wiser men than we having been deceived in this. I am afraid our eyes are bigger than our bellies, and that we have more curiosity than capacity; for we grasp at all, but catch nothing but wind.

Plato brings in Solon,—[In Timaeus.]—telling a story that he had heard from the priests of Sais in Egypt, that of old, and before the Deluge, there was a great island called Atlantis, situate directly at the mouth of the straits of Gibraltar, which contained more countries than both Africa and Asia put together; and that the kings of that country, who not only possessed that Isle, but extended their dominion so far into the continent that they had a country of Africa as far as Egypt, and extending in Europe to Tuscany, attempted to encroach even upon Asia, and to subjugate all the nations that border upon the Mediterranean Sea, as far as the Black Sea; and to that effect overran all Spain, the Gauls, and Italy, so far as to penetrate into Greece, where the Athenians stopped them: but that some time after, both the Athenians, and they and their island, were swallowed by the Flood.

It is very likely that this extreme irruption and inundation of water made wonderful changes and alterations in the habitations of the earth, as 'tis said that the sea then divided Sicily from Italy—

"Haec loca, vi quondam et vasta convulsa ruina,Dissiluisse ferunt, quum protenus utraque tellus Una foret"

["These lands, they say, formerly with violence and vast desolation convulsed, burst asunder, where erewhile were."—AEneid, iii. 414.]

Cyprus from Syria, the isle of Negropont from the continent of Beeotia, and elsewhere united lands that were separate before, by filling up the channel betwixt them with sand and mud:

"Sterilisque diu palus, aptaque remis, Vicinas urbes alit, et grave sentit aratrum."

["That which was once a sterile marsh, and bore vessels on its bosom, now feeds neighbouring cities, and admits the plough."—Horace, De Arte Poetica, v. 65.]

But there is no great appearance that this isle was this New World so lately discovered: for that almost touched upon Spain, and it were an incredible effect of an inundation, to have tumbled back so prodigious a mass, above twelve hundred leagues: besides that our modern navigators have already almost discovered it to be no island, but terra firma, and continent with the East Indies on the one side, and with the lands under the two poles on the other side; or, if it be separate from them, it is by so narrow a strait and channel, that it none the more deserves the name of an island for that.

It should seem, that in this great body, there are two sorts of motions, the one natural and the other febrific, as there are in ours. When I consider the impression that our river of Dordogne has made in my time on the right bank of its descent, and that in twenty years it has gained so much, and undermined the foundations of so many houses, I perceive it to be an extraordinary agitation: for had it always followed this course, or were hereafter to do it, the aspect of the world would be totally changed. But rivers alter their course, sometimes beating against the one side, and sometimes the other, and some times quietly keeping the channel. I do not speak of sudden inundations, the causes of which everybody understands. In Medoc, by the seashore, the Sieur d'Arsac, my brother, sees an estate he had there, buried under the sands which the sea vomits before it: where the tops of some houses are yet to be seen, and where his rents and domains are converted into pitiful barren pasturage. The inhabitants of this place affirm, that of late years the sea has driven so vehemently upon them, that they have lost above four leagues of land. These sands are her harbingers: and we now see great heaps of moving sand, that march half a league before her, and occupy the land.

The other testimony from antiquity, to which some would apply this discovery of the New World, is in Aristotle; at least, if that little book of Unheard of Miracles be his—[one of the spurious publications brought out under his name—D.W.]. He there tells us, that certain Carthaginians, having crossed the Atlantic Sea without the Straits of Gibraltar, and sailed a very long time, discovered at last a great and fruitful island, all covered over with wood, and watered with several broad and deep rivers, far remote from all terra firma; and that they, and others after them, allured by the goodness and fertility of the soil, went thither with their wives and children, and began to plant a colony. But the senate of Carthage perceiving their people by little and little to diminish, issued out an express prohibition, that none, upon pain of death, should transport themselves thither; and also drove out these new inhabitants; fearing, 'tis said, lest' in process of time they should so multiply as to supplant themselves and ruin their state. But this relation of Aristotle no more agrees with our new-found lands than the other.

This man that I had was a plain ignorant fellow, and therefore the more likely to tell truth: for your better-bred sort of men are much more curious in their observation, 'tis true, and discover a great deal more; but then they gloss upon it, and to give the greater weight to what they deliver, and allure your belief, they cannot forbear a little to alter the story; they never represent things to you simply as they are, but rather as they appeared to them, or as they would have them appear to you, and to gain the reputation of men of judgment, and the better to induce your faith, are willing to help out the business with something more than is really true, of their own invention. Now in this case, we should either have a man of irreproachable veracity, or so simple that he has not wherewithal to contrive, and to give a colour of truth to false relations, and who can have no ends in forging an untruth. Such a one was mine; and besides, he has at divers times brought to me several seamen and merchants who at the same time went the same voyage. I shall therefore content myself with his information, without inquiring what the cosmographers say to the business. We should have topographers to trace out to us the particular places where they have been; but for having had this advantage over us, to have seen the Holy Land, they would have the privilege, forsooth, to tell us stories of all the other parts of the world beside. I would have every one write what he knows, and as much as he knows, but no more; and that not in this only but in all other subjects; for such a person may have some particular knowledge and experience of the nature of such a river, or such a fountain, who, as to other things, knows no more than what everybody does, and yet to give a currency to his little pittance of learning, will undertake to write the whole body of physics: a vice from which great inconveniences derive their original.

Now, to return to my subject, I find that there is nothing barbarous and savage in this nation, by anything that I can gather, excepting, that every one gives the title of barbarism to everything that is not in use in his own country. As, indeed, we have no other level of truth and reason than the example and idea of the opinions and customs of the place wherein we live: there is always the perfect religion, there the perfect government, there the most exact and accomplished usage of all things. They are savages at the same rate that we say fruits are wild, which nature produces of herself and by her own ordinary progress; whereas, in truth, we ought rather to call those wild whose natures we have changed by our artifice and diverted from the common order. In those, the genuine, most useful, and natural virtues and properties are vigorous and sprightly, which we have helped to degenerate in these, by accommodating them to the pleasure of our own corrupted palate. And yet for all this, our taste confesses a flavour and delicacy excellent even to emulation of the best of ours, in several fruits wherein those countries abound without art or culture. Neither is it reasonable that art should gain the pre-eminence of our great and powerful mother nature. We have so surcharged her with the additional ornaments and graces we have added to the beauty and riches of her own works by our inventions, that we have almost smothered her; yet in other places, where she shines in her own purity and proper lustre, she marvellously baffles and disgraces all our vain and frivolous attempts:

> "Et veniunt hederae sponte sua melius;
> Surgit et in solis formosior arbutus antris;
> Et volucres nulls dulcius arte canunt."

> ["The ivy grows best spontaneously, the arbutus best in shady caves; and the wild notes of birds are sweeter than art can teach. —"Propertius, i. 2, 10.]

Our utmost endeavours cannot arrive at so much as to imitate the nest of the least of birds, its contexture, beauty, and convenience: not so much as the web of a poor spider.

All things, says Plato,—[Laws, 10.]—are produced either by nature, by fortune, or by art; the greatest and most beautiful by the one or the other of the former, the least and the most imperfect by the last.

These nations then seem to me to be so far barbarous, as having received but very little form and fashion from art and human invention, and consequently to be not much remote from their original simplicity. The laws of nature, however, govern them still, not as yet much vitiated with any mixture of ours: but 'tis in such purity, that I am sometimes troubled we were not sooner acquainted with these people, and that they were not discovered in those better times, when there were men much more able to judge of them than we are. I am sorry that Lycurgus and Plato had no knowledge of them; for to my apprehension, what we now see in those nations, does not only surpass all the pictures with which the poets have adorned the golden age, and all their inventions in feigning a happy state of man, but, moreover, the fancy and even the wish and desire of philosophy itself; so native and so pure a simplicity, as we by experience see to be in them, could never enter into their imagination, nor could they ever believe that human society could have been maintained with so little artifice and human patchwork. I should tell Plato that it is a nation wherein there is no manner of traffic, no knowledge of letters, no science of numbers, no name of magistrate or political superiority; no use of service, riches or poverty, no contracts, no successions, no dividends, no properties, no employments, but those of leisure, no respect of kindred, but common, no clothing, no agriculture, no metal, no use of corn or wine; the very words that signify lying, treachery, dissimulation, avarice, envy, detraction, pardon, never heard of.

> —[This is the famous passage which Shakespeare, through Florio's version, 1603, or ed. 1613, p. 102, has employed in the "Tempest," ii. 1.]

How much would he find his imaginary Republic short of his perfection?

> "Viri a diis recentes."

> ["Men fresh from the gods."—Seneca, Ep., 90.]

> "Hos natura modos primum dedit."

> ["These were the manners first taught by nature." —Virgil, Georgics, ii. 20.]

As to the rest, they live in a country very pleasant and temperate, so that, as my witnesses inform me, 'tis rare to hear of a sick person, and they moreover assure me, that they never saw any of the natives, either paralytic, bleareyed, toothless, or crooked with age. The situation of their country is along the sea-shore, enclosed on the other side towards the land, with great and high mountains, having about a hundred leagues in breadth between. They have great store of fish and flesh, that have no resemblance to those of ours: which they eat without any other cookery, than plain boiling, roasting, and broiling. The first that rode a horse thither, though in several other voyages he had contracted an acquaintance and familiarity with them, put them into so terrible a fright, with his centaur appearance, that they killed him with their arrows before they could come to discover who he was. Their buildings are very long, and of capacity to hold two or three hundred people, made of the barks of tall trees, reared with one end upon the ground, and leaning to and supporting one another at the top, like some of our barns, of which the covering hangs down to the very ground, and serves for the side walls. They have wood so hard, that they cut with it, and make their swords of it, and their grills of it to broil their meat. Their beds are of cotton, hung swinging from the roof, like our seamen's hammocks, every man his own, for the wives lie apart from their husbands. They rise with the sun, and so soon as they are up, eat for all day, for they have no more meals but that; they do not then drink, as Suidas reports of some other people of the East that never drank at their meals; but drink very often all day after, and sometimes to a rousing pitch. Their drink is made of a certain root, and is of the colour of our claret, and they never drink it but lukewarm. It will not keep above two or three days; it has a somewhat sharp, brisk taste, is nothing heady, but very comfortable to the stomach; laxative to strangers, but a very pleasant beverage to such as are accustomed to it. They make use, instead of bread, of a certain white compound, like coriander seeds; I have tasted of it; the taste is sweet and a little flat. The whole day is spent in dancing. Their young men go a-hunting after wild beasts with bows and arrows; one part of their women are employed in preparing their drink the while, which is their chief employment. One of their old men, in the morning before they fall to eating, preaches to the whole family, walking from the one end of the house to the other, and several times repeating the same sentence, till he has finished the round, for their houses are at least a hundred yards long. Valour towards their enemies and love towards their wives, are the two heads of his discourse, never failing in the close, to put them in mind, that 'tis their wives who provide them their drink warm and well seasoned. The fashion of their beds, ropes, swords, and of the wooden bracelets they tie about their wrists, when they go to fight, and of the great canes, bored hollow at one end, by the sound of which they keep the cadence of their dances, are to be seen in several places, and amongst others, at my house. They shave all over, and much more neatly than we, without other razor than one of wood or stone. They believe in the immortality of the soul, and that those who have merited well of the gods are lodged in that part of heaven where the sun rises, and the accursed in the west.

They have I know not what kind of priests and prophets, who very rarely present themselves to the people, having their abode in the mountains. At their arrival, there is a great feast, and solemn assembly of many villages: each house, as I have described, makes a village, and they are about a French league distant from one another. This prophet declaims to them in public, exhorting them to virtue and their duty: but all their ethics are comprised in these two articles, resolution in war, and affection to their wives. He also prophesies to them events to come, and the issues they are to expect from their enterprises, and prompts them to or diverts them from war: but let him look to't; for if he fail in his divination, and anything happen otherwise than he has foretold, he is cut into a thousand pieces, if he be caught, and condemned for a false prophet: for that reason, if any of them has been mistaken, he is no more heard of.

Divination is a gift of God, and therefore to abuse it, ought to be a punishable imposture. Amongst the Scythians, where their diviners failed in the promised effect, they were laid, bound hand and foot, upon carts loaded with firs and bavins, and drawn by oxen, on which they were burned to death.—[Herodotus, iv. 69.]—Such as only meddle with things subject to the conduct of human capacity, are excusable in doing the best they can: but those other fellows that come to delude us with assurances of an extraordinary faculty, beyond our understanding, ought they not to be punished, when they do not make good the effect of their promise, and for the temerity of their imposture?

They have continual war with the nations that live further within the mainland, beyond their mountains, to which they go naked, and without other arms than their bows and wooden swords, fashioned at one end like the head of our javelins. The obstinacy of their battles is wonderful, and they never end without great effusion of blood: for as to running away, they know not what it is. Every one for a trophy brings home the head of an enemy he has killed, which he fixes over the door of his house. After having a long time treated their prisoners very well, and given them all the regales they can think of, he to whom the prisoner belongs, invites a great assembly of his friends. They being come, he ties a rope to one of the arms of the prisoner, of which, at a distance, out of his reach, he holds the one end himself, and gives to the friend he loves best the other arm to hold after the same manner; which being. done, they two, in the presence of all the assembly, despatch him with their swords. After that, they roast him, eat him amongst them, and send some chops to their absent friends. They do not do this, as some think, for nourishment, as the Scythians anciently did, but as a representation of an extreme revenge; as will appear by this: that having observed the Portuguese, who were in league with their enemies, to inflict another sort of death upon any of them they took prisoners, which was to set them up to the girdle in the earth, to shoot at the remaining part till it was stuck full of arrows, and then to hang them, they thought those people of the other world (as being men who had sown the knowledge of a great many vices amongst their neighbours, and who were much greater masters in all sorts of mischief than they) did not exercise this sort of revenge without a meaning, and that it must needs be more painful than theirs, they began to leave their old way, and to follow this. I am not sorry that we should here take notice of the barbarous horror of so cruel an action, but that, seeing so clearly into their faults, we should be so

blind to our own. I conceive there is more barbarity in eating a man alive, than when he is dead; in tearing a body limb from limb by racks and torments, that is yet in perfect sense; in roasting it by degrees; in causing it to be bitten and worried by dogs and swine (as we have not only read, but lately seen, not amongst inveterate and mortal enemies, but among neighbours and fellow-citizens, and, which is worse, under colour of piety and religion), than to roast and eat him after he is dead.

Chrysippus and Zeno, the two heads of the Stoic sect, were of opinion that there was no hurt in making use of our dead carcasses, in what way soever for our necessity, and in feeding upon them too;—[Diogenes Laertius, vii. 188.]—as our own ancestors, who being besieged by Caesar in the city Alexia, resolved to sustain the famine of the siege with the bodies of their old men, women, and other persons who were incapable of bearing arms.

"Vascones, ut fama est, alimentis talibus usi Produxere animas."

["'Tis said the Gascons with such meats appeased their hunger. —Juvenal, Sat., xv. 93.]

And the physicians make no bones of employing it to all sorts of use, either to apply it outwardly; or to give it inwardly for the health of the patient. But there never was any opinion so irregular, as to excuse treachery, disloyalty, tyranny, and cruelty, which are our familiar vices. We may then call these people barbarous, in respect to the rules of reason: but not in respect to ourselves, who in all sorts of barbarity exceed them. Their wars are throughout noble and generous, and carry as much excuse and fair pretence, as that human malady is capable of; having with them no other foundation than the sole jealousy of valour. Their disputes are not for the conquest of new lands, for these they already possess are so fruitful by nature, as to supply them without labour or concern, with all things necessary, in such abundance that they have no need to enlarge their borders. And they are, moreover, happy in this, that they only covet so much as their natural necessities require: all beyond that is superfluous to them: men of the same age call one another generally brothers, those who are younger, children; and the old men are fathers to all. These leave to their heirs in common the full possession of goods, without any manner of division, or other title than what nature bestows upon her creatures, in bringing them into the world. If their neighbours pass over the mountains to assault them, and obtain a victory, all the victors gain by it is glory only, and the advantage of having proved themselves the better in valour and virtue: for they never meddle with the goods of the conquered, but presently return into their own country, where they have no want of anything necessary, nor of this greatest of all goods, to know happily how to enjoy their condition and to be content. And those in turn do the same; they demand of their prisoners no other ransom, than acknowledgment that they are overcome: but there is not one found in an age, who will not rather choose to die than make such a confession, or either by word or look recede from the entire grandeur of an invincible courage. There is not a man amongst them who had not rather be killed and eaten, than so much as to open his mouth to entreat he may not. They use them with all liberality and freedom, to the end their lives may be so much the dearer to them; but frequently entertain them with menaces of their approaching death, of the torments they are to suffer, of the preparations making in order to it, of the mangling their limbs, and of the feast that is to be made, where their carcass is to be the only dish. All which they do, to no other end, but only to extort some gentle or submissive word from them, or to frighten them so as to make them run away, to obtain this advantage that they were terrified, and that their constancy was shaken; and indeed, if rightly taken, it is in this point only that a true victory consists:

"Victoria nulla est, Quam quae confessor animo quoque subjugat hostes."

["No victory is complete, which the conquered do not admit to be so.—"Claudius, De Sexto Consulatu Honorii, v. 248.]

The Hungarians, a very warlike people, never pretend further than to reduce the enemy to their discretion; for having forced this confession from them, they let them go without injury or ransom, excepting, at the most, to make them engage their word never to bear arms against them again. We have sufficient advantages over our enemies that are borrowed and not truly our own; it is the quality of a porter, and no effect of virtue, to have stronger arms and legs; it is a dead and corporeal quality to set in array; 'tis a turn of fortune to make our enemy stumble, or to dazzle him with the light of the sun; 'tis a trick of science and art, and that may happen in a mean base fellow, to be a good fencer. The estimate and value of a man consist in the heart and in the will: there his true honour lies. Valour is stability, not of legs and arms, but of the courage and the soul; it does not lie in the goodness of our horse or our arms but in our own. He that falls obstinate in his courage—

"Si succiderit, de genu pugnat"

["If his legs fail him, he fights on his knees."—Seneca, De Providentia, c. 2.]

—he who, for any danger of imminent death, abates nothing of his assurance; who, dying, yet darts at his enemy a fierce and disdainful look, is overcome not by us, but by fortune; he is killed, not conquered; the most valiant are sometimes the most unfortunate. There are defeats more triumphant than victories. Never could those four sister victories, the fairest the sun ever be held, of Salamis, Plataea, Mycale, and Sicily, venture to oppose all their united glories, to the single glory of the discomfiture of King Leonidas and his men, at the pass of Thermopylae. Who ever ran with a more glorious desire and greater ambition, to the winning, than Captain Iscolas to the certain loss of a battle?—[Diodorus Siculus, xv. 64.]—Who could have found out a more subtle invention to secure his safety, than he did to assure his destruction? He was set to defend a certain pass of Peloponnesus against the Arcadians, which, considering the nature of the place and the inequality of forces, finding it utterly impossible for him to do, and seeing that all who were presented to the enemy, must certainly be left upon the place; and on the other side, reputing it unworthy of his own virtue and magnanimity and of the Lacedaemonian name to fail in any part of his duty, he chose a mean betwixt these two extremes after this manner; the youngest and most active of his men, he preserved for the service and defence of their country, and sent them back; and with the rest, whose loss would be of less consideration, he resolved to make good the pass, and with the death of them, to make the enemy buy their entry as dear as possibly he could; as it fell out, for being presently environed on all sides by the Arcadians, after having made a great slaughter of the enemy, he and his were all cut in pieces. Is there any trophy dedicated to the conquerors which was not much more due to these who were overcome? The part that true conquering is to play, lies in the encounter, not in the coming off; and the honour of valour consists in fighting, not in subduing.

But to return to my story: these prisoners are so far from discovering the least weakness, for all the terrors that can be represented to them, that, on the contrary, during the two or three months they are kept, they always appear with a cheerful countenance; importune their masters to make haste to bring them to the test, defy, rail at them, and reproach them with cowardice, and the number of battles they have lost against those of their country. I have a song made by one of these prisoners, wherein he bids them "come all, and dine upon him, and welcome, for they shall withal eat their own fathers and grandfathers, whose flesh has served to feed and nourish him. These muscles," says he, "this flesh and these veins, are your own: poor silly souls as you are, you little think that the substance of your ancestors' limbs is here yet; notice what you eat, and you will find in it the taste of your own flesh:" in which song there is to be observed an invention that nothing relishes of the barbarian. Those that paint these people dying after this manner, represent the prisoner spitting in the faces of his executioners and making wry mouths at them. And 'tis most certain, that to the very last gasp, they never cease to brave and defy them both in word and gesture. In plain truth, these men are very savage in comparison of us; of necessity, they must either be absolutely so or else we are savages; for there is a vast difference betwixt their manners and ours.

The men there have several wives, and so much the greater number, by how much they have the greater reputation for valour. And it is one very remarkable feature in their marriages, that the same jealousy our wives have to hinder and divert us from the friendship and familiarity of other women, those employ to promote their husbands' desires, and to procure them many spouses; for being above all things solicitous of their husbands' honour, 'tis their chiefest care to seek out, and to bring in the most companions they can, forasmuch as it is a testimony of the husband's virtue. Most of our ladies will cry out, that 'tis monstrous; whereas in truth it is not so, but a truly matrimonial virtue, and of the highest form. In the Bible, Sarah, with Leah and Rachel, the two wives of Jacob, gave the most beautiful of their handmaids to their husbands; Livia preferred the passions of Augustus to her own interest;— [Suetonius, Life of Augustus, c. 71.]—and the wife of King Deiotarus, Stratonice, did not only give up a fair young maid that served her to her husband's embraces, but moreover carefully brought up the children he had by her, and assisted them in the succession to their father's crown.

And that it may not be supposed, that all this is done by a simple and servile obligation to their common practice, or by any authoritative impression of their ancient custom, without judgment or reasoning, and from having a soul so stupid that it cannot contrive what else to do, I must here give you some touches of their sufficiency in point of understanding. Besides what I repeated to you before, which was one of their songs of war, I have another, a love-song, that begins thus:

> "Stay, adder, stay, that by thy pattern my sister may draw the fashion and work of a rich ribbon, that I may present to my beloved, by which means thy beauty and the excellent order of thy scales shall for ever be preferred before all other serpents."

Wherein the first couplet, "Stay, adder," &c., makes the burden of the song. Now I have conversed enough with poetry to judge thus much that not only there is nothing barbarous in this invention, but, moreover, that it is perfectly Anacreontic. To which it may be added, that their language is soft, of a pleasing accent, and something bordering upon the Greek termination.

Three of these people, not foreseeing how dear their knowledge of the corruptions of this part of the world will one day cost their happiness and repose, and that the effect of this commerce will be their ruin, as I presuppose it is in a very fair way (miserable men to suffer themselves to be deluded with desire of novelty and to have left the serenity of their own heaven to come so far to gaze at ours!), were at Rouen at the time that the late King Charles IX. was there. The king himself talked to them a good while, and they were made to see our fashions, our pomp, and the form of a great city. After which, some one asked their opinion, and would know of them, what of all the things they had seen, they found most to be admired? To which they made answer, three things, of which I have forgotten the third, and am troubled at it, but two I yet remember. They said, that in the first place they thought it very strange that so many tall men, wearing beards, strong, and well armed, who were about the king ('tis like they meant the Swiss of the guard), should submit to obey a child, and that they did not rather choose out one amongst themselves to command. Secondly (they have a way of speaking in their language to call men the half of one another), that they had observed that there were amongst us men full and crammed with all manner of commodities, whilst, in the meantime, their halves were begging at their doors, lean and half-starved with hunger and poverty; and they thought it strange that these necessitous halves were able to suffer so great an inequality and injustice, and that they did not take the others by the throats, or set fire to their houses.

I talked to one of them a great while together, but I had so ill an interpreter, and one who was so perplexed by his own ignorance to apprehend my meaning, that I could get nothing out of him of any moment: Asking him what advantage he reaped from the superiority he had amongst his own people (for he was a captain, and our mariners called him king), he told me, to march at the head of them to war. Demanding of him further how many men he had to follow him, he showed me a space of ground, to signify as many as could march in such a compass, which might be four or five thousand men; and putting the question to him whether or no his authority expired with the war, he told me this remained: that when he went to visit the villages of his dependence, they planed him paths through the thick of their woods, by which he might pass at his ease. All this does not sound very ill, and the last was not at all amiss, for they wear no breeches.

DISCUSSION QUESTIONS

1. What major discovery does Montaigne allude to in the opening paragraphs of the essay "Of Cannibals"? How does he use this discovery, which happened during his lifetime, to examine his own culture?

2. According to Montaigne, in "Of Cannibals," how do people of his time use the word "barbarism?" What do they generally mean by the term? Does he think the term should be applied to the natives in the newly discovered countries? Why or why not?

3. Describe the daily activities of the natives in "Of Cannibals." Does Montaigne seem to approve of their habits? How can you tell?

4. Does Montaigne justify the natives' treatment of their enemies? How does their treatment of prisoners compare to that of the Portuguese? What point is Montaigne trying to make by this comparison?

EDMUND SPENSER (C. 1552–1599)

Edmund Spenser was born in London to Elizabeth and John Spenser, a gentleman by birth, although far from wealthy. The Spensers were connected to the Spencers of Althorp, the ancestors of Princess Diana, a "house of auncient fame," as he calls it in the *Prothalamion*. He studied in the Merchant Taylors' School then at Pembroke College, Cambridge. Exceedingly well read and well versed in French, Italian, Latin, and Greek, Spenser was one of the most scholarly of the Renaissance poets, as can be seen in the wide range of allusions in his works. He took a position as a messenger with the Earl of Leicester, and through him formed a friendship with Sir Philip Sidney. His first major publication was *The Shepheardes Calendar* (1579), a pastoral poem dedicated to Sidney, which uses the 12 months of the year as its basic structure. In an unusual move for the time, Spenser chose to draw from not only classical influences, but also from native English poetry, particularly that of Chaucer. With this decision, Spenser adds a uniquely English vein to Renaissance poetry. After aiding Lord Grey de Wilton in the suppression of Irish revolts, he was given Kilcolman Castle in Cork County, where he began writing his greatest work, *The Faerie Queen*, an allegorical tribute to Queen Elizabeth I and a poetic guide to true courtly behavior. Spenser memorialized his wedding in 1594 to Elizabeth Boyle with *Amoretti*, a sonnet sequence, and *Epithalamion*, one of the greatest wedding poems in Western culture. This poem demonstrates both his use of classical sources, as it is influenced by Catullus's poetry (see Unit I), and the extraordinary richness and lyricism of his diction.

In 1598, Spenser's castle was attacked and burned by rebel forces; he and his family escaped to Cork, and from there he journeyed to London to advise the queen on the conflicts in Ireland. While there, he became ill; on January 16, 1599, he died. He is buried in Westminster Abbey, close to Chaucer.

EPITHALAMION

Ye learned sisters which have oftentimes
Beene to me ayding, others to adorne:
Whom ye thought worthy of your gracefull rymes,
That even the greatest did not greatly scorne
To heare theyr names sung in your simple layes,
But joyed in theyr prayse.
And when ye list your owne mishaps to mourne,
Which death, or love, or fortunes wreck did rayse,
Your string could soone to sadder tenor turne,
And teach the woods and waters to lament
Your dolefull dreriment.
Now lay those sorrowfull complaints aside,
And having all your heads with girland crownd,
Helpe me mine owne loves prayses to resound,
Ne let the same of any be envide:
So Orpheus did for his owne bride,
So I unto my selfe alone will sing,
The woods shall to me answer and my Eccho ring.

Early before the worlds light giving lampe,
His golden beame upon the hils doth spred,
Having disperst the nights unchearefull dampe,
Doe ye awake, and with fresh lusty hed,
Go to the bowre of my beloved love,
My truest turtle dove,
Bid her awake; for Hymen is awake,
And long since ready forth his maske to move,
With his bright Tead that flames with many a flake,
And many a bachelor to waite on him,
In theyr fresh garments trim.
Bid her awake therefore and soone her dight,
For lo the wished day is come at last,
That shall for al the paynes and sorrowes past,
Pay to her usury of long delight:
And whylest she doth her dight,
Doe ye to her of joy and solace sing,
That all the woods may answer and your eccho ring.

Bring with you all the Nymphes that you can heare
Both of the rivers and the forrests greene:
And of the sea that neighbours to her neare,
Al with gay girlands goodly wel beseene.
And let them also with them bring in hand
Another gay girland
For my fayre love of lillyes and of roses,
Bound truelove wize with a blew silke riband.
And let them make great store of bridale poses,
And let them eeke bring store of other flowers
To deck the bridale bowers.
And let the ground whereas her foot shall tread,
For feare the stones her tender foot should wrong
Be strewed with fragrant flowers all along,
And diapred lyke the discolored mead.
Which done, doe at her chamber dore awayt,
For she will waken strayt,
The whiles doe ye this song unto her sing,
The woods shall to you answer and your Eccho ring.

Ye Nymphes of Mulla which with carefull heed,
The silver scaly trouts doe tend full well,
And greedy pikes which use therein to feed,
(Those trouts and pikes all others doo excell)
And ye likewise which keepe the rushy lake,
Where none doo fishes take,
Bynd up the locks the which hang scatterd light,
And in his waters which your mirror make,
Behold your faces as the christall bright,
That when you come whereas my love doth lie,
No blemish she may spie.
And eke ye lightfoot mayds which keepe the deere,
That on the hoary mountayne use to towre,
And the wylde wolves which seeke them to devoure,
With your steele darts doo chace from comming neer,
Be also present heere,
To helpe to decke her and to help to sing,
That all the woods may answer and your eccho ring.

Wake, now my love, awake; for it is time,
The Rosy Morne long since left Tithones bed,
All ready to her silver coche to clyme,
And Phoebus gins to shew his glorious hed.
Hark how the cheerefull birds do chaunt theyr laies
And carroll of loves praise.

The merry Larke hir mattins sings aloft,
The thrush replyes, the Mavis descant playes,
The Ouzell shrills, the Ruddock warbles soft,
So goodly all agree with sweet consent,
To this dayes merriment.
Ah my deere love why doe ye sleepe thus long,
When meeter were that ye should now awake,
T'awayt the comming of your joyous make,
And hearken to the birds lovelearned song,
The deawy leaves among.
For they of joy and pleasance to you sing,
That all the woods them answer and theyr eccho ring.

My love is now awake out of her dreames,
And her fayre eyes like stars that dimmed were
With darksome cloud, now shew theyr goodly beames
More bright then Hesperus his head doth rere.
Come now ye damzels, daughters of delight,
Helpe quickly her to dight,
But first come ye fayre houres which were begot
In Joves sweet paradice, of Day and Night,
Which doe the seasons of the yeare allot,
And al that ever in this world is fayre
Doe make and still repayre.
And ye three handmayds of the Cyprian Queene,
The which doe still adorne her beauties pride,
Helpe to addorne my beautifullest bride:
And as ye her array, still throw betweene
Some graces to be seene,
And as ye use to Venus, to her sing,
The whiles the woods shal answer and your eccho ring.

Now is my love all ready forth to come,
Let all the virgins therefore well awayt,
And ye fresh boyes that tend upon her groome
Prepare your selves; for he is comming strayt.
Set all your things in seemely good aray
Fit for so joyfull day,
The joyfulst day that ever sunne did see.
Faire Sun, shew forth thy favourable ray,
And let thy lifull heat not fervent be
For feare of burning her sunshyny face,
Her beauty to disgrace.
O fayrest Phoebus, father of the Muse,
If ever I did honour thee aright,
Or sing the thing, that mote thy mind delight,
Doe not thy servants simple boone refuse,

But let this day let this one day be myne,
Let all the rest be thine.
Then I thy soverayne prayses loud will sing,
That all the woods shal answer and theyr eccho ring.

Harke how the Minstrels gin to shrill aloud
Their merry Musick that resounds from far,
The pipe, the tabor, and the trembling Croud,
That well agree withouten breach or jar.
But most of all the Damzels doe delite,
When they their tymbrels smyte,
And thereunto doe daunce and carrol sweet,
That all the sences they doe ravish quite,
The whyles the boyes run up and downe the street,
Crying aloud with strong confused noyce,
As if it were one voyce.
Hymen io Hymen, Hymen they do shout,
That even to the heavens theyr shouting shrill
Doth reach, and all the firmament doth fill,
To which the people standing all about,
As in approvance doe thereto applaud
And loud advaunce her laud,
And evermore they Hymen Hymen sing,
That al the woods them answer and theyr eccho ring.

Loe where she comes along with portly pace
Lyke Phoebe from her chamber of the East,
Arysing forth to run her mighty race,
Clad all in white, that seemes a virgin best.
So well it her beseemes that ye would weene
Some angell she had beene.
Her long loose yellow locks lyke golden wyre,
Sprinckled with perle, and perling flowres a tweene,
Doe lyke a golden mantle her attyre,
And being crowned with a girland greene,
Seeme lyke some mayden Queene.
Her modest eyes abashed to behold
So many gazers, as on her do stare,
Upon the lowly ground affixed are.
Ne dare lift up her countenance too bold,
But blush to heare her prayses sung so loud,
So farre from being proud.
Nathlesse doe ye still loud her prayses sing,
That all the woods may answer and your eccho ring.

Tell me ye merchants daughters did ye see
So fayre a creature in your towne before?

So sweet, so lovely, and so mild as she,
Adornd with beautyes grace and vertues store,
Her goodly eyes lyke Saphyres shining bright,
Her forehead yvory white,
Her cheekes lyke apples which the sun hath rudded,
Her lips lyke cherryes charming men to byte,
Her brest like to a bowle of creame uncrudded,
Her paps lyke lyllies budded,
Her snowie necke lyke to a marble towre,
And all her body like a pallace fayre,
Ascending uppe with many a stately stayre,
To honors seat and chastities sweet bowre.
Why stand ye still ye virgins in amaze,
Upon her so to gaze,
Whiles ye forget your former lay to sing,
To which the woods did answer and your eccho ring.

But if ye saw that which no eyes can see,
The inward beauty of her lively spright,
Garnisht with heavenly guifts of high degree,
Much more then would ye wonder at that sight,
And stand astonisht lyke to those which red
Medusaes mazeful hed.
There dwels sweet love and constant chastity,
Unspotted fayth and comely womenhed,
Regard of honour and mild modesty,
There vertue raynes as Queene in royal throne,
And giveth lawes alone.
The which the base affections doe obay,
And yeeld theyr services unto her will,
Ne thought of thing uncomely ever may
Thereto approch to tempt her mind to ill.
Had ye once seene these her celestial threasures,
And unrevealed pleasures,
Then would ye wonder and her prayses sing,
That al the woods should answer and your eccho ring.

Open the temple gates unto my love,
Open them wide that she may enter in,
And all the postes adorne as doth behove,
And all the pillours deck with girlands trim,
For to recyve this Saynt with honour dew,
That commeth in to you.
With trembling steps and humble reverence,
She commeth in, before th'almighties vew:
Of her ye virgins learne obedience,
When so ye come into those holy places,

To humble your proud faces;
Bring her up to th'high altar that she may,
The sacred ceremonies there partake,
The which do endlesse matrimony make,
And let the roring Organs loudly play
The praises of the Lord in lively notes,
The whiles with hollow throates
The Choristers the joyous Antheme sing,
That al the woods may answere and their eccho ring.

Behold whiles she before the altar stands
Hearing the holy priest that to her speakes
And blesseth her with his two happy hands,
How the red roses flush up in her cheekes,
And the pure snow with goodly vermill stayne,
Like crimsin dyde in grayne,
That even th'Angels which continually,
About the sacred Altare doe remaine,
Forget their service and about her fly,
Ofte peeping in her face that seemes more fayre,
The more they on it stare.
But her sad eyes still fastened on the ground,
Are governed with goodly modesty,
That suffers not one looke to glaunce awry,
Which may let in a little thought unsownd.
Why blush ye love to give to me your hand,
The pledge of all our band?
Sing ye sweet Angels, Alleluya sing,
That all the woods may answere and your eccho ring.

Now al is done; bring home the bride againe,
Bring home the triumph of our victory,
Bring home with you the glory of her gaine,
With joyance bring her and with jollity.
Never had man more joyfull day then this,
Whom heaven would heape with blis.
Make feast therefore now all this live long day,
This day for ever to me holy is,
Poure out the wine without restraint or stay,
Poure not by cups, but by the belly full,
Poure out to all that wull,
And sprinkle all the postes and wals with wine,
That they may sweat, and drunken be withall.
Crowne ye God Bacchus with a coronall,
And Hymen also crowne with wreathes of vine,
And let the Graces daunce unto the rest;
For they can doo it best:

The whiles the maydens doe theyr carroll sing,
To which the woods shal answer and theyr eccho ring.

Ring ye the bels, ye yong men of the towne,
And leave your wonted labors for this day:
This day is holy; doe ye write it downe,
That ye for ever it remember may.
This day the sunne is in his chiefest hight,
With Barnaby the bright,
From whence declining daily by degrees,
He somewhat loseth of his heat and light,
When once the Crab behind his back he sees.
But for this time it ill ordained was,
To chose the longest day in all the yeare,
And shortest night, when longest fitter weare:
Yet never day so long, but late would passe.
Ring ye the bels, to make it weare away,
And bonefiers make all day,
And daunce about them, and about them sing:
That all the woods may answer, and your eccho ring.

Ah when will this long weary day have end,
And lende me leave to come unto my love?
How slowly do the houres theyr numbers spend?
How slowly does sad Time his feathers move?
Hast thee O fayrest Planet to thy home
Within the Westerne fome:
Thy tyred steedes long since have need of rest.
Long though it be, at last I see it gloome,
And the bright evening star with golden creast
Appeare out of the East.
Fayre childe of beauty, glorious lampe of love
That all the host of heaven in rankes doost lead,
And guydest lovers through the nightes dread,
How chearefully thou lookest from above,
And seemst to laugh atweene thy twinkling light
As joying in the sight
Of these glad many which for joy doe sing,
That all the woods them answer and their echo ring.

Now ceasse ye damsels your delights forepast;
Enough is it, that all the day was youres:
Now day is doen, and night is nighing fast:
Now bring the Bryde into the brydall boures.
Now night is come, now soone her disaray,
And in her bed her lay;
Lay her in lillies and in violets,

And silken courteins over her display,
And odourd sheetes, and Arras coverlets.
Behold how goodly my faire love does ly
In proud humility;
Like unto Maia, when as Jove her tooke,
In Tempe, lying on the flowry gras,
Twixt sleepe and wake, after she weary was,
With bathing in the Acidalian brooke.
Now it is night, ye damsels may be gon,
And leave my love alone,
And leave likewise your former lay to sing:
The woods no more shal answere, nor your echo ring.

Now welcome night, thou night so long expected,
That long daies labour doest at last defray,
And all my cares, which cruell love collected,
Hast sumd in one, and cancelled for aye:
Spread thy broad wing over my love and me,
That no man may us see,
And in thy sable mantle us enwrap,
From feare of perrill and foule horror free.
Let no false treason seeke us to entrap,
Nor any dread disquiet once annoy
The safety of our joy:
But let the night be calme and quietsome,
Without tempestuous storms or sad afray:
Lyke as when Jove with fayre Alcmena lay,
When he begot the great Tirynthian groome:
Or lyke as when he with thy selfe did lie,
And begot Majesty.
And let the mayds and yongmen cease to sing:
Ne let the woods them answer, nor theyr eccho ring.

Let no lamenting cryes, nor dolefull teares,
Be heard all night within nor yet without:
Ne let false whispers, breeding hidden feares,
Breake gentle sleepe with misconceived dout.
Let no deluding dreames, nor dreadful sights
Make sudden sad affrights;
Ne let housefyres, nor lightnings helpelesse harmes,
Ne let the Pouke, nor other evill sprights,
Ne let mischivous witches with theyr charmes,
Ne let hob Goblins, names whose sence we see not,
Fray us with things that be not.
Let not the shriech Oule, nor the Storke be heard:
Nor the night Raven that still deadly yels,
Nor damned ghosts cald up with mighty spels,

Nor griesly vultures make us once affeard:
Ne let th'unpleasant Quyre of Frogs still croking
Make us to wish theyr choking.
Let none of these theyr drery accents sing;
Ne let the woods them answer, nor theyr eccho ring.

But let stil Silence trew night watches keepe,
That sacred peace may in assurance rayne,
And tymely sleep, when it is tyme to sleepe,
May poure his limbs forth on your pleasant playne,
The whiles an hundred little winged loves,
Like divers fethered doves,
Shall fly and flutter round about your bed,
And in the secret darke, that none reproves,
Their prety stelthes shal worke, and snares shal spread
To filch away sweet snatches of delight,
Conceald through covert night.
Ye sonnes of Venus, play your sports at will,
For greedy pleasure, carelesse of your toyes,
Thinks more upon her paradise of joyes,
Then what ye do, albe it good or ill.
All night therefore attend your merry play,
For it will soone be day:
Now none doth hinder you, that say or sing,
Ne will the woods now answer, nor your Eccho ring.

Who is the same, which at my window peepes?
Or whose is that faire face, that shines so bright,
Is it not Cinthia, she that never sleepes,
But walkes about high heaven al the night?
O fayrest goddesse, do thou not envy
My love with me to spy:
For thou likewise didst love, though now unthought,
And for a fleece of woll, which privily,
The Latmian shephard once unto thee brought,
His pleasures with thee wrought.
Therefore to us be favorable now;
And sith of wemens labours thou hast charge,
And generation goodly dost enlarge,
Encline thy will t'effect our wishfull vow,
And the chast wombe informe with timely seed,
That may our comfort breed:
Till which we cease our hopefull hap to sing,
Ne let the woods us answere, nor our Eccho ring.

And thou great Juno, which with awful might

The lawes of wedlock still dost patronize,
And the religion of the faith first plight
With sacred rites hast taught to solemnize:
And eeke for comfort often called art
Of women in their smart,
Eternally bind thou this lovely band,
And all thy blessings unto us impart.
And thou glad Genius, in whose gentle hand,
The bridale bowre and geniall bed remaine,
Without blemish or staine,
And the sweet pleasures of theyr loves delight
With secret ayde doest succour and supply,
Till they bring forth the fruitfull progeny,
Send us the timely fruit of this same night.
And thou fayre Hebe, and thou Hymen free,
Grant that it may so be.
Til which we cease your further prayse to sing,
Ne any woods shal answer, nor your Eccho ring.

And ye high heavens, the temple of the gods,
In which a thousand torches flaming bright
Doe burne, that to us wretched earthly clods,
In dreadful darknesse lend desired light;
And all ye powers which in the same remayne,
More then we men can fayne,
Poure out your blessing on us plentiously,
And happy influence upon us raine,
That we may raise a large posterity,
Which from the earth, which they may long possesse,
With lasting happinesse,
Up to your haughty pallaces may mount,
And for the guerdon of theyr glorious merit
May heavenly tabernacles there inherit,
Of blessed Saints for to increase the count.
So let us rest, sweet love, in hope of this,
And cease till then our tymely joyes to sing,
The woods no more us answer, nor our eccho ring.

Song made in lieu of many ornaments,
With which my love should duly have bene dect,
Which cutting off through hasty accidents,
Ye would not stay your dew time to expect,
But promist both to recompens,
Be unto her a goodly ornament,
And for short time an endlesse moniment.

DISCUSSION QUESTIONS

1. How much time does this poem cover? What is effective about using such a time frame for the poem?

2. What does he praise about his bride? What might a bride like about this poem? What might she find disturbing in it?

3. What is the refrain of the poem? What makes it effective? Would the refrain be more effective if it were exactly the same in each stanza? Why do you think Spenser altered it?

4. In stanza 17, the refrain turns negative. Why?

5. What rhyme scheme does Spenser use in each stanza? How many syllables do most lines have? Which lines have more syllables or fewer? Why would Spenser vary the line lengths?

6. In the final stanza, what does he mean when he says the poem will be "for short time an endlesse moniment?"

QUEEN ELIZABETH I (1533–1603)

Q ueen of England from 1558 to her death in 1603, Elizabeth I, daughter of King Henry VIII and his second wife, Anne Boleyn, helped to define England as a Protestant nation and world power. A crafty and courageous leader, Elizabeth outlived many assassination plots and challenges to her throne, not always in the most ethical fashion. In addition to her political roles, Elizabeth was also a patroness of the arts, helping to establish England's own Renaissance, both through her support and her own poetic contributions. In the two poems below, "The Doubt," written about 1568, and "On Monsieur's Departure" (around 1582), note how her position as sovereign permeates her thoughts, her romantic relationships, and her verse.

THE DOUBT OF FUTURE FOES

The doubt of future foes exiles my present joy,
And wit me warns to shun such snares as threaten mine annoy;
For falsehood now doth flow, and subjects' faith doth ebb,
Which should not be if reason ruled or wisdom weaved the web.
But clouds of joys untried do cloak aspiring minds,
Which turn to rain of late repent by changed course of winds.
The top of hope supposed the root upreared shall be,
And fruitless all their grafted guile, as shortly ye shall see.
The dazzled eyes with pride, which great ambition blinds,
Shall be unsealed by worthy wights whose foresight falsehood finds.
The daughter of debate that discord aye doth sow
Shall reap no gain where former rule still peace hath taught to know.
No foreign banished wight shall anchor in this port;
Our realm brooks not seditious sects, let them elsewhere resort.
My rusty sword through rest shall first his edge employ
To poll their tops that seek such change or gape for future joy.

ON MONSIEUR'S DEPARTURE

I grieve and dare not show my discontent,
I love and yet am forced to seem to hate,
I do, yet dare not say I ever meant,
I seem stark mute but inwardly do prate.
I am and not, I freeze and yet am burned,
Since from myself another self I turned.

My care is like my shadow in the sun,
Follows me flying, flies when I pursue it,
Stands and lies by me, doth what I have done.
His too familiar care doth make me rue it.
No means I find to rid him from my breast,
Till by the end of things it be supprest.

Some gentler passion slide into my mind,
For I am soft and made of melting snow;
Or be more cruel, love, and so be kind.
Let me or float or sink, be high or low.
Or let me live with some more sweet content,
Or die and so forget what love ere meant.

DISCUSSION QUESTIONS

1. In "The Doubt of Future Foes," Elizabeth I uses "doubt" as we would use the word "fear." What is she afraid of in particular? How does she answer her own fears?
2. In "On Monsieur's Departure," what lines show an unusual vulnerability for a queen?
3. In the same poem, Elizabeth makes abundant use of contrasts and contradictory images. What is the effect of these contrasts and contradictions? Why would she choose to use them?

MARY SIDNEY (1561–1621)

Selected Poems

Mary Sidney has too often been thought of primarily as the sister of Sir Philip Sidney, whose writings, as well as his heroic death from battle wounds, made him one of the most well-known poets of the English Renaissance. But Mary Sidney deserves attention for her own poetic accomplishments, which began with her completion of her brother's poetic paraphrases of the Psalms and continued with the editing and publication of other works by her brother, plus translations and the composition of her own original poetry. Because of her family's high position and connections at court and her marriage to the Earl of Pembroke in 1577, Mary had a well-rounded, humanist education and many friends in court and in the literary circles of the time. Her connections gave her a ready audience, as well as a network of writers interested in her patronage.

While the *Psalms* are a completion of a project begun by Sir Philip Sidney, and the work as a whole is a paraphrase of already existing biblical material, Mary Sidney's poetic contributions are extensive. Her brother had only completed Psalms 1–43; Mary Sidney edited the existing material and then continued the cycle through Psalm 150. She echoes key stylistic features of her brother's writing so that the entire work has continuity. In her original writings, such as "To the Angell spirit of the most excellent Sir Phillip Sidney" and "Even Now That Care," two dedicatory poems that accompany the *Psalms*, Mary Sidney's elegant diction, mastery of rhyme and meter, and humility of spirit indicate her own unique poetic voice. Because her writings were done in the name of her God, her queen, and her beloved brother, Mary Sidney was able to move in a male-dominated literary circle without transgressing the boundaries placed on women's behavior at the time.

A DIALOGUE BETWEEN TWO SHEPHERDS, THENOT AND PIERS, IN PRAISE OF ASTREA

THENOT. I SING divine Astrea's praise;
O Muses! help my wits to raise,
And heave my verses higher.
PIERS. Thou need'st the truth but plainly tell,
Which much I doubt thou canst not well,
Thou art so oft a liar.

THENOT. If in my song no more I show,
Than Heaven, and earth, and sea do know, Then truly I
have spoken.
PIERS. Sufficeth not no more to name,
But being no less, the like, the same,
Else laws of truth be broken.

THENOT. Then say, she is so good, so fair,
With all the earth she may compare,
Nota Momus' self denying.
PIERS. Compare may think where likeness holds
Nought like to her the earth enfolds:
I looked to find you lying.

THENOT. Astrea sees with wisdom's sight;
Astrea works by virtue's might;
And jointly both do stay in her.
PIERS. Nay, take from them her hand, her mind,
The one is lame, the other blind:
Shall still your lying stain her?

THENOT. Soon as Astrea shows her face,
Straight every ill avoids the place,
And every good aboundeth.
PIERS. Nay, long before her face doth show,
The last doth come, the first doth go:
How loud this lie resoundeth.

THENOT. Astrea is our chiefest joy,
Our chiefest guard against annoy,
Our chiefest wealth, our treasure.
PIERS. Where chiefest are, there others be,
To us none else but only she:
When wilt thou speak in measure?

THENOT. Astrea may be justly said,
A field in flowery robe arrayed,
In season freshly springing.
PIERS. That spring endures but shortest time,
This never leaves Astrea's clime:
Thou liest, instead of singing.

THENOT. As heavenly light that guides the day,
Right so doth shine each lovely ray
That from Astrea flieth.
PIERS. Nay, darkness oft that light enclouds:
Astrea's beams no darkness shrouds:
How loudly Thenot lieth!

THENOT. Astrea rightly term I may
A manly palm, a maiden bay,
Her verdure never dying.
PIERS. Palm oft is crooked, bay is low,
She still upright, still high doth grow:
Good Thenot leave thy lying.

THENOT. Then, Piers, of friendship tell me why,
My meaning true, my words should lie,
And strive in vain to raise her?
PIERS. Words from conceit do only rise;
Above conceit her honour flies: But silence, nought can
praise her.

TO THE ANGELL SPIRIT OF THE MOST EXCELLENT SIR PHILIP SIDNEY

(Variant printed in Samuel Daniel's 1623 *Works*)
To thee, pure spirit, to thee alone addressed
Is this joint work, by double interest thine,
Thine by his own, and what is done of mine
Inspired by thee, thy secret power impressed.
My Muse with thine, itself dared to combine

As mortal stuff with that which is divine:
Let thy fair beams give luster to the rest

That Israel's King may deign his own, transformed
In substance no, but superficial 'tire;
And English guised in some sort may aspire
To better grace thee what the vulgar formed:
His sacred tones, age after age admire;
Nations grow great in pride and pure desire
So to excel in holy rites performed.

Oh, had that soul which honor brought to rest
Too soon not left and reft the world of all
What man could show, which we perfection call,
This precious piece had sorted with the best.
But ah, wide festered wounds that never shall
Nor must be closed, unto fresh bleeding fall:
Ah, memory, what needs this new arrest?

Yet blessed grief, that sweetness can impart
Since thou art blest! Wrongly do I complain:
Whatever weights my heavy thoughts sustain
Dear feels my soul for thee. I know my part
Nor be my weakness to thy rites a stain,
Rites to aright, life-blood would not refrain:
Assist me, then, that life what thine did part.

Time may bring forth what time hath yet suppressed
In whom thy loss hath laid to utter waste;
The wrack of time, untimely all defaced,
Remaining as the tomb of life deceased,
Where, in my heart the highest room thou hast;
There, truly there, thy earthly being is placed,
Triumph of death: in life how more than blest.
Behold, oh, that thou were now to behold
This finished long perfection's part begun,
The rest but pieced, as left by thee undone.
Pardon blest soul, presumption overbold,
If love and zeal hath to this error run:
'Tis zealous love, love that hath never done,
Nor can enough, though justly here controlled.

But since it hath no other scope to go,
Nor other purpose but to honor thee,
That thine may shine, where all the Graces be;
And that my thoughts (like smallest streams that flow,
Pay to their sea, their tributary fee)

Do strive, yet have no means to quit nor free
That mighty debt of infinities I owe

To thy great worth which time to times enroll,
Wonder of men, sole born, sole of thy kind
Complete in all, but heavenly was thy mind,
For wisdom, goodness, sweetness, fairest soul:
Too good to wish, too fair for earth, refined
For heaven, where all true glory rests confined;
And where but there no life without control?

Oh, when from this account, this cast-up sum,
This reck'ning made the audit of my woe,
Sometime of rase my swelling passions know
How work my thoughts, my sense is stricken dumb
That would thee more than words could ever show,
Which all fall short. Who knew thee best do know
There lives no wit that may thy praise become.

And rest fair monuments of thy fair fame,
Though not complete. Nor can we reach, in thought,
What on that goodly piece time would have wrought
Had divers so spared that life (but life) to frame
The rest. Alas, such loss! The world hath naught
Can equal it, nor, oh, more grievance brought,
Yet what remains must ever crown thy name.

Receive these hymns, these obsequies receive,
(If any mark of thy secret spirit thou bear)
Made only thine, and no name else must wear.
I can no more: Dear Soul, I take my leave;
My sorrow strives to mount the highest sphere.

PSALM 51

O Lord, whose grace no limits comprehend;
    Sweet Lord, whose mercies stand from measure free;
To me that grace, to me that mercy send,
    And wipe, O Lord, my sins from sinful me.
    Oh, cleanse, oh, wash, my foul iniquity;
        Cleanse still my spots, still wash away my stainings,
        Till stains and spots in me leave no remainings.

For I, alas, acknowledging do know
    My filthy fault, my faulty filthiness
To my soul's eye incessantly doth show,

Which done to thee, to thee I do confess,
   Just judge, true witness, that for righteousness
      Thy doom may pass against my guilt awarded,
      Thy evidence for truth may be regarded.

My mother, lo, when I began to be,
   Conceiving me, with me did sin conceive:
And as with living heat she cherished me,
   Corruption did like cherishing receive.
   But, lo, thy love to purest good doth cleave,
      And inward truth: which, hardly else discerned,
      My truant soul in thy hid school hath learned.

Then as thyself to lepers hast assigned,
   With hyssop, Lord, thy hyssop, purge me so:
And that shall cleanse the lepry of my mind.
   Make over me thy mercy's streams to flow,
   So shall my whiteness scorn the whitest snow.
      To ear and heart send sounds and thoughts of
         gladness,
      That bruised bones may dance away their sadness.

Thy ill-pleased eye from my misdeeds avert:
   Cancel the registers my sins contain:
Create in me a pure, clean, spotless heart;
   Inspire a sprite where love of right may reign
   Ah, cast me not from thee; take not again
      Thy breathing grace; again thy comfort send me,
      And let the guard of thy free sprite attend me.

So I to them a guiding hand will be,
   Whose faulty feet have wandered from thy way,
And turned from sin will make return to thee,
   Whom turned from thee sin erst had led astray.
   O God, God of my health, oh, do away
      My bloody crime: so shall my tongue be raised
      To praise thy truth, enough cannot be praised.

Unlock my lips, shut up with sinful shame:
   Then shall my mouth, O Lord, thy honor sing.
For bleeding fuel for thy altar's flame,
   To gain thy grace what boots it me to bring?
   Burt-off'rings are to thee no pleasant thing.
      The sacrifice that God will hold respected,
      Is the heart-broken soul, the sprite dejected.

Lastly, O Lord, how so I stand or fall,
   Leave not thy loved Zion to embrace;
But with thy favor build up Salem's wall,
   And still in peace, maintain that peaceful place.
   Then shalt thou turn a well-accepting face
      To sacred fires with offered gifts perfumed:
      Till ev'n whole calves on altars be consumed.

PSALM 55

My God, most glad to look, most prone to hear,
   An open ear, oh, let my prayer find,
      And from my plaint turn not thy face away.
      Behold my gestures, hearken what I say,
   While uttering moans with most tormented mind,
My body I no less torment and tear.
For, lo, their fearful threat'nings would mine ear,
   Who griefs on griefs on me still heaping lay,
      A mark to wrath and hate and wrong assigned;
      Therefore, my heart hath all his force resigned
   To trembling pants; death terrors on me pray;
I fear, nay, shake, nay, quiv'ring quake with fear.
Then say I, oh, might I but cut the wind,
   Borne on the wing the fearful dove doth bear:
      Stay would I not, till I in rest might stay.
      Far hence, oh, far, then would I take my way
   Unto the desert, and repose me there,
These storms of woe, these tempests left behind.
But swallow them, O Lord, in darkness blind,
   Confound their counsels, lead their tongues astray,
      That what they mean by words may not appear.
      For mother Wrong within their town each where,
   And daughter Strife their ensigns so display,
As if they only thither were confined.

These walk their city walls both night and day;
   Oppressions, tumults, guiles of every kind
      Are burgesses and dwell the middle near;
      About their streets his masking robes doth wear
   Mischief clothed in deceit, with treason lined,
Where only he, he only bears the sway.
But not my foe with me this prank did play,
   For then I would have borne with patient cheer
      An unkind part from whom I know unkind,
      Nor he whose forehead Envy's mark had signed,
   His trophies on my ruins sought to rear,

From whom to fly I might have made assay.

But this to thee, to thee impute I may,
 My fellow, my companion, held most dear,
  My soul, my other self, my inward friend:
  Whom unto me, me unto whom did bind
 Exchanged secrets, who together were
God's temple wont to visit, there to pray.
Oh, let a sudden death work their decay,
 Who speaking fair such cankered malice mind,
  Let them be buried breathing in their bier;
  But purple morn, black ev'n, and midday clear
 Shall see my praying voice to God inclined,
Rousing him up, and naught shall me dismay.

He ransomed me; he for my safety fined
 In fight where many sought my soul to slay;
  He, still himself to no succeeding heir
  Leaving his empire shall no more forbear
 But at my motion, all these atheists pay,
By whom, still one, such mischiefs are designed.
Who but such caitiffs would have undermined,
 Nay, overthrown, from whom but kindness mere
  They never found? Who would such trust betray?
  What buttered words! Yet war their hearts
   bewray.
 Their speech more sharp than sharpest sword or spear
Yet softer flows than balm from wounded rind.

But my o'erloaden soul, thyself upcheer,
 Cast on God's shoulders what thee down doth weigh
  Long borne by thee with bearing pained and
  pined:
  To care for thee he shall be ever kind;
 By him the just in safety held away
Changeless shall enter, live, and leave the year:
But, Lord, how long shall these men tarry here?
 Fling them in pit of death where never shined
  The light of life, and while I make my stay
  On thee, let who their thirst with blood allay
 Have their life-holding thread so weakly twined
That it, half-spun, death may in sunder shear.

PSALM 57

Thy mercy, Lord, Lord, now thy mercy show:
  On thee I lie;
  To thee I fly.
 Hide me, hive me, as thine own,
 Till these blasts be overblown,
Which now do fiercely blow.

To highest God I will erect my cry,
  Who quickly shall
  Dispatch this all.
 He shall down from heaven send
 From disgrace me to defend
His love and verity.

My soul encaged lies with lions' brood,
  Villains whose hands
  Are fiery brands,
 Teeth more sharp than shaft or spear,
 Tongues far better edge do bear
Than swords to shed my blood.

As high as highest heav'n can give thee place,
  O Lord, ascend,
  And thence extend
 With most bright, most glorious show
 Over all the earth below,
The sunbeams of thy face.

Me to entangle every way I go
  Their trap and net
  Is ready set.
 Holes they dig but their own holes
 Pitfalls make for their own souls:
So, Lord, oh, serve them so.

My heart prepared, prepared is my heart
  To spread thy praise
  With tuned lays:
 Wake my tongue, my lute awake,
 Thou my harp the consort make,
Myself will bear a part.

Myself when first the morning shall appear,
  With voice and string
  So will thee sing:
 That this earthly globe, and all

Treading on this earthly ball,
My praising notes shall hear.

For god, my only God, thy gracious love
Is mounted far
Above each star,
Thy unchanged verity
Heav'nly wings do lift as high
As clouds have room to move.

As high as highest heav'n can give thee place,
O Lord, ascend
And thence extend
With most bright, most glorious show
Over all the earth below,
The sunbeams of thy face.

PSALM 84

How lovely is thy dwelling,
Great god, to whom all greatness is belonging!
To view thy courts far, far from any telling
My soul doth long and pine with longing
Unto the God that liveth,
The God that all life giveth,
My heart and body both aspire,
Above delight, beyond desire.

Alas, the sparrow knoweth
The house where free and fearless she resideth;
Directly to the nest the swallow goeth,
Where with her sons she safe abideth.
Oh, altars thine, most mighty
In war, yea, most almighty:
Thy altars, Lord, ah, why should I
From altars thine excluded lie?

Oh, happy who remaineth
Thy household-man and still thy praise unfoldeth!
Oh, happy who himself on thee sustaineth,
Who to thy house his journey holdeth!
Me seems I see them going
Where mulberries are growing:
How wells they dig in thirsty plain,
And cisterns make for falling rain.

Me seems I see augmented

Still troop with troop, till all at length discover
Zion, where to their sight is represented
The Lord of hosts, the Zion lover.
O Lord, O God, most mighty
In war, yea, most almighty:
Hear what I beg; hearken, I say,
O Jacob's God, to what I pray.

Thou art the shield us shieldeth:
Then, Lord, behold the face of thine anointed
One day spent in thy courts more comfort yieldeth
Than thousands otherwise appointed.
I count it clearer pleasure
To spend my age's treasure
Waiting a porter at thy gates
Than dwell a lord with wicked mates.

Thou art the sun that shineth;
Thou art the buckler, Lord that us defendeth:
Glory and grace Jehovah's hand assigneth
And good without refusal sendeth
To him who truly treadeth
The path to pureness leadeth.
O Lord of might, thrice blessed he
Whose confidence is built on thee.

PSALM 102

O Lord, my praying hear;
Lord, let my cry come to thine ear.
Hide not thy face away,
But haste, and answer me,
In this my most, most miserable day,
Wherein I pray and cry to thee.

My days as smoke are past;
My bones as flaming fuel waste,
Mown down in me, alas.
With scythe of sharpest pain.
My heart is withered like the wounded grass;
My stomach doth all food disdain.

So lean my woes me leave,
That to my flesh my bones do cleave;
And so I bray and howl,
As use to howl and bray
The lonely pelican and desert owl,

Like whom I languish long the day.

I languish so the day,
The night in watch I waste away;
Right as the sparrow sits,
Bereft of spouse, or son,
Which irked alone with dolor's deadly fits
To company will not be won.

As day to day succeeds,
So shame on shame to me proceeds
From them that do me hate,
Who of my wrack so boast,
That wishing ill, they wish but my estate,
Yet think they wish of ills the most.

Therefore my bread is clay;
Therefore my tears my wine allay.
For how else should it be,
Sith thou still angry art,
And seem'st for naught to have advanced me,
But me advanced to subvert?

The sun of my life-days
Inclines to west with falling rays,
And I as hay am dried,
While yet in steadfast seat
Eternal thou eternally dost bide,
Thy memory no years can fret.

Oh, then at length arise;
On Zion cast thy mercy's eyes.
Now is the time that thou
To mercy shouldst incline
Concerning her: O Lord, the time is now
Thyself for mercy didst assign.

Thy servants wait the day
When she, who like a carcass lay
Stretched forth in ruin's bier,
Shall so arise and live,
The nations all Jehova's name shall fear,
All kings to thee shall glory give.

Because thou hast anew
Made Zion stand, restored to view
Thy glorious presence there,

Because thou hast, I say,
Beheld our woes and not refused to hear
What wretched we did plaining pray,

This of record shall bide
To this and every age beside.
And they commend thee shall
Whom thou anew shall make,
That from the prospect of thy heav'nly hall
Thy eye of earth survey did take,

Heark'ning to prisoners' groans,
And setting free condemned ones,
That they, when nations come,
And realms to serve the Lord,
In Zion and in Salem might become
Fit means his honor to record.

But what is this if I
In the mid way should fall and die?
My God, to thee I pray,
Who canst my prayer give.
Turn not to night the noontide of my day,
Since endless thou dost ageless live.

The earth, the heaven stands
Once founded, formed by thy hands:
They perish, thou shalt bide;
They old, as clothes shall wear,
Till changing still, full change shall them betide,
Unclothed of all the clothes they bear.

But thou art one, still one:
Time interest in thee hath none.
Then hope, who godly be,
Or come of godly race:
Endless your bliss, as never ending he,
His presence your unchanged place.

PSALM 150

Oh, laud the Lord, the God of hosts commend,
Exalt his pow'r, advance his holiness:
With all your might lift his almightiness;
Your greatest praise upon his greatness spend.

Make trumpet's noise in shrillest notes ascend;

Make lute and lyre his loved fame express;
Him let the pipe, him let the tabret bless,
Him organ's breath, that winds or waters lend.

Let ringing timbrels so his honor sound,
Let sounding cymbals so his glory ring,

That in their tunes such melody be found
As fits the pomp of most triumphant king.

Conclude: by all that air or life enfold,
Let high Jehovah highly be extolled.

DISCUSSION QUESTIONS/WRITING SUGGESTION

1. Compare Sidney's versions of the Psalms to those found in the King James' version. What has she changed from the original? What is the effect of her changes?
2. In "To the Angell spirit of the most excellent Sir Phillip Sidney," what reason does Mary Sidney give for completing her brother's *Psalmes*?
3. What lines of "To the Angell Spirit" seem best to express a sister's powerful grief?

CHRISTOPHER MARLOWE (1564–1593)

Born in Canterbury, England, and educated at Cambridge University, Christopher Marlowe was one of the University Wits who contributed plays and poetry to the London literary scene in the late 1500s. His tragedies influenced Shakespeare's early plays and were the most sophisticated dramas produced in England up to that point. Although many of his plays are unequal in their quality, and some, like *Dr. Faustus*, contain scenes that seem to be written by others, all of his existing dramas contain passages of rich, memorable poetry. One of his most famous poems, "The Passionate Shepherd to His Love," a pastoral love lyric first published in 1599 in *The Passionate Pilgrim*, was imitated by other Renaissance poets and was answered by Sir Walter Raleigh in 1600 in "The Nymphs Reply to the Shepherd" (see both below).

Marlowe lived a short and unconventional life. At the age of 29, he was accused of spreading atheistic ideas and would have been arrested, but before the arrest could take place he was stabbed through the eye during a fight in a tavern. There has been some conjecture that he may have been serving as a spy for Queen Elizabeth, but that is not known for sure. What is known is that he was the first to bring English drama out of the Middle Ages successfully, thereby paving the way for Shakespeare's masterpieces.

PASSIONATE SHEPHERD TO HIS LOVE

Come live with me and be my love,
And we will all the pleasures prove,
That Valleys, groves, hills, and fields,
Woods, or steepy mountain yields.

And we will sit upon the Rocks,
Seeing the Shepherds feed their flocks,
By shallow Rivers to whose falls
Melodious birds sing Madrigals.

And I will make thee beds of Roses
And a thousand fragrant posies,
A cap of flowers, and a kirtle
Embroidered all with leaves of Myrtle;

A gown made of the finest wool
Which from our pretty Lambs we pull;
Fair lined slippers for the cold,
With buckles of the purest gold;

A belt of straw and Ivy buds,
With Coral clasps and Amber studs:
And if these pleasures may thee move,
Come live with me, and be my love.

The Shepherds' Swains shall dance and sing
For thy delight each May-morning:
If these delights thy mind may move,
Then live with me, and be my love.

DISCUSSION QUESTIONS

1. What kinds of things does the shepherd promise his love in this poem?

2. What might be the response of a rational young woman to the shepherd's offer? What might a sensible woman fear about his offer?

3. Now compare Marlowe's poem to Sir Walter Raleigh's response (see below). What fault does Raleigh's nymph find in the shepherd's offer? Do her objections make sense?

4. Return to Marlowe's poem and analyze the images he uses more closely. What are the implications and connotations of the plants he offers, such as "myrtle" and "ivy?" What properties do they have in common?

5. Where do coral and amber come from? What connotations do these materials have, given their origins? What qualities does gold have?

6. Given the characteristics of each of the shepherd's offerings, what is he implying about the nature of his love? Should the nymph respond favorably?

SIR WALTER RALEIGH

The Nymph's Reply to the Shepherd

If all the world and love were young,
And truth in every Shepherd's tongue,
These pretty pleasures might me move,
To live with thee, and be thy love.

Time drives the flocks from field to fold,
When Rivers rage and Rocks grow cold,
And *Philomel* becometh dumb,
The rest complains of cares to come.

The flowers do fade, and wanton fields,
To wayward winter reckoning yields,
A honey tongue, a heart of gall,
Is fancy's spring, but sorrow's fall.

Thy gowns, thy shoes, thy beds of Roses,
Thy cap, thy kirtle, and thy posies
Soon break, soon wither, soon forgotten:
In folly ripe, in reason rotten.

Thy belt of straw and Ivy buds,
The Coral clasps and amber studs,
All these in me no means can move
To come to thee and be thy love.

But could youth last, and love still breed,
Had joys no date, nor age no need,
Then these delights my mind might move
To live with thee, and be thy love.

WILLIAM SHAKESPEARE (1564–1616)

Not much is known about the life of William Shakespeare, which is one of the reasons for the ongoing debate about whether or not he actually wrote the plays attributed to him. Christopher Marlowe, Francis Bacon, and Edward de Vere, the 17th earl of Oxford, have all been suggested as candidates for the authorship of the plays traditionally assigned to Shakespeare because they had better educations and more court connections than Shakespeare, who never attended a university. But such theories ignore the potential of self-education and the richness of the pre-university education he would have received in Stratford-on-Avon, where he was born and raised. Since several contemporary published references to Shakespeare and his works exist from such notable writers as Ben Jonson and Robert Greene (who attacked him in print in 1592), and the First Folio edition of the plays was published under Shakespeare's name just seven years after his death, it seems valid to consider him the author of the plays traditionally attributed to him, although doubts remain about the authorship of early dramas such as *Titus Andronicus*.

The known facts of Shakespeare's adult life can be briefly summarized. Shakespeare obtained a license to marry Anne Hathaway on November 27, 1582, and six months afterward their daughter Susanna was born. Their twins, Hamnet and Judith, were born in 1585. Sometime between 1585 and 1591, the family moved to London, where Shakespeare began his career as an actor and writer. Most of his 154 sonnets were probably written in the 1590s, as Francis Meres refers to them in 1598 as "his sugred sonnets," but they were not published until 1609. As mentioned in the introductory essay to this unit, the lyricism and complex imagery of Shakespeare's sonnets make them some of the finest examples of the form. Repeatedly in these sonnets, Shakespeare raises major crises such as depression or fear of aging and death, and then in 14 lines manages to offer some resolution or comfort in the face of the problem. The tightness and efficiency of the form, the use of iambic pentameter—a rhythm that mirrors a heartbeat—and the precision of the rhymes contribute vastly to creating a harmony that in itself is a consolation in the face of troubles. In addition, the form, rhymes, and rhythms help to engrave the poems in the memory, so that they do defeat time, as Shakespeare repeatedly claims they will. His division of the sonnet's 14 lines into three quatrains and a couplet gave rise to this type of structure being called the Shakespearean (or English) sonnet.

At the same time he was writing his sonnets, Shakespeare was also penning some of his most famous comedies, tragedies, and history plays, including *A Midsummer Night's Dream*, *Henry IV*, *As You Like It*, and *Romeo and Juliet*. He wrote most of his greatest tragedies and his romance plays in the period between 1599 and 1611, including *Hamlet*, *Othello*,

King Lear, *Macbeth*, *A Winter's Tale*, and *The Tempest*. The romances such as *The Tempest*, included below, follow a similar structure as Shakespeare's comedies, with a steady increase of confusion leading to chaos that gets resolved, usually by marriage, in the conclusion. But the romances usually have a darker note of sadness and loss and often include travels and fantastic adventures. *The Tempest*, Shakespeare's final play, is often considered his farewell to the stage, and certainly some of Prospero's speeches (particularly Act IV, Scene 1, lines 148–163 and Act V, Scene 1, lines 33–57) can be seen as reflecting the sentiments of a great writer as he bids adieu to the "magic" that is his art.

While little is known of Shakespeare's life, much can be said about his influence. His plays modernized English drama by creating vivid, three-dimensional, psychologically complex characters before the term psychology was even used. Shakespeare shifts the interest of plays from *what* happens to *how* it happens, so that his dramatic works are far more based in character than in plot. While building on the themes and structures of Greek dramas, Shakespeare released plays from the restraints of the three unities that the Greek dramatists followed: unity of time, place, and action. His plays cover a much wider range of actions, times, and locales than those of his predecessors. These innovations have shaped subsequent playwrights for centuries. In addition, the beauty of Shakespeare's language has led to his being the most quoted dramatist of all time. Allusions to his plays continue to abound in plays, poems, novels, and films. Along with Sophocles, Shakespeare can be considered one of the two most influential dramatists in Western culture.

THE TEMPEST

DRAMATIS PERSONÆ.1

Alonso, King of Naples.
Sebastian, his brother.
Prospero, the right Duke of Milan.
Antonio, his brother, the usurping Duke of Milan.
Ferdinand, son to the King of Naples.
Gonzalo, an honest old Counsellor.
Adrian,
        Lords.
Francisco,

Caliban, a savage and deformed Slave.
Trinculo, a Jester.
Stephano, a drunken Butler.
Master of a Ship.
Boatswain.
Mariners.
Miranda, daughter to Prospero.

Ariel, an airy Spirit.
Iris,
Ceres,
Juno,   presented by 2 Spirits.
Nymphs,
Reapers,

Other Spirits attending on Prospero. Scene—A ship at sea: an uninhabited island.

ACT I.

Scene I. *On a ship at sea: a tempestuous noise of thunder and lightning heard.*
Enter a Ship-Master *and* a Boatswain.
Mast. Boatswain!
Boats. Here, master: what cheer?
Mast. Good, speak to the mariners: fall to't, yarely, or we run ourselves aground: bestir, bestir. *Exit.*
        Enter Mariners.

Boats. Heigh, my hearts! cheerly, cheerly, my hearts! yare, yare! Take in the topsail. Tend to the master's whistle. Blow, till thou burst thy wind, if room enough!

Enter Alonso, Sebastian, Antonio, Ferdinand, Gonzalo, *and others.*

Alon. Good boatswain, have care. Where's the master? Play the men.
Boats. I pray now, keep below.
Ant. Where is the master, boatswain?

Boats. Do you not hear him? You mar our labour: keep your cabins: you do assist the storm.
Gon. Nay, good, be patient.
Boats. When the sea is. Hence! What cares these roarers for the name of king? To cabin: silence! trouble us not.
Gon. Good, yet remember whom thou hast aboard.
Boats. None that I more love than myself. You are a Counsellor; if you can command these elements to silence, and work the peace of the present, we will not hand a rope more; use your authority: if you cannot, give thanks you have lived so long, and make yourself ready in your cabin for the mischance of the hour, if it so hap. Cheerly, good hearts! Out of our way, I say. *Exit.*
Gon. I have great comfort from this fellow: methinks he hath no drowning mark upon him; his complexion is perfect gallows. Stand fast, good Fate, to his hanging: make the rope of his destiny our cable, for our own doth little advantage. If he be not born to be hanged, our case is miserable. *Exeunt.*
Re-enter Boatswain.
Boats. Down with the topmast! yare! lower, lower! Bring her to try with main-course. [*A cry within.*] A plague upon this howling! they are louder than the weather or our office.
Re-enter Sebastian, Antonio, *and* Gonzalo.
Yet again! what do you here? Shall we give o'er, and drown? Have you a mind to sink?
Seb. A pox o' your throat, you bawling, blasphemous, incharitable dog!
Boats. Work you, then.

Ant. Hang, cur! hang, you whoreson, insolent noise-maker. We are less afraid to be drowned than thou art.

Gon. I'll warrant him for drowning; though the ship were no stronger than a nutshell, and as leaky as an unstanched wench.
Boats. Lay her a-hold, a-hold! set her two courses off to sea again; lay her off.
Enter Mariners *wet.*
Mariners. All lost! to prayers, to prayers! all lost!
Boats. What, must our mouths be cold?
Gon. The king and prince at prayers! let's assist them,
For our case is as theirs.
Seb.
      I'm out of patience.
Ant. We are merely cheated of our lives by drunkards: This wide-chapp'd rascal,—would thou mightst lie drowning
The washing of ten tides!
Gon.
      He'll be hang'd yet,
Though every drop of water swear against it,
And gape at widest to glut him.

A confused noise within: "Mercy on us!"—"We split, we split!"—"Farewell my wife and children!"—"Farewell, brother!"—"We split, we split, we split!"

Ant. Let's all sink with the king.
Seb. Let's take leave of him. *Exeunt* Ant. *and* Seb.
Gon. Now would I give a thousand furlongs of sea for an acre of barren ground, long heath, brown furze, any thing. The wills above be done! but I would fain die a dry death. *Exeunt.*

Scene II. *The island. Before* Prospero's *cell.*
Enter Prospero *and* Miranda.
Mir. If by your art, my dearest father, you have
Put the wild waters in this roar, allay them.
The sky, it seems, would pour down stinking pitch,
But that the sea, mounting to the welkin's cheek,
Dashes the fire out. O, I have suffer'd
With those that I saw suffer! a brave vessel,
Who had, no doubt, some noble creature in her,

Dash'd all to pieces. O, the cry did knock
Against my very heart! Poor souls, they perish'd!
Had I been any god of power, I would
Have sunk the sea within the earth, or ere
It should the good ship so have swallow'd and
The fraughting souls within her.
Pros.

Be collected:
No more amazement: tell your piteous heart
There's no harm done.
Mir.
O, woe the day!
Pros.

No harm.
I have done nothing but in care of thee,
Of thee, my dear one, thee, my daughter, who
Art ignorant of what thou art, nought knowing
Of whence I am, nor that I am more better
Than Prospero, master of a full poor cell,
And thy no greater father.
Mir.

More to know
Did never meddle with my thoughts.
Pros.

'Tis time
I should inform thee farther. Lend thy hand,
And pluck my magic garment from me.—So:*Lays
down his mantle.*

Lie there, my art. Wipe thou thine eyes; have comfort.
The direful spectacle of the wreck, which touch'd
The very virtue of compassion in thee,
I have with such provision in mine art
So safely order'd, that there is no soul,
No, not so much perdition as an hair
Betid to any creature in the vessel
Which thou heard'st cry, which thou saw'st sink. Sit down;
For thou must now know farther.
Mir.
You have often
Begun to tell me what I am; but stopp'd,
And left me to a bootless inquisition,
Concluding "Stay: not yet."
Pros.

The hour's now come;
The very minute bids thee ope thine ear;

Obey, and be attentive. Canst thou remember
A time before we came unto this cell?
I do not think thou canst, for then thou wast not
Out three years old.
Mir.

Certainly, sir, I can.
Pros. By what? by any other house or person?
Of any thing the image tell me that
Hath kept with thy remembrance.
Mir.

'Tis far off,
And rather like a dream than an assurance
That my remembrance warrants. Had I not
Four or five women once that tended me?
Pros. Thou hadst, and more, Miranda. But how is it
That this lives in thy mind? What seest thou else
In the dark backward and abysm of time?
If thou remember'st ought ere thou camest here,
How thou camest here thou mayst.
Mir.

But that I do not.
Pros. Twelve year since, Miranda, twelve year since,
Thy father was the Duke of Milan, and
A prince of power.
Mir.

Sir, are not you my father?
Pros. Thy mother was a piece of virtue, and
She said thou wast my daughter; and thy father
Was Duke of Milan; and his only heir
And princess, no worse issued.
Mir.

O the heavens!
What foul play had we, that we came from thence?
Or blessed was't we did?
Pros.

Both, both, my girl:
By foul play, as thou say'st, were we heaved thence;
But blessedly holp hither.
Mir.

O, my heart bleeds
To think o' the teen that I have turn'd you to.
Which is from my remembrance! Please you, farther.
Pros. My brother, and thy uncle, call'd Antonio,—
I pray thee, mark me,—that a brother should
Be so perfidious!—he whom, next thyself,
Of all the world I loved, and to him put

The manage of my state; as, at that time,
Through all the signories it was the first,
And Prospero the prime duke, being so reputed
In dignity, and for the liberal arts
Without a parallel; those being all my study,
The government I cast upon my brother,
And to my state grew stranger, being transported
And rapt in secret studies. Thy false uncle—
Dost thou attend me?
Mir.

     Sir, most heedfully.
Pros. Being once perfected how to grant suits,
How to deny them, whom to advance, and whom

To trash for over-topping, new created
The creatures that were mine, I say, or changed 'em,
Or else new form'd 'em; having both the key
Of officer and office, set all hearts i' the state
To what tune pleased his ear; that now he was
The ivy which had hid my princely trunk,
And suck'd my verdure out on't. Thou attend'st not.
Mir. O, good sir, I do.
Pros.

     I pray thee, mark me.
I, thus neglecting worldly ends, all dedicated
To closeness and the bettering of my mind
With that which, but by being so retired,
O'er-prized all popular rate, in my false brother
Awaked an evil nature; and my trust,
Like a good parent, did beget of him
A falsehood in its contrary, as great
As my trust was; which had indeed no limit,
A confidence sans bound. He being thus lorded,
Not only with what my revenue yielded,
But what my power might else exact, like one
Who having into truth, by telling of it,
Made such a sinner of his memory,
To credit his own lie, he did believe
He was indeed the duke; out o' the substitution,
And executing the outward face of royalty,
With all prerogative:—hence his ambition growing,—

Dost thou hear?
Mir.

    Your tale, sir, would cure deafness.
Pros. To have no screen between this part he play'd

And him he play'd it for, he needs will be
Absolute Milan. Me, poor man, my library
Was dukedom large enough: of temporal royalties
He thinks me now incapable; confederates,
So dry he was for sway, wi' the King of Naples
To give him annual tribute, do him homage,
Subject his coronet to his crown, and bend
The dukedom, yet unbow'd,—alas, poor Milan!—
To most ignoble stooping.
Mir.

     O the heavens!
Pros. Mark his condition, and th' event; then tell me
If this might be a brother.
Mir.

     I should sin
To think but nobly of my grandmother:
Good wombs have borne bad sons.
Pros.

    Now the condition.
This King of Naples, being an enemy
To me inveterate, hearkens my brother's suit;
Which was, that he, in lieu o' the premises,
Of homage and I know not how much tribute,
Should presently extirpate me and mine
Out of the dukedom, and confer fair Milan,
With all the honours, on my brother: whereon,
A treacherous army levied, one midnight
Fated to the purpose, did Antonio open
The gates of Milan; and, i' the dead of darkness,
The ministers for the purpose hurried thence
Me and thy crying self.
Mir.

    Alack, for pity!
I, not remembering how I cried out then,

Will cry it o'er again: it is a hint
That wrings mine eyes to't.
Pros.

    Hear a little further,
And then I'll bring thee to the present business
Which now's upon 's; without the which, this story
Were most impertinent.
Mir.

    Wherefore did they not
That hour destroy us?
Pros.

    Well demanded, wench:

My tale provokes that question. Dear, they durst not,
So dear the love my people bore me; nor set
A mark so bloody on the business; but
With colours fairer painted their foul ends.
In few, they hurried us aboard a bark,
Bore us some leagues to sea; where they prepared
A rotten carcass of a boat, not rigg'd,
Nor tackle, sail, nor mast; the very rats
Instinctively have quit it: there they hoist us,
To cry to the sea that roar'd to us; to sigh
To the winds, whose pity, sighing back again,
Did us but loving wrong.
Mir.

           Alack, what trouble
Was I then to you!
Pros.

           O, a cherubin
Thou wast that did preserve me. Thou didst smile,
Infused with a fortitude from heaven,
When I have deck'd the sea with drops full salt,
Under my burthen groan'd; which raised in me
An undergoing stomach, to bear up
Against what should ensue.
Mir.

           How came we ashore?
Pros. By Providence divine.
Some food we had, and some fresh water, that

A noble Neapolitan, Gonzalo,
Out of his charity, who being then appointed
Master of this design, did give us, with
Rich garments, linens, stuffs and necessaries,
Which since have steaded much; so, of his gentleness,
Knowing I loved my books, he furnish'd me
From mine own library with volumes that
I prize above my dukedom.
Mir.

           Would I might
But ever see that man!
Pros.

         Now I arise:*Resumes his mantle.*
Sit still, and hear the last of our sea-sorrow.
Here in this island we arrived; and here
Have I, thy schoolmaster, made thee more profit
Than other princesses can, that have more time
For vainer hours, and tutors not so careful.

Mir. Heavens thank you for't! And now, I pray you, sir,
For still 'tis beating in my mind, your reason
For raising this sea-storm?
Pros.

          Know thus far forth.
By accident most strange, bountiful Fortune,
Now my dear lady, hath mine enemies
Brought to this shore; and by my prescience
I find my zenith doth depend upon
A most auspicious star, whose influence
If now I court not, but omit, my fortunes
Will ever after droop. Here cease more questions:
Thou art inclined to sleep; 'tis a good dulness,
And give it way: I know thou canst not
choose.*Miranda sleeps.*
Come away, servant, come. I am ready now.
Approach, my Ariel, come.

         Enter Ariel.
Ari. All hail, great master! grave sir, hail! I come

To answer thy best pleasure; be't to fly,
To swim, to dive into the fire, to ride
On the curl'd clouds, to thy strong bidding task
Ariel and all his quality.
Pros.

          Hast thou, spirit,
Perform'd to point the tempest that I bade thee?
Ari. To every article.
I boarded the king's ship; now on the beak,
Now in the waist, the deck, in every cabin,
I flamed amazement: sometime I'd divide,
And burn in many places; on the topmast,
The yards and bowsprit, would I flame distinctly,
Then meet and join. Jove's lightnings, the precursors
O' the dreadful thunder-claps, more momentary
And sight-outrunning were not: the fire and cracks
Of sulphurous roaring the most mighty Neptune
Seem to besiege, and make his bold waves tremble,
Yea, his dread trident shake.
Pros.

         My brave spirit!
Who was so firm, so constant, that this coil
Would not infect his reason?
Ari.

         Not a soul
But felt a fever of the mad, and play'd

Some tricks of desperation. All but mariners
Plunged in the foaming brine, and quit the vessel,
Then all afire with me: the king's son, Ferdinand,
With hair up-staring,—then like reeds, not hair,—
Was the first man that leap'd; cried, "Hell is empty,
And all the devils are here."
Pros.

　　　　Why, that's my spirit!
But was not this nigh shore?

Ari.

　　　　Close by, my master.
Pros. But are they, Ariel, safe?
Ari.

　　　　Not a hair perish'd;
On their sustaining garments not a blemish,
But fresher than before: and, as thou badest me,
In troops I have dispersed them 'bout the isle.
The king's son have I landed by himself;
Whom I left cooling of the air with sighs
In an odd angle of the isle, and sitting,
His arms in this sad knot.
Pros.

　　　　Of the king's ship
The mariners, say how thou hast disposed,
And all the rest o' the fleet.
Ari.

　　　　Safely in harbour
Is the king's ship; in the deep nook, where once
Thou call'dst me up at midnight to fetch dew
From the still-vex'd Bermoothes, there she's hid:
The mariners all under hatches stow'd;
Who, with a charm join'd to their suffer'd labour,
I have left asleep: and for the rest o' the fleet,
Which I dispersed, they all have met again,
And are upon the Mediterranean flote,
Bound sadly home for Naples;
Supposing that they saw the king's ship wreck'd,
And his great person perish.
Pros.

　　　　Ariel, thy charge
Exactly is perform'd: but there's more work.
What is the time o' the day?
　　　　　　Ari.

　　　　Past the mid season.
Pros. At least two glasses. The time 'twixt six and
now

Must by us both be spent most preciously.
Ari. Is there more toil? Since thou dost give me pains,
Let me remember thee what thou hast promised,

Which is not yet perform'd me.
Pros.

　　　　How now? moody?
What is't thou canst demand?
Ari.
My liberty.
Pros. Before the time be out? no more!
Ari.
I prithee,
Remember I have done thee worthy service;
Told thee no lies, made thee no mistakings, served
Without or grudge or grumblings: thou didst
promise
To bate me a full year.
Pros.

　　　　Dost thou forget
From what a torment I did free thee?
Ari.

　　　　No.
Pros. Thou dost; and think'st it much to tread the
ooze
Of the salt deep,
To run upon the sharp wind of the north,
To do me business in the veins o' the earth
When it is baked with frost.
Ari.

　　　　I do not, sir.
Pros. Thou liest, malignant thing! Hast thou forgot
The foul witch Sycorax, who with age and envy
Was grown into a hoop? hast thou forgot her?
Ari. No, sir.
Pros.
　　Thou hast. Where was she born? speak; tell me.
Ari. Sir, in Argier.
Pros.

　　　　O, was she so? I must
Once in a month recount what thou hast been,
Which thou forget'st. This damn'd witch Sycorax,
For mischiefs manifold, and sorceries terrible
To enter human hearing, from Argier,
Thou know'st, was banish'd: for one thing she did
They would not take her life. Is not this true?

Ari. Ay, sir.
Pros. This blue-eyed hag was hither brought with child,

And here was left by the sailors. Thou, my slave,
As thou report'st thyself, wast then her servant;
And, for thou wast a spirit too delicate
To act her earthy and abhorr'd commands,
Refusing her grand hests, she did confine thee,
By help of her more potent ministers,
And in her most unmitigable rage,
Into a cloven pine; within which rift
Imprison'd thou didst painfully remain
A dozen years; within which space she died,
And left thee there; where thou didst vent thy groans
As fast as mill-wheels strike. Then was this island—
Save for the son that she did litter here,
A freckled whelp hag-born—not honour'd with
A human shape.
Ari.

Yes, Caliban her son.
Pros. Dull thing, I say so; he, that Caliban,
Whom now I keep in service. Thou best know'st
What torment I did find thee in; thy groans
Did make wolves howl, and penetrate the breasts
Of ever-angry bears: it was a torment
To lay upon the damn'd, which Sycorax
Could not again undo: it was mine art,
When I arrived and heard thee, that made gape
The pine, and let thee out.
Ari.

I thank thee, master.
Pros. If thou more murmur'st, I will rend an oak,
And peg thee in his knotty entrails, till
Thou hast howl'd away twelve winters.
Ari.

Pardon, master:
I will be correspondent to command,
And do my spiriting gently.
Pros.

Do so; and after two days
I will discharge thee.
Ari.

That's my noble master!
What shall I do? say what; what shall I do?

Pros. Go make thyself like a nymph o' the sea:

Be subject to no sight but thine and mine; invisible
To every eyeball else. Go take this shape,
And hither come in't: go, hence with diligence! *Exit Ariel.*
305 Awake, dear heart, awake! thou hast slept well;
Awake!
Mir.

The strangeness of your story put
Heaviness in me.
Pros.

Shake it off. Come on;
We'll visit Caliban my slave, who never
Yields us kind answer.
Mir.

'Tis a villain, sir,
I do not love to look on.
Pros.

But, as 'tis,
We cannot miss him: he does make our fire,
Fetch in our wood, and serves in offices
That profit us. What, ho! slave! Caliban!
Thou earth, thou! speak.
Cal. [*within*] There's wood enough within.
Pros. Come forth, I say! there's other business for thee:
Come, thou tortoise! when?

Re-enter ARIEL *like a water-nymph.*
Fine apparition! My quaint Ariel,
Hark in thine ear.
Ari.

My lord, it shall be done. *Exit.*
Pros. Thou poisonous slave, got by the devil himself
Upon thy wicked dam, come forth!

Enter CALIBAN.
Cal. As wicked dew as e'er my mother brush'd
With raven's feather from unwholesome fen
Drop on you both! a south-west blow on ye
And blister you all o'er!
Pros. For this, be sure, to-night thou shalt have cramps,
Side-stitches that shall pen thy breath up; urchins
Shall, for that vast of night that they may work,
All exercise on thee; thou shalt be pinch'd
As thick as honeycomb, each pinch more stinging
Than bees that made 'em.
Cal.

I must eat my dinner.
This island's mine, by Sycorax my mother,
Which thou takest from me. When thou camest first,
Thou strokedst me, and madest much of me; wouldst give me
Water with berries in't; and teach me how
To name the bigger light, and how the less,
That burn by day and night: and then I loved thee,
And show'd thee all the qualities o' th' isle,
The fresh springs, brine-pits, barren place and fertile:
Curs'd be I that did so! All the charms
Of Sycorax, toads, beetles, bats, light on you!
For I am all the subjects that you have,
Which first was mine own king: and here you sty me
In this hard rock, whiles you do keep from me
The rest o' th' island.
Pros.
　　　　Thou most lying slave,
Whom stripes may move, not kindness! I have used thee,
Filth as thou art, with human care; and lodged thee
In mine own cell, till thou didst seek to violate
The honour of my child.
Cal. O ho, O ho! would 't had been done!
Thou didst prevent me; I had peopled else

This isle with Calibans.
Pros.
　　　　Abhorred slave,
Which any print of goodness wilt not take,
Being capable of all ill! I pitied thee,
Took pains to make thee speak, taught thee each hour
One thing or other: when thou didst not, savage,
Know thine own meaning, but wouldst gabble like
A thing most brutish, I endow'd thy purposes
With words that made them known. But thy vile race,
Though thou didst learn, had that in't which good natures
Could not abide to be with; therefore wast thou
Deservedly confined into this rock,
Who hadst deserved more than a prison.
Cal. You taught me language; and my profit on't
Is, I know how to curse. The red plague rid you
For learning me your language!
Pros.

Hag-seed, hence!
Fetch us in fuel; and be quick, thou'rt best,
To answer other business. Shrug'st thou, malice?
If thou neglect'st, or dost unwillingly
What I command, I'll rack thee with old cramps,
Fill all thy bones with aches, make thee roar,
That beasts shall tremble at thy din.
Cal.
　　　　No, pray thee.
[*Aside*] I must obey: his art is of such power,
It would control my dam's god, Setebos,
And make a vassal of him.
Pros.

　　　　So, slave; hence!*Exit Caliban.*
　Re-enter Ariel, *invisible, playing and singing;*
　　　　Ferdinand*following.*

　　　　ARIEL'S *song.*
Come unto these yellow sands,
And then take hands:
Courtsied when you have and kiss'd
The wild waves whist:
Foot it featly here and there;
And, sweet sprites, the burthen bear.
Burthen [*dispersedly*]. Hark, hark!
　　　　　　　　　　　　Bow-wow.
The watch-dogs bark:
　　　　　　　　　　　　Bow-wow.
Ari. Hark, hark! I hear
The strain of strutting chanticleer
Cry, Cock-a-diddle-dow.
Fer. Where should this music be? i' th' air or th' earth?
It sounds no more: and, sure, it waits upon
Some god o' th' island. Sitting on a bank,
Weeping again the king my father's wreck,
This music crept by me upon the waters,
Allaying both their fury and my passion
With its sweet air: thence I have follow'd it.
Or it hath drawn me rather. But 'tis gone.
No, it begins again.
　　　　　　　　　ARIEL *sings.*
Full fathom five thy father lies;
Of his bones are coral made;
Those are pearls that were his eyes:
Nothing of him that doth fade,

But doth suffer a sea-change
Into something rich and strange.
Sea-nymphs hourly ring his knell:
                Burthen: Ding-dong.
Ari. Hark! now I hear them,—Ding-dong, bell.
Fer. The ditty does remember my drown'd father.
This is no mortal business, nor no sound
That the earth owes:—I hear it now above me.
Pros. The fringed curtains of thine eye advance,
And say what thou seest yond.
Mir.

        What is't? a spirit?
Lord, how it looks about! Believe me, sir,
It carries a brave form. But 'tis a spirit.
Pros. No, wench; it eats and sleeps and hath such senses
As we have, such. This gallant which thou seest
Was in the wreck; and, but he's something stain'd
With grief, that's beauty's canker, thou mightst call him
A goodly person: he hath lost his fellows,
And strays about to find 'em.
Mir.

        I might call him
A thing divine; for nothing natural
I ever saw so noble.
Pros. [*Aside*]

        It goes on, I see,
As my soul prompts it. Spirit, fine spirit! I'll free thee
Within two days for this.
Fer.

        Most sure, the goddess
On whom these airs attend! Vouchsafe my prayer
May know if you remain upon this island;
And that you will some good instruction give
How I may bear me here: my prime request,
Which I do last pronounce, is, O you wonder!
If you be maid or no?
Mir.

        No wonder, sir;
But certainly a maid.
Fer.

        My language! heavens!
I am the best of them that speak this speech,
Were I but where 'tis spoken.
Pros.

        How? the best?

What wert thou, if the King of Naples heard thee?

Fer. A single thing, as I am now, that wonders
To hear thee speak of Naples. He does hear me;
And that he does I weep: myself am Naples,
Who with mine eyes, never since at ebb, beheld
The king my father wreck'd.
Mir.

        Alack, for mercy!
Fer. Yes, faith, and all his lords; the Duke of Milan
And his brave son being twain.
Pros. [*Aside*]

        The Duke of Milan
And his more braver daughter could control thee,
If now 'twere fit to do't. At the first sight
They have changed eyes. Delicate Ariel,
I'll set thee free for this. [*To Fer.*] A word, good sir;
I fear you have done yourself some wrong: a word.
Mir. Why speaks my father so ungently? This
Is the third man that e'er I saw; the first
That e'er I sigh'd for: pity move my father
To be inclined my way!
Fer.

        O, if a virgin,
And your affection not gone forth, I'll make you
The queen of Naples.
Pros.

        Soft, sir! one word more.
[*Aside*] They are both in either's powers: but this swift business
I must uneasy make, lest too light winning
Make the prize light. [*To Fer.*] One word more; I charge thee
That thou attend me: thou dost here usurp
The name thou owest not; and hast put thyself
Upon this island as a spy, to win it
From me, the lord on't.
Fer.

        No, as I am a man.
Mir. There's nothing ill can dwell in such a temple:
If the ill spirit have so fair a house,
Good things will strive to dwell with't.
Pros.

        Follow me.

Speak not you for him; he's a traitor. Come;
I'll manacle thy neck and feet together:

Sea-water shalt thou drink; thy food shall be
The fresh-brook muscles, wither'd roots, and husks
Wherein the acorn cradled. Follow.
Fer.

No;
I will resist such entertainment till
Mine enemy has more power.*Draws, and is charmed
from moving.*
Mir.

O dear father,
Make not too rash a trial of him, for
He's gentle, and not fearful.
Pros.

What! I say,
My foot my tutor? Put thy sword up, traitor;
Who makest a show, but darest not strike, thy
conscience
Is so possess'd with guilt: come from thy ward;
For I can here disarm thee with this stick
And make thy weapon drop.
Mir.

Beseech you, father.
Pros. Hence! hang not on my garments.
Mir.

Sir, have pity;
I'll be his surety.
Pros.

Silence! one word more
Shall make me chide thee, if not hate thee. What!
An advocate for an impostor! hush!
Thou think'st there is no more such shapes as he,
Having seen but him and Caliban: foolish wench!
To the most of men this is a Caliban,
And they to him are angels.
Mir.

My affections
Are, then, most humble; I have no ambition
To see a goodlier man.
Pros.

Come on; obey:
Thy nerves are in their infancy again,
And have no vigour in them.

Fer.
So they are:
My spirits, as in a dream, are all bound up.
My father's loss, the weakness which I feel,

The wreck of all my friends, nor this man's threats,
To whom I am subdued, are but light to me,
Might I but through my prison once a day
Behold this maid: all corners else o' th' earth
Let liberty make use of; space enough
Have I in such a prison.
Pros. [*Aside*]

It works. [*To Fer.*] Come on.
Thou hast done well, fine Ariel! [*To Fer.*] Follow me.
[*To Ari.*] Hark what thou else shalt do me.
Mir.

Be of comfort;
My father's of a better nature, sir,
Than he appears by speech: this is unwonted
Which now came from him.
Pros.

Thou shalt be as free
As mountain winds: but then exactly do
All points of my command.
Ari.

To the syllable.
Pros. Come, follow. Speak not for him.*Exeunt.*

ACT II.

Scene I. *Another part of the island.*
Enter Alonso, Sebastian, Antonio, Gonzalo, Adrian,
Francisco, *and others.*
Gon. Beseech you, sir, be merry; you have cause,
So have we all, of joy; for our escape
Is much beyond our loss. Our hint of woe
Is common; every day, some sailor's wife,
The masters of some merchant, and the merchant,
Have just our theme of woe; but for the miracle,

I mean our preservation, few in millions
Can speak like us: then wisely, good
sir, weigh
Our sorrow with our comfort.
Alon.

Prithee, peace.
Seb. He receives comfort like cold porridge.
Ant. The visitor will not give him o'er so.
Seb. Look, he's winding up the watch of his wit; by
and by it will strike.
Gon. Sir,—
Seb. One: tell.
Gon. When every grief is entertain'd that's offer'd,

Comes to the entertainer—

Seb. A dollar.

Gon. Dolour comes to him, indeed: you have spoken truer than you purposed.

Seb. You have taken it wiselier than I meant you should.

Gon. Therefore, my lord,—

Ant. Fie, what a spendthrift is he of his tongue!

Alon. I prithee, spare.

Gon. Well, I have done: but yet,—

Seb. He will be talking.

Ant. Which, of he or Adrian, for a good wager, first begins to crow?

Seb. The old cock.

Ant. The cockerel.

Seb. Done. The wager?

Ant. A laughter.

Seb. A match!

Adr. Though this island seem to be desert,—

Seb. Ha, ha, ha!—So, you're paid.

Adr. Uninhabitable, and almost inaccessible,—

Seb. Yet,—

Adr. Yet,—

Ant. He could not miss't.

Adr. It must needs be of subtle, tender and delicate temperance.

Ant. Temperance was a delicate wench.

Seb. Ay, and a subtle; as he most learnedly delivered.

Adr. The air breathes upon us here most sweetly.

Seb. As if it had lungs, and rotten ones.

Ant. Or as 'twere perfumed by a fen.

Gon. Here is every thing advantageous to life.

Ant. True; save means to live.

Seb. Of that there's none, or little.

Gon. How lush and lusty the grass looks! how green!

Ant. The ground, indeed, is tawny.

Seb. With an eye of green in't.

Ant. He misses not much.

Seb. No; he doth but mistake the truth totally.

Gon. But the rarity of it is,—which is indeed almost beyond credit,—

Seb. As many vouched rarities are.

Gon. That our garments, being, as they were, drenched in the sea, hold, notwithstanding, their freshness and glosses, being rather new-dyed than stained with salt water.

Ant. If but one of his pockets could speak, would it not say he lies?

Seb. Ay, or very falsely pocket up his report.

Gon. Methinks our garments are now as fresh as when we put them on first in Afric, at the marriage of the king's fair daughter Claribel to the King of Tunis.

Seb. 'Twas a sweet marriage, and we prosper well in our return.

Adr. Tunis was never graced before with such a paragon to their queen.

Gon. Not since widow Dido's time.

Ant. Widow! a pox o' that! How came that widow in? widow Dido!

Seb. What if he had said 'widower Æneas' too? Good Lord, how you take it!

Adr. 'Widow Dido' said you? you make me study of that: she was of Carthage, not of Tunis.

Gon. This Tunis, sir, was Carthage.

Adr. Carthage?

Gon. I assure you, Carthage.

Seb. His word is more than the miraculous harp; he hath raised the wall, and houses too.

Ant. What impossible matter will he make easy next?

Seb. I think he will carry this island home in his pocket, and give it his son for an apple.

Ant. And, sowing the kernels of it in the sea, bring forth more islands.

Gon. Ay.

Ant. Why, in good time.

Gon. Sir, we were talking that our garments seem now as fresh as when we were at Tunis at the marriage of your daughter, who is now queen.

Ant. And the rarest that e'er came there.

Seb. Bate, I beseech you, widow Dido.

Ant. O, widow Dido! ay, widow Dido.

Gon. Is not, sir, my doublet as fresh as the first day I wore it? I mean, in a sort.

Ant. That sort was well fished for.

Gon. When I wore it at your daughter's marriage?

Alon. You cram these words into mine ears against
The stomach of my sense. Would I had never
Married my daughter there! for, coming thence,

My son is lost, and, in my rate, she too.
Who is so far from Italy removed
I ne'er again shall see her. O thou mine heir
Of Naples and of Milan, what strange fish
Hath made his meal on thee?
Fran.

Sir, he may live:
I saw him beat the surges under him,
And ride upon their backs; he trod the water.
Whose enmity he flung aside, and breasted
The surge most swoln that met him; his bold head

'Bove the contentious waves he kept, and oar'd
Himself with his good arms in lusty stroke
To the shore, that o'er his wave-worn basis bow'd,
As stooping to relieve him: I not doubt
He came alive to land.
Alon.

No, no, he's gone.
Seb. Sir, you may thank yourself for this great loss,
That would not bless our Europe with your daughter,
But rather lose her to an African;
Where she, at least, is banish'd from your eye,
Who hath cause to wet the grief on't.
Alon.

Prithee, peace.
Seb. You were kneel'd to, and importuned otherwise,
By all of us; and the fair soul herself
Weigh'd between loathness and obedience, at
Which end o' the beam should bow. We have lost
your son,
I fear, for ever: Milan and Naples have
More widows in them of this business' making
Than we bring men to comfort them:
The fault's your own.
Alon.

So is the dear'st o' the loss.
Gon. My lord Sebastian,
The truth you speak doth lack some gentleness,
And time to speak it in: you rub the sore,
When you should bring the plaster.
Seb.

Very well.
Ant. And most chirurgeonly.
Gon. It is foul weather in us all, good sir,
When you are cloudy.
Seb.

Foul weather?
Ant.

Very foul.
Gon. Had I plantation of this isle, my lord,—
Ant. He'ld sow't with nettle-seed.
Seb.

Or docks, or mallows.
Gon. And were the king on't, what would I do?
Seb. 'Scape being drunk for want of wine.
Gon. I' the commonwealth I would by contraries
Execute all things; for no kind of traffic
Would I admit; no name of magistrate;
Letters should not be known; riches, poverty,
And use of service, none; contract, succession,
Bourn, bound of land, tilth, vineyard, none;
No use of metal, corn, or wine, or oil;
No occupation; all men idle, all;
And women too, but innocent and pure;
No sovereignty;—
Seb.

Yet he would be king on't.
Ant. The latter end of his commonwealth forgets the
beginning.
Gon. All things in common nature should produce
Without sweat or endeavour: treason, felony,
Sword, pike, knife, gun, or need of any engine,
Would I not have; but nature should bring forth,
Of its own kind, all foison, all abundance,
To feed my innocent people.
Seb. No marrying 'mong his subjects?
Ant. None, man; all idle; whores and knaves.
Gon. I would with such perfection govern, sir,
To excel the golden age.
Seb.

'Save his majesty!
Ant. Long live Gonzalo!
Gon.

And,—do you mark me, sir?
Alon. Prithee, no more: thou dost talk nothing to
me.
Gon. I do well believe your highness; and did it to
minister occasion to these gentlemen, who are of
such sensible and nimble lungs that they always use
to laugh at nothing.
Ant. 'Twas you we laughed at.

Gon. Who in this kind of merry fooling am nothing to you: so you may continue, and laugh at nothing still.

Ant. What a blow was there given!
Seb. An it had not fallen flat-long.
Gon. You are gentlemen of brave mettle; you would lift the moon out of her sphere, if she would continue in it five weeks without changing.
   Enter ARIEL *(invisible) playing solemn music.*
Seb. We would so, and then go a bat-fowling.
Ant. Nay, good my lord, be not angry.
Gon. No, I warrant you; I will not adventure my discretion so weakly. Will you laugh me asleep, for I am very heavy?
Ant. Go sleep, and hear us.
     All sleep except Alon., Seb., and Ant.
Alon. What, all so soon asleep! I wish mine eyes
Would, with themselves, shut up my thoughts: I find
They are inclined to do so.
Seb.

     Please you, sir,
Do not omit the heavy offer of it:
It seldom visits sorrow; when it doth,
It is a comforter.
Ant.

    We two, my lord,
Will guard your person while you take your rest,
And watch your safety.
Alon.

    Thank you.—Wondrous heavy.
     Alonso sleeps. Exit Ariel.
Seb. What a strange drowsiness possesses them!
Ant. It is the quality o' the climate.
Seb.

     Why
Doth it not then our eyelids sink? I find not
Myself disposed to sleep.
Ant.

    Nor I; my spirits are nimble.

They fell together all, as by consent;
They dropp'd, as by a thunder-stroke. What might,
Worthy Sebastian?—O, what might?—No more:—
And yet methinks I see it in thy face,
What thou shouldst be: the occasion speaks thee;
and

My strong imagination sees a crown
Dropping upon thy head.
Seb.

    What, art thou waking?
Ant. Do you not hear me speak?
Seb.

    I do; and surely
It is a sleepy language, and thou speak'st
Out of thy sleep. What is it thou didst say?
This is a strange repose, to be asleep
With eyes wide open; standing, speaking, moving,
And yet so fast asleep.
Ant.

    Noble Sebastian,
Thou let'st thy fortune sleep—die, rather; wink'st
Whiles thou art waking.
Seb.

    Thou dost snore distinctly;
There's meaning in thy snores.
Ant. I am more serious than my custom: you
Must be so too, if heed me; which to do
Trebles thee o'er.
Seb.

    Well, I am standing water.
Ant. I'll teach you how to flow.
Seb.

    Do so: to ebb
Hereditary sloth instructs me.
Ant.

     O,
If you but knew how you the purpose cherish
Whiles thus you mock it! how, in stripping it,
You more invest it! Ebbing men, indeed,
Most often do so near the bottom run
By their own fear or sloth.
Seb.

    Prithee, say on:
The setting of thine eye and cheek proclaim
A matter from thee; and a birth, indeed,

Which throes thee much to yield.
Ant.

    Thus, sir:
Although this lord of weak remembrance, this,
Who shall be of as little memory
When he is earth'd, hath here almost persuaded,—
For he's a spirit of persuasion, only

Professes to persuade,—the king his son's alive,
'Tis as impossible that he's undrown'd
As he that sleeps here swims.
Seb.
I have no hope
That he's undrown'd.
Ant.
    O, out of that 'no hope'
What great hope have you! no hope that way is
Another way so high a hope that even
Ambition cannot pierce a wink beyond,
But doubt discovery there. Will you grant with me
That Ferdinand is drown'd?
Seb.
     He's gone.
Ant.
    Then, tell me,
Who's the next heir of Naples?
Seb.
     Claribel.
Ant. She that is queen of Tunis; she that dwells
Ten leagues beyond man's life; she that from Naples
Can have no note, unless the sun were post,—
The man i' the moon's too slow,—till new-born chins
Be rough and razorable; she that from whom
We all were sea-swallow'd, though some cast again,
And by that destiny, to perform an act
Whereof what's past is prologue; what to come,
In yours and my discharge.
Seb.
   What stuff is this! How say you?
'Tis true, my brother's daughter's queen of Tunis;
So is she heir of Naples; 'twixt which regions
There is some space.
Ant.
   A space whose every cubit
Seems to cry out, "How shall that Claribel
Measure us back to Naples? Keep in Tunis,
And let Sebastian wake." Say, this were death
That now hath seized them; why, they were no worse
Than now they are. There be that can rule Naples
As well as he that sleeps; lords that can prate
As amply and unnecessarily
As this Gonzalo; I myself could make
A chough of as deep chat. O, that you bore
The mind that I do! what a sleep were this

For your advancement! Do you understand me?
Seb. Methinks I do.
Ant.
And how does your content
Tender your own good fortune?
Seb.
I remember
You did supplant your brother Prospero.
Ant.
     True:
And look how well my garments sit upon me;
Much feater than before: my brother's servants
Were then my fellows; now they are my men.
Seb. But for your conscience.
Ant. Ay, sir; where lies that? if 'twere a kibe,
'Twould put me to my slipper: but I feel not
This deity in my bosom: twenty consciences,
That stand 'twixt me and Milan, candied be they,
And melt, ere they molest! Here lies your brother,
No better than the earth he lies upon,
If he were that which now he's like, that's dead;

Whom I, with this obedient steel, three inches of it,
Can lay to bed for ever; whiles you, doing thus,
To the perpetual wink for aye might put
This ancient morsel, this Sir Prudence, who
Should not upbraid our course. For all the rest,
They'll take suggestion as a cat laps milk;
They'll tell the clock to any business that
We say befits the hour.
Seb.
    Thy case, dear friend,
Shall be my precedent; as thou got'st Milan,
I'll come by Naples. Draw thy sword: one stroke
Shall free thee from the tribute which thou payest;
And I the king shall love thee.
Ant.
    Draw together;
And when I rear my hand, do you the like,
To fall it on Gonzalo.
Seb.
   O, but one word. *They talk apart.*
   Re-enter Ariel *invisible.*
Ari. My master through his art foresees the danger
That you, his friend, are in; and sends me forth,—
For else his project dies,—to keep them living.
      Sings in Gonzalo's ear.

While you here do snoring lie,
Open-eyed conspiracy
His time doth take.
If of life you keep a care,
Shake off slumber, and beware:
Awake, awake!

Ant. Then let us both be sudden.

Gon.
Now, good angels
Preserve the king!*They wake.*

Alon. Why, how now? ho, awake!—Why are you drawn?
Wherefore this ghastly looking?

Gon.
What's the matter?

Seb. Whiles we stood here securing your repose,
Even now, we heard a hollow burst of bellowing
Like bulls, or rather lions: did't not wake you?
It struck mine ear most terribly.

Alon.
I heard nothing.

Ant. O, 'twas a din to fright a monster's ear,
To make an earthquake! sure, it was the roar
Of a whole herd of lions.

Alon.
Heard you this, Gonzalo?

Gon. Upon mine honour, sir, I heard a humming,
And that a strange one too, which did awake me:
I shaked you, sir, and cried: as mine eyes open'd,
I saw their weapons drawn:—there was a noise,
That's verily. 'Tis best we stand upon our guard,
Or that we quit this place: let's draw our weapons.

Alon. Lead off this ground; and let's make further search
For my poor son.

Gon.
Heavens keep him from these beasts!
For he is, sure, i' th' island.

Alon.
Lead away.

Ari. Prospero my lord shall know what I have done:
So, king, go safely on to seek thy son.*Exeunt.*

Scene II. *Another part of the island.*
Enter CALIBAN *with a burden of wood. A noise of thunder heard.*

Cal. All the infections that the sun sucks up
From bogs, fens, flats, on Prosper fall, and make him
By inch-meal a disease! His spirits hear me,
And yet I needs must curse. But they'll nor pinch,
Fright me with urchin-shows, pitch me i' the mire,
Nor lead me, like a firebrand, in the dark

Out of my way, unless he bid 'em: but
For every trifle are they set upon me;
Sometime like apes, that mow and chatter at me,
And after bite me; then like hedgehogs, which
Lie tumbling in my barefoot way, and mount
Their pricks at my footfall; sometime am I
All wound with adders, who with cloven tongues
Do hiss me into madness.

Enter Trinculo.
Lo, now, lo!
Here comes a spirit of his, and to torment me
For bringing wood in slowly. I'll fall flat;
Perchance he will not mind me.

Trin. Here's neither bush nor shrub, to bear off any weather at all, and another storm brewing; I hear it sing i' the wind: yond same black cloud, yond huge one, looks like a foul bombard that would shed his liquor. If it should thunder as it did before, I know not where to hide my head: yond same cloud cannot choose but fall by pailfuls. What have we here? a man or a fish? dead or alive? A fish: he smells like a fish; a very ancient and fish-like smell; a kind of not of the newest Poor-John. A strange fish! Were I in England now, as once I was, and had but this fish painted, not a holiday fool there but would give a piece of silver: there would this monster make a man; any strange beast there makes a man: when they will not give a doit to relieve a lame beggar, they will lay out ten to see a dead Indian. Legged like a man! and his fins like arms! Warm o' my troth! I do now let loose my opinion; hold it no longer: this is no fish, but an islander, that hath lately suffered by a thunderbolt. [*Thunder.*] Alas, the storm is come again! my best way is to creep under his gaberdine; there is no other shelter hereabout: misery acquaints a man with strange bed-fellows. I will here shroud till the dregs of the storm be past.

Enter Stephano, *singing: a bottle in his hand.*
Ste. I shall no more to sea, to sea,

Here shall I die a-shore,—
This is a very scurvy tune to sing at a man's funeral:
well, here's my comfort.*Drinks.*
[*Sings.* The master, the swabber, the boatswain, and
I,
The gunner, and his mate,
Loved Mall, Meg, and Marian, and Margery,
But none of us cared for Kate;
For she had a tongue with a tang,
Would cry to a sailor, Go hang!
She loved not the savour of tar nor of pitch;
Yet a tailor might scratch her where'er she did itch.
Then, to sea, boys, and let her go hang!

This is a scurvy tune too: but here's my comfort.
Drinks.

Cal. Do not torment me:—O!

Ste. What's the matter? Have we devils here? Do you
put tricks upon's with savages and men of Ind, ha?
I have not scaped drowning, to be afeard now of
your four legs; for it hath been said, As proper a
man as ever went on four legs cannot make him give
ground; and it shall be said so again, while Stephano
breathes at's nostrils.

Cal. The spirit torments me:—O!

Ste. This is some monster of the isle with four legs,
who hath got, as I take it, an ague. Where the devil
should he learn our language? I will give him some
relief, if it be but for that. If I can recover him,
and keep him tame, and get to Naples with him,
he's a present for any emperor that ever trod on
neat's-leather.
Cal. Do not torment me, prithee; I'll bring my wood
home faster.
Ste. He's in his fit now, and does not talk after the
wisest. He shall taste of my bottle: if he have never
drunk wine afore, it will go near to remove his fit. If
I can recover him, and keep him tame, I will not take
too much for him; he shall pay for him that hath
him, and that soundly.

Cal. Thou dost me yet but little hurt; thou wilt anon,
I know it by thy trembling: now Prosper works upon
thee.

Ste. Come on your ways; open your mouth; here is
that which will give language to you, cat: open your
mouth; this will shake your shaking, I can tell you,
and that soundly: you cannot tell who's your friend:
open your chaps again.

Trin. I should know that voice: it should be—but
he is drowned; and these are devils:—O defend me!

Ste. Four legs and two voices,—a most delicate
monster! His forward voice, now, is to speak well
of his friend; his backward voice is to utter foul
speeches and to detract. If all the wine in my bottle
will recover him, I will help his ague. Come:—Amen!
I will pour some in thy other mouth.

Trin. Stephano!

Ste. Doth thy other mouth call me? Mercy, mercy!
This is a devil, and no monster: I will leave him; I
have no long spoon.

Trin. Stephano! If thou beest Stephano, touch me,
and speak to me; for I am Trinculo,—be not afeard,—thy good friend Trinculo.
Ste. If thou beest Trinculo, come forth: I'll pull thee
by the lesser legs: if any be Trinculo's legs, these are
they. Thou art very Trinculo indeed! How earnest
thou to be the siege of this moon-calf? can he vent
Trinculos?

Trin. I took him to be killed with a thunder-stroke.
But art thou not drowned, Stephano? I hope, now,
thou art not drowned. Is the storm overblown? I
hid me under the dead moon-calf's gaberdine for
fear of the storm. And art thou living, Stephano? O
Stephano, two Neapolitans scaped!

Ste. Prithee, do not turn me about; my stomach is
not constant.
Cal. [*aside*] These be fine things, an if they be not
sprites.
That's a brave god, and bears celestial liquor:

I will kneel to him.

Ste. How didst thou 'scape? How camest thou hither? swear, by this bottle, how thou camest hither. I escaped upon a butt of sack, which the sailors heaved o'erboard, by this bottle! which I made of the bark of a tree with mine own hands, since I was cast ashore.

Cal. I'll swear, upon that bottle, to be thy true subject; for the liquor is not earthly.

Ste. Here; swear, then, how thou escapedst.

Trin. Swum ashore, man, like a duck: I can swim like a duck, I'll be sworn.

Ste. Here, kiss the book. Though thou canst swim like a duck, thou art made like a goose.

Trin. O Stephano, hast any more of this?

Ste. The whole butt, man: my cellar is in a rock by the sea-side, where my wine is hid. How now, moon-calf! how does thine ague?

Cal. Hast thou not dropp'd from heaven?

Ste. Out o' the moon, I do assure thee: I was the man i' the moon when time was.

Cal. I have seen thee in her, and I do adore thee: My mistress show'd me thee, and thy dog, and thy bush.
Ste. Come, swear to that; kiss the book: I will furnish it anon with new contents: swear.

Trin. By this good light, this is a very shallow monster! I afeard of him! A very weak monster! The man i' the moon! A most poor credulous monster! Well drawn, monster, in good sooth!
Cal. I'll show thee every fertile inch o' th' island;
And I will kiss thy foot: I prithee, be my god.

Trin. By this light, a most perfidious and drunken monster! when's god's asleep, he'll rob his bottle.

Cal. I'll kiss thy foot; I'll swear myself thy subject.

Ste. Come on, then; down, and swear.

Trin. I shall laugh myself to death at this puppy-headed monster. A most scurvy monster! I could find in my heart to beat him,—

Ste. Come, kiss.

Trin. But that the poor monster's in drink: an abominable monster!
Cal. I'll show thee the best springs; I'll pluck thee berries;
I'll fish for thee, and get thee wood enough.
A plague upon the tyrant that I serve!
I'll bear him no more sticks, but follow thee,
Thou wondrous man.
Trin. A most ridiculous monster, to make a wonder of a poor drunkard!
Cal. I prithee, let me bring thee where crabs grow;
And I with my long nails will dig thee pig-nuts;
Show thee a jay's nest, and instruct thee how
To snare the nimble marmoset; I'll bring thee
To clustering filberts, and sometimes I'll get thee
Young scamels from the rock. Wilt thou go with me?

Ste. I prithee now, lead the way, without any more talking. Trinculo, the king and all our company else being drowned, we will inherit here: here; bear my bottle: fellow Trinculo, we'll fill him by and by again.

Cal. sings drunkenly.] Farewell, master; farewell, farewell!

Trin. A howling monster; a drunken monster!
　　Cal. No more dams I'll make for fish;
　　Nor fetch in firing
　　At requiring;
　　Nor scrape trencher, nor wash dish:
　　'Ban, 'Ban, Cacaliban
　　Has a new master:—get a new man.
Freedom, hey-day! hey-day, freedom! freedom, hey-day, freedom!

Ste. O brave monster! Lead the way. *Exeunt.*

ACT III.

Scene I. *Before* Prospero's *cell.*

Enter Ferdinand, *bearing a log.*

Fer. There be some sports are painful, and their labour
Delight in them sets off: some kinds of baseness
Are nobly undergone, and most poor matters
Point to rich ends. This my mean task
Would be as heavy to me as odious, but
The mistress which I serve quickens what's dead,
And makes my labours pleasures: O, she is
Ten times more gentle than her father's crabbed.
And he's composed of harshness.
I must remove
Some thousands of these logs, and pile them up,
Upon a sore injunction: my sweet mistress
Weeps when she sees me work, and says, such baseness
Had never like executor. I forget:
But these sweet thoughts do even refresh my labours,
Most busy lest, when I do it.

Enter MIRANDA; *and* PROSPERO *at a distance,
unseen.*

Mir.
Alas, now, pray you,
Work not so hard: I would the lightning had
Burnt up those logs that you are enjoin'd to pile!
Pray, set it down, and rest you: when this burns,
'Twill weep for having wearied you. My father
Is hard at study; pray, now, rest yourself;

He's safe for these three hours.

Fer.
O most dear mistress,
The sun will set before I shall discharge
What I must strive to do.

Mir.
If you'll sit down,
I'll bear your logs the while: pray, give me that;
I'll carry it to the pile.

Fer.
No, precious creature;
I had rather crack my sinews, break my back,
Than you should such dishonour undergo,
While I sit lazy by.

Mir.
It would become me
As well as it does you: and I should do it
With much more ease; for my good will is to it,
And yours it is against.

Pros.
Poor worm, thou art infected!
This visitation shows it.

Mir.

You look wearily.
Fer. No, noble mistress; 'tis fresh morning with me
When you are by at night. I do beseech you,—
Chiefly that I might set it in my prayers,—
What is your name?

Mir.
Miranda.—O my father,
I have broke your hest to say so!

Fer.
Admired Miranda!
Indeed the top of admiration! worth
What's dearest to the world! Full many a lady
I have eyed with best regard, and many a time
The harmony of their tongues hath into bondage
Brought my too diligent ear: for several virtues
Have I liked several women; never any
With so full soul, but some defect in her
Did quarrel with the noblest grace she owed,
And put it to the foil: but you, O you,
So perfect and so peerless, are created
Of every creature's best!

Mir.
I do not know
One of my sex; no woman's face remember,
Save, from my glass, mine own; nor have I seen
More that I may call men than you, good friend,
And my dear father: how features are abroad,
I am skilless of; but, by my modesty,
The jewel in my dower, I would not wish
Any companion in the world but you;
Nor can imagination form a shape,
Besides yourself, to like of. But I prattle

Something too wildly, and my father's precepts
I therein do forget.

Fer.
I am, in my condition,
A prince, Miranda; I do think, a king;
I would, not so!—and would no more endure
This wooden slavery than to suffer
The flesh-fly blow my mouth. Hear my soul speak:
The very instant that I saw you, did
My heart fly to your service; there resides,
To make me slave to it; and for your sake
Am I this patient log-man.

Mir.
Do you love me?
Fer. O heaven, O earth, bear witness to this sound,
And crown what I profess with kind event,
If I speak true! if hollowly, invert
What best is boded me to mischief! I,
Beyond all limit of what else i' the world,
Do love, prize, honour you.

Mir.
I am a fool
To weep at what I am glad of.

Pros.
Fair encounter
Of two most rare affections! Heavens rain grace
On that which breeds between 'em!

Fer.
Wherefore weep you?
Mir. At mine unworthiness, that dare not offer
What I desire to give; and much less take
What I shall die to want. But this is trifling;
And all the more it seeks to hide itself,
The bigger bulk it shows. Hence, bashful cunning!
And prompt me, plain and holy innocence!
I am your wife, if you will marry me;
If not, I'll die your maid: to be your fellow
You may deny me; but I'll be your servant,
Whether you will or no.

Fer.
My mistress, dearest;

And I thus humble ever.

Mir.
My husband, then?
Fer. Ay, with a heart as willing
As bondage e'er of freedom: here's my hand.
Mir. And mine, with my heart in't: and now farewell
Till half an hour hence.

Fer.
A thousand thousand!
                    Exeunt Fer. and Mir. severally.
Pros. So glad of this as they I cannot be,
Who are surprised withal; but my rejoicing
At nothing can be more. I'll to my book;
For yet, ere supper-time, must I perform
Much business appertaining.*Exit.*

Scene II. *Another part of the island.*
Enter CALIBAN, STEPHANO, *and* TRINCULO.

Ste. Tell not me;—when the butt is out, we will drink water; not a drop before: therefore bear up, and board 'em. Servant-monster, drink to me.
Trin. Servant-monster! the folly of this island! They say there's but five upon this isle: we are three of them; if th' other two be brained like us, the state totters.

Ste. Drink, servant-monster, when I bid thee: thy eyes are almost set in thyhead.
Trin. Where should they be set else? he were a brave monster indeed, if they were set in his tail.

Ste. My man-monster hath drowned his tongue in sack: for my part, the sea cannot drown me; I swam, ere I could recover the shore, five-and-thirty leagues off and on. By this light, thou shalt be my lieutenant, monster, or my standard.

Trin. Your lieutenant, if you list; he's no standard.

Ste. We'll not run, Monsieur Monster.
Trin. Nor go neither; but you'll lie, like dogs, and yet say nothing neither.

Ste. Moon-calf, speak once in thy life, if thou beest a good moon-calf.

Cal. How does thy honour? Let me lick thy shoe. I'll not serve him, he is not valiant.

Trin. Thou liest, most ignorant monster: I am in case to justle a constable. Why, thou debauched fish, thou, was there ever man a coward that hath drunk so much sack as I to-day? Wilt thou tell a monstrous lie, being but half a fish and half a monster?

Cal. Lo, how he mocks me! wilt thou let him, my lord?
Trin. 'Lord,' quoth he! That a monster should be such a natural!

Cal. Lo, lo, again! bite him to death, I prithee.

Ste. Trinculo, keep a good tongue in your head: if you prove a mutineer,—the next tree! The poor monster's my subject, and he shall not suffer indignity.

Cal. I thank my noble lord. Wilt thou be pleased to hearken once again to the suit I made to thee?

Ste. Marry, will I: kneel and repeat it; I will stand, and so shall Trinculo.

Enter ARIEL, *invisible.*

Cal. As I told thee before, I am subject to a tyrant, a sorcerer, that by his cunning hath cheated me of the island.

Ari. Thou liest.

Cal.
Thou liest, thou jesting monkey, thou:
I would my valiant master would destroy thee!
I do not lie.

Ste. Trinculo, if you trouble him any more in's tale, by this hand, I will supplant some of your teeth.
Trin. Why, I said nothing.

Ste. Mum, then, and no more. Proceed.

Cal. I say, by sorcery he got this isle;
From me he got it. If thy greatness will
Revenge it on him,—for I know thou darest,
But this thing dare not,—

Ste. That's most certain.

Cal. Thou shalt be lord of it, and I'll serve thee.

Ste. How now shall this be compassed? Canst thou bring me to the party?

Cal. Yea, yea, my lord: I'll yield him thee asleep,
Where thou mayst knock a nail into his head.

Ari. Thou liest; thou canst not.

Cal. What a pied ninny's this! Thou scurvy patch!
I do beseech thy Greatness, give him blows,
And take his bottle from him: when that's gone,
He shall drink nought but brine; for I'll not show him
Where the quick freshes are.

Ste. Trinculo, run into no further danger: interrupt the monster one word further, and, by this hand, I'll turn my mercy out o' doors, and make a stock-fish of thee.
Trin. Why, what did I? I did nothing. I'll go farther off.
Ste. Didst thou not say he lied?
Ari. Thou liest.
Ste. Do I so? take thou that. [*Beats him.*] As you like this, give me the lie another time.
Trin. I did not give the lie. Out o' your wits, and hearing too? A pox o' your bottle! this can sack and drinking do. A murrain on your monster, and the devil take your fingers!
Cal. Ha, ha, ha!
Ste. Now, forward with your tale.—Prithee, stand farther off.
Cal. Beat him enough: after a little time, I'll beat him too.
Ste. Stand farther. Come, proceed.

Cal. Why, as I told thee, 'tis a custom with him
I' th' afternoon to sleep: there thou mayst brain him,
Having first seized his books; or with a log

Batter his skull, or paunch him with a stake,
Or cut his wezand with thy knife. Remember
First to possess his books; for without them
He's but a sot, as I am, nor hath not
One spirit to command: they all do hate him
As rootedly as I. Burn but his books.
He has brave utensils,—for so he calls them,—
Which, when he has a house, he'll deck withal.
And that most deeply to consider is
The beauty of his daughter; he himself
Calls her a nonpareil: I never saw a woman,
But only Sycorax my dam and she;
But she as far surpasseth Sycorax
As great'st does least.

Ste.
Is it so brave a lass?
Cal. Ay, lord; she will become thy bed, I warrant,
And bring thee forth brave brood.
Ste. Monster, I will kill this man: his daughter and
I will be king and queen,—save our Graces!—and
Trinculo and thyself shall be viceroys. Dost thou like
the plot, Trinculo?
Trin. Excellent.

Ste. Give me thy hand: I am sorry I beat thee; but,
while thou livest, keep a good tongue in thy head.
Cal. Within this half hour will he be asleep:
Wilt thou destroy him then?
Ste.
Ay, on mine honour.

Ari. This will I tell my master.

Cal. Thou makest me merry; I am full of pleasure:
Let us be jocund: will you troll the catch
You taught me but while-ere?
Ste. At thy request, monster, I will do reason, any
reason. —Come on. Trinculo, let us sing. *Sings.*

Flout 'em and scout 'em, and scout 'em
and flout 'em;
Thought is free.

Cal. That's not the tune.
Ariel plays the tune on a tabor and pipe.
Ste. What is this same?

Trin. This is the tune of our catch, played by the
picture of Nobody.
Ste. If thou beest a man, show thyself in thy likeness:
if thou beest a devil, take't as thou list.

Trin. O, forgive me my sins!
Ste. He that dies pays all debts: I defy thee. Mercy
upon us!
Cal. Art thou afeard?
Ste. No, monster, not I.
Cal. Be not afeard; the isle is full of noises,
Sounds and sweet airs, that give delight, and hurt
    not.
Sometimes a thousand twangling instruments
Will hum about mine ears; and sometime voices,
That, if I then had waked after long sleep,
Will make me sleep again: and then, in dreaming,
The clouds methought would open, and show riches
Ready to drop upon me; that, when I waked,
I cried to dream again.

Ste. This will prove a brave kingdom to me, where I
shall have my music for nothing.
Cal. When Prospero is destroyed.
Ste. That shall be by and by: I remember the story.
Trin. The sound is going away; let's follow it, and
after do our work.
Ste. Lead, monster; we'll follow. I would I could see
this taborer; he lays it on.
Trin. Wilt come? I'll follow, Stephano. *Exeunt.*

SCENE III. *Another part of the island.*
Enter ALONSO, SEBASTIAN, ANTONIO, GONZALO,
ADRIAN, FRANCISCO, *and others.*
Gon. By'r lakin, I can go no further, sir;
My old bones ache: here's a maze trod, indeed,
Through forth-rights and meanders! By your
patience,
I needs must rest me.

Alon.
Old lord, I cannot blame thee,
Who am myself attach'd with weariness,
To the dulling of my spirits: sit down, and rest.
Even here I will put off my hope, and keep it
No longer for my flatterer: he is drown'd
Whom thus we stray to find; and the sea mocks

Our frustrate search on land. Well, let him go.

Ant. [*Aside to Seb.*] I am right glad that he's so out of hope.

Do not, for one repulse, forego the purpose
That you resolved to effect.

Seb. [*Aside to Ant.*]
The next advantage
Will we take throughly.

Ant. [*Aside to Seb.*]
Let it be to-night;
For, now they are oppress'd with travel, they
Will not, nor cannot, use such vigilance
As when they are fresh.

Seb. [*Aside to Ant.*]
I say, to-night: no more.
Solemn and strange music.

Alon. What harmony is this?—My good friends, hark!

Gon. Marvellous sweet music!

Enter PROSPERO *above, invisible. Enter several strange Shapes, bringing in a banquet: they dance about it with gentle actions of salutation; and, inviting the King, &c. to eat, they depart.*

Alon. Give us kind keepers, heavens!—What were these?

Seb. A living drollery. Now I will believe
That there are unicorns; that in Arabia
There is one tree, the phœnix' throne; one phœnix
At this hour reigning there.

Ant.
I'll believe both;
And what does else want credit, come to me,
And I'll be sworn 'tis true: travellers ne'er did lie,
Though fools at home condemn 'em.

Gon.
If in Naples
I should report this now, would they believe me?

If I should say, I saw such islanders,—
For, certes, these are people of the island,—
Who, though they are of monstrous shape, yet, note,
Their manners are more gentle-kind than of
Our human generation you shall find
Many, nay, almost any.

Pros. [*Aside*]
Honest lord,
Thou hast said well; for some of you there present
Are worse than devils.

Alon.
I cannot too much muse
Such shapes, such gesture, and such sound, expressing—
Although they want the use of tongue—a kind
Of excellent dumb discourse.

Pros. [*Aside*]
Praise in departing.
Fran. They vanish'd strangely.

Seb.
No matter, since
They have left their viands behind; for we have stomachs.—
Will't please you taste of what is here?

Alon.
Not I.

Gon. Faith, sir, you need not fear. When we were boys,
Who would believe that there were mountaineers
Dew-lapp'd like bulls, whose throats had hanging at 'em
Wallets of flesh? or that there were such men
Whose heads stood in their breasts? which now we find
Each putter-out of five for one will bring us
Good warrant of.
Alon.
I will stand to, and feed,
Although my last: no matter, since I feel
The best is past. Brother, my lord the duke,
Stand to, and do as we.

Thunder and lightning. Enter ARIEL, *like a harpy; claps his wings upon the table; and, with a quaint device, the banquet vanishes.*

Ari. You are three men of sin, whom Destiny,—
That hath to instrument this lower world
And what is in't,—the never-surfeited sea
Hath caused to belch up you; and on this island,
Where man doth not inhabit,—you 'mongst men
Being most unfit to live. I have made you mad;
And even with such-like valour men hang and drown
Their proper selves.*Alon., Seb. &c. draw their swords.*

You fools! I and my fellows
Are ministers of Fate: the elements,
Of whom your swords are temper'd, may as well
Wound the loud winds, or with bemock'd-at stabs
Kill the still-closing waters, as diminish
One dowle that's in my plume: my fellow-ministers
Are like invulnerable. If you could hurt,
Your swords are now too massy for your strengths,
And will not be uplifted. But remember,—
For that's my business to you,—that you three
From Milan did supplant good Prospero;
Exposed unto the sea, which hath requit it,
Him and his innocent child: for which foul deed
The powers, delaying, not forgetting, have
Incensed the seas and shores, yea, all the creatures,
Against your peace. Thee of thy son, Alonso,
They have bereft; and do pronounce by me:
Lingering perdition—worse than any death
Can be at once—shall step by step attend
You and your ways; whose wraths to guard you
  from,—
Which here, in this most desolate isle, else falls
Upon your heads,—is nothing but heart-sorrow
And a clear life ensuing.

He vanishes in thunder; then, to soft music, enter the Shapes again, and dance, with mocks and mows, and carrying out the table.

Pros. Bravely the figure of this harpy hast thou
Perform'd, my Ariel; a grace it had, devouring:
Of my instruction hast thou nothing bated
In what thou hadst to say: so, with good life
And observation strange, my meaner ministers
Their several kinds have done. My high charms
  work,
And these mine enemies are all knit up

In their distractions: they now are in my power;
And in these fits I leave them, while I visit

Young Ferdinand,—whom they suppose is
  drown'd,—
And his and mine loved darling.*Exit above.*
Gon. I' the name of something holy, sir, why stand
  you
In this strange stare?
Alon.
O, it is monstrous, monstrous!
Methought the billows spoke, and told me of it;
The winds did sing it to me; and the thunder,
That deep and dreadful organ-pipe, pronounced
The name of Prosper: it did bass my trespass.
Therefore my son i' th' ooze is bedded; and
I'll seek him deeper than e'er plummet sounded,
And with him there lie mudded. *Exit.*
Seb.
But one fiend at a time,
I'll fight their legions o'er.
Ant.
I'll be thy second.
Exeunt Seb. and Ant.
Gon. All three of them are desperate: their great
guilt,
Like poison given to work a great time after,
Now 'gins to bite the spirits. I do beseech you,
That are of suppler joints, follow them swiftly,
And hinder them from what this ecstasy
May now provoke them to.
Adr.
Follow, I pray you.*Exeunt.*

ACT IV.

Scene I. *Before* Prospero's *cell.*
Enter PROSPERO, FERDINAND, *and* MIRANDA.
Pros. If I have too austerely punish'd you,
Your compensation makes amends; for I
Have given you here a third of mine own life,
Or that for which I live; who once again
I tender to thy hand: all thy vexations
Were but my trials of thy love, and thou
Hast strangely stood the test: here, afore Heaven,
I ratify this my rich gift. O Ferdinand,
Do not smile at me that I boast her off,
For thou shalt find she will outstrip all praise,

And make it halt behind her.

Fer.

I do believe it

Against an oracle.

Pros. Then, as my gift, and thine own acquisition

Worthily purchased, take my daughter: but

If thou dost break her virgin-knot before

All sanctimonious ceremonies may

With full and holy rite be minister'd,

No sweet aspersion shall the heavens let fall

To make this contract grow; but barren hate,

Sour-eyed disdain and discord shall bestrew

The union of your bed with weeds so loathly

That you shall hate it both: therefore take heed,

As Hymen's lamps shall light you.

Fer.

As I hope

For quiet days, fair issue and long life,

With such love as 'tis now, the murkiest den,

The most opportune place, the strong'st suggestion

Our worser Genius can, shall never melt

Mine honour into lust, to take away

The edge of that day's celebration

When I shall think, or Phœbus' steeds are founder'd,

Or Night kept chain'd below.

Pros.

Fairly spoke.

Sit, then, and talk with her; she is thine own.

What, Ariel! my industrious servant, Ariel!

Enter ARIEL.

Ari. What would my potent master? here I am.

Pros. Thou and thy meaner fellows your last service

Did worthily perform; and I must use you

In such another trick. Go bring the rabble,

O'er whom I give thee power, here to this place:

Incite them to quick motion; for I must

Bestow upon the eyes of this young couple

Some vanity of mine art: it is my promise,

And they expect it from me.

Ari.

Presently?

Pros. Ay, with a twink.

   Ari. Before you can say, 'come,' and 'go,'

   And breathe twice, and cry, 'so, so,'

   Each one, tripping on his toe,

   Will be here with mop and mow.

   Do you love me, master? no?

Pros. Dearly, my delicate Ariel. Do not approach

Till thou dost hear me call.

Ari.

Well, I conceive.*Exit.*

Pros. Look thou be true; do not give dalliance

Too much the rein: the strongest oaths are straw

To the fire i' the blood: be more abstemious,

Or else, good night your vow!

Fer.

I warrant you, sir;

The white cold virgin snow upon my heart

Abates the ardour of my liver.

Pros.

Well.

Now come, my Ariel! bring a corollary,

Rather than want a spirit: appear, and pertly!

No tongue! all eyes! be silent. *Soft music.*

Enter IRIS.

Iris. Ceres, most bounteous lady, thy rich leas

Of wheat, rye, barley, vetches, oats, and pease;

Thy turfy mountains, where live nibbling sheep,

And flat meads thatch'd with stover, them to keep;

Thy banks with pioned and twilled brims,

Which spongy April at thy best betrims,

To make cold nymphs chaste crowns; and thy

   broom-groves,

Whose shadow the dismissed bachelor loves,

Being lass-lorn; thy pole-clipt vineyard;

And thy sea-marge, sterile and rocky-hard,

Where thou thyself dost air;—the queen o' the sky,

Whose watery arch and messenger am I,

Bids thee leave these; and with her sovereign grace,

Here on this grass-plot, in this very place,

To come and sport:—her peacocks fly amain:

Approach, rich Ceres, her to entertain.

Enter CERES.

Cer. Hail, many-colour'd messenger, that ne'er

Dost disobey the wife of Jupiter;

Who, with thy saffron wings, upon my flowers

Diffusest honey-drops, refreshing showers;

And with each end of thy blue bow dost crown

My bosky acres and my unshrubb'd down,

Rich scarf to my proud earth;—why hath thy queen

Summon'd me hither, to this short-grass'd green?

Iris. A contract of true love to celebrate;

And some donation freely to estate
On the blest lovers.

Cer.
Tell me, heavenly bow,
If Venus or her son, as thou dost know,
Do now attend the queen? Since they did plot
The means that dusky Dis my daughter got,
Her and her blind boy's scandal'd company
I have forsworn.

Iris.
Of her society
Be not afraid: I met her Deity
Cutting the clouds towards Paphos, and her son
Dove-drawn with her. Here thought they to have
   done
Some wanton charm upon this man and maid,
Whose vows are, that no bed-right shall be paid
Till Hymen's torch be lighted: but in vain;
Mars's hot minion is returned again;
Her waspish-headed son has broke his arrows,
Swears he will shoot no more, but play with
   sparrows,
And be a boy right out.

Cer.
High'st queen of state,
Great Juno, comes; I know her by her gait.

               Enter JUNO.

Juno. How does my bounteous sister? Go with me
To bless this twain, that they may prosperous be,
And honour'd in their issue. *They sing:*
Juno. Honour, riches, marriage-blessing,
Long continuance, and increasing,
Hourly joys be still upon you!
Juno sings her blessings on you.
Cer. Earth's increase, foison plenty,
Barns and garners never empty;
Vines with clustering bunches growing;
Plants with goodly burthen bowing;
Spring come to you at the farthest
In the very end of harvest!
Scarcity and want shall shun you;
Ceres' blessing so is on you.
Fer. This is a most majestic vision, and
Harmonious charmingly. May I be bold
To think these spirits?
Pros.
Spirits, which by mine art

I have from their confines call'd to enact
My present fancies.

Fer.
Let me live here ever;
So rare a wonder'd father and a wife
Makes this place Paradise.
Juno and Ceres whisper, and send Iris on employment.
Pros.
Sweet, now, silence!
Juno and Ceres whisper seriously;
There's something else to do: hush, and be mute,
Or else our spell is marr'd.
Iris. You nymphs, call'd Naiads, of the windring
   brooks,
With your sedged crowns and ever-harmless looks,
Leave your crisp channels, and on this green land
Answer your summons; Juno does command:
Come, temperate nymphs, and help to celebrate
A contract of true love; be not too late.
               Enter certain Nymphs.
You sunburnt sicklemen, of August weary,
Come hither from the furrow, and be merry:
Make holiday; your rye-straw hats put on,
And these fresh nymphs encounter every one
In country footing.
Enter certain Reapers, properly habited: they join
with the Nymphs in a graceful dance; towards the
end whereof PROSPERO *starts suddenly, and speaks;*
after which, to a strange, hollow, and confused noise,
they heavily vanish.
Pros. [*Aside*] I had forgot that foul conspiracy
Of the beast Caliban and his confederates
Against my life: the minute of their plot
Is almost come. [*To the Spirits.*] Well done! avoid;
no more!
Fer. This is strange: your father's in some passion
That works him strongly.
Mir.
Never till this day
Saw I him touch'd with anger so distemper'd.
Pros. You do look, my son, in a moved sort,
As if you were dismay'd: be cheerful, sir.
Our revels now are ended. These our actors,
As I foretold you, were all spirits, and
Are melted into air, into thin air:
And, like the baseless fabric of this vision,
The cloud-capp'd towers, the gorgeous palaces,

The solemn temples, the great globe itself,
Yea, all which it inherit, shall dissolve,
And, like this insubstantial pageant faded,
Leave not a rack behind. We are such stuff
As dreams are made on; and our little life
Is rounded with a sleep. Sir, I am vex'd;
Bear with my weakness; my old brain is troubled:
Be not disturb'd with my infirmity:
If you be pleased, retire into my cell,
And there repose: a turn or two I'll walk,
To still my beating mind.
Fer. Mir.
We wish your peace.*Exeunt.*
Pros. Come with a thought. I thank thee, Ariel:
come.

                                        Enter ARIEL.

Ari. Thy thoughts I cleave to. What's thy pleasure?
Pros.
Spirit,
We must prepare to meet with Caliban.
Ari. Ay, my commander: when I presented Ceres,
I thought to have told thee of it; but I fear'd
Lest I might anger thee.
Pros. Say again, where didst thou leave these varlets?
Ari. I told you, sir, they were red-hot with drinking;
So full of valour that they smote the air
For breathing in their faces; beat the ground
For kissing of their feet; yet always bending
Towards their project. Then I beat my tabor;
At which, like unback'd colts, they prick'd their ears,
Advanced their eyelids, lifted up their noses
As they smelt music: so I charm'd their ears,
That, calf-like, they my lowing follow'd through
Tooth'd briers, sharp furzes, pricking goss, and
    thorns,
Which enter'd their frail shins: at last I left them
I' the filthy-mantled pool beyond your cell,
There dancing up to the chins, that the foul lake
O'erstunk their feet.
Pros.
This was well done, my bird.
Thy shape invisible retain thou still:
The trumpery in my house, go bring it hither,
For stale to catch these thieves.
Ari.
I go, I go.*Exit.*
Pros. A devil, a born devil, on whose nature

Nurture can never stick; on whom my pains,
Humanely taken, all, all lost, quite lost;
And as with age his body uglier grows,
So his mind cankers. I will plague them all,
Even to roaring.

Re-enter ARIEL, *loaden with glistering apparel, &c.*

Come, hang them on this line.
PROSPERO *and* ARIEL *remain, invisible. Enter*
CALIBAN, STEPHANO, *and* TRINCULO, *all wet.*
Cal. Pray you, tread softly, that the blind mole may
    not
Hear a foot fall: we now are near his cell.
Ste. Monster, your fairy, which you say is a harmless
fairy, has done little better than played the Jack with
us.
Trin. Monster, I do smell all horse-piss; at which my
nose is in great indignation.
Ste. So is mine. Do you hear, monster? If I should
take a displeasure against you, look you,—
Trin. Thou wert but a lost monster.
Cal. Good my lord, give me thy favour still.
Be patient, for the prize I'll bring thee to
Shall hoodwink this mischance: therefore speak
    softly.
All's hush'd as midnight yet.
Trin. Ay, but to lose our bottles in the pool,—
Ste. There is not only disgrace and dishonour in that,
monster, but an infinite loss.
Trin. That's more to me than my wetting: yet this is
your harmless fairy, monster.
Ste. I will fetch off my bottle, though I be o'er ears
for my labour.
Cal. Prithee, my king, be quiet. See'st thou here,
This is the mouth o' the cell: no noise, and enter.
Do that good mischief which may make this island
Thine own for ever, and I, thy Caliban,
For aye thy foot-licker.
Ste. Give me thy hand. I do begin to have bloody
thoughts.
Trin. O King Stephano! O peer! O worthy Stephano!
look what a wardrobe here is for thee!
Cal. Let it alone, thou fool; it is but trash.
Trin. O, ho, monster! we know what belongs to a
frippery. O King Stephano!

Ste. Put off that gown, Trinculo; by this hand, I'll have that gown.

Trin. Thy Grace shall have it.

Cal. The dropsy drown this fool! what do you mean
To dote thus on such luggage? Let's alone,
And do the murder first: if he awake,
From toe to crown he'll fill our skins with pinches,
Make us strange stuff.

Ste. Be you quiet, monster. Mistress line, is not this my jerkin? Now is the jerkin under the line: now, jerkin, you are like to lose your hair, and prove a bald jerkin.

Trin. Do, do: we steal by line and level, an't like your Grace.

Ste. I thank thee for that jest; here's a garment for't: wit shall not go unrewarded while I am king of this country. 'Steal by line and level' is an excellent pass of pate; there's another garment for't.

Trin. Monster, come, put some lime upon your fingers, and away with the rest.

Cal. I will have none on't: we shall lose our time,
And all be turn'd to barnacles, or to apes
With foreheads villanous low.

Ste. Monster, lay-to your fingers: help to bear this away where my hogshead of wine is, or I'll turn you out of my kingdom: go to, carry this.

Trin. And this.

Ste. Ay, and this.

A noise of hunters heard. Enter divers Spirits, in shape of dogs and hounds, and hunt them about, PROSPERO *and* ARIEL *setting them on.*

Pros. Hey, Mountain, hey!

Ari. Silver! there it goes, Silver!

Pros. Fury, fury! there, Tyrant, there! hark, hark!

> *Cal., Ste., and Trin. are driven out.*

Go charge my goblins that they grind their joints
With dry convulsions; shorten up their sinews
With aged cramps; and more pinch-spotted make them
Then pard or cat o' mountain.

Ari.
Hark, they roar!

Pros. Let them be hunted soundly. At this hour
Lie at my mercy all mine enemies:
Shortly shall all my labours end, and thou
Shalt have the air at freedom: for a little
Follow, and do me service. *Exeunt.*

ACT V.

SCENE I. *Before the cell of Prospero.*

Enter Prospero *in his magic robes, and* Ariel.

Pros. Now does my project gather to a head:
My charms crack not; my spirits obey; and time
Goes upright with his carriage. How's the day?

Ari. On the sixth hour; at which time, my lord,
You said our work should cease.

Pros.
I did say so,
When first I raised the tempest. Say, my spirit,
How fares the king and's followers?

Ari.
Confined together
In the same fashion as you gave in charge,
Just as you left them; all prisoners, sir,
In the line-grove which weather-fends your cell;
They cannot budge till your release. The king,
His brother, and yours, abide all three distracted,
And the remainder mourning over them,
Brimful of sorrow and dismay; but chiefly
Him that you term'd, sir, "The good old lord, Gonzalo;"
His tears run down his beard, like winter's drops
From eaves of reeds. Your charm so strongly works 'em,
That if you now beheld them, your affections
Would become tender.

Pros.
Dost thou think so, spirit?

Ari. Mine would, sir, were I human.

Pros.
And mine shall.
Hast thou, which art but air, a touch, a feeling
Of their afflictions, and shall not myself,
One of their kind, that relish all as sharply,
Passion as they, be kindlier moved than thou art?
Though with their high wrongs I am struck to the quick,
Yet with my nobler reason 'gainst my fury
Do I take part: the rarer action is
In virtue than in vengeance: they being penitent,
The sole drift of my purpose doth extend
Not a frown further. Go release them, Ariel:
My charms I'll break, their senses I'll restore,
And they shall be themselves.

Ari.

I'll fetch them, sir. *Exit.*

Pros. Ye elves of hills, brooks, standing lakes, and
   groves;
And ye that on the sands with printless foot
Do chase the ebbing Neptune, and do fly him
When he comes back; you demi-puppets that
By moonshine do the green sour ringlets make,
Whereof the ewe not bites; and you whose pastime
Is to make midnight mushrooms, that rejoice
To hear the solemn curfew; by whose aid—
Weak masters though ye be—I have bedimm'd
The noontide sun, call'd forth the mutinous winds.
And 'twixt the green sea and the azured vault
Set roaring war: to the dread rattling thunder
Have I given fire, and rifted Jove's stout oak
With his own bolt; the strong-based promontory
Have I made shake, and by the spurs pluck'd up
The pine and cedar: graves at my command
Have waked their sleepers, oped, and let 'em forth
By my so potent art. But this rough magic
I here abjure; and, when I have required
Some heavenly music,—which even now I do,—
To work mine end upon their senses, that
This airy charm is for, I'll break my staff,
Bury it certain fathoms in the earth,
And deeper than did ever plummet sound
I'll drown my book. *Solemn music.*

Re-enter ARIEL *before: then* Alonso, *with a frantic
gesture, attended by* Gonzalo; Sebastian *and* Antonio
in like manner, attended by ADRIAN *and* Francisco:
they all enter the circle which Prospero *had made,
and there stand charmed; which* PROSPERO *observing, speaks:*

A solemn air, and the best comforter
To an unsettled fancy, cure thy brains,
Now useless, boil'd within thy skull! There stand,
For you are spell-stopp'd.
Holy Gonzalo, honourable man,
Mine eyes, even sociable to the show of thine,
Fall fellowly drops. The charm dissolves apace;
And as the morning steals upon the night,
Melting the darkness, so their rising senses
Begin to chase the ignorant fumes that mantle
Their clearer reason. O good Gonzalo,
My true preserver, and a loyal sir
To him thou follow'st! I will pay thy graces
Home both in word and deed. Most cruelly

Didst thou, Alonso, use me and my daughter:
Thy brother was a furtherer in the act.
Thou art pinch'd for't now, Sebastian. Flesh and
   blood,
You, brother mine, that entertain'd ambition,
Expell'd remorse and nature; who, with Sebastian,—
Whose inward pinches therefore are most strong,—
Would here have kill'd your king; I do forgive thee,
Unnatural though thou art. Their understanding
Begins to swell; and the approaching tide
Will shortly fill the reasonable shore,
That now lies foul and muddy. Not one of them
That yet looks on me, or would know me: Ariel,
Fetch me the hat and rapier in my cell:
I will discase me, and myself present
As I was sometime Milan: quickly, spirit;
Thou shalt ere long be free.

       ARIEL *sings and helps to attire him.*
Where the bee sucks, there suck I:
In a cowslip's bell I lie;
There I couch when owls do cry.
On the bat's back I do fly
After summer merrily.
Merrily, merrily shall I live now
Under the blossom that hangs on the
   bough.

Pros. Why, that's my dainty Ariel! I shall miss thee;
But yet thou shalt have freedom: so, so, so.
To the king's ship, invisible as thou art:
There shalt thou find the mariners asleep
Under the hatches; the master and the boatswain
Being awake, enforce them to this place,
And presently, I prithee.

Ari. I drink the air before me, and return
Or ere your pulse twice beat. *Exit.*

Gon. All torment, trouble, wonder and amazement
Inhabits here: some heavenly power guide us
Out of this fearful country!

Pros.
Behold, sir king,
The wronged Duke of Milan, Prospero:
For more assurance that a living prince
Does now speak to thee, I embrace thy body;
And to thee and thy company I bid
A hearty welcome.

Alon.
Whether thou be'st he or no,

Or some enchanted trifle to abuse me,
As late I have been, I not know: thy pulse
Beats, as of flesh and blood; and, since I saw thee,
The affliction of my mind amends, with which,
I fear, a madness held me: this must crave—
An if this be at all—a most strange story.
Thy dukedom I resign, and do entreat
Thou pardon me my wrongs.—But how should
Prospero
Be living and be here?

Pros.

First, noble friend,
Let me embrace thine age, whose honour cannot
Be measured or confined.

Gon.

Whether this be
Or be not, I'll not swear.

Pros.

You do yet taste
Some subtilties o' the isle, that will not let you
Believe things certain. Welcome, my friends all!
[*Aside to Seb. and Ant.*] But you, my brace of lords,
were I so minded,
I here could pluck his Highness' frown upon you,
And justify you traitors: at this time
I will tell no tales.

Seb. [*Aside*]

The devil speaks in him.

Pros.

No.
For you, most wicked sir, whom to call brother
Would even infect my mouth, I do forgive
Thy rankest fault,—all of them; and require
My dukedom of thee, which perforce, I know,
Thou must restore.

Alon.

If thou be'st Prospero,
Give us particulars of thy preservation;
How thou hast met us here, who three hours since
Were wreck'd upon this shore; where I have lost—
How sharp the point of this remembrance is!—
My dear son Ferdinand.

Pros.

I am woe for't, sir.

Alon. Irreparable is the loss; and patience
Says it is past her cure.

Pros.

I rather think
You have not sought her help, of whose soft grace
For the like loss I have her sovereign aid,
And rest myself content.

Alon.

You the like loss!

Pros. As great to me as late; and, supportable
To make the dear loss, have I means much weaker
Than you may call to comfort you, for I
Have lost my daughter.

Alon.

A daughter?
O heavens, that they were living both in Naples,
The king and queen there! that they were, I wish
Myself were mudded in that oozy bed
Where my son lies. When did you lose you daughter?

Pros. In this last tempest. I perceive, these lords
At this encounter do so much admire,
That they devour their reason, and scarce think
Their eyes do offices of truth, their words
Are natural breath: but, howsoe'er you have
Been justled from your senses, know for certain
That I am Prospero, and that very duke
Which was thrust forth of Milan; who most strangely
Upon this shore, where you were wreck'd, was
    landed,
To be the Lord on't. No more yet of this;
For 'tis a chronicle of day by day,
Not a relation for a breakfast, nor
Befitting this first meeting. Welcome, sir;
This cell's my court: here have I few attendants,
And subjects none abroad: pray you, look in.
My dukedom since you have given me again,
I will requite you with as good a thing;
At least bring forth a wonder, to content ye
As much as me my dukedom.

Here Prospero discovers FERDINAND *and* MIRANDA
playing at chess.

Mir. Sweet lord, you play me false.

Fer.

No, my dear'st love,
I would not for the world.

Mir. Yes, for a score of kingdoms you should
wrangle,
And I would call it fair play.

Alon.

If this prove
A vision of the island, one dear son
Shall I twice lose.
Seb.
A most high miracle!
Fer. Though the seas threaten, they are merciful;
I have cursed them without cause.*Kneels.*
Alon.
Now all the blessings
Of a glad father compass thee about!
Arise, and say how thou camest here.
Mir.
O, wonder!
How many goodly creatures are there here!
How beauteous mankind is! O brave new world,
That has such people in't!
Pros.
'Tis new to thee.
Alon. What is this maid with whom thou wast at play?
Your eld'st acquaintance cannot be three hours:
Is she the goddess that hath sever'd us,
And brought us thus together?
Fer.
Sir, she is mortal;
But by immortal Providence she's mine:
I chose her when I could not ask my father
For his advice, nor thought I had one. She
Is daughter to this famous Duke of Milan,
Of whom so often I have heard renown,
But never saw before; of whom I have
Received a second life; and second father
This lady makes him to me.
Alon.
I am hers:
But, O, how oddly will it sound that I
Must ask my child forgiveness!
Pros.
There, sir, stop:
Let us not burthen our remembrances with
A heaviness that's gone.
Gon.
I have inly wept,
Or should have spoke ere this. Look down, you gods,
And on this couple drop a blessed crown!
For it is you that have chalk'd forth the way

Which brought us hither.
Alon.
I say, Amen, Gonzalo!
Gon. Was Milan thrust from Milan, that his issue
Should become kings of Naples? O, rejoice
Beyond a common joy! and set it down
With gold on lasting pillars: In one voyage
Did Claribel her husband find at Tunis,
And Ferdinand, her brother, found a wife
Where he himself was lost, Prospero his dukedom
In a poor isle, and all of us ourselves
When no man was his own.

Alon. [*to Fer. and Mir.*]
Give me your hands:
Let grief and sorrow still embrace his heart
That doth not wish you joy!
Gon.
Be it so! Amen!

Re-enter ARIEL, *with the* Master *and* Boatswain *amazedly following.*
O, look, sir, look, sir! here is more of us:
I prophesied, if a gallows were on land,
This fellow could not drown. Now, blasphemy,
That swear'st grace o'erboard, not an oath on shore?
Hast thou no mouth by land? What is the news?
Boats. The best news is, that we have safely found
Our king and company; the next, our ship—
Which, but three glasses since, we gave out split—
Is tight and yare and bravely rigg'd, as when
We first put out to sea.
Ari. [*Aside to Pros.*]
Sir, all this service
Have I done since I went.
Pros. [*Aside to Ari.*]
My tricksy spirit!
Alon. These are not natural events; they strengthen
From strange to stranger. Say, how came you hither?
Boats. If I did think, sir, I were well awake,
I'ld strive to tell you. We were dead of sleep,
And—how we know not—all clapp'd under hatches;
Where, but even now, with strange and several noises
Of roaring, shrieking, howling, jingling chains,
And more diversity of sounds, all horrible,
We were awaked; straightway, at liberty;
Where we, in all her trim, freshly beheld

Our royal, good, and gallant ship; our master
Capering to eye her:—on a trice, so please you,
Even in a dream, were we divided from them,
And were brought moping hither.
Ari. [*Aside to Pros.*]
Was't well done?

Pros. [*Aside to Ari.*] Bravely, my diligence. Thou
shalt be free.
Alon. This is as strange a maze as e'er men trod;
And there is in this business more than nature
Was ever conduct of: some oracle
Must rectify our knowledge.
Pros.
Sir, my liege,
Do not infest your mind with beating on
The strangeness of this business; at pick'd leisure
Which shall be shortly, single I'll resolve you,
Which to you shall seem probable, of every
These happen'd accidents; till when, be cheerful,
And think of each thing well. [*Aside to Ari.*] Come
hither, spirit:
Set Caliban and his companions free;
Untie the spell. [*Exit Ariel.*] How fares my gracious
sir?
There are yet missing of your company
Some few odd lads that you remember not.
Re-enter ARIEL, *driving in* CALIBAN, STEPHANO, *and*
TRINCULO, *in their stolen apparel.*
Ste. Every man shift for all the rest, and let no
man take care for himself; for all is but fortune.—
Coragio, bully-monster, coragio!
Trin. If these be true spies which I wear in my head,
here's a goodly sight.
Cal. O Setebos, these be brave spirits indeed!
How fine my master is! I am afraid
He will chastise me.
Seb.
Ha, ha!
What things are these, my lord Antonio?
Will money buy 'em?
Ant.
Very like; one of them
Is a plain fish, and, no doubt, marketable.

Pros. Mark but the badges of these men, my lords,
Then say if they be true. This mis-shapen knave,

His mother was a witch; and one so strong
That could control the moon, make flows and ebbs,
And deal in her command, without her power.
These three have robb'd me; and this demi-devil—
For he's a bastard one—had plotted with them
To take my life. Two of these fellows you
Must know and own; this thing of darkness I
Acknowledge mine.
Cal.
I shall be pinch'd to death.
Alon. Is not this Stephano, my drunken butler?
Seb. He is drunk now: where had he wine?
Alon. And Trinculo is reeling ripe: where should
they
Find this grand liquor that hath gilded 'em?—
How camest thou in this pickle?
Trin. I have been in such a pickle, since I saw you
last, that, I fear me, will never out of my bones: I
shall not fear fly-blowing.
Seb. Why, how now, Stephano!
Ste. O, touch me not;—I am not Stephano, but a
cramp.
Pros. You'ld be king o' the isle, sirrah?
Ste. I should have been a sore one, then.
Alon. This is a strange thing as e'er I look'd
on.*Pointing to Caliban.*
Pros. He is as disproportion'd in his manners
As in his shape. Go, sirrah, to my cell;
Take with you your companions; as you look
To have my pardon, trim it handsomely.
Cal. Ay, that I will; and I'll be wise hereafter,
And seek for grace. What a thrice-double ass
Was I, to take this drunkard for a god,
And worship this dull fool!

Pros.
Go to; away!
Alon. Hence, and bestow your luggage where you
found it.
Seb. Or stole it, rather.*Exeunt Cal., Ste., and Trin.*
Pros. Sir, I invite your Highness and your train
To my poor cell, where you shall take your rest
For this one night; which, part of it, I'll waste
With such discourse as, I not doubt, shall make it
Go quick away: the story of my life,
And the particular accidents gone by
Since I came to this isle: and in the morn

I'll bring you to your ship, and so to Naples,
Where I have hope to see the nuptial
Of these our dear-beloved solemnized;
And thence retire me to my Milan, where
Every third thought shall be my grave.

Alon.

I long
To hear the story of your life, which must
Take the ear strangely.

Pros.

I'll deliver all;
And promise you calm seas, auspicious gales,
And sail so expeditious, that shall catch
Your royal fleet far off. [*Aside to Ari.*] My Ariel,
    chick,
That is thy charge: then to the elements
Be free, and fare thou well! Please you, draw near.

Exeunt.

EPILOGUE.

Spoken By Prospero.

Now my charms are all o'erthrown,
And what strength I have's mine own,
Which is most faint: now, 'tis true,
I must be here confined by you,
Or sent to Naples. Let me not,
Since I have my dukedom got,
And pardon'd the deceiver, dwell
In this bare island by your spell;
But release me from my bands
With the help of your good hands:
Gentle breath of yours my sails
Must fill, or else my project fails,
Which was to please. Now I want
Spirits to enforce, art to enchant;
And my ending is despair,
Unless I be relieved by prayer,
Which pierces so, that it assaults
Mercy itself, and frees all faults.
As you from crimes would pardon'd be,
Let your indulgence set me free.

NOTES.

Note I.

I. 1. 15. *What cares these roarers.* This grammatical inaccuracy, which escaped correction in the later folios, probably came from Shakespeare's pen. Similar cases occur frequently, especially when the verb precedes its nominative. For example, *Tempest*, IV. 1. 262, 'Lies at my mercy all mine enemies,' and *Measure for Measure*, II. 1. 22, 'What knows the laws, &c.' We correct it in those passages where the occurrence of a vulgarism would be likely to annoy the reader. In the mouth of a Boatswain it can offend no one. We therefore leave it.

Note II.

I. 1. 57–59. *Mercy on us!—we split, &c.* It may be doubtful whether the printer of the first folio intended these broken speeches to express 'a confused noise within.' Without question such was the author's meaning. Rowe, however, and subsequent editors, printed them as part of Gonzalo's speech. Capell was the first editor who gave the true arrangement.

Note III.

I. 2. 173. *princesses.* See Mr Sidney Walker's *Shakespeare's Versification*, p. 243 sqq. 'The plurals of substantives ending in *s*, in certain instances, in *se*, *ss*, *ce*, and sometimes *ge*, ... are found without the usual addition of *s* or *es*, in pronunciation at least, although in many instances the plural affix is added in printing, where the metre shows that it is not to be pronounced.'
In this and other instances, we have thought it better to trust to the ear of the reader for the rhythm than to introduce an innovation in orthography which might perplex him as to the sense. The form 'princesses,' the use of which in Shakespeare's time was doubted by one of our correspondents, is found in the *History of King Leir*.
Rowe's reading 'princes' might be defended on the ground that the sentiment is general, and applicable to royal children of both sexes; or that Sir Philip Sidney, in the first book of the *Arcadia*, calls Pamela and Philoclea 'princes.'

Note IV.

I. 2. 298. The metre of this line, as well as of lines 301, 302, is defective, but as no mode of correction can be regarded as completely satisfactory we have in accordance with our custom left the lines as they are printed in the Folio. The defect, indeed, in the metre of line 298 has not been noticed except by Hanmer, who makes a line thus:

'Do so, and after two days I'll discharge thee.'

Possibly it ought to be printed thus:

'Do so; and
After two days
I will discharge thee.'

There is a broken line, also of four syllables, 253 of the same scene, another of seven, 235.

There is no reason to doubt that the *words* are as Shakespeare wrote them, for, although the action of the play terminates in less than four hours (I. 2. 240 and V. 1. 186), yet Ariel's ministry is not to end till the voyage to Naples shall be over. Prospero, too, repeats his promise, and marks his contentment by further shortening the time of servitude, 'within two days,' I. 2. 420. Possibly 'Invisible' (301) should have a line to itself. Words thus occupying a broken line acquire a marked emphasis.

But the truth is that in dialogue Shakespeare's language passes so rapidly from verse to prose and from prose to verse, sometimes even hovering, as it were, over the confines, being rhythmical rather than metrical, that all attempts to give regularity to the metre must be made with diffidence and received with doubt.

Note V.

I. 2. 377, 378:

Courtsied when you have and kiss'd
   The wild waves whist.

This punctuation seems to be supported by what Ferdinand says (391, 392):

'The music crept by me upon the waters,
Allaying both their fury and my passion, &c.'

At the end of the stanza we have printed *Hark, hark! ... The watch-dogs bark* as that part of the burthen which 'sweet sprites bear.' The other part is borne by distant watch-dogs.

Note VI.

I. 2. 443. *I fear you have done yourself some wrong.* See this phrase used in a similar sense, *Measure for Measure*, I. 11. 39.

Note VII.

II. 1. 27. *Which, of he or Adrian.* 'Of' is found in the same construction, *Midsummer Night's Dream*, III. 2. 336,

'Now follow if thou darest to try whose right,
Of thine or mine, is most in Helena.'

Note VIII.

II. 1. 157. *Of its own kind.* There is no doubt, as Dr Guest has shewn, that 'it,' which is the reading of the 1st and 2nd folios, was commonly used as a genitive in Shakespeare's time, as it is still in some provincial dialects. 'Its,' however, was coming into use. One instance occurs in this play, I. 11. 95, 'in its contrary.'

Note IX.

II. 1. 241. *she that from whom.* Mr Spedding writes: 'The received emendation is not satisfactory to me. I would rather read, "She that—From whom? All were sea-swallow'd &c., i.e. from whom should she have note? The report from Naples will be that all were drowned. We shall be the only survivors." The break in the construction seems to me characteristic of the speaker. But you must read the whole speech to feel the effect.'

Note X.

II. 1. 249–251. All editors except Mr Staunton have printed in italics (or between inverted commas) only as far as '*Naples?*', but as '*keep*' is printed with a small k in the folios, they seem to sanction the arrangement given in our text.

Note XI.

II. 1. 267. *Ay, sir; where lies that? if 'twere a kibe.* Mr Singer and Mr Dyce have changed ''twere' to 'it were' for the sake of the metre. But then the first part of the line must be read with a wrong emphasis. The proper emphasis clearly falls on the first, third, and fifth syllables, 'Aý, sir; whére lies thát?' See Preface.

Note XII.

II. 2. 165. Before 'here; bear my bottle' Capell inserts a stage direction [*To Cal.*], but it appears from III. 2. 62, that Trinculo was entrusted with the office of bottle-bearer.

Note XIII.

III. 1. 15. *Most busy lest, when I do it.* As none of the proposed emendations can be regarded as certain, we have left the reading of F_1, though it is manifestly corrupt. The spelling 'doe' makes Mr Spedding's conjecture 'idlest' for 'I doe it' more probable.

Note XIV.

III. 3. 17. The stage direction, which we have divided into two parts, is placed all at once in the folios after 'as when they are fresh' [Solemne and strange Musicke; and Prosper on the top (invisible:) Enter … depart].

Pope transferred it to follow Sebastian's words, 'I say, to night: no more.'

Note XV.

III. 3. 48. *Each putter out of five for one.* See Beaumont and Fletcher, *The Noble Gentleman*, I. 1. (Vol. II. p. 261, ed. Moxon): 'The return will give you five for one.' MARINE is about to travel.

Note XVI.

IV. 1. 146. *You do look, my son, in a moved sort.* Seymour suggests a transposition: 'you do, my son, look in a moved sort.' This line however can scarcely have come from Shakespeare's pen. Perhaps the writer who composed the Masque was allowed to join it, as best he might, to Shakespeare's words, which re-commence at 'Our revels now are ended,' &c.

Note XVII.

IV. 1. 230. *Let's alone.* See Staunton's "Shakespeare," Vol. I. p. 81, note (b).

Note XVIII.

V. 1. 309. *Of these our dear-beloved solemnized.* The Folios have 'belov'd'; a mode of spelling, which in this case is convenient as indicating the probable rhythm of the verse. We have written 'beloved,' in accordance with the general rule mentioned in the Preface.

'Solemnized' occurs in four other verse passages of Shakespeare. It is three times to be accented 'sólemnized' and once (*Love's Labour's Lost*, II. 1. 41) 'solémnized.'

CRITICAL APPARATUS ("LINENOTES").

Act I: Scene 1

Sc. I. On a ship at sea] Pope.

Enter … Boatswain] Collier MS. adds 'shaking off wet.'

3. *Good,*] Rowe. *Good:* Ff. *Good.* Collier.

7. *till thou burst thy wind*] *till thou burst, wind* Johnson conj. *till thou burst thee, wind* Steevens conj.

8. Capell adds stage direction [Exeunt Mariners aloft.

11. *boatswain*] Pope. *boson* Ff.

11–18. Verse. S. Walker conj.

15. *cares*] *care* Rowe. See note (I).

31. [Exeunt] Theobald. [Exit. Ff.

33. *Bring her to try*] F$_4$. *Bring her to Try* F$_1$ F$_2$ F$_3$. *Bring her to. Try* Story conj.

33–35. Text as in Capell. *A plague*—A cry within. Enter Sebastian, Anthonio, and Gonzalo. *upon this howling.* Ff.

34–37. Verse. S. Walker conj.

43. *for*] *from* Theobald.

46. *two courses off to sea*] *two courses; off to sea* Steevens (Holt conj.).

46. [Enter …] [Re-enter … Dyce.

47. [Exeunt. Theobald.

50. *at*] *are at* Rowe.

50–54. Printed as prose in Ff.

56. *to glut*] *t' englut* Johnson conj.

57. See note (II).

59. *Farewell, brother!*] *Brother, farewell!* Theobald.

60. *with the*] Rowe. *with'* F$_1$ F$_2$. *with* F$_3$ F$_4$.

61. [Exeunt A. and S.] [Exit. Ff.

63. *furze*] Rowe. *firrs* F$_1$ F$_2$ F$_3$. *firs* F$_4$.

long heath, brown furze] *ling, heath, broom, furze* Hanmer.

65. [Exeunt] [Exit F$_1$, om. F$_2$ F$_3$ F$_4$.

Act I: Scene 2

3. *stinking*] *flaming* Singer conj. *kindling* S. Verges conj.

4. *cheek*] *heat* Collier MS. *crack* Staunton conj.

7. *creature*] *creatures* Theobald.

13. *fraughting*] Ff. *fraighted* Pope. *fraighting* Theobald. *freighting* Steevens.

15. Mir. *O, woe the day!* Pros. *No harm.*] Mir. *O woe the day! no harm?* Johnson conj.

19. *I am more better*] *I'm more or better* Pope.

24. [Lays … mantle] Pope.

28. *provision*] F$_1$. *compassion* F$_2$ F$_3$ F$_4$. *prevision* Hunter conj.

29. *soul*] *soul lost* Rowe. *foyle* Theobald. *soil* Johnson conj. *loss* Capell. *foul* Wright conj.

31. *betid*] F$_1$. *betide* F$_2$ F$_3$ F$_4$.

35. *a*] F$_1$. *the* F$_2$ F$_3$ F$_4$.

38. *thou*] om. Pope.

41. *Out*] *Full* Pope (after Dryden). *Quite* Collier MS.

44. *with*] *in* Pope (after Dryden).

53. *Twelve year … year*] *Tis twelve years … years* Pope.

58, 59. *and his only heir And princess*] *and his only heir A princess* Pope. *thou his only heir And princess* Steevens. *and though his only heir A princess*] Johnson conj.

63. *holp*] *help'd* Pope.

O, my heart] *My heart* Pope.

78. *me*] om. F$_3$ F$_4$.

80. *whom … whom*] F$_2$ F$_3$ F$_4$. *who … who* F$_1$.

81. *trash*] *plash* Hanmer.

82, 83. *'em … 'em*] *them … them* Capell.

84. *i' the state*] *i'th state* F$_1$. *e'th state* F$_2$. *o'th state* F$_3$ F$_4$. om. Pope.

88. *O, good sir … mark me.*] *Good sir … mark me then.* Pope. *O yes, good sir … mark me.* Capell.
Mir. O, … do. Pros. I … me] *I … me.* Mir. *O … do.* Steevens.

89. *dedicated*] *dedicate* Steevens (Ritson conj.).

91. *so*] F$_1$. om. F$_2$ F$_3$ F$_4$.

97. *lorded*] *loaded* Collier MS.

99. *exact, like*] *exact. Like* Ff.

100. *having into truth … of it*] *loving an untruth, and telling 't oft* Hanmer. *having unto truth … oft* Warburton. *having to untruth … of it* Collier MS. *having sinn'd to truth … oft* Musgrave conj.
telling] *quelling* S. Verges conj.

101. *Made … memory*] *Makes … memory* Hanmer. *Makes … memory too* Musgrave conj.

103. *indeed the duke*] *the duke* Steevens. *indeed duke* S. Walker conj.
out o' the] *from* Pope.

105. *his*] *is* F$_2$.

105, 106. *ambition growing*] *ambition Growing* Steevens.

106. *hear?*] *hear, child?* Hanmer.

109. *Milan*] *Millanie* F$_1$ (Capell's copy).

112. *wi' the*] Capell. *with* Ff. *wi' th'* Rowe. *with the* Steevens.

116. *most*] F$_1$. *much* F$_2$ F$_3$ F$_4$.

119. *but*] *not* Pope.

120. *Good … sons*] Theobald suggested that these words should be given to Prospero. Hanmer prints them so.

122. *hearkens*] *hears* Pope. *hearks* Theobald.

129. *Fated*] *Mated* Dryden's version.
purpose] *practise* Collier MS.

131. *ministers*] *minister* Rowe.

133. *out*] *on't* Steevens conj.

135. *to 't*] om. Steevens (Farmer conj.).
Here and elsewhere in the volume, body text has "to't" with no space, while the Notes have "to 't" with space.

138. *Wherefore*] *Why* Pope.

141. *me*] om. Pope.

146. *boat*] Rowe (after Dryden). *butt* F$_1$ F$_2$ F$_3$. *but* F$_4$. *busse* Black conj.

147. *sail*] F$_1$. *nor sail* F$_2$ F$_3$ F$_4$.

148. *have*] *had* Rowe (after Dryden).

150. *the winds*] *winds* Pope.

155. *deck'd*] *brack'd* Hanmer. *mock'd* Warburton. *fleck'd* Johnson conj. *degg'd* anon. ap. Reed conj.

162. *who*] om. Pope. *he* Steevens conj.

169. *Now I arise*] Continued to Miranda. Blackstone conj.
[*Resumes his mantle*] om. Ff. [*Put on robe again.* Collier MS.

173. *princesses*] *princesse* F$_1$ F$_2$ F$_3$. *princess* F$_4$. *princes* Rowe. *princess'* Dyce (S. Walker conj.). See note (III).

186. [*M. sleeps*] Theobald.

189. SCENE III. Pope.

190. *be't*] F$_1$. *be it* F$_2$ F$_3$ F$_4$.

193. *quality*] *qualities* Pope (after Dryden).

198. *sometime*] F$_1$. *sometimes* F$_2$ F$_3$ F$_4$.

200. *bowsprit*] *bore-sprit* Ff. *bolt-sprit* Rowe.

201. *lightnings*] Theobald. *lightning* Ff.

202. *o' the*] *of* Pope.
thunder-claps] *thunder-clap* Johnson.

205. *Seem*] *Seem'd* Theobald.

206. *dread*] F$_1$. *dead* F$_2$ F$_3$ F$_4$.
My brave] *My brave, brave* Theobald. *That's my brave* Hanmer.

209. *mad*] *mind* Pope (after Dryden).

211, 212. *vessel, … son*] *vessell; Then all a fire with me the King's sonne* Ff.

218. *sustaining*] *sea-stained* Edwards conj. *unstaining* or *sea-staining* Spedding conj.

229. *Bermoothes*] *Bermudas* Theobald.

231. *Who*] *Whom* Hanmer.

234. *are*] *all* Collier MS.
upon] *on* Pope.

239–240. Ari. *Past the mid season.* Pros. *At least two glasses*] Ari. *Past the mid season at least two glasses.* Warburton. Pros. *… Past the mid season?* Ari. *At least two glasses* Johnson conj.

244. *How now? moody?*] *How now, moody!* Dyce (so Dryden, ed. 1808).

245. *What*] F$_1$. *Which* F$_2$ F$_3$ F$_4$.

248. *made thee*] Ff. *made* Pope.

249. *didst*] F$_3$ F$_4$. *did* F$_1$ F$_2$.

264. *and sorceries*] *sorceries too* Hanmer.

267. *Is not this true?*] *Is this not true?* Pope.

271. *wast then*] Rowe (after Dryden). *was then* Ff.

273. *earthy*] *earthly* Pope.

282. *son*] F$_1$. *sunne* F$_2$. *sun* F$_3$ F$_4$.

she] Rowe (after Dryden). *he* Ff.

298. See note (IV).

301. *like*] F$_1$. *like to* F$_2$ F$_3$ F$_4$.

302. *Be subject to*] *be subject To* Malone.

but thine and mine] *but mine* Pope.

304. *in't*] *in it* Pope.

go, hence] *goe: hence* Ff. *go hence* Pope. *hence* Hanmer.

307. *Heaviness*] *Strange heaviness* Edd. conj.

312. *serves in offices*] F$_1$. *serves offices* F$_2$ F$_3$ F$_4$. *serveth offices* Collier MS.

316. *Come, thou tortoise! when?*] om. Pope.

Come] *Come forth* Steevens.

320. *come forth!*] *come forth, thou tortoise!* Pope.

321. SCENE IV. Pope.

332. *camest*] Rowe. *cam'st* Ff. *cam'st here* Ritson conj.

333. *madest*] Rowe (after Dryden). *made* Ff.

339. *Curs'd be I that*] F$_1$. *Curs'd be I that I* F$_2$ F$_3$ F$_4$. *cursed be I that* Steevens.

342. *Which*] *Who* Pope, and at line 351.

346. *thee*] om. F$_4$.

349. *would 't*] Ff. *I wou'd it* Pope.

351. Pros.] Theobald (after Dryden). Mira. Ff.

352. *wilt*] F$_1$. *will* F$_2$ F$_3$ F$_4$.

355, 356. *didst not ... Know*] *couldst not ... Shew* Hanmer.

356. *wouldst*] *didst* Hanmer.

361, 362. *Deservedly ... deserved*] *Justly ... who hadst Deserv'd* S. Walker conj. *Confin'd ... deserv'd* id. conj.

362. *Who ... prison*] om. Pope (after Dryden).

366. *thou'rt*] F$_1$ F$_2$ F$_3$. *thou art* F$_4$. *thou wer't* Rowe.

375. SCENE V. Pope.

following.] Malone.

378. *The wild waves whist*] Printed as a parenthesis by Steevens. See note (V).

380. *the burthen bear*] Pope. *bear the burthen* Ff.

381–383. Steevens gives *Hark, hark! The watch-dogs bark* to Ariel.

387. *i' th' air or th' earth?*] *in air or earth?* Pope.

390. *again*] *against* Rowe (after Dryden).

407. *owes*] *owns* Pope (after Dryden), but leaves *ow'st* 454.

408. SCENE VI. Pope.

419. *It goes on, I see,*] *It goes, I see* Capell. *It goes on* Steevens.

420. *fine spirit!*] om. Hanmer.

427. *maid*] F$_3$. *mayd* F$_1$ F$_2$. *made* F$_4$.

443. See note (VI).

444. *ungently*] F$_1$. *urgently* F$_2$ F$_3$ F$_4$.

451. *lest*] F$_4$. *least* F$_1$ F$_2$ F$_3$.

452. *One*] *Sir, one* Pope.

I charge thee] *I charge thee* [*to Ariel.* Pope.

460. Pros. prefixed again to this line in Ff.

468. *and*] *tho'* Hanmer.

469. *foot*] *fool* S. Walker conj. *child* Dryden's version.

470. *makest*] *mak'st* F$_1$. *makes* F$_2$ F$_3$ F$_4$.

471. *so*] F$_1$. om. F$_2$ F$_3$ F$_4$. *all* Pope.

478. *is*] *are* Rowe.

488. *nor*] *and* Rowe (after Dryden). *or* Capell.

489. *are*] *were* Malone conj.

Act II: Scene 1

3. *hint*] *stint* Warburton.

5. *masters*] *master* Johnson. *mistress* Steevens conj. *master's* Edd. conj.

6. *of woe*] om. Steevens conj.

11–99. Marked as interpolated by Pope.

11. *visitor*] *'viser* Warburton.

him] om. Rowe.

15. *one*] F$_1$. *on* F$_2$ F$_3$ F$_4$.

16. *entertain'd ... Comes*] Capell. *entertain'd, That's offer'd comes*] Ff. Printed as prose by Pope.

27. *of he*] Ff. *of them, he* Pope. *or he* Collier MS. See note (VII).

35. Seb. *Ha, ha, ha!—So you're paid*] Theobald. Seb. *Ha, ha, ha!* Ant. *So you'r paid* Ff. Ant. *So you've paid* Capell.

81, 82. Seb. *His ... too*] Edd. Ant. *His ... harp.* Seb. *He ... too* Ff.

88. *Ay.*] *I.* Ff. *Ay?* Pope.

96. *sir, my doublet*] F$_1$. *my doublet, sir* F$_2$ F$_3$ F$_4$.

113. *stroke*] F$_1$ F$_2$ F$_3$. *strokes* F$_4$.

124. *Weigh'd*] *Sway'd* S. Verges conj.

at] *as* Collier MS.

125. *o' the*] *the* Pope.

should] *she'd* Malone.

129. *The fault's your own*] *the fault's your own* (at the end of 128) Capell. *the fault's Your own* Malone.

137. *plantation*] *the plantation* Rowe. *the planting* Hanmer.

139. *on't*] *of it* Hanmer.

144. *riches, poverty*] *wealth, poverty* Pope. *poverty, riches* Capell.

145. *contract, succession*] *succession, Contract* Malone conj. *succession, None* id. conj.

146. *none*] *olives, none* Hanmer.

157. *its*] F$_3$ F$_4$. *it* F$_1$ F$_2$. See note (VIII).

162. *'Save*] F$_1$ F$_2$ F$_3$. *Save* F$_4$. *God save* Edd. conj.

175. Enter … invisible … music.] Malone. Enter Ariel, playing solemn music. Ff. om. Pope. [Solemn music. Capell.

181. [All sleep … Ant.] Stage direction to the same effect, first inserted by Capell.

182–189. Text as in Pope. In Ff. the lines begin *Would … I find … Do not … It seldom … We two … While … Thank.*

189. [Exit Ariel] Malone.

192. *find not*] Pope. *find Not* Ff.

211. *so too, if heed*] *so too, if you heed* Rowe. *so, if you heed* Pope.

212. *Trebles thee o'er*] *Troubles thee o'er* Pope. *Troubles thee not* Hanmer.

222. *throes*] Pope. *throwes* F$_1$ F$_2$ F$_3$. *throws* F$_4$.
Thus, sir] *Why then thus Sir* Hanmer.

226. *he's*] *he'as* Hanmer. *he* Johnson conj.

227. *Professes to persuade*] om. Steevens.

234. *doubt*] *drops* Hanmer. *doubts* Capell.

241. *she that from whom*] Ff. *she from whom* Rowe. *she for whom* Pope. *she from whom coming* Singer. *she that—from whom?* Spedding conj. See note (IX).

242. *all*] om. Pope.

243. *And … to perform*] *May … perform* Pope. *And by that destin'd to perform* Musgrave conj. *(And that by destiny) to perform* Staunton conj.

244. *is*] F$_1$. *in* F$_2$ F$_3$ F$_4$.

245. *In*] *Is* Pope.

250. *to*] F$_1$. *by* F$_2$ F$_3$ F$_4$.
Keep] *Sleep* Johnson conj.

251. See note (X).

267. *'twere*] *it were* Singer.

267–271. Pope ends the lines with *that? … slipper … bosom … Milan … molest … brother.*

267. See note (XI).

269. *twenty*] *Ten* Pope.

270. *stand*] *stood* Hanmer.
candied] *Discandy'd* Upton conj.

271. *And melt*] *Would melt* Johnson conj. *Or melt* id. conj.

273, 274. *like, that's dead; Whom I, with*] *like, whom I With* Steevens (Farmer conj.).

275. *whiles*] om. Pope.

277. *morsel*] *Moral* Warburton.

280, 281. *business … hour.*] *hour … business.* Farmer conj.

282. *precedent*] Pope. *president* Ff.

287. *O*] om. Pope.
[They talk apart] Capell.
Re-enter Ariel invisible.] Capell. Enter Ariel with music and song. Ff.

289. *you, his friend,*] *these, his friends* Steevens (Johnson conj.).

289, 290. *friend … project dies … them*] *friend … projects dies … you* Hanmer. *friend … projects die … them* Malone conj. *friend … project dies … thee* Dyce.

298. [They wake.] Rowe.

300. *this*] *thus* Collier MS.

307. *Gonzalo*] om. Pope.

312. *verily*] *verity* Pope.
upon our guard] *on guard* Pope.

Act II: Scene 2

4. *nor*] F$_1$ F$_2$. *not* F$_3$ F$_4$.

15. *and*] *now* Pope. *sent* Edd. conj. (so Dryden).

21. *foul*] *full* Upton conj.

35. [Thunder] Capell.

38. *dregs*] *drench* Collier MS.

40. SCENE III. Pope.
[a bottle in his hand] Capell.

46. *and Marian*] *Mirian* Pope.

56. *savages*] *salvages* Ff.

60. *at's nostrils*] Edd. *at 'nostrils* F$_1$. *at nostrils* F$_2$ F$_3$ F$_4$. *at his nostrils* Pope.

78. *you, cat*] *you Cat* Ff. *a cat* Hanmer. *your cat* Edd. conj.

84. *well*] F$_1$ om. F$_2$ F$_3$ F$_4$.

115, 116. Steevens prints as verse, *I'll … thy True … earthly.*

118. *swear, then, how thou escapedst*] *swear then: how escapedst thou?* Pope.

119. *Swum*] *Swom* Ff.

131. *and thy dog, and thy bush*] *thy dog and bush* Steevens.

133. *new*] F₁. *the new* F₂ F₃ F₄.

135. *weak*] F₁. *shallow* F₂ F₃ F₄.

138. *island*] F₁. *isle* F₂ F₃ F₄.

150–154, 157–162, printed as verse by Pope (after Dryden).

162. *scamels*] *shamois* Theobald. *seamalls, stannels* id. conj.

163. *Ste.*] F₁. *Cal.* F₂ F₃ F₄.

165. Before *here; bear my bottle* Capell inserts [To Cal.]. See note (XII).

172. *trencher*] Pope (after Dryden).
trenchering Ff.

175. *hey-day*] Rowe. *high-day* Ff.

Act III: Scene 1

1. *and*] *but* Pope.

2. *sets*] Rowe. *set* Ff.

4, 5. *my … odious*] *my mean task would be As heavy to me as 'tis odious* Pope.

9. *remove*] *move* Pope.

14. *labours*] *labour* Hanmer.

15. *Most busy lest*] F₁. *Most busy least* F₂ F₃ F₄. *Least busy* Pope. *Most busie-less* Theobald. *Most busiest* Holt White conj. *Most busy felt* Staunton. *Most busy still* Staunton conj. *Most busy-blest* Collier MS. *Most busiliest* Bullock conj.

Most busy lest, when I do (*doe* F₁ F₂ F₃) *it*] *Most busy when least I do it* Brae conj. *Most busiest when idlest* Spedding conj. *Most busy left when idlest* Edd. conj. See note (XIII).

at a distance, unseen] Rowe.

17. *you are*] F₁. *thou art* F₂ F₃ F₄.

31. *it is*] *is it* Steevens conj. (ed. 1, 2, and 3). om. Steevens (ed. 4) (Farmer conj.).

34, 35. *I do beseech you,—Chiefly*] *I do beseech you Chiefly* Ff.

59. *I therein do*] *I do* Pope. *Therein* Steevens.

62. *wooden*] *wodden* F₁.

than to] *than I would* Pope.

72. *what else*] *aught else* Malone conj. (withdrawn).

80. *seeks*] *seekd* F₃ F₄.

88. *as*] F₁. *so* F₂ F₃ F₄.

91. *severally*] Capell.

93. *withal*] Theobald. *with all* Ff.

Act III: Scene 2

SCENE II. Another …] Theobald. The other … Pope.

Enter …] Enter S. and T. reeling, Caliban following with a bottle. Capell. Enter C. S. and T. with a bottle. Johnson.

8. *head*] F₁. *heart* F₂ F₃ F₄.

13, 14. *on. By this light, thou*] on, by this light thou Ff. on, by this light.—Thou Capell.

25. *debauched*] *debosh'd* Ff.

37. *to the suit I made to thee*] *the suit I made thee* Steevens, who prints all Caliban's speeches as verse.

60. Johnson conjectured that this line was spoken by Stephano.

68. *farther*] F₁ *no further* F₂ F₃ F₄.

72. [Beats him.] Rowe.

84. *there*] *then* Collier MS.

89. *nor*] *and* Pope.

93. *deck*] *deck't* Hanmer.

96. *I never saw a woman*] *I ne'er saw woman* Pope.

99. *great'st does least*] *greatest does the least* Rowe.

115, 116] Printed as verse in Ff.

115. *any*] F₁. *and* F₂ F₃ F₄.

117. *scout 'em, and scout 'em*] Pope. *cout 'em and skowt 'em* Ff.

125. *sins*] *sin* F₄.

132. *twangling*] *twanging* Pope.

133. *sometime*] F₁. *sometimes* F₂ F₃ F₄.

137. *that*] om. Pope.

147. Trin. *Will come? I'll follow, Stephano*] Trin. *Wilt come?* Ste. *I'll follow.* Capell. Ste. … *Wilt come?* Trin. *I'll follow, Stephano.* Ritson conj.

Act III: Scene 3

2. *ache*] *ake* F₂ F₃ F₄. *akes* F₁.

3. *forth-rights*] F₂ F₃ F₄. *fourth rights* F₁.

8. *flatterer*] F₁. *flatterers* F₂ F₃ F₄.

17. Prospero above] Malone. Prosper on the top Ff. See note (XIV).

20. *were*] F₁ F₂ F₃. *are* F₄.

26. *'tis true*] *to 't* Steevens conj.
did lie] *lied* Hanmer.

29. *islanders*] F₂ F₃ F₄. *islands* F₁.

32. *gentle-kind*] Theobald. *gentle, kind* Ff. *gentle kind* Rowe.

36. *muse*] F₁ F₂ F₃. *muse,* F₄. *muse;* Capell.

48. *of five for one*] Ff. *on five for one* Theobald. *of one for five* Malone, (Thirlby conj.) See note (XV).

49–51. *I will … past*] Mason conjectured that these lines formed a rhyming couplet.

53. SCENE IV. Pope.

54. *instrument*] *instruments* F_4.

56. *belch up you*] F_1 F_2 F_3. *belch you up* F_4. *belch up* Theobald.

60. [… *draw their swords*] Hanmer.

65. *dowle*] *down* Pope.

plume] Rowe. *plumbe* F_1 F_2 F_3. *plumb* F_4.

67. *strengths*] *strength* F_4.

79. *wraths*] *wrath* Theobald.

81. *heart-sorrow*] Edd. *hearts-sorrow* Ff. *heart's-sorrow* Rowe. *heart's sorrow* Pope.

82. *mocks*] *mopps* Theobald.

86. *life*] *list* Johnson conj.

90. *now*] om. Pope.

92. *whom*] *who* Hanmer.

93. *mine*] *my* Rowe.

[*Exit above*] Theobald.

94. *something holy, sir,*] *something, holy Sir,* F_4.

99. *bass*] Johnson. *base* Ff.

106. *do*] om. Pope.

Act IV: Scene 1

3. *a third*] *a thread* Theobald. *the thread* Williams conj.

4. *who*] *whom* Pope.

7. *test*] F_1. *rest* F_2 F_3 F_4.

9. *off*] F_2 F_3 F_4. *of* F_1.

11. *do*] om. Pope.

13. *gift*] Rowe. *guest* Ff.

14. *but*] F_1. om. F_2 F_3 F_4.

25. *'tis*] *is* Capell.

30. *Phœbus'*] *Phœbus* F_1. *Phœdus* F_2 F_3. *Phœduus* F_4.

34. SCENE II. Pope.

41. *vanity*] *rarity* S. Walker conj.

48. *no?*] *no.* Rowe.

53. *abstemious*] *abstenious* F_1.

60. SCENE III. A MASQUE. Pope.

thy] F_1. *the* F_2 F_3 F_4.

64. *pioned*] *pionied* Warburton. *peonied* Steevens.

twilled] *tulip'd* Rowe. *tilled* Capell (Holt conj.). *lilied* Steevens.

66. *broom-groves*] *brown groves* Hanmer.

68. *pole-clipt*] *pale-clipt* Hanmer.

72. After this line Ff. have the stage direction, '*Juno descends.*'

74. *her*] Rowe. *here* Ff.

83. *short-grass'd*] F_3 F_4. *short gras'd* F_1 F_2. *short-grass* Pope.

96. *bed-right*] *bed-rite* Singer.

101. *High'st*] *High* Pope.

102. Enter JUNO] om. Ff.

110. Cer.] Theobald. om. Ff.

foison] F_1 *and foison* F_2 F_3 F_4.

114. *Spring*] *Rain* Collier MS.

119. *charmingly*] *charming lay* Hanmer. *charming lays* Warburton. *Harmoniously charming* Steevens conj.

121. *from their*] F_1. *from all their* F_2 F_3 F_4.

123. *wife*] F_1 (var.). Rowe. *wise* F_1 (var.) F_2 F_3 F_4.

124. *Makes*] *make* Pope.

sweet, now, silence] *now, silence, sweet* Hanmer.

124. In Ff. the stage direction [Juno, &c. follows line 127. Capell made the change.

128. *windring*] *winding* Rowe. *wand'ring* Steevens.

129. *sedged*] *sedge* Collier MS.

136. *holiday*] *holly day* F_1 F_2 F_3. *holy-day* F_4.

139. SCENE IV. Pope.

143. *This is*] *This'* (for This 's) S. Walker conj.

strange] *most strange* Hanmer.

145. Ff put a comma after *anger*. Warburton omitted it.

146. *do*] om. Pope. See note (XVI).

151. *this*] F_1. *their* F_2 F_3 F_4. *th' air visions* Warburton.

156. *rack*] F_3 F_4. *racke* F_1 F_2. *track* Hanmer. *wreck* Dyce (Malone conj.).

163. *your*] F_1 F_2 F_3. *you* F_4.

164. *I thank thee, Ariel: come.*] *I thank you:—Ariel, come.* Theobald.

169. *Lest*] F_4. *Least* F_1 F_2 F_3.

170. *Say again*] *Well, say again* Capell.

180. *furzes*] Rowe. *firzes* Ff.

181. *shins*] *skins* Warburton conj. (note, V. 1. p. 87).

182. *filthy-mantled*] *filthy mantled* Ff. *filth-ymantled* Steevens conj.

184. *feet*] *fear* Spedding conj.

190. *all, all*] *are all* Malone conj.

193. *them on* Rowe. *on them* Ff. Prospero … invisible. Theobald, Capell. om. Ff.

194. SCENE V. Pope.

230. *Let's alone*] *Let's along* Theobald. *Let it alone* Hanmer. *Let 't alone* Collier. See note (XVII).

246. *to apes*] om. *to* Pope.

255. Stage direction added by Theobald.

256. *they*] F_1 F_3 F_4. *thou* F_2.

261. *Lie*] Rowe. *lies* Ff.

Act V: Scene 1

7. *together*] om. Pope.

9. *all*] *all your* Pope.

10. *line-grove*] *lime-grove* Rowe.

11. *your*] F₁ F₂. *you* F₃ F₄.

15. *sir*] om. Pope.

16. *run*] *runs* F₁.

winter's] *winter* F₄.

23. F₁ F₂ put a comma after *sharply*. F₃ F₄ omit it.

24. *Passion*] *Passion'd* Pope.

26. *'gainst*] Pope. *gainst* F₁ F₂. *against* F₃ F₄.

33. SCENE II. Pope.

37. *green sour*] *green-sward* Douce conj.

46. *strong-based*] Rowe. *strong-bass'd* Ff.

58. SCENE III. Pope.

and] om. Capell.

60. *boil'd*] Pope. *boile* F₁ F₂. *boil* F₃ F₄.

62. *Holy*] *Noble* Collier MS.

63. *show*] *shew* Ff. *flow* Collier MS.

64. *fellowly*] *fellow* Pope.

68. *O*] *O my* Pope. *O thou* S. Walker conj.

69. *sir*] *servant* Collier MS.

72. *Didst*] F₃ F₄. *Did* F₁ F₂.

74. *Sebastian. Flesh and blood,*] *Sebastian, flesh and blood.* Theobald.

75. *entertain'd*] *entertaine* F₁.

76. *who*] Rowe. *whom* Ff.

82. *lies*] F₃ F₄. *ly* F₁ F₂.

83. *or*] *e'er* Collier MS.

84. Theobald gives as stage direction "Exit Ariel and returns immediately."

88. *suck*] *lurk* Theobald.

90. *couch*] *crowch* F₃ F₄.

Capell punctuates *There I couch: when owls do cry,*

92. *summer*] *sun-set* Theobald.

106. *Behold,*] *lo!* Pope.

111. *Whether thou be'st*] *Where thou beest* Ff. *Be'st thou* Pope. *Whe'r thou be'st* Capell.

112. *trifle*] *devil* Collier MS.

119. *my*] *thy* Collier MS.

124. *not*] F₃ F₄. *nor* F₁ F₂.

132. *fault*] *faults* F₄.

136. *who*] F₂ F₃ F₄. *whom* F₁.

145. *and,*] *sir, and* Capell.

supportable] F₁ F₂. *insupportable* F₃ F₄. *portable* Steevens.

148. *my*] *my only* Hanmer.

A daughter] *Only daughter* Hanmer. *Daughter* Capell.

156. *eyes*] F₁. *eye* F₂ F₃ F₄.

their] *these* Capell.

172. SCENE IV. Pope.

Here Prospero discovers ...] Ff. SCENE opens to the entrance of the cell. Here Prospero discovers ... Theobald. Cell opens and discovers ... Capell.

172. *dear'st*] *dearest* Ff.

179. [Kneels] Theobald.

191. *advice*] F₄. *advise* F₁ F₂ F₃.

199, 200. *remembrances with*] *remembrance with* Pope. *remembrances With* Malone.

213. *When*] *Where* Johnson conj.

216. SCENE V. Pope.

sir, look, sir] *sir, look* F₃ F₄.

is] *are* Pope.

221. *safely*] *safe* F₃ F₄.

230. *of sleep*] *a-sleep* Pope.

234. *more*] Rowe. *mo* F₁ F₂. *moe* F₃ F₄.

236. *her*] Theobald (Thirlby conj.). *our* Ff.

242–245. Given to Ariel in F₂ F₃ F₄.

247. *leisure*] F₁. *seisure* F₂. *seizure* F₃ F₄.

248. *Which shall be shortly, single*] Pope. *(which shall be shortly single)* Ff.

253. [Exit Ariel] Capell.

256. SCENE VI. Pope.

258. *Coragio*] *corasio* F₁.

268. *mis-shapen*] *mis-shap'd* Pope.

271. *command, without her power.*] *command. Without her power,* anon. conj.

without] *with all* Collier MS.

280. *liquor*] *'lixir* Theobald.

282–284. Printed as verse in Ff.

289. *This is*] F₁ F₂. *'Tis* F₃ F₄.

a strange] *as strange a* Capell.

e'er I] *I ever* Hanmer.

[Pointing to Caliban.] Steevens.

299. [Exeunt ... Trin.] Capell.

308. *nuptial*] *nuptiall* F₁. *nuptials* F₂ F₃ F₄.

309. See note (XVIII).

Epilogue

EPILOGUE ... PROSPERO.] advancing, Capell.

1. *Now*] *Now, now* F₃ F₄.

3. *now*] *and now* Pope.

13. *Now*] *For now* Pope.

DISCUSSION QUESTIONS ON *THE TEMPEST*

1. Why are Prospero and Miranda on the island, and why does Prospero use his magic to wreck the ship?

2. There are three different betrayal plots in *The Tempest*. What are they? Why would Shakespeare repeat the betrayal motif three times?

3. How do those betrayed respond to the betrayals in the end? What does Shakespeare seem to be suggesting is necessary for a happy ending to occur? (Note in particular Act 5, scene 1, lines 25–32 and lines 115–133).

4. Who are Ariel and Caliban? What is their connection to Prospero?

5. Numerous critics have pointed out that Shakespeare wrote *The Tempest* shortly after a pamphlet called "A Discovery of the Bermudas, Otherwise Called the Isle of Devils" was printed, describing how a Virginia Company flagship heading for Jamestown landed on the island of Bermuda, which turned out to be far more hospitable than reports had suggested. What parallels can you find between the discovery of Prospero's island in the play and the discovery of Bermuda in the New World? Do any speeches seem particularly tailored to remind readers or listeners of the New World discovery?

6. Why does Prospero treat Ferdinand harshly? What is his plan? Does it work?

7. Why do you think Shakespeare has Prospero ask the audience for "pardon" and "indulgence" in the last two lines of the play?

SUGGESTION FOR WRITING

1. Trace connections between the character of Prospero and Shakespeare himself. Analyze the connections seen in specific speeches, themes, and plot elements.

SONNETS

XVIII

Shall I compare thee to a summer's day?
Thou art more lovely and more temperate:
Rough winds do shake the darling buds of May,
And summer's lease hath all too short a date:
Sometime too hot the eye of heaven shines,
And often is his gold complexion dimm'd,
And every fair from fair sometime declines,
By chance, or nature's changing course untrimm'd:
But thy eternal summer shall not fade,
Nor lose possession of that fair thou ow'st,
Nor shall death brag thou wander'st in his shade,
When in eternal lines to time thou grow'st,
So long as men can breathe, or eyes can see,
So long lives this, and this gives life to thee.

XXIX

When in disgrace with fortune and men's eyes
I all alone beweep my outcast state,
And trouble deaf heaven with my bootless cries,
And look upon myself, and curse my fate,
Wishing me like to one more rich in hope,
Featur'd like him, like him with friends possess'd,
Desiring this man's art, and that man's scope,
With what I most enjoy contented least;
Yet in these thoughts my self almost despising,
Haply I think on thee,— and then my state,
Like to the lark at break of day arising
From sullen earth, sings hymns at heaven's gate;
For thy sweet love remember'd such wealth brings
That then I scorn to change my state with kings.

LV

Not marble, nor the gilded monuments
Of princes, shall outlive this powerful rhyme;
But you shall shine more bright in these contents
Than unswept stone, besmear'd with sluttish time.
When wasteful war shall statues overturn,
And broils root out the work of masonry,
Nor Mars his sword, nor war's quick fire shall burn
The living record of your memory.
'Gainst death, and all-oblivious enmity
Shall you pace forth; your praise shall still find room
Even in the eyes of all posterity
That wear this world out to the ending doom.

So, till the judgment that yourself arise,
You live in this, and dwell in lovers' eyes.

LX

Like as the waves make towards the pebbled shore,
So do our minutes hasten to their end;
Each changing place with that which goes before,
In sequent toil all forwards do contend.
Nativity, once in the main of light,
Crawls to maturity, wherewith being crown'd,
Crooked eclipses 'gainst his glory fight,
And Time that gave doth now his gift confound.
Time doth transfix the flourish set on youth
And delves the parallels in beauty's brow,
Feeds on the rarities of nature's truth,
And nothing stands but for his scythe to mow:
And yet to times in hope, my verse shall stand.
Praising thy worth, despite his cruel hand.

LXXIII

That time of year thou mayst in me behold
When yellow leaves, or none, or few, do hang
Upon those boughs which shake against the cold,
Bare ruin'd choirs, where late the sweet birds sang.
In me thou see'st the twilight of such day
As after sunset fadeth in the west;
Which by and by black night doth take away,
Death's second self, that seals up all in rest.
In me thou see'st the glowing of such fire,
That on the ashes of his youth doth lie,
As the death-bed, whereon it must expire,
Consum'd with that which it was nourish'd by.
This thou perceiv'st, which makes thy love more strong,
To love that well, which thou must leave ere long.

CXVI

Let me not to the marriage of true minds
Admit impediments. Love is not love
Which alters when it alteration finds,
Or bends with the remover to remove:
O, no! it is an ever-fixed mark,
That looks on tempests and is never shaken;
It is the star to every wandering bark,
Whose worth's unknown, although his height be taken.
Love's not Time's fool, though rosy lips and cheeks
Within his bending sickle's compass come;
Love alters not with his brief hours and weeks,

But bears it out even to the edge of doom.
If this be error and upon me prov'd,
I never writ, nor no man ever lov'd.

CXXX

My mistress' eyes are nothing like the sun;
Coral is far more red, than her lips red:
If snow be white, why then her breasts are dun;
If hairs be wires, black wires grow on her head.
I have seen roses damask'd, red and white,
But no such roses see I in her cheeks;
And in some perfumes is there more delight
Than in the breath that from my mistress reeks.
I love to hear her speak, yet well I know
That music hath a far more pleasing sound:
I grant I never saw a goddess go,—
My mistress, when she walks, treads on the ground:
And yet by heaven, I think my love as rare,
As any she belied with false compare.

DISCUSSION QUESTIONS

1. In Sonnets 18 and 55, which subject seems to concern the poet the most—his lover or his poetry? Explain your answer.

2. In Sonnet 18 ("Shall I compare thee"), the couplet reads: "So long as men can breathe or eyes can see, / So long lives this, and this gives life to thee." Does the speaker make a hollow boast in this couplet, or is his claim valid? Explain your answer.

3. Sonnet 29 expresses feelings of depression. What images does Shakespeare use to convey this feeling? What helps the speaker out of his dark mood?

4. What is worrying the speaker in Sonnet 60? What provides him with comfort in the midst of his worries?

5. What are the three main images that Shakespeare uses in Sonnet 73 to describe his time of life? What do these images imply about his powers?

6. Do the three main images in Sonnet 73 share any characteristics in common? What are the connotations of these characteristics? Is there an implied consolation in these images for aging and death?

7. What is Shakespeare's definition of love, according to Sonnet 116?

8. In Sonnet 130, why does the speaker resist describing his lover's eyes as being like the sun or her lips as being like coral? What is the speaker's tone in this poem? Why is this poem ultimately *not* insulting to the lover?

SUGGESTION FOR WRITING

1. Select one or two sonnets and analyze how the rhymes and rhythms of the poems help to reinforce the poem's meaning and underscore the consolation that the speaker offers.

JOHN DONNE (C. 1572–1631)

Selected Poems

J ohn Donne was born into a Catholic family at a time when Catholics were being persecuted in England. Although he studied at Oxford and Cambridge and entered Lincoln's Inn to pursue law, his career would probably have been hampered by his religion, which may explain why he renounced Catholicism in the 1590s. In 1598, he became secretary to Sir Thomas Egerton, but when his secret marriage to Lady Egerton's 17-year-old niece, Ann More, was discovered, Donne was imprisoned briefly and spent the next decade piecing together employment so he could take care of his family. He still found favor with some members of the aristocracy and wrote poems in honor of Sir Robert Drury's daughter (*The Anniversaries*). But his position was not secure until King James forcefully encouraged him to become an Anglican minister, which he did in 1615. Noted for his brilliant sermons, many of which have survived, Donne's career in the church prospered, and he was made dean of St. Paul's Cathedral in London in 1621.

Whether Donne was writing erotic love poetry or holy sonnets, he approached his subject with great passion, energy, and a penetrating intellect. He rejected the clichés of love poetry and used instead much fresher and more challenging images, such as the compass in "Valediction: Forbidding Mourning." His use of everyday speech patterns and word choices makes his poetry seem lively and immediate, even to 21st-century readers. Consider the opening line of "The Canonization"—"For God's sake hold your tongue, and let me love" —or the first lines of "The Good-Morrow"—"I wonder, by my troth, what thou and I/Did, till we loved?" Donne's refusal to be restricted by set metrical patterns or poetic structures also adds to the natural sound of his poetry, although, like Shakespeare, he made brilliant use of the sonnet form, as can be seen below, in addition to developing his own stanza structures. Some critics have faulted Donne for his informal diction and irregular meter, but these faults contribute to the liveliness of his verse.

Although Donne's poetry circulated among friends during his life, most of it was not published until 1633, after his death, as it might have injured his reputation as a religious leader. His verse greatly influenced poets such as George Herbert and Andrew Marvell (sometimes referred to, along with Donne, as the "metaphysical" poets). But his poetry fell out of fashion in the following two centuries, only to be brought back into attention in the late 19th and early 20th centuries with new editions of his poetry.

THE GOOD-MORROW.

I WONDER by my troth, what thou and I
Did, till we loved ? were we not wean'd till then?
But suck'd on country pleasures, childishly?
Or snorted we in the Seven Sleepers' den?
'Twas so; but this, all pleasures fancies be ;
If ever any beauty I did see,
Which I desired, and got, 'twas but a dream of thee.
And now good-morrow to our waking souls,
Which watch not one another out of fear;
For love all love of other sights controls,
And makes one little room an everywhere.
Let sea-discoverers to new worlds have gone;
Let maps to other, worlds on worlds have shown;
Let us possess one world; each hath one, and is one.
My face in thine eye, thine in mine appears,
And true plain hearts do in the faces rest;
Where can we find two better hemispheres
Without sharp north, without declining west?
Whatever dies, was not mix'd equally;
If our two loves be one, or thou and I
Love so alike that none can slacken, none can die.

THE SUN RISING.

BUSY old fool, unruly Sun,
  Why dost thou thus,
Through windows, and through curtains, call on us?
Must to thy motions lovers' seasons run?
  Saucy pedantic wretch, go chide
  Late school-boys and sour prentices,
  Go tell court-huntsmen that the king will ride,
  Call country ants to harvest offices;
Love, all alike, no season knows nor clime,
Nor hours, days, months, which are the rags of time.
  Thy beams so reverend, and strong
  Why shouldst thou think?
I could eclipse and cloud them with a wink,
But that I would not lose her sight so long.

If her eyes have not blinded thine,
  Look, and to-morrow late tell me,
  Whether both th' Indias of spice and mine
  Be where thou left'st them, or lie here with me.
Ask for those kings whom thou saw'st yesterday,
And thou shalt hear, "All here in one bed lay."

  She's all states, and all princes I;
  Nothing else is;
Princes do but play us ; compared to this,
All honour's mimic, all wealth alchemy.
  Thou, Sun, art half as happy as we,
  In that the world›s contracted thus;
  Thine age asks ease, and since thy duties be
  To warm the world, that›s done in warming us.
Shine here to us, and thou art everywhere;
This bed thy center is, these walls thy sphere.

THE CANONIZATION.

FOR God's sake hold your tongue, and let me love;
  Or chide my palsy, or my gout;
  My five gray hairs, or ruin'd fortune flout;
With wealth your state, your mind with arts improve;
  Take you a course, get you a place,
  Observe his Honour, or his Grace;
Or the king's real, or his stamp'd face
  Contemplate; what you will, approve,
  So you will let me love.
Alas ! alas ! who's injured by my love?
  What merchant›s ships have my
  sighs drown'd?
  Who says my tears have overflow'd his ground?
When did my colds a forward spring remove?
  When did the heats which my veins fill
  Add one more to the plaguy bill?
Soldiers find wars, and lawyers find out still

Litigious men, which quarrels move,

Though she and I do love.
Call's what you will, we are made such by love ;
  Call her one, me another fly,
  We're tapers too, and at our own cost die,
And we in us find th' eagle and the dove.
  The phoenix riddle hath more wit
  By us ; we two being one, are it;
So, to one neutral thing both sexes fit.
  We die and rise the same, and prove
  -Mysterious by this love.

We can die by it, if not live by love,
  And if unfit for tomb or hearse
  Our legend be, it will be fit for verse;
And if no piece of chronicle we prove,
  We'll build in sonnets pretty rooms;
  As well a well-wrought urn becomes
The greatest ashes, as half-acre tombs,
  And by these hymns, all shall approve
  Us canonized for love ;
And thus invoke us, "You, whom reverend love
  Made one another›s hermitage ;
  You, to whom love was peace, that now is rage ;
Who did the whole world's soul contract, and drove
  Into the glasses of your eyes ;
  So made such mirrors, and such spies,
That they did all to you epitomize—
  Countries, towns, courts beg from above
  A pattern of your love."

A VALEDICTION FORBIDDING MOURNING.

AS virtuous men pass mildly away,
  And whisper to their souls to go,
Whilst some of their sad friends do say,
  "Now his breath goes," and some say, "No."
So let us melt, and make no noise,
  No tear-floods, nor sigh-tempests move ;
'Twere profanation of our joys
  To tell the laity our love.

Moving of th' earth brings harms and fears ;
  Men reckon what it did, and meant ;
But trepidation of the spheres,
  Though greater far, is innocent.
Dull sublunary lovers' love
  —Whose soul is sense—cannot admit
Of absence, 'cause it doth remove
  The thing which elemented it.
But we by a love so much refined,
  That ourselves know not what it is,
Inter-assurèd of the mind,
  Care less, eyes, lips and hands to miss.
Our two souls therefore, which are one,
  Though I must go, endure not yet
A breach, but an expansion,
  Like gold to aery thinness beat.
If they be two, they are two so
  As stiff twin compasses are two ;
Thy soul, the fix'd foot, makes no show
  To move, but doth, if th' other do.
And though it in the centre sit,
  Yet, when the other far doth roam,
It leans, and hearkens after it,
  And grows erect, as that comes home.
Such wilt thou be to me, who must,
  Like th' other foot, obliquely run ;
Thy firmness makes my circle just,
  And makes me end where I begun.

ELEGY XIX. TO HIS MISTRESS GOING TO BED

COME, Madam, come, all rest my powers defy,
Until I labour, I in labour lie.
The foe oft-times having the foe in sight,
Is tir'd with standing though he never fight.
Off with that girdle, like heaven's Zone glistering,
But a far fairer world encompassing.
Unpin that spangled breastplate which you wear,
That th'eyes of busy fools may be stopped there.
Unlace yourself, for that harmonious chime,
Tells me from you, that now it is bed time.

Off with that happy busk, which I envy,
That still can be, and still can stand so nigh.
Your gown going off, such beauteous state reveals,
As when from flowery meads th'hill's shadow steals.
Off with that wiry Coronet and shew
The hairy Diadem which on you doth grow:
Now off with those shoes, and then safely tread
In this love's hallow'd temple, this soft bed.
In such white robes, heaven's Angels used to be
Received by men; Thou Angel bringst with thee
A heaven like Mahomet's Paradise; and though
Ill spirits walk in white, we easily know,
By this these Angels from an evil sprite,
Those set our hairs, but these our flesh upright.

    Licence my roving hands, and let them go,
Before, behind, between, above, below.
O my America! my new-found-land,
My kingdom, safeliest when with one man mann'd,
My Mine of precious stones, My Empirie,
How blest am I in this discovering thee!
To enter in these bonds, is to be free;
Then where my hand is set, my seal shall be.

    Full nakedness! All joys are due to thee,
As souls unbodied, bodies uncloth'd must be,
To taste whole joys. Gems which you women use
Are like Atlanta's balls, cast in men's views,
That when a fool's eye lighteth on a Gem,
His earthly soul may covet theirs, not them.
Like pictures, or like books' gay coverings made
For lay-men, are all women thus array'd;
Themselves are mystic books, which only we
(Whom their imputed grace will dignify)
Must see reveal'd. Then since that I may know;
As liberally, as to a Midwife, shew
Thy self: cast all, yea, this white linen hence,
There is no penance due to innocence.

    To teach thee, I am naked first; why then
What needst thou have more covering than a man.

HOLY SONNETS.
X.

Death, be not proud, though some have called thee
Mighty and dreadful, for thou art not so;
For those, whom thou think'st thou dost overthrow,
Die not, poor Death, nor yet canst thou kill me.
From rest and sleep, which but thy picture[s] be,
Much pleasure, then from thee much more must flow,
And soonest our best men with thee do go,
Rest of their bones, and soul's delivery.
Thou'rt slave to Fate, chance, kings, and desperate men,
And dost with poison, war, and sickness dwell,
And poppy, or charms can make us sleep as well,
And better than thy stroke; why swell'st thou then?
One short sleep past, we wake eternally,
And Death shall be no more; Death, thou shalt die.

HOLY SONNETS.
XIV.

Batter my heart, three-person'd God; for you
As yet but knock; breathe, shine, and seek to mend;
That I may rise, and stand, o'erthrow me, and bend
Your force, to break, blow, burn, and make me new.
I, like an usurp'd town, to another due,
Labour to admit you, but O, to no end.
Reason, your viceroy in me, me should defend,
But is captived, and proves weak or untrue.
Yet dearly I love you, and would be loved fain,
But am betroth'd unto your enemy;
Divorce me, untie, or break that knot again,
Take me to you, imprison me, for I,
Except you enthrall me, never shall be free,
Nor ever chaste, except you ravish me.

JOHN DONNE (C. 1572–1631) | 435

DISCUSSION QUESTIONS

1. What are some of the effects of love that the speaker lists in "The Good-Morrow?" Which seem to you to be particularly original ideas?

2. Which images in "The Good-Morrow" seem to reflect major Renaissance events or discoveries?

3. In "The Sun Rising," what is the speaker's feeling about the sun? What is unusual about this attitude, and why does he have it?

4. According to the speaker in "The Sun Rising," he and his lover have greater powers than the sun. How does he prove this?

5. Compare "The Good-Morrow" and "The Sun Rising." What images, themes, and sentiments do they share in common? How are they different?

6. In "The Canonization," why does the speaker feel that he and his lover should be canonized for their love?

7. In "Valediction: Forbidding Mourning," how does the speaker feel that he and his lover should express their sorrow upon being separated from each other for a while? What reasons does he give for his suggestions?

8. In the same poem, what two images does the speaker offer to describe the state of their souls when the lovers are apart? Which image is more effective? Why?

9. In "Elegy 19. Going to Bed," what is the speaker asking his lover to do? What is his tone as he makes his commands? Which lines strike you as particularly humorous? Which, if any, seem shocking?

10. What is the rhyme scheme in Elegy 19? Why is it appropriate?

11. In Holy Sonnet 10, Donne writes that death shouldn't be proud. Why not?

12. In Holy Sonnet 14, what does the speaker compare himself to? What does he want God to do to him? Why does he need God to be violent?

BEN JONSON (1572–1637)

Selected Poems

M ore renowned for his writings in his own day than was his contemporary, William Shakespeare, Jonson was a poet, playwright, critic, translator and eventually poet laureate in 1616, the year of Shakespeare's death. Educated at Westminster School, he became a soldier and fought valiantly in Flanders against the Spanish. After he returned to England, he worked as an actor but was arrested for killing another actor in a duel and converted to Catholicism while in jail, a dangerous move in such anti-Catholic days. He later returned to the Anglican Church.

Jonson's comic plays, *Every Man in His Humour*, *Volpone*, *The Alchemist*, and *Bartholomew Fair*, satirize human weaknesses and were very popular in his day and continue to be produced today. He also wrote masques, theatricals that emphasize spectacle and flattery of royalty, which no doubt aided his career. His poetry ranges from epitaphs and elegies, to bawdy verse, and to tributes to friends (see the ones to Donne and Shakespeare below). Jonson published his collected works in 1616 (*The Works of Ben Jonson*), a common practice today but unheard of at the time. His self-promotion helped establish some respectability for the profession of author, and his fame was extended by his many followers, including Robert Herrick, below.

ON MY FIRST DAUGHTER

Here lies, to each her parents' ruth,
Mary, the daughter of their youth;
Yet, all heaven's gifts, being heaven's due,
It makes the father less to rue.
At six months' end, she parted hence,
With safety of her innocence;
Whose soul heaven's queen, whose name she bears,
In comfort of her mother's tears,
Hath placed amongst her virgin-train;
Where, while that severed doth remain,
This grave partakes the fleshly birth;
Which cover lightly, gentle earth!

TO JOHN DONNE

Donne, the delight of Phoebus and each Muse
Who, to thy one, all other brains refuse;
Whose every work of thy most early wit
Came forth example, and remains so yet;
Longer a-knowing than most wits do live;
And which no affection praise enough can give!
To it, thy language, letters, arts, best life,
Which might with half mankind maintain a strife.
All which I meant to praise, and yet I would;
But leave, because I cannot as I should!

TO CELIA

Drink to me only with thine eyes,
  And I will pledge with mine;
Or leave a kiss but in the cup,
  And I'll not look for wine.
The thirst that from the soul doth rise
  Doth ask a drink divine:
But might I of Jove's nectar sup,
  I would not change for thine.
I sent thee late a rosy wreath,
  Not so much honouring thee,
As giving it a hope that there

It could not withered be.
But thou thereon didst only breathe,
  And sent'st it back to me:
Since when it grows, and smells, I swear,
  Not of itself, but thee.

ON MY FIRST SON

Farewell, thou child of my right hand, and joy;
My sin was too much hope of thee, loved boy;
Seven years thou wert lent to me, and I thee pay,
Exacted by thy fate, on the just day.
Oh! could I lose all father, now! for why,
Will man lament the state he should envy?
To have so soon 'scaped world's, and flesh's rage,
And, if no other misery, yet age!
Rest in soft peace, and, asked, say here doth lie
Ben Jonson his best piece of poetry;
For whose sake, henceforth, all his vows be such,
As what he loves may never like too much.

SIMPLEX MUNDITIIS (STILL TO BE NEAT)

Still to be neat, still to be dressed,
As you were going to a feast;
Still to be powdered, still perfumed:
Lady, it is to be presumed,
Though art's hid causes are not found,
All is not sweet, all is not sound.

Give me a look, give me a face,
That makes simplicity a grace;
Robes loosely flowing, hair as free:
Such sweet neglect more taketh me
Than all the adulteries of art;
They strike mine eyes, but not my heart.

DISCUSSION QUESTIONS

1. Compare Jonson's tributes to his daughter and son in "On My First Daughter," and "On My First Son." What consolation for his own loss does Jonson offer in his poems?

2. The first line of "Song: To Celia" is one of the most famous in all of English poetry: "Drink to me only with thine eyes ... " What does this line and the following one mean? Why do you think this line has been so often repeated? What makes it effective?

3. In "To John Donne," what is it that Jonson admires about Donne? What is ironic about his tribute to Donne?

4. In "Still to Be Neat," what does Jonson mean by "neat?" Why does he object to the artifice women use to adorn themselves? Why would he refer to such neatness as "th' *adulteries* of art?"

ROBERT HERRICK (1591–1674)

Selected Poems

S on of a London goldsmith, Robert Herrick graduated from Cambridge and accepted a position in a parish in Devon. His interests leaned more to poetry than church affairs, however, and he preferred living in London, as can be seen in "His Return to London," where he writes, "London my home is, though by hard fate sent/ Into a long and irksome banishment." His verse often focuses on imaginary mistresses named Julia, Corinna, etc., following the lead of his Latin models. He also follows the lead of his contemporary inspiration, Ben Jonson, whom he refers to as "Saint Ben" in "His Prayer to Ben Jonson," in which he asks Jonson to aid him in his writing. Herrick's poems frequently address the *carpe diem* or "seize the day" theme, as can be seen in "Corinna's Going A-Maying" and most famously in "To the Virgins, to Make Much of Time," with its famous imperative, "Gather ye rosebuds while ye may,/ Old time is still a-flying."

Because Herrick sided with the king during the English Civil War, the Puritans removed him from his position in the church in 1647. He returned to his beloved London where he published his only book of poems, *Hesperides and Noble Numbers* (the two titles reflecting the secular and the sacred poems). The book received little notice. When the monarchy was restored in 1660, Herrick returned to his position in Devon. In his couplet "To His Book's End," he offered a fitting summary of his life and writings: "To his book's end this last line he'd have placed:/ Jocund his muse was, but his life was chaste."

TO THE VIRGINS, TO MAKE MUCH OF TIME.

GATHER ye rosebuds while ye may,
  Old time is still a-flying :
And this same flower that smiles to-day
  To-morrow will be dying.

The glorious lamp of heaven, the sun,
  The higher he's a-getting,
The sooner will his race be run,
  And nearer he's to setting.

That age is best which is the first,
  When youth and blood are warmer ;
But being spent, the worse, and worst
  Times still succeed the former.

Then be not coy, but use your time,
  And while ye may go marry :
For having lost but once your prime
  You may for ever tarry.

UPON JULIA'S CLOTHES.

WHENAS in silks my Julia goes,
Then, then, methinks, how sweetly flows
That liquefaction of her clothes.

Next, when I cast mine eyes and see
That brave vibration each way free ;
O how that glittering taketh me !

DELIGHT IN DISORDER.

A SWEET disorder in the dress
Kindles in clothes a wantonness :
A lawn about the shoulders thrown
Into a fine distraction :
An erring lace which here and there
Enthrals the crimson stomacher :
A cuff neglectful, and thereby
Ribbons to flow confusedly :
A winning wave (deserving note)
In the tempestuous petticoat :
A careless shoe-string, in whose tie
I see a wild civility :
Do more bewitch me than when art
Is too precise in every part.

DISCUSSION QUESTIONS

1. "To the Virgins, to Make Much of Time" is written in ballad form, which means that it's divided into quatrains whose first and third lines are in iambic tetratmeter (four accents per line) and second and fourth lines are in iambic trimeter (three accents per line). Discuss how this form reflects the subject Herrick is discussing (in other words, why is it effective in reference to his *carpe diem* theme to start with a line with more syllables and follow it with a line with fewer?)

2. All ballads, such as "To the Virgins," can be sung to melodies written for ballads, such as "Greensleaves." Try this on your own. How would the popularity and prevalence of the ballad as a musical form help preserve Herrick's poem?

3. What are the connotations of the "rosebud" image in the first line of "To the Virgins?"

4. Why does Herrick take delight in disorder, as he states in the poem of the same name? Why might "precise" art "bewitch" him less?

5. What is the form of "Delight in Disorder?" Does Herrick follow a strict rhythmic pattern in this poem? Why or why not?

6. Compare "Upon Julia's Clothes" to "Delight in Disorder." What is similar about the theme of each? Compare both to Jonson's poem, "Still to Be Neat," printed above. How do these poems go against the aesthetic tastes of the period (see General Introduction to this unit)?

JOHN MILTON (1608–1674)

J ohn Milton was born in Cheapside and educated at St. Paul's School and Christ's College, Cambridge, where he earned a B.A. in 1629 and an M.A. in 1632. After graduating, he spent six years in quiet self-education, culminated by a year of traveling on the continent. Milton's first published poem, included below, is *Lycidas* (1638), written in honor of a friend, Edward King (the Lycidas of the title), who drowned in 1637 when crossing the Irish Sea. *Lycidas* is considered by many to be the greatest elegy in English literature, and while Milton follows many pastoral elegy traditions in the poem—such as allusions to shepherds, gods and beasts from classical mythology—he transcends literary conventions with his inventive language and his mastery of poetic meter and rhyme.

The middle years of Milton's life were shaped by the Civil War in England and Milton's support of Cromwell, who overthrew the monarchy. When Milton's first wife, Mary Powell, the daughter of a supporter of the king, left him after only a few weeks of marriage, Milton turned to publishing pamphlets in favor of divorce in the case of incompatibility. These pamphlets added to his reputation as a radical, as did *Areopagitica*, his defense of the freedom of the press. In 1645, his wife returned to him and gave birth to three daughters over the next seven years. She died in 1652, and in 1656 he married Katherine Woodcock, who died giving birth two years later.

With the beheading of Charles I in 1649 and the establishment of the Commonwealth, Milton became the most literate defender of the new government until its last days, both in his position as Latin secretary to Cromwell's Council of State and in various pamphlets supporting the new government. During these years, he began to go blind, but was able to continue his duties with assistance. When the Commonwealth failed in 1660 and Charles II took the throne, Milton was taken into custody and fined. That he escaped execution was probably due to the intervention of friends, Andrew Marvell among them. Blind, impoverished, and deeply disappointed, he spent the rest of his life in quiet retirement working on his epic masterpiece, *Paradise Lost* (1667), which he hoped would "justify the ways of God to men" through its recounting of the stories of Adam, Eve, and Lucifer. In 1671, the sequel, *Paradise Regained*, dealing with Christ's temptation in the wilderness, was published, as was the closet drama, *Samson Agonistes*. This play's depiction of Samson's restored powers at the end of his life suggests that at the end of Milton's life, he still felt the potential of his own poetic abilities and perhaps even had hopes for the restoration of the Commonwealth that he had worked so hard to support.

In this Monody the Author bewails a learned Friend, unfortunately drown'd in his Passage from *Chester* on the *Irish* Seas, 1637. And by occasion fortels the ruine of our corrupted Clergy then in their height.

LYCIDAS

Yet once more, O ye Laurels, and once more
Ye Myrtles brown, with Ivy never-sear,
I com to pluck your Berries harsh and crude,
And with forc'd fingers rude,
Shatter your leaves before the mellowing year.
Bitter constraint, and sad occasion dear,
Compels me to disturb your season due:
For *Lycidas* is dead, dead ere his prime
Young *Lycidas*, and hath not left his peer:
Who would not sing for *Lycidas*? he knew
Himself to sing, and build the lofty rhyme.
He must not flote upon his watry bear
Unwept, and welter to the parching wind,
Without the meed of som melodious tear.
    Begin, then, Sisters of the sacred well,
That from beneath the seat of *Jove* doth spring,
Begin, and somwhat loudly sweep the string.
Hence with denial vain, and coy excuse,
So may som gentle Muse
With lucky words favour my destin'd Urn,
And as he passes turn,
And bid fair peace be to my sable shrowd.
For we were nurst upon the self-same hill,
Fed the same flock, by fountain, shade, and rill.
    Together both, ere the high Lawns appear'd
Under the opening eye-lids of the morn,
We drove a-field, and both together heard
What time the Gray-fly winds her sultry horn,
Batt'ning our flocks with the fresh dews of night,
Oft till the Star that rose, at Ev'ning, bright
Toward Heav'ns descent had slop'd his westering wheel.
Mean while the Rural ditties were not mute,
Temper'd to th'Oaten Flute;
Rough *Satyrs* danc'd, and *Fauns* with clov'n heel,
From the glad sound would not be absent long,
And old *Damætas* lov'd to hear our song.
    But O the heavy change, now thou art gon,
Now thou art gon, and never must return!
Thee Shepherd, thee the Woods, and desert Caves,
With wilde Thyme and the gadding Vine o'ergrown,
And all their echoes mourn.

The Willows, and the Hazle Copses green,
Shall now no more be seen,
Fanning their joyous Leaves to thy soft layes.
As killing as the Canker to the Rose,
Or Taint-worm to the weanling Herds that graze,
Or Frost to Flowers, that their gay wardrop wear,
When first the White thorn blows;
Such, *Lycidas*, thy loss to Shepherds ear.
    Where were ye Nymphs when the remorseless deep
Clos'd o're the head of your lov'd *Lycidas*?
For neither were ye playing on the steep,
Where your old Bards, the famous *Druids* ly,
Nor on the shaggy top of *Mona* high,
Nor yet where *Deva* spreads her wisard stream:
Ay me, I fondly dream!
Had ye bin there—for what could that have don?
What could the Muse her self that *Orpheus* bore,
The Muse her self, for her inchanting son
Whom Universal nature did lament,
When by the rout that made the hideous roar,
His goary visage down the stream was sent,
Down the swift *Hebrus* to the *Lesbian* shore.
    Alas! What boots it with uncessant care
To tend the homely slighted Shepherds trade,
And strictly meditate the thankles Muse,
Were it not better don as others use,
To sport with *Amaryllis* in the shade,
Or with the tangles of *Næra's* hair?
Fame is the spur that the clear spirit doth raise
(That last infirmity of Noble mind)
To scorn delights, and live laborious dayes;
But the fair Guerdon when we hope to find,
And think to burst out into sudden blaze,
Comes the blind *Fury* with th'abhorred shears,
And slits the thin-spun life. But not the praise,
Phœbus repli'd, and touch'd my trembling ears;
Fame is no plant that grows on mortal soil,
Nor in the glistering foil
Set off to th'world, nor in broad rumour lies,
But lives and spreds aloft by those pure eyes,
And perfet witnes of all judging *Jove*;
As he pronounces lastly on each deed,

Of so much fame in Heav'n expect thy meed.
  O fountain *Arethuse,* and thou honour'd floud,
Smooth-sliding *Mincius,* crown'd with vocall reeds,
That strain I heard was of a higher mood:
But now my Oate proceeds,
And listens to the Herald of the Sea
That came in *Neptune's* plea,
He ask'd the Waves, and ask'd the Fellon winds,
What hard mishap hath doom'd this gentle swain?
And question'd every gust of rugged wings
That blows from off each beaked Promontory,
They knew not of his story,
And sage *Hippotades* their answer brings,
That not a blast was from his dungeon stray'd,
The Ayr was calm, and on the level brine,
Sleek *Panope* with all her sisters play'd.
It was that fatall and perfidious Bark
Built in th'eclipse, and rigg'd with curses dark,
That sunk so low that sacred head of thine.
  Next *Camus,* reverend Sire, went footing slow,
His Mantle hairy, and his Bonnet sedge,
Inwrought with figures dim, and on the edge
Like to that sanguine flower inscrib'd with woe.
Ah! Who hath reft (quoth he) my dearest pledge?
Last came, and last did go,
The Pilot of the *Galilean* lake,
Two massy Keyes he bore of metals twain,
(The Golden opes, the Iron shuts amain)
He shook his Miter'd locks, and stern bespake,
How well could I have spar'd for thee young swain,
Anow of such as for their bellies sake,
Creep and intrude, and climb into the fold?
Of other care they little reck'ning make,
Then how to scramble at the shearers feast,
And shove away the worthy bidden guest.
Blind mouthes! that scarce themselves know how to hold
A Sheep-hook, or have learn'd ought els the least
That to the faithfull Herdmans art belongs!
What recks it them? What need they? They are sped;
And when they list, their lean and flashy songs
Grate on their scrannel Pipes of wretched straw,
The hungry Sheep look up, and are not fed,
But swoln with wind, and the rank mist they draw,
Rot inwardly and foul contagian spread:

Besides what the grim Woolf with privy paw
Daily devours apace, and nothing sed,
But that two-handed engine at the door,
Stands ready to smite once, and smite no more.
Return *Alpheus*, the dread voice is past,
That shrunk thy streams; Return *Sicilian* Muse,
And call the Vales, and bid them hither cast
Their Bels, and Flourets of a thousand hues.
Ye valleys low where the milde whispers use,
Of shades and wanton winds, and gushing brooks,
On whose fresh lap the swart Star sparely looks,
Throw hither all your quaint enameled eyes,
That on the green terf suck the honied showres,
And purple all the ground with vernal flowres.
Bring the rathe Primrose that forsaken dies.
The tufted Crow-toe, and pale Gessamine,
The white Pink, and the Pansie freakt with jeat,
The glowing Violet.
The Musk-rose, and the well attir'd Woodbine,
With Cowslips wan that hang the pensive hed,
And every flower that sad embroidery wears:
Bid *Amaranthus* all his beauty shed,
And Daffadillies fill their cups with tears,
To strew the Laureat Herse where *Lycid* lies.
For so to interpose a little ease,
Let our frail thoughts dally with false surmise.
Ay me! Whilst thee the shores, and sounding Seas
Wash far away, where ere they bones are hurld,
Whether beyond the stormy *Hebrides*,
Where thou perhaps under the whelming tide
Visit'st the bottom of the monstrous world;
Or whether thou to our moist vows deny'd,
Sleep'st by the fable of *Bellerus* old,
Where the great vision of the guarded Mount
Looks toward *Namancos* and *Bayona's* hold;
Look homeward Angel now, and melt with ruth.
And, O ye *Dolphins,* waft the haples youth.
  Weep no more, woful Shepherds weep no more,
For *Lycidas* your sorrow is not dead,
Sunk though he be beneath the watry floar,
So sinks the day-star in the Ocean bed,
And yet anon repairs his drooping head,
And tricks his beams, and with new spangled Ore,
Flames in the forehead of the morning sky:

So *Lycidas* sunk low, but mounted high,
Through the dear might of him that walk'd the waves,
Where other groves, and other streams along,
With *Nectar* pure his oozy Lock's he laves,
And hears the unexpressive nuptiall Song,
In the blest Kingdoms meek of joy and love.
There entertain him all the Saints above,
In solemn troops, and sweet Societies
That sing, and singing in their glory move,
And wipe the tears for ever from his eyes.
Now *Lycidas* the Shepherds weep no more;
Hence forth thou art the Genius of the shore,
In they large recompense, and shalt be good
To all that wander in that perilous flood.
    Thus sang the uncouth Swain to th'Okdes and rills,
While the still morn went out with Sandals gray,
He touch'd the tender stops of various Quills,
With eager thought warbling his *Dorick* lay:
And now the Sun had stretch'd out all the hills,
And now was dropt into the Western bay;
At last he rose, and twitch'd his Mantle blew:
To morrow to fresh Woods, and Pastures new.

ON SHAKESPEAR. 1630.

What needs my Shakespear for his honour'd Bones,
The labour of an age in piled Stones,
Or that his hallow'd reliques should be hid
Under a Star-ypointing *Pyramid*?
Dear son of memory, great heir of Fame,
What need'st thou such weak witnes of thy name?
Thou in our wonder and astonishment
Hast built thy self a live-long Monument.
For whilst to th' shame of slow-endeavouring art,
Thy easie numbers flow, and that each heart
Hath from the leaves of thy unvalu'd Book
Those Delphick lines with deep impression took,
Then thou our fancy of it self bereaving,
Dost make us Marble with too much conceaving;
And so Sepulcher'd in such pomp dost lie,
That Kings for such a Tomb would wish to die.

WHEN I CONSIDER HOW MY LIGHT IS SPENT

When I consider how my light is spent,
  Ere half my days, in this dark world and wide,
    And that one Talent which is death to hide
    Lodged with me useless, though my Soul more bent
To serve therewith my Maker, and present
  My true account, lest he returning chide;
    "Doth God exact day-labour, light denied?"
    I fondly ask. But patience, to prevent
That murmur, soon replies, "God doth not need
  Either man's work or his own gifts; who best
    Bear his mild yoke, they serve him best. His state
Is Kingly. Thousands at his bidding speed
  And post o'er Land and Ocean without rest:
  They also serve who only stand and wait."

SONNET XXIII.

ON HIS DECEASED WIFE.

METHOUGHT I saw my late espoused saint
  Brought to me like Alcestis, from the grave,
  Whom Jove's great son to her glad husband gave,
  Rescued from death by force, though pale and faint.
Mine, as whom wash'd from spot of child-bed taint
  Purificationin the old Law did save,
  And such, as yet once more I trust to have
  Full sight of her in Heaven without restraint,
Came vested all in white, pure as her mind:
  Her face was veil'd; yet to my fancied sight
  Love, sweetness, goodness, in her person shin'd
So clear, as in no face with more delight.
  But O, as to embrace me she inclin'd,
  I wak'd; she fled; and day brought back my night.

PARADISE LOST (1674)/BOOK I

Of Man's first disobedience, and the fruit
Of that forbidden tree whose mortal taste
Brought death into the World, and all our woe,
With loss of Eden, till one greater Man
Restore us, and regain the blissful seat,
Sing, Heavenly Muse, that, on the secret top
Of Oreb, or of Sinai, didst inspire
That shepherd who first taught the chosen seed
In the beginning how the heavens and earth
Rose out of Chaos: or, if Sion hill
Delight thee more, and Siloa's brook that flowed
Fast by the oracle of God, I thence
Invoke thy aid to my adventurous song,
That with no middle flight intends to soar
Above th' Aonian mount, while it pursues
Things unattempted yet in prose or rhyme.
And chiefly thou, O Spirit, that dost prefer
Before all temples th' upright heart and pure,
Instruct me, for thou know'st; thou from the first
Wast present, and, with mighty wings outspread,
Dove-like sat'st brooding on the vast Abyss,
And mad'st it pregnant: what in me is dark
Illumine, what is low raise and support;
That, to the height of this great argument,
I may assert Eternal Providence,
And justify the ways of God to men.

Say first—for Heaven hides nothing from thy view,
Nor the deep tract of Hell—say first what cause
Moved our grand parents, in that happy state,
Favoured of Heaven so highly, to fall off
From their Creator, and transgress his will
For one restraint, lords of the World besides.
Who first seduced them to that foul revolt?

Th' infernal Serpent; he it was whose guile,
Stirred up with envy and revenge, deceived
The mother of mankind, what time his pride
Had cast him out from Heaven, with all his host
Of rebel Angels, by whose aid, aspiring
To set himself in glory above his peers,

He trusted to have equalled the Most High,
If he opposed, and with ambitious aim
Against the throne and monarchy of God,
Raised impious war in Heaven and battle proud,
With vain attempt. Him the Almighty Power
Hurled headlong flaming from th' ethereal sky,
With hideous ruin and combustion, down
To bottomless perdition, there to dwell
In adamantine chains and penal fire,
Who durst defy th' Omnipotent to arms.

Nine times the space that measures day and night
To mortal men, he, with his horrid crew,
Lay vanquished, rolling in the fiery gulf,
Confounded, though immortal. But his doom
Reserved him to more wrath; for now the thought
Both of lost happiness and lasting pain
Torments him: round he throws his baleful eyes,
That witnessed huge affliction and dismay,
Mixed with obdurate pride and steadfast hate.
At once, as far as Angels ken, he views
The dismal situation waste and wild.
A dungeon horrible, on all sides round,
As one great furnace flamed; yet from those flames
No light; but rather darkness visible
Served only to discover sights of woe,
Regions of sorrow, doleful shades, where peace
And rest can never dwell, hope never comes
That comes to all, but torture without end
Still urges, and a fiery deluge, fed
With ever-burning sulphur unconsumed.
Such place Eternal Justice has prepared
For those rebellious; here their prison ordained
In utter darkness, and their portion set,
As far removed from God and light of Heaven
As from the centre thrice to th' utmost pole.
Oh how unlike the place from whence they fell!
There the companions of his fall, o'erwhelmed
With floods and whirlwinds of tempestuous fire,
He soon discerns; and, weltering by his side,
One next himself in power, and next in crime,
Long after known in Palestine, and named

John Milton, "Book I," *Paradise Lost.* Copyright in the Public
Domain.

Beelzebub. To whom th' Arch-Enemy,
And thence in Heaven called Satan, with bold words
Breaking the horrid silence, thus began:—
"If thou beest he—but O how fallen! how changed
From him who, in the happy realms of light
Clothed with transcendent brightness, didst outshine
Myriads, though bright!—if he whom mutual league,
United thoughts and counsels, equal hope
And hazard in the glorious enterprise
Joined with me once, now misery hath joined
In equal ruin; into what pit thou seest
From what height fallen: so much the stronger proved
He with his thunder; and till then who knew
The force of those dire arms? Yet not for those,
Nor what the potent Victor in his rage
Can else inflict, do I repent, or change,
Though changed in outward lustre, that fixed mind,
And high disdain from sense of injured merit,
That with the Mightiest raised me to contend,
And to the fierce contentions brought along
Innumerable force of Spirits armed,
That durst dislike his reign, and, me preferring,
His utmost power with adverse power opposed
In dubious battle on the plains of Heaven,
And shook his throne. What though the field be lost?
All is not lost—the unconquerable will,
And study of revenge, immortal hate,
And courage never to submit or yield:
And what is else not to be overcome?
That glory never shall his wrath or might
Extort from me. To bow and sue for grace
With suppliant knee, and deify his power
Who, from the terror of this arm, so late
Doubted his empire—that were low indeed;
That were an ignominy and shame beneath
This downfall; since, by fate, the strength of Gods,
And this empyreal substance, cannot fail;
Since, through experience of this great event,
In arms not worse, in foresight much advanced,
We may with more successful hope resolve
To wage by force or guile eternal war,
Irreconcilable to our grand Foe,
Who now triumphs, and in th' excess of joy
Sole reigning holds the tyranny of Heaven."

So spake th' apostate Angel, though in pain,
Vaunting aloud, but racked with deep despair;

And him thus answered soon his bold compeer:—

"O Prince, O Chief of many throned Powers
That led th' embattled Seraphim to war
Under thy conduct, and, in dreadful deeds
Fearless, endangered Heaven's perpetual King,
And put to proof his high supremacy,
Whether upheld by strength, or chance, or fate,
Too well I see and rue the dire event
That, with sad overthrow and foul defeat,
Hath lost us Heaven, and all this mighty host
In horrible destruction laid thus low,
As far as Gods and heavenly Essences
Can perish: for the mind and spirit remains
Invincible, and vigour soon returns,
Though all our glory extinct, and happy state
Here swallowed up in endless misery.
But what if he our Conqueror (whom I now
Of force believe almighty, since no less
Than such could have o'erpowered such force as ours)
Have left us this our spirit and strength entire,
Strongly to suffer and support our pains,
That we may so suffice his vengeful ire,
Or do him mightier service as his thralls
By right of war, whate'er his business be,
Here in the heart of Hell to work in fire,
Or do his errands in the gloomy Deep?
What can it then avail though yet we feel
Strength undiminished, or eternal being
To undergo eternal punishment?"

Whereto with speedy words th' Arch-Fiend replied:—
"Fallen Cherub, to be weak is miserable,
Doing or suffering: but of this be sure—
To do aught good never will be our task,
But ever to do ill our sole delight,
As being the contrary to his high will
Whom we resist. If then his providence
Out of our evil seek to bring forth good,
Our labour must be to pervert that end,
And out of good still to find means of evil;
Which ofttimes may succeed so as perhaps
Shall grieve him, if I fail not, and disturb
His inmost counsels from their destined aim.
But see! the angry Victor hath recalled
His ministers of vengeance and pursuit
Back to the gates of Heaven: the sulphurous hail,

Shot after us in storm, o'erblown hath laid
The fiery surge that from the precipice
Of Heaven received us falling; and the thunder,
Winged with red lightning and impetuous rage,
Perhaps hath spent his shafts, and ceases now
To bellow through the vast and boundless Deep.
Let us not slip th' occasion, whether scorn
Or satiate fury yield it from our Foe.
Seest thou yon dreary plain, forlorn and wild,
The seat of desolation, void of light,
Save what the glimmering of these livid flames
Casts pale and dreadful? Thither let us tend
From off the tossing of these fiery waves;
There rest, if any rest can harbour there;
And, re-assembling our afflicted powers,
Consult how we may henceforth most offend
Our enemy, our own loss how repair,
How overcome this dire calamity,
What reinforcement we may gain from hope,
If not, what resolution from despair."

Thus Satan, talking to his nearest mate,
With head uplift above the wave, and eyes
That sparkling blazed; his other parts beides
Prone on the flood, extended long and large,
Lay floating many a rood, in bulk as huge
As whom the fables name of monstrous size,
Titanian or Earth-born, that warred on Jove,
Briareos or Typhon, whom the den
By ancient Tarsus held, or that sea-beast
Leviathan, which God of all his works
Created hugest that swim th' ocean-stream.
Him, haply slumbering on the Norway foam,
The pilot of some small night-foundered skiff,
Deeming some island, oft, as seamen tell,
With fixed anchor in his scaly rind,
Moors by his side under the lee, while night
Invests the sea, and wished morn delays.
So stretched out huge in length the Arch-fiend lay,
Chained on the burning lake; nor ever thence
Had risen, or heaved his head, but that the will
And high permission of all-ruling Heaven
Left him at large to his own dark designs,
That with reiterated crimes he might
Heap on himself damnation, while he sought
Evil to others, and enraged might see
How all his malice served but to bring forth

Infinite goodness, grace, and mercy, shewn
On Man by him seduced, but on himself
Treble confusion, wrath, and vengeance poured.

Forthwith upright he rears from off the pool
His mighty stature; on each hand the flames
Driven backward slope their pointing spires, and, rolled
In billows, leave i' th' midst a horrid vale.
Then with expanded wings he steers his flight
Aloft, incumbent on the dusky air,
That felt unusual weight; till on dry land
He lights—if it were land that ever burned
With solid, as the lake with liquid fire,
And such appeared in hue as when the force
Of subterranean wind transports a hill
Torn from Pelorus, or the shattered side
Of thundering Etna, whose combustible
And fuelled entrails, thence conceiving fire,
Sublimed with mineral fury, aid the winds,
And leave a singed bottom all involved
With stench and smoke. Such resting found the sole
Of unblest feet. Him followed his next mate;
Both glorying to have scaped the Stygian flood
As gods, and by their own recovered strength,
Not by the sufferance of supernal Power.

"Is this the region, this the soil, the clime,"
Said then the lost Archangel, "this the seat
That we must change for Heaven?—this mournful gloom
For that celestial light? Be it so, since he
Who now is sovereign can dispose and bid
What shall be right: farthest from him is best
Whom reason hath equalled, force hath made supreme
Above his equals. Farewell, happy fields,
Where joy for ever dwells! Hail, horrors! hail,
Infernal world! and thou, profoundest Hell,
Receive thy new possessor—one who brings
A mind not to be changed by place or time.
The mind is its own place, and in itself
Can make a Heaven of Hell, a Hell of Heaven.
What matter where, if I be still the same,
And what I should be, all but less than he
Whom thunder hath made greater? Here at least
We shall be free; th' Almighty hath not built
Here for his envy, will not drive us hence:
Here we may reign secure; and, in my choice,
To reign is worth ambition, though in Hell:

Better to reign in Hell than serve in Heaven.
But wherefore let we then our faithful friends,
Th' associates and co-partners of our loss,
Lie thus astonished on th' oblivious pool,
And call them not to share with us their part
In this unhappy mansion, or once more
With rallied arms to try what may be yet
Regained in Heaven, or what more lost in Hell?"

So Satan spake; and him Beelzebub
Thus answered:—"Leader of those armies bright
Which, but th' Omnipotent, none could have foiled!
If once they hear that voice, their liveliest pledge
Of hope in fears and dangers—heard so oft
In worst extremes, and on the perilous edge
Of battle, when it raged, in all assaults
Their surest signal—they will soon resume
New courage and revive, though now they lie
Grovelling and prostrate on yon lake of fire,
As we erewhile, astounded and amazed;
No wonder, fallen such a pernicious height!"

He scarce had ceased when the superior Fiend
Was moving toward the shore; his ponderous shield,
Ethereal temper, massy, large, and round,
Behind him cast. The broad circumference
Hung on his shoulders like the moon, whose orb
Through optic glass the Tuscan artist views
At evening, from the top of Fesole,
Or in Valdarno, to descry new lands,
Rivers, or mountains, in her spotty globe.
His spear—to equal which the tallest pine
Hewn on Norwegian hills, to be the mast
Of some great ammiral, were but a wand—
He walked with, to support uneasy steps
Over the burning marl, not like those steps
On Heaven's azure; and the torrid clime
Smote on him sore besides, vaulted with fire.
Nathless he so endured, till on the beach
Of that inflamed sea he stood, and called
His legions—Angel Forms, who lay entranced
Thick as autumnal leaves that strow the brooks
In Vallombrosa, where th' Etrurian shades
High over-arched embower; or scattered sedge
Afloat, when with fierce winds Orion armed
Hath vexed the Red-Sea coast, whose waves o'erthrew
Busiris and his Memphian chivalry,

While with perfidious hatred they pursued
The sojourners of Goshen, who beheld
From the safe shore their floating carcases
And broken chariot-wheels. So thick bestrown,
Abject and lost, lay these, covering the flood,
Under amazement of their hideous change.
He called so loud that all the hollow deep
Of Hell resounded:—"Princes, Potentates,
Warriors, the Flower of Heaven—once yours; now lost,
If such astonishment as this can seize
Eternal Spirits! Or have ye chosen this place
After the toil of battle to repose
Your wearied virtue, for the ease you find
To slumber here, as in the vales of Heaven?
Or in this abject posture have ye sworn
To adore the Conqueror, who now beholds
Cherub and Seraph rolling in the flood
With scattered arms and ensigns, till anon
His swift pursuers from Heaven-gates disern
Th' advantage, and, descending, tread us down
Thus drooping, or with linked thunderbolts
Transfix us to the bottom of this gulf?
Awake, arise, or be for ever fallen!"

They heard, and were abashed, and up they sprung
Upon the wing, as when men wont to watch
On duty, sleeping found by whom they dread,
Rouse and bestir themselves ere well awake.
Nor did they not perceive the evil plight
In which they were, or the fierce pains not feel;
Yet to their General's voice they soon obeyed
Innumerable. As when the potent rod
Of Amram's son, in Egypt's evil day,
Waved round the coast, up-called a pitchy cloud
Of locusts, warping on the eastern wind,
That o'er the realm of impious Pharaoh hung
Like Night, and darkened all the land of Nile;
So numberless were those bad Angels seen
Hovering on wing under the cope of Hell,
'Twixt upper, nether, and surrounding fires;
Till, as a signal given, th' uplifted spear
Of their great Sultan waving to direct
Their course, in even balance down they light
On the firm brimstone, and fill all the plain:
A multitude like which the populous North
Poured never from her frozen loins to pass
Rhene or the Danaw, when her barbarous sons

Came like a deluge on the South, and spread
Beneath Gibraltar to the Libyan sands.
Forthwith, from every squadron and each band,
The heads and leaders thither haste where stood
Their great Commander—godlike Shapes, and Forms
Excelling human; princely Dignities;
And Powers that erst in Heaven sat on thrones,
Though on their names in Heavenly records now
Be no memorial, blotted out and rased
By their rebellion from the Books of Life.
Nor had they yet among the sons of Eve
Got them new names, till, wandering o'er the earth,
Through God's high sufferance for the trial of man,
By falsities and lies the greatest part
Of mankind they corrupted to forsake
God their Creator, and th' invisible
Glory of him that made them to transform
Oft to the image of a brute, adorned
With gay religions full of pomp and gold,
And devils to adore for deities:
Then were they known to men by various names,
And various idols through the heathen world.

Say, Muse, their names then known, who first, who last,
Roused from the slumber on that fiery couch,
At their great Emperor's call, as next in worth
Came singly where he stood on the bare strand,
While the promiscuous crowd stood yet aloof?

The chief were those who, from the pit of Hell
Roaming to seek their prey on Earth, durst fix
Their seats, long after, next the seat of God,
Their altars by his altar, gods adored
Among the nations round, and durst abide
Jehovah thundering out of Sion, throned
Between the Cherubim; yea, often placed
Within his sanctuary itself their shrines,
Abominations; and with cursed things
His holy rites and solemn feasts profaned,
And with their darkness durst affront his light.
First, Moloch, horrid king, besmeared with blood
Of human sacrifice, and parents' tears;
Though, for the noise of drums and timbrels loud,
Their children's cries unheard that passed through fire
To his grim idol. Him the Ammonite
Worshiped in Rabba and her watery plain,
In Argob and in Basan, to the stream

Of utmost Arnon. Nor content with such
Audacious neighbourhood, the wisest heart
Of Solomon he led by fraud to build
His temple right against the temple of God
On that opprobrious hill, and made his grove
The pleasant valley of Hinnom, Tophet thence
And black Gehenna called, the type of Hell.
Next Chemos, th' obscene dread of Moab's sons,
From Aroar to Nebo and the wild
Of southmost Abarim; in Hesebon
And Horonaim, Seon's real, beyond
The flowery dale of Sibma clad with vines,
And Eleale to th' Asphaltic Pool:
Peor his other name, when he enticed
Israel in Sittim, on their march from Nile,
To do him wanton rites, which cost them woe.
Yet thence his lustful orgies he enlarged
Even to that hill of scandal, by the grove
Of Moloch homicide, lust hard by hate,
Till good Josiah drove them thence to Hell.
With these came they who, from the bordering flood
Of old Euphrates to the brook that parts
Egypt from Syrian ground, had general names
Of Baalim and Ashtaroth—those male,
These feminine. For Spirits, when they please,
Can either sex assume, or both; so soft
And uncompounded is their essence pure,
Not tried or manacled with joint or limb,
Nor founded on the brittle strength of bones,
Like cumbrous flesh; but, in what shape they choose,
Dilated or condensed, bright or obscure,
Can execute their airy purposes,
And works of love or enmity fulfil.
For those the race of Israel oft forsook
Their Living Strength, and unfrequented left
His righteous altar, bowing lowly down
To bestial gods; for which their heads as low
Bowed down in battle, sunk before the spear
Of despicable foes. With these in troop
Came Astoreth, whom the Phoenicians called
Astarte, queen of heaven, with crescent horns;
To whose bright image nightly by the moon
Sidonian virgins paid their vows and songs;
In Sion also not unsung, where stood
Her temple on th' offensive mountain, built
By that uxorious king whose heart, though large,
Beguiled by fair idolatresses, fell

To idols foul. Thammuz came next behind,
Whose annual wound in Lebanon allured
The Syrian damsels to lament his fate
In amorous ditties all a summer's day,
While smooth Adonis from his native rock
Ran purple to the sea, supposed with blood
Of Thammuz yearly wounded: the love-tale
Infected Sion's daughters with like heat,
Whose wanton passions in the sacred porch
Ezekiel saw, when, by the vision led,
His eye surveyed the dark idolatries
Of alienated Judah. Next came one
Who mourned in earnest, when the captive ark
Maimed his brute image, head and hands lopt off,
In his own temple, on the grunsel-edge,
Where he fell flat and shamed his worshippers:
Dagon his name, sea-monster, upward man
And downward fish; yet had his temple high
Reared in Azotus, dreaded through the coast
Of Palestine, in Gath and Ascalon,
And Accaron and Gaza's frontier bounds.
Him followed Rimmon, whose delightful seat
Was fair Damascus, on the fertile banks
Of Abbana and Pharphar, lucid streams.
He also against the house of God was bold:
A leper once he lost, and gained a king—
Ahaz, his sottish conqueror, whom he drew
God's altar to disparage and displace
For one of Syrian mode, whereon to burn
His odious offerings, and adore the gods
Whom he had vanquished. After these appeared
A crew who, under names of old renown—
Osiris, Isis, Orus, and their train—
With monstrous shapes and sorceries abused
Fanatic Egypt and her priests to seek
Their wandering gods disguised in brutish forms
Rather than human. Nor did Israel scape
Th' infection, when their borrowed gold composed
The calf in Oreb; and the rebel king
Doubled that sin in Bethel and in Dan,
Likening his Maker to the grazed ox—
Jehovah, who, in one night, when he passed
From Egypt marching, equalled with one stroke
Both her first-born and all her bleating gods.
Belial came last; than whom a Spirit more lewd
Fell not from Heaven, or more gross to love
Vice for itself. To him no temple stood

Or altar smoked; yet who more oft than he
In temples and at altars, when the priest
Turns atheist, as did Eli's sons, who filled
With lust and violence the house of God?
In courts and palaces he also reigns,
And in luxurious cities, where the noise
Of riot ascends above their loftiest towers,
And injury and outrage; and, when night
Darkens the streets, then wander forth the sons
Of Belial, flown with insolence and wine.
Witness the streets of Sodom, and that night
In Gibeah, when the hospitable door
Exposed a matron, to avoid worse rape.

These were the prime in order and in might:
The rest were long to tell; though far renowned
Th' Ionian gods—of Javan's issue held
Gods, yet confessed later than Heaven and Earth,
Their boasted parents;—Titan, Heaven's first-born,
With his enormous brood, and birthright seized
By younger Saturn: he from mightier Jove,
His own and Rhea's son, like measure found;
So Jove usurping reigned. These, first in Crete
And Ida known, thence on the snowy top
Of cold Olympus ruled the middle air,
Their highest heaven; or on the Delphian cliff,
Or in Dodona, and through all the bounds
Of Doric land; or who with Saturn old
Fled over Adria to th' Hesperian fields,
And o'er the Celtic roamed the utmost Isles.

All these and more came flocking; but with looks
Downcast and damp; yet such wherein appeared
Obscure some glimpse of joy to have found their Chief
Not in despair, to have found themselves not lost
In loss itself; which on his countenance cast
Like doubtful hue. But he, his wonted pride
Soon recollecting, with high words, that bore
Semblance of worth, not substance, gently raised
Their fainting courage, and dispelled their fears.
Then straight commands that, at the warlike sound
Of trumpets loud and clarions, be upreared
His mighty standard. That proud honour claimed
Azazel as his right, a Cherub tall:
Who forthwith from the glittering staff unfurled
Th' imperial ensign; which, full high advanced,
Shone like a meteor streaming to the wind,

With gems and golden lustre rich emblazed,
Seraphic arms and trophies; all the while
Sonorous metal blowing martial sounds:
At which the universal host up-sent
A shout that tore Hell's concave, and beyond
Frighted the reign of Chaos and old Night.
All in a moment through the gloom were seen
Ten thousand banners rise into the air,
With orient colours waving: with them rose
A forest huge of spears; and thronging helms
Appeared, and serried shields in thick array
Of depth immeasurable. Anon they move
In perfect phalanx to the Dorian mood
Of flutes and soft recorders—such as raised
To height of noblest temper heroes old
Arming to battle, and instead of rage
Deliberate valour breathed, firm, and unmoved
With dread of death to flight or foul retreat;
Nor wanting power to mitigate and swage
With solemn touches troubled thoughts, and chase
Anguish and doubt and fear and sorrow and pain
From mortal or immortal minds. Thus they,
Breathing united force with fixed thought,
Moved on in silence to soft pipes that charmed
Their painful steps o'er the burnt soil. And now
Advanced in view they stand—a horrid front
Of dreadful length and dazzling arms, in guise
Of warriors old, with ordered spear and shield,
Awaiting what command their mighty Chief
Had to impose. He through the armed files
Darts his experienced eye, and soon traverse
The whole battalion views—their order due,
Their visages and stature as of gods;
Their number last he sums. And now his heart
Distends with pride, and, hardening in his strength,
Glories: for never, since created Man,
Met such embodied force as, named with these,
Could merit more than that small infantry
Warred on by cranes—though all the giant brood
Of Phlegra with th' heroic race were joined
That fought at Thebes and Ilium, on each side
Mixed with auxiliar gods; and what resounds
In fable or romance of Uther's son,
Begirt with British and Armoric knights;
And all who since, baptized or infidel,
Jousted in Aspramont, or Montalban,
Damasco, or Marocco, or Trebisond,

Or whom Biserta sent from Afric shore
When Charlemain with all his peerage fell
By Fontarabbia. Thus far these beyond
Compare of mortal prowess, yet observed
Their dread Commander. He, above the rest
In shape and gesture proudly eminent,
Stood like a tower. His form had yet not lost
All her original brightness, nor appeared
Less than Archangel ruined, and th' excess
Of glory obscured: as when the sun new-risen
Looks through the horizontal misty air
Shorn of his beams, or, from behind the moon,
In dim eclipse, disastrous twilight sheds
On half the nations, and with fear of change
Perplexes monarchs. Darkened so, yet shone
Above them all th' Archangel: but his face
Deep scars of thunder had intrenched, and care
Sat on his faded cheek, but under brows
Of dauntless courage, and considerate pride
Waiting revenge. Cruel his eye, but cast
Signs of remorse and passion, to behold
The fellows of his crime, the followers rather
(Far other once beheld in bliss), condemned
For ever now to have their lot in pain—
Millions of Spirits for his fault amerced
Of Heaven, and from eternal splendours flung
For his revolt—yet faithful how they stood,
Their glory withered; as, when heaven's fire
Hath scathed the forest oaks or mountain pines,
With singed top their stately growth, though bare,
Stands on the blasted heath. He now prepared
To speak; whereat their doubled ranks they bend
From wing to wing, and half enclose him round
With all his peers: attention held them mute.
Thrice he assayed, and thrice, in spite of scorn,
Tears, such as Angels weep, burst forth: at last
Words interwove with sighs found out their way:—

"O myriads of immortal Spirits! O Powers
Matchless, but with th' Almighty!—and that strife
Was not inglorious, though th' event was dire,
As this place testifies, and this dire change,
Hateful to utter. But what power of mind,
Forseeing or presaging, from the depth
Of knowledge past or present, could have feared
How such united force of gods, how such
As stood like these, could ever know repulse?

For who can yet believe, though after loss,
That all these puissant legions, whose exile
Hath emptied Heaven, shall fail to re-ascend,
Self-raised, and repossess their native seat?
For me, be witness all the host of Heaven,
If counsels different, or danger shunned
By me, have lost our hopes. But he who reigns Monarch
in Heaven till then as one secure
Sat on his throne, upheld by old repute,
Consent or custom, and his regal state
Put forth at full, but still his strength concealed—
Which tempted our attempt, and wrought our fall.
Henceforth his might we know, and know our own,
So as not either to provoke, or dread
New war provoked: our better part remains
To work in close design, by fraud or guile,
What force effected not; that he no less
At length from us may find, who overcomes
By force hath overcome but half his foe.
Space may produce new Worlds; whereof so rife
There went a fame in Heaven that he ere long
Intended to create, and therein plant
A generation whom his choice regard
Should favour equal to the Sons of Heaven.
Thither, if but to pry, shall be perhaps
Our first eruption—thither, or elsewhere;
For this infernal pit shall never hold
Celestial Spirits in bondage, nor th' Abyss
Long under darkness cover. But these thoughts
Full counsel must mature. Peace is despaired;
For who can think submission? War, then, war
Open or understood, must be resolved."
He spake; and, to confirm his words, outflew
Millions of flaming swords, drawn from the thighs
Of mighty Cherubim; the sudden blaze
Far round illumined Hell. Highly they raged
Against the Highest, and fierce with grasped arms
Clashed on their sounding shields the din of war,
Hurling defiance toward the vault of Heaven.

There stood a hill not far, whose grisly top
Belched fire and rolling smoke; the rest entire
Shone with a glossy scurf—undoubted sign
That in his womb was hid metallic ore,
The work of sulphur. Thither, winged with speed,
A numerous brigade hastened: as when bands
Of pioneers, with spade and pickaxe armed,

Forerun the royal camp, to trench a field,
Or cast a rampart. Mammon led them on—
Mammon, the least erected Spirit that fell
From Heaven; for even in Heaven his looks and thoughts
Were always downward bent, admiring more
The riches of heaven's pavement, trodden gold,
Than aught divine or holy else enjoyed
In vision beatific. By him first
Men also, and by his suggestion taught,
Ransacked the centre, and with impious hands
Rifled the bowels of their mother Earth
For treasures better hid. Soon had his crew
Opened into the hill a spacious wound,
And digged out ribs of gold. Let none admire
That riches grow in Hell; that soil may best
Deserve the precious bane. And here let those
Who boast in mortal things, and wondering tell
Of Babel, and the works of Memphian kings,
Learn how their greatest monuments of fame
And strength, and art, are easily outdone
By Spirits reprobate, and in an hour
What in an age they, with incessant toil
And hands innumerable, scarce perform.
Nigh on the plain, in many cells prepared,
That underneath had veins of liquid fire
Sluiced from the lake, a second multitude
With wondrous art founded the massy ore,
Severing each kind, and scummed the bullion-dross.
A third as soon had formed within the ground
A various mould, and from the boiling cells
By strange conveyance filled each hollow nook;
As in an organ, from one blast of wind,
To many a row of pipes the sound-board breathes.
Anon out of the earth a fabric huge
Rose like an exhalation, with the sound
Of dulcet symphonies and voices sweet—
Built like a temple, where pilasters round
Were set, and Doric pillars overlaid
With golden architrave; nor did there want
Cornice or frieze, with bossy sculptures graven;
The roof was fretted gold. Not Babylon
Nor great Alcairo such magnificence
Equalled in all their glories, to enshrine
Belus or Serapis their gods, or seat
Their kings, when Egypt with Assyria strove
In wealth and luxury. Th' ascending pile
Stood fixed her stately height, and straight the doors,

Opening their brazen folds, discover, wide
Within, her ample spaces o'er the smooth
And level pavement: from the arched roof,
Pendent by subtle magic, many a row
Of starry lamps and blazing cressets, fed
With naptha and asphaltus, yielded light
As from a sky. The hasty multitude
Admiring entered; and the work some praise,
And some the architect. His hand was known
In Heaven by many a towered structure high,
Where sceptred Angels held their residence,
And sat as Princes, whom the supreme King
Exalted to such power, and gave to rule,
Each in his Hierarchy, the Orders bright.
Nor was his name unheard or unadored
In ancient Greece; and in Ausonian land
Men called him Mulciber; and how he fell
From Heaven they fabled, thrown by angry Jove
Sheer o'er the crystal battlements: from morn
To noon he fell, from noon to dewy eve,
A summer's day, and with the setting sun
Dropt from the zenith, like a falling star,
On Lemnos, th' Aegaean isle. Thus they relate,
Erring; for he with this rebellious rout
Fell long before; nor aught aviled him now
To have built in Heaven high towers; nor did he scape
By all his engines, but was headlong sent,
With his industrious crew, to build in Hell.
Meanwhile the winged Heralds, by command
Of sovereign power, with awful ceremony
And trumpet's sound, throughout the host proclaim
A solemn council forthwith to be held
At Pandemonium, the high capital
Of Satan and his peers. Their summons called
From every band and squared regiment
By place or choice the worthiest: they anon
With hundreds and with thousands trooping came
Attended. All access was thronged; the gates

And porches wide, but chief the spacious hall
(Though like a covered field, where champions bold
Wont ride in armed, and at the Soldan's chair
Defied the best of Paynim chivalry
To mortal combat, or career with lance),
Thick swarmed, both on the ground and in the air,
Brushed with the hiss of rustling wings. As bees
In spring-time, when the Sun with Taurus rides,
Pour forth their populous youth about the hive
In clusters; they among fresh dews and flowers
Fly to and fro, or on the smoothed plank,
The suburb of their straw-built citadel,
New rubbed with balm, expatiate, and confer
Their state-affairs: so thick the airy crowd
Swarmed and were straitened; till, the signal given,
Behold a wonder! They but now who seemed
In bigness to surpass Earth's giant sons,
Now less than smallest dwarfs, in narrow room
Throng numberless—like that pygmean race
Beyond the Indian mount; or faery elves,
Whose midnight revels, by a forest-side
Or fountain, some belated peasant sees,
Or dreams he sees, while overhead the Moon
Sits arbitress, and nearer to the Earth
Wheels her pale course: they, on their mirth and dance
Intent, with jocund music charm his ear;
At once with joy and fear his heart rebounds.
Thus incorporeal Spirits to smallest forms
Reduced their shapes immense, and were at large,
Though without number still, amidst the hall
Of that infernal court. But far within,
And in their own dimensions like themselves,
The great Seraphic Lords and Cherubim
In close recess and secret conclave sat,
A thousand demi-gods on golden seats,
Frequent and full. After short silence then,
And summons read, the great consult began.

DISCUSSION QUESTIONS

1. Which lines of "Lycidas" strike you as most poignant and expressive? Discuss why they are effective.
2. Which lines of "Lycidas" seem to stray the most from the subject of his grief? Why would Milton have included these passages?
3. What qualities is Lycidas celebrated for?
4. In Sonnet XIX, what problem is the speaker discussing in the first two stanzas? Where does the "turn," or change of tone, in the poem occur? What consolation or solution to the problem does Milton offer in the last two stanzas?
5. How is the structure and movement of Sonnet XXIII different from the tradition as established by Petrarch and Shakespeare? (Note, for instance, where the turn comes and what it brings.) Does this poem offer any consolation for grief and fear of death?
6. In Book 1 of *Paradise Lost*, how does Milton characterize Satan? What are your first impressions of him? Does he exhibit any admirable characteristics?
7. How does Milton describe hell in Book 1? Do his descriptions arouse pity for the fallen angels?
8. What is ironic about Satan's statement that, "The mind is its own place, and in itself/Can make a Heav'n of Hell, a Hell of Heav'n" (Bk. 1, lines 254–55)?

WRITING SUGGESTION

1. Compare Milton's and Dante's versions of hell and Satan (see Unit 2). What are the chief differences? What might account for their vastly different characterizations of Satan?

ANNE DUDLEY BRADSTREET (1612–1672)

B orn in Northampton, England, Anne Dudley married Simon Bradstreet in 1628 and emigrated with him in 1630 to America, where her husband later became governor of Massachusetts. Her first book of poetry was published in 1650 in London, making her the first female American writer. Her poetry is distinguished by its domestic images and its fresh and informal diction, which gives it an effective sense of directness and intimacy. The following poems reflect her concerns for her family, but also for her poetry, which she addresses as a child in "The Author to Her Book."

THE AUTHOR TO HER BOOK

Thou ill-formed offspring of my feeble brain,
Who after birth did'st by my side remain,
Till snatcht from thence by friends, less wise than true,
Who thee abroad exposed to public view,
Made thee in rags, halting to th' press to trudge,
Where errors were not lessened (all may judge).
At thy return my blushing was not small,
My rambling brat (in print) should mother call.
I cast thee by as one unfit for light,
The visage was so irksome in my sight,
Yet being mine own, at length affection would
Thy blemishes amend, if so I could.
I washed thy face, but more defects I saw,
And rubbing off a spot, still made a flaw.
I stretcht thy joints to make thee even feet,
Yet still thou run'st more hobbling than is meet.
In better dress to trim thee was my mind,
But nought save home-spun cloth, i' th' house I find.
In this array, 'mongst vulgars may'st thou roam.
In critic's hands, beware thou dost not come,
And take thy way where yet thou art not known.
If for thy father askt, say, thou hadst none;
And for thy mother, she alas is poor,
Which caused her thus to send thee out of door.

BEFORE THE BIRTH OF ONE OF HER CHILDREN

All things within this fading world hath end,
Adversity doth still our joys attend;
No ties so strong, no friends so dear and sweet,
But with death's parting blow are sure to meet.
The sentence past is most irrevocable,
A common thing, yet oh, inevitable.
How soon, my Dear, death may my steps attend,
How soon't may be thy lot to lose thy friend,
We both are ignorant, yet love bids me
These farewell lines to recommend to thee,
That when the knot's untied that made us one,
I may seem thine, who in effect am none.
And if I see not half my days that's due,
What nature would, God grant to yours and you;
The many faults that well you know I have
Let be interred in my oblivious grave;
If any worth or virtue were in me,
Let that live freshly in thy memory
And when thou feel'st no grief, as I no harmes,
Yet love thy dead, who long lay in thine arms,
And when thy loss shall be repaid with gains
Look to my little babes, my dear remains.
And if thou love thyself, or loved'st me,
These O protect from stepdame's injury.
And if chance to thine eyes shall bring this verse,
With some sad sighs honor my absent hearse;
And kiss this paper for thy dear love's sake,
Who with salt tears this last farewell did take.

DISCUSSION QUESTIONS

1. In "The Author to Her Book," what kind of child does she describe her book as? What are its faults?

2. In the same poem, which images of a child's body work particularly well as metaphors for Bradstreet's poetry? What do these metaphors suggest about her sense of her abilities as a poet? Do you think this poem expresses her true feelings about her verses? Why or why not?

3. What is the rhyme scheme in this poem? Is it effective? Why or why not?

4. Who is the poet addressing in "Before the Birth of One of Her Children?" What motivated her to write the poem?

5. What specific threat is she concerned about her children facing?

WRITING SUGGESTION

1. Compare Bradstreet's attitude toward her poetry to Shakespeare's in any of the sonnets in which he refers to his verse. What might account for the differences? Can you find any similarities? If so, what are they?

ANDREW MARVELL (1621–1678)

Selected Poems

B orn in Yorkshire, Andrew Marvell studied at Trinity College, Cambridge. After several appointments as a tutor (including his tutoring of William Dutton, the ward of Oliver Cromwell), Marvell became an assistant to Milton in 1657 and later a member of Parliament in the Commonwealth government. Even after the restoration of the monarchy, he remained faithful to the Commonwealth and convinced that monarchy must be eliminated. He wrote most of his poetry before the Restoration; afterward, he turned his attention primarily to politics.

Marvell's poetry abounds in natural imagery and garden images in particular, as can be seen in both "The Garden" and his famous carpe diem poem, "To His Coy Mistress," printed below. His verse is also characterized by its wit and playfulness, although his description of the worms taking his mistress's virginity in "To His Coy Mistress" deserves to be ranked as one of the most grotesque and sinister in the English language.

TO HIS COY MISTRESS

Had we but world enough and time,
This coyness, lady, were no crime.
We would sit down, and think which way
To walk, and pass our long love's day.
Thou by the Indian Ganges' side
Shouldst rubies find; I by the tide
Of Humber would complain. I would
Love you ten years before the flood,
And you should, if you please, refuse
Till the conversion of the Jews.
My vegetable love should grow
Vaster than empires and more slow;
An hundred years should go to praise
Thine eyes, and on thy forehead gaze;
Two hundred to adore each breast,
But thirty thousand to the rest;
An age at least to every part,
And the last age should show your heart.
For, lady, you deserve this state,
Nor would I love at lower rate.

  But at my back I always hear
Time's wingèd chariot hurrying near;
And yonder all before us lie
Deserts of vast eternity.
Thy beauty shall no more be found;
Nor, in thy marble vault, shall sound
My echoing song; then worms shall try
That long-preserved virginity,
And your quaint honour turn to dust,
And into ashes all my lust;
The grave's a fine and private place,
But none, I think, do there embrace.

  Now therefore, while the youthful hue
Sits on thy skin like morning dew,
And while thy willing soul transpires
At every pore with instant fires,
Now let us sport us while we may,
And now, like amorous birds of prey,
Rather at once our time devour
Than languish in his slow-chapped power.
Let us roll all our strength and all
Our sweetness up into one ball,
And tear our pleasures with rough strife
Thorough the iron gates of life:
Thus, though we cannot make our sun
Stand still, yet we will make him run.

THE GARDEN

How vainly men themselves amaze
To win the palm, the oak, or bays,
And their uncessant labours see
Crown'd from some single herb or tree,
Whose short and narrow verged shade
Does prudently their toils upbraid;
While all flow'rs and all trees do close
To weave the garlands of repose.

Fair Quiet, have I found thee here,
And Innocence, thy sister dear!
Mistaken long, I sought you then
In busy companies of men;
Your sacred plants, if here below,
Only among the plants will grow.
Society is all but rude,
To this delicious solitude.

No white nor red was ever seen
So am'rous as this lovely green.
Fond lovers, cruel as their flame,
Cut in these trees their mistress' name;
Little, alas, they know or heed
How far these beauties hers exceed!
Fair trees! wheres'e'er your barks I wound,
No name shall but your own be found.

When we have run our passion's heat,
Love hither makes his best retreat.
The gods, that mortal beauty chase,
Still in a tree did end their race:
Apollo hunted Daphne so,
Only that she might laurel grow;
And Pan did after Syrinx speed,
Not as a nymph, but for a reed.

What wond'rous life in this I lead!
Ripe apples drop about my head;

The luscious clusters of the vine
Upon my mouth do crush their wine;
The nectarine and curious peach
Into my hands themselves do reach;
Stumbling on melons as I pass,
Ensnar'd with flow'rs, I fall on grass.
Meanwhile the mind, from pleasure less,
Withdraws into its happiness;
The mind, that ocean where each kind
Does straight its own resemblance find,
Yet it creates, transcending these,
Far other worlds, and other seas;
Annihilating all that's made
To a green thought in a green shade.
Here at the fountain's sliding foot,
Or at some fruit tree's mossy root,
Casting the body's vest aside,
My soul into the boughs does glide;
There like a bird it sits and sings,
Then whets, and combs its silver wings;

And, till prepar'd for longer flight,
Waves in its plumes the various light.
Such was that happy garden-state,
While man there walk'd without a mate;
After a place so pure and sweet,
What other help could yet be meet!
But 'twas beyond a mortal's share
To wander solitary there:
Two paradises 'twere in one
To live in paradise alone.
How well the skillful gard'ner drew
Of flow'rs and herbs this dial new,
Where from above the milder sun
Does through a fragrant zodiac run;
And as it works, th' industrious bee
Computes its time as well as we.
How could such sweet and wholesome hours
Be reckon'd but with herbs and flow'rs!

DISCUSSION QUESTIONS

1. "To His Coy Mistress" has three stanzas, each with a distinct tone and theme. Paraphrase the main theme of each stanza, and describe the differences in each stanza's tone.

2. Which lines of the first stanza strike you as comic? What is the source of the comedy in these lines?

3. Why would the speaker refer to worms taking his mistress's virginity?

4. In the last two lines of the same poem, what does the speaker mean when he says that they will make the sun run? What is his overall purpose in this poem?

5. In "The Garden," what positive characteristics does the speaker attribute to the garden (or to any natural retreat, for that matter)?

6. Which stanza of "The Garden" seems comical? What is the nature of the comedy in this stanza? What is the effect of this stanza on the poem as a whole?

7. In the last line of the sixth stanza, what does the speaker mean by a "green thought in a green shade?"

8. According to the speaker, what would make "Two paradises ... in one?"

IMAGE CREDITS

Unit 1

Section opener: Copyright © 2007 Steve F-E-Cameron / Wikimedia Commons / CC BY-SA 3.0

1. Epidaurus Theater: Copyright © 2007 User:Olecorre / Wikimedia Commons / CC BY-SA 3.0

2. Copyright © 2009 Eve Andersson / CC BY-SA 3.0

3. Dionysus in a Boat: User:Bibi Saint-Pol / Wikimedia Commons / Public Domain.

4. Herakles Fighting Busiris: Copyright © 2005 Marsyas / Wikimedia Commons / CC BY-SA 2.5

5. New Your Kouros: Copyright © 2005 Yair Talmor / Wikimedia Commons / CC BY-SA 3.0

6. Kroisos Kouros: User:Mountain / Wikimedia Commons / Public Domain

7. Doryphoros: Copyright © 2012 Marie-Lan Nguyen / Wikimedia Commons / CC BY 2.5

8. Portrait Bust of a Man: Copyright © 2009 Jorge Elías / Wikimedia Commons / CC BY 2.0

9. Greek Orders: Pearson Scott Foresman / Wikimedia Commons / Public Domain

10. Discobolus: Copyright © 2007 Steve F-E-Cameron / Wikimedia Commons / CC BY-SA 3.0

11. Parthenon from West: User:Mountain / Wikimedia Commons / Public Domain

12. Augustus of Prima Porta: Copyright © 2007 Till Niermann / Wikimedia Commons / CC BY-SA 3.0

13. Bedroom from the Villa: Copyright © 2007 Ad Meskens / Wikimedia Commons / CC BY-SA 3.0

14. Ara Pacis: Copyright © 2006 User:Sailko / Wikimedia Commons / CC BY-SA 3.0

15. View of the Pont du Gard: Copyright © 2011 Les Portes du Temps / Wikimedia Commons / CC BY-SA 3.0

16. The Colosseum: Copyright © 2007 Paul Zangaro / Wikimedia Commons / CC BY-SA 3.0

Unit 2

17. Theodora: Basilica of St. Vitale / Public Domain

18. Basilique Saint Remi: User:Vassil / Wikimedia Commons / Public Domain

19. Arche Saint-Sernin: Copyright © 2011 User:Léna / Wikimedia Commons / CC BY 3.0

20. Saint-Denis Cathedral: Copyright © 2005 User:Beckstet / Wikimedia Commons / CC BY-SA 3.0

21. Lindisfarne Evangeliarium: User:Jpemery / Wikimedia Commons / Public Domain

22. The Virgin and Child Enthroned: Cimabue / National Gallery, London / Public Domain

23. The Mourning of Christ: Giotto di Bondone / Cappella Scrovegni, Padua / Public Domain

Unit 3

Section opener: Copyright © 2012 Depositphotos / Maugli

24. Trinity Scheme: Masaccio / Public Domain

25. Florence Cathedral: Copyright © 2007 User:Bonus Onus / Wikimedia Commons / CC BY 2.5

26. Versailles Chateau: Copyright © 2007 Marc Vassal / Wikimedia Commons / CC BY-SA 3.0

27. Holy Trinity: Masaccio / Santa Maria Novella, Florence / Public Domain

CPSIA information can be obtained at www.ICGtesting.com
Printed in the USA
LVOW02s2239040914

402289LV00018B/42/P